# LEADING

# ORGANIZATIONS

*To my friends and colleagues*
*in the Kellogg Leadership Studies Project, 1992–1997*

# LEADING
# ORGANIZATIONS
## PERSPECTIVES FOR A
## NEW ERA

## GILL ROBINSON HICKMAN
Editor

SAGE Publications
*International Educational and Professional Publisher*
Thousand Oaks  London  New Delhi

*For information:*

SAGE Publications, Inc.
2455 Teller Road
Thousand Oaks, California 91320
E-mail: order@sagepub.com

SAGE Publications Ltd.
6 Bonhill Street
London EC2A 4PU
United Kingdom

SAGE Publications India Pvt. Ltd.
M-32 Market
Greater Kailash I
New Delhi 110 048 India

Printed in the United States of America

*Library of Congress Cataloging-in-Publication Data*

Main entry under title:

Leading organizations: Perspectives for a new era / edited by Gill
    Robinson Hickman.
        p. cm.
        Includes bibliographical references and index.
        ISBN 0-7619-1422-6 (cloth: acid-free paper)
        ISBN 0-7619-1423-4 (pbk.: acid-free paper)
        1. Organizational behavior. 2. Organizational effectiveness.
        3. Leadership. I. Hickman, Gill Robinson.
    HD58.7 .L4 1998
    658.4'06—ddc21
                                                98-25335

98  99  00  01  02  03  04  7  6  5  4  3  2  1

| | |
|---|---|
| *Acquiring Editor:* | Marquita Flemming |
| *Editorial Assistant:* | MaryAnn Vail |
| *Production Editor:* | Diana E. Axelsen |
| *Editorial Assistant:* | Denise Santoyo |
| *Permissions Editor:* | Jennifer Morgan |
| *Typesetter/Designer:* | Christina M. Hill |
| *Cover Designer:* | Candice Harman |

# Contents

# Preface

Organizations are entering a century marked by unprecedented changes in technology, political and economic systems, and societal demands. The nature of these changes calls for leadership that can develop an organization's human capacity, structure, and functions to perform effectively in a highly dynamic environment. In this environment, organizations are being challenged further to serve as new integrating mechanisms that must balance the purpose for which they exist with the interrelated needs of other institutions and societal responsibilities.[1] Leadership is the critical factor in helping organizations.

This book focuses on the roles and responsibilities of leaders and participants in new-era organizations and links contemporary leadership concepts and theories to the organizational context. The study of organizational leadership presents a major challenge because the literature on this topic is dispersed across multiple disciplines. Consequently, this text brings together knowledge from varied fields and provides a framework for examining and integrating issues pertaining to organizational leadership. Its framework and content emerged over a 4-year period through the development and refinement of a newly created course on leadership in organizations. The book is intended for those who study this phenomenon and those who serve in the roles of leaders and participants. These are the individuals who can make a differ-ence in the processes and outcomes of organizations in the future.

Participation in the Kellogg Leadership Studies Project (KLSP), which brought together leadership scholars and practitioners from throughout the country, contributed considerably to the development and refinement of this book. The works of the KLSP participants along with the writings of other prominent contributors provide a wealth of rich scholarship on organizational leadership throughout the book.

## Acknowledgments

Many colleagues, mentors, and friends contributed their time, effort, advice, and support to help create this edited book. I would especially like to thank James MacGregor Burns, Georgia Sorenson, Barbara Kellerman, and Larraine Matusak, who served as my mentors in the KLSP and continue to be wonderful friends and colleagues. I truly appreciate the strong endorsements for this project from my colleagues and friends Bruce Avolio, Barry Posner, and Bernard Bass. Your enthusiastic support made it possible for the book to be considered for publication. My sincere thanks and appreciation go to my editor Marquita Flemming, who truly believed in this project and made it happen.

To my faculty mentors and dean, Richard Couto, Joanne Ciulla, and John Rosenblum at the Jepson School of Leadership Studies, I owe a huge debt of gratitude for shepherding me through the tenure process while I finished this book. You are extraordinary friends and colleagues. I also want to thank Karin Klenke, a former member of the Jepson School, for serving as the inspiration for this book. Without her prompting, I would never have started this venture. Endless appreciation goes to Amy Keown, who secured all the permissions, provided technical editing, and constantly pushed the process along. Without her exceptional organizational skills and diligent work, there would be no book. I sincerely want to thank Judy Mable, who took my crude sketches and turned them into wonderful graphic illustrations of the concepts that are now conveyed in each of the ten sections. She remained cheerful and wonderfully supportive no matter how many times I added, deleted, or revised each graphic. To all the students in both sections of my Spring 1998 Leadership in Organizations course, thank you for using and critiquing the draft of this text so that other student and faculty users could benefit from your insights.

Most of all to my husband, Michael Hickman, thank you for withstanding all the time I spent in front of the computer and in the library completing this project, and for all the flowers, cards, and expressions of support. A very special thank-you goes to my mother, Beatrice Price, my daughter Kimberly, and my grandson Ryan for their constant love and understanding.

### Note

1. See Peter Drucker's chapter, "The Age of Social Transformation," in Part IX of this text.

# Introduction

Leadership can and does make a meaningful difference in every aspect of organizations. The current proliferation of writing about leadership is indicative of our urgent need for good leadership that is competent, purposeful, intelligent, and caring. This form of leadership is critical to create organizations that are better and more responsive than ever before. A primary assumption underlying this book is that new-era organizations can become better by focusing on the development of human capacity—qualitative enhancements of participants' abilities, competencies, and capabilities for continuous learning. A further assumption is that new-era organizations can become better and more responsive by basing their actions on a foundation of values and ethics. A major role of leadership in this context is to engage participants in the adaptive work of identifying, developing, and employing these values and ethics.[1]

These assumptions imply leadership based on intentional acts that affect people and outcomes. Given these assumptions, organizations will need to consciously align their leadership philosophy and behavior with their purpose, values, ethics, responsibilities, and commitment to their participants. The leadership philosophy of an organization is more than a style. It is the essence of an organization's integrity—a clear demonstration of its beliefs in action. Determining the tenets of organizational philosophy requires the combined efforts of leaders and participants. Accordingly, leadership concepts and theories are incorporated in the book to advance purposeful creation of leadership philosophy and beliefs.

The figure on p. xiv depicts a holistic framework for understanding and analyzing the role of leadership in new-era organizations. The first component of this framework identifies the leadership role with regard to sensing and analyzing change that emerges in the external environment. Change in the environment is incorporated in the organization through vital processes of interaction between leaders and participants. The overlapping circles in the center of the framework represent these processes. They are the core of leadership and permeate all sectors of organizational life.

In the interaction between leaders and participants, leaders are initiators who take the first step toward change based on motivation and self-confidence, and communicate with other potential participants to gain a positive response.[2] Participants are highly motivated critical thinkers and actors who perform equal but different roles than leaders to meet their mutual goals.[3]

The fluidity of these roles is a fundamental shift in the philosophy and functioning of leadership in organizations. Individuals move from participant to leader or leader to participant based on capabilities, expertise, motivation, ideas, and circumstances, not solely on position or authority. In

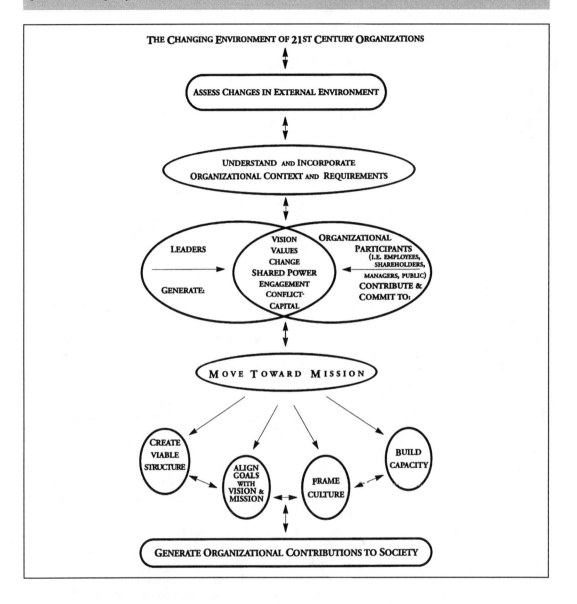

new-era organizations, leadership starts with formal leaders (appointed authorities) in concert with other organizational participants and stakeholders, *and* leadership originates with participants without formal authority. The concept of leadership as a process of initiation and involvement does not negate formal authority. Participants share formal authority broadly in contemporary structures such as self-directed work teams or virtual office projects.

In the figure, the factors in the intersection of the two circles identify the challenging work of leaders and participants—forming vision, values, change, shared power, engagement, and conflict capital.[4] Based on these factors, leaders and participants determine how the organization will respond to its external environment and how it will align its purpose in light of new information. These critical factors guide the creation and achievement of organizational mission, structure, goals, culture, and capacity building.

The last component of the framework identifies the role of new-era organizations with regard to the larger society. Organizational leaders and participants take activist roles to tackle issues such as the environment, inner-city renewal, homelessness, and education in addition to traditional forms of philanthropy. They are in highly advantageous positions to facilitate unprecedented advances for society and resolve complex problems based on their collective capacity to mobilize human, technical, and economic resources.

In its entirety, the framework provides an approach to conceptualizing and guiding leadership in new-era organizations. The book follows this framework throughout and the selected literature provides meaning and depth to each component. The text contains several parts with an overview by the editor on leadership and organizational issues for each segment. Part I examines the impact of major changes in the external environment on new-era organizations and describes the forces that are driving these changes including irreversible change, technology, highly skilled knowledge workers, multiple bottom lines including social responsibility, and globalization. In Part II the focus shifts internally to contemporary perspectives on the inherent requirements, responsibilities, and obstacles that organizations place on appointed leaders. Several readings emphasize the leadership challenges involved in transforming old organizational concepts to meet new visions and requirements. Part III begins by distinguishing between leadership and management roles. Beyond these distinctions, this section examines leadership concepts and theories as they apply to the organizational context. Part IV explores factors that contribute to effective leader-participant relationships in organizations. The chapters in this section focus on issues of shared power and engagement, and analyze how relationships between leaders and participants are generated and maintained. Part V emphasizes the critical role of vision in organizational leadership. It distinguishes factors that comprise strong visions and identifies fallacies in misguided

ones. This section further describes the role of mission, goals, and environmental scanning in relation to vision. Part VI considers the impact of leadership on organizational design and structure, and examines various alternatives for new-era organizations. Part VII looks at the essential responsibilities of leadership for framing the culture of an organization. It specifically focuses on values, ethics, work-family issues, and diversity. Part VIII highlights individual and organizational capacity building through development of personal mastery, organizational change, conflict capital, and recognition of participants' contributions. Part IX looks at the new work of leaders and participants in the area of social enterprise with regard to organizational contributions toward improving difficult and complex conditions in the larger society. Finally, Part X provides an organizational framework for leadership in the new millennium and presents a futuristic perspective on the larger role and purpose of leadership in society.

Altogether, the book strives to provide more than a collection of engaging readings. Its intent is to provide an integrated perspective for facilitating good leadership of organizations so that they are well suited for the demands of a highly complex and changing environment.

### Notes

1. See Ronald Heifetz's chapter, "Values in Leadership" in Part VII of this text.

2. See James M. Burns, "Empowerment for Change: A Conceptual Working Paper," Kellogg Leadership Studies Project, College Park, MD, September 1996.

3. See Robert Kelley, "In Praise of Followers," *Harvard Business Review,* 1988, Vol. 88, No. 6, pp. 142-148.

4. Conflict capital is conceived as a substantially enhanced outcome that results from the effort to bring about change among leaders and participants with diverse perspectives. This concept will be discussed more fully in the section on leadership and capacity building.

# The Changing Environment of 21st-Century Organizations

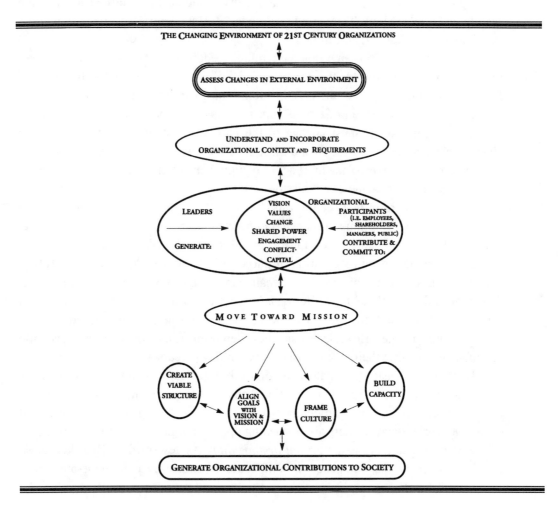

Part I focuses on the impact of a rapidly changing external environment on organizations. As we move into the 21st century, organizations are major participants in an environment of unprecedented change. The environment is so dynamic that the ground and ground rules are changing steadily while other transformations are occurring all around. In a 5-year span, we witnessed the fall of the Berlin Wall, reconfiguration of the former Soviet Union, and the rise of struggling democracies and warring factions in many previously communist societies. Events such as these link people and organizations globally in an environmental context of turbulence, unpredictability, and quantum change.

Added to these political changes are numerous other factors that affect organizational functioning. Warren Bennis and Burt Nanus identify several forces that shape leadership in 21st-century organizations—the speed and turbulence of technological change, the influx of knowledge workers, a global and multicultural workplace, and new organizational designs that reflect changes in communications and decision making facilitated by technology. They provide a model of 21st-century leadership to address the changes that beset organizations.

The dynamism of this environment requires leadership that continuously assesses the external environment for the purpose of identifying or creating opportunities and lessening potential threats to the organization. This environmental complexity cannot be ignored, reduced, or minimized, as appealing as those options may seem. Instead, leaders and participants must engage in the hard work of determining what these changes mean to the organization and must generate new approaches and resources to meet external challenges. They must act or realign their actions in accordance with the organization's vision, values, and mission.

All the chapters in this section raise issues concerning how this environmental context has and will continue to change traditional concepts of organizational purpose, structure, functioning, and leadership. Toffler's classic work indicates that organizations are "experiencing a deep redefinition of purposes." Bergquist adds support to Toffler and describes an irreversible process of change in a poignant statement about modern-day organizations: "We are now entering an era of fire, during which old organizational forms, structures, and processes will be consumed and new forms, structures, and processes will emerge." He indicates that these newly emerging organizations have little resemblance to either their premodern or modern-day precursors.

Tapscott and Caston postulate a paradigm shift generated by information technology. This shift has created a new international business environment consisting of open, networked enterprise. They proclaim that "as walls are falling in the political and economic world, today's enterprise is opening up." One organizational embodiment of this new information era is the *virtual organization.* As described by Bleecker, these collaborative networks, composed of combinations of local-area and wide-area computer and communications networks, allow businesses to form, interact, and dissolve relationships instantly. With the use of technology, a single worker can perform the tasks of multiple individuals in an international context without barriers of time and geographic location.

Each author acknowledges that implications for leadership are immense. This uncharted territory requires unparalleled innovative leadership that cannot be an extension or revision of the old models. The authors cause us to consider the question, What forms should this new leadership take to rise to the challenge of the new environment and its accompanying paradigm shift in organizations? Bennis and Nanus's model suggests that the form of leadership that succeeds will be accomplished by those individuals throughout the organization who (a) set direction during turbulent times; (b) manage change while still providing exceptional customer service and quality; (c) attract resources and forge new alliances to accommodate new constituencies; (d) harness diversity on a global scale; (e) inspire a sense of optimism, enthusiasm, and commitment among their followers; and (f) become a leader of leaders, especially regarding knowledge workers.

The challenge for organizational participants is to determine how to develop and prepare individuals for this new model of leadership and effect such leadership with credibility and authenticity. Subsequent sections of the book address leadership theories and concepts on which organizations can base their overall philosophy and approaches as well as leader-participant relations that are appropriate for this new environment.

# 1

# Toward the New Millennium

WARREN BENNIS
BURT NANUS

To this point, we've been examining the lessons of our ninety leaders. We set out to distill the essence of what worked for them as they gained their experience and honed their skills over the past several decades. To mine this lode of information, we've been digging in the past, albeit the recent past. But what's next? What new demands are likely to be made upon leaders in the early part of the next century? Will leaders need new skills and values, and how might they begin to prepare for them?

Here we move to less solid ground, as we speculate on future trends and their implications. Let's start by assuming that leadership will continue to be concerned with marshaling the commitment, energies, and resources of an organization to move it in a particular direction. We expect that most of the time-tested personal characteristics identified in this book—vision, passion, integrity, self-knowledge, empowerment, doing things right—will continue to be important, but perhaps there'll be other factors as well.

The key driver in the twenty-first century is likely to be the speed and turbulence of technological change—a virtual tsunami of change. It makes the future tense. Already we feel the rumbles of a new round of technological eruptions in fields as diverse as genetics, communications, materials, oceanography, medicine, microminiaturization, and entertainment. Technology explodes like nuclear fission, with every new breakthrough triggering others in an accelerating cascade of changes. The effects are pervasive. It's hard to think of any industry or government agency that won't find itself heavily dependent on technology in their operations, products, or services.

The implications for leaders could be profound. Increasingly, they'll have to place high-stakes bets on emerging technologies whose benefits and consequences can be only partly understood in advance, and with considerable uncertainty. But that's just the beginning. As Will Rogers said, "It isn't enough to be on the right track. If you aren't moving you can still get hit by a train."

New technologies begin to grow old the day they're installed. They need constant care and feeding, development, and improvement until the day of reckoning, when a new batch comes on-line. Thus, nurturing technological change and facilitat-

SOURCE: "Toward the New Millennium" from *Leaders: The Strategies for Taking Charge* by Warren Bennis and Burt Nanus (1985). Reprinted by permission of Harper Collins Publishers, Inc.

ing transitions from one generation of product and process technologies to another is likely to become a major challenge and potential cost trap for twenty-first-century leaders.

Bill Gates at Microsoft and Andrew Grove at Intel may only be the leading edge of a new generation of technologically savvy leaders who feel comfortable making these kinds of decisions. Certainly, few leaders will be able to survive without being able to create and sustain organizational cultures in which new technologies are embraced and implemented quickly—time after time. They may well find themselves repeating this prayer from an African-American church: "Lord, we're not what we want to be, we're not what we need to be, we're not what we are going to be, but thank God Almighty, we're not what we used to be."[1]

As Peter Drucker and others have been predicting for some time, most organizations will be filled with knowledge workers. They'll have substantial expertise in their own areas, often beyond that of their so-called leaders, and they'll expect to be free to make decisions in their own areas of competence. They'll exercise considerable influence over their own work and often set their own schedules. Many of them will be leaders themselves, heading project teams or programs, so top executives will have to become what our colleague James O'Toole calls "leaders of leaders."[2] In such a setting, decisions are shaped far less by leadership authority than by collaboration, shared values, and mutual respect.

As the half-life of new knowledge decreases, workers may feel they're constantly being bombarded by changes. Along with added responsibility to act on the organization's behalf, they'll have fewer middle-management buffers to insulate them from the turbulence they experience daily both at work and at home—and fewer safety nets to protect them against the consequences of their mistakes and those of others. All this will make their organizational lives interesting, but also confusing, uncertain, risky, and stressful.

Therefore, the challenge to leaders will be to act as compassionate coaches, dedicated to reducing stress by ensuring that the whole team has everything it needs—from human and financial resources to emotional support and encourage-

ment—to work together effectively and at peak performance most of the time. Recognizing, developing, and celebrating the distinctive skills of each individual will become critically important to organizational survival. In the new global, multicultural workplace where employees have different languages, values, and loyalties, this may well challenge leaders to new heights of interpersonal sensitivity, understanding, and commitment to the best that human diversity has to offer.

Some of the technological changes, especially in computers and communications, could shatter traditional organizational designs. Already we appear to be entering a centrifugal age that is spinning power and decision making out to the perimeters of organizations, wherever in the world an employee "interfaces" with a customer, supplier, or joint-venture partner. Activities are being distributed over space and time, with work going on not just around the clock but around the globe. Increasingly, transactions occur in cyberspace, with information transmitted instantly and simultaneously to all who need to know. Organizations are becoming flatter, less hierarchical, and more intricately networked than ever before.

With these forces at work, people's energies, actions, and ambitions would fly off in every direction without a shared vision to provide a field that can align the many disparate and distributed tasks and units. It will no longer be enough for leaders to issue pious platitudes about innovation while they eviscerate their research departments. Slogans of the week just won't cut it. Leaders will have to be architects and cheerleaders for change—true visionaries who are able to point to destinations that are so desirable and credible that workers will enthusiastically sign on to become partners in making it happen. Though this will be much tougher amid the technologically driven turbulence of the next few decades, it is likely to become the indispensable litmus test of twenty-first-century leadership.

Today, leaders are prized for their ability to downsize, streamline, and turn around organizations that have grown bloated and unwieldy. Tomorrow, they will be expected to create totally new organizational forms that position their enterprises in anticipation of future changes. They'll preside

**TABLE 1.1** Likely Model of Twenty-First-Century Leadership

| *From* | *To . . .* |
|---|---|
| Few leaders, mainly at the top; many managers | Leaders at every level; fewer managers |
| Leading by goal-setting; e.g., by near-term profits, ROI | Leading by vision—new directions for long-term business growth |
| Downsizing, benchmarking for low cost, high quality | Also creating domains of uniqueness, distinctive competencies |
| Reactive/adaptive to change | Anticipative/futures-creative |
| Designer of hierarchical organizations | Designer of flatter, distributed, more collegial organizations; leader as social architect |
| Directing and supervising individuals | Empowering and inspiring individuals, but also facilitating teamwork |
| Information held by few decision makers | Information shared with many, both internally and with outside partners |
| Leader as boss, controlling processes and behaviors | Leader as coach, creating learning organizations |
| Leader as stabilizer, balancing conflicting demands and maintaining the culture | Leader as change agent, creating agenda for change, balancing risks, and evolving the culture and the technology base |
| Leader responsible for developing good managers | Leader also responsible for developing future leaders; serving as leader of leaders |

over endless experiments to discover ways to deliver new benefits or services to clients who may not even know they need them yet. Since no organization can possibly be all things to all people, the leader will be constantly challenged to forge major alliances and partnerships with others to achieve mutual goals. Thus the role of leader as social architect will be expanded, and skills such as negotiation, technology assessment, and design of organizational cultures could grow in importance for aspiring leaders.

All these changes, as summarized in Table 1.1, will create a need for millions of new leaders in the future. In the end, the leaders who succeed best will be those who are best able to (1) set direction during turbulent times; (2) manage change while still providing exceptional customer service and quality; (3) attract resources and forge new alliances to accommodate new constituencies; (4) harness diversity on a global scale; (5) inspire a sense of optimism, enthusiasm, and commitment among their followers; and (6) be a leader of leaders, especially regarding knowledge workers. Leadership in the twenty-first century is not a job for wimps, but then, it never was.

### Notes

1. Cited in Lovett H. Weems, Jr., *Church Leadership* (Nashville: Abingdon Press, 1993), p. 38.

2. James O'Toole, *Leading Change* (San Francisco: Jossey-Bass, 1995).

# 2

# The Corporate
# Identity Crisis

ALVIN TOFFLER

The big corporation was the characteristic business organization of the industrial era. Today several thousand such behemoths, both private and public, bestride the earth, producing a large proportion of all the goods and services we buy.

Seen from the outside they present a commanding appearance. They control vast resources, employ millions of workers, and they deeply influence not merely our economies but our political affairs as well. Their computers and corporate jets, their unmatched ability to plan, to invest, to execute projects on a grand scale, make them seem unshakably powerful and permanent. At a time when most of us feel powerless, they appear to dominate our destinies.

Yet that is not the way they look from the inside, to the men (and a few women) who run these organizations. Indeed, many of our top managers today feel quite as frustrated and powerless as the rest of us. For exactly like the nuclear family, the school, the mass media, and the other key institutions of the industrial age, the corporation is being hurled about, shaken and transformed by the Third Wave of change. And a good many top managers do not know what has hit them.

## Kabuki Currency

The most immediate change affecting the corporation is the crisis in the world economy. For three hundred years Second Wave civilization worked to create an integrated global marketplace. Periodically these efforts were set back by wars, depressions, or other disasters. But each time the world economy recovered, emerging larger and more closely integrated than before.

Today a new crisis has struck. But this one is different. Unlike all previous crises during the industrial era, it involves not only money but the entire energy base of the society. Unlike the crises of the past, it brings inflation and unemployment

SOURCE: From "The Corporate Identity Crisis," in *The Third Wave,* by Alvin Toffler. Copyright © 1980 by Alvin Toffler. By permission of William Morrow & Company, Inc.

simultaneously, not sequentially. Unlike those of the past, it is directly linked to fundamental ecological problems, to an entirely new species of technology, and to the introduction of a new level of communications into the production system. Finally, it is not, as Marxists claim, a crisis of capitalism alone, but one that involves the socialist industrial nations as well. It is, in short, the general crisis of industrial civilization as a whole.

The upheaval in the world economy threatens the survival of the corporation as we know it, throwing its managers into a wholly unfamiliar environment. Thus from the end of World War II until the early 1970s the corporation functioned in a comparatively stable environment. Growth was the key word. The dollar was king. Currencies remained stable for long periods. The postwar financial structure laid in place at Bretton Woods by the capitalist industrial powers, and the COMECON system created by the Soviets, seemed solid. The escalator to affluence was still ascending, and economists were so confident of their ability to predict and control the economic machine that they spoke casually about "fine tuning" it.

Today the phrase evokes only derisive snorts. The President wisecracks that he knows a Georgia fortune-teller who is a better forecaster than the economists. A former Secretary of the Treasury, W. Michael Blumenthal, says that "the economics profession is close to bankruptcy in understanding the present situation—before or after the fact." Standing in the tangled wreckage of economic theory and the rubble of the postwar economic infrastructure, corporate decision-makers face rising uncertainties.

Interest rates zigzag. Currencies gyrate. Central banks buy and sell money by the carload to damp the swings, but the gyrations only grow more extreme. The dollar and the yen perform a Kabuki dance, the Europeans promote their own new currency (quaintly named the "ecu"), while Arabs frantically off-load billions of dollars worth of American paper. Gold prices break all records.

While all of this is occurring, technology and communications restructure world markets, making transnational production both possible and necessary. And to facilitate such operations, a jet-age money system is taking form. A global electronic banking network—impossible before the computer and satellite—now instantaneously links Hong Kong, Manila, or Singapore with the Bahamas, the Cayman Islands, and New York.

This sprawling network of banks, with its Citibanks and Barclays, its Sumitomos and Narodnys, not to mention Crédit Suisse and the National Bank of Abu Dhabi, creates a balloon of "stateless currency"—money and credit outside the control of any individual government—which threatens to blow up in everyone's face.

The bulk of this stateless currency consists of Eurodollars—dollars outside the United States. In 1975, writing about the accelerated growth of Eurodollars, I warned that this new currency has a wild card in the economic game. "Here the 'Euros' contribute to inflation, there they shift the balance of payments in another place they undermine the currency—as they stampede from place to place" across national boundaries. At that time there were an estimated 180 billion such Eurodollars.

By 1978 a panicky *Business Week* was reporting on "the incredible state" of the international finance system and the 180 billion had mushroomed into some 400 billion dollars worth of Eurodollars, Euromarks, Eurofrancs, Euroguilders, and Euroyen. Bankers dealing with the supranational currency were free to issue unlimited credit and—not being required to hold any cash reserves—were able to lend out at bargain-basement rates. Today's estimates put the Eurocurrency total as high as a trillion dollars.

The Second Wave economic system in which the corporation grew up was based on national markets, national currencies, and national governments. This nation-based infrastructure, however, is utterly unable to regulate or contain the new transnational and electronic "Euro-bubble." The structures designed for a Second Wave world are no longer adequate.

Indeed, the entire global framework that stabilized world trade relations for the giant corporations is rattling and in danger of coming apart. The World Bank, the International Monetary Fund (IMF), and the General Agreement on Tariffs and Trade are all under heavy attack. Europeans scramble to bolt together a new structure to be controlled by them. The "less developed countries" on one side, and the Arabs brandishing their petrodollars on the other, clamor for influence in the financial system of tomorrow and speak of creating their own counterparts to the IMF. The dollar is dethroned, and jerks and spasms rip through the world economy.

All this is compounded by erratic shortages and gluts of energy and resources; by rapid changes in the attitudes of consumers, workers, and managers; by rapidly shifting imbalances of trade; and above all by the rising militancy of the nonindustrial world.

This is the volatile, confusing environment in which today's corporations struggle to operate. The managers who run them have no wish to relinquish corporate power. They still battle for profits, production, and personal advancement. But faced with soaring levels of unpredictability, with mounting public criticism and hostile political pressures, our most intelligent managers are questioning the goals, structure, responsibility, the very *raison d'être* of their organizations. Many of our biggest corporations are experiencing something analogous to an identity crisis as they watch the once stable Second Wave framework disintegrate around them.

## The Accelerative Economy

This corporate identity crisis is intensified by the speed at which events are moving. For the very speed of change introduces a new element into management, forcing executives, already nervous in an unfamiliar environment, to make more and more decisions at a faster and faster pace. Response times are honed to a minimum.

At the financial level the speed of transactions is accelerating as banks and other financial institutions computerize. Some banks even relocate geographically to take advantage of time zone differences. Says *Euromoney,* the international bankers' journal, "Time zones can be used as a competitive edge."

In this hotted-up environment, the big corporations are driven almost willy-nilly to invest and borrow in various currencies not on an annual, a ninety-day, or even a seven-day basis, but literally on an overnight or minute-to-minute basis. A new corporate officer has appeared in the executive suite—the "international cash manager," who remains plugged into the worldwide electronic casino twenty-four hours a day, searching for the lowest interest rates, the best currency bargains, the fastest turnaround.[1]

In marketing, a similar acceleration is evident. "Marketers must respond quickly in order to insure survival for tomorrow," declares *Advertising Age,* reporting that "Network TV programmers . . . are accelerating their decisions on killing new TV series that show rating weaknesses. No more waiting six or seven weeks, or a season. . . . Another example: Johnson & Johnson learns that Bristol-Myers is determined to undersell J&J's Tylenol . . . Does J&J adopt a wait-and-see attitude? No. In an amazingly short time, it moves to cut Tylenol's prices in the stores. No more weeks or months for procrastination." The very prose is breathless.

In engineering, in manufacture, in research, in sales, in training, in personnel, in every department and branch of the corporation the same quickening of decision-making can be detected.

And once more we see a parallel process, though less advanced, in the socialist industrial nations. COMECON, which used to revise prices every five years when it issued its five-year plan, has been forced to revise its prices annually in an attempt to keep up with the faster pace. Before long it will be six months, then even less.

The results of this generalized speedup of the corporate metabolism are multiple: shorter product life-cycles, more leasing and renting, more frequent buying and selling, more ephemeral consumption patterns, more fads, more training time for workers (who must continually adjust to new procedures), more frequent changes in contracts, more negotiations and legal work, more pricing changes, more job turnover, more dependence on data, more ad hoc organization—all of it exacerbated by inflation.

The result is a high-stakes, high-adrenaline business environment. Under these escalating pressures it is easy to see why so many businessmen, bankers, and corporate executives wonder what exactly they are doing and why. Brought up with Second Wave certainties, they see the world they knew tearing apart under the impact of an accelerating wave of change.

## The De-Massified Society

Even more mystifying and upsetting for them is the crack-up of the industrial mass society in which they were trained to operate. Second Wave managers were taught that mass production is the most advanced and efficient form of production . . . that a mass market wants standardized goods . . . that mass distribution is essential . . . that "masses" of uniform workers are basically all alike and can be motivated by uniform incentives. The effective manager learned that synchronization, centralization, maximization, and concentration are necessary to achieve his goals. And in a Second Wave environment these assumptions were basically correct.

Today, as the Third Wave strikes, the corporate manager finds all his old assumptions challenged. The mass society itself, for which the corporation was designed, is beginning to de-massify. Not merely information, production, and family life, but the marketplace and the labor market as well are beginning to break into smaller, more varied pieces.

The mass market has split into ever-multiplying, ever-changing sets of mini-markets that demand a continually expanding range of options, models, types, sizes, colors, and customizations. Bell Telephone, which once hoped to put the same black telephone in every American home—and very nearly succeeded—now manufactures some one thousand combinations or permutations of telephone equipment from pink, green, or white phones to phones for the blind, phones for people who have lost the use of their larynx, and explosion-proof phones for construction sites. Department stores, originally designed to massify the market, now sprout "boutiques" under their roofs, and Phyllis Sewell, a vice president of Federated Department Stores, predicts that "we will be going into greater specialization . . . with more different departments."

The fast-increasing variety of goods and services in the high-technology nations is often explained away as an attempt by the corporation to manipulate the consumer, to invent false needs, and to inflate profits by charging a lot for trivial options. No doubt, there is truth to these charges. Yet something deeper is at work. For the growing differentiation of goods or services also reflects the growing diversity of actual needs, values, and lifestyles in a de-massified Third Wave society.

This rising level of social diversity is fed by further divisions in the labor market, as reflected in the proliferation of new occupations, especially in the white-collar and service fields. Newspaper want ads clamor for "Vydec Secretary" or "Minicomputer Programmer," while at a conference on the service professions I watched a psychologist list 68 new occupations from consumer advocate, public defender, and sex therapist to psychochemotherapist and ombudsman.

As our jobs become *less* interchangeable, people do too. Refusing to be treated as interchangeable, they arrive at the workplace with an acute consciousness of their ethnic, religious, professional, sexual, subcultural, and individual differences. Groups that throughout the Second Wave era fought to be "integrated" or "assimilated" into mass society now refuse to melt their differences. They emphasize instead their unique characteristics. And Second Wave corporations, still organized for operation in a mass society, are still uncertain how to cope with this rising tide of diversity among their employees and customers.

Though sharply evident in the United States, social de-massification is progressing rapidly elsewhere as well. In Britain, which once regarded itself as highly homogeneous, ethnic minorities, from Pakistanis, West Indians, Cypriots, and Ugandan Asians to Turks and Spaniards, now intermingle with a native population itself becoming more heterogeneous. Meanwhile, a tidal influx of Japanese, American, German, Dutch, Arab, and African visitors leave in their wake American hamburger stands, Japanese tempura restaurants, and signs in store windows that read "Se Habla Español."

Around the world, ethnic minorities reassert their identities and demand long-denied rights to jobs, income, and advancement in the corporation. Australian Aborigines, New Zealand Maoris, Canadian Eskimos, American Blacks, Chicanos, and even Oriental minorities once regarded as politically passive are on the move. From Maine to the Far West, Native Americans assert "Red Power," demand the restoration of tribal lands, and dicker with the OPEC countries for economic and political support.

Even in Japan, long the most homogeneous of the industrial nations, the signs of de-massification are mounting. An uneducated convict overnight emerges as spokesman for the small minority of Ainu people. The Korean minority grows restless, and sociologist Masaaki Takane of Sophia University says, "I have been haunted by an anxiety . . . Japanese society today is quickly losing its unity and is disintegrating."

In Denmark scattered street fights break out between Danes and immigrant workers and between leather-jacketed motorcyclists and long-haired youth. In Belgium the Walloons, the Flemish, and the Bruxelloises reactivate ancient, indeed preindustrial, rivalries. In Canada Quebec threatens to secede, corporations padlock their headquarters in Montreal, and English-speaking executives throughout the country take crash courses in French.

The forces that made mass society have suddenly been thrown into reverse. Nationalism in the high technology context becomes regionalism instead. The pressures of the melting pot are replaced by the new ethnicity. The media, instead of creating a mass culture, de-massify it. In turn all these developments parallel the emerging diversity of energy forms and the advance beyond mass production.

All these interrelated changes create a totally new framework within which the production organizations of society, whether called corporations or socialist enterprises, will function. Executives who continue to think in terms of the mass society are shocked and confused by a world they no longer recognize.

### Redefining the Corporation

What deepens the identity crisis of the corporation still further is the emergence, against this already unsettling background, of a worldwide movement demanding not merely modest changes in this or that corporate policy that a deep redefinition of its purposes.

In the United States, writes David Ewing, an editor of the *Harvard Business Review,* "public anger at corporations is beginning to well up at a frightening rate." Ewing cites a 1977 study by a research affiliate of the Harvard Business School whose findings, he says, "sent tremors throughout the corporate world." The study revealed that about half of all consumers polled believe they are getting worse treatment in the marketplace than they were a decade earlier; three fifths say that products have deteriorated; over half mistrust product guarantees. Ewing quotes a worried businessman as saying, "It feels like sitting on a San Andreas fault."

Worse yet, Ewing continues, "growing numbers of people are not simply disenchanted, irritated or angry, but . . . irrationally and erratically afraid of new technologies and business ventures."

According to John C. Biegler, an executive of Price Waterhouse, one of the giant blue-chip accounting firms, "Public confidence in the American corporation is lower than at any time since the Great Depression. American business and the accounting profession are being called on the carpet for a kind of zero-based rejustification of just about everything we do. . . . Corporate performance is being measured against new and unfamiliar norms."

Similar tendencies are visible in Scandinavia, Western Europe, and even, *sotto voce,* in the socialist industrial nations. In Japan, as Toyota's official magazine puts it, "A citizens' movement of a type never before seen in Japan is gradually gathering momentum, one that criticizes the way corporations disrupt everyday life."

Certainly corporations have come under scorching attack at other times in their history. Much of today's clamor of complaint, however, is crucially different and arises from the emerging values and assumptions of Third Wave civilization, not the dying industrial past.

Throughout the Second Wave era corporations have been seen as economic units, and the attacks on them have essentially focused on economic issues. Critics assailed them for underpaying workers, overcharging customers, forming cartels to fix prices, making shoddy goods, and a thousand other economic transgressions. But no matter how violent, most of these critics accepted the corporation's self-definition: They shared the view of the corporation as an inherently economic institution.

Today's corporate critics start from a totally different premise. They attack the artificial divorce of economics from politics, morality, and the other dimensions of life. They hold the corporation increasingly responsible, not merely for its economic performance but for its side effects on everything from air pollution to executive stress. Corporations are thus assailed for asbestos poisoning, for using poor populations as guinea pigs in drug testing, for distorting the development of the nonindustrial world, for racism and sexism, for secrecy and deception. They are pilloried for supporting unsavory regimes or political parties, from the fascist generals in Chile and the racists in South Africa to the Communist party in Italy.

What is at issue here is not whether such charges are justified—all too often they are. What is far more important is the concept of the corporation they imply. For the Third Wave brings with it a rising demand for a new kind of institution altogether—a corporation no longer responsible simply for making a profit or producing goods but for simultaneously contributing to the solution of extremely complex ecological, moral, political, racial, sexual, and social problems.

Instead of clinging to a sharply specialized economic function, the corporation, prodded by criticism, legislation, and its own concerned executives, is becoming a multipurpose institution.

## A Pentagon of Pressures

The redefinition is not a matter of choice but a necessary response to five revolutionary changes in the actual conditions of production. Changes in the physical environment, in the lineup of social forces, in the role of information, in government organization, and in morality are all pounding the corporation into a new, multifaceted, multipurposeful shape.

The first of these new pressures springs from the biosphere.

In the mid-1950s, when the Second Wave reached its mature stage in the United States, world population stood at only 2.75 billion. Today it is over 4 billion. In the mid-1950s the earth's population used a mere 87 quadrillion Btu of energy a year. Today we use over 260 quadrillion. In the mid-50s, our consumption of a key raw material like zinc was only 2.7 million metric tons a year. Today it is 5.6 million.

Measured any way we choose, our demands on the planet are escalating wildly. As a result the biosphere is sending us alarm signals—pollution, desertification, signs of toxification in the oceans, subtle shifts in climate—that we ignore at the risk of catastrophe. These warnings tell us we can no longer organize production as we did during the Second Wave past.

Because the corporation is the main organizer of economic production, it is also a key "producer" of environmental impacts. If we want to continue our economic growth—indeed if we wish to survive— the managers of tomorrow will have to assume responsibility for converting the corporation's environmental impacts from negatives into positives. They will assume this added responsibility voluntarily or they will be compelled to do so, for the changed conditions of the biosphere make it necessary. The corporation is being transformed into an environmental, as well as an economic, institution—not by do-gooders, radicals, ecologists, or government bureaucrats, but by a material change in the relationship of production to the biosphere.

The second pressure springs from a little-noticed change in the social environment in which the corporation finds itself. That environment is now far more organized than before. At one time each firm operated in what might be termed an underorganized society. Today the socio-sphere, especially in the United States, has leaped to a new level of organization. It is packed with a writhing, interacting mass of well-organized, often well-funded, associations, agencies, trade unions, and other groupings.

In the United States today, some 1,370,000 companies interact with well over 90,000 schools and universities, 330,000 churches, and hundreds of thousands of branches of 13,000 national organizations, plus countless purely local environmental, social, religious, athletic, political, ethnic, and civic groups, each with its own agenda and priorities. It takes 144,000 law firms to mediate all these relationships!

In this densely crowded socio-sphere, every corporate action has repercussive impacts not merely on lonely or helpless individuals but on organized groups, many of them with professional staffs, a press of their own, access to the political system, and resources with which to hire experts, lawyers, and other assistance.

In this finely strung socio-sphere, corporate decisions are closely scrutinized. "Social pollution" produced by the corporation in the form of unemployment, community disruption, forced mobility, and the like is instantly spotted, and pressures are placed on the corporation to assume far greater responsibility than ever before for its social, as well as economic "products."

A third set of pressures reflects the changed info-sphere. Thus, the de-massification of society means that far more information must be exchanged between social institutions—including the corporation—to maintain equilibrial relationships among them. Third Wave production methods further intensify the corporation's hunger for information as raw material. The firm thus sucks up data like a gigantic vacuum cleaner, processes it, and disseminates it to others in increasingly complex ways. As information becomes central to production, as "information managers" proliferate in industry, the corporation, by necessity, impacts on the informational environment exactly as it impacts on the physical and social environment.

The new importance of information leads to conflict over the control of corporate data—battles over disclosure of more information to the public, demands for open accounting (of oil company production and profit figures, for example), more pressures for "truth in advertising," or "truth in lending." For in the new era, "information impacts" become as serious a matter as environmental and social impacts, and the corporation is seen as an information producer as well as an economic producer.

A fourth pressure on the corporation arises from politics and the power-sphere. The rapid diversification of society and the acceleration of change are everywhere reflected in a tremendous complexification of government. The differentiation of society is mirrored in the differentiation of government, and each corporation must therefore interact with more and more specialized units of government. These units, badly coordinated and each with its own priorities, are, moreover, in a perpetual turmoil of reorganization.

Jayne Baker Spain, a senior vice-president of Gulf Oil, has pointed out that as recently as ten or fifteen years ago, "There was no EPA. There was no EEOC. There was no ERISSA. There was no OSHA. There was no ERDA. There was no FEA." All these and many other government agencies have sprouted up since then.

Every company thus finds itself increasingly ensnarled in politics—local, regional, national, or even transnational. Conversely, every important corporate decision "produces" at least indirect political effects along with its other output, and is increasingly held responsible for them.

Finally, as Second Wave civilization wanes and its value system shatters, a fifth pressure arises, affecting all institutions—including the corporation. This is a heightened moral pressure. Behavior once accepted as normal is suddenly reinterpreted as corrupt, immoral, or scandalous. Thus the Lockheed bribes topple a government in Japan. Olin Corporation is indicted for shipping arms to South Africa. Gulf Oil's chairman is forced to resign in the wake of a bribery scandal. The reluctance of Distillers Company in Britain to repay the victims of Thalidomide adequately, the failures of McDonnell Douglas with respect to the DC-10—all trigger tidal waves of moral revulsion.

The ethical stance of the corporation is increasingly seen as having a direct impact on the value system of the society, just as significant to some as the corporation's impact on the physical environment or the social system. The corporation is increasingly seen as a "producer" of moral effects.

These five sweeping changes in both the material and nonmaterial conditions of production makes untenable the Second Wave school-book notion that a corporation is nothing but an economic institution. Under the new conditions the corporation can no longer operate as a machine for maximizing some economic function—whether production or profit. The very definition of "production" is being drastically expanded to include the side, as well as the central, effects, the long-range as well as the immediate effects, of corporate action. Put simply, every corporation has more "products" (and is now held responsible for more) than Second Wave managers ever had to consider—environmental, social, informational, political, and moral, not just economic products.

The purpose of the corporation is thus changed from singular to plural—not just at the level of rhetoric or public relations but at the level of identity and self-definition as well.

In corporation after corporation we can expect to see an internal battle between those who cleave to the single-purpose corporation of the Second Wave past and those who are ready to cope with the Third Wave conditions of production and to fight for the multipurpose corporation of tomorrow.

### The Multipurpose Corporation

Those of us brought up in Second Wave civilization have a difficult time thinking of institutions in this way. We find it hard to think of a hospital as having economic as well as medical functions, a school as having political as well as educational functions—or a corporation as having powerful noneconomic or "trans-economic" functions. That recently retired exemplar of Second Wave thinking, Henry Ford II, insists that the corporation "is a specialized instrument designed to serve the economic needs of society and is not well equipped to serve social needs unrelated to its business operations." But while Ford and other defenders of the Second Wave resist the redefinition of the production organization, many firms are, in fact, altering both their words and their policies.

Lip service and public relations rhetoric often substitute for real change. Fancy promotional brochures proclaiming a new era of social responsibility very often camouflage a robber-baron rapacity. Nevertheless, a fundamental "paradigm shift"—a reconceptualization—of the structure, goals, and responsibilities of the corporation is taking place

in response to new pressures brought by the Third Wave. The signs of this change are numerous.

Amoco, a leading oil company, for example, states that "it is the policy of our company, with respect to plant locations, to supplement the routine economic evaluation with a detailed exploration of the social consequences. . . . We look at many factors, among them the impact on the physical environment, the impact on public facilities . . . and the impact on local employment conditions, particularly with respect to minorities." Amoco continues to weight economic considerations most heavily, but it assigns importance to other factors as well. And where alternative locations are similar in economic terms but "different in terms of the social impact," these social factors can prove decisive.

In the event of a merger proposal, the directors of Control Data Corporation, a top U.S. computer manufacturer, explicitly take into account not merely financial or economic considerations but "all relevant" factors—including the social effects of the merger and its impact on employees and the communities in which Control Data operates. And while other companies have been racing into the suburbs, Control Data has deliberately built its new plants in inner-city areas of Washington, St. Paul, and Minneapolis, to help provide employment for minorities and to help revive urban centers. The corporation states its mission as "improving the quality, equality, and potential of people's lives"—*equality* being an unorthodox goal for a corporation.

In the United States, the advancement of women and nonwhites has become a long overdue matter of national policy, and some companies go so far as to reward their managers financially for meeting "affirmative action" targets. At Pillsbury, a leading food company, each of its three product groups must present not only a sales plan for the following year but a plan relating to the hiring, training, and promotion of women and minority group members. Executive incentives are linked to the attainment of these social goals. At AT&T all managers are evaluated annually. Fulfillment of affirmative action objectives counts as part of a positive appraisal. At Chemical Bank in New York, 10 to 15 percent of a branch manager's job performance appraisal is based on her or his social performance—sitting on community agency boards, making loans to not-for-profit organizations, hiring and upgrading minorities. And at the Gannett chain of newspapers, chief executive Allen Neuharth brusquely tells editors and local publishers that "a major portion" of their bonuses will "be determined on the basis of progress in these . . . programs."

Similarly, in many top corporations we see a distinct upgrading of the status and influence of executives concerned with the environmental consequences of corporate behavior. Some now report directly to the president. Other companies have set up special committees on the board of directors to define the new corporate responsibilities.

This social responsiveness of the corporation is not all substance. Says Rosemary Bruner, director of community affairs at Hoffmann-LaRoche's American subsidiary, "Some of this is pure public relations, of course. Some is self-serving. But much of it actually does reflect a changed perception of corporate functions." Grudgingly, therefore, driven by protests, lawsuits, and fear of government action as well as by more laudable motives, managers are beginning to adapt to the new conditions of production and are accepting the idea that the corporation has multiple purposes.

### Many Bottom Lines

The multipurpose corporation that is emerging demands, among other things, smarter executives. It implies a management capable of specifying multiple goals, weighting them, interrelating them, and finding synergic policies that accomplish more than a single goal at a time. It requires policies that optimize not for one, but for several variables simultaneously. Nothing could be further from the single-minded style of the traditional Second Wave manager.

Moreover, once the need for multiple goals is accepted we are compelled to invent new measures of performance. Instead of the single "bottom line" on which most executives have been taught to fixate, the Third Wave corporation requires attention to multiple bottom lines—social, environmental, informational, political, and ethical bottom lines—all of them interconnected.

Faced with this new complexity, many of today's managers are taken aback. They lack the intellectual tools necessary for Third Wave management. We know how to measure the profitability of a corporation, but how do we measure or evaluate the achievement of noneconomic goals? Price Waterhouse's John C. Biegler says, managers "are being asked to account for corporate behavior in areas where no real standards of accountability have been established—where even the language of accountability has yet to be developed."

This explains today's efforts to develop a new language of accountability. Indeed, accounting itself is on the edge of revolution and is about to explode out of its narrowly economic terms of reference.

The American Accounting Association, for example, has issued reports of a "Committee on Non-Financial Measures of Effectiveness" and of a "Committee on Measures of Effectiveness for Social Programs." So much work is being done along these lines that each of these reports lists nearly 250 papers, monographs, and documents in its bibliography.

In Philadelphia, a consulting firm called the Human Resources Network is working with twelve major U.S. corporations to develop cross-industry methods for specifying what might be called the "trans-economic" goals of the corporation. It is trying to integrate these goals into corporate planning and to find ways of measuring the company's trans-economic performance. In Washington, meanwhile, the Secretary of Commerce, Juanita Kreps, raised a storm of controversy by suggesting that the government itself should prepare a "Social Performance Index," which she described as a "mechanism companies could use to assess their performance and its social consequences."

Parallel work is under way in Europe. According to Meinolf Dierkes and Rob Coppock of the Berlin-based International Institute for Environment and Society, "Many large and medium-sized companies in Europe have been experimenting with [the social report] concept. . . . In the Federal Republic of Germany, for example, about 20 of the largest firms now publish social reports regularly.

In addition, more than a hundred others draw up social reports for internal management purposes."

Some of these reports are no more than puff-accounts of the corporation's "good works," carefully overlooking controversial problems like pollution. But others are remarkably open, objective, and tough. Thus a social report issued by the giant Swiss food firm, Migros-Genossenschafts-Bund, self-critically confesses that it pays women less than men, that many of its jobs are "extremely boring," and that its nitrous dioxide emissions have risen over a four-year period. Says the company's managing director, Pierre Arnold, "It takes courage for an enterprise to point out the differences between its goals and its actual results."

Companies like STEAG and the Saarbergwerke AG have pioneered the effort to relate company expenditures to specific social benefits. Less formally, companies like Bertelsmann AG, the publishers; Rank Xerox GmbH, the copier firm; and Hoechst AG, the chemical manufacturer, have radically broadened the kind of social data they make available to the public.

A much more advanced system is employed by companies in Sweden and Switzerland and by Deutsche Shell AG in Germany. The latter, instead of publishing an annual report, now issues what it calls an *Annual and Social Report* in which both economic and trans-economic data are interrelated. The method used by Shell, termed "goal accounting and reporting" by Dierkes and Coppock, stipulates concrete economic, environmental, and social goals for the corporation, spells out the actions taken to achieve them, and reports the expenditures allocated to them.

Shell also lists five overall corporate goals—only one of which is to achieve a "reasonable return on investment"—and specifically states that each of the five goals, economic and noneconomic, must "carry the same weight" in corporate decision-making. The goal accounting method forces companies to make their trans-economic objectives explicit, to specify time periods for their attainment, and to open this up to public review.

On a broader theoretical level, Trevor Gambling, professor of accounting at the University of Birmingham in the United Kingdom, in a book called *Societal Accounting* has called for a radical reformulation of accounting that begins to integrate the work of economists and accountants with that of the social scientists who have developed social indicators and methods of social accounting.

In Holland the Dean of the Graduate School of Management in Delft, Cornelius Brevoord, has designed a set of multidimensional criteria for monitoring corporate behavior. This is made necessary, he suggests, by deep value changes in the society, among them the change from "an economic production orientation" in society to "a total well-being orientation." Similarly, he notes a shift from "functional specialization to an interdisciplinary approach." Both these changes strengthen the need for a more rounded concept of the corporation.

Brevoord lists 32 different criteria by which a corporation must measure its effectiveness. These range over its relationships with consumers, shareholders, and unions to those with ecology organizations and its own management. But, he points out, even these 32 are only "a few" of the parameters along which the emerging corporation of the future will test itself.

With the Second Wave economic infrastructure in a shambles, with change accelerating as de-massification spreads, with the bio-sphere sending danger signals, with the level of organization in society rising, and the informational, political, and ethical conditions of production changing, the Second Wave corporation is obsolete.

What is happening, therefore, is a thoroughgoing reconceptualization of the meaning of production and of the institution that, until now, has been charged with organizing it. The result is a complex shift to a new-style corporation of tomorrow. In the words of William Halal, professor of management at American University, "Just as the feudal manor was replaced by the business corporation when agrarian societies were transformed into industrial societies, so too should the older model of the firm be replaced by a new form of economic institution." This new institution will combine economic and trans-economic objectives. It will have multiple bottom lines.

The transformation of the corporation is part of the larger transformation of the socio-sphere as a whole, and this in turn parallels the dramatic changes in the techno-sphere and info-sphere. Taken together, they add up to a massive historical shift. But we are not merely altering these giant structures. We are also changing the way ordinary people, in their daily lives, behave. For when we change the deep structure of civilization, we simultaneously rewrite all the codes by which we live.

## *Note*

1. Nor is this function trivial. Like farmers who make more from selling land than from growing food, some major corporations are making more profit—or racking up greater losses—from currency and financial manipulation than from actual production.

*3*

# From the Pendulum to the Fire

## Coming to Terms With Irreversible Change

WILLIAM BERGQUIST

If Western Civilization does go down, irrevocably, the last figures to be seen above the floodwaters will have pencil and notebook in hand, as they busily conduct an investigation of what is happening. No. We need to understand our ailing visions in order to know what to reject and what to accept in them, but all our study is only a preliminary clearing of the decks for the urgent vision-work of creating tomorrow. Self-analysis is only meaningful if it liberates us to choose our own destiny. Man has the capacity to dream finer dreams than he has ever succeeded in dreaming. He has the capacity to build a finer society than he has ever succeeded in building. We have always known this. Must this knowledge paralyze us? Here lies the real challenge! There are among us even now dreamers and builders ready to repeat the age-old process of splitting the atom of time, to release the Western world from its too-long imprisonment in the present. Then man will once again be free to "seek the city which is to come."

*Fred Polak, The Image of the Future*

SOURCE: From *The Postmodern Organization: Mastering the Art of Irreversible Change,* by William Bergquist, pp. 1-14. Copyright 1993 Jossey-Bass Inc., Publishers. Reprinted with permission.

Contemporary organizational theory—for that matter, most organizational theory of the past century—is built on a solid, mechanistic foundation. Organizations operate like other systems; they import resources from the outside (such as raw materials, employees, capital, sales orders, and customers), effect some sort of transformation on them (such as converting iron to automobiles or untrained children to properly educated citizens), and export the transformed products to other organizations located in the external world. Under the best of circumstances, organizations operate like a carefully designed and crafted Swiss watch. At other times, unfortunately, organizations appear ill managed and ill equipped to deal with a highly turbulent world. Nevertheless, even under conditions of turbulence, we expect contemporary organizations to somehow come to terms with this external world, and we speak of searching for equilibrium and homeostasis in a volatile environment.

The mechanistic organization, in essence, runs like a pendulum, which epitomizes elegance and simplicity in motion. We can disrupt the course of the pendulum by giving it an added push or by bumping into it and slowing it down. In either case, the pendulum will adjust its course and continue swinging back and forth at a greater or lesser magnitude. The pendulum, in modern systems theory terms, always returns to a homeostatic balance, retaining its basic form or pathway.

According to many contemporary theorists, organizations are homeostatic in nature. They tend to return to their previous form and function after disruptions and interferences. While the contemporary organization may seem to be chaotic and in disarray, we are merely witnessing a long-term process of homeostatic readjustment, with an ultimate return to a former state or style of functioning.

### Fire and Second-Order Change in Organizations

Is this mechanistic analogy to the pendulum still accurate for contemporary organizations? Was it ever very accurate, for that matter? Ilya Prigogine, a Nobel Prize-winning scientist, suggests that many processes in nature do not work mechanisti-cally—as much as scientists throughout the ages have wanted the world to resemble the orderly pendulum or Swiss watch (Prigogine and Stengers, 1984). Rather, many processes of the world more likely resemble the phenomenon we call fire.

Fire is an enduring problem in the history of science. Prigogine (Prigogine and Stengers, 1984) notes that modern scientists, in an effort to create a coherent mechanistic model of the world, have tended to ignore the complex, transformative processes of fire, concentrating on only one of its properties: the capacity to generate heat. Fire became a heat-producing machine for scientists and was thus treated in a mechanistic manner.

Fire, however, has many fascinating properties. Most important, it is an irreversible process: it consumes something that cannot be reconstructed. Homes lost in a fire can never be unburned; a community destroyed by fire can never be readjusted. There is only the construction of new homes and a new community, which will never exactly replicate the old homes or community. Many other processes of change and transformation are similarly irreversible. Avalanches can never be undone, nor can Pandora's box ever be closed once the lid is opened and the evil spirits have escaped.

The process of change in organizations often operates like fire. We blurt out organizational truths in moments of frustration or anger and can never cover them up again. We tentatively consider a change in organizational structure, but the word gets out and we are soon stuck with the change whether we like it or not. Equilibrium has been disturbed, chaos often follows, and we ourselves are not the same as we were before. Time moves in one direction and cannot be reversed.

A second remarkable characteristic of fire is its ephemeral nature. It is all process and not much substance. As Prigogine notes, the Newtonian sciences concentrated on substances and the ways in which various forces operated on various substances. The Newtonian world was governed by a "science of being." Fire, by contrast, is a "science of becoming" (Prigogine and Stengers, 1984, p. 209). A science of being, argues Prigogine, focuses on the states of a system, whereas a science of becoming focuses on temporal changes—such as the flickering of a flame. Fire demands a focus not on the outcomes of a process but rather on the nature of the process itself.

Much as children focus on their process of drawing when showing their parents a picture they have made, so must we focus on organizational processes, for example, ways in which decisions are made in organizations or styles used to manage employees, rather than focusing on the final decisions that are made or the relative success of an employee's performance. Unfortunately, organizational processes (like fires) are elusive. They are hard to measure and even harder to document in terms of their ultimate impact on an organization.

Pendulums operate in a quite different manner from fires. First of all, the movement of a pendulum is quite predictable, whereas that of fire is unpredictable (as in the case of most dynamic systems). Once we know the initial parameters of the pendulum (length of stem, force applied when pendulum is first pushed in a specific direction, and so forth), we can predict virtually everything of importance about this mechanistic and relatively closed system. Even without any initial information, we can readily predict the future movement of the pendulum after observing its trajectory once or twice.

A second important feature of the pendulum—one that makes it a particular favorite of many modern scientists—is its primary connection to one of the central building blocks of Newtonian science: gravity. While fire seems to defy or at least be indifferent to gravity, flickering about apparently weightless and formless, our noble pendulum provides clear evidence that gravity is present and that it operates in a uniform and predictable manner on objects of substance. The pendulum is a tool that is readily transformed into a technology (for example, the Swiss watch), based on its dependability and conceptual accessibility. Fire, by contrast, can burn and rage uncontrolled. Once started, fires tend to take on a life of their own, seemingly defying the laws of entropy. Pendulums are domestic and obey the laws of entropy. They stop when they receive inadequate attention and never rage out of control.

A third feature of the pendulum is the reversibility of its process. The pendulum swings back and forth, repeatedly moving back to a space that it occupied a short time before. The pendulum, like many mechanistic systems, frequently undoes what has already been done in order for the system to remain in equilibrium and in operation. A pendulum that swung in only one direction (to but not fro) would soon be replaced by one that works properly.

Organizations that operate like pendulums seem to be everywhere (though they are becoming less common). An organization shifts in one direction, then soon corrects itself and shifts back in the opposite direction. Large inventories are soon corrected by a drop in production orders. Later, production orders are increased to make up for a drop in inventory. In organizations that resemble pendulums, homeostasis is always preserved—eventually. The organization keeps returning to an ideal or at least minimally acceptable state. Homeorhesis (a Greek word referring to the tendency to return to a common pathway or style) is also preserved. The organization monitors, reviews, and readjusts its mode of operation in order to return to a desired path, style, or strategy.

Gregory Bateson (1979), the exceptional biologist and anthropologist, speaks of this process as "first-order" change. In essence, a first-order change occurs when people in an organization do more of something that they are already doing or less of something that they are already doing as a way of returning to some desired state of being (homeostasis). We spend more money on a computer system in order to reduce our customer response time to a former level. We reduce the cost of a specific product in order to restore our competitive edge in the marketplace. We pay our employees higher wages in order to bring back high-level morale and productivity to the company. First-order changes are always reversible because we can go back to the drawing board and repeatedly readjust our change effort, using feedback systems that provide us with information about how we are performing relative to our standard or goal.

Bateson identifies "second-order" change as a process that is irreversible. A second-order change occurs when we decide to (or are forced to) do something different from what we have done before, rather than just doing more or less of what we have already been doing. A second-order change occurs when an organization chooses to provide a new kind of compensation, rather than merely increasing or decreasing current levels and rates of compensation. Rather than paying more money or less money, I pay my employees with something other than money (for example, stock in the company, greater autonomy, or a new and more thoughtful mode of personal recognition and appreciation). Second-order change happens when I choose not to increase or decrease my rate of communication with my subordinates (first-order change), but rather to communicate something different to my subordinates from what I have ever communicated to them before. In other words, rather than talking more or talking less about something, I talk about something different.

In the case of any second-order change, there is a choice point when an organization begins to move in a new direction. Once this choice point (what systems theorists call the point of "bifurcation" and what poets call the "fork in the road"), is traversed, there is no turning back. Once the fire has begun, one cannot unburn what has already been consumed. One can extinguish the fire, but a certain amount of damage has already been done and a certain amount of warmth has already been generated. Once I have changed the way in which I compensate my employees, there is no turning back (as many leaders have found in their unionized organizations).

In summary, the idea of reversibility and irreversibility of organizational change relates directly to the concepts of pendulums and fires, and first- and second-order change. just as some changes are first order and others are second order, and some look like the period adjustment of a pendulum while others look like fire, so it is the case that some changes appear to be reversible and others are irreversible. Those organizational change processes that are reversible involve the restoration of balance or style. They typically are first order in nature and resemble the dynamics of a pendulum. Other organizational change processes are irreversible. They bring about transformation and parallel the combustive processes of fire, rather than the mechanical processes of the pendulum. Second-order change is typically associated with these irreversible processes of combustion.

Throughout this book, I explore the nature of irreversible, second-order changes in our emerging postmodern world. The implications of organizational irreversibility are profound, for major problems often emerge when organizational fires are mistaken for organizational pendulums. The 1991 Soviet coup, for instance, appears to exemplify an irreversible, combustible form of change. Whereas the coup leaders thought that the Soviet Union would continue to operate as a pendulum, with each new group of leaders restoring the government to its previous state, the people on the streets saw an opportunity to kindle a fire—a second-order change. Their new order of things was not one of restoration, but rather one of transformation. Whatever happens in the old Soviet Union, there will never be a return to the prior order. The toothpaste can't be shoved back into the tube. The story cannot be untold.

## Poised on the Edge of Order and Chaos

In a recent article, Stuart Kauffman (1991) introduces a new concept of chaos and order. He describes three different categories—or states—in which many systems (perhaps even organizations) can be placed. One of these states is highly ordered and structured. Kauffman uses an analogy between this state and the solid state that water takes when it is frozen. A second state is highly chaotic and disorderly. Kauffman equates this state with the gaseous form water takes when it is evaporating. The third (most interesting) state is one of transition between order and chaos, which Kauffman identifies with the liquid state of water (though he notes that true liquids are not transitory in nature but are instead a distinct form of matter). The differentiation between solid, gaseous, and liquid networks can be of significant value in setting the context for any discussion of postmodernism in organizations—and, in particular, the irreversibility of many organizational processes. We must look not only at ordered networks (the so-called solid state) and at chaotic networks (the so-called gaseous state) but also at liquid networks that hover on the brink of chaos if we are to understand and influence our unique postmodern institutions.

The third (liquid) state holds particularly great potential when we examine and seek to understand confusing and often elusive organizational phenomena such as mission, leadership, and communication. Turbulent rivers, avalanches, shifting weather patterns, and other conditions that move between order and chaos typify the liquid state. Liquid systems contain chaotic elements as well as elements of stability. There are both quiet pools and swirling eddies in a turbulent river; mountain avalanches consist not only of rapidly moving volumes of snow but also of stable snowpacks; stable and chaotic weather patterns intermingle to form overall climatic patterns on our planets. The liquid state is characterized by edges and shifting boundaries. A liquid, edgy state is filled with the potential for learning.

How is a liquid state formed? At certain points in the life of solid-state systems, the system reaches a supercritical state and can no longer adjust to additional change or variation in pattern. The snowpack grows larger with each additional snowflake. At some critical point, the snowpack can no longer grow larger. At this point, the system becomes fluid and an avalanche occurs. Once the avalanche has stopped, the snowpack (now further down the hill) assumes a new form (as a function of the landscape at this location on the hill) and is once again stable. The system (snowpack) can once again adjust to the addition of a few changes or alterations in pattern (additional snowflakes).

I suggest that most organizations exist in the liquid state, poised on the edge of chaos. Furthermore, organizations are mechanisms that can learn and adjust (through first-order change). Yet, at a supercritical stage, organizations can no longer adjust; they can no longer accept even one additional change or one additional crisis. An avalanche begins, and the organization changes in a profound manner (a second-order change). The theory of self-organized criticality (Bak and Chen, 1991), or weak chaos, suggests that small events (first-order changes), such as a shift in leadership, will usually produce only minor alterations in the structure and dynamics of the organization (the snowpack will grow a bit wider or a bit deeper with each new snowflake). Sometimes, however, a change in leadership will create a major second-

order alteration (an avalanche). Furthermore, while the outcomes are dramatically different, Bak and Chen propose that the same processes initiate both the minor and major changes and that the onset of the major event cannot be predicted—in part because the same process brings about both outcomes (one snowflake will add to the snowpack, while a second snowflake will precipitate an avalanche).

The liquid state and the edge are places of leadership and innovation ("the leading edge"). They are settings where things get done, often in the context of a very challenging and exhausting "white water" environment (Vaill, 1989; Quehl, 1991). Edges have no substance; they come to a point and then disappear. Perhaps this is what the new postmodern edginess—what Milan Kundera (1984) calls "the unbearable lightness of being"— is all about.

We must learn how to live and work in this new world of edges. Perhaps we need to listen to the architects and prophets of postmodernism, for they may provide some valuable clues as to how this world might best be faced. These architects and prophets come in many different forms: deconstructionists, feminists, chaos theorists, structuralists. This book is devoted, in part, to the examination of these postmodernists as they might help inform and revise our assumptions about the nature, purpose, and dynamics of the organizations in which we live and work.

I propose that we are poised on the edge of order and chaos in our contemporary organizations— that an avalanche has already taken place and the new form of the snowpack is already defined (though obviously some major adjustments are still occurring as the snowpack settles into the new landscape). We may have entered a new, distinct, and long-lasting postmodern era that in many ways—like the avalanche—is irreversible. Alternatively, we may be living in a short-term transitional period, having left the modern era forever; the avalanche, in other words, is now under way and we are living in it. If this is the case, then we have not yet settled into a new era but are instead living temporarily in an intermediate stage on the edge of something that we cannot yet know, let alone describe.

Regardless of which perspective one wishes to take, the process seems to be irreversible. While the past fifty years might best be described as an era of adjustment (the modern-day organizational pendulum), we are now entering an era of fire, during which old organizational forms, structures, and processes will be consumed and new forms, structures, and processes will emerge, like the phoenix, from the ashes of fiery consumption. This new era, however, will not be composed entirely of new organizational elements; rather, it will offer a blend of very old, premodern elements of our society, modern-day elements of out society (as exemplified by many organizations that reached their zenith during the second half of the twentieth century), and newly emerging elements that bear little similarity to either their premodern or modern-day precursors.

### Poised on the Edge of Postmodernism

We are currently poised on the edge of a newly emerging, complex world that many social observers have labeled *postmodern*. This is a particularly exciting and challenging time, for the edges of large social systems have always been the primary source of activity and information in defining the nature of cultures and societies. We can best understand an organization—or any other large or small social system—by examining its edges and the ways it interacts with other components of its environment. Consider the "edginess" of the emerging postmodern era to be not simply a restatement of the modern-day "age of anxiety" but rather as a sign of the potential that confronts us in our information-rich world.

Postmodernists encourage us to identify differences that truly make a difference in our world. We must discard that which is superficially interesting but transitory and determine that which we individually and collectively should attend to at any point in time. Information derived from the identification of differences becomes critical to any leader or manager in a postmodern organization. Many organizational theorists are coming to recognize the importance of detecting change and difference. When change and differences are very grad-

ual or when they are noticed after considerable delay, it is often too late to respond to them, leaving the organization in an exceptionally vulnerable position. We have only to look at the American auto industry or, more broadly, the world's ecology to appreciate the devastating effect of delayed recognition of a problematic change. The need for sensitivity to change and to differences-that-make-a-difference offers a considerable challenge for many men and women in postmodern organizations, given that we have been trained and rewarded primarily for noticing and encouraging nondifferences (that is, conformity to preestablished standards). In this book, I focus on differences that I believe do make a difference. These are differences not only in terms of premodern, modern, and postmodern elements of contemporary organizations but also in terms of alternative perspectives in examining the essential nature and purpose of all organizations at any point in time.

We also find the edges of postmodernism in the complex interplay between order and chaos. Everywhere we look in contemporary organizational life, we find order and chaos existing side by side. Sometimes organizations seem to make sense. The policies and procedures look right (at least on paper), and things seem to be moving along in a predictable manner. At other times, everything seems to be fragmented and chaotic. Nothing makes any sense in the organization, and one wonders if the center can hold. Postmodern theorists (especially those who are studying chaotic systems) suggest that these seemingly contradictory observations are actually a result of examining the organization at different levels (a spatial perspective) and at different points in its history (a temporal perspective).

Organizations (like virtually all other systems) contain layers and moments of both chaos and order. When confronted with a seemingly chaotic and unpredictable organization, we have only to move up one level (to greater abstraction) or down one level (to greater specificity) if we wish to find order. Alternatively, we have only to move backward or forward in time to find either order or chaos. For instance, the behavior of members of a specific department may make more sense if we examine the overall dynamics of the department, rather than just looking at their individual behavior. Organizational theorists now tell us about the deskilling of personnel that often occurs in organizations and the ways in which this deskilling contributes to stability. We have only to look back through the history of the organization and its culture to understand the orderly nature of and reason for this deskilling.

Similarly, we can move up or down levels of analysis to find chaos in an organization that seems to be orderly. The operation of a ballet or theater company, for example, may look very orderly from the rather limited perspective of a member of the audience. At a higher level, however, everything may look quite chaotic (inadequate funding, props that never arrive, recalcitrant performers), just as at the level of the individual performer we will find stage fright, confusion, rivalry, and other forms of "nonrational" and chaotic behavior that are never seen by the appreciative audience. Certainly, in many large organizations, the customers (and perhaps even corporate board members) are never allowed to witness such pervasive chaos.

Leaders of this edgy postmodern world must somehow navigate a turbulent "white water" environment, one filled with unpredictability and requiring both short-term survival tactics and long-term strategies based on broad visions and deeply embedded values. Leaders must be sources of integration in postmodern organizations. They perform this integrative role through the creation and sustenance of community and through acting in the role of servant to those with whom they work. The notions of community and servanthood, in turn, lead us away from the traditional (both premodern and modern) notions of a society based on dominance to a society based on partnership and collaboration—styles of leadership more commonly found among women than among men. This model of leadership calls into question much of the traditional managerial training of leaders and many of the motives that guide men and women to seek positions of leadership in our society.

While organizational transformations during the postmodern era may often seem thunderous, individual men and women during this period will come silently into the world of personal transformation. Postmodern conditions usually require small steps toward renewal rather than elaborate plans. These conditions also require a shift to different levels of understanding and modes of learning. In the modern world, boundaries (and identities defined by roles and rules) serve as containers of anxiety. In the postmodern world, we must look to an inner sense of self and to an outer structure of support and community for shelter, stability, and insight in an edgy and turbulent world.

In the postmodern world, we must find commitment within the context of faith and doubt. We must discover ways to make commitments and take action, while keeping a relativistic stance in a world that no longer allows for simple values or answers or for a stable ground of reference. We must often look to that which is old and that with which we disagree to find the balance and the kernel of truth we need to navigate successfully in our turbulent and confusing postmodern world. We return to the wisdom found in virtually all premodern cultures concerning the facade of progress and the ephemeral nature of planning. While standing on the edge of a postmodern world, we must discover wisdom in the patience and persistence of premodern man. We must return to premodern perspectives regarding the sacred nature of human organizations and once again listen to enlightening stories regarding our own human history and destiny. Only in this way can we successfully tend the complex and irreversible fires of the postmodern world.

## References

Bak, P., and Chen, K. "Self-Organized Criticality." *Scientific American,* January 1991, pp. 46-53.

Bateson, G. *Mind and Nature: A Necessary Unity.* New York: Dutton, 1979.

Kauffman, S. "Antichaos and Adaptation." *Scientific American,* August 1991, pp. 78-84.

Kundera, M. *The Unbearable Lightness of Being.* New York: HarperCollins, 1984.

Polak, F. *The Image of the Future.* San Francisco: Jossey-Bass, 1972.

Prigogine, I., and Stengers I. *Order Out of Chaos.* New York: Bantam, 1984.

Quehl, G. "The Inner World of Leadership." Unpublished essay, Orinda, California, 1991.

Vaill, P. *Managing as a Performing Art: New Ideas for a World of Chaotic Change.* San Francisco: Jossey-Bass, 1989.

# 4

# *Paradigm Shift*

## *Introduction*

DON TAPSCOTT
ART CASTON

### *What on Earth Will Happen Next?*

It happens to you at various points throughout the day—starting with reading the morning newspaper and ending with watching the late night news. The staggering changes taking place in the world and their implications for our professional and personal lives are relentless, changes unimagined just a few years, months, or weeks ago. There is a new openness and volatility that seem rich with opportunity and fraught with danger for humanity, your country, your organization, and you. As you read the headlines, you often find yourself shaking your head: What on earth will happen next!

When news of the collapse of the Berlin Wall reverberated around the globe at the end of the 1980s, even the most diehard cold warriors realized that the world was changing. The assumptions that had directed the economic and political events of the world since 1945 suddenly had to be questioned

and reconsidered. The status quo of more than four decades was quickly disappearing. Authors of East-West espionage thrillers, such as John LeCarré, admitted that their work was quickly becoming dated.

The Berlin Wall, the physical and symbolic barrier that had separated two countries, two ideologies, and divided a continent, was dismantled and its pieces sold as souvenirs of another time. Its demise, to people all over the globe, was the beginning of a new decade and a new world. Its destruction symbolized the birth of an uncertain but exciting new era and a profound shift in the structure of world order.

The Berlin bulldozer engines were still warm when Saddam Hussein—freed of the constraints of a bygone, bipolar world—boldly set out to exploit the new world situation. He was followed, in turn, by George Bush, who sought to define and establish a new world order. The United States and the

SOURCE: From *Paradigm Shift: The New Promise of Information Technology,* by D. Tapscott and A. Caston. New York: McGraw-Hill. Copyright 1993. Reproduced with permission of The McGraw-Hill Companies.

Soviet Union stood side by side. Old rules and alliances were quickly swept away. New alliances and rules were forged. Six months and tens of thousands of deaths later the world had seen a first glimpse of the dark side of a new era.

Other dramatic changes continue as the twentieth century draws to a close. With the postwar era and its economic, political, and social barriers collapsing, changes in economic and political relations are affecting countries everywhere and challenging traditional ways of thinking. Whether they be concrete blocks in Berlin or tariff barriers in Europe and North America, physical, economic, cultural, and political barriers are tumbling. There is a growing awareness of the interdependency of nations, individual countries no longer operating as island states if they hope to survive, let alone prosper.

Countries, whether they be in southeast Asia, western Europe, North America, South America, Africa, or the Middle East, have become integral parts of a world trading market. Through economic necessity as well as political and social pressures, attitudes are rapidly changing. As the world prepares to enter the twenty-first century, there is a new openness among countries and cultures and a freer flow of information, goods, and ideas.

As more and more of the traditional postwar barriers fall, a new era bringing upheaval, unprecedented change, and major political and economic realignments continues to unfold. The stunning disintegration of Stalinism in eastern Europe and the breakup of the Soviet Union clearly constitute one of the most significant developments in the century (ranking with the "10 days that shook the world" in October 1917) and arguably in human history.

Information and information technology are at the center of this opening. Faxes provide students demonstrating in Tienanmen Square with information about what is happening in their own country and enable them to communicate their story with the world. People around the world view the Iraqi war from live television feeds in besieged Baghdad. Debates once restricted to the Soviet underground *samizdat* rage in the pages of Russian newspapers, presenting views that a few years ago would have qualified most authors for a one-way trip to a psychiatric hospital. Smart bombs enter 6 $foot^2$ windows, and thousands of networked personal computers become key battlefield weapons. Global telecommunications networks energize the metabolism of world commerce and move us inexorably toward Marshall McLuhan's global village.

There are new opportunities, but there are also potential perils for nations, cultures, economies, and people. The growth of political, economic, and technological openness and interdependence is occurring alongside rapidly growing nationalism, cultural reaffirmation, and radicalism which have both positive and negative dynamics. Witness the continually shifting relationship of forces between democratic, ultranationalist, neofascist, Islamic fundamentalist, Stalinist, and other factions in the countries of the former Soviet Union. Who will win out in each of these countries? What will become of the region and the continent?

The transformation of world economics has produced massive casualties, and these are not confined to eastern Europe or the countries of the former Soviet Union. Many countries are stalled economically. Canada continues to reel from an increasingly distorted economy and volatile national differences. Although buoyed by the 1992 European Community unification, many countries in western Europe are up and down or stalled. Even the Japanese industrial behemoth shows signs of weakness.

The heartland of free enterprise—the United States—is in serious trouble, by most accounts. Economic growth has been lackluster to say the least. It is estimated that 25 million Americans—20 percent of the work force—were unemployed at some point in 1991.[1] The United States has lost ground in key industrial sectors—for example, the loss of the consumer electronics and car manufacturing hegemony to the Japanese. Today, the United States imports over $30 billion per year in automobiles and parts and over $25 billion in consumer electronics. The federal debt tripled from $1.3 to $3.6 trillion during the 1970s and 1980s (in part a legacy of the cold war with its military buildup). The annual cost of servicing this debt is $360 billion—more than the cost of the war in Iraq. The United States was once the world's largest creditor. It now is the world's largest debtor.

Today's American children will be the first generation in U.S. history to experience a lower standard of living than their parents. Infant mortality ranks with some third world countries despite much higher per capita health care costs compared with other Western economies. The infrastructure of roads, sewers, and the like is in serious decay. Homelessness is an international disgrace. Substantial numbers of people are socially and economically marginalized, as the growth of drug use and drug-oriented economies and subcultures indicates. The dream of home ownership is becoming just a dream for millions of young people. Productivity of knowledge and service workers is a huge problem.[2]

There is growing awareness of the seriousness of this situation. For example, Barlett and Steele's stunning indictment of the American decline entitled *America: What Went Wrong?* rose to the top of the nonfiction best-seller list in 1992. Among other things, the book documents the dismantling of the American middle class, leaving a two-class society of rich and poor.[3] The 1992 Los Angeles riots were a wake-up call to the nation, notwithstanding widely divergent interpretations of the origins and causes of unrest.

## The New Business Environment

The titles of new management and business books by leading thinkers at the turn of the decade tell a story of changing business conditions linked to the global political and economic changes: *The Borderless World, Power and Strategy in the Interlinked Economy* by Kenichi Ohmae,[4] *The New Realities in Government and Politics/in Economics and Business/in Society and World View* by Peter F. Drucker,[5] *Megatrends 2000, Ten New Directions for the 1990s* by Patricia Aburdene and John Naisbitt,[6] *Cracking the Global Market, How to Do Business Around the Corner and Around the World* by Jack Nadel,[7] and *The Competitive Advantage of Nations* by Michael E. Porter.[8] All discuss the fundamental shifts in the world economic situation, the nature of business, and the need for a new paradigm—a fundamentally new approach and way of thinking to understand and deal with the new realities.

Businesses face a paradox. They have unprecedented opportunities to tap new markets. Meanwhile, traditional markets are changing dramatically, shrinking or becoming intensely competitive. Additionally, reduced profit margins along with rising customer demands for quality products and services are placing unrelenting pressures on many enterprises.

A pressing reality of the new global environment is the emergence of a new era of competition. Competition is arising not only from traditional adversaries in traditional markets, or from new entrants to a specific industry or economic sector, but also from the disintegration of barriers to previously insulated and protected markets. Enterprises no longer limit their growth to traditional customer bases. Bankers offer insurance and brokerage services. Credit card companies enter territory previously reserved for banks. Insurance companies market financial services. High-technology companies sell consumer goods. Even national postal services are becoming heavily involved in direct mail and retailing.

On the other hand, some other companies that had expanded into new markets have retrenched as the pressures of the early 1990s recession force them to "stick to their knitting." For example, American Express, which expanded aggressively into a wide range of financial and related businesses, has more recently refocused on its core credit card business.

The barriers that separated economic and vertical market sectors and the companies that operated within them are quickly falling. Competition can arise unexpectedly from anywhere. This means that enterprises can no longer be overconfident about their market shares and their competitive positions. For businesses faced with shrinking profit margins, the ability to lower unit operating costs and overheads in these highly competitive markets has become a key concern. No longer are the minor gains in efficiencies of a few percentage points experienced over the last two decades sufficient to meet the cost-containment demands of the 1990s.

The opening of world marketplaces has caused many corporations to reel—resulting in massive restructuring in virtually every business sector. According to its chairman, the General Motors of the mid- to late 1990s will be half the size of the General Motors of the mid- to late 1980s. IBM is becoming a network of autonomous businesses. Citibank is completely transforming its organization. All are restructuring their cost bases through severe downsizing.

The restructuring of national economies is relentless, largely driven by advances in information technology. Although there is a transition from the old industrial economy, the terms *service economy* and, to some extent, *information economy* are misleading. The planet, and even the Western world, still relies on agriculture and industrial production for the creation of wealth and the meeting of basic human needs. You can't eat or live on information. Humanity is a long way from an economic structure based on tourism, leisure, government services, software, and fast food. Just as industrial production was applied to the previous (agricultural) economy, *information technology* (IT) is being applied to all aspects of production, and in turn agriculture. Information, as a result, has become a capital good. It is becoming similar in value to labor, materials, and financial resources. Furthermore, the IT sector itself is undergoing explosive growth.

For example, in 1992 the IT and communications sector had grown to close to 10 percent of the gross domestic product in the United States. The computer equipment and services sector alone was larger than auto, steel, mining, petrochemical, and natural gas combined.

Information technology is also penetrating every other sector in ways that are stunning. If you purchase a new car this year, you'll find more computer power under the hood than Neil Armstrong had in his lunar lander.

With markets and their players constantly changing, the possibility of enterprises establishng a sustainable competitive advantage no longer exists. No organization can afford to rest on its laurels; each must constantly innovate to compete.

## Seven Key Drivers of the New Business Environment

Since the 1990s will be a decade of major transition in the way business is conducted, this is a time to get serious about implementing strategic programs focused on business development and survivability and to begin building the future enterprise.

A number of recurring business themes are emerging in today's strategic plans as enterprises reengineer themselves for the new environment: Each of these is demanding a new technology paradigm.

### Productivity of Knowledge and Service Workers

A critical business challenge facing our clients is the need to significantly improve the productivity of knowledge and service workers. Peter Drucker argues that the single greatest challenge facing managers in the West today is to raise the productivity of knowledge and service workers. He says that productivity will dominate management thinking for many decades. It will ultimately determine the competitive performance of companies, the quality of life in every industrialized nation, and the very fabric of society.[9]

Drucker goes on to compare and contrast this need for productivity in the information age with that of the industrial age. Productivity in manufacturing, farming, mining, construction, and transportation has improved at a combined annual rate of 3 to 4 percent, resulting in a phenomenal 45-fold improvement over the last 120 years! These improvements continue today; however, their impact on the economy is diminishing since their relative proportion of the economy is shrinking. These outstanding productivity gains were the result of the effective application of scientific methods, advanced engineering, and management sciences. The capital and technology of the industrial age focused on industrial productivity. The capital and technology of the information age is focused on knowledge and service worker productivity. Information technology is the foremost tool for making the substantial and ongoing productivity gains that will shape the leaders (individuals, companies, institutions, and countries) of the twenty-first century.

For many organizations this means a restructuring of their cost base. No longer are minor gains in efficiencies (of a few percentage points here and there) adequate to meet the cost-containment demands of the 1990s. The focus is now shifting to major business transformations where entire processes (both production and management) are streamlined. Paper-based systems, bureaucratic approval processes, labor-intensive clerical activities, batch processing cycles, and multilayered decision-making processes are being replaced by source data capture, integrated transaction processing, electronic data interchange, real-time systems, on-line decision support, document management systems, and expert systems.

Another important trend is a shift in the focus of productivity programs from cost cutting to improving organizational performance and effectiveness. This trend is occurring for two reasons. Many cost restructuring programs have failed, permanently weakening a company in its market and compromising its chances for survival.[10] Moreover, the enabling effect of information technology is leading to completely new high-performance work-system models. Human energy is reinvested in new things as opposed to being eliminated through head count reductions. You will read in subsequent chapters how this can be achieved.

## Quality

In many manufacturing and production operations today, quality problems can back up an entire plant and cause a chain reaction along the supplier network. This is primarily due to the integrated nature of production processes, and can be exacerbated by such things as just-in-time inventory. Failures in shipped products often result in expensive outages for customers, costly repairs, and, most regrettably, dissatisfied customers.

Product and service quality programs have moved from manufacturing operations to knowledge and service work. Service industries are faced with similar client and competitive drivers for im-

proved quality of services and means of delivery. Quality expectations continue to rise. By building a corporate culture around quality, many companies such as Federal Express have been able to achieve significant success. Quality has become a broad theme, encompassing the notions of consistency, predictability, employee motivation, supplier involvement, and performance measurement.

## Responsiveness

The need to react to rapidly changing market conditions, competitive threats, and customer demands is another growing challenge to enterprises. The time from product/service innovation to delivery to the market is rapidly shrinking in most business and industrial sectors.

For example, programs for "mass customization" are beginning in several sectors. The clothing industry in the United States has implemented integrated solutions to capture purchasing trends by area at the point of sale and to feed back this information to the manufacturing and distribution operations.

The ability to react and the time to react are key considerations in setting strategies and enabling organizations to become more market driven and opportunistic. In global markets there is a need to eliminate, or at least reduce, time and space dependencies.

The old saying "Better late than never" has been turned around to "Better never than late." It is often better not to have started to develop a product than to get to the market after a competitor, or after the market has changed.

## Globalization

With the emphasis on the expansion of free trade zones and the removal of access barriers, another common strategic theme is the globalization of markets, operations, and competition. This often involves mergers, acquisitions, and alliances to gain market knowledge and presence.

Operations often extend to 24 hours a day with worldwide networks linking customers, suppliers, and the supporting business infrastructure (financial, customs, shippers, etc.).

Globalization also brings new competitive threats to the "home" market. Aggressive new entrants can seriously disrupt established markets and set new standards. The consumer electronics and automotive markets in North America are good illustrations of this factor.

Linked to this is an erosion in the ability of national governments to shelter inefficient industries. As world economies become more interdependent, protectionism will increasingly fail.

## Outsourcing

There is a paradox occurring around the role of key suppliers to an organization. As the ability to integrate the production facilities and support resources of suppliers into our own production and management processes increases, the same infrastructures enable the off-loading of previously internal processes to outside suppliers.

We are experiencing a resurgence in interest for outsourcing certain aspects of production, distribution, sales, service, and support functions. The interest is on focusing the resources of an organization on key areas of value-added capability and not diluting attention to these areas by overloading the capabilities of the organization.

In the past, organizations attempted to be self-sufficient through vertical integration within the enterprise. The streamlined enterprise of the 1990s has shifted the focus to vertical and horizontal integration across organizations, including alliance partners, sales and distribution agencies, key suppliers, support organizations, and other divisions, within their own company. As Joe Brophy, president of the Travelers insurance company told us, "Outsourcing is ready to take off." The Travelers will focus on its unique competencies and partner with others to provide additional services.

## Partnering

Companies that previously had little in common are merging or forming joint ventures to go after both new and traditional business opportunities. Many businesses are positioning themselves to function in the growing worldwide marketplace by establishing alliances and joint ventures with other key players in both similar and disparate markets. Others are forming strategic alliances with governments to meet specific market needs. These partnerships (which involve enterprises of all sizes) can involve the creation of research and development consortia, joint ventures, and cross-licensing arrangements. They are providing many of these organizations with the financial, human, and other resources required to compete in diverse and sometimes volatile markets.

The Japanese *keiretsu*—the association of a number of industries centered on a bank—has proved to be devastatingly effective in reducing time to market and creating long-term competitiveness. Variants of the keiretsu have now sprung up in North America and Europe as important companies such as Ford and IBM acquire equity positions in suppliers, participate in various consortia, and in other ways become partners with external organizations.

The enterprise is becoming "extended"—based on new kinds of relationships with suppliers, customers, affinity groups, and even competitors. Such relationships enable organizations to develop comprehensive approaches to markets, jointly fund large efforts in their common interests, respond quickly to new or ephemeral opportunities, get access to each other's customers without acquiring each other, create new markets, share information, combine as interest groups or lobbies, rapidly expand geographically, etc.

## Social and Environmental Responsibility

Due to changing and growing expectations by employees, business partners, and customers, today's enterprise must act responsibly in its relationships with others. The *sleaze* factor of the 1980s has resulted in a responsibility backlash. The 1990s have become the decency decade. Customers want to purchase goods from companies that are ethical, good corporate citizens, and green. The triumph of the Body Shop tells the story. The company presented itself convincingly as one that created healthy, environment-friendly products developed without animal testing and that championed various causes with corporate profits. The result was a huge international success.

In the new business environment, employees and groups must be empowered and motivated to cooperate for success. A prerequisite for such change is employer responsibility toward staff who expect fair treatment, some control over decision making, a stake in the success of the group and enterprise, and proper tools to do their jobs and collaborate effectively.

## The New Enterprise

You can read about it everywhere. Management lecturers talk about it. Business schools debate it. But as Bob Dylan once wrote, "You don't need a weatherman to know which way the wind blows." The traditional, hierarchical organization is in deep trouble. The reason is that the old enterprise is poorly equipped to respond to the new business needs. The command-and-control hierarchy has its roots in the church and military bureaucracies of a previous time. It separates people into two groups—the governed and the governors. At one end of the chain of command is the supreme governor. At the other end are the supremely governed. In between there exists a chain of people who alternately act as governor or governed. These middle managers act as transmitters of the communications that come down from the top. Communication the other way is limited, except through formal labor-management relations. Communication either way can take the form of meetings, telephone calls, or memos.

You were an employee, nested somewhere in the hierarchy of an organization owned by someone else. Your goal was to move up the hierarchy and have more people reporting to you. You were motivated by material rewards and fear of punishment. Your work goals were determined by your boss, and his or her goals by his or her boss—all the way up to the top—where decisions were made. You were focused internally rather than on the customer. Innovation and creativity (for example, in giving better customer service or creating products) were typically not part of the picture. Often you found yourself taking credit for the work of those below you in the hierarchy, or in seemingly never-ending "turf" battles and organizational poli-

tics. You hung in with the company until you retired or were fired. You were the "organization man."

While this picture may seem stereotypical, especially given the changes occurring in organizations today, this was the traditional model of the enterprise. Today there is growing acceptance that this structure stifles creativity, self-motivation, commitment, and responsiveness to market demands, not to mention failing to meet the human needs for fulfilling work. Fundamental changes—in fact, the transformation of the nature of our organizations and the way business is undertaken—are required.

Just as walls are falling in the political and economic world, today's enterprise is opening up.

Many companies have begun a transition to the new enterprise. Others are struggling with what to do. Virtually none has actually achieved a comprehensive implementation of the new model. There is no handbook or guide for the new approach. There are also many dimensions of change, and organizations tend to move at different paces along some or all dimensions. Yet, conceptually, some strong themes are emerging. In total, these themes create an image of what we refer to as the open networked organization. These are illustrated in Figure 4.1.

The structure of the new enterprise is shifting from a multilayered hierarchy to flatter networks or relatively autonomous businesses. The responsive, entrepreneurial business team is becoming a key organizational entity rather than the traditional department locked into a traditional organization chart.

The concept of the organization is being expanded to include links with external business partners-suppliers and customers. The resource focus is shifting from capital to human and information resources. Rather than remain static and stable, the enterprise must be dynamic and constantly changing. The professional, not the manager, is emerging as the central player—often working in multidisciplinary teams that cut across traditional organizational boundaries. Interpersonal commitment, rather than traditional reward and punishment mechanisms, is becoming the desired basis for organizational cohesion and stability.

The new team is self-managed. Team members are united by a common vision that cascades across

| | Closed Hierarchy | | Open Networked Organization |
|---|---|---|---|
| Structure | Hierarchical | → | Networked |
| Scope | Internal/closed | → | External/open |
| Resource focus | Capital | → | Human, information |
| State | Static, stable | → | Dynamic, changing |
| Personnel/focus | Managers | → | Professionals |
| Key drivers | Reward and punishment | → | Commitment |
| Direction | Management commands | → | Self-management |
| Basis of action | Control | → | Empowerment to act |
| Individual motivation | Satisfy superiors | → | Achieve team goals |
| Learning | Specific skills | → | Broader competencies |
| Basis for compensation | Position in hierarchy | → | Accomplishment, competence level |
| Relationships | Competitive (my turf) | → | Cooperative (our challenge) |
| Employee attitude | Detachment (It's a job.) | → | Identification (It's my company.) |
| Dominant requirements | Sound management | → | Leadership |

**Figure 4.1.** The Open Networked Organization

the enterprise. Individuals are empowered to act, and do so responsibly and creatively. Freed from bureaucratic control, they take initiatives and even risks to get closer to customers and work more productively. They are motivated by one another to achieve team goals rather than to satisfy superiors. With common interests that are immediate and clear, cooperation flourishes.

This is a working-learning environment where individuals develop strong specialized expertise and broader competencies, not just specific skills. The notion of learning job skills that require periodic updating is replaced with the notion of lifelong learning. Income is tied to level of competence and accomplishments rather than to position in the hierarchy. The enterprise holds a sense of social responsibility, and people identify with it. Rather than good management, leadership and vision are becoming the dominant requirements for success in a changing and volatile business environment.

It is generally accepted that all of this is achievable, because the new enterprise is becoming information-based. It is assumed that information technology provides the means whereby organizations that have remained fundamentally unchanged for decades, and arguably for centuries, can be transformed. The theory (and it is often just that) is that the new structure is possible when each member understands the team vision; has the competencies required; has the trust of others; and, very important, has access to the information and tools required for functioning and collaborating within the team in a broader context.[11]

Information technology has enabled a reduction of the middle layers of management who are "relays—human boosters for the faint, unfocused signals that pass for communication in the traditional preinformation organization."[12] The old organization also needed separate departments that housed specialized information and knowledge. This assumption can now be challenged. For example, it was unthinkable that a plant worker could (or should) be involved in any marketing activities. However, with technology able to provide information regarding production, shipping, warehousing, and sales along with tools for marketing such as telemarketing workstations—all within a plant—it is possible to build a different kind of organization structure. Perhaps a team approach could provide variety for plant workers, get them closer to the customer, reduce interpersonal friction, and build commitment.

However, until recently, technology to deliver the new structure did not really exist.

### The New Paradigm in Information Technology

Through what technology and by what means will this shift to the new enterprise occur? It is clear that a new paradigm in the *world geopolitical situation* is occurring. This is creating a new paradigm in the *international business environment.* The rise of the new open, networked enterprise constitutes a *new organizational paradigm.*

Just as the organizational structures, business environments, and old world order are being dramatically altered by ongoing global changes, the first era of information technology is experiencing a similar fate. Technology walls are falling. Old computing architectures are being overthrown. The nature and purpose of computing are being radically altered. Like traditional cold war thinking, the old approach to technology is proving to be inadequate to deal with the new world.

A series of DMR syndicated studies investigated a number of critical changes taking place in the use of technology and in the technology itself. The research confirmed that a paradigm shift is occurring. A new technology era is unfolding—an era that parallels and is inextricably linked to changes in organizations and to the broader world changes. We are entering a *second era of information technology* in which the business applications of computers, the nature of the technology itself, and the leadership for use of technology are all going through profound change. Organizations that cannot understand the new era and navigate a path through the transition are vulnerable and will be bypassed.

For its first few decades (1950s, 1960s, and 1970s) data processing was pursued primarily to reduce clerical costs. As one insurance company executive told us, "We were after clerical heads." Today, however, technology has moved to the front line in most organizations. It has become strategic

in the sense that it is a necessary component in the execution of a business strategy. Countless books and articles discuss the innovative use of computers to achieve temporary competitive advantage or parity. For example, many banks felt the sting of losing customers to better information services such as Merrill Lynch's Cash Management Account. These banks and others in similar circumstances have scrambled to expand computing beyond back-room data processing to the front-line delivery of business services and products to customers.

A change has also occurred in terms of who uses computers. In the first era the focus was on technical specialists, professionals, and managers who designed, implemented, managed, controlled, and usually owned the computing infrastructure of the enterprise. With the transition to the new era, business users of technology have moved to the fore. They number in the tens of millions and are more sophisticated and more demanding. They are also no longer content to depend on management information systems departments to achieve the benefits that technology can bring. Users want to shape the technology that is implemented in their organizations. They want to control its use and determine the effect it will have on their own work. They are rapidly understanding that their effective use of technology coupled with a change in how they do business will determine their personal and organizational success. They have become the vanguard of an information technology revolution that is quickly altering the old ways of organizational computing.

### Three Critical Shifts in the Application of Information Technology

There are three fundamental shifts now occurring in the application of computers in business, each affecting a different level of business opportunity. Information technology enables enterprises to have a *high performance team structure,* to function as *integrated businesses* despite high business unit autonomy, and to reach out and develop *new relationships with external* organizations—to

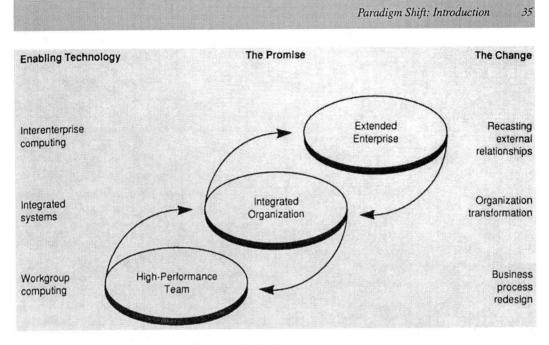

**Figure 4.2.** The Enabling Effect of Information Technology

become an "extended enterprise." These levels are depicted in Figure 4.2.

### Shift 1: From Personal to Work-Group Computing.

Personal computers (PCs) have percolated throughout organizations to touch almost every job. However, their impact can rarely be described as strategic. The main limiting factor is that the stand-alone PC does not work the way that people do—in communication with others, especially within a work group. The new thrust appreciates the importance of the business team as the cornerstone organizational unit and the huge opportunities to support teams within the execution of business functions.

Work-group computing provides personal and work-group tools, in formation, and capabilities to directly support all categories of people in the information sector of the economy. If well conceived and implemented, work-group systems can be a focal point for the redesign of business processes and jobs. This can result in spectacular improvements in productivity and responsiveness. Rather than improving the efficiency of a task such as writing a report or preparing a budget, the goal is to improve the effectiveness and performance of the group.

Work-group systems enable users to streamline a work process and change the nature of jobs in a business unit. The results are typically a reduction in the turnaround time for creating work products. Staff are also able to save time, which can be reinvested in doing more important activities. For example, a West Coast electric utility's process to complete a customer order had a 7-week cycle time. An investigation revealed this was completely unrelated to the actual work time required to execute the process. A reengineering program, enabled by information technology, reduced the cycle time to several hours.

As another example, Citibank Corporate Real Estate marketing personnel were able to save hours a day, freeing them to spend more time in direct customer contact. This was achieved through redesign of work processes, the implementation of work-group computing, and the building of high-performance work teams. The result was a dramatic increase in revenue and profit, and, interestingly, quality of work life for employees.

## Shift 2: From System Islands to Integrated Systems

Traditionally, information technology was used to help manage and control costs of three resources: physical assets, financial resources, and people. As a result, separate system islands sprung up through the organization in three areas.

1. *Management and control of physical assets and facilities.* These included a broad range of sensor-based or real-time control systems associated with production and process control; systems involved with more efficient storage and movement of raw materials and intermediate or finished goods; and systems dealing with improved management, operation, and protection of facilities and equipment that included plant sites, sales and distribution points, vehicles, and offices.

2. *Financial management and control systems.* These systems formed the origins of the data-processing department and dealt with the automation of the bookkeeping end of business transactions. They were oriented toward reducing clerical overhead and increasing the efficiency of processing business transactions. Data-processing systems grew beyond financial applications to address broader information such as customers and insurance policies.

3. *Technologies to manage and support the human resource.* These technologies were intended to support management and other employees in fulfilling their various job functions. They included administrative technologies such as photocopiers; office automation systems such as word processing, records management, and library systems and office communications including telephone, telex, electronic mail, and facsimile; and human resource applications such as benefits administration and skills inventories.

In the first era of information technology, organizations were forced to keep these areas separate and independent, because of the immaturity of the technology and our ability to exploit it. This strategy resulted in the creation of isolated islands of technology. Separate areas of the organization (engineering departments, the information systems function, and the administrative function) took responsibility for these three different types of systems applications. Unfortunately, the result was often systems that were not integrated, that were highly fragmented, that overlapped in function and content, and that were costly to maintain.

Because of the maturity of technology standards, it is now possible to plan an entire enterprise architecture, rather than to continue to add another room on the farmhouse as required.

Enterprise architectures provide the backbone for the new open, networked enterprise; in fact, they are a key prerequisite. They enable moving beyond the organizational hierarchy, as layers of management are not required when information is instantly available electronically. Such architectures can enable the enterprise to function better as a cohesive organization, providing corporatewide information for decision making and new competitive enterprise applications that transcend autonomous business units.

A good example is Federal Express (FEDEX), which has built an integrated, and very competitive, company on an enterprise architecture. Integrated systems at FEDEX enable tracking of a parcel in *real time* and provide detailed information regarding minute-by-minute parcel movements for the management of quality. The architecture integrates systems capabilities to manage the three resources—physical, financial, and human.

At the same time, such architectures provide a platform for entrepreneurial innovation in the use of computers by business teams—while maintaining an enterprise capability. As a transitional step, many companies are building links between various systems to enable an enterprise capability. For example, Phillips Petroleum, Frito-Lay, and Northern Telecom have implemented management support systems to provide information from a variety of disparate systems for executive decision making.

## Shift 3: From Internal to Interenterprise Computing

In the first era, systems were viewed as being internal to the organization—reflecting the walls that existed between enterprises. Computer systems are now extending the reach of organizations outward to link enterprises with their suppliers, distribution channels, and consumers. Insurance companies and airlines link with agents. Governments provide information kiosks for the public. Banks provide on-line access to customers. Manufacturers tie in to terminals in the trucks of a distributor. The research found that such systems can strengthen customer loyalty, lock out competitors, speed up distribution of goods and customer service, and save money (to name just a few examples).

Technology is becoming a vehicle for creating links between business partners—both suppliers and consumers of products and services. Early systems, such as American Airlines' SABRE reservation system and the American Hospital Supply customer order system, have become legends in how to use technology to link with customers to defeat the competition. However, they were really the tip of the iceberg.

The new technology of *extended reach* enables the recasting of relationships with external organizations. Computer systems between enterprises are beginning to talk to each other. The manual value chain from suppliers to consumers is becoming an *electronic value network* that also links to affinity groups (such as business partners) and even competitors. Corporate computing is becoming interenterprise computing, enabling the rise of the "interenterprise."

The emerging technologies include interenterprise databases, voice response systems, electronic messaging, and new point-of-sale technologies. Standards such as electronic data interchange (EDI)—the computer-to-computer interchange of business documents between companies—are transforming the ways companies work together. For example, when large auto manufacturers demand that their suppliers communicate with them using EDI, one of the objectives is to make suppliers more productive, profitable, and therefore stable. Auto manufacturers acquire an interest in the profitability of their suppliers and can contribute through EDI. New extended enterprises are being born.

Overall, then, information technology can be viewed as classes of systems from the personal level to interenterprise systems. *Personal* applications directly support and are controlled by the end user. *Work-group* applications are shared by a team or function that may be centrally located or widely dispersed throughout the enterprise. *Corporate* or *enterprise applications* support a broad range of users across the enterprise and may involve many divisions or departments. *Public* or *interenterprise* applications involve interaction with users and systems that are external to the organization.

## *Eight Critical Technology Shifts*

The DMR research shows that the computing environments of the last few decades are now failing to deliver the goods required for success in the new business environment. The high-performance business team, the integrated organization, and the extended enterprise cannot be achieved with first-era technology. The old technology cannot respond to the main requirements of today's world—globalization, quality, productivity, responsiveness, partnering, outsourcing, and cost control.

Simultaneously with the demand pull for a new kind of technology, the maturation of computing and telecommunications is creating a technology push for a paradigm shift. Rather than attempting to extend their current platforms, leading organizations are setting out on a course of migration to fundamentally new and different IT infrastructure.

The problem is that today's enterprises are locked into the technology of the past—isolated systems based on outmoded host computers. These systems are costly, poorly integrated, hard to maintain, and difficult to learn and use. Such system islands are also self-perpetuating as new software applications are built on the old platform. The need to address this problem is urgent, for the longer an enterprise waits, the greater are the inertia and investment in its legacy systems.

What are the themes of the new paradigm? Following are eight shifts that are revolutionizing information technology today (depicted in Figure 4.3).

### Network Computing

*Shift 1: From Traditional Semiconductors to Microprocessor-Based Systems.* The microprocessor—

|  | Era I |  | Era II |
|---|---|---|---|
| *Network Computing* |  |  |  |
| Processing | Traditional semiconductor | → | Microprocessors |
| System | Host-based | → | Network-based |
|  |  |  |  |
| *Open Systems* |  |  |  |
| Software standards | Vendor-proprietary | → | Vendor-neutral |
| Information forms | Separate data, text, voice, image | → | Multimedia |
| Vendor-customer relationships | Account control | → | Multivendor partnerships |
|  |  |  |  |
| *Industrial Revolution in Software* |  |  |  |
| Software development | Craft | → | Engineered |
| User interface | Alphanumeric character set | → | Graphical |
| Applications | Stand-alone | → | Integrated |

**Figure 4.3.** Eight Critical Technology Shifts

computer on a chip—is at the center of the new paradigm. Traditional semiconductor technology, which fills the massive cabinets of the mainframe and minicomputers in your corporate data centers, is going the way of the dinosaur. Microprocessors are beginning to dominate leading-edge computers of every size. Since 1988, desktop machines costing under $20,000 have outperformed the multimillion dollar mainframes that preceded them. Similarly, when comparing the speed of computers today, a unit of performance costs hundreds of dollars on a microprocessor-based system compared with tens of thousands of dollars on mainframe systems. Systems that combine many microprocessors into a single large computer can dramatically outperform mainframes in sheer power.

The advantage of the microprocessor will continue to grow. The capacity of traditional semiconductor computers is growing at around 20 percent per year. The number of transistors on a microprocessor chip, however, has grown from around 30,000 in 1980 to an anticipated 100 million by 1999—a compound annual growth rate of over 150 percent. In addition, we can anticipate that well before the end of the 1990s, a single microprocessor chip will pass today's mainframe in raw power.

The microprocessor is the precondition for a new approach to computing, which (like organizational empowerment) moves intelligence out into the enterprise where the action is (for example, at the point of sale, customer service, research and development laboratory, or marketing department). It enables organizations to have *empowered architectures* that exploit the superior price/performance of microprocessor technology. Even IBM has recognized this shift, announcing a development effort to build a supercomputer based on *massively parallel* microprocessors.

*Shift 2: From Host-Based to Network-Based Systems.* Era I systems were based on large host mainframe or minicomputers each supporting an attached network of local or remote terminals. These hosts were optimized for efficiency given the high cost of traditional semiconductor technology. The terminals were typically "dumb" with a cryptic user interface. Only data-processing specialists (often viewed as "gurus") could make changes to the system. New applications that made their way to the front of the queue seemed to take forever to build. Systems from different manufacturers and often those from within one manufacturer did not talk to one another.

By the early 1980s, two forces were at work to dislodge the degree of centralized control implicit in era I architectures. The first was distributed computing—the concept of moving some of the computing resources closer to the operational areas of the business. This typically involved departmental computing using various sizes of low-end mainframes or minicomputers usually incompatible with the central mainframe environment. There was often great resistance to these approaches by the data-processing department, resulting in many renegade user departments going their own way. Minicomputers and distributed computing became a force to be reckoned with.

The second force was the arrival of the personal computer. This brought distributed computing down to the desktop and ultimately the briefcase. More important, the relatively low cost of PCs opened up many new application areas, especially for knowledge workers, who had not been well served by era I applications. The rapid proliferation of PCs could not be constrained by the centralized data-processing department. When host attachment and networking requirements emerged, some of the underlying architecture issues and opportunities became apparent. The transition to the second era was on.

Now, because of the spectacular power of the microprocessor and the maturity of networking technology and standards, a fundamentally different style of computing is emerging. It goes by different names, such as network computing, cooperative processing, and client/server architectures. Regardless of the name, the new approach provides the potential for users to access a wide range of data, applications, and computing resources without worrying about where they are or how they are connected.

Most important, software is processed not only on a host but wherever it makes most sense. It does not even have to be limited to one machine, but can be processed cooperatively on various computers on the network. The computer becomes the network, and the network becomes the computer. To use a human analogy, thoughts are processed in the minds of many people in an office—not just in the mind of the person with the biggest brain. And the results are communicated as required to meet the requirements of the collective process.

The advantages of this shift are huge. Network computing exploits the inherent power of the microprocessor. It more efficiently uses computing power as unused devices on the network can be brought to bear on a problem as required. It enables information and applications to be processed where they should be—close to the user, such as in the case of a work-group application.

**Open Systems**

*Shift 3: From Vendor Proprietary Software to Open Software Standards.* In the early days, computers used software created specifically for that computer—*one computer, one vendor.* When a larger computer was needed, the software had to be re-created at huge cost to the customer. In the 1960s vendors introduced the concept of *scalability* with software that would work on different-sized computers—*one vendor, multiple computers.* However, each vendor had a unique product architecture. Software, whether purchased from that vendor or developed in house, worked only on the hardware of that vendor. Consequently, the organization was locked in to that vendor, as it was too costly to move the software to another vendor's equipment.

Now the computer industry (like the construction industry of seventeenth-century Boston, the railroad industry of the nineteenth century, and the electric bulb and automobile industries of the twentieth century) has matured to the point where it is consolidating around standards. Open systems, based on industry standards that are not controlled by any one vendor, are transforming the computer industry and presenting a monumental challenge to commercial organizations. Standards are arising in all areas of computing including communications, databases, user interfaces, computer operating systems, and software development tools. By 1992, every major computer vendor had adopted open systems as its main approach to technology.

Open systems result in information and software being portable, that is, run on hardware regardless of size or brand. Such standards also enable systems of different sizes and brands to interoperate, that is, communicate with one another.

DMR's research showed that open systems have far-reaching advantages over the traditional approach. They are significantly less expensive as a result of their exploitation of microprocessors, lower vendor margins due to customer freedom, and use of shrink-wrapped, as opposed to home-grown, software—to name a few. More important, the leading organizations had concluded that industry standards were necessary to enable them to adopt the new computing paradigm. Standards in general, and open systems in particular, do not simply provide benefits. They are becoming imperative in order to create the kind of modular, flexible, powerful, networked computing architectures required by the new business environment.

*Shift 4: From Single to Multimedia—Data, Text, Voice, and Image.* In the first era, the immaturity of technology and the absence of open standards meant that these four forms of information were separate, each with separate technologies to manage them. Data-processing systems handled data. Word-processing systems and telex handled text. Telephone and dictation systems handled voice. Photocopiers and microform systems handled image. As the information contained in these systems becomes digitized, and as standards grow, the opportunity unfolds to integrate them. Today, for example, two professionals in different parts of the globe can exchange (at the speed of light) computerized or *digital* documents that contain all four forms of information. A document on a workstation screen may have text surrounding a digitized photograph and a so-called screen live spreadsheet with another's voice (requesting clarification from the recipient) attached to certain parts of the document. This compound document can be filed electronically, retrieved, altered, and communicated as appropriate without ever being transformed into paper. Again, the research showed that the benefits can be striking.

An example extension of such integration which is getting a lot of press these days is virtual reality. This technology creates an artificial reality for the integration of not only visual and audio information but also information from other senses in three-dimensional, interactive real time. The foreshadow of such systems was the Spatial Data Man-

agement System developed at MIT in the 1970s, in which a user sat in a chair and, through touching small screens on the side, "navigated" around through "dataland" on a giant color screen facing the chair. The next step was flight simulation systems that enable pilots to lose all their engines in a training situation without losing their lives. With virtual reality the user actually wears some kind of clothing such as a glove (Nintendo already has a commercial product), goggles, and headset. The user sits in hyperspace, experiencing a simulated world.

Sound like science fiction? Entertainment applications will make a critical mass of users—leading to commercial viability for commercial applications in the mid-1990s. Petroleum engineers will penetrate the earth. Doctors will navigate through your cardiovascular system. Researchers will browse through a library. Students will go for a stroll on the moon. Auto designers will sit in the back seat of a car they are creating to see how it feels and examine the external view. By the end of this decade, the home computer, television, and telephone will have converged into multimedia devices delivering a vast array of applications that currently are provided by separate telecommunications, entertainment, publishing, computing, and home electronics industries.

*Shift 5: From Account Control to Computer Vendor—Customer Partnerships Based on Free Will.* In the first era, customers were locked in to a given vendor's products. This allowed the vendor to have account control over the customer. The good news was that vendors typically provided reasonable service and support. However, there were problems. The vendor could also charge high margins for products because the customer in the account relationship didn't really have a lot of choice. Customers also lacked the freedom to take advantage of new technology coming from unpredictable sources. They just hoped that they had chosen the right vendor.

When asked to describe their IT architecture, customers would typically respond, "We're a System 370 architecture," or "We've adopted the VAX VMS architecture." Both of these architectures are product architectures, rather than a disciplined organization of the IT resource to achieve a business vision.

More recently when we asked Dave Carlson, the chief information officer at Kmart, to describe his company's architecture, he responded: "We have the Kmart architecture." It is based on vendor-neutral standards. "We say to vendors 'don't tell me how good your products are. Tell me how you comply with my architecture or how you could make it better.' "

In the open systems market, the account relationship breaks down. Vendors must now work to seek partnerships with their customers based on customer choice. Although this is a difficult transition for many vendors to face, in the long run it will benefit everyone.

**The Industrial Revolution in Software**

*Shift 6: Software Development—From Craft to Factory.* Like the preindustrial creation of guns, software development in the first era was a craft. The quality and cost of software was a function of the skills and creativity of the professionals developing it. Typically, programs from within the same organization—even running on the same computer and developed by individuals within a team—were as different in style, utility, and cost as the weapons of early America. When a gun broke, a craftsman had to fix it, as there were no interchangeable parts.

As significant as the move to the industrial design and production of rifles, software is going through a fundamental transformation. It is becoming an engineered profession using factory-of-the-future production techniques. This is an important issue given the huge investment in software made by any medium or large organization.

Because computers are now the basic delivery systems for products and services, companies need new computer applications in days or weeks, rather than months or years. For example, some financial products in the banking industry have a competitive life span of a few weeks. Leading enterprises have concluded that the traditional model of custom software development on traditional computing platforms was too expensive and too slow.

Developers use and reuse modules or parts that are standardized and that work together. *Computer-aided software engineering* (CASE) tools (after much ballyhoo and delay) are finally showing their potential to radically improve the way software is created—not unlike the automated industrial production line.

Interestingly, it is wrong to conjure up images of Orwellian servitude for programmers. DMR research showed that programmers working in this production environment tend to love it. They are freed from the alienating work of reinventing the wheel every time they create a program. They also have better collaboration with other team members. Developer workbenches facilitate the management of projects and communication among team members. Repositories of information about the software being developed give programmers a better handle on what they are doing, enabling large complex processes to be undertaken in a more managed and coordinated fashion. This also facilitates the reuse of previously developed modules.

*Shift 7: From Alphanumeric to Graphical, Multiform User Interface.* To describe the user interfaces of the first era as unfriendly is to be charitable. Terse cryptic interfaces using numbers and letters were, more often than not, "user-vicious." Semantics and user feedback told the tale; "system dead," "illegal entry" (a felony), "abort," "fatal error," "kill," and "execute" were the vocabulary of a time when systems were designed by computer specialists to be used by computer specialists.

The personal computer, standards, and network computing are changing all this. With computing power on the desktop and with industry standards for software developers, the alphanumeric user interface is disappearing. In its place is the *graphical user interface,* known affectionately by programmers as the GUI (pronounced "gooey"). This technology was popularized by Apple. Users work with the computer by manipulating graphical images or icons on the screen. Various files or tools are contained in windows on the screen which can be changed in size or closed. Activities on the computer can be performed by pointing to them. Images can be captured, displaced, and processed on the screen, as can voice information.

Again the research showed huge advantages of GUIs over traditional alphanumeric interfaces.

People learn to use computers much more easily and quickly. They retain capabilities longer. They can perform computer functions faster, and they choose to use the computer for longer proportions of the business day. For the first time, computers are becoming usable by the general population.

*Shift 8: From Stand-Alone to Integrated Software Applications.* A number of changes now make it possible to integrate the system islands of the first era. Software programs are becoming more modular, like Lego blocks, built to standards that make them more interchangeable and integratable. For example, a standard GUI facilitates the creation of a similar look and feel for software applications. Open systems means that software programs can be moved to different vendors' hardware, again undermining the isolation of systems. DMR's research showed that the integration of these technology islands was being driven by business needs for new classes of information and new types of applications demanded by the competitive business environment.

## The New Challenges

The fundamental changes in today's business environment coupled with the rise of the new technology paradigm are beginning to present a major challenge to organizations. While many complex and significant technical issues must be overcome, the research showed that the main difficulties were not in the area of technology. Rather, the organizational structures for managing computing, along with the knowledge, skills, resource base, approaches to systems planning, and even organizational culture, were being challenged by the new era. Moreover, the basic nature of business operations which have been essentially unchanged for decades needed to be questioned.

The challenge is one of managing change. Back in 1976, Marilyn Ferguson, in her book *The Aquarian Conspiracy—Personal and Social Transformation in Our Time,* was one of the first to popularize the notion of a paradigm shift.[13] She wrote that a paradigm shift involves dislocation, conflict, confusion, uncertainty. New paradigms

are nearly always received with coolness, even mockery or hostility. Those with vested interests fight the change. The shift demands such a different view of things that established leaders are often the last to be won over, if at all.

## How Will This Shift Occur?

How will the shift to the second era of information technology occur within your organization?

The research undertaken by DMR produced another very striking finding. Today's enterprise is typically faced with a crisis of leadership. Many traditional *information systems* (IS) professionals and managers are so buried in fighting the brushfires of the old IS world that they are unable to lead in the creation of the new. For example, three-quarters of the IS managers surveyed in one of the DMR studies frankly admitted that their organizations did not have the knowledge to understand and evaluate the relative merits of moving to open systems. Those IS executives who appreciate the change required are typically struck by the enormity of the challenge as they survey their legacy investments in outmoded technology and their armies of IS professionals whose entire experience, skills, and knowledge rest with the old paradigm.

Leadership is often not forthcoming from the technology vendors either. In the past, as part of the traditional account relationship, they shaped the evolution of first-era technology in customer organizations, providing leadership, complete support, and a safety net. The enterprise of today has relationships with multiple vendors. Today, technology standards mean that the providers of hardware are often commodity suppliers who deliver the best box for the cheapest price. Customers who want their cake (commodity price/performance) and want to eat it too (account relationship support and leadership) are typically a disappointed lot.

Nor is leadership forthcoming from third parties such as consultants, value-added resellers, and the like. Old approaches, knowledge, methods, and attitudes die hard, even (and perhaps especially) among the leaders of the old view. And leadership is a challenge for the CEO, the business unit executives, and the user community who traditionally have been cynical about the claims, arcane lan-

guage, and perceived territorial motives of IS professionals. Many business managers have, until
relatively recently, left technology to the tech-
nologists and feel that they lack the confidence
and knowledge to engineer a change of this magnitude.

The premise of this book is that leadership is
your personal challenge, whatever your organizational role. The research showed that critical
leadership to manage change and achieve the spectacular results that have been identified came from
every conceivable place in every conceivable type
of organization. From secretaries to the chairman
of the board, across every industry sector, from line
business units to the central IS function, from both
IT vendors and commercial enterprises, leaders are
beginning to appear.

*Paradigm Shift: The New Promise of Informa-
tion Technology* was written to provide nascent
leaders with a framework for understanding the
transition facing them. Rather than seeking to exploit a shopping list of opportunities and avoid a
field of random mines, it will be helpful to know
that you are setting out to lead a transition to a new
way of doing business. This book synthesizes some
lessons from those who have been most successful
and others who have failed. Their experiences are
worth heeding.

## Notes

1. *Newsweek,* January 9, 1992.

2. Peter F. Drucker, "The New Productivity Challenge,"
*Harvard Business Review,* November-December 1991.

3. Donald L. Barlett and James B. Steele, *America: What
Went Wrong?* Andrews & McMeel, Kansas City, 1992.

4. Kenichi Ohmae, *The Borderless World, Power and
Strategy in the Interlinked Economy,* HarperCollins, New York,
1990.

5. Peter F. Drucker, *The New Realities in Government and
Politics/in Economics and Business/in Society and World View,*
Harper & Row, New York, 1989.

6. Patricia Aburdene and John Naisbitt, *Megatrends 2000,
Ten New Directions for the 1990s,* William Morrow, New York,
1990.

7. Jack Nadel, *Cracking the Global Market, How to Do
Business Around the Corner and Around the World,* American
Management Association, New York, 1987.

8. Michael E. Porter, *The Competitive Advantage of Nations,* Free Press, New York, 1990.

9. Drucker, "The New Productivity Challenge."

10. Jerry White, from a presentation describing research
conducted by Ernst and Young. A longitudinal study of companies that had undertaken massive cost-cutting programs showed
revenue erosion, marketplace decline, and ironically creeping
cost increases necessary for survival.

11. D. Quinn Mills, *Rebirth of the Corporation,* Wiley, New
York, 1991, pp. 34-36.

12. Drucker, *The New Realities in Government and Politics/
in Economics and Business/in Society and World View,* p. 209.

13. Marilyn Ferguson, *The Aquarian Conspiracy—Personal and Social Transformation in Our Time,* St Martin's, New
York, 1976.

# 5

# The Virtual Organization

SAMUEL E. BLEECKER

Look around. The corporations you see today on the business landscape are changing rapidly in structure and function and will be, within a few decades, almost entirely new entities.

What is evolving are virtual enterprises. Using integrated computer and communications technologies, corporations will increasingly be defined not by concrete walls or physical space, but by collaborative networks linking hundreds, thousands, even tens of thousands of people together.

These collaborative, or consultative networks—combinations of local-area and wide-area computer and communications networks—allow businesses to form and dissolve relationships at an instant's notice and thus create new corporate ecologies. They also allow a single worker to seem like an army of workers and for work to collapse time and space.

For example, let's suppose you head a large company. It's Christmastime, and you need to add 100 customer representatives to the payroll. It doesn't make sense to keep 100 offices with 100 computers open all year long just to accommodate one month's rush of business. Instead, it makes sense to hire 100 people who work at home and

have their own computers. These "virtual workers" can be in Hong Kong or Singapore or Cincinnati. It makes no difference. They dial into the company's database and become an extension of the company. When a customer calls in, all information about that person is flashed on the computer screen of the temporary worker, wherever located. The widely scattered workers can operate as if they were all at company headquarters.

A prelude to virtual enterprising appeared in one state's efforts to find jobs for the homeless. Colorado's dilemma was this: How do you locate a homeless person to tell him or her that a job interview has been scheduled or an opportunity for work has opened up? After all, the homeless have no addresses, no telephones. The state decided to establish individual voice mailboxes accessible by toll-free telephone numbers for each homeless person in the program. The individuals simply call their personalized numbers to get their messages. And it works. So far, more than 75% of the homeless people enrolled in this program have found jobs.

In the future, virtual enterprising will follow Colorado's example by operating without walls.

SOURCE: Originally appeared in the March/April 1994 issue of *The Futurist*. Used with permission from the World Future Society, 7910 Woodmont Avenue, Suite 450, Bethesda, Maryland 20814. 301/656-8274; http://www.wfs.org/wfs.

These collaborative networks make it possible to draw upon vital resources as needed, regardless of where they are physically and regardless of who "owns" them—supplier or customer.

"Collaborative networks deliver better products, higher quality, improved time-to-market, and higher returns to the bottom line," says Gordon Bridge, president of AT&T's messaging company. "They leverage the strengths of each link in the value chain, improve efficiencies, reduce expenses, and focus on the interoperability of processes and supporting systems."

## *"Virtual" Trends in the Marketplace*

Several factors are driving businesses toward virtual enterprising.

*Pace.* As Alvin Toffler predicted more than two decades ago, businesses now run at warp speeds, demanding immediate responses anywhere, anytime. Today, "it's survival of the fastest, not the fittest," he notes.

*Cost.* The cost of market entry is often smaller than previously, especially in the information services and other technology-driven industries, where even undercapitalized startups can have an enormous impact on innovation.

*Personalization.* Computerized manufacturing has made it economical to produce assembly-line product runs of a few dozen items instead of a few thousand. This has meant that corporations are now driven more by customer demands than by internal needs. Today, customers get what they want or go elsewhere.

*Globalization.* Businesses no longer compete only with their nearest rivals, but internationally.

In the recent past, businesses could count on a steady stream of profit from a product line because a product's life cycle stretched ahead for years. Current product cycles have dropped to 18 months or less for some products. For example, the time it takes to conceive, design, manufacture, and sell

386-chip-based computers lasts maybe 18 months. If a company wants to recoup its R&D investments, it must truly be nimble.

As a result, large corporations are under pressure to drastically cut the time it takes to deliver a product from the engineer's workbench to the showroom floor. If they can't, they'll lose millions of dollars in investment to a faster competitor.

What has insulated many corporations from this reality, particularly in the United States, has partially been the high cost of entry into well-entrenched distribution networks. For years, U.S. car manufacturers could ignore consumer demands because it was too costly for a foreign competitor with a better idea or a better-made vehicle to enter the U.S. market.

All that changed when new technologies and political realities blurred national borders. GM, Ford, and Chrysler sprang to their feet when well-financed Japanese and German auto manufacturers started penetrating American barriers and delivering cheaper and better-designed cars.

Other industries besides car manufacturers are also getting the message. Giants like AT&T and IBM are reengineering themselves to be more agile. They are using their cash, extensive marketing machinery, and manufacturing might to form relationships with faster, less-encumbered companies—even startups. Recently, the business news pages are bloated with reports of joint ventures between IBM and Apple, US West and Time Warner (to deliver new home entertainment services via fiber-optic cables), and AT&T and startups, such as the Go Corporation, which develops pen-based operating software, and EO, which manufactures pen-based palmtop computers.

Many corporations are also motivated to form alliances by marketing and manufacturing considerations. Some form joint ventures with foreign partners (or even competitors) simply to gain better coverage of international markets or to take advantage of reduced labor and delivery charges in other countries.

As a result, business is no longer local or even national. It's global. For example, I know of a Spanish-speaking person who drives an "American" Ford designed in Europe, with a Japanese-built engine, assembled in Korea, and sold in Con-

### BOX 5.1
## Agile Manufacturing

Only 40% of U.S. manufacturers are electronically linked to share data with their suppliers, according to the National Center for Manufacturing Sciences.

Yet, data sharing is increasingly viewed as critical to the future of manufacturing and other enterprises. The goal of data sharing, says David Greenstein of General Motors, is to increase the agility of manufacturing enterprises.

"Manufacturing information systems are undergoing significant changes," says Greenstein, who is GM's manager of the Agile Manufacturing Information System (AMIS) project, a consortium of 23 U.S. manufacturers, including users of information technology, vendors who will provide the technology, and systems integrators who will build the system. "We view the largest improvement to manufacturing in the future will be contributed by information systems."

A goal of the AMIS project is to coordinate the use of distributed data throughout the manufacturing network, says Greenstein. "The entire philosophy of manufacturing has changed, and information systems architecture has evolved as a result. Hierarchical, vertical systems cannot fulfill the long-term needs of the market and serve the market correctly," he concludes.

### Size of Virtual Enterprises

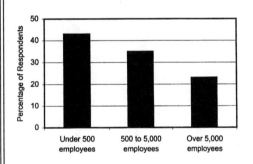

**Left:** American manufacturers believe that smaller organizations will be most likely to benefit from becoming "virtual" corporations. The biggest obstacle to becoming virtual is the corporate culture, said the respondents in a National Center for Manufacturing Sciences survey.

**Below:** This chart shows how American manufacturers currently use electronic networks between their operations and their suppliers.

### Uses for Existing Networks

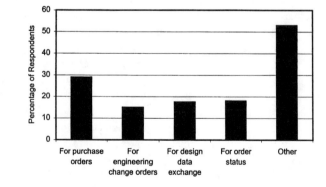

SOURCE: *Focus* (October 1993). National Center for Manufacturing Sciences, 3025 Boardwalk, Ann Arbor, Michigan 48108. Telephone: (313) 995-0300.

necticut. Getting that car developed, assembled, delivered, and sold required important structural changes in business.

## Mobile Knowledge Workers

Increasingly, the "office" is where the worker is—not the other way around. Today, 45 million U.S. workers now spend more of their time on the road than at their desks. This new mobile work force demands new tools that both untether them from the workplace and, at the same time, allow them to stay in touch anytime, anyplace, and (very importantly) in any way-via phone, computer, fax, pager, videoconference, and so on.

The new, ultra-mobile work force, nicknamed "road warriors," are message-intensive. They talk on the go and go where the action is. Road warriors need new tools as they go on their "infoquests" into the offices, factories, and homes of their clients.

As Intel's Andy Grove says, we are in the midst of a major paradigm shift in both the computer industry and the workplace itself. The new mobile work force doesn't so much need computer devices that communicate as they need communications devices that compute. We are at the brink of un-tethered communications. It is the dawn of a new era—the era of universal devices—when your pen-based palmtop PC becomes your personal communicator, serves as your mailbox, your fax machine, your notebook, and even your electronic secretary. This single device will manage and store your electronic communications, becoming, in essence, your "briefcase office."

Yet, for this revolution in work and workplace to materialize, an invisible worldwide infrastructure of new hardware tools, wireless links, and land-based communications superhighways are needed for high-speed and broadband data transfer of high-definition documents, such as medical X-rays or multimedia presentations.

Increasingly, we will see a host of personal digital assistants (PDAs), also known as "pocket pals" or "personal communicators." These handy devices feature built-in wireless telephones and modems, voice-recognition and voice-synthesis capabilities, and have photographic-quality, touch-sensitive screens. Increasingly, companies will build their telecommunications operations around virtual networks, such as AT&T's Software Defined Network, which allows a company to piggy-back on a private virtual network that has the intelligence and reach of AT&T's global public telephone network.

Once armed with these new tools, businesses will reengineer themselves. Powerful personal communicators are expected to trigger new applications in data collection so that, for example, an insurance claims adjuster can collect data in the field, complete an application or an accident report, and have it sent back to the office immediately.

Personal communicators will also allow vital information to be wirelessly downloaded to the field. For example, that same claims adjuster might need a diagram of an older-model car to be sent directly to his or her personal communicator for the accident report to be completed. Salespeople, too, can get immediate answers to customers' questions or price quotes downloaded wirelessly from head-quarters and thus close a sale on the spot rather than having to postpone the sale until information is available.

With electronic messaging and wireless commu-nications, the road warrior can now also have a universal mailbox. Colleagues need not follow his or her movements because they can deliver their communications—memos, faxes, presentations—directly to the mobile worker anywhere by address-ing his or her universal mailbox. And, wherever the worker is—on the road, on a plane, in a hotel, or at a client's office—those messages are waiting. And if there's no fax machine handy, the mobile worker can read messages on the computer through elec-tronic messaging.

## Unwiring Society

In the 1980s we noted proudly that we were a wired society. Soon we can proudly say we are an unwired society. It's the age of emancipation. Time and space will collapse, and the barriers to commu-nications will fall away. It won't matter if you're in America and your trading partner is in Bulgaria. You will be truly connected—linked to one another

---

**BOX 5.2**
## Virtual Products

The virtual enterprise is emerging largely because a new kind of product is seeing increased demand: the virtual product.

Overnight package delivery, prescription eyeglasses and high-quality photograph developing in less than an hour, instant movies from tiny camcorders, and custom-made tacos in 20 seconds are just a few of the dazzling array of virtual products leading the way.

"What these products and services have in common is that they deliver instant customer gratification in a cost-effective way," write William H. Davidow and Michael S. Malone in *The Virtual Corporation.*" "The ideal virtual product or service is one that is produced instantaneously and customized in response to customer demand."

Products and services that were once never thought capable of meeting such enormous demands are being "virtualized." The automobile, for instance, is being virtualized by Japanese manufacturers who aim to meet a domestic order within 72 hours.

"Not only will virtual products have great value for the customer, but the ability to make them will determine the successful corporations of the next century," the authors conclude.

SOURCE: *The Virtual Corporation: Structuring and Revitalizing the Corporation for the 21st Century* by William H. Davidow and Michael S. Malone. HarperBusiness, 1992. Available from the Futurist Bookstore for $23.

---

by an invisible web of communications networks and intelligent, integrated appliances: the electronic virtual office.

Traditional offices, on the other hand, will shrink to mere landing sites, where mobile workers dock for an hour or so at a communal electronic desk. Here, you will plug in your personal communicator, or personal digital assistant, and download all the data you've collected into a single unit—an integrated intelligent document-processing and management appliance combining fax, copier, printer, and scanner all in a machine no larger than your current laser printer.

In the future, this intelligent peripheral will not only receive, store, and transmit data, but also manage your work flow. Truly an intelligent personal assistant, such a device will even turn your notes into desktop published reports, including graphs, facts, and figures. It will sort through your files for the references you include and insert them where instructed.

It will also store and index information so that you can retrieve it instantly without intervention of a secretary. When you're on the road, it will receive your correspondence and, if the information is urgent enough, track you down and e-mail or fax your messages to you. Right now, several e-mail software developers are working on such intelligent assistants, including Lotus's *Notes* and Beyond's *Mail.*

### Winning the Business War

Business is war. We *battle* our competition. We call our work force an *army.* We call our mobile work force *road warriors.* We *invade* markets. And, during crises, we call the conference room the *war room.* So what will make the virtual enterprise of tomorrow the most productive—that is, competitive—is *warware.* Computers without it will be little more than expensive paperweights.

Warware is strategic simulation software that allows executives to manage complexity, to create virtual realities (or virtual enterprises) on the computer screen, and to watch the results of their scenarios as they replay the parameters. It's not new. The Pentagon has been doing it for years.

Even civilian PC users have been doing it. With *SimCity,* they play town manager; with *Gettysburg,* they fight again and again the famous American battle.

But we haven't gone far enough. When computers get smart enough, business executives will be charting reorganizations on computers, not on paper. They will make fewer mistakes and grow greater profits. They will assign project management to computers, not to line personnel. With warware, executives will open new markets, anticipate economic shifts, and play currency markets. They will have a strategic edge because they will be able to simulate business scenarios free of risk and will come away less bloodied when actions are taken later in the real world.

In addition to corporate warware, however, there will also be personal software that increases an executive's capabilities. It's this sort of software that will cause executives to embrace hardware as never before. Contrary to popular myth, CEOs *do* use computers, but they're called vice presidents. The next generation of software will replace the VP as the CEO's intelligent assistant by mimicking the VP's activities. It will anticipate an executive's needs, learn from experience, conduct self-directed searches, synthesize data, provide analysis, and tailor-make reports.

Right now, the software isn't smart enough, and computers aren't powerful enough, so human vice presidents are still needed. But two developments will help change all that: parallel processing and fuzzy logic.

Parallel processing will allow software designers and systems experts to consider the workplace as a large number of independent processors acting in a coordinated fashion. By assigning rule-based operations to each processor and orchestrated actions to the whole, parallel processing will help more accurately simulate the corporation and anticipate the consequences of any corporate actions or policy changes.

To "think" like a person, however, computers must not only think faster, but differently. In many cases, the answer to a question or solution to a problem is not yes or no, but maybe; not good or bad, but okay; not hot or cold, but temperate. Fuzzy sets and fuzzy logic reject the binary notion that the world is entirely discrete and accepts a continuum of values. As a result, fuzzy logic will enable computers to think more like people do and to create real-world simulations.

Once we've accepted the preeminence of communication rather than location for winning enterprises, we will have come a long way toward reshaping corporations. Virtual enterprises will develop not in the image of the factory floor of 100 years ago, but as a new business ecosystem characterized by flexible relationships formed electronically at a moment's notice.

*II*

# *The Inherent Leadership Context*

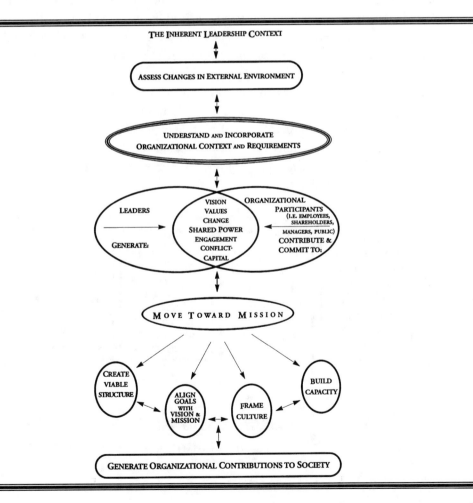

This section focuses on requirements and responsibilities that are inherent components of leadership in organizations. Figure II.1 identifies four major areas that impact the functioning of organizational leadership—power, purpose, structure, and performance.

These inherent factors in the organizational context identify "what" leaders and participants are responsible for overseeing, not "how" these factors should be accomplished. Old concepts of power, purpose, structure, and performance were appropriate to meet the needs of the industrial era and its accompanying environment. Their enduring presence lead many organizational participants to believe falsely that these approaches are permanently etched in the essence of organizational functioning.

When an individual is appointed to an executive leadership position, he or she is granted legitimate power to act on behalf of the organization's interest and the authority to accomplish its functions. Executive leaders are expected to accomplish the organization's purpose and continually move their institutions toward accomplishing its mission and goals. Leaders are expected to establish an organizational structure that allows participants to accomplish the work of their institutions effectively and expeditiously.

Leaders of large-scale corporate and public sector organizations, during the earlier part of the 20th century, used *bureaucratic* structures to accomplish the work of their institutions. Gardner indicates that organizational leaders did not heed the warnings of Max Weber, originator of the bureaucratic model, who predicted that society might not like the "iron cage" it was constructing for itself by adopting bureaucracies uncritically. Burns and Gardner point out the constraints and anomalies of bureaucratic structures on leadership in organizations. Burns asserts vehemently that bureaucratic organizations are incompatible with the goals and purpose of certain forms of leadership—specifically *transforming* leadership.

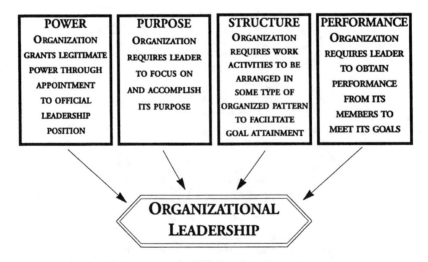

**Figure II.1.** Impact of Organizational Context on Leadership

In the latter portion of the 20th century and into the 21st century, changes in the external environment identified in Part I, such as explosive technology, globalization, changing economies, and sociocultural shifts, are moving organizations and their leadership to new structures and ways of functioning. Brunsson and Olsen describe efforts to reform public sector institutions, which are viewed traditionally as the most resistant institutions to change. Finally, Barach and Eckhardt explore 10 leadership paradoxes that they view as inherent in the role of executive leadership:

1. Autonomy versus dependence;
2. Empowering others versus power to command;
3. Titular, formal authority versus that granted by the governed;
4. Manager and managee—all bosses and leaders report to someone;
5. Archetype of group norms and values versus agent for changing them;
6. Power—use it or lose it versus abuse it and lose it;
7. Being "one of us" versus appearing larger than life;
8. Information—share to get loyalty versus keep the power of knowledge;
9. Leadership supplied by followers; and
10. Privilege—role versus person.

Although leadership must still address issues of power, purpose, structure, and performance, the complex realities described earlier raise some critical questions. What are the new requirements and challenges for leadership with regard to the inherent context of organizations? How can leaders and participants overcome the constraints and obstacles of large-scale public and private institutions to meet these new requirements and challenges?

As we examine the remaining sections of this text, numerous writers attest to a transformation in how the inherent requirements of leadership are being accomplished. Concepts of power in new-era organizations are shifting from tightly held authority to power sharing among self-managed organizational participants. Organizational purpose is expanding to include the needs and wants of organizational participants, customers, public service recipients, and the larger society. Structures and work design are shifting from hierarchical forms to flatter arrangements including teams, networks, and webs of interdependent relationships among colleagues within and across organizations. Performance is no longer viewed solely as meeting job description requirements but is based on using vision, values, purpose, and long-term goals to guide the work of individuals and groups. Leadership requires bold actions and necessitates the courage to change systems, patterns of human interactions, and organizational outcomes. The challenges of this new era dictate that old concepts be transformed to meet new realities.

# 6

# *Bureaucracy Versus Leadership*

JAMES MacGREGOR BURNS

On the face of it, a bureaucratic organization would appear to embody leadership characteristics opposite to those of the small group and transactional leadership. The bureaucratic organization seems to be the product of a conscious decision by leadership to organize human and material resources for a carefully defined goal, while the small group is viewed as the more or less spontaneous, autonomous outgrowth of social conditions. Bureaucratic leadership would appear to have the formal and actual authority to organize and reorganize employees in hierarchical relations for both its continuing and its changing purposes. The small group may follow goals that may be ill defined, conflicting, and susceptible to group change; its leadership may lack formal legitimacy and perhaps external credibility and be peculiarly vulnerable to the shifting loyalties and purposes of followers. It may be nonhierarchical. However tough and durable a small group may be, according to these perceptions, it draws these qualities from its own resources and not from formal or legal structures or

authority. All this contrasts with stereotypes about bureaucracy.

Bureaucracy is the world of explicitly formulated goals, rules, procedures, and givens that define and regulate the place of its "members," a world of specialization and expertise, with the roles of individuals minutely specified and differentiated. Its employees are organized by purpose, process, clientele, or place. It is a world that prizes consistency, predictability, stability, and efficiency (narrowly defined) more than creativity and principle. Roles and duties are prescribed less by superiors (leaders) than by tradition, formal examinations, and technical qualifications. Careers and job security are protected by tenure, pensions, union rules, professional standards, and appeal procedures. The structure, Robert Merton notes, is one that "approaches the complete elimination of personalized relationships and nonrational considerations (hostility, anxiety, effectual involvements, etc.)." The more these personalized relationships are eliminated, the less potential there is for reci-

SOURCE: "Bureaucracy Versus Leadership" from *Leadership* by James MacGregor Burns. Copyright © 1978 by James MacGregor Burns. Reprinted by permission of HarperCollins Publishers, Inc.

procity, response to wants, needs, and values—that is, transactional leadership.

Bureaucratic behavior as characterized in this archetype is antithetical to leadership as defined in this volume. Through its methodical allotment of tasks, its mediating and harmonizing and "adjustment" procedures, its stress on organizational ethos, goals, and authority, bureaucracy assumes consensus and discounts and discredits clash and controversy, which are seen as threats to organizational stability. Bureaucracy discourages the kind of power that is generated by the tapping of motivational bases among employees and the marshaling of personal—as opposed to organizational—resources. Bureaucracy pursues goals that may as easily become separated from a hierarchy of original purposes and values as from human needs. And bureaucracy, far from directing social change or serving as a factor in historical causation, consciously or not helps buttress the status quo.

In this theoretical description of bureaucracy, authority is substituted for power. Bureaucratic authority is formal power that has been vested in persons by virtue of their holding certain positions, that is, vested in the positions themselves; the exercise of power under such authority is recognized both by rulers and decision makers and by those subject to the rules and decisions. The personal characteristics of superior and subordinate and the virtue or good sense of the rules or decisions are held to be irrelevant. Such authority may be used to influence subordinates under a system of rewards and penalties, but authority is typically accepted because the subordinate is motivated to respect its credibility and legitimacy. Formal authority does not acknowledge other motivational bases. Reliability and conformity are the hallmarks of bureaucracy; hence, Merton observes "the fundamental importance of discipline which may be as highly developed in a religious or economic bureaucracy as in the army."

Under this model "the bureaucratization of the world"—whether in democracies, dictatorships, or developing nations"—has been so widely noted as to appear to be a universal or at least a dominant phenomenon. Max Weber observed, however, that bureaucratic authority historically was not the rule but the exception. Even in large political systems such as those of the ancient Orient, the Germanic and Mongolian empires of conquest, and many feudal structures of state, he noted, rulers carried out key measures through their inner circles of personal trustees, table companions, and servants of the court. In certain cultures, on the other hand, bureaucracies were the dominant basis of organization—as in Egypt during the new empire; the later Roman principate; the Roman Catholic Church, especially since the thirteenth century; China during most of its recent history; and the modern European state and the large complex capitalistic enterprise. To Weber, development of the money economy was a precondition for the establishment of pure bureaucratic organization. The shifting of the authority to tax and to allocate revenue from lord or satrap to central authority was crucial to the rise of central administration. The purchase of offices, commissions, and sinecures gave way to more impersonal, fixed, and "regular" ways of staffing governments. The most notable sphere of bureaucratization was *war*. As late as the Thirty Years' War the soldier still had personal ownership of his weapon, horses, and uniforms, the rank of officer was obtained through purchase of a commission, and the regiment served as an economic and managerial organization operating under the colonel as entrepreneur. War became bureaucratized when it was "nationalized" by the state, much as railways and utilities were later taken over by socialist governments.

Bureaucratization of society brought early reactions against its seeming impersonality and rigidity and against a collective arbitrariness that often exceeded the personal capriciousness of the ruler of old. Tocqueville warned of "an immense and tutelary power" that extended its arm over the whole community, covering "the surface of society with a network of small complicated rules, minute and uniform, through which the more original minds and the most energetic characters cannot penetrate, to rise above the crowd." The fact that this "humanitarian bureaucracy," as Robert Nisbet called it, was a product of mass democracy and egalitarianism made it seem no less threatening and insidious in the modern world.

Whether the reaction against bureaucracy takes the form of grumbling at the endless forms and waiting lines of Soviet officialdom, of complaining about the bottomless "paperwork" of large public and private bureaucracies in the United States, or of protesting the procedures in new nations associated with British and other colonial rule that are often exceeded by new native officials, that reaction is almost as universal as the process of bureaucratization itself. Reasoned repugnance toward bureaucracy is based mainly on two considerations. One is the fear that the individual is swallowed up in the machine, separated from tools, alienated from work, and ultimately, as Thorstein Veblen contended, trained into incapacity: Organization Man and Woman, anti-human, anti-individualistic, anti-their own real nature. The other fear, closely related, is that the original human *ends* of work or administration come to be submerged in organizational *means.* Once-rational procedure becomes foolish routine. Paperwork designed to enhance communication now blocks or distorts it. What was a considered hierarchy of ends and means is overturned as instrumental values are substituted for ultimate or terminal values. A change in motives on the part of the bureaucrat goes hand in hand with a displacement of goals, resulting in rigidity and ritualism.

These bureaucratic tendencies might seem far removed from the turbulent world of leadership, transformational or transactional, and especially of democratic politics. But one of the most searching dissections of bureaucracy took as its subject the seemingly most dynamic, popular, and goal-minded institution of democracy, the mass political party. Writing of trade unions as well as parties, Robert Michels enunciated a general rule that "the increase in the power of the leaders is directly proportional with the extension of the organization." Thus the "iron law of oligarchy" inverted the relation of leaders and led. The kind of political party that had been designed to challenge the old aristocratic or autocratic political organizations had itself bureaucratized political organization and stifled political action.

Michels's application of the iron law to political parties, Weber's thesis that the demos never "governs" larger associations but rather that the mass of people are governed by executives and administrators, the contention of a multitude of analysts

that bureaucracy subordinates employees to rigid authority—such concepts pose a paradox for the study of leadership and bureaucracy. On the one hand, bureaucracy would seem to be, as we have noted, the very distillation of leadership, since administrative means are carefully organized to carry out explicit ends; if some of the directives may appear to be outmoded or anachronistic, leadership has the authority to change them. On the other hand, the classic stereotype of bureaucracy—rigidity, oligarchy, deference, impersonality, specialization, lack of reciprocal relationship of wants, needs, motives, and values between leaders and followers—would seem to represent the negation of leadership. To the extent that bureaucracy is *in practice* the simple application of authority from the top down, it is not leadership. To the extent that it exemplifies conflict, power, values, and change in accordance with leader-follower needs, it embodies leadership.

Even the outwardly most disciplined and unified bureaucracy may harbor latent and overt conflict. Analysis of an industrial organization will typically identify not only employer-employee tension but power struggles among top managers, between line and staff personnel, and among members with different affiliations or kinds of expertness, and other tensions that shade into the personal and the idiosyncratic. The most disciplined army is full of grumbling, jockeying, intramural competition, and criticism. Conflict is often sharper in public bureaucracies because of their legal obligations to respond to clientele groups which in turn exert pressures on them (e.g., taxpayer groups and contractors in relation to defense departments). Conflict between individual need systems and environmental demands, Warren Bennis postulates, occurs in all segments of organization; the degree of conflict "depends primarily on the level of aspiration of the individual as determined by his reference groups and personality factors, and of need satisfaction rather than the environmental conditions." Conflict may vary with the location of positions: Robert L. Kahn noted that positions deep in an organizational structure were relatively conflict free, while positions located near the "skin or boundary" of the organization were likely to be conflict ridden. Conflict within public bureaucracies is also affected by the political culture and climate—the extent, for example, to which the free play and combat of interests are stifled, permitted, or encouraged in the outside world. The question is not the existence of conflict within public bureaucracies but its character, intensity, and the manner in which it is expressed, channeled, or camouflaged.

At the root of bureaucratic conflict lies some kind of struggle for power and prestige. This struggle pervades the bureaucracy because it engages persons who tap one another's motivational and need bases and who have various power resources (withdrawal of services, denial of esteem to others, widening the area of conflict by such devices as giving "confidential" stories to the press, appeals up the line to superiors or unions or professional associations) that they can employ or mobilize in this process. This is the "real" authority that lies behind the "legitimate" authority of executives and foremen. The authorities are supposed to have a monopoly of sanctions and hence of formal power in bureaucracies, but since sanctions are as variegated as the human wants and needs that activate them, sanctions may be widely distributed throughout the bureaucracy. While the actual extent of the distribution will vary broadly from organization to organization depending on a host of internal and external factors, the analysis of power in bureaucracy cannot be confined within the boundaries of formal authority.

In bureaucracy, as in other social entities, power is arbitrary and feckless unless guided by purpose. What objectives, intentions, or goals, measured by what values, inform the uses of institutional power? The answers, again, are as varied as the motives of administrative leaders and followers. If bureaucracies were rationally organized and led, administrators would act according to a hierarchy of ends and means, a comprehensive and integrated scale of values. In actual behavior, Herbert A. Simon writes, "a high degree of conscious integration is seldom attained. Instead of a single branching hierarchy, the structure of conscious motives is usually a tangled web or, more precisely, a disconnected collection of elements only weakly and incompletely tied together, and the integration of these elements becomes progressively weaker as the higher levels of the hierarchy—the more final

ends—are reached." This does not mean that bureaucrats are utterly lost in a maze of immediate motives and ultimate values. Particularly in public bureaucracies, where the agency is committed by statute to certain objectives, officials may make more than a token effort to realize those objectives.

Often we find in even sharper form the ambivalence noted between the pursuit of personal ends such as income and job security and the pursuit of broader, more collective ends such as the established goals of the agency. While every organization embraces both sets of values, usually in the same person, the allegiance to more general ends is typically greater in a public than in a private bureaucracy (such as a business enterprise) because in the latter the institutional ethic and the commercial subculture around it support an unembarrassed pursuit of higher profits, more pay, and better working conditions. To be sure, in public bureaucracies perhaps more than in private, rules originally conceived as means to ends become transformed into ends-in-themselves as Merton has pointed out, and instrumental values become terminal values, but at least the broader purposes and values remain there to be invoked by political authority and leadership. Ultimately, as both Weber and Parsons have insisted, organizations must be tested and defined by purpose.

And change? The stereotyped view of bureaucracy is one of an institution braced against change. As a Harvard professor during the 1960s, Henry Kissinger wrote an article that lamented the stifling influence of the foreign policy bureaucracy on creative diplomacy. "Attention tends to be diverted from the act of choice—which is the ultimate test of statesmanship—to the accumulation of facts. Decisions can be avoided until a crisis brooks no further delay, until the events themselves have removed the element of ambiguity. But at that point the scope for constructive action is at a minimum. Certainty is purchased at the cost of creativity." Not surprisingly, when Kissinger became White House foreign policy adviser and then secretary of state, he circumvented the structure of department bureaucracy and process in a way some would castigate as "Lone Ranger diplomacy."

Certainly the great administrative agencies in virtually all societies encompass powerful forces that guard the ramparts against threats to the status quo. But this protective and rigidifying tendency is not universal and inevitable. If potential or actual conflict exists in the bureaucracy, if bureaucrats respond to wider sets of values than the narrow organization norms, if these dynamic forces engage persons' needs and motives and hence manifest themselves in new power patterns and alignments, then the bureaucracy may become more a seedbed for change than an arena for *stasis*.

This process will vary with the type of change. At the least the bureaucracy may respond to internal innovative forces, in the case of the coming to power of a new executive leader who can mobilize support within the bureaucracy on the basis of legitimacy as the new leader, the appeal of the program to some bureaucratic elements, and the power to reward friends and penalize foes in the agency. This was the case when Kissinger took the helm of the State Department in 1973. Yet as Kissinger and countless others have discovered, the administrator may find these powers inadequate in dealing with encrusted routines and widespread resistance and hence may have to find other ways of mobilizing administrative resources. More typically, even hostile bureaucrats change to at least some degree in response to external pressure because of the need to survive and the civil service ethic of neutrality. Radicals and revolutionaries may feel the need to transform the structure of the entire bureaucracy or to abolish it to fulfill their goals. Successful revolutionaries usually replace the old with a new form of bureaucracy.

Another type of change is generated internally. Certain bureaucratic elements, reflecting both their developing needs and external societal influences, serve as forces of change within some administrative enclaves, and the spirit of change may be contagious. Still another type of change is anticipatory; as Louis Gawthrop says, the force of change may be anticipated by the organization, which is then in a position to "respond" to the change even before an external or internal group makes the specific demand for the change. The test of change is not passive adaptation but policy and organizational innovation and creativity, and these depend, as Victor Thompson and others have contended, on the maintenance within bureau-

cracies of legitimized conflict and a "pluralized babble."

"Not I, but ten thousand clerks, rule Russia," sighed an eighteenth-century czar. In bureaucracy Weber saw the possibility for both freedom and despotism—for the liberation of humankind through collective reason, and for the dehumanization of people through the conversion of bureaucratic means into ends. Less grandiosely, we can see potentials for both ossification and innovation in most public bureaucracies. The potential for bureaucratic leadership is at its fullest when these forces are somewhat evenly balanced in conflict. By responding to this conflict, by engaging the forces that play on and in the organization, by remaining sensitive to the distribution of power within the agency, bureaucratic leadership can be an important part of the broader forces of party, legislative, and executive leadership that bring change to the entire society. Public bureaucracies participate in genuine leadership if, recognizing that they themselves are instrumentalities to external ends, they respond to reciprocal relationships with the individuals and groups they exist to serve.

Bureaucracy has had a bad name because the reciprocal relationship is often forgotten or distorted—bureaucracies may lead, but they are also followers, "servants of the people." Too often bureaucracies acknowledge only their internal reciprocity and the transactional relationship between managers and employees and in consequence respond to their own mutual wants, needs, motives, and values without acknowledging the *primary* relationship, which is external. Thus bureaucracies may make their own survival the terminal value rather than an instrumental one. Welfare recipients or "clients," students, patients, constituents of private and religious organizations, customers, often find themselves regarded as irrelevant nuisances by those hired to serve them. Public bureaucracies may be more vulnerable to this distortion than private retail business because they often lack competition, demand for accountability of performance, and dependency on the client for job security and advancement. Private business may also be vulnerable the further it gets from its customers and the more monopolistic it becomes.

# 7

# Large-Scale Organized Systems

JOHN W. GARDNER

So far in our discussion, despite an occasional acknowledgment of historical and cultural context, we have given little attention to the fact that today's world is characterized by vast and interdependent organized systems.

If one calls to mind ancient images of leadership—Moses leading the Israelites out of Egypt, Leonidas leading the Spartans in the defense of Thermopylae—and then reflects on the kind of leadership required to get anything done today, one might wonder whether the same word should be used for such spectacularly different activities. I am for keeping the word, even though the changes have been extraordinary.

*The first thing that strikes one as characteristic of contemporary leadership is the necessity for the leader to work with and through extremely complex organizations and institutions*—corporations, government agencies at all levels, the courts, the media of communication, and so on. Leaders must understand not only the intricate organizational patterns

of their own segment but also the workings of neighboring segments. Business leaders must understand how our political system works. Political leaders must understand our economic system.

The leaders who succeed in making large and complex systems work may not achieve fame. Although their success is noted by those in the particular field in which they function, generally they do not achieve the "figure against the sky" visibility that they might have gained as individual performers. Some hire public relations people to pump them up and occasionally it works, but it is not a natural outcome.

Steven Muller, president of Johns Hopkins University and one of the wisest, most effective leaders in higher education today, points out how difficult it is to play a highly visible role nationally and still do justice to leadership of a great contemporary university with its size, complexity, huge investments in research, and so on. "We . . . are builders. Our task is to help to remodel our institutions for tomorrow."[1] If we want our complicated world to work, we had better revise our conception of leaders to make room for the Steven Mullers.

## Large-Scale Organization

Many years ago, Max Weber, the great German sociologist, provided the first authoritative description of the bureaucratic form of organization that has dominated both governmental and corporate life throughout the twentieth century.[2] He pointed out that it was more efficient than the preindustrial modes it displaced, but warned that ultimately society might not like the "iron cage" it was constructing for itself. Not many people heard the warning. The division of labor, the specialization, and the rational allocation of functions characteristic of bureaucracy lent themselves to modern purposes, and the industrial societies proceeded hell-bent down that road.

One factor that blinded us to the difficulties that lay ahead was our belief that the word *bureaucracy* applied only to government agencies; we did not see that the problems were present in all large organizations, corporate as well as governmental.

### A New Trend in Industry

There were some who looked at large-scale organization with a more perceiving and prophetic eye.[3] Alfred P. Sloan of General Motors recognized early that as systems increase in size and complexity, thought must be given to dispersing leadership and management functions throughout the system.

But most corporate leaders were not listening. They were against bureaucratic centralization by government, but embraced it unthinkingly in their own companies.

In the 1970s American industry was shaken to its foundations by the emergence of Japan as an immensely effective competitor, and we set out to examine the organizational practices behind Japan's phenomenal performance. The reexamination soon broadened to include every aspect of our own organizational functioning. And other segments of the society beyond industry began to reexamine their own practices. It is quite likely that

historians will see the last half of the twentieth century as a time when we undertook a revolutionary reevaluation of large-scale organization and the sources of organizational vitality.

### Problems of Large Organizations

We have come to recognize that the sheer size of an organization can create grave problems for the leader interested in vitality, creativity, and renewal. We cannot escape the necessity for large-scale systems of organized human endeavor. A complex society—to say nothing of a complex world—requires such systems, but we now know that we can design them so that they do not suffer the worst ailments of size. There are ways of making them flexible and adaptive. There are ways of breaking them up into smaller subsystems.

All large-scale systems develop certain characteristic failings, some of which are destructive of organizational vitality. Largeness leads top executives to create huge headquarters staffs to monitor and analyze. Substructures proliferate, an elaborate organization chart emerges, and obsessive attempts to coordinate follow. Creative leaders work to reduce complexity, slim down central staff, eliminate excessive layering, and create units of manageable size.

In large organizations the chain of command becomes excessively long. Decisions are slowed and adventurous moves blocked by too many screening points and multiple sign-offs. As one production executive put it, "If I can get an idea past my boss and his boss and the financial vice-president and the general counsel, it's probably too feeble an idea to change anything."

The industrial community has in recent years expended great effort to accomplish the deeper involvement of workers in their jobs—through job redesign, autonomous working groups, schemes for feedback on performance, and various ways of providing recognition for work well done. Since sheer size creates problems in the organizational environment, some corporations have worked to counter the trend toward larger units. The chief executive officer of Hewlett-Packard Company, John Young, was recently rated as the most admired leader in the high-tech industries. He says, "Having small divisions is not the only way to organize a company, but having organizations that people can run like a small business is highly motivational.... Keeping that spirit of entrepreneurship is very important to us."[4]

Recognizing that the impersonality (some say dehumanization) of large-scale organization leaves many people feeling anonymous, powerless, and without a sense of their relationship to the whole, effective leaders create a climate that encourages two-way communication, participation, and a sense of belonging. They pay attention to people. They eliminate conditions that suppress individuality.

The goal is to give the individual employee and the lower levels of supervisors and district managers the conviction that their voices are heard, their participation welcomed. Everyone recognizes that autocratic practices work against this. Not everyone recognizes that depersonalization of the society may be a greater enemy than autocracy. My boss may be autocratic, but if he gets sore when I make a suggestion, at least I know he heard me. When a sense of impersonality pervades an organization, the conviction spreads that any suggestion I make will surely be lost in the complex processes of the organization.

### The Turf Syndrome

Everyone who has worked in a large organization has memories of one or another zealous bureaucratic infighter. In the late 1940s, when I was serving as consultant to a large government agency, I had my first opportunity to observe over a considerable period a prime example of the species. Too timid to lead, too vain to follow, his game was turf defense. He was a master of the hidden move and the small betrayal. He understood with a surgeon's precision the vulnerabilities of his colleagues, and he masked calculated unresponsiveness in a thousand innocent guises. As a young observer eager to understand bureaucracy, I found him an open textbook.

Predictable characteristics of large-scale organization include a complex division of labor, specialization, fixed roles, and careful definitions of rank and status. Equally predictable are the proliferation of defined subsystems, increasingly rigid boundaries between subsystems and emergence of the turf syndrome. Rivalry and conflict develop, and effective internal communication is diminished. Referring to conflicts among his chief lieutenants, Henry Ford II once told me, "I try to remind them that the enemy is not the guy across the hall. It's the guys out there selling Chevys or Hondas."

All of this hampers adaptability, creativity, and renewal. The organization most likely to renew itself enjoys good internal communication among its diverse elements. Effective leaders tear down internal walls and bureaucratic enclaves, counter segmental loyalties through the creation of working groups that cut across boundaries, and foster informal exchange throughout the organization.

### The Informal Organization

As everyone knows, the formal channels of communication and influence as defined by the organization chart do not constitute a complete description of what goes on. There are complex patterns of communication and influence that are generally spoken of as the *informal organization*. Because it is not one coherent system, it might be more accurate to speak of *informal groups* and *informal networks*.

Call them what you will, they are essential to the functioning of the system. They carry the bulk of communication relating to the organization's internal politics. They are the haunts of gossips and grumblers, sycophants and saboteurs, but they are also favored instruments of the natural leaders and power brokers scattered throughout every organization. Flexible and disrespectful of boundaries, the informal networks can serve the purposes of leaders shrewd enough to use them.

### *Communication*

Communication is at the very heart of the leader-follower or leader-constituent relationship. The greater the size and complexity of the systems, the harder it is to ensure the kinds of two-way communication necessary to effective functioning.

## Communication Downward

Our political system assumes that constituents are adequately informed to make sound judgments. But those who exercise political power generally find it much to their short-term advantage to withhold certain kinds of information. It is not a tendency that can be remedied once and for all. Citizens face the certainty of a never-ending battle to obtain necessary information. And top leaders must recognize that even if they themselves favor a free flow of information, many at the second, third, and fourth levels will act to block, filter, or distort the downward flow.

The problem is not peculiar to the political system. It exists in all large, organized systems. A high-ranking air force general once said to me: "The intentions of the chief of staff get reinterpreted as they pass down through each level. The colonels who really run this place [the Pentagon] make the final interpretation, and it may bear little resemblance to the original."

## Communication Upward

Middle- and upper-level executives should recognize that they are dependent on information that has been filtered, analyzed, abstracted, sorted, and condensed by other segments of the organization. It is hard for them to stay in touch with unprocessed reality. Every official must periodically step outside the executive cocoon and experience the basic realities that the system is presumably designed to deal with.

Every organization has its frontline activities—selling, fighting, healing, teaching—and its bureaucratic or executive-level activities. Both are important, but the frontline activities take place far from the executive's swivel chair. The frontline people who wrestle with action problems every day know a lot more than anyone ever asks them.

The layers of middle and upper management can be a formidable filter against creative ideas generated below, and there have been many attempts to

create alternative opportunities for communication upward, such as the suggestion box and the inspector general. But there is probably no substitute for creating a culture—a set of attitudes, customs, and habits throughout the organization—that favors easy two-way communication, in and out of channels, among all layers of the organization. Two key messages should be implicit in such a culture: (1) "You will know what's going on," and (2) "Your voice will be heard."

## Lateral Communication

In any large-scale organization, over time each of the component parts tends to create its own distinctive culture and to establish boundaries that are less permeable than one might wish. Enlightened executives work continuously to correct such insularity—through cross-boundary transfers of personnel, cross-boundary working groups, and reorganization.

In communities there are fewer bureaucratic boundaries, yet the problem of lateral communication among different segments (ethnic, occupational, socioeconomic) is just as real. People live in different worlds and are out of touch with one another in essential matters.

## The Media

The means at our disposal for communicating with other human beings are unimaginably greater than ever before. But the needs that drive people to communicate seem limitless, so that the flow of messages expands as rapidly as the opportunities. Result: hubbub.

So despite the wonders of modern communication, the leader with a serious message has a problem. It is a big, noisy society. The leader has to compete with popular entertainment, skillfully crafted commercial messages, the drama and violence of the news, and so on.

Another problem is that though the means of bombarding people with messages seem to expand without limit, the capacity of individuals to receive and absorb messages seems to remain about the same. Result: overload.

So it is immensely frustrating for serious contemporary leaders to try to get their messages across. Constituents not only suffer from overload, but they also have notoriously short attention spans. And their alertness or deafness is influenced by the fashions or anxieties of the moment. During the oil shortage of the 1970s even fairly dull stories on alternate sources of energy commanded attention. A half dozen years later, a genuinely exciting story on the subject drew editorial ho-hums.

The most effective means of gaining access to the media is to spend money, and the impact of that simple fact on the political process has been profound. Politicians scramble for dollars because they simply must have them to compete in the television era—and in the process they tend to become accountable to donors rather than constituents.

It is easy to indict the media. But for anyone who has observed the devastating consequences of a controlled press, the bottom line is clear. Throughout our history our free press has made an overwhelmingly positive contribution.

Dorothea Dix's successful nineteenth-century campaign to reform the treatment of the mentally ill would never have resulted in effective legislation without the collaboration of the press in every state in which she worked. The Pure Food and Drug Act of 1906 owed almost everything to Upton Sinclair's exposure of the meatpacking industry in *The Jungle,* and the dissemination of his revelations through the press. And in more recent times, exposure of the Watergate scandals was a triumph of effective journalism.

## *Dispersion*

### Conflicting Impulses

In the history of this country there has been a tug-of-war between two conflicting intentions. One is to disperse power, to create pluralistic arrangements, to design systems in which initiative and responsibility are widely shared. Our Founding Fathers expressed that intention in the separation of powers, the reservation of powers to the states, and other features of our political system. The intention is vividly reflected in our private sector today; both its profit and nonprofit segments exhibit extraordinary diversity and dispersion of initiative.

The other intention is to centralize in the name of efficiency, coherence, and order. Among the Founding Fathers, Alexander Hamilton symbolized the impulse.

Conflict between the two approaches is ancient and at the same time quite contemporary. The corporate headquarters in New York City tries to decide how much freedom to give the branch manager in Tucson, Arizona. The parent in Tallahassee, Florida, worries that the federal government is trying to control the schools. Both are expressions of the same crucial question for any social system: to what extent are power and initiative to be dispersed throughout the system? The answer arrived at will profoundly affect patterns of leadership.

The impulse to centralize, latent or manifest in all societies always, gained strength in our society in the late nineteenth and early twentieth centuries. Far-flung organized systems are nothing new; the Roman Empire was such a system. But technological advances, particularly in transportation and communication, have made central control possible to a degree never before envisaged. Caesar did not have to arrange a teleconference with the Roman Senate before his raid on Britain.

### Our Preference for Dispersion

Compared with other Western democracies, the United States has leaned toward dispersion—and we think with good reasons. Dispersion ranks second only to the rule of law as a means of domesticating power and ensuring liberty.

Beyond that, dispersion suits our style. We believe that a society should be vital in all its parts and not just at the center; that ideas, initiative, and creativity should flow both ways between the center and the periphery. We believe that social controls should not emanate solely from the top but also out of the community, neighborhood, family—and not least out of self-discipline. We believe that individuals throughout the system should have a keen sense of responsibility—not just for their own behavior but for the larger good.

## Allocation of Functions

Top managers in large systems, seeking to govern the behavior of people they will never see face to face, create a dense thicket of rules and regulations. But excessive central rule-making leads to overstandardization—too many rules over too wide a territory.

In every large national organization, the truly effective local manager solves many problems by bending the rules. Not long ago the local manager for a famous national corporation pointed out to me the inappropriateness of the latest edict from headquarters. "I don't really blame them," he said. "What do they know about conditions here in San Francisco? I just do a little judicious reinterpreting and it all works out." Top-level decision making on certain matters is absolutely essential, but most matters can be settled far below the top, many at the grass roots.

When Don Peterson was elected president of Ford Motor Company in 1980, the corporation was sustaining huge losses and the quality of its product was distressingly low. In 1986—by this time Peterson was the chief executive officer—Ford's earnings exceeded those of General Motors for the first time in sixty years, and it was producing the most reliable American-made cars. Peterson says that the company pushes decision making "as far down in the organization as we think we possibly can, on the very sound principle that the farther down you get, the closer you're getting to where there's true knowledge about the issues."[5]

In 1988-1989 I served on the National Commission on the Public Service, chaired by Paul Volcker, former chairman of the Federal Reserve Board. In its final report the commission came out strongly for devolution of initiative and responsibility within the vast federal establishment.

To pose the issue as a choice between centralization and decentralization is misleading. An ill-conceived decentralizing can be disastrous. Some functions and decisions are best made at the periphery of the system, some at the center. It is a matter of allocating functions to the appropriate level.

## State and Local Government

In examining the dispersion of initiative and responsibility in our own society, one is bound to consider the role of state and local government. Given the pluralistic tradition with which this nation began, one might suppose that state and local governments would have flourished from the beginning, but the record is poor. There have been brilliant exceptions, to be sure. Wisconsin in the days of LaFollette exhibited great vigor. Pittsburgh, under the beneficent team leadership of Richard King Mellon and Mayor David Lawrence, set a remarkable standard for urban leadership. One could mention other shining examples, but for most of our history state and local governments have not been an effective countervailing force to the centralizing trends in American life.

Then in the 1960s, there began a slow but unmistakable reassertion of vitality at state and local levels. The Supreme Court's reapportionment decisions—*Baker v. Carr* (1962) and *Reynolds v. Sims* (1964)—broke the grip of rural constituencies and opened the way to a wave of state legislative reform. During the same period, both state and city administrations grew stronger as they found themselves charged with administering very large federal grants.

The valuable strengthening of state and local government should not lead, as some ideologues would have it, to a withering away of the federal government. This huge and complex society cannot do without a vigorous and effective federal government. What is wanted is the optimum balance of federal, state, and local initiative on each particular issue. The civil rights advances of 1954-1968 would never have occurred without action at the federal level.

## Motivation and Initiative

As I suggested in the preceding chapter, to maintain a high level of motivation it is essential that the largest possible number of individuals within the system feel that they share ownership of the problem (to use the currently popular phrase) and that they themselves are part of the solution. One of the root difficulties of large-scale organization is that those far from the top are insufficiently motivated. Daniel Yankelovich reports that fewer than 25 percent of workers today say that they work at full potential, and about 60 percent believe they do not work as hard as they once did.[6] Roughly 75 percent say they could be significantly more effective than they are now.

The large-scale organization must ask a great deal of its lower-level people. It needs their local knowledge, their initiative, their problem-solving skills, their intimate grasp of realities on the firing line. Unfortunately, some supervisors do not welcome eager subordinates. In a recent cartoon the boss said, "Of course you're worth more than you're getting, Dobbins. Why don't you let up a bit?"

The same considerations apply when we ask how the whole society can be made to function effectively. A great many individuals down through the system must take action at their level, reweaving connections between warring subsystems and proposing redesign of malfunctioning processes. If it were not for this wide dispersal of leadership, our kind of society could not function.

There is bound to be a certain trade-off between the need to push initiative and autonomy out to the constituent parts of the organization and the need for the cohesion that every system must have in some degree. And in seeking a solution, executives will find that a widely shared understanding of the organization's goals and values will do much to ensure cohesiveness even when the various parts of the organization are given considerable autonomy.

### The Leader's Advantage

Just about everything in large-scale organization seems to militate against leadership. All the intricate processes slow the leader down. Innumerable system manipulators push their particular agendas and block the leader's initiatives in untraceable ways. Cyert and March point out that an organization is generally a coalition of individuals and

groups with diverse goals, engaged in continuous bargaining for power.[7] Elective officials have multiple constituencies that further complicate leadership.

But no matter how numerous the frustrations, leaders have advantages. They have a centrality that heightens their capacity to make strategic moves. Unless they have foolishly isolated themselves, they are privy to more kinds of information than anyone else in the organization. They have many ways of granting or withholding favors and almost invariably have veto power over many decisions within the organization.

The leader generally has the power to set the agenda. I have known a number of mayors who essentially had no more power than any other member of the city council, but had the right to set the council's agenda. That, plus shrewd use of access to the media, enabled them to lead very effectively.

Leaders have the capacity to mobilize lower-level leaders within the system and to reach out to potential allies at all levels. With respect to most of the initiatives the leader wishes to take, there will be numbers of individuals down through the organization who are wholehearted allies, and the leader can often activate them regardless of intervening resistance in the chain of command. Leaders can turn on green lights throughout the organization with a minimum expenditure of energy.

Bennis and Nanus say that a major task of leadership is the management of attention.[8] The symbolic role of leaders, coupled with their privileges as the prime source of official information, gives them voice and visibility.

### Notes

1. Steven Muller, "The University Presidency Today," *Science, 237,* 14 August 1987.

2. Max Weber, *The Theory of Social and Economic Organization,* trans. A. M. Henderson and Talcott Parsons (New York: Oxford University Press, 1947).

3. For example, Elton Mayo, an industrial psychologist at the Harvard School of Business, did pioneering work on the morale and motivation of workers. In 1938, Chester Barnard, in his book *The Functions of the Executive* (republished by Harvard University Press in 1984), contributed importantly to a new

understanding. In the 1950s and 1960s writers such as Rensis Likert, *New Patterns of Management* (New York: McGraw-Hill, 1961), and Douglas McGregor, *The Professional Manager* (New York: McGraw-Hill, 1967), pursued the same questions.

4. *Business Week,* 6 December 1982.

5. *Forbes Magazine,* 30 May 1988.

6. Daniel Yankelovich, *Work and Human Values* (New York: Public Agenda Foundation, 1983).

7. Richard M. Cyert and James G. March, *A Behavioral Theory of the Firm* (Englewood Cliffs, NJ: Prentice Hall, 1963).

8. Warren Bennis and Burt Nanus, *Leaders* (New York: Harper and Row, 1965).

*8*

# The Paradoxes
# of Leadership

JEFFREY A. BARACH
D. REED ECKHARDT

*Le cœur a ses raisons que la raison ne connait point.*

—*Pascal*

Leadership is inherently paradoxical. It has to be. Any time people deal with their feelings—and the feelings of others—logic and rationality are tossed out the window. As defined in Chapter 1, leadership focuses on "the emotional side of directing organizations." Because it is so personal, so symbolic, so affected by charisma, so inspirational, not only is leadership difficult to grasp, but also it sometimes seems as if one is gripping polar opposites at the same time. Anyone who has been involved in leadership knows this. One day that person is required by circumstances to act one way; the next day he or she is acting in the absolute opposite. Yet, somehow, it all seems to make sense.

A couple of examples might help to demonstrate some of the mystery.

James Kouzes and Barry Posner wrote about the nature of a leader's authority: "Your challenge is to give your power away. If you get power and then hold and covet it, you will eventually be corrupted by it. The intriguing paradox of power is that the more you give away to others, the more you get for yourself."[1]

Give power to get power? Such is the paradoxical nature of leadership.

Again, listen to Kouzes and Posner discuss a survey that found 87 percent of Americans rating newsman Walter Cronkite "believable" compared with then-President Ronald Reagan's 62 percent: "What this study makes evident is that when a leader takes a position on issues when he or she has a clear point of view and a partisan sense of where the country or the organization ought to be headed—that individual will be seen as less believable than someone who takes no stand. . . . We demand that our leaders be credible, but also contribute to undermining their credibility by expecting them to focus on a clear direction for the future."[2]

Leaders must take a stand, articulate a vision; yet, when they do, they become less believable to their followers. To do nothing is to be more believable. It's another one of those paradoxes of leadership that seem so nonsensical to the rational mind. However, again, leadership is not only an issue of logic but also a matter of feelings, and feelings often go where rationality fears to tread.

One path to understanding leadership is to abandon, at least temporarily, logical rules and organization for a Grecian perspective, in which questions become more the focus than the answers. It is here that the riddles of the Sphinx hold the meaning of life. Philosopher Gerald Heard said the five riddles of the Sphinx were: What is Power? "How to exercise force." What is Wealth? "The production and distribution of wealth." What is Love? "The issue and variety of psycho-physical love." What is your Word? "The problem of the word." What is your Thought? "The deep riddle of the levels of thought."[3] The answers to these riddles are the flow of life. They represent a constancy of reasking the same questions and getting an enormous variety of specific answers. It's like traveling the Mississippi River. There, the grey-brown water and the green-brown willow trees lining the banks seem constant and similar; yet, each bend, each twisting mile is a different challenge to the pilots who must navigate there.

Paradoxes cannot be studied the same way rationally organized concepts can. They are like wisdom, which is a combination of knowledge and experience that cannot be learned the same way as knowledge. To grow in leadership potential, focus on the key questions rather than the key answers. The answers will be discovered on a case-by-case basis, one day one way, the next day another,

perhaps opposite, way. Joseph Fletcher said that to ask what was absolutely right or wrong was an illusion, like Oscar Wilde's dead mackerel in the moonlight: it glitters but it stinks. One must ask about a specific case.[4] Recognize that this is how the learning of leadership must be approached, then an organization can be imposed on the subject without obscuring the fact that we are really raising questions. The answers will emerge only from experience. Even then, those answers will be crucial only in that situation.

Here then, are ten paradoxes of leadership. As a person lives leadership, he or she may discover others.

## Paradox of Parenting— Autonomy Versus Dependence

This is the granddaddy of all the paradoxes. Its essence is the simultaneous need of children for both autonomy and dependence.

All parents experience this paradox almost from the time their children begin to crawl. A perfect example is how young ones learning to walk will wander away to explore, only to come rushing back to make sure mother is there. The decisions only get harder as the young ones grow and enter their teenage years. In fact, this paradox seems to be particularly acute in children's later years as they seem to swing between the poles demanding autonomy or showing dependence—if not actually being at both ends at the same time.

Every parent has his or her favorite stories about being caught in this paradoxical whipsaw. One tells of the time when his son was about seven years old. The child asked his father for help with a picture puzzle. Dad sat down at the card table and placed a piece in the puzzle. His son's reaction: "Don't put my pieces in for me!"

This paradox is part of all superior-subordinate relationships, so it is at the heart of leadership. This is not to imply that leaders are the "adults" and subordinates are the "children," but anyone who has served in a leadership role knows that the people they lead look to be independent and at the same time retain some measure of dependency. As mentioned above, how the leader parcels out independence, when, and in what amount depend on circumstances. The subordinate who demands independence today is the same one who can't seem to make a decision on even the smallest matter tomorrow.

An additional way of looking at this paradox is through the conventional wisdom that entrepreneurs make poor managers, and vice versa. Although it is possible to come up with lots of counterexamples (Sam Walton comes to mind), the fact still exists: entrepreneurs often are lousy managers, and vice versa. Why? Perhaps the paradox of parenting—and its attendant problems—are at the root of it.

One crucial reason for entrepreneurs' managerial weaknesses is that they are comfortable with horizontal, adult-adult relationships, such as subcontractors. The entrepreneur contracts with someone in Hong Kong to make his product. He strikes a deal that pleases both him and the subcontractor. Neither person is otherwise obligated—the entrepreneur has his company; the subcontractor has his. Now the entrepreneur contacts a woman who, as a consultant, designs his marketing program. He pays her, and that's it. He hires a sales rep firm and deals with independent wholesalers. His company is little more than a post office box to which people send money—but it's all his. When he deals with someone else, each person can cancel that relationship if he or she doesn't like it. The entrepreneur doesn't give orders; he negotiates, he persuades. All of this is very adult behavior.

In contrast, the corporate manager usually owns his resources. He has employees who are dependent on them. If he fired them, they would be desperate. Consequently, he can give orders. He is obeyed. His employees are dependent on him, just as children are dependent on parents. The particular skills of good managers are those of someone who can keep adults in a childlike relationship with the manager. At the same time, the manager must keep watch on his own career by being a good child-adult in reporting to his boss. A lot of people, particularly entrepreneurs, rankle at being a child again, and they don't have the manners and subtlety to keep their own employees happy. Further-

more, the family-like mutual dependency between employee and employer may make the entrepreneur nervous about having high-level employees inside his very own firm.

Some might argue that, through a series of conditional rules (if *a* then *b*), one might map one's way through this paradox of parenting, but those who are or have been parents know that it works much better to just accept the paradoxical nature of parenting and take an opportunistic approach to satisfying both these contradictory needs in one or another way. Remember the father whose son wanted help with the puzzle? His theory on autonomy was to accept the changing nature of it and roll with the punches. Every six months he would ask his son what issue was particularly important for him to have autonomy about. The father recognized that, if he could provide some slack in that area, usually different from what had been "most important" just months previous, his son would have less trouble accepting rules in other areas. A key aspect of this paradox is the next.

### *Paradox of Delegation— Empowering Others Versus Power to Command*

How much power do leaders retain and how much do they extend to their subordinates? That is the question here. What makes the situation particularly paradoxical is that, by giving power away, a leader can accrue more power to himself.

Jack Telnak, chief design executive for the Ford Motor Company, expressed this when he said, "I had to give power to gain power."[5]

This can be accomplished in a context of shared goals, when, for example, management sets goals and conditions ("painting the box") so that subordinates do not feel the limits to their autonomy while management has assured that subordinates' actions are within desired parameters. This hearkens back to the paradox of parenting. Imagine a baby is playing in the yard while mama supervises from the back steps. Baby has lots of freedom to roam but is under the eagle eye of mama. The telephone rings, and mama puts baby in the play-pen and goes inside. Now, baby is operating totally on his own—but only in a three-foot by three-foot space.

Managers' trust in subordinates' goals, values, and competencies is crucial in delegation; without it, managers are unlikely to take the risk involved in delegating. Of course, the greater the manager's trust, the larger the area that will be delegated. The time may eventually arrive that, when mama goes in the house, the child will be allowed to roam free, though he or she still will be accountable to mama's rules and regulations.

The head of one of the United States' largest companies said during a lecture that he believed in delegation to the greatest extent possible. When asked what happened when his subordinates did not do what he desired, the CEO replied, "That never happens." His reply was greeted with general laughter. The paradox remains, but it is possible for excellent managers to make it happen that way.

### *Paradox of the Source of Authority— Titular, Formal Authority Versus That Granted by the Governed*

Legitimate power (also called "formal" or "positional" power, i.e., power granted by title or organizational position) cannot be exercised at will, even though it has been granted to leaders by their title or their box on the organizational chart. The paradox is that, even though one has been granted authority, he or she might not be able to use it. Anyone who has ever been exasperated enough by an unwilling subordinate to shout, "But I am the boss!" knows just how limited formal authority can be.

The degree to which positional power can be exercised over the objection of those who are governed depends on

1. The power any boss has. What are his or her capacities to reward, sanction, or otherwise coerce? Has the boss any other kind of power to bolster his or her position? Discussing the bases of power a leader uses to get what he or she wants done, J. Schermerhorn, J. Hunt, and R. Osborn wrote, "*Reward power* is the extent to which a manager can use extrinsic and intrinsic rewards to control other people . . . *coercive power* is the extent to which a manager can deny rewards or administer punishment to control other people . . . *legitimate power* [is the] extent to which a manager can use subordinates' internalized values or beliefs that the 'boss' has the 'right to command' to control their behavior. . . . *Expert power* is the ability to control another's behavior through the possession of knowledge, experience or judgment that the other person does not have but needs. . . . *Referent power* is the ability to control another's behavior because of wanting to identify with the power source."[6] Middle-level managers often find themselves with a title but lacking much power. They live this paradox of power daily.

2. The structure of authority. Was the leader chosen through the indirect selection of the employees' boss, by a superior boss or board of directors, or through something more empowering, such as direct, town hall government? More on this in a moment.

3. The concentration or diffusion of what E. P. Hollander called the boss's "idiosyncratic credits."[7] These essentially are psychological "chits" that allow a leader to act outside the bounds of normal group behavior, providing him or her with necessary legitimacy to exercise power. (More on this is in the paradox of norms.)

The general conclusion of the experts is that power ultimately rests with the governed rather than with a formal title or position. The recent overthrow of communist rule in the Eastern Bloc and in the former U.S.S.R. certainly reasserts the truth of that—if our own separation from England were not enough. However, the Boston Tea Party notwithstanding, how come it took so long for the oppressed peoples of eastern Europe to assert their power? What about the War between the States (a terminological middle ground between the more common name and what Louisiana friends call the "War of the Northern Aggression")? Just as revolutions prove the theory, years of oppression all over the world give an ironic meaning to the word "ultimately."

### *Paradox of the Manager and Managee— All Bosses and Leaders Report to Someone*

It is patently obvious that every managee has a manager, and every manager has a managee. It is the yin and yang of management. At the same time, every manager is also a managee. CEOs and chairmen of boards answer to shareholders and fellow board members. Even entrepreneurs who own 100 percent of their firms answer to bankers and customers. Congressmen and presidents answer to their constituents.

This paradox is related to the paradox of authority, in that, ultimately, even dictators answer to their people. Mussolini was hung upside down as a corpse by the citizens of Italy. King John of Magna Charta fame found out that he worked for the nobles he ruled. Machiavelli, in the *Prince,* counsels often that the prince must court powerful nobles and common subjects if he wants their support and if he wants them to fight his wars. As Stan Freberg said, Julius Caesar was stabbed eight times in the rotunda—a very painful place.[8]

To stay in charge, leaders must pay attention to their "bosses." These include superiors; key peers (internal and external); the organization; and even their subordinates, who, by their performance or lack of it, can make or break their leader's success.

About this last—the power of subordinates—a little explanation. In management, responsibility always exceeds authority. The only time the general manager's authority and responsibility are equal is if there is a fire and the general manager takes a place in the bucket brigade. Inevitably, anyone in charge can be undermined completely by subordinates. Hence, William Oncken's quip: "When a boss wants something real bad, that's usually how he gets it."[9] A newly appointed cabinet secretary in Washington is an extreme example of this: 90 percent of the secretary's subordinates are career civil servants who have seen or will see many secretaries come and go. Getting a federal agency to do anything new or different is a gargantuan challenge for its top executives.

### *Paradox of Norms— Archetype of Group Norms and Values Versus Agent for Changing Them*

Leaders of groups are expected to reflect the norms and values of their groups and to do that to an exemplary degree. Leaders are followed by members of a "culture" and must pay their dues to that culture. Iconoclasts do not lead establishment groups. They lead small bands of other iconoclasts.

At the same time, it is the leaders of groups who are in a uniquely favorable position to change the group's culture. Groups have strong centripetal forces to maintain their norms and values. Nonconformists often are dealt with severely. Therefore, few people within a group are in a position to change its character. If anyone can, it is the leader. To that leader, the group entrusts the management of its culture. The key role of leadership, according to author Philip Selznick, is to infuse the organization with value: "The institutional leader . . . *is primarily an expert in the promotion and protection of values.*"[10] However, how can a creature who, perhaps more than anyone else in the group, exemplifies its norms and values be the one to change them? That is the paradox.

One key to unlocking this paradox is the leader's excess of idiosyncratic credits[11] over debits, that is, leaders so archetypically represent some values and norms that their atypical, social debits are overwhelmed. The concentration of a leader's idiosyncratic credits in a few areas can give an incongruent perception of the leader's group-centered legitimacy.

An example: In 1966, a fledgling assistant professor who had just grown a moustache and goatee—then a nonconformist thing to do—and a senior professor from another university were talking at a convention. This senior professor was a most outrageous individual, a studied nonconformist. By way of giving advice to the younger man, he said, "The only reason I can get away with all the outrageous stuff I do is because I outpublish everyone on my faculty by a wide margin."

Political candidates also wrestle with the paradox of norms. Most of them run with the intention of altering the present system: witness Bill Clinton's calls for "change" in the 1992 presidential campaign. However, before a candidate can gain that opportunity, he or she first must conform to key values and behaviors of the electorate. Successful candidates know that sharing people's values is a source of potential power for them, that they must represent the concerns and values of the electorate if they want to get elected.

Part of this paradox for politicians is that, when leaders use the group's words, they simply reflect the followers. When they are no more than the electorate's representative, why should anyone follow them? Newt Gingrich, congressman from Georgia, says: listen, learn, help, lead. If a leader listens to people hard enough to really learn what their needs are, then he or she can help them. After that, they will follow the leader. On the other hand, if the leader already is in a position of power, he or she has the power of incumbency and can use that office to help someone. That increases the power—it amounts to idiosyncratic credits that can be used to accomplish group goals or change group behavior.

A classic way that these credits and debits are balanced is by providing a new, revolutionary, charismatic vision to solve a problem. The uniqueness and revolutionary nature of the vision is a debit—it is in conflict with present group norms that the leader is supposed to be upholding. However, the degree to which the new vision gives meaning to the followers that reflects the values, norms, and beliefs of the group—it supports essential elements of the culture—the newness can be accepted. It makes the balance.

Jack Rogers, chief executive of United Parcel Service, is a good example of a leader who, by representing group norms, built up enough idiosyncratic credits that, when it was time for change, he was able to move the "brown bloods" at United Parcel Service in new directions. Paul Oberkotter, one of Rogers's predecessors, said as much when he discussed the firm's policy of internal development:

It's an intangible sort of thing. Everything we do to develop managers is in support of it. Individuals learn to get along and manage through personal influence and credibility of experience rather than through title and coercion. For example, we tracked Jack Rogers

through 50 different types of permanent assignments and short-term projects. . . . Over time he became known throughout the organization. No one was frightened when he was named chief executive officer. He could make substantial changes in this business without worrying about the security or the continuation of the culture.[12]

Leaders do need to be different from their groups. Yet, the paradox is that they must not be more than three paces ahead of their troops. If they get too far ahead, few will follow them. The horse must be hitched to the cart. At the same time that they infuse their values into the organization, they are responsible for changing the norms and values of those they lead. They are not identical to the group, or they would not be seen as worthy to lead.

Few leaders are celebrated for being just like everyone else in every degree. Such conformists are called group "regulars," not "leaders." Again, the paradox of leaders is that they must not incur the idiosyncratic or nonconformist reputation that labels them "deviants" or, in the more extreme case, "isolates."[13]

### Paradox of Power—Use It or Lose It Versus Abuse It and Lose It

Leaders demonstrate that they deserve power by being strong and confident enough to use it. They ride the stallion. They live in the White House. Jean Riboud of Schlumberger Ltd., a high-tech, multinational company that produces tools used by oil companies to drill for oil, was held in awe because of his periodic ruthlessness. One company executive said Riboud ran Schlumberger "like an absolute, constitutional monarch." Another, Felix Rohatyn, said, "His authority is as absolute as any executive I've seen."[14]

If it is not used, power can, indeed, be lost. For example, laws that are not regularly enforced can become unenforceable. An ordinance forbidding overnight parking on the streets of Cambridge, Massachusetts, was enforced about once a year, and an acquaintance, who was in law school at the time, used that fact to have his ticket nullified. The law had lost its power through lack of use.

At the same time, tyranny begets opposition. The abuse of power carries with it the risk of losing it. Machiavelli warns the prince not to rape his female subjects if the prince wants his subjects to fight for him.[15] From *Sic semper tyrannis!* to "Give me liberty or give me death!" the evidence is overwhelming that the gross abuse of power risks the loss of it. One need only think back to the previous discussion on the paradox of the source of authority to be reminded why. If power ultimately rests with the governed and the governor abuses his power, the governed will find themselves a new leader.

On an everyday basis, subtleties in the use—and abuse—of power abound. In the early 1980s, a new dean was appointed to a nationally respected business school. He quickly replaced his predecessor's fancy office furniture with a desk, conference table, and chairs more fitting to his own personality. At the same time, he obtained a state-of-the-art personal computer for use at his home, where he did substantial school-related work on weekends and evenings. There was little objection to spending scarce resources on new furniture, but a number of faculty felt that the computer (for which a better need-based argument could be made than for the furniture) represented an abuse of power.

At the GOP convention in 1988, a day was spent with a friend who was an influential congressman. The representative could be observed entering restricted areas without a pass, assuming that he would be recognized. When asked about perks and exercises of power, he replied earnestly: "Have you seen me do anything that could be interpreted as an *abuse* of power?" The honest response was no, he had not. Obviously, the congressman knew both sides of this paradox.

### Paradox of Kinship—Being "One-of-Us" Versus Appearing Larger Than Life

When organizations become so large that the leaders cannot have individual, personal relationships with each member, leaders build symbolic personal relationships, a kinship with followers. Sometimes it's as simple as using "we" rather than "I" in conversation. This creates a feeling that success is mutual, not something done exclusively by the hands of the leader. Irwin Frederman, president of Monolithic Memories, demonstrated this mindset when asked in an interview how he was able to save his company. He replied, "I didn't turn the company around. I presided over it. The people in this company turned it around. I was the captain of the ship, but they were doing all the rowing."[16]

However, even as they are building kinship, that "one of us" feeling with their followers, leaders also must build a mystery around themselves. This is done through symbolic acts, mass promotion of key acts, and using the entourage of those close to the leader to build larger-than-life myths. One beneficiary of this myth-building is Seymour Cray, whose company, Cray Research, is a world-class innovator in supercomputers. Listen to John Rollwagen, president and CEO of Cray Research:

> Maybe 90% of our employees have never met Seymour, but everyone knows Seymour stories. There's the one about Seymour building a new sailboat each spring, sailing it over the summer and then burning it at the end of the season so he wouldn't be bound by that year's mistakes when he designs a more perfect craft the following year. That's the way Seymour approaches computer design. It says a great deal about innovation. Some of the Seymour stories probably aren't true, but I wouldn't deny them for the world.[17]

When a person has great status, when someone occupies a towering leadership role, then evidence of the leader's humanity can provide a sense of kinship. President George Bush exercised symbolic kinship when he announced that his mother had always made him eat broccoli, even though he didn't like it. Now that he was president, Bush said, he wasn't going to eat it any more. He built the bridge between the president and the "folks." This was not a trivial remark: the Broccoli Growers Association picketed in front of the House of Representatives' office buildings for the next three months. Now, suppose Bush had told the story of having been made to eat broccoli *before* he was elected president. The same story that humanized the president might have hurt his candidacy by undermining the voters' confidence that he was presidential timber.

This paradox requires a delicate mixture of hero and kinship. The stakes can be high. Followers have expectations of how heroes behave, and the hero can be toppled by showing too much humanity. Some leaders have been hurt by discovery of marital infidelity; some have not. Catherine the Great of Russia carried on outrageously with little attempt at discretion. Dwight Eisenhower, Nelson Rockefeller, and John Kennedy were much more discreet about their alleged amorous affairs.

Another leader who is able to demonstrate kinship is Larry E. Wilner, who was called upon as general manager of Western Union to turn that division around. In an interview, he explained that, when he took over the helm, he came in saying, "I hope you guys know how this division works, because we are going to have to do this together." He never used the word "personnel," as if employees were assets under his care; he used the word "people" instead. His key technique was to treat people as individuals, to be in personal contact with them, and to keep them informed about as much as possible in a timely manner. The results: the division's turnover rate dropped from 15 percent to 4 percent in a year, and he raised the gross margin to 40 percent, the net margin to over 16 percent.

### Paradox of Information— Share to Get Loyalty Versus Keep the Power of Knowledge

Part of what made Wal-Mart's Sam Walton a legend was his willingness to share information with his "associates" (employees). Company financial results and individual store results were posted in Wal-Marts across the nation. In a 1991 interview, Walton told *Fortune* magazine, "What sets us apart is that we train people to be merchants. We let them see the numbers so they know exactly how they're doing within the store and within the company; they know their cost, their mark-up, their overhead and their profit. It's a big responsibility and a big opportunity."[18] It made thousands of loyal Wal-Mart employees feel like "associates."

Then, there is the impact on morale and loyalty when employees find out critical changes in their company in the daily newspaper before they hear

it from management directly. The likely response: "They treat me like a corporate mushroom: they keep me in the dark and feed me bullshit!" Sharing information helps employees buy into corporate goals and increases empowerment. Denying information makes people feel that management couldn't care less about them.

However, the other side of this paradox is this: one source of authority is information the boss has that others do not. Knowledge is power. In terms of organizational dynamics, knowing things others do not know is power. It leads to respect, often the kind of respect people expect their leaders to deserve.

Bosses with little capacity for leadership can hold onto power by zealously guarding their sources of information and trading the needed information they possess for demonstrations of obsequiousness; that is the opposite of leadership by sharing power. This is the paradox at work for bosses who want to show leadership. However, even looking strictly at leaders, rather than managers, the paradox persists. Leaders want to be revered for their fountain of knowledge, their capacity to use their sources, and their network. That adds to the status followers need to give to their leaders. To give it away can undo leadership capacity.

Good leaders must strike a balance in response to changing conditions and particular situations between the information they share and that which they release carefully. The goal is to retain and enhance the leaders' power and the aura of respect it gives them, yet maintain the morale advantages of openness.

### Paradox of Followership— Leadership Supplied by Followers

No matter how hard they might try, leaders cannot do it all. At times, bosses who do not possess leadership skills adequate to the task set before them are bailed out by their followers. For any number of reasons—organizational survival, morale, accomplishment of mission—members of organizations often assist their leaders by suggesting or supplying behavior that articulates or exercises leadership.

Those offering the help may be the informal leaders of the group, or they may be other subordinates who are in positions to set an inspiring example, to articulate a vision, or to write powerful prose that builds emotional commitment to goals, policies, and actions. Subordinate divisions may have general managers who build strong teams and shared goals. It may be the sum of the impact of these subordinate general managers that fills the leadership gap.

A strong example of this can be seen in the movie *Twelve O'Clock High.*[19] When a beloved but ineffective commander of an early B-17 bomber group in England during WWII is replaced by General Savage, an archetype of impersonal toughness who hides his emotions and rules by the book, a crisis of morale quickly becomes a catastrophe. All the pilots under the general ask for transfers! Savage would have been finished before he got a chance to start if it had not been for the company adjutant, whose loyalty was to the bomber group. It was this man, Major Stovall, who saved the day by offering to stall the paperwork on the pilots' transfers. Stovall also rescued Savage from a morale disaster concerning a rash demotion by the general: Stovall assigned the poor soldier to be the general's driver, a position that justified his former rank. There are five or six more explicit examples of leadership exercised by subordinates in this extraordinary film, which was based closely on actual people and events. Followers made Savage an acceptable leader. They do it in other places and contexts as well.

In industry and in organizations of all kinds, leadership often is exercised by followers in order to save the group from setbacks. Sometimes an incompetent boss is kept in office long after his lack of qualification is obvious because his employees save his backside. Perhaps they fear a worse disaster if the organization's failure were to become headless. Sometimes the motivation is just to make the group succeed. In all cases, good bosses and good leaders often are helped by real leadership exercised by those who work for them.

Some bosses abandon many of the challenges available to them to be leaders, but in other cases, bosses who are excellent managers delegate and empower sufficiently so that followers have the initiative to cause leadership to emerge from within. This makes the boss appear to be more of a leader than he or she is (this certainly was the result with Savage, though it was not motivated by any efforts toward good management on his part).

Walton was famous for advocating this kind of servant leadership. Listen in on this conversation between the late retailing giant and an associate at Store No. 950 in Memphis when he dropped in for one of his famous unannounced visits:

> A manager rushes up with an associate in tow.
> "Mr. Walton, I want you to meet Renee. She runs one of the top ten pet departments in the country."
> "Well, Renee, bless your heart. What percentage of the store [sales] are you doing?"
> "Last year it was 3.1%," Renee says, "but this year I'm trying for 3.3%."
> "Well, Renee, that's amazing," says Sam. "You know our average pet department only does about 2.4%. Keep up the great work."[20]

Leaders, in their capacity as leaders, create empowerment through inspiration, by creating missions with meaning for people, by developing shared goals and values. Given enough management skills to delegate and empower and the leadership courage to let people stumble as they try new things, leadership will emerge from within. Because inspiration implies action by the inspired, this part of leadership is creating subordinate leaders. One of the stated goals of the software company Intuit, which created the home financial package Quicken, was to design a package that was so usable that it would create not just users, but "apostles." A business professor who regularly teaches a case study on Intuit polls his class: "How many have Quicken?" (Most do.) "How many got it from a recommendation?" (Most did.) "How many have recommended it to others?" (Most have.) Those are apostles—leadership by leader-inspired followers.

It takes many people at many levels to make a culture real in an organization. The same is true for a vision of a strategy, a mission: it works best if it is widely shared. Sharing a vision seldom involves only one-to-many communication. Groups sign on, become passionate about the mission, and share it with their subordinates persuasively. This cascading of commitment is evidence of leadership exercised at all levels of the organization.

## Paradox of Privilege— Role Versus Person

Is the ability to lead derived from the role that leaders are given—their title or position on the organizational chart—or does it come from their personal qualities? Obviously, neither is enough: having the role without the ability to lead guarantees failure, but without a role, a potential leader cannot act. So the question then becomes, how much power comes from the office, and how much from the person? The answer: it depends. Such is the paradoxical nature of leadership.

Political perks are a good example of this paradox of role versus person. Politicians have big offices, but they do not own them. They receive many ceremonial gifts that they can't keep. To some extent, leaders must reject personalizing their power by giving the power to the role. Yet, they must still fill the role, take ownership of it, and personalize it. An example of this was when Caesar rejected the crown three times and then took it for his own.

If the role holder does not personalize the role, he or she may not be able to hold it. It's much like a wolf in the forest marking a tree, even though it isn't the wolf's tree. Woe to leaders who act like the role is theirs to keep and use as they will.

The system promotes followers and loyalty to the institution. Soldiers are taught to salute all officers. "Honor the chain of command" is the rule in the military as well as in many businesses and bureaucracies. Titular, formal authority, the power of the role, generally belongs to the person in that role only as long as the person has the role.

Bosses without significant leadership skill often hide behind their role. Leaders have a harder time doing this because of the need to personalize their role, to offer their followers more than a box in an organizational chart. However, this involves the risk that they will, or will be perceived to, assume the power is theirs independently. It often hurts a

leader to take advantage of perks. A good example of that was demonstrated by Archie McCardell, CEO of International Harvester. He took a bonus that he had earned for past successes in a year of corporate hardship in which others, including the union rank and file, were asked to take cuts.

This paradox of privilege is related to the paradox of kinship in that roles make severe demands on those who hold them. The vestal virgin cannot fool around. The Catholic priest cannot marry. One's humanity is somewhat limited by the demands of filling a distinct role; yet, leadership power is enhanced when role holders are human, real people. Professors, ministers, and mental health practitioners often have psychological power over their students, parishioners, and patients. It is highly unethical for these professionals to use this power to gain repeated and flagrant sexual favors.

This paradox is also related to the paradox of power. It is important to keep in mind that fine line between using one's power—such as taking advantage of perks—and the perception that one is abusing that power. (People think tightrope walkers have a tough job!)

Obviously, there is overlap among most of these ten paradoxes, and nowhere is it written in stone there be only ten. However, the strong fact remains that there is much that is truly paradoxical about leadership. The crucial point is that leadership is a skill involving judgment and wisdom, which is distinct from knowledge. Wisdom and judgment are the marrying of knowledge with experience. With leadership, the questions must be understood so the answers can be found in individual situations. There are very few "if *a*, then *b*" solutions. Rather, it is "if *a*, then *b*" when faced with today's circumstances. Tomorrow it very well could be "if *a*, then *c* or *d* or *e* or *f* or . . . "

There is another way in which the meaning of leadership can be lost: when it is taken out of context. This is crucial to the study of leadership. Being a leader is only part of the job of being an effective executive. The challenge of being in command is much broader than what this book means by leadership.

Although leadership is invaluable to successful executives, it is just one of seven key roles they must play. In order to understand the part that leadership plays, it is imperative to understand it in the context of the challenge facing executives, whether in industry, government, not-for-profit organizations, health care, the professions, or the military.

## Notes

1. James M. Kouzes and Barry Z. Posner, *The Leadership Challenge* (San Francisco, Calif.: Jossey-Bass Publishers, 1991), p. 182.

2. Ibid., p. 24.

3. Gerald Heard, "Ethics in Business," speech, Harvard Business School, Boston, Mass., 1961.

4. Joseph Fletcher, *Situation Ethics* (Philadelphia, Pa.: Westminster Press, 1966), p. 142.

5. Jack Telnack, Ford Motor Company, in Kouzes and Posner, *The Leadership Challenge,* p. 164.

6. J. Schermerhorn, J. Hunt, and R. Osborn, *Managing Organizational Behavior* (New York: John Wiley and Sons, 1991), p. 431.

7. E. P. Hollander, "Conformity, Status and Idiosyncratic Credit," *Psychological Review* 65 (1958): 124.

8. Said by Stan Freberg in a routine in which a Sam Spade-type detective is hired by Brutus to catch Caesar's murderer.

9. William Oncken, Jr., "Quotations of Benjamin Franklin's Grandfather," *Managing Management Time* (transcript of video and audio tape series) (Dallas, Tex.: William Oncken Corporation, 1973), p. 225.

10. Philip Selznick, *Leadership in Administration* (New York: Harper & Row, 1957), pp. 17, 22, 26-27 and passim; quote, p. 28.

11. Hollander, "Conformity, Status and Idiosyncrasy Credit," p. 124.

12. Jeffrey Sonnenfeld and Meredith Lazo, "United Parcel Service," case study 9-488-016, Harvard Business School, 1992, p. 9.

13. See A. Zaleznik, C. R. Christensen, and F. J. Roethlisberger, *The Motivation, Productivity and Satisfaction of Workers: A Prediction Study* (Boston, Mass.: Division of Research, Harvard Business School, 1958), for the classification of group members as social leaders, task leaders, regulars, deviants, and isolates.

14. E. Tatum Christiansen, "Schlumberger, Ltd.: Jean Riboud Excerpts from 'A Certain Poetry' by Ken Aluetta," case study 384-087, Harvard Business School, 1983, 1984 (excerpted from Ken Aluetta, "A Certain Poetry—Parts I and II," *The New Yorker,* 1983), in Joseph L. Bower, Christopher A. Bartlett, C. Roland Christensen, Andrall E. Pearson, and Kenneth R. Andrews, *Business Policy: Text and Cases,* 7th ed. (Homewood, Ill.: Richard D. Irwin, 1991), p. 405.

15. Niccolò Machiavelli, *The Prince* (trans. Thomas G. Bergin) (New York: Appleton-Century-Crofts, 1947), p. 48.

16. As quoted in "A Bean Counter With a Heart," *San Jose Mercury News,* November 24, 1986, p. C1, by Kouzes and Posner, *The Leadership Challenge,* p. 153.

17. Francis J. Aguilar and Caroline Brainard, "Cray Research, Inc.," Harvard Business School, case study 9-385-011, 1985, p. 11.

18. John Huey, "America's Most Successful Merchant," *Fortune,* September 23, 1991, p. 50.

19. Sy Bartlett and Beime Lay, Jr., *Twelve O'Clock High* (movie) (Twentieth Century Fox, 1949).

20. Huey, "America's Most Successful Merchant," p. 30.

# 9

# Reforming Institutionalized Organizations

NILS BRUNSSON
JOHAN P. OLSEN

For decades governments worldwide have provided students of public administration with ample opportunity to study the processes of reform. Though there have been cycles of enthusiasm and disappointment, governments seem to remain convinced that public administration can be improved by means of explicit choice and design. In recent years, many governments have embarked on a new round of reforms. Working on an assumption that major surgery is needed, they have put comprehensive administrative reform on the national political agenda, formulating policies both to reshape the public sector and to redraw the boundary between the public and the private sectors. Across a range of political, economic, and cultural settings, there is a great deal of overlap in the problems that have been identified and the solutions that have been proposed.

Public administration is generally criticized for being too complex, centralized, interventionist, powerful, bureaucratic, rigid, and incompetent. It is thought to be inadequately responsive to elected leaders and citizens, and too sensitive to pressure from organized interests and groups, while devoting too little attention to cost-effectiveness, results, efficiency, and productivity. There is a general disenchantment with the performance, structures, and processes of public administration, which has arisen after numerous attempts over a long period to modernize and rationalize the structures of public administration. We must therefore question whether the ideas, concepts, and theories underlying those reforms have been adequate (Brunsson 1985, 1989; Olsen 1986, 1988a, 1989b; Knott and Miller 1987; Kooiman and Eliassen 1987; Sjöblom and Ståhlberg 1987; Campbell and Peters 1988; Crozier 1988; Dente and Kjellberg 1988; Peters 1988a; Brunsson et al. 1989; Egeberg 1989a; March and Olsen 1989).

SOURCE: From *The Reforming Organization*, by N. Brunsson and J. P. Olsen. London: Routledge, 1993. Reprinted with permission.

For most of its history, public administration has been a practical art rather than a theoretical discipline. In administrative reform, applied, institution-specific knowledge and political pressure have been more influential than theoretical models (Sjøblom and Ståhlberg 1987). Advisers have seldom accounted explicitly for their assumptions and methods (Scharpf 1977). Yet progress in explaining change and inertia in political institutions is likely to depend on the development of better theoretical ideas and concepts in order to understand the nature of reforms as explicitly designed and controlled modifications in organizational structure in order to achieve pre-stated goals.

Recent reform programmes may encourage a return to some old and central questions in political theory concerning the role of administration. They might also help to restore government structure and administrative variables as legitimate focuses of research (Campbell and Peters 1988). Recent reform programmes provide students of comparative public administration with the opportunity to update their theoretical framework for analysing organizations and their formation. Do the structures of governmental and political institutions matter? If so, what are the effects of different organizational forms? Why have the current forms developed? How can we explain their origins, development, and endurance?

This chapter explores how modernization programmes are affected by the characteristics of existing institutions. First, we argue that contemporary modernization programmes are based on an instrumental view of organizational decision-making and change. The following section elaborates one part of the alternative perspective, namely, the idea that organizations are institutionalized. Then we examine some of the implications of this idea for the study of modernization programmes. Finally, we show that while the instrumental view of organizations dominates the way reformers talk and write about modernization, an institutional approach is a better explanatory tool in analysing the activities of reformers and the outcomes of reform efforts.

## Modernization, Rational Adaptation, and Competitive Selection

What does it mean to be, or to become, modern? Modernization as a concept suggests a society heading towards a better state, a development towards progress and maturity (Bendor 1977; Eckstein 1982; Offe 1987). "Modern" society, as compared with "traditional" or "primitive," implies a rational approach, effectiveness, efficiency, and improvement. Ideas of reform defined as modern are difficult to challenge. Individuals who resist reform are easily labelled old-fashioned, outmoded, obsolete, obstructive, irrational, or reactionary. For change to be embarked upon, a country's public sector should be seen to be "lagging behind" the public administration in other countries or the private sector.

Modernization is a disputed term, but there seems to be agreement on two basic issues related to decision-making and organizations. The first is that modernization implies individual choice based on utilitarian calculation, which is extended at the expense of rule-prescribed behaviour derived from custom, habit, and prescriptive roles. The underlying principle of behaviour in modern society is the choice of optimum means (including organizational forms, processes, leaders, and time allocation) in pursuit of self-determined goals.

The second area of broad agreement regarding organizations is that the sphere of formal organizations, as deliberately designed instruments for the attainment of specified goals, grows at the expense of traditional bonds and forms of social organization like the family, the local community, and the religious community. Formal organizations are seen as the most rational and efficient form of social organization. They are fundamental to modern civilization, an expression of the high value modern society places on means-end rationality, effectiveness, and productivity (Etzioni 1964). Because the rational and the traditional are seen as opposites, breaking with the past becomes a central aspect of modern culture. In order to be effective and productive it is necessary to be able to adapt to changing circumstances, whether past or anticipated. Change is normal and a sign of modernity.

Whereas public administration traditionally pursued absolute organizational principles, the structure-performance hypothesis of organizational theory suggests that structures are contingent on circumstance. Depending on the aims and the environment of an organization, some structures are more effective and efficient than others. Success depends on constructing appropriate links between an organization's structure and its shifting context. Thus, the problem of organizational design is to improve adaptability to changing conditions (Lawrence and Lorsch 1967; Galbraith 1973, 1977). Organizational effectiveness becomes one of the main determinants of structure, and the organizational forms which exist in a society are the ones that are most effective and efficient within that society (Basu et al. 1987). Increasingly efficient interaction with the broad environment is attained through one of two processes: rational adaptation or competitive selection.

### Efficient Reform and Rational Adaptation

In this section, our focus is on single organizations. We start from the premise that organizational forms can deliberately be chosen. Changes in structure are explained as willed design.

Organizations are consciously planned to seek specific goals. They continually evaluate their activities and respond to new opportunities and challenges by means of deliberate restructuring (Etzioni 1964). Organizations may either adapt to resource dependencies (Pfeffer and Salancik 1978) or to norms and beliefs in their environment (Meyer and Rowan 1977), or they may restructure themselves in order to reduce transaction costs (Williamson 1975, 1985). Reformers are assumed not only to know what they want but to be able to diagnose what is wrong with the organization and its performance; to be able to dictate how structures should be changed in order to meet objectives, as well as to have the authority and power to implement reforms.

### Efficient Environments and Competitive Selection

Here we consider changes within a population of organizations. The survival of an organizational form or an individual organization depends on how well they match their environment. Yet within this tradition individual organizations are seen as prisoners of their past with no capacity to transform themselves. Alternatively, changes have little adaptive value, in that they do not improve an organization's performance or its chances of survival. Structural change and variation are dictated by the environment, and better matches are achieved through the development of new, individual organizations and organizational forms which, over time, replace older and less well-adapted ones (Stinchcombe 1965; Hannan and Freeman 1977, 1984). Assuming a context of efficient, competitive selection, neo-classical economists see particular structures as optimal outcomes of the current balance of competing forces. In explaining variations in structure, the static equilibrium theory of maximizing behaviour under perfect competition need not consider the past, the process through which a structure is generated, or the characteristics of reformers trying to adapt an organization to its environment (Basu et al. 1987).

How helpful are the ideas of rational adaptation and competitive selection when it comes to understanding change and reforms in public administration? There is no reason to suppose either that reformers are always successful in adapting organizations to contingencies or that competition and selection mechanisms are always effective in weeding out organizations that are not optimal. The next section argues that when adaptation and selection processes are inefficient, it is more productive to view political organizations as institutions than as instruments.

### *Bounded Morality, Intelligence, and Power, and the Relevance of Institutions*

It is easy to imagine conditions under which reformers or environments are inefficient. Reformers may be unable to formulate precise, consistent, and stable goals. Their analytical capabilities may be overwhelmed by the complexity of a situation or by the pace of change. They may lack the power to implement their choices. At the opposite extreme, contextual constraints on administrative reforms may be overestimated. It might require time to achieve equilibrium, or there may possibly be a number of different equilibria. An institutional analysis of political organizations must consider the boundedness of morality, intelligence, and power.

## Bounded Morality

The concept of bounded morality challenges the idea that organizational improvement can be evaluated on the basis of a shared purpose or fixed individual preferences. Organizations routinely make decisions without the kind of preferences that would satisfy models of rational choice and rational adaptation (March 1981a). Individuals may maintain goals for an organization, but goal ambiguity and goal conflict are normal. Individuals can coordinate their actions and cooperate without agreeing on goals (Cyert and March 1963; Keeley 1988). Organizational structure and decision-making also affect goals, and changing (endogenous) preferences make it difficult to apply the Coase theorem (1937, 1960), which suggests that organizational structures are to be evaluated by their contributions to lowering transaction costs. One implication of endogenous preferences is that it becomes more difficult to evaluate the performance and improvement of organizations (March 1978; von Weizsäcker 1984).

## Bounded Intelligence

While the idea of bounded rationality is well known, the problems of experiential learning have only recently been explored in studies of formal organizations (March and Olsen 1975; Levitt and March 1988). Both ideas seem relevant to the study of public administration, in which the paucity of evidence stands in sharp contrast to the firmly held ideological convictions aroused by alternative organizational proposals. There is still no firm theo-

retical basis for organizational design, and proposals for change therefore tend to be contradictory (Simon 1957; Kaufman 1977; Seidman 1980). When research indicates that structure affects participation, patterns of interaction, response levels, the nature of conflicts, the balance of power within organizations or their capacity for innovation, the authors usually emphasize the tentative and provisional nature of their findings. Others are more disillusioned, and point to the scarcity of testable hypotheses and generalizable explanations as well as to the problems of describing, measuring, and classifying today's mixed organizational structures. The essence is captured by Peters (1988a), who argues that the structure of administrative systems is the most frequently manipulated and perhaps the least understood aspect of public administration. Reformers themselves are rarely interested in a thorough evaluation of what reforms have achieved (Brown 1979; Feldman and March 1981; Steinman and Miewald 1984; Røvik 1987; Levitt and March 1988).

## Bounded Power

Structural change is often resisted because those affected do not perceive it as beneficial and progressive. Instead, reform proposals are regarded as being disruptive, painful, and threatening, and a drain on resources, especially in its effects on the organization's internal structures regulating status, power, and policy.

Organizational reform is an exercise in the acquisition or use of political power (Peters 1988b), and it is unlikely that conflicts can always be resolved by reference to "the presence of one or more power centres which control the concerted efforts of the organization and direct them toward its goals" (Etzioni 1964: 3). It is also unlikely that conflicts can always be resolved by the overriding influence of competition and selection. Environments may be more or less competitive, complex or simple, benign or harsh. They may change slowly or rapidly. Organizations vary as to their power to select, influence, or survive within their environments. Where there are large numbers of incompatible interests, and thus multiple variables with conflicting design implications, a public organization must choose which part of the environment to adapt to (Child 1977; Child and Kieser 1981; Nystrom and Starbuck 1981). Government, in particular, is in the business of forming its environment rather than adapting to it (Hood 1979). Thus, creating commitment and winning support are key aspects of reform processes. We need to study the institutional arrangements and the interests, resources, cleavages, and alliances organized around modernization issues, as well as the value-, interest-, and power bases of organizations to be reformed.

### Organizations as Institutions

In a world of bounded morality, intelligence, and power, political organizations may be conceptualized as institutions rather than as instruments. When political organizations are analysed as institutions, they are seen to be collections of rules. These rules define legitimate participants and agendas, prescribe the rules of the game, and create sanctions against deviations, as well as establishing guidelines for how the institution may be changed. Institutions create a temporary and imperfect order. They influence and simplify the way we think and act, what we observe, how we interpret what we observe, our standards of evaluation and how we cope with conflicts.

The specific perspective on institutional analysis suggested here differs in important ways from an instrumental perspective in (a) its interpretation of how decisions are made, (b) what is at stake in organizational reform efforts, (c) how change takes place, and (d) when structures are likely to change.

Within that perspective (March and Olsen 1989):

• Political actors are driven by a logic of appropriateness built into standard operating procedures, conventions, and rules of thumb rather than (or in addition to) a logic of calculated self-interest.
• Organizations are built around the construction of meaning as well as (or instead of) making choices. Reforms may have as much to do with affecting the interpretations of participants and onlookers as with affecting effectiveness and efficiency.

• Organizational structures cannot easily be metamorphosed to any arbitrary form. Adaptations to environments are not instantaneous or efficient, and equilibrium between environmental contingencies and organizational structures are rare. An organization may survive in spite of the fact that it would not be chosen if decision-makers could select without the constraints of the organization's origin and history (Basu et al. 1987). It may persist even though no individual benefits from it (Akerlof 1976).

The assumption of organizational inertia is a priori not more useful than the assumption of perfect flexibility through rational adaptations or competitive selection. There is a need for history-dependent process models which could explain both flexibility and change. There is still an inadequate understanding of when structures change and what stimulates change. The institutional analysis we present here suggests that major structural change takes place at long intervals. It arises as a consequence either of crises, related to declining performance or increasing expectations, or of conflict between the rights and duties granted by different institutional rule systems. The next section addresses some possible implications of this view: implications for when change will take place, which parts of an organization will change more easily than others, who are most likely to be successful reformers, and what are the likely results of reform efforts.

### *Implications for Studies of Modernization Programmes*

The structures of public administration are simultaneously both stable and fluid. Political organizations are not entirely rigid; nor are they immortal. Nevertheless, comprehensive reforms often fail. Change takes place without explicit decisions to change: there is no prearranged plan and there are no architects (Sait 1938). Change is sometimes explained by means of a life-cycle analogy associated with the birth, maturation, decline, and death of organic systems (Kimberly and Miles 1980; Cameron et al. 1988). Changes occur before decisions are taken. Decision-making does not produce change, or it leads to unanticipated, unintended, or unforeseen changes (March and Olsen 1976, 1983; March 1981b; Romanow 1981).

In order to understand the intricacies of organizational inertia, change, and reform, we need to analyse the interaction of the intentions of reformers, organizational structures, and transformations in society. Organizational change is shaped by neither reformers' intentions nor environmental transformations, though both have a role to play. This view is reflected in the debate of to what extent organizational change depends on the normative match between reform programmes and established organizations, the match between reform programmes and the normative drift in society, the degree to which reform intentions are well-defined or ambiguous, and the organization of reform processes.

## The Normative Matching Between Reforms and Institutionalized Organizations

Organizational responses to external reform efforts are affected by the degree of consistency between the value basis and beliefs underlying a proposed reform and the value basis and beliefs of an organization (March and Olsen 1975). Organizations have their own dynamics. Incremental transformations through routinized processes which relate the organization to its environment (March 1981b) will succeed as long as they are consistent with the established institutional identity of the organization. Organizations mobilize their resources and their allies to resist external efforts to change those parts of their structures which relate closely to their institutional identities. Similarly, individuals who identify with established organizations—because, for example, they have been in power for extended periods and are seen as the architects of current structures—are unlikely to propose and seek to introduce comprehensive reform programmes inconsistent with established institutional identities. For them, creating new agencies will be more attractive than changing an established institutional identity. Since creating new organizations is easiest in times of slack resources, reforming existing organizations becomes

a likely response to performance crises, primarily in periods with little slack.

The more an organization is integrated into a larger political order so that changes in one organization require changes in several others, the less it is likely that deliberate change will occur (Krasner 1988). Constitutional reforms, that is, those affecting the political order regulating the exercise of public authority and power, are difficult to achieve.

## The Normative Matching Between Reforms and Society

Reformers are more likely to succeed if they try to change organizations in ways consistent with long-term trends in society, both international and national, than if they try to go against the tide. Modernization, democratization, bureaucratization, and professionalization represent aggregate processes which constrain the options available to reformers. Moreover, the normative drift of society is not necessarily consistent. In the most extreme case, reformers may try to adapt public administration to conflicting trends or demands that are not reconcilable.

What can be achieved in reforming organizations is a long-standing question in political theory. One view is that people should be taken as they are, with their self-chosen values and individual choices. As argued by Madison (Hamilton et al. 1787-1788/1964), if men were angels no government would be necessary. But humanity is not angelic, and it is neither possible nor even desirable to eradicate all evil from the face of earth. Therefore we need to design political institutions which control and regulate the negative effects of human selfishness and immoral choices by individuals by letting selfish ambition counteract selfish ambition through competition.

A contending idea in political philosophy since Aristotle is that public organizations and laws are not adequate in themselves to ensure virtue. Civic education is necessary to establish moral standards of justice and fairness and to balance principles of public virtue against self-interest (Morrisey 1986; Goldwin 1986). Thus, an alternative to changing public organizations is to change individuals and the demands they make upon public administrations. The weaker civic education is in a society, the more likely it is that public administration will be asked to do things which cannot be done whatever organizational form is adopted. Reform cannot be successful.

## The Ambiguity of Intentions

The outcome of modernization programmes depends on the intentions of the reformers as well as on organizational responses and environmental factors. Reformers are more likely to succeed if their plans are focused and well defined rather than broad and general.

When there is a poor match between reform aims, institutional identities of organizations, and environments, reformers will confront conflicting demands. As a result, they will find it hard to take the initiative and present their plans clearly. More generally, the aims of a reform may themselves be uncertain because the merits of that reform appear to be ambiguous. Politics and public administration reflect a precarious balance between the need for change versus the need for stability. The recent government obsession with change has to be held up against the traditional concern in political analysis for order, predictability, and reliability, and the destructive effects of institutional decline or breakdown (Wolin 1960; Leazes 1987).

There is a dramatic scenario in which reform attempts create conflict and lead to the breakdown of established values, identities, and relationships. It is more common for the search for new structures to conflict with an organization's capacity to perform predictably and accountably. There is a balance to be found between exploiting known structures and exploring the potential benefits of new ones (March 1989). The results of organizations that undergo frequent or protracted reorganizations may be limited, and those organizations have little chance of survival (Hannan and Freeman 1984). Governments in particular may be unwilling to devote much time and energy to introducing comprehensive reforms as opposed to debating the need for change. This is the case when the expected adaptive value is modest because means-end relationships are uncertain, the environment is ambiguous, performance is difficult to measure or evaluate, opposition is likely, or it takes a long time to transform a structure.

The tensions and contradictions inherent in modernization programmes may also affect the willingness of governments to embark on such efforts. For example, representativeness, neutral competence, and executive leadership are competing values in the organization of public agencies. Improvement in one sphere often makes it difficult to improve on the others. One period's horror story of bureaucracy is the next period's ideal. While the reformers of public administration in one period focus on creating incentives for initiative, innovation, and willingness to take responsibility, the bureaucrats of a later one are expected to act in accordance with political dictates rather than in an entrepreneurial style (Kaufman 1956; Jacobsen 1964, 1966).

Why then do reformers keep trying if the improvements in terms of effectiveness and efficiency are so unpredictable and difficult to achieve? Citizens will support a set of norms, beliefs, and practices embodied in public administration, and reform programmes may be a part of the creation of meaning or even as propaganda (March and Olsen 1976, 1983, 1989; Brunsson 1985, 1989). It is often difficult to legitimize reforms by demonstrating that particular decisions will produce appropriate results. Thus, legitimacy depends as much on the willingness to reform, on rhetoric, and on the nature of the reform process as it does on eventual outcomes. Structural, process, or personnel measures are treated as surrogates for outcome measures, and it becomes of vital importance for organizations to maintain normatively approved forms (Meyer and Rowan 1977).

Modernization programmes may be seen as part of a long-term redefinition of politics and society. On the one hand, legitimacy effects may be valuable, independent of structural changes, making reformers more interested in rhetoric than in implementation. On the other hand, ignoring the constraints of bounded morality, intelligence, and power can create unrealistic expectations and overselling the need for reform. Reformers may exaggerate the defects of existing forms and overrate the benefits of new proposals. Possibly, reforms cannot successfully be marketed unless they promise more than they can deliver (Schick 1977).

Using rhetoric to change people's attitudes and beliefs in order to create a normative climate may however also facilitate future structural change. While Marx (1845/1976) viewed the interpretation of history and the changing of history as opposites, it is possible that the two processes are closely related. Debates about reform programmes may alter the values of the state, the purpose and meaning of governmental actions, the rationale and legitimacy of organizational boundaries, the way in which conflict is regulated, and the conditions under which different interests can be pursued (Poggi 1984; Dyson 1980).

**The Organization of Reform**

To succeed, comprehensive reform requires the backing of a strong organization capable of maintaining support for the reform and of overcoming resistance. Any goals of comprehensive reforms that are not apparent in the organization of the reform process itself are unlikely to succeed.

Change can occur when the inherent authority and power of the public administration does not conform to actual influence and control, that is, cannot cope with critical contingencies (Pfeffer 1978). But public administration does not respond instantly to minor deviations in power: it tends to maintain the status quo until the external demands for change are substantial. Comprehensive reforms in public administration are likely to succeed only if there are significant inefficiencies in the historical development of those organizations, that is, if the authority and power exercised by policy makers deviate markedly from the levels they would have held in a state of equilibrium (a "clearance of the power market"; March and Olsen 1989).

Political leaders have succeeded in introducing reforms where reorganizations have been given top priority and ordinary procedures have been bypassed (Roness 1979; Christensen 1987; Egeberg 1984, 1987, 1989a). However, such successes have generally been restricted to the reform of specific governmental agencies. Comprehensive reforms tend to attract more opposition and trigger processes with complex and unforeseen conse-

quences. If the organizational structure cannot protect reform efforts from short-term fluctuations in attention, comprehensive reforms are more likely to become "garbage can" processes and to be derailed or defeated (March and Olsen 1983).

The process of change itself may to a certain extent be institutionalized and rule-bound. In addition, organizations are likely to resist what they see as inappropriate reform procedures. If comprehensive reform presupposes a perceived performance crisis, political pressure and confrontation may, under some conditions, be more productive than merely defining reform as a technical issue. Where there is a history of gradual, consensual reform (such as in the Nordic countries), governments may be less successful in introducing reform under these conditions.

In the next section these speculations are assessed in the light of evidence from some recent reform attempts. To date, there is no comparative study of modernization programmes in a representative sample of countries. The case studies available from single countries or specific organizations have not yet been reviewed and analysed, nor will they be here. Instead, our theoretical speculations are illustrated by specific observations, primarily from studies of modernization efforts in Britain and in the Nordic countries. Given our focus upon normative matches, it is interesting to compare British reforms after the Thatcher victory in 1979 with the reform efforts of the Social Democratic governments of Norway and Sweden.

## *Some Observations*

While some have announced the coming of a postmodern era, modernization programmes are strongly influenced by a vision of modernity, including a conception of organizations as instruments and change as deliberate policy. Such programmes assume that the problems of public administration can be solved by reorganization. Comprehensive administrative policies imply that governments, in order to achieve their political ends, can apply a coherent set of ideas and practices to the organizational structures and processes of public administration. This entails two assumptions: first, that organizational form is a significant determinant of administrative performance; and, second, that choices made by political leaders are important determinants of organizational forms.

The latter concept emphasizes that human will, reason, effort, and power are all involved in the transformation of society. The former represents a view of public administration as part of modern technology, as illustrated by the use of such mechanical metaphors as "instrument," "tool," "apparatus," and "machinery" of governance (Olsen 1988a). In general, the normative world of modernization programmes is characterized by rationality and control. The enthusiasm for rational management techniques remains high although they have produced few striking successes and several failures in the public sector (Landau and Stout 1979; Wittrock and Lindström 1984; Goodsell 1985).

In contrast, the behavioural world of modernizers is more complex and less easy to predict or control. There is a marked lack of alternative organizational models and uncertainty about their effects. For instance, there is a scarcity of literature on the distinctions between public and private organizations, or between centralized or decentralized structures. Reformers often argue that administrative policies should be seen as experimental and conscious attempts to learn from experience. Nevertheless, changes are seldom followed by systematic efforts to assess successes and failures:

> Little information has been made available by any reporting country on the evaluation of results of their modernization efforts. . . . Most countries have yet to incorporate full-scale evaluation in their reform efforts. (OECD 1989: 9)

Modernization programmes (at least in OECD countries) are collections of reform ideas rather than coherent doctrines with a unified strategy of change. Yet the international tendency in the 1980s was neo-liberal and was critical of many of the developments in the post-World War II (Social Democratic) welfare state. This was replaced with "more managerial thinking and market mentality" (OECD 1987: 117). The private sector became the role model, and public administration was seen as a service to citizens as clients and consumers. Programmes reflected both the penetration of the macroeconomic, cost-benefit approach to public administration (Colvin 1985; Downs and Larkey 1986) and the renewed interest in the economics of organizations (Moe 1984).

There was widespread agreement among governments regarding the need to reshape the public sector in order to increase efficiency and improve public services. The goals of public administration were to be specified precisely, and better methods for monitoring results and measuring efficiency and productivity were to be sought. Citizens' desires were to be met through prices and markets rather than by means of formal representation, advocacy, and rules. The introduction of market-style forms in the public sector would create more competition and increase the citizen's freedom of choice. The administrative culture was to be transformed. There was little support for the Weberian idea that bureaucracy was the most modern, rational, and efficient form of administration (Weber et al. 1924/1978). What was to be achieved was more important than how (in terms of procedures and rules), and incentives and performance were to be more closely linked. A modern public administration was supposed to delegate and decentralize in order to improve its flexibility. The possible benefits of stability and the trade-offs between stability and adaptability were barely considered. The programmes also reflected a strong belief in the value of information technology and electronic data-processing equipment.

Modernization programmes varied in their proposals for redrawing the boundaries between the public and the private sectors. Some governments wanted to reduce public sector expenditure and employment; others were "pragmatic" or reluctant to commit themselves on this point, but none advocated major growth in the public sector.

From the viewpoint of normative matching, these observations are not surprising. While a concern with economy and efficiency is common to most governments, the issue of privatization was linked to a major cleavage in the organizing politics of many countries. It was predictable that the Thatcher government, with its neo-liberal goals and negative attitudes towards the public sector, should be in the forefront of modernization efforts. It is not surprising that this government emphasized both privatization and value-for-money.

As expected, the Social Democratic governments in Norway and Sweden showed little enthusiasm for reforming public administration along neo-liberal lines. Social Democratic programmes focused upon reforming the public sector in order to make it perform better, rather than upon privatization. The Swedish programme more than any other accentuated the need to widen democratic participation. Yet even in Sweden the private sector became the role model for civil servants (Czarniawska 1985) and for the symbols and logos employed by the state (Petersson and Fredén 1987).

Modernization programmes tended to lack explicit structural analyses, for instance, of what organizational options were available to reformers in modern society. When options were discussed, they were usually seen as dependent upon economic developments. The idea of a normative mismatch between reforms and general trends in society may, however, help explain why it is often difficult for reformers to deregulate (Christensen 1989) or to implement the management-by-objectives features of some modernization programmes.

Modernization, involving as it does a reduction in the effectiveness of informal control via shared standards of appropriateness, creates a need for more detailed, formal rules and more powerful enforcement mechanisms. As society becomes more fragmented and specialized, with less common socialization, less frequent contacts between social groups, and more utilitarian calculation and strategic behaviour, there will be a wider demand for formal rules and contracts in order to resolve conflicts (North 1984). It follows that attempts to reduce the number of formal rules may be unlikely to succeed in modern society. Many of those likely to lose out in bargaining over private contracts may prefer public regulation. Similarly, techniques like management-by-objectives may be difficult to implement in modern society because the participants do not share common goals. In a plural society, one group of actors cannot easily force its goals upon another.

Recent reform efforts are responses to a situation where many public programmes have built-in, quasi-mechanical increases in expenditure, where citizens-as-taxpayers are seemingly unwilling to pay more, and yet citizens-as-clients and consumers demand new services as well as higher service efficiency and quality (OECD 1989). The idea that a proper response is to reform public administration and thereby provide better services for less money has to be attractive to elected politicians. However, it is not obvious that this idea is viable, that is, that better services for less money can be achieved simultaneously in any public organization.

It is quite probable that, through the long period of growth in public administration, some organizations accumulated excess resources and became inefficient. However, it is unclear how much waste there is in public administration today (Kelman 1985). Improving efficiency may also be relatively unimportant in the context of solving a nation's economic problems. The running costs of government departments are small in comparison with expenditure on public programmes (Fry 1988). As it is uncertain what can be achieved through reorganization, modern society may need to consider the possibility of coping with the current demands through civic education and of initiating public debate about the realism and legitimacy of those demands.

The conflicts between the international neo-liberal trend and their own ideologies and traditions have created difficulties for the Social Democratic governments in the Nordic countries in clearly defining their intentions as well as their criteria for improvement and success in public administration. Reform programmes promised better service, a better and more efficient economy, improved workplaces for employees, and greater democracy through increasing the influence of elected leaders and the public generally. Programmes were founded on a rhetorical claim of serving common, apolitical goals of economy and efficiency. They retreated from politically divisive issues like privatization and whether reforms would serve particular groups. For instance, the Danish government promised that life would improve for Danish citizens. The Swedish government said it would take the citizens' part against bureaucratic inefficiency. What was lacking in such statements was any explicit consideration of whether the goals appeared consistent and achievable in light of the dilemmas and conflicts inherent in comprehensive administrative reforms. The programmes primarily addressed how public administration could improve its practices in choosing means. There was little assessment of the values being pursued or of the particular concept of welfare underlying the modernization programmes (Mellbourn 1986; Olsen 1988a, 1988b; Bentzon 1988; Hansen 1989).

By contrast, the intentions of the Thatcher government were clearer, although at first even this government had difficulty stating precisely what it wanted to do. There was no blueprint for action, no master plan. Goals evolved over time. Neither were there any ready-made, reliable indicators of performance. It was difficult to develop measures that were not ambiguous, misleading, or open to manipulation, to define aims and to measure the value of services and programmes, as well as to measure the efficiency with which resources were used. In short, it was difficult to say whether citizens were getting good value for their money (Beeton 1987; Harrison and Gretton 1987).

During this period, reform ideas were not universally accepted. Governmental processes in the Nordic countries and Britain differ both in how they cope with conflict and how they organize reforms. In the Nordic countries, modernization efforts provide illustrations of the limitations of parliamentarian and ministerial hierarchy. Governments were reluctant to spend large sums on administrative reform. Reform agencies were politically weak and of low status. Resources crucial to the success of administrative policy were often controlled by other state organizations. The ambitious aim of a comprehensive administrative policy was not built into the reform process (Mellbourn 1986; Olsen 1988a). In contrast, in Britain secretariats attached to the Prime Minister's office directed and coordinated reforms from the highest level of political authority.

Similarly, there were differences in reform styles. In the Nordic countries, where there was a commitment to consensus, conflict was avoided. This was particularly so where opponents claimed

that reform proposals broke with the post-World War II development of the welfare state and raised constitutional questions (March and Olsen 1989).

The Thatcher government, on the other hand, employed a confrontational and ideological style, making its era a traumatic one for the career civil service and the trade unions (Hastings and Levie 1983; Metcalf and Richards 1987; Fry 1988). There were profound changes, and it was claimed that the Thatcher reforms constituted a turning point in the evolution of British government from which there would be no going back (LeGrand and Robinson 1984; Gray and Jenkins 1985; Wass 1985; Harrison and Gretton 1987; Metcalf and Richards 1987). It was less clear whether the promised improvements in efficiency were achieved, and in particular there were doubts about the benefits of changing public monopolies into private monopolies (Kay and Thompson 1986).

Since 1945 the Nordic countries have shown a considerable capacity for reform, although it is difficult to determine what has really been achieved in terms of structural change (Mellbourn 1986; Winther 1987; Bentzon 1988; Olsen 1988a, 1988b; Hansen 1989). The concepts and data employed in the modernization process have been more appropriate to rhetoric and image-building than to rational analysis and choice. If we see reform processes as part of a struggle for control over people's minds, the efforts to date can be regarded as attempts to create a new consensus about the role and organization of public administration. On the other hand, the debate about modernization may have prepared the ground for major changes in public attitudes towards and understanding about the public sector, so perhaps facilitating future structural change.

## Postscript

Although the observations offered in this chapter do not provide a strong test of the theoretical speculations we have presented, we believe they show some promise. In a world of bounded morality, intelligence, and power, public organizations may be understood as institutions, rather than as instruments deliberately designed and redesigned. Processes of rational adaptation and competitive selection would not therefore dictate the form of public administration, but they would be relevant in institutional transformation. History could have direction even if it is not determined or directed by the intention and explicit choices of reformers. To argue that public administration can change but that it is not easily transformed to any arbitrary form is not to assert that political leadership through explicit choice and design is impossible.

In the remainder of this book, we discuss three main issues in relation to administrative reforms: their origins, contents, and implementation. These issues must be analysed in order to answer the question we posed in the first chapter as to the freedom of action and power of reformers. Control over reforms consists of the power to initiate them, to determine their content, and to implement them so that they have the desired effects. When discussing these themes it is important to consider the institutional qualities of organizations analysed in this chapter. But in the next four chapters we will also describe how organizational environments are institutionalized and how this phenomenon affects the conditions of reform.

Determining the origins of reform involves asking why reforms are ever initiated in organizations and what makes reforms such frequent phenomena in modern organizations. This is the subject of the next chapter. In Chapters 4, 5, and 6 we discuss how the content of reforms emerges. Chapters 7 to 11 deal with the implementation of reforms. In the final chapter we use the analyses offered in the previous chapters to draw some conclusions as to power over reforms. We argue that reformers are much less powerful than is supposed in the reform idea.

## References

Akerlof, George A. (1976). "The economics of caste and of the rat race and other woeful tales," *Quarterly Journal of Economics* 90: 599-617.

Basu, K., Jones, E. and Schlicht, E. (1987). "The growth and decay of custom: The role of the New Institutional Economics in economic history," *Explorations in Economic History* 24: 1-21.

Beeton, D. (1987). "Measuring departmental performance," in A. Harrison and J. Gretton (eds.), *Reshaping Central Government*, New Brunswick/London: Transaction Books, 77-89.

Bendor, J. (1977). "Confusion between developmental and evolutionary theories," *Administration and Society* 8(4): 481-514.

Bentzon, K. H. (1988). *Fra vækst til omstilling—modernisering af den offentlige sektor*, Copenhagen: Nyt fra Samfundsviden skabeme.

Brown, R. G. (1979). *Reorganizing the National Health Service: A Case Study in Administrative Change*, Oxford: Blackwell/Robertson.

Brunsson, N. (1985). *The Irrational Organization: Irrationality as a Basis for Organizational Action and Change*, Chichester: Wiley.

Brunsson, N. (1989). *The Organization of Hypocrisy: Talk, Decisions and Actions in Organizations*, Chichester: Wiley.

Brunsson, N., Forssell, A. and Winberg, H. (1989). *Reform som tradition*, Stockholm: EFI.

Cameron, K. S., Sutton, R. I. and Whetten, D.A. (eds.). (1988). *Readings in Organizational Decline*, Cambridge, MA: Ballinger.

Campbell, C. and Peters, B. G. (eds.). (1988). *Organizing Governance, Governing Organizations*, Pittsburgh, PA: University of Pittsburgh Press.

Child, J. (1977). "Organizational design and performance: Contingency theory and beyond," in E. H. Burach and A. R. Negandhi, *Organization Design, Theoretical Perspectives and Empirical Findings*, Kent, OH: Kent State University Press.

Child, J. and Kieser, A. (1981). "Development of organizations over time," in P. C. Nystrom and W. H. Starbuck (eds.), *Handbook of Organizational Design* (vol. 1), Oxford: Oxford University Press, 28-64.

Christensen, T. (1987). "How to succeed in reorganizing: The case of the Norwegian Health Administration," *Scandinavian Political Studies* 10(1): 61-77.

Christensen, T. (1989). "Forutsetninger og effekter: restruktureringcn av den sentrale helseadministrasjonen i Norge," in M. Egeberg (ed.), *Institusjonspolitikk og forvaltningsutvikling: Bidrag til en anvendt statsvitenskap*, Oslo: Tano, 186-206.

Coase, R. H. (1937). "The nature of fun," *Economica* 5: 386-405.

Coase, R. H. (1960). "The problem of social cost," *Journal of Law and Economics* 3: 1-44.

Colvin, P. (1985). *The Economic Ideal in British Government*, Manchester: Manchester University Press.

Crozier, M. (1988). *Comment réformer l'Etat?* Paris: La Documentation Française.

Cyert, R. M. and March, J. G. (1963). *A Behavioral Theory of the Firm*, Englewood Cliffs, NJ: Prentice Hall.

Czarniawska, B. (1985). "The ugly sister: On relationships between the private and the public sectors in Sweden," *Scandinavian Journal of Management Studies* 2(2): 83-103.

Dente, B. and Kjellberg, F. (eds.). (1988). *The Dynamics of Institutional Change*, London: Sage.

Downs, G. W. and Larkey, P. D. (1986). *The Search for Government Efficiency: From Hubris to Helplessness,* Philadelphia, PA: Temple University Press.

Dyson, K. (1980). *The State Tradition in Western Europe,* Oxford: Martin Robertson.

Eckstein, H. (1982) "The idea of political development: From dignity to efficiency," *World Politics* 34: 451-486.

Egeberg, M. (1984). *Organisasjonsutforming i offentlig virksomhet,* Oslo: Aschehougfranum, Nordli.

Egeberg, M. (1987). "Designing public organizations," in J. Kooiman and K. A. Eliassen (eds.), *Managing Public Organizations: Lessons From Contemporary European Experience,* London: Sage, 142-157.

Egeberg, M. (ed.). (1989a). *Instilusjonspolitikk og forvaltningsutvikung: Bidrag til anvendt statsvitenskap,* Oslo: Tano.

Etzioni, A. (1964). *Modern Organizations,* Englewood Cliffs, NJ: Prentice Hall.

Feldman, M. S. and March, J. G. (1981). "Information in organizations as signal and symbol," *Administrative Science Quarterly* 26: 171-186.

Fry, G. K. (1988). "The Thatcher Government: The Financial Management Initiative and the "New Civil Service." *Public Administration* 66: 1-20.

Galbraith, J. R. (1973). *Designing Complex Organizations,* Reading, MA: Addison-Wesley.

Galbraith, J. R. (1977). *Organization Design,* Reading, MA: Addison-Wesley.

Goldwin, R. A. (1986). "Of men and angels: A search for morality in the Constitution," in R.H. Horwitz (ed.), *The Moral Foundations of the American Republic* (3rd ed.), Charlottesville, VA: University Press of Virginia, 24-41.

Goodsell, C. T. (1985). *The Case for Bureaucracy,* Chatham, NJ: Chatham House.

Gray, A. and Jenkins, W. I. (1985). *Administrative Politics in British Government,* London: Harvester.

Hamilton, A., Jay, J. and Madison, J. (1787-1788/1964 ed.). *The Federalist Papers,* New York: Pocket Books.

Hannan, M. T. and Freeman, J. (1977). "The population ecology of organizations," *American Journal of Sociology* 82: 929-964.

Hannan, M. T. and Freeman, J. (1984). "Structural inertia and organizational change," *American Sociological Review* 49: 149-164.

Hansen, H. Foss (1989). "Moderniseringens effektivilet," *Nordisk Administrativt Tidsskrift* 2: 199-212.

Harrison, A. and Gretton, J. (1987). *Reshaping Central Government,* New Brunswick/Oxford: Transaction Books.

Hastings, S. and Levie, H. (eds.). (1993). *Privatization,* Nottingham: Spokesman.

Hood, C. (1979). *The Machinery of Government Problem* (Studies in Public Policy No. 28), Glasgow: University of Glasgow.

Jacobsen, K. D. (1964). *Teknisk hjelp ogpolitiskstruktur,* Oslo: Universitetsforlaget.

Jacobsen, K. D. (1966). "Public administration under pressure: The role of the expert in the modernization of traditional agriculture," *Scandinavian Political Studies* 1: 159-193.

Kaufman, H. (1956). "Emerging conflicts in the doctrine of American public administration," *American Political Science Review* 50: 1057-1073.

Kaufman, H. (1977). "Reflections on administrative reorganization," in J. A. Pechman (ed.), *Setting National Priorities: The 1978 Budget,* Washington, DC: Brookings.

Kay, D. A. and Thompson, D. J. (1986). "Privatisation: A policy in search of a rationale," *The Economic Journal* 90: 18-32.

Keeley, M. (1988). *A Social-Contract Theory of Organizations,* Notre Dame, IN: Notre Dame University Press.

Kelman, S. (1985). "The Grace Commission: How much waste in government?" *The Public Interest* 78: 62-82.

Kimberly, J. R. and Miles, R. H. et al. (1980). *The Organizational Life Cycle,* San Francisco, CA: Jossey-Bass.

Knott, J. H. and Miller, G. J. (1987). *Reforming Bureaucracy,* Englewood Cliffs, NJ: Prentice Hall.

Kooiman, J. and Eliassen, K. A. (eds.). (1987). *Managing Public Organizations: Lessons From Contemporary European Experience,* London: Sage.

Krasner, S. D. (1988). "Sovereignty: An institutional perspective," *Comparative Political Studies* 21: 66-94.

Landau, M. and Stout, R. (1979). "To manage is not to control, or the folly of Type II errors," *Public Administration Review* 39: 148-156.

Lawrence, P. and Lorsch, J. (1967). *Organization and Environment,* Cambridge, MA: Harvard University Press.

Leazes, Jr., F. J. (1987). *Accountability and the Business State,* New York: Praeger.

LeGrand, J. and Robinson, R. (1984). *Privatization and the Welfare State,* London: Allen & Unwin.

Levitt, B. and March, J. G. (1988). "Organizational Learning," *Annual Review of Sociology* 14: 319-340.

March, J. G. (1978). "Bounded rationality, ambiguity, and the engineering of choice," *Bell Journal of Economics* 9: 587-608.

March, J. G. (1981a). "Decisions in organizations and theories of choice," in A. Van de Ven and W. Joyce (eds.), *Perspectives on Organizational Design and Performance,* New York: Wiley, 205-244.

March, J. G. (1981b). "Footnotes to organizational change," *Administrative Science Quarterly* 26(4): 563-577.

March, J. G. (1989). "Exploration and exploitation in organizational learning," Stanford, CA: Stanford University, manuscript.

March, J. G. and Olsen, J. P. (1975). "The uncertainty of the past: Organizational learning under ambiguity," *European Journal of Political Research* 3: 147-171.

March, J. G. and Olsen, J. P. (1976). *Ambiguity and Choice in Organizations,* Bergen: Universitetsforlaget.

March, J. G. and Olsen, J. P. (1983). "Organizing political life: What administrative reorganization tells us about government," *American Political Science Review* 77(2): 281-297.

March, J. G. and Olsen, J. P. (1989). *Rediscovering Institutions: The Organizational Basis of Politics,* New York: Free Press.

Marx, K. (1845/1976). "Theses on Feuerbach," in K. Marx and P. Engels, *Collected Works* (vol. 5), London: Lawrence & Wishart, 3-5.

Mellbourn, A. (1986). *Bortom det starka samhället,* Stockholm: Carlsson Bokförlag.

Metcalf, L. and Richards, S. (1987). *Improving Public Management,* London: Sage.

Meyer, J. W. and Rowan, B. (1977). "Institutionalized organizations: Formal Structure as myth and ceremony," *American Journal of Sociology* 83: 340-363.

Moe, T. (1984). "The new economics of organizations," *American Journal of Political Science* 28: 739-781.

Morrisey, W. (1986). "The moral foundations of the American Republic: An introduction," in R. H. Horwitz (ed.), *The Moral Foundations of the American Republic* (3rd ed.), Charlottesville, VA: University Press of Virginia, 1-23.

North, D. C. (1984). "Transaction costs, institutions, and economic history," in E. G. Furubotn and R. Richter (eds.), *Zeitschrift für die Gesamte Staatswissenschaft (Journal of Institutional and Theoretical Economics)* 140(1): 7-17.

Nystrom, P. C. and Starbuck, W. H. (1981). *Handbook of Organizational Design,* Oxford: Oxford University Press.

OECD. (1987). *Administration as Service: The Public as Client,* Paris: OECD.

OECD. (1989). *Survey of Public Management Developments 1988,* Paris: OECD.

Offe, C. (1987). "The utopia of the zero-option modernity and modernization as normative political criteria," *Praxis International* 7: 1-24.

Olsen, J. P. (1986). "Foran en ny offentlig revolusjon," *Nytt Norsk Tidsskrift* 3: 3-15.

Olsen, J. P. (1988a). "The modernization of public administration in the Nordic countries: Some research questions," *Hallinnon Tutkimus (Administrative Studies),* Finland: 2-17.

Olsen, J. P. (1988b). "Administrative reform and theories of organization," in C. Campbell and B. G. Peters (eds.), *Organizing Governance, Governing Organizations,* Pittsburgh, PA: University of Pittsburgh Press, 233-254.

Peters, B. G. (1988a). *Comparing Public Bureaucracies: Problems of Theory and Method,* Tuscaloosa, AL: University of Alabama Press.

Peters, B. G. (1988b). "Introduction," in C. Campbell and B. G. Peters (eds.), *Organizing Governance, Governing Organizations,* Pittsburgh: University of Pittsburgh Press, 3-15.

Petersson, O. and Fredén, J. (1987). *Statens symbokr,* Uppsala: Maktutredningen.

Pfeffer, J. (1978). *Organizational Design,* Arlington Heights, IL: ARM Publishing.

Pfeffer, J. and Salancik, G. R. (1978). *The External Control of Organizations: A Resource Dependence Perspective,* New York: Harper & Row.

Poggi, G. (1984). *The Development of the Modern State,* Stanford, CA: Stanford University Press.

Romanow, A. (1981). "Case studies of organizational change: A review," Stanford, CA: Stanford University, manuscript.

Roness, P. G. (1979). *Reorganisering av departementa: Eit politisk styringsmiddel?* Bergen: Universitetsforlaget.

Røvik, K. A. (1987). "Læringssystemer og læringsatferd i offentlig forvaltning: en studie av styringens kunnskapsgrunniag," Tromsø: Institutt for samfunnsvitenskap, manuscript.

Sait, E. McChesney. (1938). *Political Institutions: A Preface,* New York: Appleton-Century-Crofts.

Scharpf, F. W. (1977). "Does organization matter? Task structure and interaction in the ministerial bureaucracy," in E. H. Burack and A. R. Negandhi (eds.), *Organization Design: Theoretical Perspectives and Empirical Findings,* Kent, OH: Kent State University.

Schick, A. (1977). "Zero-base budgeting and sunset: Redundancy or symbioses," *The Bureaucrat* 6: 12-32.

Seidman, H. (1980). *Politics, Position and Power: The Dynamics of Federal Organization* (3rd ed.), New York: Oxford University Press.

Simon, H. A. (1957). *Administrative Behavior: A Study of Decision-Making Processes in Administrative Organization,* New York: Macmillan.

Sjøblom, S. and Ståhlberg, K. (1987). "Att utveckla förvaltningen: en beskrivning av förvaltningsreformskommittéer i Finland åren 1975-1987," *Hallinnon Tutkimus* 4: 263-272.

Steinman, M. and Miewald, R. (1984). "Administrative reform: Introduction," in R. Miewald and M. Steinman (eds.), *Problems in Administrative Reform,* Chicago, IL: Nelson-Hall, 1-9.

Stinchcombe, A. L. (1965). "Social structure and organizations," in J. G. March (ed.), *Handbook of Organizations,* Chicago, IL: Rand McNally.

Wass, D. (1985). "The civil service at the crossroads," *Political Quarterly* 50(3): 227-241.

Weber, M., Roth, G. and Wittich, C. (eds.). (1924/1978). *Economy and Society,* translated by E. Fischoff et al., Berkeley, CA: University of California Press.

Weizsäcker, C. C. von (1984). "The influence of property rights on tastes," *Zolischrift für die Gesamte Staatswissenschaft (Journal of Institutional and Theoretical Economics)* 140(1): 90-95.

Williamson, O. E. (1975). *Markets and Hierarchies: Analysis and Antitrust Implications,* New York: Free Press.

Williamson, O. E. (1985). *The Economic Institutions of Capitalism,* New York: Free Press.

Winther, S. (1987). "Reorganisering og modernisering—en introduksjon," *Politika* 19(4): 374-384.

Wittrock, B. and Lindström, S. (1984). *De stora programmens tid: Forskning och energi,* Stockholm: Akademilitteratur.

Wolin, S. (1960). *Politics and Vision: Continuity and Innovation in Western Political Thought,* Boston: Little, Brown.

# III

# Leadership Concepts and Theories in Organizations

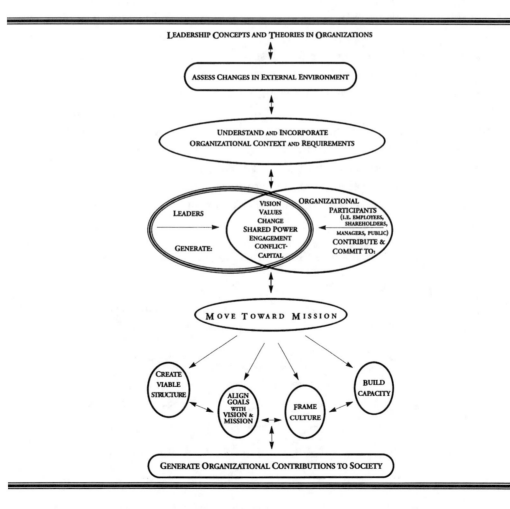

The essential question for this section is, What type of leadership do new-era organizations require? The kind of leadership philosophy and approaches that an organization adopts provides the impetus for how leaders and participants exemplify their beliefs in action, interact with each other, and carry out the organization's purpose. Scholars in this section provide a rich array of leadership theories and concepts that contribute insight into the forms of leadership that can invigorate new-era organizations.

Joseph Rost begins the dialogue by addressing the distinctions between leadership and management. He contends that the two concepts are fundamentally different, but their distinctions do not and should not imply the denigration of management to ennoble leadership. As illustrated in Figure III.1, leadership and management have different focuses but function interdependently to produce outcomes that sustain integrity, vision, values, and wholeness while meeting the goals for which the organization was established.

Beyond these leadership-management distinctions, this section focuses on leadership theories as they apply to organizations. Greenleaf and DePree examine *servant leadership* in their respective chapters. This theory characterizes the leader as steward. The needs of participants are the foremost priority for servant leaders whose role is to pave the way and provide support for participants to function at their best. Greenleaf contends that "the business then becomes a serving institution—serving those who produce and those who use." These kinds of organizations and their leadership produce meaningful work for those in the institution and serve society in the process.

In 1978, James MacGregor Burns's classic definitions of *transactional* and *transforming* leadership provided the conceptual foundation for revolutionary thinking about the role and purpose of leadership. Bernard Bass imported Burns's concepts from the political and social movement arena into the context of organizations.[1] In the organiza-

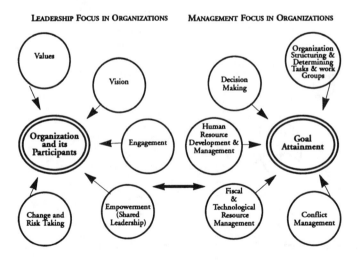

**Figure III.1.** Leadership and Management Focus in Organizations

tional context, Burns's link to social change is separated from the theory of transforming leadership leaving the focal point of transformation on leader-participant interactions. Bass adopted Burns's definition of transactional leadership and expanded the concepts to what he termed *transformational* leadership. Bass and coauthor Avolio's research reveals that a qualitative change in performance and relationships occurs in transformational leadership to the benefit of the individual and the organization. Four critical factors comprise this form of leadership: idealized influence, inspirational motivation, intellectual stimulation, and individualized consideration.

Hughes, Ginnett, and Curphy present an overview of *contingency* theories of leadership. Although there are several different contingency theories, the authors maintain that, in general, these theories purport that leadership effectiveness is maximized when leaders correctly make their behavior "contingent" on certain situational and follower characteristics.

Howell and Avolio describe *charismatic* leaders as achieving heroic feats in organizations by "powerfully communicating a compelling vision of the future, passionately believing in their vision, relentlessly promoting their beliefs with boundless energy, propounding creative ideas, and expressing confidence in followers' abilities to achieve high standards." The authors warn, however, that those who act on behalf of organizations must understand the distinction between ethical and unethical charismatic leadership when searching for leaders who can turn around ailing corporations, revitalize aging bureaucracies, or launch new enterprises.

*Chaos* theory is based on the premise of self-organizing systems. It encourages a view of organizations as whole systems with nonlinear activity. Wheatley contends that leaders in a chaotic world are called on to shape their organizations through concepts and governing principles, which emphasize guiding visions, strong values, and organizational beliefs. These, say Wheatley, are "the few rules individuals can use to shape their own behavior." When problems occur, leadership is exercised by maintaining focus, trusting the workings of chaos, and stepping back to look for naturally occurring themes and patterns that lead to solutions.

Each of the authors in this section describes forms of leadership that have great value in the context of new-era organizations. The challenge is to determine how to configure leadership throughout the organization to effectively and ethically attain the vision, mission, and goals that organizational participants intend. This consideration requires movement away from a singular focus on executive-level, positional leadership to a view of multileadership that serves various functions, purposes, and levels throughout the organization.

## Note

1. See Bernard Bass, *Leadership and performance beyond expectations.* New York: Free Press, 1985.

# 10

# *Leadership and Management*

JOSEPH C. ROST

Confusing leadership and management and treating the words as if they were synonymous have a long and illustrious history in leadership studies. The practice is pervasive in the mainstream literature of leadership. It is pervasive in all academic disciplines where one can find the literature of leadership. As has been shown in the discussion of the definitions of leadership since the 1930s, leadership scholars instilled the values from the industrial paradigm into their understanding of leadership and equated leadership with good management. Many scholars and practitioners went even further and equated leadership with management.

Some scholars, including myself, have had serious conceptual problems with using leadership and management as synonymous words. These authors have written books, chapters, and articles in which they have argued that leadership is not the same as management, but these works have had little impact on the mainstream of literature or practice of leadership. The melding of these concepts and understanding leadership as good management still dominated leadership studies at the end of the 1980s (see Badaracco & Ellsworth, 1989; Bennis,

1989a, 1989b; Cohen, 1990; Conger, 1989a; De-Pree, 1989; Hunt, Baliga, Dachler, & Schriesheim, 1988; Immegart, 1988; Janis, 1989; Kotter, 1988; Nanus, 1989; Ridge, 1989; Sergiovanni, 1990; Smith & Peterson, 1988; Yukl, 1989; Zaleznik, 1989). The industrial paradigm of leadership is still holding strong.

A postindustrial school of leadership must come to terms with this issue, and that is the purpose of this chapter. After some discussion of previous attempts to distinguish between leadership and management, most of which have not been successful, I propose a new framework that uses the essential elements of the definitions of leadership and management to make a clear separation between the two concepts.

### *Some Attempts to Distinguish Between Leadership and Management*

There were only a few serious attempts to deal with the leadership is management syndrome prior to 1978, when Burns rethought the concept of leadership, and the late 1980s, when a number of scholars called for a different approach to understanding leadership.

The first such attempt I have found was by Selznick (1957) in his marvelous little book *Leadership in Administration.* He wrote:

*Leadership is not equivalent to office-holding or high prestige or authority or decision-making.* It is not helpful to identify leadership with whatever is done by people in high places. The activities we have in mind may or may not be engaged in by those who are formally in positions of authority. This is inescapable if we are to develop a theory that will be useful in diagnosing cases of inadequate leadership on the part of persons in authority. If this view is correct, it means that only some (and sometimes none) of the activities of decision-makers are leadership activities. Here again, understanding leadership requires understanding of a broader social process. If some types of decisions are more closely related to leadership activities than others, we should learn what they are. To this end in this analysis let us make a distinction between "routine" and "critical" decision making. (p. 24)

Selznick devoted an entire chapter in the book to fleshing out the distinction between routine and critical decision making, between management and leadership.

Jacobs (1970), in a very thoughtful book that was not widely read but should have been, devoted considerable space to distinguishing between leadership and management. Toward the end of this book, he wrote: "Perhaps the most important conclusion reached in this work is the importance of distinguishing between the concepts of leadership, power, and authority and of identifying superordinate role behaviors that constitute each" (p. 341). Jacobs gave one-sentence definitions of each of the terms, and they contained discrete elements that an analyst could use to distinguish among them. "Authority [management] resides in the relationships between positions in an organization, and is derived from consensually validated role expectations for the position incumbents involved" (p. 231). "Leadership is taken as an interaction between persons in which one presents information of a sort and in such a manner that the other becomes convinced that his outcomes (benefits/costs ratio) will be improved if he behaves in the manner suggested or desired" (p. 232). "Power is defined . . . as the capacity to deprive another needed satisfaction or benefits, or to inflict 'costs' on him for noncompliance with an influence attempt" (p. 230).

Katz and Kahn (1966/1978) articulated a distinction between leadership and management that has had some currency among leadership scholars, especially psychologists: "One common approach to the definition of leadership is to equate it with the differential exertion of influence. . . . We maintain . . . that every act of influence on a matter of organizational relevance is to some degree an act of leadership. . . . We consider the essence of organizational leadership to be the influential increment over and above mechanical compliance with routine directives of the organization" (pp. 302-303). Management, obviously, is the mechanical compliance of people in organizations with routine directives. A variation in this theme is that leadership is the use of influence and management is the use of authority. In the 1970s, quite a few authors actually used this distinction in their works, but they often failed to remain true to their definitions in their research and in their discussion of leadership after the definitions were given.

Graham (1988) followed up on this distinction.

Definitions of leader-follower relationships typically draw a distinction between voluntary acceptance of another's influence, on the one hand, and coerced compliance, on the other (Graham, 1982; Hunt, 1984; Jacobs, 1971 [*sic*]; Jago, 1982; Katz & Kahn, 1966/1978). That distinction rests on the degree of free choice exercised by followers. Specific instances of obedience which stem from fear of punishment, the promises of rewards, or the desire to fulfill contractual obligations are examples not of voluntary followership but of subordination, and the range of free choice available to subordinates is relatively small. Appropriate labels for the person giving orders, monitoring compliance, and administering performance contingency rewards and punishments include "supervisor" and "manager," but *not* "leader." (p. 74)

Zaleznik (1977) attempted to distinguish between leaders and managers in a celebrated article published in the *Harvard Business Review.* In that article as well as his 1989 book, he equates management with managers and leadership with leaders, so his distinction between management and leadership is based on the personality differences of managers and leaders. "Managers and leaders differ fundamentally in their world views. The dimensions for assessing these differences include managers' and leaders' orientations toward their goals, their work, their human relations, and their selves" (1977, p. 69). Using William James's two basic personality types, Zaleznik suggested that managers are "once-born" and leaders are "twice-born." He used a trait approach to distinguish between leaders and managers, and consequently between leadership and management.

There are contextual indications in Burns (1978) that he did distinguish between leadership and management, but they are more or less hidden in the text. The index in his book does not contain an item labeled "management" or one labeled "leadership and management." There is a section titled "Bureaucracy Versus Leadership" (pp. 295-302), but the material in those pages is not helpful in trying to distinguish between leadership and management (or authority, as Burns called it).

Several commentators, including myself, have reinterpreted Burns's model of leadership to be, in reality, a model of management *and* leadership. This reinterpretation states quite simply that Burns's transactional leadership is management, and his transformational leadership is leadership, and the difference between the two is the distinction between leadership and management. Enochs (1981), in a very popular article in the *Phi Delta Kappan,* stated this reinterpretation very well: "Transactional leadership is managerial and custodial; it is competent but uninspired care-taking for a quiet time. Transformational leadership is a more lofty undertaking. It is not a trade-off for survival between leader and followers during good times, but rather a process for achieving fundamental changes in hard times" (p. 177).

The same point was made in a reaction paper by Jill Graham (1988) to Avolio and Bass's presentation on transformational leadership and charisma at a leadership symposium:

The distinction between transactional and transformational leadership in the Avolio & Bass chapter bears a striking resemblance to what is now a well-established difference between supervision and leadership. Certainly, a transactional leader's use of contingent reinforcements is nothing more than supervision. Research on supervision, moreover, is in the same conceptual category as theories of organizational control and the operant paradigm for employee motivation (Jago, 1982, p. 330). Only transformational leadership occupies a conceptual category that is independent of these topics, that is, leadership standing alone. (pp. 74-75)

In personal conversations with Burns in 1989, he made it very clear to me that he does not agree with this reinterpretation of his conceptual framework of leadership. He has continued to hold the view that transactional leadership is leadership, not management, and his views on that subject are quite strongly held.

Dubin wrote a stinging critique of leadership research in 1979 that to some extent dealt with the distinction between leadership and management.

Another observation: 3) the ease with which the concept of *leadership* is treated as a synonym for *management and supervision.* This is amazing. My knowledge of organizational behavior has led me to the conclusion that effective organization can be managed and supervised and *not* led, while some ineffective organizations can be led into their difficulties without the benefit of management and supervision.

This leads to my first conclusion: Leadership is a rare phenomenon, not a common one in organizational behavior. Those who proposed to *observe* leadership behavior as their methodology for study to gain knowledge (an orientation I applaud), will find that tracking managers to record their every behavior will produce relatively little data on leadership. . . . The first cut at such data mass will consist of sorting it into two piles; the small stack of leadership acts, and the very large pile of acts of managing and supervising.

. . . In my view, the central problem has to do with the reluctance, or inability, to specify the dimensionality of the leadership phenomena. We have even succeeded in confusing "leadership" with other social behaviors as my predecessor in this "overview" role, Miner, did when he boldly proposed to substitute "control" for the concept of leadership (Miner, 1975). We have failed in handling the dimensionality problem by focusing on some of the wrong dimensions of leadership and ignoring others.

One major problem that has preoccupied American social science has been the formulation of leadership as an interpersonal phenomenon. This has been a major shortcoming in the study of leadership. . . . There are face-to-face relations between a leader and followers. But it should also be evident that there are situations of leadership which do not involve face-to-face relations with followers. Furthermore, there are many face-to-face relations between supporters and subordinates that *do not* involve leadership in the ongoing interaction. . . .

I believe that the primary emphasis of the work in this volume is on leadership in face-to-face relationships. I will boldly propose: There may be many significant findings among the studies [in this book], but in the broad span of human affairs, they are largely trivial findings because they fail to address leadership *of* organization. (pp. 225-227)

Tucker (1981) used the Selznick dichotomy to distinguish between leadership and management. Defining a political leader as "one who gives direction, or meaningfully participates in the giving of direction, to the activities of a political community" (p. 15), Tucker suggested that "one might argue that even in ordinary, day-to-day group life, when no great uncertainties exist, groups are in need of being directed. But such routine direction might better be described as *management,* reserving the term *leadership* for the directing of a group at times of choice, change, and decision, times when deliberation and authoritative decision occur, followed by steps to implement decisions reached" (p. 16).

Bennis has long held that leadership is different from management. In 1977 he wrote: "Leading does not mean managing; the difference between the two is crucial. I know many institutions that are very well managed and very poorly led" (p. 3). Similar statements appear in many of his other articles and books. In their 1985 book, Bennis and Nanus wrote:

The problem with many organizations, and especially the ones that are failing, is that they tend to be over-managed and underled. . . . They may excel in the ability to handle the daily routine, yet never question whether the routine should be done at all. There is a profound difference between management and leadership, and both are important. "To manage" means "to bring about, to accomplish, to have change of or responsibility for, to conduct." "Leading" is "influencing, guiding in direction, course, action, opinion." The distinction is crucial. *Managers are people who do things right and leaders are people who do the right thing.* The difference may be summarized as activities of vision and judgment—*effectiveness* versus activities of mastering routines—*efficiency.* (p. 21)

Other paragraphs on other pages in the book deliver essentially the same message.

A persistent theme of the 1980s literature on leadership is an attempt to label as leadership those management processes which produce excellence in organizational outcomes and which leave the meaning of management to include all the other management processes that produce less than excellent outcomes. Leadership is excellence management; management is doing anything less than excellence. This distinction, of course, is simply a restatement of the industrial paradigm of leadership that upgrades good management to excellent management.

### An Evaluation of the Attempts to Distinguish Leadership From Management

While the attempts to distinguish between leadership and management listed in the last section are admirable, and while a few scholars actually get at substantive differences, the attempts are as a whole more or less weak in giving scholars and practitioners the conceptual ability to make such a distinction. Generally, the distinctions are perfunctory and poorly constructed, and the criteria given to make the distinction are often too general and too ambiguous for people to use with any accuracy in real life or in research. Another problem is that many of the distinctions given by scholars are distinctions of personality traits and behaviors of leaders and managers, not differences in the processes or relationships that get at the nature of leadership and management. There is a pervasive tendency among these scholars to equate leadership with leaders, confusing a process with a person, which, in the end, doubles the confusion present in the use of the words *leadership* and *management* as synonyms.

The other problem, of course, is that these scholars were swimming against the tide of the mainstream concept of leadership as embedded in the industrial paradigm: Leadership is good management. These authors had a very difficult time making their case. They were generally ignored, and so the distinctions were not pursued and developed. They had a difficult time gaining collaborators. And, it is important to remember that leadership as a field of study was often a sideline for these scholars; their main scholarly interest was more connected to their primary academic discipline.

Worse yet is that most of the authors mentioned have paid little attention to their own distinction. It was not uncommon for an author to make the distinction in an early chapter and then ignore it in the other chapters of the book. Using Argyris's (1976) framework to make sense of such inconsistencies, one could state that these authors developed theories of leadership that espoused a difference between leadership and management, but their theories-in-use reflected the industrial paradigm, which equated leadership with good management. Selznick and Jacobs are the major exceptions; they were able to use the words *leadership* and *management* consistently throughout their books.

Bryman (1986) noted the same tendency, and he criticized leadership scholars for not paying attention to the distinction.

> It would seem important to maintain a distinction between a leader who is in a leadership position and who has power and authority vested in his or her office, and leadership as an influence process which is more than the exercise of power and authority. . . . However, . . . a great deal of leadership research rides roughshod over these distinctions. Studies abound on the subject of the behavior of leaders in which the strategy involves discerning the activities of people in positions of leadership, with little reference to how these activities might be indicative of leadership *per se* as distinct from the exercise of power and authority. (p. 4)

Unfortunately, Bryman ignored his own critique: "It is necessary to hold many of these terminological difficulties in abeyance and the remainder of the book will focus on what, in the author's view, is generally taken to be the study of leadership in organizations" (p. 16).

Wilpert (1982) did the same kind of turnaround in response to three papers at a leadership symposium.

> What should be noted right at the outset . . . is the terminological uncertainty in all three contributions [papers presented at the symposium] with respect to the use of the terms "leader" and "manager." Although some difference of kind is even implied in the titles of two of the presentations (Steward; Lombard & McCall), not one of the three contributions elaborate [*sic*] the distinctions, in fact, all use the two terms synonymously. So I will follow suit and assume for purposes of discussion that managers always perform some leadership function due to their organizational position. (pp. 68-69)

Schon (1984) did exactly the same thing in his presentation at another symposium. "Leadership and management are not synonymous terms, one can be a leader without being a manager. . . . Conversely, one can manage without leading. . . . Nonetheless, we generally expect managers to lead, and criticize them if they fail to do so. Hence, for the purposes of this essay, I shall treat management and leadership as though they were one" (p. 36).

Lombardo and McCall (1982) show how much the industrial concept of leadership has penetrated even highly sophisticated centers on leadership. They worked at the Center for Creative Leadership in Greensboro, North Carolina during the 1980s. (McCall left the Center in the late 1980s.) The Center is a multimillion-dollar operation that employs some 100 professional researchers and trainers "to encourage and develop creative leadership and effective management for the good of society overall" (from the Center's mission statement).

In the early 1980s, Lombardo and McCall produced an elaborate simulation called "Looking Glass, Inc.," which has been one of the cornerstones of the Center's leadership/management training programs. The authors made a presentation at the 1982 leadership symposium in which they stated:

> This chapter is based on a day in the life of a glass manufacturing company and the 30 leaders who run it. . . .
>
> It was with this inherent belief—that management or leadership only makes sense when viewed in its entirety—that a complex simulation was designed for use in leadership research. Its goals were both clear and fuzzy: to mirror as realistically as possible the demands of a typical managerial job in a complex organization, to have actual managers run the simulated company as they chose, and to bring multiple methods to bear on learning something new about leadership. By watching a day in the life of managers dealing with the complexity and chaos of organizations, we hoped to develop some more pertinent questions to guide future research on what leadership is, and how and when it matters. (pp. 50-51)

Notice the equation of leaders with managers, and the equation of leadership with what managers do. Lombardo and McCall clearly state that if a person studies a day (or several days) in the life of a manager (or several managers), he/she will certainly understand leadership better. The industrial concept of leadership has seldom been articulated more forcefully.

Actually, the brochures from the Center for Creative Leadership publicizing the Looking Glass simulation are considerably more accurate in describing the simulation.

> Looking Glass, a robust simulation of managerial action, is beginning its second decade and gaining worldwide use for one critical reason: It teaches the lessons that matter. What lessons? How managers react to constantly changing environments. How they make decisions, set priorities, network and communicate to get the job done. . . . Looking Glass puts managers in the middle of the chaos of managerial life and lets them . . . examine how well they did and how they might do better. (Center for Creative Leadership, n.d., p. 1)

Notice that the words *leader* and *leadership* are never used in the description.

The same cannot be said about the trainers who use Looking Glass in the Center-sponsored work-

shops. I attended a one-day, introductory session of the Looking Glass simulation in 1989, and the equation of management and leadership was pervasive. The simulation as I experienced it on that day had almost nothing to do with leadership as I define the word. The whole thing was relatively straightforward and the simulation delivered exactly what the brochure promised: insights into enlightened management. However, the trainers had a different view entirely. They thought that they were delivering insights into enlightened leadership (since they were imbued with the industrial view that leadership is good management), and they definitely wanted the workshop participants to take home the idea that the Looking Glass simulation was about leadership.

Allison (1984) took another strategy in articulating the industrial view of leadership. He rejected outright the notion that scholars need to distinguish leadership from management, and then proceeded to ignore any definitional problems that position might have on his understanding of leadership. After discussing five "leadership" authors who claimed to have discovered "the essence of the concept" of leadership, Allison opined that "one might conclude that 'administrative leadership' is, in fact, an oxymoron—a contradiction in terms" (p. 215). Then, he concluded: "I find the claims of these authors to have isolated the 'real thing' ultimately unpersuasive" (p. 217). So what does Allison do?

> For the purpose of this discussion, I cannot hope to surmount these formidable obstacles [definitional problems]. Thus, this paper will attempt to circumvent them by taking a less abstract, more simplistically empirical path: focusing on people playing lead roles in administrative settings. . . . Following Webster I will use the term "lead" to mean "to show the way by going in advance; to conduct, escort, or direct." Those who lead in administrative settings, I will call managers. Again, following Webster, I will use the term "management" to mean the "purposive organization and direction of resources to achieve a desired outcome." (p. 218)

The upshot of these approaches to the concepts of leadership and management is a cultural acceptance in the research community (and ultimately in the popular press and among practitioners) of sloppy scholarship and practice, which produce conceptual frameworks that use different terms interchangeably. In a very real sense, the culture of permissiveness goes like this: "Since other scholars and practitioners confuse leadership and management, since other scholars have not come up with a definition of leadership that distinguishes it from management, I am free to do the same thing. I will also use the words *leadership* and *management, leader* and *manager,* as synonymous terms. I will also equate *leadership* with *leader* and *management* with *manager,* so that there are four terms that I will equate with one another."

Some scholars defend this practice by calling it diversity of thought or academic freedom. I once challenged Fiedler at an Academy of Management conference about his view that leaders and managers are the same, a view he has consistently held since the 1960s. I asked: "How can you be sure that the managers you study in your research are actually leaders?" His answer went something like this: "My definition of a leader is as good as your definition or that of any other researcher. I believe that managers are leaders and so the managers in my studies are leaders."

Schriesheim, Hunt, and Sekaran (1982) ended the leadership symposium of that year with a ringing defense of definitional diversity. "We cherish diversity and see it as needed for our collective endeavor.... Our values and beliefs suggest that . . . if we are to advance the field . . . we should . . . encourage diversity.... We want to be able to enjoy our enterprise and, at the same time, to serve constituencies of our own choosing, with products compatible with their own needs and ours" (pp. 297-298). While this statement is a stirring defense of the free market of ideas, scholarship brings with it the responsibility to critically analyze the ideas in the free market. It seems that Schriesheim, Hunt, and Sekaran want to be able to use the words *leadership* and *management* interchangeably so as to serve the self-esteem needs of the corporate manager, who, they seem to think, need to view themselves as leaders simply because they are managers. Such a position is equivalent to accepting the age-old assumption undergirding the free market framework: Let the buyer beware. I believe that scholars have more responsibility than that.

So do practitioners. Burack (1979) summarized the interviews he had with four executives, and the interviews indicate they had some of the same difficulties with leadership research.

> Past SIU symposia, whatever their academic and intellectual merits, have been so far removed from the pressure on the practitioner as to be useless to anyone running training programs or to anyone in leadership positions. (p. 27)
>
> The implications of this observation [given in previous paragraphs, that only 25 percent of the people in any group have leadership skills] should be quite clear by now. . . . It leads to Moses' Commandment which is . . . "Thou shalt study leaders who are first *accurately identified* as leaders before attempting to build theories of leadership behavior."
>
> . . . much of our research is based on available (translate that to mean the easiest to obtain) measures. . . . There does not seem to have been a serious effort to obtain adequate samples of leaders in most of the research studies purporting to be evaluating leaders. Rather, one studies what is available. Sometimes these are college sophomores, sometimes these are managers—rarely, however, are the subjects of intensive analysis evaluated to determine if they have the skills we are trying to study. (p. 32)

The leadership research reported in the 1982 symposium did not pass the Bill and Barbara test developed by Mintzberg (1982) from the feedback of two practitioner colleagues. What bothered Barbara the most, she wrote, "was the gnawing suspicion that the research was being carried out as an end in itself. Hence relevance was really a side issue." Bill concluded that the researchers "seemed more interested in studying the subtleties of a particular research approach—or even worse, studying other studies—than they are in contributing to a real understanding of leadership itself" (p. 243).

Evidently Barbara and Bill, as well as the four executives on whom Burack reported, thought that leadership researchers had a professional responsibility which included more than enjoying themselves and serving their own self-interests. At the same time, they stated very strongly that the products of these researchers did not meet their needs, which goes to the heart of the argument Schriesheim, Hunt, and Sekaran (1982) used to support the free market of ideas approach to leadership studies.

Hosking and Hunt (1982) delivered a stinging critique of leadership literature at the end of the symposium. "A pervasive . . . theme [of the speakers at the symposium] concerned the meaning of the terms 'leaders' and 'leadership.' It was very apparent that people used them to mean totally different things but on the whole . . . did not seem to see this as a problem. Indeed we saw little evidence of any desire to develop a common language." On the other hand, a few other speakers "felt it was essential to distinguish clearly different aspects of leadership and between such related terms as leadership and management" (p. 280).

Later in this chapter, Hosking and Hunt summarized the approaches of the U.S. scholars to the study of leadership. First, "there seems very little interest in developing models or theories of leadership. . . . Second, when theoretical propositions are tested, they are typically concerned with the distribution of control and decision-making authority within organizations, little or no reference being made to 'leadership.' Third, there is relatively little concern with getting down to definitional problems: by not studying leaders and leadership it is possible to focus on members of organizations (usually appointed officials)" (p. 288). The coauthor of these words is the same Hunt who argued for diversity in leadership studies in the concluding chapter of the same book (Schriesheim, Hunt, and Sekaran, 1982) wherein leadership studies is likened to an ice cream manufacturer who serves up different flavors of ice cream to satisfy the varied needs of the customers. The only trouble with the metaphor is this: Ice cream manufacturers know the differences between ice cream and sherbet or frozen yogurt, but I see no evidence, even by 1990, that leadership researchers know the differences between leadership and management. The differences are in the natures of the processes (such as the differences in the nature of ice cream, sherbet, and frozen yogurt) and not in the people—their traits, styles, and behaviors—who do the processes

(not in the colors and flavors of the ice cream, sherbet, and frozen yogurt).

Increasingly, however, scholars have insisted that the old order is not good enough. Foster (1986b) flatly stated that "leadership is a construct which must be dismantled and rebuilt. The dismantling is necessary because it would appear that the future of leadership studies in social science research is bleak" (p. 3). In another book, Foster (1986a) wrote: "The concept of leadership often receives poor treatment from scholars and educators alike. Often, it is mistaken for the ability to manage small groups in accomplishing tasks; at other times, as a means for improving production. We shall argue that both views adopt a fundamentally mistaken approach to leadership insofar as they identify leadership with aspects of management" (p. 169).

Two British researchers have taken the bull by the horns, so to speak. Hosking and Morley (1988) made a serious attempt to reconstruct the concept of leadership, as Foster insisted we must do:

Our opening argument was for taking the concept of leadership seriously. This requires an explicit definition that can be employed to interpret existing literature and to direct subsequent research and theory. We argue for a definition of leaders as those who consistently contribute certain kinds of acts to leadership processes. More precisely, we define participants as leaders when they (1) consistently make effective contributions to social order and (2) are both expected and perceived to do so by fellow participants. . . . This conceptualization has three general and important implications. The first is that we prefer *not* to follow the common practice of using the terms *leader* and *manager* interchangeably. . . . In our view, studies of managerial behavior should not be assumed necessary to inform our understanding of leadership. Of course they may; however, it is always necessary to establish that the managers concerned were also leaders in the sense the term is used here. . . .

The second and related point is that the only sure means of identifying leaders is through the analysis of leadership processes. The reason, quite simply, is that leaders achieve the status as a result of their contributions, and the ways these are received, relative to the contributions of others. . . . In other words, to study leaders must be to study leadership, that is, the process by which "social order" is constructed and changed.

Third, and last, our conceptualization recognizes that significant leadership contributions may come from a minority, including a minority of one; equally, they may be expected and contributed by the majority. (p. 90)

By our definition, it is necessary to study the processes by which particular acts come to be perceived as contributions to social order, and therefore come to be perceived as leadership acts. . . . Our conceptualization implies that these processes are endemic to leadership whether or not there are appointed managers involved. In other words, the position taken here is that leadership, properly conceived, is emergent. (p. 91)

The entire chapter must be read by anyone interested in reconstructing leadership by taking it out of its industrial moorings. This short quotation shows how differently leadership can be conceptualized when one takes the concept seriously by distinguishing between leadership and management and then putting that distinction to work consistently in a conceptual framework of leadership.

### *Denigrating Management to Ennoble Leadership*

In 1985 I wrote a paper (Rost, 1985) called "Distinguishing Leadership and Management: A New Consensus," in which I suggested that there was a new consensus among the leadership scholars of the 1980s, namely, that leadership is fundamentally different from management and that the two words should not be used synonymously. Then I explicated a conceptual model that contrasted leadership and management according to twelve different criteria. In each case, I suggested that there is a fundamental difference between the two processes.

I presented the paper for the first time at the Organizational Development Network National Conference in 1985, and I received a largely positive response from an overflow crowd. I gave the paper at several other national conventions, and I received the same positive response. I also used it in my leadership classes, and the doctoral students generally approved of the model, many of them using it in their own training activities in various organizations.

Unfortunately, the paper was problematic on both of its major points. As the 1980s wore on and the leadership literature continued to pour off the presses, it became increasingly obvious that the predictive force of the paper was in error. A new consensus was not developing around the reinterpretation of Burns's model of leadership (transactional leadership is really management and transformational leadership is leadership). If anything, as suggested in Chapter 4, the 1980s consensus developed around a very old idea of leadership, the great man/woman theory of leadership (do the leader's wishes), and not a reconstructed notion of leadership as transformation.

Second—and the leadership doctoral students were the first to identify this problem—the twelve differences between leadership and management developed in the paper were different more in degree than in fundamental nature. Several of the twelve contrasting elements did hit upon essential elements of each process, but the overall model gave the impression that the people practicing leadership were the "good guys in white hats" and the people practicing management were the mediocre types bungling the job, the "bad guys in black hats." (*Guys* is a slang expression that in common practice is used to refer to both women and men.)

The model has a third problem. Traits and behaviors were used to explain some of the differences between leadership and management. I was very conscious of using them in writing the piece. While I didn't like using them, I didn't know of any way around that problem. This feature of the model, however, did not bother the large majority of those who read the paper because traits and behaviors were what they were used to reading about in leadership books and articles.

The good guy/bad guy scenario, however, did bother some thoughtful critics a great deal, and in the end it caused me to completely rethink the model and eventually to reject it. I had written the piece with the express purpose of not raising up leadership and putting down management, but the paper ended up giving that impression anyway, mostly in covert ways. Such is the nature of deeply held background assumptions, even when a person expresses the opposite view to him/herself and consciously believes the opposite view.

Indeed, the good guy/bad guy view of leadership/management is pervasive in the 1980s literature on leadership. The most recent and overtly stated example of this view is in Zaleznik's (1989) book. The title of the book states the point succinctly: *The Managerial Mystique: Restoring Leadership in Business.* The managerial mystique is the bad guy, the cause of U.S. business problems in the 1980s. Leadership is the good guy, and restoring leadership is the solution to the United States' business problems. Zaleznik's book is only the most recent of such tracts. Leadership was consistently viewed as excellent management in the 1980s. That, in a nutshell, is what the excellence movement is all about.

United Technologies stuck a responsive chord with an advertisement published in numerous magazines in 1984. It was titled: "Let's Get Rid of Management," and its message was that "people don't want to be managed, they want to be led." (The advertisement was reprinted in Bennis & Nanus, 1985, p. 22.) H. Ross Perot is quoted in Kouzes and Posner (1987, p. xv) as expressing the same thought: "People cannot be managed. Inventories can be managed, but people must be led." The view of leadership and management presented in the advertisement and in the Perot quotation are great for symbolic mythmaking, but as a conceptual framework for understanding both leadership and management, it is dead wrong.

First of all, the universal human experience, at least in the Western world in the last few centuries, is that people do like to be managed—as long as management is not equated with dictatorship. If you want to find out how much people love management, try these simple strategies:

- Deliver the payroll checks late.
- Decrease the supplies people need to do their jobs.
- Stop any utility service people need to live or work.
- Have the buses, trains, airplanes run late.

- Eliminate stop lights on city streets.
- Deliver unworkable products to consumers.
- Tie promotions or salary raises to idiosyncratic criteria such as pleasing the whims of a supervisor.

The list could go on to include thousands of items that people have come to expect from being managed. We literally live in a managed society; management is what the industrial era is all about, and much of it is not going to change in the postindustrial era. Our civilization is so complex, it has to be managed. We have no other choice. As the saying goes, "We want our trains to run on time." And that epitomizes what managers and subordinates do when they manage.

Effective managers are a joy to behold and a pleasure to work with in any organization. People love to work for well-organized managers who facilitate getting the job done by coordinating the work of various people, and they hate to work for managers who are ineffective, uncoordinated, or incompetent. Most human beings crave order, stability, well-run programs, coordinated activity, patterned behavior, goal achievement, and the successful operation of an organization. They take pride in their ability to produce and deliver quality goods and services to consumers, and they are generally unhappy when the opposite conditions prevail. People generally like some predictability in their lives concerning the basic elements of living. That is the attraction of having the trains run on time. On the other hand, people become frustrated when they encounter poor or ineffective management, when the proverbial trains do not run on time. They vent their frustrations in many ways, from passivity and anomie to sabotage and revolution.

An example of this frustration with poor management can be seen in the revolutions in Eastern Europe in 1989-1990. The major causes of these revolutions will probably be debated for years to come. I heard a persuasive argument recently that the root cause of all the yearning for democracy was ethnic unrest. The Eastern European nations under Communist rule have never succeeded, this professor suggested, in gaining a real commitment to national unity from the various ethnic groups through some kind of melting pot strategy. The peoples in these countries identify with their ethnic group first and with their nation second. The cry for democracy has been a cry for ethnic freedom.

Another explanation may be just as persuasive. Despite, or maybe because of, the Communist belief in a planned economy and centralized (even dictatorial) control of society and business organizations, the Eastern bloc countries were badly managed. As a result, quality goods and services wanted and needed were not delivered at all. Thus, the revolution against the Communist system could be interpreted as a revolt against bad management and the effects that it has on people's lives and work. Under the Communist system, the people had no alternatives, since everything was strictly controlled by a few people at the top. Thus, they could not replace bad managers with good managers, nor could they replace a bad system of management with a good one. The cry for freedom, then, was a cry for the freedom to select, among other things, the managers and the system of management that would provide them with the basic goods and services they had come to expect from life (and that they could easily see on television that the people of neighboring countries enjoyed). With freedom came the ability to choose one management system over another, rather than being forced to accept a management system that obviously has not been working.

If that analysis is even somewhat accurate, it shows that effective management is highly valued by people. If people are willing to risk life and limb to get rid of bad management, if people believe that the ability to obtain wanted goods and services from the effective management of business and government organizations in their societies is essential to the good life, and if they engineer revolutions, in part, to throw out bad managers and a bad management system and to have the freedom to replace them with good managers and a better management system, then management is indeed a powerful process in our societies. Management is a process highly valued by people who do not have it operating effectively and do not have the power to change either the managers or the management stem. Effective management is so widely expected as the normal operating procedure in highly devel-

oped countries that it is often taken for granted. The people in Eastern Europe found they could not take it for granted.

It is time to stop the denigration of management and begin to rethink the nature of management and its necessity to the operation of our complex societies and the organizations that help make these societies function. The view that management is less than satisfactory if it is not infused with leadership is unacceptable as a conceptual framework to understand either management or leadership. That view contributes to the confusion over what leadership is and what management is. If we cannot manage effectively without leading, then certainly there is no fundamental distinction between leadership and management.

Scholars do not have to glamorize the concept of management by equating it (or good management) with the more popular concept of leadership. Management, pure and simple, is necessary and essential to the good life as we have come to experience it, and as such it has as much going for it as leadership does. It should be highly valued for what it is, not for what some authors want to make of it. Devaluing management in favor of leadership has disastrous effects in the everyday world of work and play. Human beings depend on the effective and efficient management of organizations hundreds of times every day, and that basic fact of life alone should make us want to understand the essential nature of management so as to promote and foster its widespread use in operating our organizations effectively and efficiently. Down with management and up with leadership is a bad idea.

Thus, I want to say quite forcefully that I reject the following views of leadership and management.

1. Management is ineffective unless it is equated with or infused with leadership.
2. Management is bad, leadership is good.
3. Management is a necessary but inadequate process in operating organizations. Leadership is needed at all times to operate any organization effectively.
4. Management is okay, but leadership is what makes the world go round.
5. Management is what got the United States into the mess that it is in vis-à-vis Japan and Germany and

other international go-getters. Leadership is what will get the United States out of the mess. Or, management is what got the federal government into the mess that it is in with regard to the budget deficit, and leadership is what will get the federal government out of the mess. Or, management is what got the public schools into the mess they are in regarding low student learning, dropouts, and so on, and leadership is what will get the public schools out of the mess. And so on.

The difficulty with all of these statements is that they, one and all, denigrate management and enno-ble leadership. Leadership is not the answer to all the ills of our societies or their institutions and organizations. Leadership may, in some cases, be part of the answers. (Note the plural!) But manage-ment, properly understood, is also part of the an-swers. Any concept of leadership that dignifies leadership at the expense of management has to be defective. Exalting leadership by casting asper-sions on management is an inherently flawed approach to understanding the nature of either concept.

The second problem with these statements is that they assume leadership is always good, effective, and helpful. There is, according to this view, no such thing as bad or ineffective leadership. Bad leadership is an oxymoron. Again, this approach to leadership may be adequate for symbolic myth-making, but it does not square with the lived expe-rience of human beings since the word *leadership* came into common usage. Including an effective-ness dimension in our understanding of leadership creates all kinds of conceptual and practical prob-lems in any attempt to come to terms with the nature of leadership. The same is true of manage-ment, except that most people do not automatically equate management with being good or effective. In both the scholarly and the popular press and among practitioners, there *is* a notion of bad man-agement. There is no similar notion of bad leader-ship in most of the leadership literature and among practitioners, especially in the 1980s.

The practical results of requiring leadership to be effective or good are readily apparent. It does not work when we try to make sense out of the distinction between leadership and management.

The conceptual result of such a view is that either (1) management cannot be effective, since when-ever it becomes effective, it turns into leadership, or (2) leadership must include management be-cause leadership is management that is good. At the very least, management becomes a necessary but inadequate element in defining leadership. What, then, happens to the definition when people experience leadership in a relationship wherein no one is a manager and the process of management is not occurring? The definition quickly loses its validity.

The practical result of such a view is to require every manager to be a leader because leaders are an absolutely essential element in all notions of leadership. Being only a manager means that one is relegated to being an ineffective professional person. Thus, being a leader becomes essential to the self-concept of every manager; clearly an im-possible task, if not an inhuman requirement, for many people.

Finally, such a view in effect makes leadership as a concept redundant. If leadership is good man-agement, the concept of leadership is superfluous because management as a construct had a lengthy and illustrious linguistic history long before people started talking and writing about leadership. As we have seen, leadership as a concept is relatively new, whereas the concept of authority or management is ages old. There must be something more to leader-ship as a concept than redundancy.

## Defining Management

If leadership is an influence relationship among leaders and followers who intend real changes that reflect their mutual purposes, what is manage-ment? Taking a cue from the four essential ele-ments of the definitions of leadership, I would like to suggest a corresponding definition of manage-ment. *Management is an authority relationship between at least one manager and one subordinate who coordinate their activities to produce and sell particular goods and/or services.*

From this definition, a person can identify four essential elements for a phenomenon to be labeled management:

1. Management is an authority relationship.
2. The people in this relationship include at least one manager and one subordinate.
3. The manager(s) and subordinate(s) coordinate their activities.
4. The manager(s) and subordinate(s) produce and sell particular goods and/or services.

Some discussion of each of these essential elements follows. Since my purpose is to explicate the difference between leadership and management, not to explicate a full-blown model of management, the discussion is limited to what is necessary to distinguish between leadership and management.

**Authority Relationship**

The first element is that management is a relationship based on authority. This element contains two points.

Management is a relationship. Many management scholars do not view management as a relationship but conceive of it as either (1) a manager doing certain behaviors, such as organizing, planning, staffing, communicating, motivating, controlling, and decision making, or (2) the process whereby a manager gets the job (whatever that job is) done efficiently and effectively. In both of these models of management, as well as others that could be cited, management is what the manager does. Management is not what both the manager and subordinate do, only what the manager does.

The behavior of managers is a necessary but insufficient explanation of the nature of management as a concept. The behaviors of managers make no sense without the corresponding behaviors of subordinates, and so I view management as a relationship.

The distinguishing feature of this relationship is that it is based on authority. Authority is a contractual (written, spoken, or implied) relationship wherein people accept superordinate or subordinate responsibilities in an organization. By its very nature, authority includes the use of both coercive and noncoercive actions. The contract allows the managers to tell the subordinates what to do, and some of the telling is coercive. Management as a

concept is built on such telling: "Sell this product for $3.95"; "Put a half-inch nut on this bolt on this part of the product"; "Do these five problems for homework tonight"; "Be at work at 7:30 A.M."; "Stop at all stop lights when they are red"; "Pay a percentage of your income for Social Security"; "Take this patient to the lab for an X-ray"; "Enter the name of the product in these 25 spaces on the bill of sale"; and so on.

Not all the behaviors in any management relationship are coercive. The point is that many of them are (while many of them may not be), and the second point is that coercive behaviors are perfectly acceptable to both managers and subordinates. While subordinates may resent some coercive behaviors—for instance, a police officer giving a person a ticket for running a red light—most subordinates accept the general pattern of coercive action in the management of organizations—for instance, a law requiring everyone to stop at red lights and police officers to enforce the law.

**Manager and Subordinate**

The people in the relationship called management are at least one manager and one subordinate. This is the second essential element in the definition.

Both words are in the singular because it takes at least two people to have a relationship, and we know from information readily available to anyone who looks for it that some organizations are actually managed by only two people, one being a manager and the other being a subordinate. Such organizations are not very typical any more, but they are a reality. If management actually happens in such organizations, and I believe it does, the definition must be worded to include them.

Generally speaking, however, most management relationships include one manager and several subordinates or, even more typical, numerous managers and even more numerous subordinates.

Both of these words (manager and subordinate) indicate positions within an organization. It is easy to identify who is a manager and who is a subordinate in an organization because they are positions identified on the organization chart or in a contract.

A manager is a person who is contracted to manage an organization or some part of one; a subordinate is a person who reports to the manager and is contractually required to obey the manager. To make things complicated, some people are both managers and subordinates in an organization. Teachers, for instance, are subordinates in relationship to the principal or superintendent, but they are managers in relationship to the students.

If both the manager and the subordinate are part of the relationship called management, it follows that they both are involved in management. A relationship cannot exist unless both parties contribute to it.

The contributors, however, are not necessarily equal. In fact, in management the component parts of the relationship are inherently unequal, with the manager having the dominant part and the subordinate—as the name indicates—having the subordinate part. Management is a two-way relationship that is primarily top-down as to the directives given and bottom-up as to the responses given. In more democratic or flat organizations, the two-way relationship may be more horizontal than hierarchical.

**Coordination of Activities**

The third essential element in the definition of management is that manager and subordinate coordinate their activities. The coordination of activities is necessary if the relationship is to achieve its purpose—the production and sale of goods and/or services. Coordinating their activities is the means whereby the manager(s) and subordinate(s) achieve their goal. Without some coordination, goods or services could not produced or sold. The goods and/or services are the result of the coordinated activities of the manager(s) and subordinate(s) who enter into the authority relationship.

**Production and Sale of Particular Goods and/or Services**

The manager and subordinate are in a relationship to produce and sell particular goods and/or services.

Producing and selling are the raison d'être of management. They are the heart of the relationship

called management. Both are essential. Producing is the expense, and selling is the income. While some people in public organizations may think that selling is not part of the management of their organizations, since many clients or consumers might not pay for the services specifically rendered to them, such a view of public management is inaccurate. Public management involves the selling of services to the public because income to cover the expenses of the services is required for the organization not only to exist but also to prosper.

Producing and selling are the purpose of the relationship that is management. They are why people enter into the relationship. They are what the people in the relationship do. They identify what the relationship is all about. Management is a relationship established in organizations so that people can produce and sell particular goods and/or services.

Goods and/or services are also what the people in the relationship produce by their coordinated activities. Management is essential to their production. However, the relationship goes further than just production. The people in the relationship also sell these goods and/or services because they understand that focusing only on production will get them nowhere. Thus, the relationship is incomplete unless the products are sold.

The word *particular* precedes goods and/or services in the definition because the manager(s) and subordinate(s) coordinate their activities to produce and sell only certain goods and/or services, not any or all goods and services.

*And/or* is used in the definition because I am not certain that all managerial relationships involve both goods and services. Its use allows for some managerial relationships to produce and sell one or the other, not both. My guess is that the large majority of managerial relationships involve both.

*Leadership and Management*

The definition given above does not require management to be effective or ineffective, good or bad, efficient or inefficient, excellent or mediocre, and so on. All of these words are adjectives that people can apply to particular managerial relationships when they evaluate the management of an organization according to stated criteria. These evaluative criteria are different from the essential elements analysts should use as criteria to determine if the phenomenon is management. Thus, there is a two-step process. First, one must determine if the phenomenon is management. Second, the analyst can then determine if the relationship that is management is effective or ineffective, good or bad, efficient or inefficient, excellent or mediocre.

The same statement can be made about leadership. The definition of leadership given in Chapter 5 does not require leadership to be effective or ineffective, good or bad, efficient or inefficient, excellent or mediocre, and so on. All of these words are adjectives that people can apply to a particular relationship that is determined to be leadership when they evaluate that relationship according to predetermined criteria. That evaluation comes after the analyst determines if the phenomenon is actually leadership. The two-step process is the same as that for evaluating management.

The essential nature of management as a relationship and that of leadership as a relationship are neutral to all such evaluative criteria. Management that is ineffective, bad, inefficient, or mediocre is still management. Leadership that is ineffective, bad, inefficient, or mediocre is still leadership. Management that is effective, good, efficient, or excellent is still management. These qualities do not transform management into leadership. The idea that good management is leadership destroys any possible clear definition of both leadership and management. Leadership as good management mixes both management and leadership into a mishmash of conceptual confusion. Out of that confusion comes our inability to distinguish leadership from management (and vice versa) and our inability to intelligently understand either concept.

## *Distinguishing Between Management and Leadership*

Using the essential elements of the two definitions, four substantive differences between leadership and management can be ascertained. The first

**TABLE 10.1** Distinguishing Leadership From Management

| Leadership | Management |
|---|---|
| Influence relationship | Authority relationship |
| Leaders and followers | Managers and subordinates |
| Intend real changes | Produce and sell goods and/or services |
| Intended changes reflect mutual purposes | Goods/services result from coordinated activities |

three are clear and distinct, and scholars and practitioners can easily use them to distinguish between leadership and management. The last difference is perhaps less distinctive and is, therefore, more difficult to use in distinguishing leadership from management.

Table 10.1 presents the four differences between leadership and management in short statements. A discussion of each of these differences follows.

### Influence vs. Authority Relationship

The difference is that leadership is an influence relationship and management is an authority relationship. The differences in these two kinds of relationships have to do with (1) use of coercion and (2) directionality of the attempts to impact on people.

Influence requires that coercion not be used, at least as a regular and patterned form of behavior. Authority allows the use of coercion as a regular and patterned form of behavior.

Attempts to influence other people in a leadership relationship are multidirectional. Leaders influence other leaders and followers while followers influence other followers and leaders. Attempts to use authority in a managerial relationship are unidirectional and top-down. Managers use authority to impact on subordinates, who then respond to the authoritative directive, producing the two-way relationship. While there may be more democratic relationships between managers and subordinates these days, the basic and fundamental relationship remains top-down.

## Leaders and Followers vs. Managers and Subordinates

Leaders and followers are the people involved in a leadership relationship. Subordinates can be leaders, as can managers. Managers can be followers, as can subordinates. Leaders and followers can have a relationship that includes no managers and no subordinates.

Managers and subordinates are the people involved in a managerial relationship. Followers can be managers, as can subordinates. Leaders can be subordinates, as can followers. Managers and subordinates can be involved in a relationship that includes no leaders and no followers.

The two sets of words are not synonymous. Leaders are not the same as managers. Followers are not the same as subordinates. Managers may be leaders, but if they are leaders, they are involved in a relationship different from management. Subordinates may be followers, but if they are followers, they are involved in a relationship different from management. Leaders need not be managers to be leaders. Followers need not be subordinates to be followers.

People in authority positions—presidents, governors, mayors, CEOs, superintendents, principals, administrators, supervisors, department heads, and so on—are not automatically leaders by virtue of their holding a position of authority. Being a leader must not be equated with being in a position of authority. The definition of a leader cannot include a requirement that the person be in a position of authority. Such a definition of a leader is totally inconsistent with the definition of leadership given in Chapter 5.

On the other hand, people in authority positions are automatically managers because that is the definition of a manager: a person who holds a position of authority. Being a manager must not be equated with being a leader. The definition of a manager cannot include a requirement that the person be a leader. Such a definition of a manager is totally inconsistent with both the definition of

leadership presented in Chapter 5 and the definition of management given above.

A distinction between leadership and management requires that the words *leader* and *manager, follower* and *subordinate,* be defined differently. The two sets of words cannot be used interchangeably.

## Intending Real Change vs. Producing and Selling Goods and/or Services

Leaders and followers intend real changes, while managers and subordinates produce and sell goods and/or services.

Leadership involves an intention on the part of leaders and followers. Management involves the production and sale on the part of managers and subordinates. Intending is very different from producing and selling.

Leadership involves (intending) real changes. Management involves (producing and selling) goods and services. Leaders and followers join forces to attempt to really change something. Managers and subordinates join forces to really change the ways they produce and sell their goods/services, or really change the kind of goods/services they produce and sell, those managers and subordinates may have transformed their managerial relationship into a leadership relationship. (I say *may* because the three other essential elements must be present for there to be leadership.)

## Mutual Purpose vs. Coordinated Activities

The intended changes must reflect the mutual purposes of the leaders and followers. The goods and/or services result from the coordinated activities of the managers and subordinates.

There is nothing in the definition of management about mutual purposes, so when one sees mutual purposes being forged in a relationship, that is a cue that leadership is happening. (Again, the three other essential elements have to be present.) Mutual purposes are more than independent goals mutually held. They are common purposes developed over time as followers and leaders interact in a noncoercive relationship about the changes they intend. Leaders and followers are constantly in the process of developing mutual purposes, and their commitment to that development makes the leadership relationship different from the management relationship.

Coordinated activities, on the other hand, allow for independent goals mutually agreed upon by managers and subordinates in order to get the job done, in order to produce and sell particular goods and/or services. Coordinated activities include negotiated agreements, exchanges, transactional accommodations, and compromises. They also include telling subordinates what to do: "Barbara and Bill will watch the children eating in the cafeteria while John and Jane monitor them on the playground and Mary and Mark organize games for them in the field so that six other faculty members can eat lunch." Coordinated activities include staffing and other ways of deploying resources, making decisions about how goods are going to be made and sold and about how services are going to be delivered and sold.

None of those activities are necessary to leadership as a relationship, primarily because leadership is not about producing and selling goods and/or services. Some of these activities may not even be helpful to particular leaders and followers who intend real changes. The leadership relationship allows for a great many activities that would not be classified as coordinated activities in the ordinary sense of the term: revolution, reform, demonstration, rallies, breaking unjust laws, charismatic behaviors, intuitive decisions, behaving according to new governing assumption, ad hoc committees, disrupting coordinated activities, unplanned actions, and so on. These kinds of activities may be clues that leadership is happening and that management is not.

Of course, a leadership relationship may involve coordinated activities, but the crucial point is that these coordinated activities are not essential to leadership. They are, however, essential to management. It is impossible to conceive of people in a management relationship producing and selling goods and/or services without coordinated activities.

## References

Allison, G. T. (1984). Public and private administrative leadership: Are they fundamentally alike in all unimportant respects? In T. J. Sergiovanni & J. E. Crobally (Eds.), *Leadership and organizational culture* (pp. 214-239). Urbana: University of Illinois Press.

Argyris, C. (1976). *Increasing leadership effectiveness.* New York: Wiley.

Badaracco, J. L., Jr., & Ellsworth, R. R. (1989). *Leadership and the quest for integrity.* Boston: Harvard Business School Press.

Bennis, W. G. (1977, March-April). Where have all the leaders gone? *Technological Review,* pp. 3-12.

Bennis, W. G. (1989a). *On becoming a leader.* Reading, MA: Addison-Wesley.

Bennis, W. G. (1989b). *Why leaders can't lead.* San Francisco: Jossey-Bass.

Bennis, W. G., & Nanus, B. (1985). *Leaders: The strategy for taking charge.* New York: Harper & Row.

Bryman, A. (1986). *Leadership and organizations.* London: Routledge & Kegan Paul.

Burack, E. H. (1979). Leadership findings and applications: The viewpoint of four from the real world—David Campbell, Joseph L. Moses, Paul J. Patinka, and Blanchard B. Smith. In J. G. Hunt & L. L. Larson (Eds.), *Crosscurrents in leadership* (pp. 25-46). Carbondale: Southern Illinois University Press.

Burns, J. M. (1978). *Leadership.* New York: Harper & Row.

Center for Creative Leadership. (n.d.). *Looking Glass, Inc.: A management simulation of a day in the life of top management.* Greensboro, NC: Author.

Cohen, W. A. (1990). *The art of the leader.* Englewood Cliffs, NJ: Prentice Hall.

Conger, J. A. (1989a). *The charismatic leader.* San Francisco: Jossey-Bass.

DePree, M. (1989). *Leadership is an art.* New York: Doubleday.

Dubin, R. (1979). Metaphors of leadership: An overview. In In J. G. Hunt & L. L. Larson (Eds.), *Crosscurrents in leadership* (pp. 225-238). Carbondale: Southern Illinois University Press.

Enochs, J. C. (1981, November). Up from management. *Phi Delta Kappan,* pp. 175-178.

Foster, W. F. (1986a). *Paradigms and promises.* Buffalo, NY: Prometheus.

Foster, W. F. (1986b). *The reconstruction of leadership.* Victoria, Australia: Deakin University Press.

Graham, J. W. (1982, August). *Leadership: A critical analysis.* Paper presented at the 42nd annual meeting of the Academy of Management, New York City.

Graham, J. W. (1988). Transformational leadership: Fostering follower autonomy, not automatic followership. In J. G. Hunt, B. R. Baliga, H. P. Dachler, & C. A. Schriesheim (Eds.), *Emerging leadership vistas* (pp. 73-79). Lexington, MA: Lexington Books.

Hosking, D. M., & Hunt, J. G. (1982). Leadership research and the European connection: An epilogue. In J. G. Hunt, U. Sekaran, & C. A. Schriesheim (Eds.), *Leadership: Beyond establishment views* (pp. 278-289). Carbondale: Southern Illinois University Press.

Hosking, D. M., & Morley, I. E. (1988). The skills of leadership. In J. G. Hunt, B. R. Baliga, H. P. Dachler, & C. A. Schriesheim (Eds.), *Emerging leadership vistas* (pp. 89-106). Lexington, MA: Lexington Books.

Hunt, J. G. (1984a). *Leadership and managerial behavior.* Chicago: Science Research Associates.

Hunt, J. G., Baliga, B. R., Dachler, H. P., & Schriesheim, C. A. (Eds.). (1988). *Emerging leadership vistas.* Lexington, MA: Lexington Books.

Immegart, G. L. (1988). Leadership and leader behavior. In N. J. Boyan (Ed.), *Handbook of research on educational administration* (pp. 259-277). New York: Longman.

Jacobs, T. O. (1970). *Leadership and exchange in formal organizations.* Alexandria, VA: Human Resources Research Organization.

Jago, A. G. (1982). Leadership: Perspectives in theory and research. *Management Science, 28,* 315-336.

Janis, I. L. (1989). *Crucial decisions: Leadership in policymaking and crisis management.* New York: Free Press.

Katz, D., & Kahn, R. L. (1978). *The social psychology of organizations* (2nd ed.). New York: Wiley. (Original work published 1966)

Kotter, J. P. (1988). *The leadership factor.* New York: Free Press.

Kouzes, J. M., & Posner, B. Z. (1987). *The leadership challenge.* San Francisco: Jossey-Bass.

Lombardo, M. M., & McCall, M. W., Jr. (1982). Leaders on line: Observations from a simulation of managerial work. In J. G. Hart, U. Sekaran, & C. A. Schriesheim (Eds.), *Leadership: Beyond establishment views* (pp. 50-67). Carbondale: Southern Illinois University Press.

Miner, J. B. (1975). The uncertain failure of the leadership concept: An overview. In J. G. Hunt & L. L. Larson (Eds.), *Leadership frontiers* pp. 197-208). Kent, OH: Kent State University Press.

Mintzberg, H. (1982). If you're not serving Bill and Barbara, then you're not serving leadership. In J. G. Hart, U. Sekaran, & C. A. Schriesheim (Eds.), *Leadership: Beyond establishment views* (pp. 239-250). Carbondale: Southern Illinois University Press.

Nanus, B. (1989). *The leader's edge.* Chicago: Contemporary Press.

Ridge, W. J. (1989). *Follow me.* New York: AMACOM.

Rost, J. C. (1985, October). *Distinguishing leadership and management: A new consensus.* Paper presented at the Organizational Development Network National Conference, San Francisco.

Schon, D. A. (1984). Leadership as reflection in action. In T. J. Sergiovanni & J. E. Corbally (Eds.), *Leadership and organizational culture* (pp. 36-63). Urbana: University of Illinois Press.

Schriesheim, C. A., Hunt, J. G., & Sekaran, U. (1982). Conclusion: The leadership management controversy revisited. In J. G. Hunt, U. Sekaran, & C. A. Schriesheim (Eds.), *Leadership: Beyond establishment views* (pp. 290-298). Carbondale: Southern Illinois University Press.

Selznick, P. (1957). *Leadership in administration: A sociological interpretation.* Evanston, IL: Row, Peterson.

Sergiovanni, T. J. (1990). *Value-added leadership.* San Diego, CA: Harcourt Brace Jovanovich.

Smith, P. B., & Peterson, M. F. (1988). *Leadership, organizations and culture.* Beverly Hills, CA: Sage.

Tucker, R. C. (1981). *Politics as leadership.* Columbia: University of Missouri Press.

Wilpert, B. (1982). Commentary on part 1: Various paths beyond establishment views. In J. G. Hunt, U. Sekaran, & C. A. Schriesheim (Eds.), *Leadership: Beyond establishment views* (pp. 68-74). Carbondale: Southern Illinois University Press.

Yukl, G. A. (1989). *Leadership in organizations* (2nd ed.). Englewood Cliffs, NJ: Prentice Hall.

Zaleznik, A. (1977). Managers and leaders: Are they different? *Harvard Business Review, 15*(3), 67-84.

Zaleznik, A. (1989). *The managerial mystique: Restoring leadership in business.* New York: Harper & Row.

# 11

# Servant Leadership in Business

ROBERT K. GREENLEAF

Perhaps I reflect the influence of my own vocational choice when I say that, in the next few years, more will be learned in business than in any other field about how to bring servant leadership into being as a major social force. In my view, businesses not only do as well with their obligations now, under the conditions imposed on them, as other kinds of institutions do with theirs, but businesses are more questioning of their own adequacy, they are more open to innovation, and they are disposed to take greater risks to find a better way.

The three statements that comprise this chapter, one given to a general audience and two addressed to specific businesses—one large and one small—give a fair sample of what contemporary business people are willing to think about. What these three quite different pieces have in common, and they were written between 1958 and 1974, is a call to a new business ethic—a striving for excellence. Businesses are asked not only to produce better goods and services but to become greater social assets as institutions.

It is important for the non-business reader to note that government attitudes, reflecting, no doubt, the prevailing popular view toward privately owned businesses, are different from those taken toward other types of institutions. By law, with criminal sanctions, profit-making businesses are required to compete as the principal means for compelling them to serve. This is a crude and cumbersome and ambiguous approach, By implication, public policy is saying that if profit is an aim, the institution will not serve unless it is compelled to. The practical consequence of this decision has been to impose, and surround with an aura of sanctity, the law of the jungle. Necessarily, I believe, business schools teach more about how to survive and prosper in the jungle than how, through excellence, to help build a better society. This is a questionable mission for a university.

SOURCE: From *Servant Leadership* by Robert K. Greenleaf © 1977 by Robert K. Greenleaf; © 1991 by The Robert K. Greenleaf Center. Used by permission of Paulist Press.

It is not the purpose here to argue the merits of this approach, or to suggest that there is not a problem of some businesses not serving well. But, in my view, the problem of not serving well is no greater in business than with schools, churches, hospitals, philanthropies, and government itself.

In addressing businesses, therefore, with the intent of encouraging a greater *voluntary* striving for excellence as servant, I am mindful of the special conditions under which businesses operate, as distinguished from other institutions. A principle is suggested: *When any action is regulated by law, the incentive for individual conscience to govern is diminished—unless the law coincides with almost universally held moral standards.* We should have learned this out of our experience with alcoholic prohibition. The U.S. Constitution was amended, after World War I, in order to suppress the acknowledged (by the majority) evil of alcohol. In 1933 the amendment was repealed, not because of a change in view about the evil, but because so many disregarded the law that the nation would be destroyed in trying to enforce it. We are repeating this error now with marijuana (although we have recently begun a retreat from it), and the logic which says that marijuana is evil seems less persuasive than with alcohol.

I cite the examples of prohibition on alcohol and marijuana because they suggest that, before we pass a law, we should weigh the possible consequences of diminishing voluntary ethical striving toward the same end, unless, as I have said, the ethical norm is already almost universally accepted. Before the prohibition on alcohol was enacted into law, substantial progress was being made (in the United States) toward containing the evil of alcohol with a voluntary ethic. We seem to have lost much of that ethic by the passage of the law. *We cannot have it both ways.*

In making this point I am not arguing for anarchy, for no law. My point is that we in the United States are more naive than most about what can be done with law, especially with the labyrinth of law with which business is surrounded. It comes out better if one persuades rather than compels.

Let me suggest to the reader that the assumptions be examined—both about the making of profit and about undertaking to compel service by law. Is all that we want from profit-making business the lowest price we can exact? In my own efforts to help business to become more serving I feel that I am contending with a popular view that *price is all.* Personally, I would prefer to pay a considerably higher price *if,* thereby, the institution could become substantially more serving to all who are touched by its actions.

Having said all of this, I recognize the problem of so much of business not serving well. But the core of the problem, as I see it, is not in business institutions; rather it is in the attitudes, concepts, and expectations regarding business held by the rest of society. People in churches, universities, government, and social agencies *do not love* business institutions. As a consequence, many inside business do not love them either. Businesses, despite their crassness, occasional corruption, and unloveliness, *must be loved* if they are to serve us better. They are much too large a presence in the lives of all of us to have them in our midst and not serve us better.

But how, one may ask, can one love this abstraction called the corporation? One doesn't! One loves *only the people* who are gathered to render the service for which the corporation is enfranchised. *The people are the institution!*

## Ethics and Manipulation

*(A paper presented at the Conference on "The Manipulation of Man, The Gottlieb Dutweiler Institute, Zurich, Switzerland, February 26, 1970)*

Part of the problem of dealing with our subject, "Ethics and Manipulation," is that the words *manipulation* and *management* have a common root in *manus,* hand, and both words imply shaping other people's destinies. Whereas *manipulation* of people has long been taken as bad because it implies moving them without their knowing fully what is going on, until recently *management* has been accepted as legitimate. Now, as I read the signs, we are in a period of radical transition regarding power, authority, and decision everywhere, and a cloud has settled over all leadership and management in any form. All institutions are affected by these trends, and institutional leadership is now quite different from what it was a few years ago. I expect these trends to continue.

There has emerged from this ferment the expectation, held by many, that a manipulation-free society is a possibility—a "leaderless" society that is governed by a continuing consensus with full participation and with every motive behind every action fully exposed. I respect the motives of those who advocate this ideal state and admit to occasional utopian dreams of life in an influence-free society. But, realistically, I do not see such a society in prospect, and I will deal here with the institution of American business as I know it in my own experience—a state of affairs in which strong, able people must lead, and therefore manipulate, if the goods and services expected are to emerge. Some of us would do better with less goods, though we need more services—health care, for instance. But whatever the level of goods and services, institutions will be required to deliver them. These institutions, if they are to rise above mediocrity, will have their ablest people as leaders, and those leaders will manipulate.

The issue then, as I see it, is not whether all manipulation can be banished as evil, but rather: Can some manipulation be made legitimate? By what standards, and how? What ethic should govern for these times? Before I conclude, I will speculate on what one new business ethic might be.

I cannot visualize a world without leaders, without those who better see the path ahead taking the risks to lead and show the way. What reason is there for accepting the constraints of a society except that therein the more able serve the less able? One way that some people serve is to lead. And anyone who does this *manipulates* others because one literally helps shape their destinies without fully revealing either one's motives or the direction in which one is leading them. Leaders may be completely honest about their conscious intent. But the essential artistry in their leadership, that which makes them more dependable and trustworthy than most, is their intuitive insight which cannot be fully explained. We have it from the great French jurist, Saleilles, that a judge makes decisions intuitively, and then devises the fine legal reasoning to justify them—after the fact. So it is with the scientist on the growing edge of discovery. And so it is with the leader—whether one be a business person, administrator, politician, clergyman, or teacher. I cannot conceive of a duller, less creative world than one in which everything can be fully and rationally explained.

My search, therefore, day by day, is for a path through the maze along which people are accepted as they are and which leads to a world that is more benign. As I look out through my particular window on the world I realize that I do not see all. Rather I see only what the filter of my biases and attitudes of the moment permits me to see. Therefore if, in the course of this discussion, I make a declaration without appending "it seems to me," please assume such a qualification on everything I say.

Traveling this path, I see the field of American business is almost without professional standards. It is not much supported by sentiment, there is no aura of professional sanctity to mask its shortcomings, and, because it is one of the least restrained—by a professional ethic—of all fields of practice, at the low end of the scale there is much that is corrupt and very bad, while at the high end there is much at a level of excellence that is truly distinguished. The spread between the two extremes is wide.

Performance in any field or calling should be judged in reference to the obligations assumed for society, which differ from field to field. I know something of what goes on in the fields of education, government, religion, philanthropy, and health services. In my judgment, businessmen do as well by their obligations as do the others. None does very well.

The world of practice in all fields, as I see it through my particular window, is, on the average, mediocre. No field does very well when judged by what is reasonable and possible with available resources. This is what makes the subject of manipulation, or almost any other dimension of modern Western society, so interesting. How can we do better? We have the resources to do so much better, far better than the mediocre level that now prevails because so much leadership is poor.

The problem of doing better in the modern world, as I see it, is: How can people perform better in, and be better served by, *institutions*—especially large ones?

In my country at least, where business practice is shaped more by the influence of large institutions, and where there is a wide range of choice as to what a business may be like, as a subculture, there is much to be found that is relevant to our theme, "The Manipulation of Man," by exploring briefly how our big businesses came to be what they are—and how they may be different in the future.

Let me use the three largest American businesses in their fields as examples. Each of them is what it is today because each, at a critical period in its history, was headed by a building genius (not the founding owner) who gave the institution the stamp of his personal values. Each of these building geniuses was an adequate leader and manager for his day, but each brought unusual conceptual powers—in defining the institution and establishing his values as its values.

In General Motors, our largest manufacturing concern, the genius was Alfred Sloan, whose unique gift was remarkable organizational insight and the growing of managers; in Sears Roebuck, our largest merchandising company, the genius was Julius Rosenwald, who brought unusual humanness and trust; in American Telephone and Telegraph Company, our largest public utility (and my old company), the genius was Theodore N. Vail, who gave it dedication to service supported by relentless technical innovation. Although Vail has been gone fifty years (he was the earliest of the three), AT&T is still his business—his personal values still dominate it. There has been an erosion, of course, but fifty years is a long time for one man's recognizable influence to last in something as transient as a business or in an institution as large as this one. It is the same with Sloan and Rosenwald, who came later. General Motors and Sears are still "their" companies. These three companies rose above the level of mediocrity because three great leader-builders brought them there.

I do not cite these companies as paragons or models for the future. They have the same faults and frailties common to all human institutions at this stage of their development. But each of these, at a critical period in its growth, made a lunge forward and contributed something to the art of institution building. Whether it can be done again depends on the quality of the people who emerge, inside, to serve and lead.

The test of leadership has not changed: What does the scorekeeper (or the several scorekeepers) say? The scorekeeper's rules have changed a bit, and they will change even more. There are more "publics" demanding satisfaction, and the intensity of their scrutiny has increased. Business institutions have grown larger and much more complex and the pace of innovation is sometimes breathtaking. Dealing with these conditions, large business leadership has become a sophisticated calling, and the leaders are much more concerned with building strength and bringing sharpness of focus to many people and building a dependable staff rather than with deciding everything themselves. Contemporary business leaders are just as much determined institution builders as their predecessors, but they work differently and their role is more difficult to understand—from the outside.

The role of top leadership in large American business is shifting away from that of the dominant decision-maker to that of manager of the information system. Leadership depends more on the pull of the overarching goals plus building the competence and sustaining the autonomy of many decision-makers. This, in turn, is supported by wide access to reliable and comprehensive information. The sanctions pressing on individuals for good performance are, first, their own pride and conscience framed within adequate information that guides them and tells them how they are doing; second, the social pressure of peers whose own performance is interlinked with theirs and who have access to the common pool of information so that they know how their colleagues are doing; and, finally, the last-resort authority of the superior officer, which, in a good institution, is rarely used. The value of coercive power is inverse to its use.

This is a hopeful and encouraging trend. It is made possible by a wide scope of freedom for quite autonomous institutions under the shelter of political democracy. But, in my country, the model for it has not been set by the government, nor is it the product of democratization within the firm. Rather it is the result of the growth of knowledge, relentless market pressures, and the emergence of some unusual business builders. Political democracy is a necessary condition, but it does not guarantee anything. The only assurance of a good result is the encouragement of the culture for incremental thrusts by large numbers of strong, free, able people as they serve and lead. Individual people doing the right things give a society its moral stature. This does not make a perfect society, but this is how such goodness as it has is built.

Earlier I said that I believed that the decisive creative response to the challenge of the contemporary ferment, the response that is more likely to turn things around than any other I know about, will come from the business firm. I see the tentative first steps already being made.

How then will businesses respond to the new conditions? How can they perform their expected functions in a way that the charge of manipulation recedes as a serious issue?

I have confidence that, after a bit of confusion, a new business ethic will emerge. And the best I can do at this point is to speculate on what that ethic might be. I will confine my speculation to only one facet of the total problem of business ethics—those who work within business. There are many parts of the total business ethic that need attention, but the one I will deal with seems the more basic.

What might the new ethic be? (Not a new idea but new as a firmly held business ethic.)

Looking at the two major elements, the work and the person, the new ethic, simply but quite completely stated, will be: *the work exists for the person as much as the person exists for the work.* Put another way, the business exists as much to provide meaningful work to the person as it exists to provide a product or service to the customer.

The business then becomes a serving institution—serving those who produce and those who use. At first, the new ethic may put these two on a par. But as the economy becomes even more productive and people get more sensible and settle for fewer "things," in the new ethic service to those who produce may rise in priority above service to those who use, and the significance of work will be more the joy of the doing rather than the goods and services produced. There must, of course, be goods and services at some level, but in an era of abun-

dance they need not be the top priority. This view of it not only will make a better society, but, in the future, this may be the only way the consumer can be well served—by accepting that serving is more important than being served, and that the mere possession of money does not give one an unqualified right to command the service of another. (We are partly there already.) Furthermore, users will be better served if they find a way to communicate this belief to those who serve. A new consumer ethic will need to evolve alongside the new business ethic. I am close enough to this restless generation of young people in my country to believe that the more able and discerning among them will not settle for less than this as the prevailing ethic for the future. And they will enforce their view simply by too many of the abler ones refusing to work on any other terms.

I have said that the idea is not new but that its adoption as a firmly held business ethic will be new in our time. In fact, as an idea, it is very old—at least twenty-five hundred years. Its first formulation, to my knowledge, is in the Buddhist ethic, as one step in the noble eightfold path—right vocation, or right livelihood—as given in the famous sermon at Benares.

Speaking to those in business who presume to manage, it is important that this principle be embraced as an ethic and not simply as a "device" to achieve harmony or increase productivity or reduce turnover. Some popular procedures, such as participation or work enlargement or profit sharing, may be manipulative devices if they do not flow naturally out of a comprehensive ethic. "Participative democracy" in industry as it is now advocated in Europe may, in practice, be another such device, especially in a large industry. I do not think it will flourish in my country. Our unions are too astute to permit it, and involvement with it will divert attention from more basic matters.

Manipulative devices, and manipulation as a concept, are attacked because they are visible targets. However, just removing the evidences of manipulation (assuming it can be done) will not produce meaning and significance in individual lives. In an overcrowded industrial society this can only be done by the institutions we now have, where most people spend their working lives, adopting an ethic in which meaning and significance are the goal—at least on a parity with other goals. And to bring it to parity, it must, for a while at least, be the primary goal. This means that business institutions must adopt this goal, and its accomplishment rests on the ability of builders, leaders, to move these institutions (while keeping them intact and functioning), from where they are, with the heavy emphasis on production, to where they need to be, with the heavy emphasis on growing people. And they will do this while meeting all of the other performance criteria that society imposes for institutional survival.

When George Fox gave the seventeenth-century English Quaker businessmen a new business ethic (truthfulness, dependability, fixed prices—no haggling), he did it because his view of right conduct demanded it, not because it would be more profitable. It did, in fact, become more profitable because those early Quaker businessmen quickly emerged out of the seamy morass of that day as people who could be trusted. But the new ethic was a radical demand on those people and they must have had apprehensions about it when it was urged upon them.

The ethic suggested here is a radical one too, and businessmen will probably be apprehensive about it. Those who are moved to act on it are not likely to move so much in response to the moral imperative simply because the moral leader with sufficient stature to persuade them (as George Fox did with his followers) doesn't seem to be around. The new ethic will come, if it comes, as an acknowledgment (or in anticipation) of the relentless pressure of the revolution in values.

Very soon, across the whole gamut of our institutions, we may know how many determined builders there are who can move creatively with these times in which powerful new forces for integrity are operating. I wager that in American business we have a few leaders who will rise to the challenge. But they will not choose to announce, with great fanfare, a new ethic to deal with the new conditions. If they are wise they will not announce *anything*. There is an ancient moral injunction which tells us to "practice what we preach." A few businessmen have learned the hard way to follow the modern version of that advice which says:

"Don't practice what you preach; just practice!" Consequently the wise businessmen will simply start the slow process of converting the large numbers of people within the institution who must share this view if it is to be viable. It will be noticed only in practice, and that gradually.

It will take some courage for a large business to make this ethical shift, but only one of them need make the shift initially. When Henry Ford set up his assembly line to manufacture automobiles, ultimately everybody in that kind of business had to convert. So it may be with the new business ethic.

The process has already started in some businesses with the effort to accommodate the very able young people who have a clear individualistic style that they are determined to preserve and who need the excitement of a dynamic purpose. Such very able individuals are quickly given a track of their own to run on so that they can have the satisfaction of personal achievement. This is easier to do in a small business, but larger firms are learning to decentralize in a way that creates a variety of environments in which different styles of able people will flourish and be themselves. The corporate leader and his staff provide a context for all of this so that individuals can have a clear focus of purpose, so that they can be supported when they need it and feel a part of a larger purpose without losing their individuality, and so that all the parts can contribute to the total strength of the enterprise. (If some people want to make their career with a large business and keep their individuality, then they should choose a strong business.) This is the first step—to accommodate the wide differences and needs of the very able. A few strong businesses are well along with this step. The test? They have many able young people but it is difficult to "raid" them and lure them away.

The second step, and the more difficult, is to exert a strong pull for growth on *all* in the enterprise who have unrealized potential and who want to grow. More people will want to grow when the climate is encouraging. Most large businesses have the staff resources to redesign the work so as to capitalize on individual strengths. Sometimes it means taking on a product or service that is not particularly profitable just because someone needs it. The specific imperative that brings this about will probably be the pressure from the *able* young people within the firm who are recruited under arrangements mentioned in the preceding paragraph.

Motivation then becomes what people generate for themselves when they experience growth. Whereas the usual assumption about the firm is that it is in business to make a profit and serve its customers and that it does things for and to employees to get them to be productive, the new ethic requires that *growth* of those who do the work is the primary aim, and the workers then see to it that the customer is served and that the ink on the bottom line is black. It is *their* game. The art, of course, is how to do this in a firm that employs many thousands.

It won't be easy. But neither will it be any harder than other difficult things that large businesses have to do. And this one, ultimately, they will accept that they *have* to do. With that acceptance will come the belief that it is right, which makes it an ethic.

If done well, the change will come slowly, and those who demand instant perfection will probably say that nothing at all is happening. To stay alive and meet all of the other criteria that must be met, a business will probably continue to operate the old way while moving toward the new. There will be inevitable confusion. But this is what makes business leadership interesting.

In my country we are well on the way to accepting that the world owes every person a living. The next step may be to acknowledge that every person is entitled to work that is meaningful in individual terms and that it is the obligation of employers, in toto, to provide it. Whereas "a living" can be dispensed via money through a relief agency, "meaningful work" is likely to be delivered only within an employing institution that is living by a new ethic. And the practice of this ethic is a positive move toward a holistic society.

Except for a few esoteric scholars, the case for the university as a place set apart from the world of work rests on tenuous grounds. Perhaps, experimentally at least, we should move toward a new institution that embraces both work and learning—learning in a deep and formal sense and all of the school influence most people need. This requires a

new type of leader, one who can conceptualize such an institution, generate enthusiasm so that many good and able people want to be a part of it, and provide the strong focus of purpose that builds dynamic strength in many. Great things happen when able leaders create these conditions. There are some able leaders in American business who can rise to the challenge to create these conditions. All that is needed is enough incentive to make them want to do it. Our young people are busy building that incentive.

To those who do not know intimately the inner workings of large American businesses it may be difficult to appreciate what a profound effect on the business culture a new ethic like this will have. When the business manager who is fully committed to this ethic is asked, "What are you in business for?" the answer may be: "*I am in the business of growing people*—people who are stronger, healthier, more autonomous, more self-reliant, more competent. Incidentally, we also make and sell at a profit things that people want to buy so we can pay for all this. We play that game hard and well and we are successful by the usual standards, but that is really incidental. I recall a time when there was a complaint about manipulation. We don't hear it anymore. We manage the business about the same way we always did. We simply changed our aim. Strong, healthy, autonomous, self-reliant, and competent people don't mind being manipulated. In fact they take it as a game and do a little of it themselves. Consequently, as an institution, we are terribly strong. In fact, we are distinguished. How do I know we are distinguished? Because the best young people want to work for us. We select the best of the best and, once inside, they never want to leave. Any business that can do that is a winner."

Utopian?

No, I don't think so. Most of our large American businesses have the capability and the resources to embrace a new ethic like this and act resolutely on its implications. And I believe that among them there are several that have sufficient foresight and creative drive that they will prefer to run ahead of the changing ethic rather than be run over by it. Such is the way that new ethics are made.

In the long perspective of history, this period of the 1970s may be seen as one in which, in the course of coming to grips with the moral issues of power, authority, *and* manipulation, a new view of how people are best served by institutions may emerge. Institutions are not necessarily more benign when they protest their idealistic motives, nor are they necessarily less benign when they admit to crass commercialism. One should not be surprised that a Ralph Waldo Emerson who could see "the good of evil born" would observe, when he was weighing his words carefully, that "the greatest meliorator of the world is selfish, huckstering trade."

I predict that, under the pressures of the times, the typical American business, because it is more flexible, more adaptive, more human, more openly responsive to market forces, and because, in business, integrity of service (or lack of it) is more vividly and concretely demonstrated than in other types of institutions, will more quickly resolve the issues of manipulation—in all of their manifestations. And it will accomplish this not by banishing manipulation but by sublimating it, and, out of the alchemy, it may contribute something significantly new to the evolving knowledge of how people can better live and work together in societies.

If this proves in practice to be generally recognized, then there may be a radical realignment of expectations from institutions, and what society has traditionally expected from businesses, churches, schools, governments, and philanthropic foundations may be considerably scrambled. If this happens, I wager that, out of this scrambling, the business type of institution will emerge with a considerably larger role than heretofore. Witness the agitation in my country to take the Post Office out of the Civil Service and into a public corporation, and the vigorous entry of a few of our aggressive private business firms into the "learning" field. This is happening not because of any inherent virtue in business, but simply because, the way institutions have evolved, businesses are more adaptive and more responsive to opportunity.

Despite the ideological tensions in the world today, when any society really wants to accomplish something, it tends to draw on whatever works best. The builders find the useful pieces wherever they are, and they invent new ones when needed, all without regard to ideological coloration. "How

do you get the right things done?" comes to be the watchword of the day—every day.

I admit a bias. If I were young again, I would again cast my lot with a large American business. I would do it because my country is a business-dominated society (not in a formal power sense but simply by the sheer mass of the business presence) and any social advance will move, in part, from forces generated inside business. From my own experience there is enough integrity in the typical business that I would be more useful and my personal growth would be better nourished by working *inside* rather than by trying to influence it from the outside. I would choose to join a large business firm because there would be more satisfaction in being where the action is (the *action,* not just the excitement)—at the point where some of the critical issues of society must be resolved if the work of the world is to be done. And I would do it because I believe that if I accept the challenge to cope with the inevitable manipulation within an institution that is responding sensibly and creatively to issues and situations that require new ethics, I will emerge at the end of my career with a better personal value system than I would have if I had chosen a work where I was more on my own and, therefore, freer from being manipulated.

This is the ultimate test: What values govern one's life—at the end of it?

Manipulation, as I see it, is one of the imperfections of an imperfect world. It is a social problem, but it is not first priority, and the reformer's zeal will blunt its point by attacking it as primary. *Mediocrity* (including self-serving) in positions of influence *is* primary, and it cannot be dealt with by eliminating influence, as in the "leaderless society." Mediocrity will still be there.

Reducing mediocrity is a slow, difficult, person-by-person process in which the less able learn to identify and trust the more able who will diligently and honestly serve them. *It is also a process in which able, honest, serving people prepare themselves to lead and accept the opportunity to lead when offered.*

Reducing mediocrity in positions of influence by replacing the less qualified with more able, honest serving people is a manageable task with our available resources. It can be done. And I am confident that it will be done on a substantial scale when the people and institutions that have the good of society at heart bring a clearer focus to their efforts and concentrate on the one thing that will turn us about the quickest: excellence in place of mediocrity.

## Memo on Growing From Small to Large

*(The following memorandum was written for the chief executive and principal owner of a small company that has achieved the reputation for unusual quality of product and service. It has grown rapidly to its present size and has the potential for becoming a distinguished large institution if it can maintain its present quality as it continues to grow. That could be done, it seemed to me, if the head of it, to whom this memo was addressed, could (1) change his role from sole manager of a small enterprise to leader of a collective of many able people who would administer a large enterprise, and (2) see to it that each work group in the company becomes a positive social force.)*

The line that separates a large business from a small one might be drawn at that point where the business can no longer function well under the direct oversight of one individual. If the business has been built largely on one person's drive, imagination, taste, and judgment, as yours seems to have been, it may be difficult to recognize when that point has been reached. The signals that would tell you may not be unmistakably clear. The most immediate risk in your present way of operating may be that you could not be replaced, if there should be a need of that. Another risk is that the day-to-day demands on your leadership may become more taxing at a time when you may wish that they become less so. But the greatest risk may be that the company cannot grow and keep its present quality. I assume that you would like to minimize all of these risks.

I would guess, from our conversation, that your business is on the verge of becoming large in the sense that these risks loom as real possibilities, and it may be timely to consider an alternative that would permit the company to continue to grow while reducing these risks. The alternative I suggest is that you begin to shift your personal effort toward *building an institution* in which you become more the *manager of a process* that gets the job done and less the *administrator of day-to-day operations*. This might be the first step toward the ultimate optimal long-term performance as a large business that is managed by a board of directors who act as trustees and is administered by a team of equals who are led by a *primus inter pares*. The result would be an institution that would have the best chance of attracting and holding in its service the large number of able people who will be required to give it strength, quality, and continuity. This would require a shift in goals for you, a move from a preoccupation with building and operating the business day to day, to one of building an institution that has an autonomy of its own, that will do as well on a large scale what you have been able to do so well on a smaller scale, and that will have a life span, as a large and exceptional business, that is far beyond what it is likely to have if you continue in your present role.

I do not underestimate the difficulty of doing this. As I told you, I have watched another who has built a unique business as you have, and who accepted, intellectually, the need to transform it into an institution, but who faltered when faced with the practical steps this required. It is not realistic to expect people like you to hand over the control of a business you have built to others who are not as experienced, perhaps not basically as able, as your self. Yet, if you stay as you are, that is precisely what you will be forced to do—sometime.

If you accept the goal named above as desirable, what then do you do? It seems to me that you take one initial step now, within your present way of operating, that will be the first of a series of steps that move you gradually toward the role of institution builder. Each step should give you a base for a prudent next step so that you can move steadily toward a new role without ever contemplating a move that presents an unwarranted risk to what you have already built.

A possible first step, as I see it, emerged in our conversation. You have a problem which you put to me as a consultant who presumably has ideas on such things. You want to know what you should do to keep at least eighty percent of the able, high potential young people you have hired recently. I responded that I did not think any consultant could give you an answer to that question. The search for an answer is something you should assign to one of your best people as a staff problem.

As I have reflected on our discussion of this idea, I concluded that this may be as good an issue as any on which to make your first move toward building an institution. As long as you see your role in terms of the person who wants a consultant to give you an answer to a question like that, you are standing in your old role of the one-person builder and operator of the business, whereas, if you move on this as a problem for one of your best people to solve as an explicit, and perhaps as an exclusive staff assignment, then you have taken a big step toward building an institution out of a successful small businesses. Instead of being the seeker of solutions, directly from a consultant to you (which is all that the manager of a small business can do), you will be moving toward being the *manager of the process* by which the best solution can be found. And by continuing to take such steps you will be shifting your role from one-person manager of a small business to builder of a large institution in which (as I think is evolving) directors (under a strong chairman) *manage* and the operating executives administer. Let me supply some reasoning that may help to qualify this suggestion as a sound first step:

• Such an assignment to one of your most able people will enable you to get the right question in focus. Maybe you should not keep eighty percent of the people you have hired recently who are presumed to have high potential. Maybe you should lose eighty percent of them. I am not suggesting that this is the case, but I have a suspicion that the necessary staff work has not been done to establish that these are the people you should have hired. And there are too many of them for you to know them well enough personally to make that judgment. So you need to get the question framed in a way that I suspect has not yet been done. The right person assigned to this, after a little work, can tell you whether you are asking the right question.

• When you get the question settled, then you may want to provide some consulting help to the person you assign to get the answer. There may be many useful inputs from consulting sources, but probably none that will provide the complete answer—one that is best for your company at this time. Your own staff person will have to work that out.

• Probably the main reason you should assign this problem to one of your best people rather than seek an answer from a consultant is that, in an area like this, getting the right answer into practice in your company is likely to be much more difficult than finding the right answer in the first place. It is possible, on some legal, technical, or financial questions, to get dependable expert advice that may be readily put to use. But anything that cuts deep into the culture, like a new procedure for the future staffing of your executive group, is much more difficult to install than it is to discover. The outside consultant, even if lucky enough to recommend the right answer, would not be able to get it installed.

• The safest way I know for changing the character of any institution is through building a staff of very able people who will get their greatest creative fulfillment in finding and installing good solutions to critical problems. They may be happier doing that than they would be if they were administering part of the business, and they may be more valuable to the business in these roles. Such a group of effective staff people would probably become the core of the administration of the business—its most valuable asset. You can always find capable operating administrators for a business, *provided* that you have a strong staff that can find and install good solutions for its problems. Furthermore, the building and directing of such a staff may be one of the best preparations for a person to move from the one-person management of a small business to board chairman of a large business.

• By taking such issues one at a time you can gradually shift your role from that of the finder and installer of answers to that of the administrator of the process by which this takes place. When you have accomplished this, you can then be replaced by a competent professional administrator and move into the board chairman position, keeping (as you say you want to keep) the research function under your wing. I suspect, though, that if you take this route you may find institution building (including vitalizing the trustee function) to be such an interesting creative challenge that you may choose to leave research, as you now conceive it, as a part of the operating administration of the business.

In Chapters II and III, "The Institution as Servant" and "Trustees as Servants," I have summarized my best thinking about the structure of both the operating administration and the board of trustees of large institutions. But I know of no single model where all that I have suggested above is to be seen in operation. If there were such, there would be no need for me to write this memo; it would be available in manual form. But everything noted here has its roots somewhere in my experience and I urge it with confidence that if all of it is put into practice, it will make a superior model.

However, what I have suggested above deals only with the top structure of the business. If you want to make your present distinguished small business into a distinguished large one, you will need also to attend to the bottom structure of the business, the work group, and make of it something that is as congenial to the times in which it will be judged as I believe the top structure I have recommended will prove to be. And on this, the nature of the optimal work group of the future, I can only speculate.

I am reasonably familiar with current experiments with work and the work group in this country and in Europe, and I do not believe that an adequate philosophy of work has yet been stated, one that you can accept as a guide for the design of the optimal work group for the years ahead. Therefore I suggest that all those in a spot like yours, people who are actively building the model for the viable future business, will need to state the philosophy, based upon their own experience in following their own reliable intuitive judgment. The intuition of the institution builder will originate the experiment; the philosophy will emerge as the experi-

ment is studied. What follows, then, is not a recommendation. Rather it is food to nourish your own intuitive process as you plot your course into virgin territory—with confidence.

Twenty-five years ago the late Professor Fritz Roethlisberger of Harvard Business School wrote a provocative article entitled "The Foreman, Master and Victim of Double Talk." This article describes the impossible situation of the typical foreman: impossible as a vocation for a person and impossible for the company because of the unrealistic expectations of what the person in that role should do. The foreman is the one at the end of the chain of command, the one who has to get the work done—somehow—according to someone else's design. The foreman must deal with the union steward who is sometimes a member of the work group and is viewed as a hostile adversary. The foreman is often responsible for only part of an integrated process, and must deal, first hand, with the growing disenchantment with the demands of work. Professor Roethlisberger's article evoked wide comment in industrial circles but not much was done about the problem that was identified at that time. Now, I believe, if one is to build the distinguished business of the future, especially a large business, one will need to do something about work and the work group and the leadership of that group. Let me suggest something.

First there will be, and should be, a labor union. Several large American industries still manage to operate without a union and they tend to consider it as a notable achievement. Others who have unions sometimes dream of the ideal situation in which they do not have one. In sharp contrast with this attitude, the builder of the distinguished business of the future will accept the union as indispensable to the optimal work group, and, as the leader of a big company, will learn to deal with a big union so as to make of the work group a constructive force for the individual worker, for the company, and for society at large.

In saying this I am not approving of unions as they now stand, any more than I approve of corporations as they now stand. Both have much to do to become the servants of society that their roles make possible, and that influential critics will demand with greater insistence. I simply say that if you want to lead your present distinguished small business to become a distinguished large one, then you should do this in a way that helps a union to evolve as a responsible part of the enterprise.

I believe that you need to assume that work, all work, exists as much for the enrichment of the life of the worker as it does for the service of the one who pays for it. This does not mean that work will not be hard, demanding, and sometimes frustrating. It is just that the workers' life goals (quite apart from the money they earn) will be served by doing the work, and that is at least half the reason the work is there to be done. The implications of this assumption, if you choose to make it, are enormous and I will not try to trace all of them.

Movement guided by this assumption will begin, I believe, by taking the foreman out of management and arranging the work so that, as far as possible, it will be done by cohesive work groups or teams that are small enough that the group members become a community. The design of the work groups might be done jointly between the administration of the company and the union, with the exception that neither the work leader (who replaces the foreman) nor the union steward will be regarded as an agent of the parent group in contentions that may arise between the union and the company. This is essential if they are not to be regarded as adversaries within the work group. If there is contention between the union and the company (as there is likely to be at times), neither the work leader nor the union steward will be involved.

The essential concept is that the task belongs to the group. Both the work leader and the union steward are designated as persons who are acceptable to the group and who further its growth as a human community. If the product (goods or services) or the arrangements that affect people are not satisfactory, the problem becomes a matter for joint concern of the administration and the union. The administration assumes the primary concern to see that those who pay for the product or service are well served. The union assumes the primary obligation to see that those who do the work are adequately rewarded, psychically and materially. But each has a minor share of the other's primary obligation. If these two parties cannot resolve an issue, then it may be given to an arbitrator to decide, as is sometimes done now, or the ultimate sanction of a strike or a lockout may be resorted to. But whatever happens, the work group remains a cohesive community which includes the work leader and the union steward as full participating members, and all are insulated from the larger controversy.

This kind of thinking conceives of administration as the agent of the owners—whether they be shareholders, government, or trustees—and of beneficiaries of the effort: clients, patrons, or customers. The union is then seen as guardian of the workers' personal stake in the enterprise, psychic and material, and their channel into the political process. Both are made legitimate by the integrity of the work group. Work groups are the foundation stones of the whole structure of institutions.

The above thoughts on work groups, as I stated earlier, are not given as a plan of action. Rather they are offered to suggest that you set aside conventional wisdom and begin to think of a wholly new design for a business. If you can build a new structure of administrative leadership, as outlined earlier in this memo, and if you can arrange the work so that strong communities evolve to do it, you may find that you do not need much of the elaborate intermediate structure that has become so burdensome (and sometimes obstructive) in large institutions.

In summary, I am suggesting that a person like you who has been so successful in building a distinguished small business might, at your age, find an even more exciting challenge in transforming this one-person business into an institution that has autonomy and creative drive as a collective of many able people and that has the capacity for expansion into a large business without losing, and perhaps even enhancing, the claim to distinction it has achieved as a small one.

### Business Directors Initiate Social Policy

*For years I made the strongest pleas I could for our major institutions to become affirmative (as opposed to passive or reactive) servants of society. Surely there was a trustee of a university, business, or church who was ready to move in this direction.*

*In 1974 the first unequivocal response came to me, saying: "We would like to know how to be that kind of institution."*

*This response did not come from where the casual observer might guess—a church, a university, a hospital, a social agency. It came from where I expected it—from a business, a large multinational business. I expected this not because I impute any special virtue to business as such, but because, as I know institutions, businesses are least lulled to complacency by idealistic pretensions and the support of sentiment, and they have fewer professional hang-ups than the others. When the heads of eleemosynary institutions are confronted with evidence of a deficiency they cannot deny, they sometimes seem to put on sackcloth and ashes and go in for self-flagellation, but they do not do anything about it. Businesses, when similarly confronted, sometimes stoutly assert their innocence and proclaim their virtue, but then they quietly take some remedial action.*

*The directors of this company had read my pamphlet version of the earlier chapter on "The Institution as Servant" and decided that they wanted to explore how they could move toward being a more socially responsible company. The chairman got in touch with me and arranged for me to have separate conversations with each of the directors. At the conclusion of these conversations, I wrote the following proposal for the directors. With minor changes, it was given to the operating administrators of the company.*

## Note to Directors

The attached memorandum is suggested as a first communication from the directors concerning the establishment of a new social policy for the company, with accountability, in detail, to the directors.

As a first such policy statement, it contains a minimum of prescriptive direction. Most of it deals with the start of a new information flow to the directors concerning the social performance of the company. This will provide the directors with the data to guide later and more explicit statements of social policy.

The customary outline of items for a social audit are omitted at this time. This can better be constructed for the several divisions of the company after the directors have had the opportunity to study the opinions and attitudes of the major constituencies who normally judge the behavior of the company. The directors will then have a sound basis for establishing reasonable social performance standards for the company.

The aim is that within one year sufficient data will be assembled and analyzed so that agreement can be reached among directors on what social performance it is reasonable to expect from the company in the foreseeable future.

## Social Policy for the Company

As a general policy, the company is to be economically successful (both long term and short term) and it is to be regarded as socially responsible by all interested parties: employees (including administrators), vendors, owners, customers, suppliers, church, university, and appropriate agencies of government. Social performance is to be separately judged in each country where the company operates.

The criteria for economic success are well established and the economic performance of the company as a whole is currently good. This is to be maintained.

The criteria for judging social performance, heretofore, have not been made explicit. This first policy statement is a step toward making these criteria more explicit in the company and its subsidiaries, together with procedures for assessing performance.

1. The company will be concerned to develop a leading role in social matters, and hence will take care not only to follow the spirit of existing legal requirements, but even to keep ahead of them, by elaborating and applying original measures ahead of legal requirements.

In this respect, each major division of the company will present to the directors, for the first time in July 1975, an annual report for the past twelve months giving: (1) a description of all new laws or regulations governing social performance that became effective in that period; and (2) the position of the company as far as these new laws or regulation are concerned, indicating also the new measures taken voluntarily in this field by the company.

2. The central office of the company will devise a general system for assessing the attitudes toward, and opinions about, the social performance of the company by all eight of the constituencies named above. These will be adapted as appropriate in each of the countries where the company has a substantial operation, but the central office of the company will maintain a sufficient knowledge of variations so that a company-wide assessment can be made. After a review of these findings by the top administrators of the company, they will be reported to the directors not later than July 1, 1975. The directors, with the aid of professional consultants responsible to them, will analyze these reports and will determine whether the data from these surveys give a sufficient basis for the design of a procedure for a social audit. Further detailed policy determinations will emerge from these deliberations.

3. Coincident with the above, each major division of the company will establish a task force study team of five workers and five administrators who will be relieved of their regular duties for three months to conduct a study of opportunities for greater participation of workers in decisions that affect them. The purpose of these studies will be to provide the data that will give the basis for prudent arrangements for effective worker participation that will be appropriate for each location. After reviewing their findings with the top administrators of the company, all study teams will report in person to the directors not later than January 1, 1976. The directors, with the aid of professional consultants responsible to them, will analyze these reports and will formulate explicit policies, appropriate to each subsidiary company, for worker participation.

4. A study team of ten key administrators from as many divisions of the company will be established. These administrators will be relieved of their regular duties for three months to study the structure of power and authority at all levels of the company. Particularly, the team will study the practical functioning of the top executive groups in the company and its subsidiaries with reference to the proposals set forth in the essay on "The Institution as Servant," and it will reach conclusions about the feasibility of top administrative groups composed of governing councils of equals that are led by a *primus inter pares*. After having reviewed its findings with the top administrators of the company, this study team will report its findings in person to the directors not later than January 1, 1976. The directors, with the aid of professional consultants responsible to them, will analyze the reports and will formulate explicit policies regarding the structure of power and authority in the company.

5. The central office of the company will provide staff help to the study teams described in the previous two paragraphs to assist both in the organization of the studies and in the writing of their reports and recommendations. But such support will not be used to influence the substance of the reports and recommendations, which will be reviewed by the top administrators of the company, but which will be reported in person to the directors for their use in formulating policy. The directors will, of course, take into account the views of top administrators in making their policy decisions.

6. Each major division of the company is expected (1) to be aware of trends and developments in other businesses and other institutions in matters covered by the foregoing paragraphs, (2) to participate in associations and consultations concerning these matters in the countries where they have substantial operations, and (3) to report to the directors on each July 1 on such involvements during the previous year, plus any conclusions reached regarding the application of what is learned to the company.

## Concluding Note to Directors

These recommendations are made, as I said at the outset, primarily to start a new and regular flow of information to the directors. The procedures suggested here will establish that the interpretation of these data which the directors need for their policy decisions is different from what administrators need for their operating decisions. Therefore, the directors should begin to build their own independent source of advice to help them interpret the new data. Taking these steps (asking for the data and securing independent advice) will probably be disturbing to administrators, initially. But once the practice is established, and with regular discussions between directors and administrators about it, the administrators will realize that they can operate with greater assurance if the directors establish policy—clearly, firmly, and prudently.

If directors want a more socially responsible company (and this is written with the understanding that you, as directors, do want this) they should start the process by becoming more responsible directors. This will require some adjustment from administrators who are accustomed to nominal (and, therefore, less responsible) directors. Directors should accept that when they move to their proper role they create a problem, and that they should deal with it as a problem. The heightened quality of the company that will result will be to everybody's benefit, including the administrators who will be disturbed by the adjustment they must make.

# 12

# *What* Is *Leadership?*

MAX DePREE

The first responsibility of a leader is to define reality. The last is to say thank you. In between the two, the leader must become a servant and a debtor. That sums up the progress of an artful leader.

Concepts of leadership, ideas about leadership, and leadership practices are the subject of much thought, discussion, writing, teaching, and learning. True leaders are sought after and cultivated. Leadership is not an easy subject to explain. A friend of mine characterizes leaders simply like this: "Leaders don't inflict pain; they bear pain."

The goal of thinking hard about leadership is not to produce great or charismatic or well-known leaders. The measure of leadership in not the quality of the head, but the tone of the body. The signs of outstanding leadership appear primarily among the followers. Are the followers reaching their potential? Are they learning? Serving? Do they achieve the required results? Do they change with grace? Manage conflict?

I would like to ask you to think about the concept of leadership in a certain way. Try to think about a leader, in the words of the gospel writer Luke, as "one who serves." Leadership is a concept of ow-ing certain things to the institution. It is a way of thinking about institutional heirs, a way of thinking about stewardship as contrasted with ownership. Robert Greenleaf has written an excellent book about this idea, *Servant Leadership.*

The art of leadership requires us to think about the leader-as-steward in terms of relationships: of assets and legacy, of momentum and effectiveness, of civility and values.

*Leaders should leave behind them assets and a legacy.* First, consider assets; certainly leaders owe assets. Leaders owe their institutions vital financial health, and the relationships and reputation that enable continuity of that financial health. Leaders must deliver to their organizations the appropriate services, products, tools, and equipment that people in the organization need in order to be accountable. In many institutions leaders are responsible for providing land and facilities.

But what else do leaders *owe?* What are artful leaders responsible for? Surely we need to include people. People are the heart and spirit of all that counts. Without people, there is no need for leaders. Leaders can decide to be primarily concerned

SOURCE: From *Leadership Is an Art* by Max DePree. Copyright © 1987 by Max DePree. Used by permission of Doubleday, a division of Bantam Doubleday Dell Publishing Group, Inc.

with leaving assets to their institutional heirs or they can go beyond that and capitalize on the opportunity to leave a legacy, a legacy that takes into account the more difficult, qualitative side of life, one which provides greater meaning, more challenge, and more joy in the lives of those whom leaders enable.

Besides owing assets to their institutions, leaders owe the people in those institutions certain things. Leaders need to be concerned with the institutional value system which, after all, leads to the principles and standards that guide the practices of the people in the institution. Leaders owe a clear statement of the values of the organization. These values should be broadly understood and agreed to and should shape our corporate and individual behavior. What is this value system based on? How is it expressed? How is it audited? These are not easy questions to deal with.

Leaders are also responsible for future leadership. They need to identify, develop, and nurture future leaders.

Leaders are responsible for such things as a sense of quality in the institution, for whether or not the institution is open to influence and open to change. Effective leaders encourage contrary opinions, an important source of vitality. I am talking about how leaders can nurture the roots of an institution, about a sense of continuity, about institutional culture.

Leaders owe a covenant to the corporation or institution, which is, after all, a group of people. Leaders owe the organization a new reference point for what caring, purposeful, committed people can be in the institutional setting. Notice I did not say what people can do—what we can do is merely a consequence of what we can be. Corporations, like the people who compose them, are always in a state of becoming. Covenants bind people together and enable them to meet their corporate needs by meeting the needs of one another. We must do this in a way that is consonant with the world around us.

Leaders owe a certain maturity. Maturity as expressed in a sense of self-worth, a sense of belonging, a sense of expectancy, a sense of responsibility, a sense of accountability, and a sense of equality.

Leaders owe the corporation rationality. Rationality gives reason and mutual understanding to programs and to relationships. It gives visible order. Excellence and commitment and competence are available to us only under the rubric of rationality. A rational environment values trust and human dignity and provides the opportunity for personal development and self-fulfillment in the attainment of the organization's goals.

Business literacy, understanding the economic basis of a corporation, is essential. Only a group of people who share a body of knowledge and continually learn together can stay vital and viable.

Leaders owe people space, space in the sense of freedom. Freedom in the sense of enabling our gifts to be exercised. The need to give each other the space to grow, to be ourselves, to exercise our diversity. We need to give each other space so that we may both *give* and *receive* such beautiful things as ideas, openness, dignity, joy, healing, and inclusion. And in giving each other the gift of space, we need also to offer the gifts of grace and beauty to which each of us is entitled.

Another way to think about what leaders owe is to ask this question: What is it without which this institution would not be what it is?

*Leaders are obligated to provide and maintain momentum.* Leadership comes with a lot of debts to the future. There are more immediate obligations as well. Momentum is one. Momentum in a vital company is palpable. It is not abstract or mysterious. It is the feeling among a group of people that their lives and work are intertwined and moving toward a recognizable and legitimate goal. It begins with competent leadership and a management team strongly dedicated to aggressive managerial development and opportunities. This team's job is to provide an environment that allows momentum to gather.

Momentum comes from a clear vision of what the corporation ought to be, from a well-thought-out strategy to achieve that vision, and from carefully conceived and communicated directions and plans that enable everyone to participate and be publicly accountable in achieving those plans.

Momentum depends on a pertinent but flexible research and development program led by people with outstanding gifts and unique talents. Momentum results when a corporation has an aggressive, professional, inspired group of people in its marketing and sales units. Momentum results when the operations group serves its customers in such a way that the customer sees them as their best supplier of tools, equipment, and services. Underlying these complex activities is the essential role of the financial team. They provide the financial guidelines and the necessary ratios. They are responsible for equity among the various groups that compose the corporate family.

*Leaders are responsible for effectiveness.* Much has been written about effectiveness—some of the best of it by Peter Drucker. He has such a great ability to simplify concepts. One of the things he tells us is that efficiency is doing the thing right, but effectiveness is doing the right thing.

Leaders can delegate efficiency, but they must deal personally with effectiveness. Of course, the natural question is "how." We could fill many pages dealing with how to be effective, but I would like to touch on just two ways.

The first is the understanding that effectiveness comes about through enabling others to reach their potential—both their personal potential and their corporate or institutional potential.

In some South Pacific cultures, a speaker holds a conch shell as a symbol of a temporary position of authority. Leaders must understand who holds the conch—that is, who should be listened to and when. This makes it possible for people to use their gifts to the fullest for the benefit of everyone.

Sometimes, to be sure, a leader must choose who is to speak. That is part of the risk of leadership. A leader must assess capability. A leader must be a judge of people. For leaders choose a person, not a position.

Another way to improve effectiveness is to encourage roving leadership. Roving leadership arises and expresses itself at varying times and in varying situations, according to the dictates of those situations. Roving leaders have the special gifts or the special strengths or the special temperament to lead in these special situations. They are acknowledged by others who are ready to follow them. (See "Roving Leadership.")

*Leaders must take a role in developing, expressing, and defending civility and values.* In a civilized institution or corporation, we see good manners, respect for persons, an understanding of "good goods," and an appreciation of the way in which we serve each other.

Civility has to do with identifying values as opposed to following fashions. Civility might be defined as an ability to distinguish between what is actually healthy and what merely appears to be living. A leader can tell the difference between living edges and dying ones.

To lose sight of the beauty of ideas and of hope and opportunity, and to frustrate the right to be needed, is to be at the dying edge.

To be a part of a throwaway mentality that discards goods and ideas, that discards principles and law, that discards persons and families, is to be at the dying edge.

To be at the leading edge of consumption, affluence, and instant gratification is to be at the dying edge.

To ignore the dignity of work and the elegance of simplicity, and the essential responsibility of serving each other, is to be at the dying edge.

Justice Oliver Wendell Holmes is reported to have said this about simplicity: "I would not give a fig for the simplicity this side of complexity, but I would give my life for the simplicity on the other side of complexity." To be at the living edge is to search out the "simplicity on the other side of complexity."

In a day when so much energy seems to be spent on maintenance and manuals, on bureaucracy and meaningless quantification, to be a leader is to enjoy the special privileges of complexity, of ambiguity, of diversity. But to be a leader means, especially, having the opportunity to make a meaningful difference in the lives of those who permit leaders to lead.

# 13

# Transactional and Transforming Leadership

JAMES MacGREGOR BURNS

Some define leadership as leaders making followers do what *followers* would not otherwise do, or as leaders making followers do what the *leaders* want them to do; I define leadership as leaders inducing followers to act for certain goals that represent the values and the motivations—the wants and needs, the aspirations and expectations—of *both leaders and followers*. And the genius of leadership lies in the manner in which leaders see and act on their own and their followers' values and motivations.

Leadership, unlike naked power-wielding, is thus inseparable from followers' needs and goals. The essence of the leader-follower relation is the interaction of persons with different levels of motivations and of power potential, including skill, in pursuit of a common or at least joint purpose. That interaction, however, takes two fundamentally different forms. The first I will call *transactional* leadership. . . . Such leadership occurs when one person takes the initiative in making contact with others for the purpose of an exchange of valued things. The exchange could be economic or political or psychological in nature: a swap of goods or of one good for money; a trading of votes between candidate and citizen or between legislators; hospitality to another person in exchange for willingness to listen to one's troubles. Each party to the bargain is conscious of the power resources and attitudes of the other. Each person recognizes the other as a *person*. Their purposes are related, at least to the extent that the purposes stand within the bargaining process and can be advanced by maintaining that process. But beyond this the relationship does not go. The bargainers have no enduring purpose that holds them together; hence they may go their separate ways. A leadership act took place, but it was not one that binds leader and follower together in a mutual and continuing pursuit of a higher purpose.

Contrast this with *transforming* leadership. Such leadership occurs when one or more persons *engage* with others in such a way that leaders and followers raise one another to higher levels of motivation and morality. . . . Their purposes, which might have started out as separate but related, as in the case of transactional leadership, become fused. Power bases are linked not as counterweights but as mutual support for common purpose. Various names are used for such leadership, some of them derisory: elevating, mobilizing, inspiring, exalting, uplifting, preaching, exhorting, evangelizing. The relationship can be moralistic, of course. But transforming leadership ultimately becomes *moral* in that it raises the level of human conduct and ethical aspiration of both leader and led, and thus it has a transforming effect on both. Perhaps the best modern example is Gandhi, who aroused and elevated the hopes and demands of millions of Indians and whose life and personality were enhanced in the process. Transcending leadership is dynamic leadership in the sense that the leaders throw themselves into a relationship with followers who will feel "elevated" by it and often become more active leaders themselves, thereby creating new cadres of leaders. Transcending leadership is leadership *engagé*. Naked power-wielding can be neither transactional nor transforming; only leadership can be.

# 14

# Improving Organizational Effectiveness Through Transformational Leadership

## Introduction

BERNARD M. BASS
BRUCE J. AVOLIO

### Executive Summary

The purpose of this book is to show how the concepts of the full range of leadership—transactional and transformational—can apply to specific areas of leadership, management, and organizational development. Transactional and transformational leadership are introduced within the framework of a full-range model of leadership that includes the highly inactive and ineffective laissez-faire (LF) leadership to the highly active and effective inspirational and, ideally, influential leadership. This model is concisely applied to research, development, and training that have already appeared. Brief summaries of the chapters that follow are provided.

When a human resources director for a newly organized assembly plant was asked how the new organization came about, he said it began with a vision. The vision was subsequently modified and shared by management and employees. The director was describing one aspect of transformational leadership: the new leadership that must accompany good management but goes beyond the importance of leaders simply getting the work done with their followers and maintaining quality relationships with them.

During the last two decades, theories about transformational leadership have taken shape. Evidence about these theories has been amassed for all levels of organization and society and not just for charismatic leaders of social movements and organizations.

In physics, a new theory is usually tested by colleagues within a few years, sometimes even within a few months. Applications may appear in new technologies shortly afterward. In social science, theories are seldom adequately tested. They are likely to hang around as long as the originator is active. Adaptations take decades. Thus the theories of team participation that originated in the 1930s resulted in a mass of research in the 1950s; for the most part, they are just now being applied to the wholesale restructuring of many industrial firms.

One exception has occurred with transformational leadership. First mention of it appeared in Downton's *Rebel Leadership* (1973), a sociological treatise, and independently in James MacGregor Burns's seminal 1978 conceptualization.[1] In 1985, Bass presented a formal theory of transformational leadership as well as models and measurements of its factors of leadership behavior.[2] These were refined further by Bass and Avolio and their colleagues from a variety of evaluative investigations and the development of a model— the full range of leadership development—and an assessment and training program in transformational leadership.[3]

Meanwhile, at least 25 independent dissertations and numerous other research projects were completed in the United States and elsewhere.[4] And, starting in 1989, just four years after the appearance of *Leadership and Performance Beyond Expectations,* Fiat, an Italian multinational conglomerate of 250,000 employees, launched programs to present the *full range of leadership program* (FRLP) to 200 of its *alta direcciones* (top executives) and many of its 4,000 *direcciones* (middle managers) and 20,000 supervisors. A parallel program supported by the Kellogg Foundation also was initiated at the Center for Leadership Studies; by 1993, it was completed with close to 400 leaders. These leaders were drawn from all sectors of local communities, including education, health care, arts, industry, and government.

*Transformational* leadership is seen when leaders:

- stimulate interest among colleagues and followers[5] to view their work from new perspectives,
- generate awareness of the mission or vision of the team and organization,
- develop colleagues and followers to higher levels of ability and potential, and
- motivate colleagues and followers to look beyond their own interests toward those that will benefit the group.

Transformational leaders motivate others to do more than they originally intended and often even more than they thought possible. They set more challenging expectations and typically achieve higher performances.

Transformational leadership is an expansion of *transactional* leadership. Transactional leadership emphasizes the transaction or exchange that takes place among leaders, colleagues, and followers. This exchange is based on the leader discussing with others what is required and specifying the conditions and rewards these others will receive if they fulfill those requirements.

Transformational leaders do more with colleagues and followers than set up simple exchanges or agreements. They behave in ways to achieve superior results by employing one or more of the "Four I's":[6]

1. *Idealized influence.* Transformational leaders behave in ways that result in their being role models for their followers. The leaders are admired, respected, and trusted. Followers identify with the leaders and want to emulate them. Among the things the leader does to earn this credit is considering the needs of others over his or her own personal needs. The leader shares risks with followers and is consistent rather than arbitrary. He or she can be counted on to do the right thing, demonstrating high standards of ethical and moral conduct. He or she avoids using power for personal gain and only when needed.

2. *Inspirational motivation.* Transformational leaders behave in ways that motivate and inspire those around them by providing meaning and challenge to their followers' work. Team spirit is aroused. Enthusiasm and optimism are displayed. The leader gets followers involved in envisioning attractive future states. The leader creates clearly

communicated expectations that followers want to meet and also demonstrates commitment to goals and the shared vision.

3. *Intellectual stimulation.* Transformational leaders stimulate their followers' efforts to be innovative and creative by questioning assumptions, reframing problems, and approaching old situations in new ways. Creativity is encouraged. There is no public criticism of individual members' mistakes. New ideas and creative problem solutions are solicited from followers, who are included in the process of addressing problems and finding solutions. Followers are encouraged to try new approaches, and their ideas are not criticized because they differ from the leaders' ideas.

4. *Individualized consideration.* Transformational leaders pay special attention to each individual's needs for achievement and growth by acting as coach or mentor. Followers and colleagues are developed to successively higher levels of potential. Individualized consideration is practiced as follows: New learning opportunities are created along with a supportive climate. Individual differences in terms of needs and desires are recognized. The leader's behavior demonstrates acceptance of individual differences (e.g., some employees receive more encouragement, some more autonomy, others firmer standards, and still others more task structure). A two-way exchange in communication is encouraged, and "management by walking around" work spaces is practiced. Interactions with followers are personalized (e.g., the leader remembers previous conversations, is aware of individual concerns, and sees the individual as a whole person rather than as just an employee). The *individually considerate* leader listens effectively. The leader delegates tasks as a means of developing followers. Delegated tasks are monitored to see if the followers need additional direction or support and to assess progress; ideally, followers do not feel they are being checked on.

Several thousand leaders in the private sector and community leaders in the public sector have been trained using the model of the full range of leadership.[7] This model includes the Four I's of transformational leadership as well as transactional leadership behavior and laissez-faire or nonleadership behavior.

Transactional leadership occurs when the leader rewards or disciplines the follower depending on the adequacy of the follower's performance. Transactional leadership depends on contingent reinforcement, either positive *contingent reward* (CR) or the more negative active or passive forms of *management-by-exception* (MBE-A or MBE-P). CR has been found to be reasonably effective, although not as much as the Four I's, in motivating others to achieve higher levels of development and performance. With this method, the leader assigns or gets agreement on what needs to be done and promises rewards or actually rewards others in exchange for satisfactorily carrying out the assignment.

Management-by-exception tends to be more ineffective but required in certain situations. In MBE-A the leader arranges to actively monitor deviances from standards, mistakes, and errors in the follower's assignments and to take corrective action as necessary. MBE-P implies waiting passively for deviances, mistakes, and errors to occur and then taking corrective action. The LF style is the avoidance or absence of leadership and is, by definition, the most inactive—as well as the most ineffective according to almost all research on the style. As opposed to transactional leadership, laissez-faire represents a nontransaction.

Fundamental to the full-range leadership training effort is that every leader displays each style to some degree. An optimal profile is shown in Figure 14.1. The third dimension of this model (depth) represents how frequently an individual displays a particular style of leadership. The active dimension helps clarify the style, and the effectiveness dimension broadly represents the impact of the leadership style on performance.

In Figure 14.1, the leader infrequently displays LF leadership and increasing frequencies of the transactional leadership styles of MBE-P, MBE-A, and CR. This optimal profile shows the transformational Four I's as they are most frequently displayed.

In contrast, the poorly performing leader's profile, tending toward inactivity and ineffectiveness, is opposite that of optimal leaders (see Figure 14.2).

Many research studies have been completed in business and industry, government, the military, educational institutions, and nonprofit organizations, all of them showing that transformational

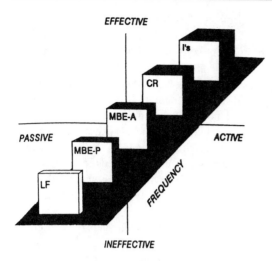

**Figure 14.1.** Optimal Profile

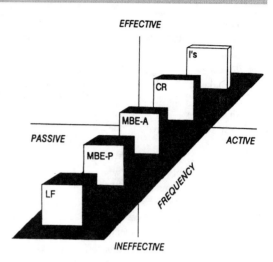

**Figure 14.2.** Suboptimal Profile

leaders, as measured by the survey instruments derived from the Bass and Avolio model, were more effective and satisfying as leaders than transactional leaders, although the best of leaders frequently do some of the latter but more of the former. Follow-up investigations have shown that developing transformational leadership with training in the Four I's can enhance effectiveness and satisfaction as a leader.[8] Hence, the optimal and suboptimal models depicted in Figures 14.1 and 14.2 represent the full range of styles and the impact on effectiveness found in these previous investigations.

This book shows how transformational leadership is expected to contribute to an organization's efforts to improve its operations and the best use of its human resources. (These innovations are even seen to occur in organizations that do not explicitly recognize that transformational leadership is involved.)

Each chapter deals with a different aspect of the organization and how it is affected by influence processes that are associated especially with frequent transformational leadership. In each instance, the end goal is to develop a highly committed work force that is more eager and willing to take on the challenges in the last decade of this century and into the next millennium. As we will see, employee commitment, involvement, and loyalty, coupled with enlightened management, are fundamental to long-range organizational improvement.

In Chapter 2, Karl Kuhnert focuses attention on the delegation process. He shows, as with transformational leadership in general, the connection of the delegation process with the moral development of the leader. The concept of delegation is expanded beyond traditional definitions and is included as part of the overall developmental strategy for elevating the needs and potential of both leader and follower in the organization.

We have found transformational leadership to varying degrees at every level in the organization from the informal leadership that takes place in team activities to the leadership displayed by chief executive officers. Moreover, as we move up the organizational pyramid, such leadership can indirectly influence increasing numbers of both levels and employees. In Chapter 3, Francis Yammarino describes how leadership may cascade downward in the organization through many levels as well as bypass levels. As a consequence, the transformational leader can exert influence indirectly at an organizational distance by the behaviors and actions that serve as role models and by the culture that is developed to support the leader's vision and mission. Moreover, such indirect influence is also exerted upward in the system in ways described by Yammarino.

Organizations increasingly are coming to depend on self-managed but fully led multifunctional teams to get tasks done effectively. In Chapter 4, David Atwater and Bernard Bass lay out what a half century of research on small group behavior tells the team leader who would be transformational. In Chapter 5, David Waldman reviews current examples of how transformational leadership of multifunctional teams more effectively promotes research, innovation, and change.

In Chapter 6, Bernard Bass considers the linkages between transformational leadership and decision making in teams and organizations.[9] He connects his model of organizational decision making with the Avolio and Bass model of transformational leadership. This combined leadership and decision-making framework highlights the impact of transformational leadership on the information-processing strategies of leaders, teams, and followers in the organization. The framework also shows the procedures that leaders, teams, and followers go through to make effective decisions.

The authorities, Deming and Juran, heavily emphasize the importance of leadership to total quality improvement but do not say much about the actual or specific leadership required. In Chapter 7, Bruce Avolio supplies the linkages between transformational and transactional leadership and quality-improvement programs, offering strategies for merging these respective areas to enhance the leadership and quality-improvement efforts under way today in many firms, agencies, and institutions.

The last three chapters expand into detailed examinations of what firms are doing to promote innovation and change in their human resources programs and policies that can contribute to the emergence of more transformational leadership. In Chapter 8, Leanne and David Atwater review organizational change efforts, current innovations, and selected benchmark companies. In addition to reviewing these successful organizational efforts, the authors also detail the criteria for change that are used by these respective organizations and the methods used for such appraisals.

K. Galen Kroeck in Chapter 9 further examines the principles and applications of the transformational leadership model, focusing attention on ex-

amples of reorganizing, "right-sizing" efforts and accompanying human resources programs and practices. His chapter focuses on redirecting organizations from managing work force numbers to a longer-term strategy of human resource staffing whereby the organization continuously "right sizes" its work force to the organization's current demands and future aspirations.

The chapter that follows Kroeck's deals with applications of transformational leadership and related innovations; these are relevant to the diffusion of transformational leadership that seeks to improve organizational performance in the 1990s. In Chapter 10, Avolio and Bass sum up the efforts of the preceding chapters. To remain competitive in a world of rapidly changing technology, changing work force expectations, and cheaper off-shore labor, leadership—particularly transformational leadership—is required at all levels in the firm and must be diffused into more traditional areas of organizational functioning to have the best effect. Avolio and Bass add a special concern for the role of training and development in the diffusion effort and the integration of individual development and organizational development.

The full-range model of transformational, transactional, and nontransactional leadership has been introduced in this chapter. In the following chapters, the model generates implications for development and change in the individual leader and his or her associates, the team, the organization, and the full range of leadership. We begin now by examining the delegation process as it appears at different levels of the full range of leadership as a contribution to the development of leaders and their associates.

## Notes

1. Burns, J. M. (1978). *Leadership.* New York: Harper & Row; Downton, J. V. (1973). *Rebel leadership: Commitment and charisma in the revolutionary process.* New York: Free Press.

2. Bass, B. M. (1985). *Leadership and performance beyond expectations.* New York: Free Press.

3. Bass, B. M. & Avolio, B. J. (1990). *Multifactor leadership questionnaire.* Palo Alto, CA: Consulting Psychologist Press.

4. For example, see Deluga, R. J. (1988). Relationship of transformational and transactional leadership with employee influencing strategies. *Group & Organization Studies, 13,* 456-467.

5. *Follower* will be used in this chapter in its most general sense. In formal organizations, those who are influenced by leaders may include subordinates, supervisees, and direct reports, as well as colleagues. *Associates* will imply followers or colleagues or both. If the influence is upward in the organization, then the follower is the leader's boss. In social and political movements, followers may include constituents, adherents, disciples, partisans, and supporters.

6. Avolio, B. J., Waldman, D. A., & Yammarino. F. J. (1991). Leading in the 1990s: The Four I's of transformational leadership. *Journal of European Industrial Training, 15*(4), 9-16.

7. See Bass (1983), Chapter 9, and Avolio. B. J., & Bass, B. M. (1990). *The full range of leadership program: Basic and advanced manual.* Binghamton, NY: Bass, Avolio, & Associates.

8. Bass, B. M., & Avolio, B. J. (1990). The implications of transactional and transformational leadership for individual, team, and organizational development. *Research in Organizational Change and Development, 4,* 231-272.

9. Bass, B. M. (1983). *Organizational decision making.* Homewood, IL: Irwin.

# 15

# *Contingency Theories of Leadership*

RICHARD L. HUGHES
ROBERT C. GINNETT
GORDON J. CURPHY

### *The Situational Leadership Theory*

It seems fairly obvious that leaders do not interact with all followers in the same manner. For example, a leader may give general guidelines or goals to her highly competent and motivated followers but spend considerable time coaching, directing, and training her unskilled and unmotivated followers. Or leaders may provide relatively little praise and assurances to followers with high self-confidence but high amounts of support to followers with low self-confidence. Although leaders often have different interactional styles when dealing with individual followers, is there an optimum way for leaders to adjust their behavior with different followers and thereby increase their likelihood of success? And if there is, on what factors should the leader base his behavior? The follower's intelligence? Personality traits? Values? Preferences?

Technical competence? Hersey and Blanchard (1969, 1977, 1982) developed *situational leadership theory* (SLT) to answer these two important leadership questions.

### Leader Behaviors

Situational leadership theory has evolved over time. Its roots are in the Ohio State studies, in which the two broad categories of leader behaviors, initiating structure and consideration, were initially identified. As SLT evolved, so did the labels (but not the content) for the two leadership behavior categories. Initiating structure changed to *task behaviors,* which were defined as the extent to which the leader spells out the responsibilities of an individual or group. Task behaviors include telling people what to do, how to do it, when to do it, and who is to do it. Similarly, consideration changed to

SOURCE: From *Leadership: Enhancing the Lessons of Experience,* by R. Hughes, R. Ginnett, and G. Curphy. Chicago: Irwin. Copyright 1996. Reproduced with permission of The McGraw-Hill Companies.

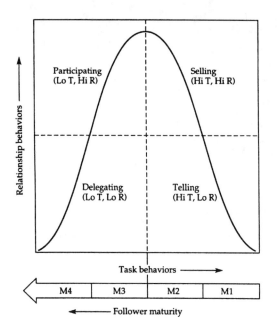

**Figure 15.1.** The SLT Prescriptions for the Most
Appropriate Leader Behaviors Based on Follower
Maturity

SOURCE: Paul Hersey and Kenneth Blanchard, *Management of Organizational Behavior: Utilizing Human Resources,* 4th ed., © 1982,
p. 152, Prentice Hall, Englewood Cliffs, NJ.
    The model in Figure 15.1 no longer represents the current views of
the authors. For current information, contact The Center for Leadership
Studies, 230 West Third Avenue, Escondido, CA 92025-4180.

*relationship behaviors,* or how much the leader
engages in two-way communication. Relationship behaviors include listening, encouraging,
facilitating, clarifying, and giving socioemotional
support.
    There was little evidence to show that these two
categories of leader behavior were consistently
related to leadership success. As with traits, the
relative effectiveness of these two behavior dimensions often depended on the situation. Hersey and
Blanchard (1969, 1977, 1982) proposed a model to
explain why leadership effectiveness varied across
these two behavior dimensions and situations.
First, they arrayed the two orthogonal dimensions
as in the Ohio State studies and then divided each
of them into high and low segments (see Figure
15.1). According to Hersey and Blanchard, depict-
ing the two leadership dimensions this way indi-

cated that certain combinations of task and relationship behaviors may be more effective in some
situations than in others. For example, in some
situations high levels of task but low levels of
relationship behaviors were effective; in other situations, just the opposite was true. So far, however,
we have not considered the key follower or situational characteristics with which these combinations of task and relationship behaviors were most
effective. Hersey and Blanchard stated that these
four combinations of task and relationship behaviors would increase leadership effectiveness if they
were made contingent on the maturity level of the
individual follower.

**Maturity of the Follower**

    Follower maturity is comprised of two compo-
nents: *job maturity* and *psychological maturity.* Job
maturity is the amount of *task-relevant* knowledge,
experience, skill, and ability that the follower possesses. In a sense, job maturity is much the same
as technical expertise. Psychological maturity is
the follower's self-confidence, commitment, motivation, and self-respect *relative to the task* at hand.
Notice that both of these elements of maturity are
meaningful only with regard to a particular task.
Someone with a medical degree and years of experience as a surgeon might be rated as extremely
mature at performing open-heart surgery. That
same person might have virtually no job or psychological maturity for the tasks of designing and
building a house, piloting a hot-air balloon, or
counseling a suicidal patient. It is impossible to
assess either job or psychological maturity if the
task is unknown. Similarly, because most of us
perform multiple tasks, there is no universal level
of maturity. Both job and psychological maturity
vary according to the task at hand.

**Prescriptions of the Theory**

    Now that the key contingency factor, follower
maturity, has been identified, let us move on to
another aspect of the figure—combining follower
maturity levels with the four combinations of
leader behaviors described earlier. The horizontal
bar or arrow in Figure 15.1 depicts follower matur-

ity as increasing from right to left (not in the direction we are used to seeing). There are four segments along this continuum, ranging from M1 (the least mature) to M4 (the most mature). Along this continuum, however, the assessment of follower maturity can be fairly subjective. A follower who possesses high levels of both job and psychological maturity relative to the task would clearly fall in the M4 category, just as a follower with neither job nor psychological maturity would fall in M1. The discriminating factors for categories M2 and M3 are less clear, however.

To complete the model, Hersey and Blanchard (1982) added a curved line that represents the leadership behavior that will most likely be effective given a particular level of follower maturity. In order to use SLT, leaders should first assess the maturity level (M1-M4) of the follower relative to the task to be accomplished. Next, a vertical line should be drawn from the center of the maturity level up to the point where it intersects with the curved line in Figure 15.1. The quadrant in which this intersection occurs represents the level of task and relationship behavior that has the best chance of producing successful outcomes. For example, imagine you are a fire chief and have under your command a search-and-rescue team. One of the team members is needed to rescue a backpacker who has fallen in the mountains, and you have selected a particular follower to accomplish the task. What leadership behavior should you exhibit? Assuming this is a responsible and psychologically mature follower who has both substantial training and experience in this type of rescue, you would assess his maturity level as M4. A vertical line from M4 would intersect the curved line in the quadrant where both low task and low relationship behaviors by the leader are most apt to be successful. As the leader, you should exhibit a low level of task and relationship behaviors and delegate this task to the follower. On the other hand, you may have a brand-new member of the fire department who still has to learn the ins and outs of firefighting. Because this particular follower has low job and psychological maturity (M1), SLT maintains that the leader should use a high level of task and a low level of relationship behaviors when initially dealing with this follower.

Hersey and Blanchard suggest one further step leaders wish to consider. The model described above helps the leader select the most appropriate behaviors given the current level of follower maturity. However, there may be cases when the leader would like to see the followers increase their level of maturity. Because more mature followers are generally more effective than less mature followers, leaders may wish to implement a series of *developmental interventions* to help boost follower maturity levels. The process would begin by first assessing the follower's current level of maturity and then determining the leader behavior that best suits that follower in that task. Instead of using the behavior prescribed by SLT, however, the leader would select the next higher leadership behavior. Another way of thinking about this would be for the leader to select the behavior pattern that would fit the follower if that follower were one level higher in maturity. This intervention is designed to help followers in their maturity development; hence its name (see Box 15.1 on developmental interventions).

**Concluding Thoughts About the Situational Leadership Theory**

In Figure 15.2, we can see how the factors in SLT fit within the L-F-S framework. In comparison to the Vroom and Yetton model, there are fewer factors to be considered in each of the three elements. The only situational consideration is knowledge of the task, and the only two follower factors are job and psychological maturity. On the other hand, the theory goes well beyond decision making, which was the sole domain of the normative decision model. In fact, Hersey and Blanchard have suggested that their model can even be extended to other applications, such as parenting.

Situational leadership theory is usually appealing to students and practitioners because of its commonsense approach as well as its ease of understanding. Unfortunately, there is little research to support the predictions of SLT in the workplace (Vecchio, 1987; Yukl & Van Fleet, 1992). Moreover, follower maturity is poorly defined (Graeff, 1983), and the model provides inadequate rationale or sufficiently specific guidance

**BOX 15.1**
**A Developmental Intervention Using SLT**

Dianne is a resident assistant in charge of a number of students in a university dorm. One particular sophomore, Michael, has volunteered to work on projects in the past but never seems to take the initiative to get started on his own. Michael seems to wait until Dianne gives him explicit direction, approval, and encouragement before he will get started. Michael can do a good job, but he seems to be unwilling to start without some convincing that it is all right and making explicit the steps to be taken. Dianne has assessed Michael's maturity level as M2, but she would like to see him develop, both in task maturity and in psychological maturity. The behavior most likely to fit Michael's current maturity level is selling, or high task, high relationship. But Dianne has decided to implement a developmental intervention to help Michael raise his maturity level. Dianne can be most helpful in this intervention by moving up one level to participating or low task, high relationship. By reducing the amount of task instructions and direction while encouraging Michael to lay out a plan on his own and supporting his steps in the right direction, Dianne is most apt to help Michael become an M3 follower. This does not mean the work will get done most efficiently, however. Just as we saw in the Vroom and Yetton model earlier, if part of the leader's job is development of followers, then time may be a reasonable and necessary trade-off for short-term efficiency.

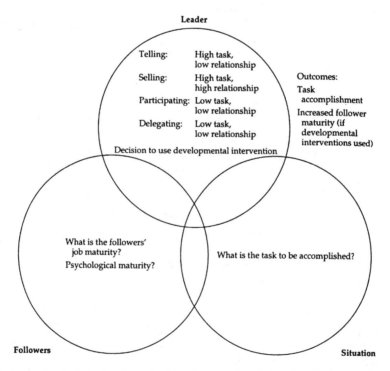

**Figure 15.2.** Factors From the Situational Leadership Theory and the Interactional Framework

about *why* or *how* particular levels of task and relationship behaviors correspond to each of the follower maturity levels (Yukl, 1989). Furthermore, Hersey and Blanchard have simply defined leadership effectiveness as those leader behaviors that match the prescriptions of SLT. They have not presented any evidence that leaders who behave according to the model's prescriptions actually have higher unit performance indices, better performing or more satisfied subordinates, or a more favorable organizational climate (Vecchio, 1987). Nevertheless, even with these shortcomings, SLT is a useful way to get leaders to think about how leadership effectiveness may depend somewhat on being flexible with different subordinates, not on acting the same way toward them all.

## *The Contingency Model*

Although leaders may be able to change their behaviors toward individual subordinates, leaders also have dominant behavioral tendencies. Some leaders may be generally more supportive and relationship oriented, whereas others may be more concerned with task or goal accomplishment. The contingency model (Fiedler, 1967) recognizes that leaders have these general behavioral tendencies and specifies situations where certain leaders (or behavioral dispositions) may be more effective than others.

Fiedler's (1967) *contingency model* of leadership is probably the earliest, most well known contingency theory and is often perceived by students to be almost the opposite of SLT. In comparing the contingency model to SLT, SLT emphasizes flexibility in leader behaviors, whereas the contingency model maintains that leaders are much more consistent (and consequently less flexible) in their behavior. Situational leadership theory maintains that leaders who *correctly base their behaviors* on follower maturity will be more effective, whereas the contingency model suggests that leader effectiveness is primarily determined by *selecting the right kind of leader for certain situations or changing the situation* to fit the particular leader's style. Another way to say this is that leadership effectiveness depends on both the leader's style and the

favorableness of the leadership situation. Some leaders are better than others in some situations but less effective in other situations. To understand contingency theory, therefore, we need to look first at the critical characteristics of the leader and then at the critical aspects of the situation.

### The Least Preferred Co-Worker Scale

In order to determine a leader's general style or tendency, Fiedler developed an instrument called the *least preferred co-worker (LPC) scale.* The scale instructs a leader to think of the single individual with whom he has had the greatest difficulty working (i.e., the least preferred co-worker) and then to describe that individual in terms of a series of bipolar adjectives (e.g., friendly-unfriendly, boring-interesting, sincere-insincere). Those ratings are then converted into a numerical score.

In thinking about such a procedure, many people assume that the score is determined primarily by the characteristics of whatever particular individual the leader happened to identify as his least preferred co-worker. In the context of contingency theory, however, it is important to understand that the score is thought to *represent something about the leader, not the specific individual the leader evaluated.*

The current interpretation of these scores is that they identify a leader's motivation hierarchy (Fiedler, 1978). Based on their LPC scores, leaders are categorized into two groups: *low LPC leaders* and *high LPC leaders.* In terms of their motivation hierarchy, low LPC leaders are primarily motivated by the task, which means that these leaders primarily gain satisfaction from task accomplishment. Thus, their dominant behavioral tendencies are similar to the initiating structure behavior described in the Ohio State research or the task behavior of SLT. However, if tasks are being accomplished in an acceptable manner, then low LPC leaders will move to their secondary level of motivation, which is forming and maintaining relationships with followers. Thus, low LPC leaders will focus on improving their relationships with followers after they are assured that assigned tasks are being satisfactorily accomplished. As soon as tasks are no longer being accomplished in an acceptable manner, however, low LPC leaders will refocus their efforts on task accomplishment and persist with these efforts until task accomplishment is back on track.

In terms of motivation hierarchy, high LPC leaders are primarily motivated by relationships, which means that these leaders are primarily satisfied by establishing and maintaining close interpersonal relationships. Thus, their dominant behavioral tendencies are similar to the consideration behaviors described in the Ohio State research or the relationship behaviors in SLT. If high LPC leaders have established good relationships with their followers, then they will move to their secondary level of motivation, which is task accomplishment. As soon as leader-follower relations are jeopardized, however, high LPC leaders will cease working on tasks and refocus their efforts on improving relationships with followers.

It may help to think in terms of an analogy with a motivational theory—Maslow's hierarchy of needs. You can think of the LPC scale as identifying two different sorts of leaders with their respective motivational hierarchies depicted in Figure 15.3. As with Maslow's hierarchy of needs, lower-level needs must be satisfied first. Low LPC leaders will move "up" to satisfying relationship needs when they are assured the task is being satisfactorily

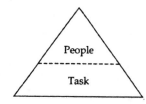

Low LPC Leader motivational hierarchy

High LPC Leader motivational hierarchy

**Figure 15.3.** Motivational Hierarchies for Low and High LPC Leaders

accomplished. High LPC leaders will move "up" to emphasizing task accomplishment when they have established good relationships with their followers.

Because all tests have some level of imprecision, Fiedler (1978) suggested that the LPC scale cannot accurately identify the motivation hierarchy for those individuals with certain intermediate scores. Research by Kennedy (1982) suggests an alternative view. Kennedy has shown that individuals within the intermediate range of LPC scale scores may more easily or readily switch between being task- or relationship-oriented leaders than those individuals with more extreme scale scores. They may be equally satisfied by working on the task or establishing relationships with followers.

### Situational Favorability

The other critical variable in the contingency model is situational favorability, which is the amount of control the leader has over the followers. Presumably, the more control a leader has over followers, the more favorable the situation is, at least from the leader's perspective. Fiedler included three subelements in situation favorability. These were leader-member relations, task structure, and position power.

*Leader-member relations* is the most powerful of the three subelements in determining overall situation favorability. It involves the extent to which relationships between the leader and followers are generally cooperative and friendly or antagonistic and difficult. Leaders who rate leader-member relations as high would feel they had the support of their followers and could rely on their loyalty.

*Task structure* is second in potency in determining overall situation favorability. Here the leader would objectively determine task structure by assessing whether there were detailed descriptions of work products, standard operating procedures, or objective indicators of how well the task is being accomplished. The more questions one could answer affirmatively, the higher the structure of the task.

*Position power* is the weakest of the three elements of situation favorability. Position power is

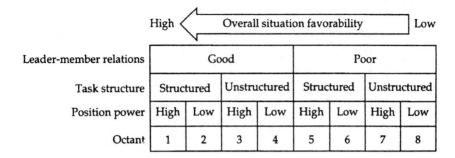

**Figure 15.4.** Contingency Model Octant Structure for Determining Situation Favorability

similar to legitimate power, and leaders who have titles of authority or rank, the authority to administer rewards and punishments, and the legitimacy to conduct follower performance appraisals have greater position power than leaders who lack them.

The relative weights of these three subelements, when added together, can be used to create a continuum of situational favorability. When using the contingency model, leaders are first asked to rate items that measure the strength of leader-member relations, the degree of task structure, and their level of position power. These ratings are then weighted and combined to determine an overall level of situational favorability facing the leader (Fiedler & Chemers, 1982). Any particular situation's favorability can then be plotted on a continuum, which Fiedler divided into octants representing distinctly different levels of situational favorability. The relative weighting scheme for the subelements and how they make up each of the eight octants can be seen in Figure 15.4.

You can see that the octants of situation favorability range from 1 (highly favorable) to 8 (very unfavorable). The highest levels of situational favorability occur when leader-member relations are good, the task is structured, and position power is high. The lowest levels of situational favorability occur when there are high levels of leader-member conflict, the task is unstructured or unclear, and the leader does not have the power to reward or punish subordinates. Moreover, the relative weighting of the three subelements can easily be seen by their order of precedence in Figure 15.4, with leader-member relations appearing first, followed by task structure and then position power.

For example, because leader-member relations carry so much weight, it is impossible for leaders with good leader-member relations to have anything worse than moderate situational favorability, regardless of their task structure or position power. In other words, leaders with good leader-member relations will be in a situation that has situational favorability no worse than octant 4; leaders with poor leader-member relations will be facing a leadership situation with situational favorability no better than octant 5.

**Prescriptions of the Model**

Fiedler and his associates have conducted numerous studies to determine how different leaders (as described by their LPC scores) have performed in different situations (as described in terms of situational favorability). Figure 15.5 describes which type of leader (high or low LPC) Fiedler found to be most effective, given different levels of situation favorability. The solid, dark line represents the relative effectiveness of a low LPC leader, and the dashed line represents the relative effectiveness of a high LPC leader. It is obvious from the way the two lines cross and recross that there is some interaction between the leader's style and the overall situation favorability. If the situation favorability is moderate (octants 4, 5, 6, or 7), then those groups led by leaders concerned with establishing and maintaining relationships (high LPC leaders) seem to do best. However, if the situation is either very unfavorable (octant 8) or highly favorable (octants 1, 2, or 3), then those groups led

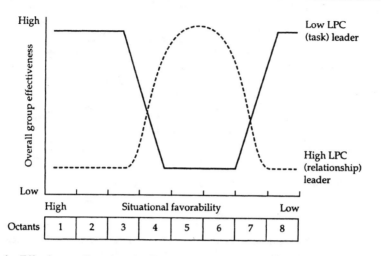

**Figure 15.5.** Leader Effectiveness Based on the Contingency Between Leader LPC Score and Situation Favorability

by the task-motivated (low LPC) leaders seem to do best.

Fiedler suggested that leaders will try to satisfy their primary motivation when faced with unfavorable or moderately favorable situations. This means that low LPC leaders will concentrate on the task and high LPC leaders will concentrate on relationships when faced with these two levels of situational favorability. Nevertheless, leaders facing highly favorable situations know that their primary motivations will be satisfied and thus will move to their secondary motivational state. This means that *leaders will behave according to their secondary motivational state only when faced with highly favorable situations* (see Box 15.2).

There are several interesting implications of Fiedler's (1967) model worthy of additional comment. Because leaders develop their distinctive motivation hierarchies and dominant behavior tendencies through a lifetime of experiences, Fiedler believed these hierarchies and tendencies would be difficult to change through training. He maintained it was naive to believe that sending someone to a relatively brief leadership training program could substantially alter any leader's personality or typical way of acting in leadership situations; after all, such tendencies had been developed over many years of experience. Instead of trying to change the leader, Fiedler concluded, training would be more

effective if it showed leaders how to recognize and change key situational characteristics to better fit their personal motivational hierarchies and behavioral tendencies. Thus, according to Fiedler, the content of leadership training should emphasize situational engineering rather than behavioral flexibility in leaders. Relatedly, organizations could become more effective if they matched the characteristics of the leader (in this case, LPC scores) with the demands of the situation (i.e., situational favorability) than if they tried to change the leader to fit the situation. These suggestions imply that high or low LPC leaders in mismatched situations should either change the situation or move to jobs that better match their motivational hierarchies and behavioral patterns. Although the idea of fitting the characteristics of the leader to the demands of the situation is very similar to earlier suggestions made about improving the usefulness of personality traits in leadership selection, the suggestions for leadership training are almost the opposite of those put forth by the other theories in this chapter.

### Concluding Thoughts About the Contingency Model

Before reviewing the empirical evidence, perhaps a clearer understanding of the contingency

## BOX 15.2
### High and Low LPC Leaders and the Contingency Model

Suppose we had two leaders, Tom Low (a low LPC or task motivated leader) and Brenda High (a high LPC or relationship motivated leader). In unfavorable situations, Tom will be motivated by his primary level and will thus exhibit task behaviors. In similar situations, Brenda will also be motivated by her primary level and as a result will exhibit relationship behaviors. Fiedler found that in unfavorable situations, task behavior will help the group to be more effective, so Tom's behavior would better match the requirements of the situation. Group effectiveness would not be aided by Brenda's relationship behavior in this situation.

Moving to situations with moderate favorability, both Tom and Brenda are still motivated by their primary motivations, so their behaviors will be precisely the same as described: Tom will exhibit task behaviors and Brenda will exhibit relationship behaviors. Because the situation has changed, however, group effectiveness no longer requires task behavior. Instead, the combination of situational variables leads to a condition where a leader's relationship behaviors will make the greatest contribution to group effectiveness. Hence, Brenda will be the most effective leader in situations of moderate favorability. In highly favorable situations, the explanation provided by Fiedler gets more complex. When leaders find themselves in highly favorable situations, they no longer have to be concerned about their primary motivations being satisfied (they already are). In highly favorable situations, leaders switch to satisfying their secondary motivations. Because Tom's secondary motivation is to establish and maintain relationships, in highly favorable situations he will exhibit relationship behaviors.

Similarly, Brenda will also be motivated by her secondary motivation, so she would manifest task behaviors in highly favorable situations. Fiedler believed that leaders who manifested relationship behaviors in highly favorable situations helped groups to be more effective. In this case, Tom is giving the group what they need to be more effective.

model can be attained by examining it through the L-F-S framework. As seen in Figure 15.6, task structure is a function of the situation and LPC scores are a function of the leader. Because position power is not a characteristic of the leader but of the situation the leader finds him- or herself in, it is included in the situational circle. Leader-member relations is a joint function of the leader and the followers; thus, it best belongs in the overlapping intersection of the leader and follower circles.

As opposed to the dearth of evidence for Hersey and Blanchard's (1969, 1982) situational theory, Fiedler and his fellow researchers have provided considerable evidence that the predictions of the model are empirically valid, particularly in laboratory settings (Fiedler, 1978; Fiedler & Chemers, 1982; Peters, Hartke, & Pohlmann, 1985; Strube &

Garcia, 1981). However, a review of the studies conducted in field settings yielded only mixed support for the model (Peters, Hartke, & Pohlmann, 1985). Moreover, researchers have criticized the model for the uncertainties surrounding the meaning of LPC scores (Kennedy, 1982; Rice, 1978; Schriesheim & Kerr, 1977); the interpretation of situational favorability (Jago & Ragan, 1986a, 1986b); and the relationship between LPC scores and situational favorability (Jago & Ragan, 1986a, 1986b; Vecchio, 1983).

Recent research by Ayman and Chemers (1991) may provide a partial explanation for why some studies failed to support certain hypotheses of the contingency model. These researchers assessed leaders' motivational hierarchies (via LPC scores) and situational favorability levels as well as lead-

**Figure 15.6.** Factors From Fiedler's Contingency Theory and the Interactional Framework

ers' standing on the trait of self-monitoring. Ayman and Chemers found that those leaders who were low in self-monitoring performed poorly when there was not a match between their LPC scores and situational favorability. However, in the same mismatches between LPC score and situation favorability, high self-monitors performed significantly better than the model predicted. Apparently, those leaders who were good at reading social cues from their followers and modifying their behavior according to those cues had higher-performing groups, even when the leaders' motivational hierarchies did not match the needs of the situation. Thus, Fiedler's explanation of behavior determinism may be less applicable to high self-monitors than it is to low self-monitors.

The latter finding by Ayman and Chemers (1991) makes an important point that concerns all four of the theories in this chapter. Even though the contingency theories are more comprehensive than any of the other leadership models or theories

previously described in this text, even these four theories are still extremely limited with respect to the myriad of leader, follower, and situational factors that affect the leadership process. For example, none of the theories really considers the variety of leadership traits found to be related to leadership effectiveness (like self-monitoring); the leader's and followers' values, attitudes, and preferences; the cohesiveness, norms, or size of the group; or the task, organizational design and culture, or environmental factors that can affect the leadership process. Because many of the latter variables can and do vary in field settings (and often have a greater effect on the leadership process than the variables considered by the theories described in this chapter), finding any support for those theories outside controlled laboratory experiments is fairly remarkable. Thus, although many of the criticisms of Fiedler's contingency model remain unanswered, the theory has been thoroughly tested in laboratory settings and has found some degree of empirical support in field settings. Furthermore, like any good theory, the contingency model has stimulated considerable research, and even if this research did not always lend support to the model, the findings still contributed to our knowledge of the leadership process.

## *The Path-Goal Theory*

Perhaps the most sophisticated (and comprehensive) of the four contingency models is *path-goal theory.* The underlying mechanism of path-goal theory is not particularly new or complicated. In fact, we discussed the "engine" of path-goal theory when we described expectancy theory. You may recall that expectancy theory was a cognitive theory of motivation where people calculated effort-to-performance probabilities ("If I study for 12 hours, what is the probability I will get an A on the final exam?"), performance-to-outcome probabilities ("If I get an A on the final, what is the probability of getting an A in the course?"), and assigned valences or values to outcome ("How much do I value a higher GPA?"). Theoretically at least, people were assumed to make these calculations on a rational basis, and the theory could be used to predict what tasks people will put their energies into, given some finite number of options.

Path-goal theory uses the same basic assumptions of expectancy theory. At the most fundamental level, the effective leader will provide or ensure the availability of valued rewards for followers (the "goal") and then help them find the best way of getting there (the "path"). Along the way, the effective leader will help the followers identify and remove roadblocks and avoid dead ends; the leader will also provide emotional support as needed. These "task" and "relationship" leadership actions essentially involve increasing followers' probability estimates for effort-to-performance and performance-to-reward expectancies. In other words, the leader's actions should strengthen followers' beliefs that if they exert a certain level of effort they will be more likely to accomplish a task, and if they accomplish the task they will be more likely to achieve some valued outcome.

Although not very complicated in its basic concept, the model added more variables and interactions over time. Evans (1970) is credited with the first version of path-goal theory, but we will focus on a later version developed by House and Dessler (1974). Their conceptual scheme is ideally suited to the L-F-S framework because they described three classes of variables, which include leader behaviors, followers, and the situation. We will examine each of these in turn.

### Leader Behaviors

The four types of leader behavior in path-goal theory can be seen in Box 15.3. Like SLT, path-goal theory assumes that leaders not only may use varying styles with different subordinates but might very well use differing styles with the same subordinates in different situations. Path-goal theory suggests that depending on the followers and the situation, these different leader behaviors can increase followers' acceptance of the leader, enhance their level of satisfaction, and raise their expectations that effort will result in effective performance, which in turn will lead to valued rewards.

### The Followers

Path-goal theory contains two groups of follower variables. The first relates to *satisfaction of followers,* and the second relates to *the followers' perception of their own abilities* relative to the task to be accomplished. In terms of followers' satisfaction, path-goal theory suggests that leader behaviors will be acceptable to the followers to the degree followers see the leader's behavior as either an immediate source of satisfaction or as directly instrumental in achieving future satisfaction. In other words, followers will actively support a leader as long as they view the leader's actions as a means for increasing their own levels of satisfaction. However, there is only so much a leader can do to increase followers' satisfaction levels, as satisfaction also depends on characteristics of the followers themselves.

A frequently cited example of how followers' characteristics influence the impact of leader behaviors on followers' levels of satisfaction involves

---

**BOX 15.3**
**The Four Leader Behaviors of Path-Goal Theory**

*Directive leadership.* These leader behaviors are very similar to the task behaviors from SLT. They include telling the followers what they are expected to do, how to do it, when it is to be done, and how their work fits in with the work of others. This behavior would also include setting schedules, establishing norms, and providing expectations that followers will adhere to established procedure and regulations.

*Supportive leadership.* Supportive leadership behaviors include courteous and friendly inter-actions, expressing genuine concern for the followers' well-being and individual needs, and re-maining open and approachable to followers. These behaviors, which are very similar to the relationship behaviors in SLT, also are marked by attention to the competing demands of treating followers equally while recognizing status differentials between the leader and the followers.

*Participative leadership.* Participative leaders engage in the behaviors that mark the consultative and group behaviors described by Vroom and Yetton (1973). As such, they tend to share work problems with followers; solicit their suggestions, concerns, and recommendations; and weigh these inputs in the decision-making process.

*Achievement-oriented leadership.* Leaders exhibiting these behaviors would be seen as both demanding and supporting in interactions with their followers: They would set up very challenging goals for group and follower behavior, continually seek ways to improve performance en route, and expect the followers to always perform at their highest levels. However, they would support these behaviors by exhibiting a high degree of ongoing confidence that subordinates can put forth the necessary effort; will achieve the desired results; and, even further, will assume even more responsibility in the future.

---

the trait of locus of control. Mitchell, Smyser, and Weed (1975) found that follower satisfaction was not directly related to the degree of participative behaviors manifest by the leader (i.e., followers with highly participative leaders were not any more satisfied than followers with more autocratic leaders). However, when followers' locus of control scores were taken into account, a contingency relationship was discovered. As can be seen in Figure 15.7, internal-locus-of-control followers, who believed outcomes were a result of their own decisions, were much more satisfied with leaders who exhibited participative behaviors than they were with directive leaders. Conversely, external-locus-of-control followers were more satisfied with di-

rective leader behaviors than they were with participative leader behaviors.

Followers' perceptions of their own skills and abilities to perform particular tasks can also affect the impact of certain leader behaviors. Followers who believe they are perfectly capable of performing a task are not as apt to be motivated by, or as willing to accept, a directive leader as they would a leader who exhibits participative behaviors. Using the same rationale as for locus of control, one can predict the opposite relationship for followers who do not perceive they have sufficient abilities to perform the task. Once again, the acceptability of the leader and the motivation to perform are in part determined by followers' characteristics.

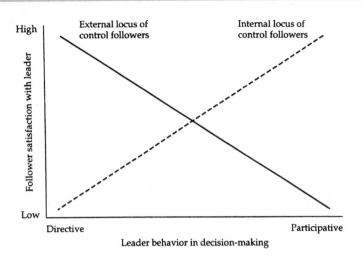

**Figure 15.7.** Interaction Between Followers' Locus of Control Scores and Leader Behavior in Decision Making
SOURCE: Adapted from T. R. Mitchell, C. M. Smyser, and S. E. Weed, "Locus of Control: Supervision and Work Satisfaction," *Academy of Management Journal 18* (1975), pp. 623-30.

Thus, path-goal theory suggests that both leader behaviors and follower characteristics are important in determining outcomes.

**The Situation**

Path-goal theory considers three situational factors that impact on moderate the effects of leader behavior can follower attitudes and behaviors. These include the *task,* the *formal authority system,* and the *primary work group.* Each of these three factors has been described earlier in this text, and each can influence the leadership situation in one of three ways. These three factors can serve as an independent motivational factor, a constraint on the behavior of followers (which may be either positive or negative in outcome), or as a reward. For example, it may be recalled that the task itself could be motivational (if it involved a high level of skill variety and task significance), constraining (if it had a high level of task interdependence), or delegated as a reward (if it had a high level of autonomy).

However, it should also be increasingly apparent that these variables can often affect the impact of various leader behaviors. For example, if the task is very structured and routine, the formal authority system has constrained followers' behaviors, and the work group has established clear norms for performance, then leaders would be serving a redundant purpose by manifesting directive or achievement-oriented behaviors. These prescriptions are similar to some of those noted in substitutes for leadership theory (Kerr & Jermier, 1978), as everything the follower needs in order to understand the effort-to-performance and performance-to-reward links is provided by the situation. Thus, redundant leader behaviors might be interpreted by followers as either a complete lack of understanding or empathy by the leader, or an attempt by the leader to exert excessive control. Neither of these interpretations is likely to enhance the leader's acceptance by followers or increase their motivation.

Although we have already described how follower characteristics and situational characteristics can affect leader behaviors, path-goal theory also maintains that follower and situational variables can affect each other. In other words, situational variables, such as the task performed, can also affect the influence of followers' skills, abilities, or personality traits on followers' satisfaction. Although this seems to make perfect sense, you should by now see how complicated path-goal

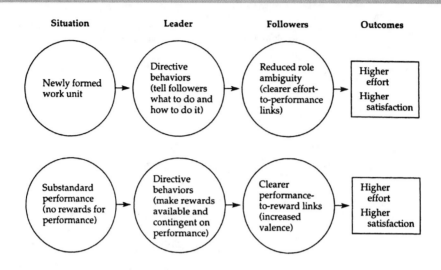

**Figure 15.8.** Examples of Applying Path-Goal Theory

theory can be when one starts considering how situational variables, follower characteristics, and leader behaviors interact in the leadership process. Because these interactions can become extremely complicated and are beyond the scope of this text, readers who wish to learn more about the intricacies of path-goal theory are encouraged to read House and Dessler (1974).

**Prescriptions of the Theory**

In general, path-goal theory maintains that leaders should first assess the situation and select a leadership behavior appropriate to situational demands. By manifesting the appropriate behaviors, leaders can increase followers' effort-to-performance expectancies, performance-to-reward expectancies, or valences of the outcomes. These increased expectancies and valences will improve subordinates' effort levels and the rewards attained, which in turn will increase subordinates' satisfaction and performance levels and the acceptance of their leaders. Perhaps the easiest way to explain this fairly complicated process is through the use of an example. Suppose we have a set of followers who are in a newly created work unit and do not have a clear understanding of the requirements of their positions. In other words, the followers have a reasonably high level of role ambiguity. According-

ing to path-goal theory, leaders should exhibit a high degree of directive behaviors in order to reduce the role ambiguity of their followers. The effort-to-performance link will become clearer when leaders tell followers what to do and how to do it in ambiguous situations, which in turn will cause followers to exert higher effort levels. Because role ambiguity is assumed to be unpleasant, these directive leader behaviors and higher effort levels should eventually result in higher satisfaction levels among followers. Figure 15.8 provides a graphic representation of this process. Similarly, leaders may look at the leadership situation and note that followers' performance levels are not acceptable. The leader may also conclude that the current situation offers few, if any, incentives for increased performance. In this case, the leader may use directive behaviors to increase the value of the rewards (or valence), which in turn will increase followers' effort levels and performance.

**Concluding Thoughts About the Path-Goal Theory**

Before getting into the research surrounding path-goal theory, it may be useful to examine the theory using the L-F-S framework. As seen in Figure 15.9, the components of path-goal theory fit quite nicely into the L-F-S model. The four leader

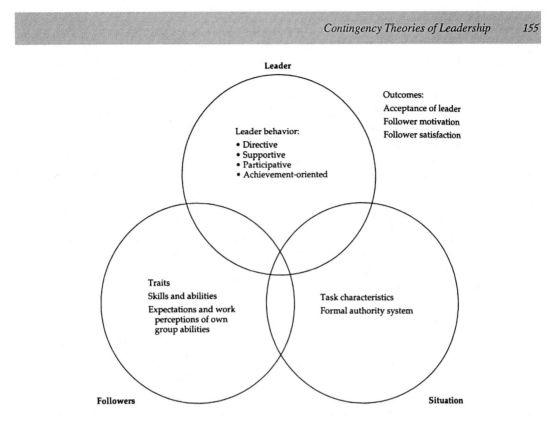

**Figure 15.9.** Factors From Path-Goal Theory and the Interactional Framework

behaviors fit squarely in the leader circle, the characteristics of the followers fit into the follower circle, and the task and formal authority system fit into the situation circle. Of all the components of path-goal theory, the only "mismatch" with the L-F-S model deals with the primary workgroup. The norms, cohesiveness, size, and stage of development of groups is considered to be part of the follower function in the L-F-S model but is part of the situation function in path-goal theory. In that regard, we hasten to note we use the L-F-S framework primarily for heuristic purposes. Ultimately, the concepts described in these four theories are sufficiently complex and ambiguous that there probably is no "right" answer to any single depiction.

In terms of research, the path-goal theory has received only mixed support to date (Schriesheim & DeNisi, 1981; Schriesheim & Kerr, 1977; Yukl, 1989). Although many of these mixed findings may be due to the fact that the path-goal theory

excludes many of the variables found to affect the leadership process, they may also be due to problems with the theory. Yukl (1989) maintained that most of these criticisms deal with the methodology used to study path-goal theory and the limitations of expectancy theory. Moreover, the path-goal theory assumes that the only way to increase performance is to increase followers' motivation levels. The theory ignores the roles leaders play in selecting talented followers, building their skill levels through training, and redesigning their work (Yukl & Van Fleet, 1992).

Nonetheless, path-goal theory is useful for illustrating two points. First, as noted by Yukl (1989), "path-goal theory has already made a contribution to the study of leadership by providing a conceptual framework to guide researchers in identifying potentially relevant situational moderator variables" (p. 104). Path-goal theory also illustrates that as models become more complicated, they may be more useful to researchers and less appealing to practitioners. Our experience is that pragmatically oriented students and in-place leaders want to take something from a model that is understandable and can be applied in their work situation right away. This does not mean they prefer simplicity to validity—they generally appreciate the complexity of the leadership process—but neither do they want a model that is so complex as to be indecipherable.

## Summary

This chapter is designed to provide an overview of four of the more well-known contingency theories of leadership, which include the normative decision model (Vroom & Yetton, 1973), the situational leadership model (Hersey & Blanchard, 1982), the contingency model (Fiedler, 1967), and the path-goal theory (House & Dressler, 1974). All four models are fairly similar in that they specify that leaders should make their behaviors contingent on certain aspects of the followers or the situation in order to improve leadership effectiveness. In addition, all four theories implicitly assume that leaders can accurately assess key follower and situational factors. However, it is entirely possible that two leaders in the same situation may reach very different conclusions about followers' level of knowledge, maturity, the strength of leader-follower relationships, the degree of task structure, or the level of role ambiguity being experienced by followers. These differences in perception could lead these two leaders to reach different conclusions about the situation, which may in turn cause them to take very different actions in response to the situation. Furthermore, these actions may be in accordance or in conflict with the prescriptions of any of these four theories, and leaders whose perceptions may have caused them to act in a manner not prescribed by a particular model may be an underlying reason why these four theories have reported conflicting findings, particularly in field settings.

Another reason why these theories have generally found mixed support in field settings concerns the fact that they are all fairly limited in scope. Many of the factors that affect leader and follower behaviors in workgroup, team, or volunteer com-

mittee settings are not present in laboratory studies but often play a substantial role in field studies. For example, none of the models takes into account how levels of stress, organizational culture and climate, working conditions, technology, economic conditions, or type of organizational design affect the leadership process. Nevertheless, the four contingency theories have been the subject of considerable research, and even if only mixed support for the models has been found, this research has succeeded in adding to our body of knowledge about leadership and has given us a more sophisticated understanding of the leadership process.

## References

Ayman, R., and M. M. Chemers. "The Effect of Leadership Match on Subordinate Satisfaction in Mexican Organizations: Some Moderating Influences on Self-Monitoring." *Applied Psychology: An International Review* 40 no. 3 (1991), pp. 229-314.

Evans, M. G. "The Effects of Supervisory Behavior on the Path-Goal Relationship." *Organizational Behavior and Human Performance* 5 (1970), pp. 277-298.

Fiedler, F. E. *A Theory of Leadership Effectiveness.* New York: McGraw-Hill, 1967.

———. "The Contingency Model and the Dynamics of the Leadership Process." In *Advances in Experimental Social Psychology,* ed. L. Berkowitz. New York: Academic Press, 1978.

Fiedler, F. E., and M. M. Chemers. *Improving Leadership Effectiveness: The Leader Match Concept.* 2nd ed. New York: Wiley, 1982.

Graeff, C. L. "The Situational Judgment Theory: A Critical Review." *Academy of Management Journal* 8 (1983), pp. 285-296.

Hersey, P., and K. H. Blanchard. "Life Cycle Theory of Leadership." *Training and Development Journal* 23 (1969), pp. 26-34.

———. *Management of Organizational Behavior: Utilizing Human Resources.* 3rd ed. Englewood Cliffs, NJ: Prentice Hall, 1977.

———. *Management of Organizational Behavior: Utilizing Human Resources.* 4th ed. Englewood Cliffs, NJ: Prentice Hall, 1982.

House, R. J., and G. Dressler. "The Path-Goal Theory of Leadership: Some Post Hoc and A Priori Tests." In *Contingency Approaches to Leadership,* ed. J. G. Hunt and L. L. Larson. Carbondale, IL: Southern Illinois University Press, 1974.

Jago, A. G., and J. W. Ragan. "The Trouble With Leader Match Is That It Doesn't Match Fiedler's Contingency Model." *Journal of Applied Psychology* 71 (1986a), pp. 555-559.

————. "Some Assumptions Are More Troubling Than Others: Rejoinder to Chemers and Fiedler." *Journal of Applied Psychology* 71 (1986b), pp. 564-565.

Kennedy, J. K. "Middle LPC Leaders and the Contingency Model of Leader Effectiveness." *Organizational Behavior and Human Performance* 30 (1982), pp. 1-14.

Kerr, S., and J. M. Jermier. "Substitutes for Leadership: Their Meaning and Measurement." *Organizational Behavior and Human Performance* 22 (1978), pp. 375-403.

Mitchell, R. R., C. M. Smyser, and S. E. Weed. "Locus of Control: Supervision and Work Satisfaction." *Academy of Management Journal* 18 (1975), pp. 623-630.

Peters, L. H., D. D. Hartke, and J. T. Pohlmann. "Fiedler's Contingency Theory of Leadership: An Application of the Meta-Analytic Procedures of Schmidt and Hunter." *Psychological Bulletin* 97 (1985), pp. 274-285.

Rice, R. W. "Construct Validity of the Least Preferred Co-Worker Score." *Psychological Bulletin* 85 (1978), pp. 1199-1237.

Schriesheim, C. A., and A. S. DeNisi. "Task Dimensions as Moderators of the Effects of Instrumental Leadership: A Two Sample Replicated Test of Path-Goal Leadership Theory." *Journal of Applied Psychology* 66 (1981), pp. 589-597.

Schriesheim, C. A., and S. Kerr. "Theories and Measures of Leadership: A Critical Appraisal of Current and Future Directions." In *Leadership: The Cutting Edge,* ed. J. G. Hunt and L. L. Larson. Carbondale, IL: Southern Illinois University Press, 1977.

Strube, M. J., and Garcia, J. E. "A Meta-Analytic Investigation of Fiedler's Contingency Model of Leadership Effectiveness." *Psychological Bulletin 90,* pp. 307-321.

Vecchio, R. P. "Assessing the Validity of Fiedler's Contingency Model of Leadership Effectiveness: A Closer Look at Strube and Garcia." *Psychological Bulletin* 93 (1983), pp. 404-408.

————. "Situational Leadership Theory: An Examination of a Prescriptive Theory." *Journal of Applied Psychology* 72 (1987), pp. 444-451.

Vroom, V. H., and P. W. Yetton. *Leadership and Decision Making.* Pittsburgh: University of Pittsburgh Press, 1973.

Yukl, G. A. *Leadership in Organizations.* 2nd ed. Englewood Cliffs, NJ: Prentice Hall, 1989.

Yukl, G. A., and D. D. Van Fleet. "Theory and Research on Leadership in Organizations." In *Handbook of Industrial & Organizational Psychology,* ed. M. D. Dunnette and L. M. Hough. Vol. 3. Palo Alto, CA: Consulting Psychologists Press, 1992, pp. 1-51.

# 16

# Chaos and the Strange Attractor of Meaning

MARGARET J. WHEATLEY

> Thus before all else, there came into being the Gaping Chasm, Chaos, but there followed the broad-chested Earth, Gaia, the forever-secure seat of the immortals . . . and also Love, Eros, the most beautiful of the immortal gods, he who breaks limbs.
>
> —*Hesiod*

Several thousand years ago, when primal forces haunted human imagination, great gods arose in myths to explain the creation of all beings. At the very beginning was Chaos, the endless, yawning chasm devoid of fern or fullness, and Gaia, the mother of the earth who brought forth form and stability. In Greek consciousness, Chaos and Gaia were partners, two primordial powers engaged in a duet of opposition and resonance, creating everything we know.

These two mythic figures again inhabit our imaginations and our science. They have taken on new life as scientists explore more deeply the workings of our universe. I find this return to mythic wisdom both intriguing and comforting. It signifies that a new relationship with Chaos is available, even in the midst of increasing turbulence. Like ancient Gaia, we need to appreciate the necessity for Chaos, understanding it as the life source of our creative power. From his great chasm comes support and opposition, creating the "light without which no form would be visible" (Bonnefoy 1991, 369-70). We, the generative force, give birth to form and meaning, dispelling Chaos with

SOURCE: Reprinted with permission of the publisher. From *Leadership and the New Science: Learning About Organization From an Orderly Universe,* copyright © 1994 by Margaret J. Wheatley, Berrett-Koehler Publishers, Inc., San Francisco, CA. All rights reserved.

our creative expression. We fill the void with worlds of our creation and turn our backs on him. But we must remember, so the Greeks and our science tell us, that deep within our Gaian centers lives always the dark heart of Chaos.

The heart of chaos has been revealed with modern computers. Watching chaos emerge on a computer screen is a mesmerizing experience. The computer tracks the evolution of a system, recording a moment in the system's state as a point of light on the screen. With the speed typical of computers, we can soon observe millions of moments in the system's history. The system careens back and forth with violent unpredictability, never showing up in the same spot twice. This chaotic movement is seen as rapidly moving lines zooming back and forth across the screen. But as we watch, the lines weave their strands into a pattern, and an order to this disorder emerges. The chaotic movements of the system have a shape. The shape is a "strange attractor," and what has appeared on the screen is the order inherent in chaos.

Chaos has always had a shape—a concept contradictory to our common definition of chaos—but until we could see it through the eyes of computers, we saw only turbulence, energy without predictable form or direction. Chaos is the final state in a system's movement away from order. Not all systems move into chaos, but if a system is dislodged from its stable state, it moves first into a period of oscillation, swinging back and forth between different states. If it moves from this oscillation, the next state is full chaos, a period of total unpredictability. But in the realm of chaos, where everything should fall apart, the strange attractor comes into play. (Science uses other attractors. These particular ones were named *strange* by two scientists, David Ruelle and Floris Takens, who felt the name was deeply suggestive [Gleick 1987, 131]. As Ruelle said, "The name is beautiful and well-suited to these astonishing objects, of which we understand so little [in Coveney and Highfield 1990, 204].)

A strange attractor is a basin of attraction, an area displayed in computer-generated phase space that the system is magnetically drawn into, pulling the system into a visible shape. Computer phase space is multidimensional, allowing scientists to

see a system's movement in more dimensions than had been possible previously. Shapes that were not visible in two dimensions now become apparent. In a chaotic system, scientists now can observe movements that, though random and unpredictable, never exceed finite boundaries. "Chaos," says planning expert T. J. Cartwright, "is order without predictability" (1991, 44). The system has infinite possibilities, wandering wherever it pleases, sampling new configurations of itself. But its wandering and experimentation respect a boundary.

Ruelle, like many chaos scientists, reaches for poetic language to describe these strange attractors: "These systems of curves, these clouds of points, suggest sometimes fireworks or galaxies, sometimes strange and disquieting vegetal proliferations. A realm lies there of forms to explore, of harmonies to discover" (in Coveney and Highfield, 1990, 206).

Briggs and Peat, in describing the computer images of systems wandering between orderly and chaotic states, paint a similarly compelling picture of this dance between turbulence and order:

> Evidently familiar order and chaotic order are laminated like bands of intermittency. Wandering into certain bands, a system is extruded and bent back on itself as it iterates, dragged toward disintegration, transformation, and chaos. Inside other bands, systems cycle dynamically, maintaining their shapes for long periods of time. But eventually all orderly systems will feel the wild, seductive pull of the strange chaotic attractor. (1989, 76-77)

In much of new science, we are challenged by paradoxical concepts—matter that is immaterial, disequilibrium that creates global equilibrium, and now chaos that is nonchaotic. Yet the paradox of chaos was known anciently, in its mythic pairing with order. In every system lurks the potential for chaos, "a creature slumbering deep inside the perfectly ordered system" (Briggs and Peat 1989, 62). But chaos, when it erupts, will never exceed the bounds of its strange attractor. This mirror world of order and disorder challenges us to look, once again, at the whole of the system. Only when we step back to observe the shape of things can we see

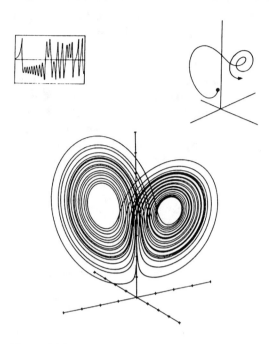

**Figure 16.1.**

SOURCE: Gleick, 1987; used with permission.

NOTE: This wonderful, well-ordered butterfly or owl-shaped image of a chaotic system was not visible to scientists until they developed a way to plot the development of a system using multiple variables. Traditional plots of one variable (upper left) show a system in chaos—total unpredictability. However, in phase space, three variables are plotted simultaneously; as the system wanders chaotically, the location of the system can be plotted in three-dimensional space (upper right). This perspective shows the emergence of a strange attractor, the boundaries that contain chaos. The system never lands in the same place twice, yet it never exceeds certain boundaries. As the attractor takes shape, it contains layer upon layer of trajectories that never intersect.

the patterns of movement from chaos to order and from order to chaos. "Here," recalls chaos scientist Doyne Farmer, "was one coin with two sides. Here was order, with randomness emerging, and then one step further away was randomness with its own underlying order" (in Gleick 1987, 252).

Chaos of this nature (known as deterministic chaos) is created by iterations in a nonlinear system, information feeding back on itself and changing in the process. (This process of iteration also characterizes the self-organization observed in biological and chemical systems.) Nonlinearity has been described by Coveney and Highfield as "getting more than you bargained for" (1990, 184). Very slight variances in the conditions of the equation, variances so small as to be indiscernible, amplify into unpredictable results when they are fed back on themselves. If the system is nonlinear, iterations can take the system in any direction, away from anything we might expect. The proverbial straw that broke the camel's back is one familiar example of nonlinearity: A very small change had an impact far beyond what could have been predicted.

Until recently, we discounted the effects of nonlinearity, even though it abounds in life. We had been trained to believe that small differences averaged out, that slight variances converged toward a point, and that approximations would give us a fairly accurate picture of what could happen. But chaos theory ended all that. In a dynamic, changing system, the *slightest* variation can have explosive results. Hypothetically, were we to create a difference in two values as small as rounding them off to the thirty-first decimal place (calculating numbers this large would require a computer of astronomical size), after only one hundred iterations the whole calculation would go askew. The paths of the two systems would have diverged in unpredictable ways. Even infinitesimal differences are far from inconsequential. "Chaos takes them," physicist James Crutchfield says, "and blows them up in your face" (in Briggs and Peat 1989, 73).

Scientists now emphasize the very small differences at the beginning of a system's evolution that make prediction impossible; this is termed "sensitive dependence on initial conditions." Edward Lorenz, a meteorologist, first drew modern-day attention to this with his "butterfly effect." (At the end of the nineteenth century, mathematician, physicist, and philosopher Henri Poincaré had called attention to chaos in dynamic systems and its impact on prediction, but it was chaos science late in this century that revived his findings.) Does the flap of a butterfly wing in Tokyo, Lorenz queried, affect a tornado in Texas (or a thunderstorm in New York)? Though unfortunate for the future of accurate weather prediction, his answer was "yes."

Science has been profoundly affected by this new relationship with the nonlinear character of our world. Many of the prevailing assumptions of scientific thought have had to be recanted. As the scientist Arthur Winfree expresses it:

The basic idea of Western science is that you don't have to take into account the falling of a leaf on some planet in another galaxy when you're trying to account for the motion of a billiard ball on a pool table on earth. Very small influences can be neglected. There's a convergence in the way things work, and arbitrarily small influences don't blow up to have arbitrarily large effects. (Gleick 1987, 15)

But chaos theory has proved these assumptions false. The world is far more sensitive than we had ever thought. We may harbor the hope that we will regain predictability as soon as we can learn how to account for all variables, but in fact no level of detail can ever satisfy this desire. Iteration creates powerful and unpredictable effects in nonlinear systems. In complex ways that no model will ever capture, the system feeds back on itself, enfolding all that has happened, magnifying slight variances, encoding it in the system's memory—and prohibiting prediction, ever.

Chaos theory is based on Newtonian mechanical principles, but in its unpredictability, it shares the uncertainty experienced at the quantum level. In both sciences, uncertainty arises because the *wholeness* of the universe resists being studied in pieces. Briggs and Peat, in their intriguing exploration of the mirror world of chaos and order, suggest that wholeness is "what rushes in under the guise of chaos whenever scientists try to separate and measure dynamical systems as if they were composed of parts. . . . The whole shape of things depends upon the minutest part. The part *is* the whole in this respect, for through the action of any part, the whole in the form of chaos or transformative change may manifest" (1987, 74-75). The strange attractors that form on our screens, Briggs and Peat suggest, are not the shape of chaos. They are the shape of wholeness.

Iteration launches a system on a journey that visits both chaos and order. The most beautiful images of iteration are found in the artistry of fractals, computer-generated models drawn by the iteration of a few equations. The equations change as they are fed back on themselves. After countless iterations, their tracks materialize into form, creating detailed shapes at finer and finer levels. Everywhere in this minutely detailed fractal landscape,

there is self-similarity. The shape we set at one magnification we will see at all others. No matter how deeply we look, peering down through very great magnifications, the same forms are evident. There is pattern within pattern within pattern. There is no end to them, no scale small enough that these intricate shapes cease to form. Because the formations go on forever, there is no way to ever gain a finite measurement of them. We could follow the outline of forms forever, and at ever smaller levels, there would always be something more to measure.

Fractals entered our world through the research of Benoit Mandelbrot of IBM. In discovering them, he gave us a language, a form of geometry, that allowed us to understand nature in new ways. Fractals are everywhere around us, in the patterns by which nature forms clouds, landscapes, circulatory systems, trees, and plants. We observe fractals daily, but until recently, we lacked a means for understanding them or how they were created.

Fractals, as common as they are, teach some new and important things. For example, it is impossible to ever know the precise measurement of a fractal. Mandelbrot's seminal fractal exercise was a simple question posed to colleagues and students. "How long is the coast of Britain?" As his colleagues soon learned, there is no final answer to this question. The closer you zoom in on the coastline, the more there is to measure.

Since there can be no definitive measurement, what is important in a fractal landscape is to note the *quality* of the system—its complexity and distinguishing shapes, and how it differs from other fractals. If we ignore these qualitative factors and focus on quantitative measures, we will always be frustrated by the incomplete and never-ending information we receive. Fractals, in stressing *qualitative* measurement, remind us of the lessons of wholeness we encountered in the systems realm. What we *can* know, and what is important to know, is the shape of the whole—how it develops and changes, or how it compares to another system.

In organizations, we are very good at measuring activity. In fact, that is primarily what we do. Fractals suggest the futility of searching for ever finer measures of discrete parts of the system. There is never a satisfying end to this reductionist search, never an end point where we finally know everything about even one part of the system. When we study the individual parts or try to understand the system through its *quantities,* we get lost in a world we can never fully measure nor appreciate. Scientists of chaos study shapes in motion; if we were to approach organizations in a similar way, what would constitute the shape and motion of an organization?

We have started edging toward an answer to this question in our growing focus on studying organizations as whole systems rather than our old focus on discrete tasks. Organizations that are using complex system modeling are experimenting with these skills. In other organizations, this newer awareness of dynamic shape may occur simply in how problems are approached. Is there an attempt to step back from the problem, to gain enough perspective so that its shape emerges out of the myriad variables that influence it? Are people encouraged to look for themes and patterns, rather than isolated causes? Some of the analytic tools introduced in corporate quality programs, although relying initially on diverse and minute mathematical information, eventually prove effective because they allow people to appreciate the complex and ever-changing shape of the organization, and how multiple forces work together to form it.

Fractal principles have given us valuable insight into how nature creates the shapes we observe. Mountains, rivers, coastlines, vegetables, lungs, circulatory systems—all of these (and millions more) are fractal, replicating a dominant pattern at several smaller levels of scale. The scientist Michael Barnsley was intrigued to see if he could recreate the shapes of natural objects by deducing the initial equations that described their forms. He invented the "Chaos Game," in which he decoded objects to derive the number rules that expressed certain global information about their shapes (his first attempt was with a fern). These numbers captured only essential information about the shape. They were surprisingly simple, devoid of the levels of precise prescriptive information we might expect. Barnsley then interjected randomness, setting the numbers loose to feed back on themselves. They were allowed to follow their own iterative wanderings, working at whatever scale they chose.

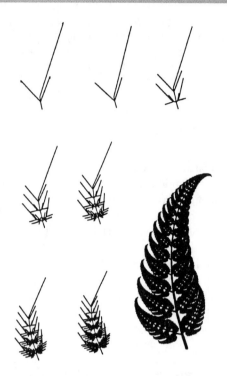

**Figure 16.2.**
SOURCE: Drawing by Linda Garcia, 1991 (*The Fractal Explorer,* Dynamic Press, Santa Cruz, CA); used with permission.
NOTE: Creating complexity from simplicity. Strange as it seems, the basic shape of a fern is captured in a simple stick drawing (top left). To make a fern of curving, intricate complexity, all that is required is this stick shape, or "seed," and a few basic rules. The only rules are that the seed shape is free to repeat itself at many different levels of scale, that it is placed in an upright direction, and that it connects with what is already on the page. From this combination of a few simple rules and high levels of autonomy—of order and chaos working in tandem—emerges the beautiful complexity of a fern. (This process can be used to create other complex fractal objects, such as trees or intricate patterns, once the basic shape is abstracted.)

With this approach, he successfully reproduced an entire computer garden of plant shapes.

His work with "random fractals" and the chaos game are very instructive. First, Barnsley shows us that predictability still exists. The shapes that he created are predictable, built into the numbers. But indeterminism (randomness) also plays a key role. It is randomness that leads to the creation of the pattern at different levels of scale. The same shapes appear predictably everywhere with only simple levels of instruction and large amounts of freedom. It seems that with a few simple guidelines, left to develop and change randomly, nature creates the complexity and harmony of form we see everywhere.

Many disciplines have seized upon fractals, testing whether self-similar phenomena occur at different levels of scale in both natural and manmade systems. For example, business forecasters and stock analysts have observed a fractal quality to stock market behaviors and have seen patterns that resemble one another in daily and monthly market fluctuations.

And I believe that fractals also have direct application for the leadership of organizations. The very best organizations have a fractal quality to them. An observer of such an organization can tell what the organization's values and ways of doing business are by watching anyone, whether it be a production floor employee or a senior manager. There is a consistency and predictability to the quality of behavior. No matter where we look in these organizations, self-similarity is found in its people, in spite of the complex range of roles and levels.

How is this quality achieved? The potent force that shapes behavior in these fractal organizations, as in all natural systems, is the combination of simply expressed expectations of acceptable behavior and the freedom available to individuals to assert themselves in nondeterministic ways. Fractal organizations, though they may never have heard the word *fractal,* have learned to trust in natural organizing phenomena. They trust in the power of guiding principles or values, knowing that they are strong enough influencers of behavior to shape every employee into a desired representative of the organization. These organizations expect to see similar behaviors show up at every level in the organization because those behaviors were patterned into the organizing principles at the very start.

Fractals and strange attractors echo the principles evidenced in the globally stable, locally changing structures we observed in self-organizing systems. In both realms, whether it be a biological system or a mathematical rendering of a chaotic system, the structure is capable of maintaining its overall shape and a large degree of independence from the environment because each part of the system is free to express itself within the context of that system. Fluctuations, randomness, and un-predictability at the local level, in the presence of guiding or self-referential principles, cohere over time into definite and predictable form. It was this odd combination of predictability and self-determination that attracted some early scientists of chaos. The science seemed to explain how free will could be expressed and have value in an orderly universe. "The system is deterministic, but you can't say what it's going to do next" (Gleick 1987, 251).

These ideas speak with a simple clarity to issues of effective leadership. They bring us back to the importance of simple governing principles: guiding visions, strong values, organizational beliefs—the few rules individuals can use to shape their own behavior. The leader's task is to communicate them, to keep them ever-present and clear, and then allow individuals in the system their random, sometimes chaotic-looking meanderings.

This is no simple task. Anytime we see systems in apparent chaos, our training urges us to interfere, to stabilize and shore things up. But if we can trust the workings of chaos, we will see that the dominant shape of our organizations can be maintained if we retain clarity about the purpose and direction of the organization. If we succeed in maintaining focus, rather than hands-on control, we also create the flexibility and responsiveness that every organization craves. What leaders are called upon to do in a chaotic world is to shape their organizations through concepts, not through elaborate rules or structures.

Ever since my imagination was captured by the phrase "strange attractor," I have wondered if we could identify such a force in organizations. Is there a magnetic force, a basin for activity, so attractive that it pulls all behavior toward it and creates coherence? My current belief is that we *do* have such attractors at work in organizations and that one of the most potent shapers of behavior in organizations, and in life, is *meaning.* Our main concern, writes Viktor Frankl in his presentation of logotherapy, "is not to gain pleasure or to avoid pain but rather to see a meaning in . . . life" (1959, 115).

I became aware of the call of meaning in our organizational lives when I worked with a number of incoherent companies that had been tipped into chaos by reorganizations or leveraged buyouts. They had lost any purpose beyond the basic struggle to survive. Yet under these circumstances, I saw some employees who continued to work hard and contribute to the organization even when the organization could offer them nothing, not even the promise of a job in the future. Most employees had, more predictably, checked out psychologically, just putting in their time, waiting for the inevitable. But others stayed creative and focused on creating new services, even with the great uncertainty of the future. This puzzled me greatly.

I assumed at first that they were simply denying reality. But when I talked to these employees, it became evident that something else much more important was going on. They were staying creative, making sense out of non-sense, because they had taken the time to create a meaning for their work, one that transcended present organizational circumstances. They wanted to hold onto motivation and direction in the midst of turbulence, and the only way they could do this was by investing the current situation with meaning. Frankl, in *Man's Search for Meaning,* points out very clearly that meaning saved lives in the concentration camps of Germany. The one thing that can never be taken from us, he writes, is our attitude toward a situation. If we search to create meaning, we can survive and even flourish. In chaotic organizations, I observed just such a phenomenon. Employees were wise enough to sense that personal meaning-making as their only route out of chaos. In some ways, the future of the organization became irrelevant. They held onto personal coherence because of the meaning attractor they created. Maybe the organization didn't make sense, but their lives did.

I have also seen companies make deliberate use of meaning to move through times of traumatic change. I've seen leaders make great efforts to speak forthrightly and frequently to employees about current struggles, about the tough times that lie ahead, and about what they dream of for the future. These conversations fill a painful period with new purpose, giving reasons for the current need to sacrifice and hold on. In most cases, given this kind of meaningful information, workers respond with allegiance and energy.

All of us want so much to know the "why" of what is going on. (How often have you heard yourself or others say, "I just wish they would tell me *why* we're doing this"?) We instinctively reach out to leaders who work with us on creating meaning. Those who give voice and form to our search for meaning, and who help us make our world purposeful, are leaders we cherish, and to whom we return gift for gift.

The formative powers of meaning echo back, at least in my own thinking, to a lesson I learned from self-organizing systems, where the principle of self-reference or self-consistency plays such a critical role. A self-organizing system has the freedom to grow and evolve, guided only by one rule: It must remain consistent with itself and its past. The presence of this guiding rule allows for both creativity and boundaries, for evolution and coherence, for determinism and free will.

When I think about meaning as a strange attractor, I see links to these sciences. Meaning or purpose serves as a point of reference. As long as we keep purpose in focus in both our organizational and private lives, we are able to wander through the realms of chaos, make decisions about what actions will be consistent with our purpose, and emerge with a discernible pattern or shape to our lives.

When a meaning attractor is in place in an organization, employees can be trusted to move freely, drawn in many directions by their energy and creativity. There is no need to insist, through regimentation or supervision, that any two individuals act in precisely the same way. We know they will be affected and shaped by the attractor, their behavior never going out of bounds. We trust that they will heed the call of the attractor and stay within its basin. We believe that little else is required except the cohering presence of a purpose, which gives people the capacity for self-reference.

The science of strange attractors can be linked back, in its images and teachings, to other sciences in many ways. Chaos theory, based on Newtonian mechanics and applicable to the world of large objects, conjures up visions of unseen forces that create order and manage coherence. The fields of quantum space speak of energy that takes form when two subatomic fields intersect. The fields of biological morphogenesis describe physical forms shaped by invisible geometries. It is important to keep the distinctions between these sciences clear (at least for now), but it is also important to note a resonant similarity. Each attempts to describe the presence of nonvisible influences that facilitate orderly processes of creation and change.

In chaos theory it is axiomatic that you can never tell where the system is headed until you've observed it over time. This is also true for organizations, and it is what makes trusting something as ethereal as a strange attractor difficult. It takes time to see if a meaning-rich organization really works. A few are already out there, bright beacons to the future. But if they have not been part of our own experience, we are back to acts of faith. As the universe keeps revealing more of these invisible allies, perhaps we will grow in the belief that systems can evolve into an orderly shape when they center around clear points of self-reference.

We can use our own lives as evidence for this because they evolve in just such a fashion. By the end of our lifetime, we are able to discern our individual basins of attraction. What has been the shape of our life? What has made seemingly random events now appear purposeful? What has made "chance" meetings fit smoothly into the movement of our lives? We discover that we have been influenced by a meaning that is wholly and uniquely our own. We experience a deeper knowledge of the purpose that structured all of our activities, many times invisibly and without our awareness. Whether we believe that we create this meaning in a restrospective attempt to make sense of our lives, or that we discover meaning as the preexistent creation of a purposeful universe, it is, at the end, only meaning that we seek. Nothing else is attractive, nothing else has the power to cohere an entire lifetime of activity. We become like ancient Gaia who boldly embraced the void, knowing that from Chaos' dark depths she would always pull forth order.

## References

Bonnefoy, Yves. *Mythologies*. Chicago: University of Chicago Press, 1991.

Briggs, John, and F. David Peat. *Turbulent Mirror: An Illustrated Guide to Chaos Theory and the Science of Wholeness*. New York: Harper and Row, 1989.

Cartwright, T. J. "Planning and Chaos Theory." *APA Journal* (Winter 1991): 44-56.

Coveney, Peter, and Roger Highfield. *The Arrow of Time: A Voyage Through Science to Solve Time's Greatest Mystery*. New York: Fawcett Columbine, 1990.

Frankl, Viktor. *Man's Search for Meaning*. Boston: Beacon Press, 1959.

Gleick, James. *Chaos: Making a New Science*. New York: Viking, 1987.

# 17

# The Ethics of Charismatic Leadership

## Submission or Liberation?

JANE HOWELL
BRUCE J. AVOLIO

Wanted: Corporate Leaders. Must have vision and ability to build corporate culture. Mere managers need not apply.[1]

Charismatic leaders are celebrated as the heroes of management. By turning around ailing corporations, revitalizing aging bureaucracies, or launching new enterprises, these leaders are viewed as the magic elixir to cure organizational woes and change the course of organizational events. Charismatic leaders achieve these heroic feats by powerfully communicating a compelling vision of the future, passionately believing in their vision, relentlessly promoting their beliefs with boundless energy, propounding creative ideas, and expressing confidence in followers' abilities to achieve high standards. Charismatic leaders are typically viewed as effective leaders: leaders who inspire

SOURCE: "The Ethics of Charismatic Leadership," by Jane M. Howell and Bruce J. Avolio, *Academy of Management Executive,* Vol. 6, No. 2, 1992. Reprinted with permission of Academy of Management. The authors are indebted to Leanne Atwater, Bernard Bass, Joseph DiStefano, Jeffrey Gandz, two anonymous reviewers, and Associate Editor [of *Academy of Management Executive*] Kathryn Bartol for their helpful comments.

extraordinary performance in followers as well as build their trust, faith, and belief in the leader.[2] But is charisma a desirable force for leading an organization? While the virtues of charismatic leaders are extolled in the popular management press, and in a growing number of studies, the potential dark side of these leaders is often ignored.

Charismatics can be very effective leaders, yet they may vary in their ethical standards. The label charismatic has been applied to very diverse leaders in politics (Adolf Hitler, Benito Mussolini, Franklin Delano Roosevelt), in religious spheres (Jesus Christ, Jim Jones), in social movement organizations (Mahatma Gandhi, Martin Luther King, Jr., Malcolm X) and in business (Lee Iacocca, Mary Kay Ash, John DeLorean). This list underscores that the term "charisma" is value neutral: it does not distinguish between good or moral and evil or immoral charismatic leadership. This means the risks involved in charismatic leadership are at least as large as the promises. Charisma can lead to blind fanaticism in the service of megalomaniacs and dangerous values, or to heroic self-sacrifice in the service of a beneficial cause.[3] An awareness of this risk is missing from most of the current popular writings on charismatic leadership, which may be interpreted by executives and managers as an unqualified recommendation of such leadership. In this chapter, we argue that rather than dismiss charisma on the grounds of its associated risks, we need to understand the differences between ethical and unethical charismatic leaders so managers can make informed decisions about recruiting, selecting, and promoting their future organizational leaders who will pursue visions that benefit their organizations rather than simply building their own power base at the expense of the organization.

To understand the ethics of charismatic leadership, we interviewed and surveyed more than 150 managers in 25 large Canadian organizations.[4] Based on these managers' descriptions of their bosses, we identified twenty-five charismatic leaders for in-depth study. Each leader was interviewed for two hours about his or her philosophy, values, and attitudes towards followers and completed a questionnaire measuring various personality characteristics and leadership behaviors. To determine whether a charismatic leader was ethical or unethical, interview transcripts were content analyzed for the presence of themes related to whether the leader attacked moral abuses, confronted and resolved dilemmas, encouraged pursuits of ideals, cultivated an ethically responsible culture, and fostered and rewarded those with moral integrity.[5] We draw on these interviews and questionnaire responses, as well as popular accounts of well-known charismatic leaders, to highlight the key characteristics and behaviors of ethical and unethical charismatic leaders.

We first describe the key behaviors and moral standards that differentiate ethical from unethical charismatic leaders. The impact of ethical and unethical charismatic leaders on their followers' development is discussed next. Finally, we outline how managers can nurture ethical charismatic leadership in their organizations.

## Charismatic Leaders: Some Uncommon Denominators

Many charismatic leaders incorporate their followers' hopes, dreams, and aspirations in their vision. These leaders develop creative, critical thinking in their followers, provide opportunities for them to develop, welcome positive and negative feedback, recognize the contributions of others, share information with followers, and have moral standards that emphasize collective interests of the group, organization, or society. We call these leaders "ethical charismatics." Other charismatic leaders are interested in pursuing their own personal vision. These charismatic leaders control and manipulate their followers, promote what is best for themselves rather than their organizations, and have moral standards that promote self-interests. We call these leaders "unethical charismatics."

We now examine the marks of ethical and unethical charismatic leaders to see how those who seek to be leaders might avoid the often attractive traps associated with unethical leadership, while cultivating the characteristics of genuinely ethical leadership. As illustrated in Exhibit 1 [Exhibit 1 omitted] and described below, ethical and unethical charismatic leaders are distinguished by five key behaviors: exercising powers, creating visions, communicating with followers, intellectually stimulating followers, developing followers, and moral standards.

## Exercising Power

Exercising power or influence varies among ethical and unethical charismatic leaders. Ethical charismatic leaders use power in socially constructive ways to serve others. They are genuinely concerned about contributing to the welfare of followers. Leadership that stresses serving rather than dominance, status, or prestige is reflected in the construction services company Townsend and Bottum, Inc.'s Plan for Continuity:

It shall be an organization operating with the highest principles of integrity, service to society and clients, in an environment of trust which will nurture growth and development of employees so that they become stronger, more autonomous, and more serving of their fellow men and women.[6]

In contrast, unethical charismatics exercise power in dominant and authoritarian ways to serve their self-interests, to manipulate others for their own purposes, and to win at all costs. Power is used for personal gain or impact. Exercising power in a dominant and controlling manner was captured in the words of an invited speaker at an American Management Association Conference for presidents: "I want men that are vicious, grasping, and lusting for power. He who has the gold makes the rules."[7]

## Creating the Vision

Ethical and unethical charismatic leaders differ in how they create and express their vision. Ethical charismatic leaders express goals that are follower driven; their visions are ultimately responsive to the interests and desires of their followers. Followers actively contribute to and develop the vision further so that it is shared. In the words of one of the charismatic leaders we interviewed:

My job is to transfer some of the dream so others think it's as neat as I think it's neat. I use all of the emotional

trigger words to get people to buy into the concept. You don't want manipulation because you really do want their best creative efforts on it. So it's really exciting them with the potential to get them to buy in. So you have to spend a lot of time talking and transferring the potential notions so that they own a piece of it.

President and CEO Bill O'Brien of the Hanover Insurance Companies strongly believes in the power of a shared vision:

In my first year as president, I went across the country and I talked to every single employee in every branch of the company. I told them what my vision was for The Hanover Insurance Company. Now a vision is an intensely personal thing. Your vision gets you out of bed to go to work in the morning. My vision gets me working. My vision doesn't do a lot for you. So, we don't have a lot of meetings on what should be the vision of the company or what should be the vision of a department. We encourage our people if they run an operation to have a vision for it. And then, when they are facing live, real situations, act in a visionary way. I have never seen a vision come out of a committee. I have heard people say, "Here is what I believe and here is what I think we can do. What do you think?" That kind of process will build some visions. We encourage every single department to build its own vision of what it wants to become. When we first did it, everybody thought we were going to have chaos. But there is remarkable harmony between what a branch or department envisions and what a company sees.[8]

While ethical charismatic leaders develop their visions partly through interaction with followers, unethical charismatic leaders derive their visions solely from within themselves. Unethical charismatic leaders communicate goals that promote their own personal agenda often to the disadvantage of others. In the extreme, the leader's goals are pursued without question. As one leader remarked to us: "The key thing is that it is my idea, and I am going to win with it at all costs."

## Communicating With Followers

To set agendas that represent the interests of their followers, ethical charismatic leaders continuously seek out their viewpoints on critical issues. Such leaders listen to the ideas, needs, aspirations, and wishes of followers and then, within the context of their own well-developed system of beliefs, respond to these in an appropriate way. They invite two-way communication with subordinates, while still promoting a sense of knowing what they are doing. This sense of mutual interaction is captured in one charismatic leader's comment: "If you don't walk the plant, you don't know what's going on. You have to work at it."

Open communication with employees is a key principle at Wal-Mart Stores, the highly successful retailing giant.[9] To stay in touch with employees, or "associates" in Wal-Mart's language, the charismatic founder Sam Walton relies on a highly elaborate communication system ranging from a six-channel satellite system to a private airforce of eleven planes. Says CEO David Glass, "We believe nothing constructive happens in Bentonville (the company's headquarters). Our grass-roots philosophy is that the best ideas come from people on the firing line."

Similarly, Bill O'Brien of the Hanover Insurance Companies promotes the values of openness and localness. Within Hanover, information is widely disseminated. In Bill O'Brien's words: "My reports to the board, for instance, go right down into the middle management of our branches. They are available to anyone."[10] Localness means that a decision is made or an action taken at the lowest level of the organization that is competent to do so. Interference by higher levels is inappropriate and demoralizing according to this Hanover value.

What do unethical charismatics do in contrast? They are one-way communicators, close-minded to input and suggestions from others. For a time, Ken Olsen at Digital Equipment Corporation created a culture that completely discouraged a reexamination of old strategies. Telling the founder of a successful organization that the nature of the game had changed and that his vision must be updated was very difficult. How do you tell the creator to reevaluate his creation, particularly when you have a very strong and outspoken leader? Many of his key advisers avoided discussions about changes that were necessary to Digital's

marketing strategy, because of the negative reaction they anticipated from him.[11]

## Accepting Feedback

Ethical charismatic leaders are realistic in their appraisal of their own abilities and limitations. They learn from criticism, rather than being fearful of it. This requires them to be open to advice and willing to have their initial judgments challenged.

In his discussion of the art of leadership, Max DePree, CEO of Herman Miller, a highly profitable furniture design and manufacturing company, asserts that leaders who are clear about their own beliefs (assumptions about human nature, the role of the organization, and the measurement of performance, for example) have the self-confidence to encourage contrary opinions and can enhance themselves through the strengths of others.

Unethical charismatic leaders have an inflated sense of self-importance, thriving on attention and admiration from others and shunning contrary opinions. Such leaders attract and gravitate towards loyal and uncritical followers. As one former disciple of Michael Milken, the junk bond king, said, "If he walked off the cliff, everyone in that group would have followed him."[12] Successful followers quickly learn to offer the leader information that he or she wants to hear, whether that information is correct or not.

Creating loyal supporters and eliminating dissenters were characteristic of Texas Instruments (TI) President J. Fred Bucy and CEO Mark Shepard, Jr.'s leadership style. Both men turned TI's low-cost policy into a fanatical obsession by building in control mechanisms that completely squashed any opportunity for individual initiative, thought, or innovation. Both were unwilling to have their strategies questioned no matter how disastrous the results. Both were intolerant and intimidating bosses.

Over time, TI employees spent more time telling Shepard and Bucy what they wanted to hear, rather than what was important or even critical to operations. This destructive behavior was exemplified by TI employees who withheld critical information from Bucy and Shepard about the disastrous slump in the home computer division until inventory had piled up in the aisles.[13]

Lee Avery at Montgomery Ward practiced a similar brand of leadership. If anyone was foolish enough to differ with Avery he vowed to throw them out the window. After a major purge of his corporate executives he remarked, "I have never lost anyone I wanted to keep."[14]

## Stimulating Followers Intellectually

Another important characteristic that differentiates ethical and unethical charismatic leaders is the intellectual development of their followers. Unethical charismatic leaders expect and even demand that their decisions be accepted without question. Ethical charismatic leaders encourage their followers to view the world from different perspectives which they themselves may not have previously considered. They ask their followers to question the "tried and true" ways to solving problems by reevaluating the assumptions they used to understand and analyze the problem. As one leader commented: "You want the best creativity, the best ideas to give you the biggest success."

## Developing Followers

Ethical and unethical charismatic leaders differ in the strategies they use to develop followers. Unethical charismatic leaders are insensitive and unresponsive to followers' needs and aspirations, while ethical charismatic leaders focus on developing people with whom they interact to higher levels of ability, motivation, and morality. "I enjoy developing people from the standpoint of seeing more potential in them than they see in themselves. I try to bring that potential out in people," said one leader in our study. They also express confidence in followers' capabilities to achieve the vision. And when the vision is met, ethical charismatic leaders share recognition with others. "I'd rather transfer the recognition to my people and make them feel that it's their project, it's their contribution, and it's their result," stated one leader. According to another leader: "You certainly share the center of applause. You make sure you share as much of the success and excitement as you can."

## Moral Standards

Charismatic leaders differ widely in their moral standards which influences their decisions of what's right or wrong. Ethical charismatic leaders follow self-guided principles which may go against the majority opinion. Such leaders are not swayed by popular opinion unless it is in line with their principles. They promote a vision that inspires followers to accomplish objectives that are constructive for both the organization and society. Their vision is driven by "doing what's right" as opposed to "doing the right thing." Through the personal values they espouse, ethical charismatic leaders develop the moral principles, standards, and conduct of their followers.[15]

Ethical charismatic leaders possess three primary virtues: courage, a sense of fairness or justice, and integrity. Courage enables leaders to assume reasonable risks. When they believe something is wrong they speak up. Considering and balancing stakeholder claims underlies the virtue of justice. Just leaders respect others' rights and interests and honor principles. Leaders with strong integrity are characterized by internal consistency, acting in concert with their values and beliefs.

Jeff Furnam, chief financial officer of Ben and Jerry's Ice Cream, described Ben and Jerry as leaders who were using their success in business to show other leaders that they could maximize profit, while still having a positive social impact on society. Their attempt to get other U.S. companies to donate pretax profits for social programs is just one example of their overall strategy to create a higher moral standard for other business leaders to follow.

Integrity is a key value at Herman Miller. While executives at other companies were preoccupied with "looking out for number one" by arranging golden parachutes for themselves, in 1986 Herman Miller introduced silver parachutes for all its employees with more than two years of service.[16] In the event of a hostile takeover of Herman Miller that led to termination of employment, the silver parachute plan would offer a soft landing for employees whose welfare is often ignored in corporations.

Adherence to ethical principles is also accorded a high profile at Johnson & Johnson.[17] CEO Ralph

Larsen enjoys telling employees at Johnson & Johnson about his days as a trainee in one of the company's baby shampoo factories. He recalls attending a management meeting where a great debate ensued about whether to ship a large batch of shampoo that was safe but did not meet Johnson & Johnson's "no tears" standard. The ultimate decision was to absorb the loss. Similarly, in the tragic Tylenol case in which eight people died by swallowing poisoned capsules, the product was quickly recalled, mistakes were admitted, and the company lost $240 million in earnings. Says Larsen: "If we keep trying to do what's right, at the end of the day we believe the marketplace will reward us."

Behind these ethical decisions at Johnson & Johnson lies the Credo, a forty-four year old statement created by Robert Wood Johnson, son of the founder. The Credo emphasizes honesty, integrity, and respect for people—phrases common to most such statements. The difference is that senior executives at Johnson & Johnson devote considerable time and energy to ensuring that employees live by those words. Every few years, senior managers gather to debate the Credo's contents, a process used to keep ideas current. On his tours Larsen always mentions the document. "I tell employees they have to be prepared to take the short hit, in the end they'll prosper." In symbol and deeds the ethical standards of the leader and company are clearly articulated.

Unethical charismatic leaders follow standards if they satisfy their immediate self-interests. They are adept at managing an impression that what they are doing conforms to what others consider "the right thing to do." By applying their enormous skills of communication, they can manipulate others to support their personal agenda.

A striking example of the values espoused by unethical charismatic leaders is Ross Johnson, the former chief executive officer and president of RJR Nabisco.[18] Over his career, Johnson gained the reputation as a glib, self-serving, "win at all costs" executive with "a patina of charisma." He would fire executives with no remorse, especially those who fell from his favor. Responsible for scattering one of America's largest, most venerable corporations to the winds through a massive leveraged buyout, Johnson was renown for his notoriously

bloated expense accounts and lavish perks. He failed to investigate, and even protected, flagrant violations of spending by senior company executives. In one instance, he condoned payments from the company's international operations to a dummy corporation, which appeared to be billing the company for thousands of dollars of a senior executive's personal expenses. Johnson's reaction was to fire the people who uncovered the unethical activities and to promote the executive to president, despite an internal investigation which revealed that the executive had exercised poor judgment.

In this section, we have examined how two very different leaders who have been labeled charismatic can differ markedly in their use of power, creation of visions, communication style, tolerance of opposing views, sensitivity to the needs of others, and moral standards. We now discuss how the distinctive qualities of ethical and unethical charismatic leaders impact on followers.

### *The Impact of Charismatic Leaders: Developing or Enslaving Followers?*

The double-edged sword of charismatic leadership is readily seen in the impact on followers. Ethical charismatic leaders convert followers into leaders. By expressing confidence in followers' abilities to accomplish collective goals, and by encouraging followers to think on their own and to question the established ways of doing things, they create followers who are more capable of leading themselves. According to Max DePree, this is the essence of leadership: "liberating people to do what is required of them in the most effective and humane way possible."[19] Followers feel independent, confident, powerful, and capable. They eventually take responsibility for their own actions, gain rewards through self-reinforcement, and like their leader, establish a set of internal standards to guide their actions and behavior.[20]

The magnitude of impact that charismatic leaders can have on followers was shown many years after the death of Walt Disney. Almost two decades after his death, managers would continually quote Disney to justify their decisions. Disney's strategy and policies were seen as unalterable and God help anyone who tried to change them![21]

Unethical charismatic leaders select or produce obedient, dependent, and compliant followers. They undermine followers' motivation and ability to challenge existing views, to engage in self-development, and to develop independent perspectives. Ultimately, followers' self-worth becomes inextricably linked to supporting the achievement of the leader's vision. . . . Since the leader is the moral standard bearer, followers can rationalize even the most destructive actions and behaviors. Michael Milken is a recent example of an unethical charismatic leader who abused power. Milken was terribly arrogant. He rarely had the patience to listen to other viewpoints. As one Drexel executive declared, "What he wanted was bodies—but loyal bodies. Disciples."[22]

The impact of charismatic leaders on followers is often more extreme during periods of crisis. For the unethical charismatic leader, a crisis situation is often ripe for gaining or solidifying his or her power base. This power base can then be used to secure the leader's personal vision and to minimize dissent among followers. Followers easily become dependent on the leader who provides a clear action plan to pursue. "So strong is the belief in the leader's charismatic powers that the followers place their destinies in his or her hands. It is as if they have fallen under a magical spell; they become submissive, obedient, enraptured, and blind in their absolute loyalty."[23] The leader's authority over them seems boundless.

After the crisis subsides, followers increasingly rely on the leader for direction. Over time, they lose their self-confidence to question the leader's thinking and decisions, magnifying their dependence on the leader.

Followers of the ethical charismatic leader enter crises with a greater willingness to analyze the problem and offer solutions to the leader. The ethical charismatic leader works assiduously to develop followers' self-esteem, so that during a crisis followers are able to offer counsel to the leader to help resolve problems. They provide the needed checks and balances concerning the leader's decisions. Since followers have trust and faith in their leader, they will rally behind the

leader's decision when there is no longer time to deliberate. Crises are not used by ethical charismatic leaders to blame followers for their inadequacies. Rather, crises are used to develop strength and a sense of purpose in the mission and vision. Crises often underscore the leader's intention to do what's right.

Ethical charismatic leaders use the crisis as a learning experience, once the crisis has passed. They point to the need for followers to develop their own capabilities so that future crises can be avoided, dealt with more effectively, or handled by followers themselves, when the leader is unavailable.

## The Failure of Success

First suggested by Camille Cavour, then articulated by Lord Acton, absolute power corrupts absolutely. The trap that awaits charismatic leaders who have a successful track record partially lies in the accolades that accompany their accomplishments. If they readily believe the praises heaped upon them, they can be seduced by delusions of invincibility and greatness. Rather than focusing on the next challenge, they become preoccupied with maintaining an aura of greatness. Image management replaces active, meaningful contribution to the organization.

Ethical charismatic leaders have developed a value system that will help avoid the trappings of success. Moreover, the promotion of followers to higher stages of development provides the ethical charismatic leader with critical input that may keep them from straying down the wrong path.

Don Burr, founder, president, and CEO of the now defunct People Express Airline, exemplifies a recent example of the corruptive influence of success.[24] During the airline's formative years, Burr was heralded as an invincible charismatic leader. His accomplishments were widely praised in boardrooms, in the airline industry, and the management press. Touted as an entrepreneurial legend, Burr brought his company from a standing start in 1981 to $1 billion in revenues by 1984. The rapid growth was largely attributed to Burr's innovative management policies, hinging on employees being major stockholders in the company, opportunities for personal and professional growth through continuing education, cross-utilization and job rotation, promotion from within the company, security of lifetime employment, and compensation higher than other companies paid for similar skills and experience. However, after achieving their market niche, rather than nurturing the growth of People Express, Burr went on a spending spree, acquiring other airlines. As the airline's growth failed to keep up with Burr's rapid expansion of routes and schedules, he shifted his consultative leadership style to an executive who fired anyone who challenged his views. Burr became a masterful manipulator and dictator, unreceptive to criticism or challenges. Employees lost their sense of family and gained a sense of alienation. Key management people left the company and fear pervaded the organization, ultimately resulting in its demise.

It is unclear whether Don Burr had the seeds of unethical charismatic leadership, or if he changed as a consequence of the crisis confronting his organization. What is apparent from this example is that he failed to take advantage of followers' input and the input of others outside the organization during a critical stage in the company's life cycle, unfortunately resulting in its demise.

A charismatic leader from our interview study, who had established a highly successful track record, was also keenly aware of the corruption of multiple successes. He was determined to avoid it.

> Over the course of my career I've become more concerned with getting my people to buy-in and let them have a large piece of success than I might have done as a young Turk. You use less brute strength and more intelligence. But then that's just a function of living. You have to stay humble. If you think what you are doing today is important, all you have to do is put it in context of how it will be in 500 million years. I keep a "humble-izer" in my pocket—an arcopod— little sea urchin that lived in Arcona that's 500 million years old. It reminds me to stay humble.

Thomas J. Watson, Sr. was keenly aware of the trap of success as exemplified in a speech delivered to a group of IBM managers in Paris during the height of the Great Depression.[25] "People often speak to me about our successful business. I always correct them. We have not made a success, but I do feel IBM is succeeding. We want you to also feel that you have not succeeded. We want you to feel that you are aiming for success but you are never going to catch up with it, for if you do, you are finished." Perhaps, the key distinction is to encourage all members of the organization to think more about what they can do to continuously improve the organization, always questioning the reasons for success. Leaders who fear changes might disrupt their strategies used to achieve success, are showing the early sign of leadership paralysis. Often such leaders abuse their power in the spirit of maintaining the status quo.

### Creating and Maintaining Ethical Charismatic Leadership

> Beware charisma! . . . But to beware does not necessarily mean or entail "Avoid!" . . . Be aware! Then choose.[26]

"As a transforming force, charisma is charged with explosive, unpredictable potential that, like the genie when released from the bottle, is beyond our control."[27] Executives and managers need to be aware of the risks of unleashing its darker side as well as the promises of cultivating its brighter side. Without awareness of the key behaviors, moral standards, and effects distinguishing ethical and unethical charismatic leaders, appointing a charismatic to a leadership position can be dangerous. The attributes which contribute to the unethical charismatic leader's success in aggressively ascending the corporate ladder may contribute to his or her ultimate failure as a leader.

How can the risks associated with charismatic leadership be diminished and the promises be enhanced? Clearly, managers and executives need to carefully select and promote their charismatic leaders. While the bright charismatic stars can be readily identified in organizations, should they be promoted to senior positions? We believe that the acid test for promotion is whether the candidate meets each of the key ethical charismatic behaviors outlined in Exhibit 1. If the candidate fails to meet any of these dimensions, he or she should not be promoted.

More generally, given the importance of ethical charismatic leaders for developing future leadership potential within organizations, how can ethical charismatic leaders themselves be created and sustained in organizations? What kinds of organizational policies, procedures, and processes can increase ethical charismatic leaders' probability of emergence and ultimate success? To answer these questions we asked our ethical charismatic leaders what top management needs to do to support their behavior. Six key factors were identified.

- Top management commitment to a clearly stated code of ethical conduct that is continually enforced helps establish acceptable standards or boundaries for employee conduct.[28]
- Recruiting, selecting, and promoting managers with high moral standards are ways of creating a culture of ethical responsibility.
- Developing performance standards and rewards that emphasize, for example, respect for people as individuals.
- Providing leaders with education and training that teaches them how to integrate diverse points of view. Being able to see the interrelationships among new perspectives and old lies at the source of moral development.[29]
- Training individuals with the necessary personality characteristics, social skills, and motivation to acquire ethical charismatic leader behaviors.[30] Training in ethical leadership skills must be consistent with the philosophy of the top leadership in the company and the company culture.
- Identifying heroes or heroines who exemplify high moral conduct. Such heroes or heroines need to be heralded by top management as essential to the long-term success of the organization.[31]

In conclusion, building internal ethical standards in leaders is a challenging undertaking which requires formal codes of ethical conduct, top management who subscribe to and practice ethical behavior, systems that reinforce ethical behavior, and role models who exemplify high moral standards. In fact, our ethical charismatic leaders reported that

the most significant factor influencing their development of values and priorities was role models with whom they had very direct personal contact.

## A Look Towards the Future

Ethical charismatic leaders in the end deserve this label only if they create transformations in their organizations so that members are motivated to follow them and to seek organization objectives not simply because they are ordered to do so, and not merely because they calculate that such compliance is in their self-interest, but because they voluntarily identify with the organization, its standards of conduct and willingly seek to fulfill its purpose.[32]

In the period of time that we currently operate, and with the values of employees entering our organizations today, the successful organization will be a place where individual needs are recognized and enhanced rather than brought into conformity with the old ways of doing things.[33] Leaders will know that the best form of leadership builds followers into leaders who eventually take responsibility for their own ethical behavior, development, and performance.

## Notes

1. Quote from W. Kiechel III, "Wanted: Corporate Leaders," *Fortune,* May 30, 1983, 135.

2. For nontechnical reading about charismatic leadership, the following are suggested: B. M. Bass's *Leadership and Performance Beyond Expectations* (New York: Free Press, 1985); and "Leadership: Good, Better, Best," *Organizational Dynamics,* 1985; W. G. Bennis and B. Nanus's *Leaders: The Strategies for Taking Charge* (New York: Harper & Row, 1985); J. M. Kouzes and B. Z. Posner's *The Leadership Challenge: How to Get Extraordinary Things Done in Organizations* (San Francisco: Jossey-Bass, 1987). Early writings on charisma include M. Weber, *The Theory of Social and Economic Organizations* (R. A. Henderson and T. Parsons, Trans.), (New York: Free Press, 1947); P. Selznick, *Leadership in Administration* (Evanston: Row, Peterson, 1957); and A. Etzioni, *A Comparative Analysis of Complex Organizations* (New York: Free Press). More recent literature on charismatic leadership in organizations includes a chapter by R. J. House, "A 1976 Theory of Charismatic Leadership" in *Leadership: The Cutting Edge,*

edited by J. G. Hunt & L. L. Larson (Carbondale, IL: Southern Illinois University Press, 1977), 189-204, which traces the historical significance of the topic as well as describes the personality characteristics, behaviors, and effects of such leaders.

3. For more on charismatic leadership that is prosocial or antisocial, see J. M. Howell's "Two Faces of Charisma: Socialized and Personalized Leadership in Organizations" in *Charismatic Leadership: The Elusive Factor in Organizational Effectiveness* (San Francisco: Jossey-Bass, 1988), edited by J. A. Conger and R. N. Kanungo; B. M. Bass "The Two Faces of Charismatic Leadership," *Leaders Magazine*, 12, 4, 44-45; R. J. House, J. M. Howell, B. Shamir, B. J. Smith, and W. D. Spangler's "Charismatic Leadership: A 1990 Theory and Five Empirical Tests," Unpublished Manuscript, The Wharton School, University of Pennsylvania; and J. M. Howell and R. J. House's "Socialized and Personalized Charisma: An Essay on the Bright and Dark Sides of Leadership," Unpublished manuscript, School of Business Administration, University of Western Ontario.

4. For more information about the method and findings of this study, see J. M. Howell and C. A. Higgins, "Champions of Technological Innovation," *Administrative Science Quarterly*, 1990, 35, 317-341.

5. In their recent book *Good Management: Business Ethics in Action* (Toronto, Prentice Hall, 1991), F. Bird and J. Gandz discuss in detail ethical leadership.

6. Quote from J. E. Liebig, *Business Ethics: Profiles in Civic Virtue* (Golden, CO: Fulcrum, 1990), 174.

7. Quote from M. DePree, *Leadership Is an Art* (New York: Dell, 1989), 68.

8. Quote from J. E. Liebig, *Business Ethics: Profiles in Civic Virtue*, 134-135.

9. The description of the excellent quality of management at Wal-Mart Stores is drawn from S. Smith, "Leaders of the Most Admired," *Fortune*, January 29, 1990, 46.

10. Quote from J. E. Liebig, *Business Ethics: Profiles in Civic Virtue*, 136.

11. For a discussion of controlling leadership see D. Miller, *The Icarus Paradox: How Exceptional Companies Brag About Their Own Downfall* (New York: HarperBusiness, 1990).

12. For more information on Milken's life, refer to *The Predator's Ball* by Connie Bruck.

13. For a review of Texas Instruments' downward slide, refer to Brian O'Reilly, "Texas Instruments: New Boss, Big Job," *Fortune*, July 8, 1985.

14. For a discussion of Lee Avery's leadership style, see D. Miller, *The Icarus Paradox: How Exceptional Companies Brag About Their Own Downfall* (New York: HarperBusiness, 1990).

15. For more on values and ethics of leaders, see K. Andrews, "Ethics in Practice," *Harvard Business Review*, September-October 1989, 99-104, and F. Bird and J. Gandz, *Good Management: Business Ethics in Action* (Toronto, Prentice Hall, 1991).

16. See M. DePree, *Leadership Is an Art* (New York, Dell, 1989), xviii.

17. The description of the outstanding corporate citizenship of Johnson & Johnson is drawn from B. Dumaine, "Leaders of the Most Admired," *Fortune*, January 29, 1990, 50, 54.

18. The best-selling book *Barbarians at the Gate* by B. Burrough and J. Helyar (New York: Harper & Row, 1990) documents the fight to control RJR Nabisco and the central role played by CEO Ross Johnson.

19. Quote from M. DePree, *Leadership Is an Art*, 1.

20. For more information on the impact of leadership on follower development, refer to B. J. Avolio and T. Gibbons, "Developing Transformational Leaders: A Lifespan Approach" in *Charismatic Leadership: The Elusive Factor in Organizational Effectiveness*, edited by I. A. Conger and R. N. Kanungo (San Francisco: Jossey-Bass, 1988).

21. See I. Ross, "Disney Gambles on Tomorrow," *Fortune*, October 4, 1982.

22. See *The Predator's Ball* by Connie Bruck for further details about Michael Milken.

23. Quote from N. C. Roberts and R. T. Bradley's "Limits of Charisma" in *Charismatic Leadership: The Elusive Factor in Organizational Effectiveness* (San Francisco: Jossey-Bass, 1988), edited by J. A. Conger and R. N. Kanungo.

24. Accounts tracing the rise and fall of Donald Burr's People Express Airline include J. A. Byrne, "Up, Up and Away?" *Business Week*, November 25, 1985, 80-94; J. R. Norman, "People Is Plunging, but Burr Is Staying Cool," *Business Week*, July Academy of Management Executive 7, 1986, 31-32; E. M. Garrett, "The Troops Are Restless at People Express," *Venture*, 1986, 8, 102-104.

25. Quote was taken from a speech delivered by Thomas J. Watson, Sr. on July 29, 1930 entitled, "Growing Man" in *As a Man Thinks*, by Thomas J. Watson, Sr.

26. Quote from C. Hodgkinson, *The Philosophy of Leadership* (New York: St. Martin's Press, 1983), 187.

27. Quote from N. C. Roberts and R. T. Bradley's "Limits of Charisma," 273.

28. The value of an organizational ethics policy for reducing unethical decision behavior was reported by W. H. Hegarty and H. P. Sims, Jr., "Organizational Philosophy, Policies, and Objectives Related to Unethical Decision Behavior: A Laboratory Experiment," *Journal of Applied Psychology*, 1979, 64, 331-338.

29. Ways of enhancing ethical decision making in organizations are discussed by L. K. Trevino, "Ethical Decision Making in Organizations: A Person-Situation Interactionist Model," *Academy of Management Review*, 1986, 11, 601-617. The impact of education and training on moral development is discussed by G. D. Baxter and C. A. Rarick, "Education for the Moral Development of Managers: Kohlberg's Stages of Moral Development and Integrative Education," *Journal of Business Ethics*, 1987, 6, 243-248.

30. Charismatic leadership training and its related caveats are described in J. M. Howell and P. B. Frost's "A Laboratory Study of Charismatic Leadership," *Organizational Behavior and Human Decision Processes*, 1989, and in B. M. Bass and B. J. Avolio's "OD and Transformational Leadership: Organizational and Individual Applications" in *Research in Organiza-*

*tional Change and Development,* edited by R. W. Woodman and R. Passmore (Greenwich: JAI Press, 1990).

31. W. A. Kahn, "Toward an Agenda for Business Ethics Research," *Academy of Management Review,* 1990, 15, 311-328.

32. See F. Bird and J. Gandz, *Good Management: Business Ethics in Action* (Toronto: Prentice Hall, 1991), 166.

33. A discussion of future organizations and their workforce was reported by L. R. Offermann and M. K. Gowing, "Organizations of the Future: Challenges and Changes," *American Psychologist,* 1990, 45, 95-108.

# IV

# *Leader–Participant Relationships in Organizations*

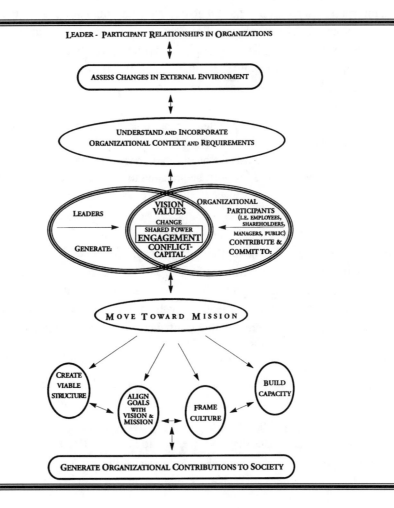

The focus of this section is on relationships between leaders and participants internally and relationships with external stakeholders including customers and public sector service recipients. Diligent attention to the quality and integrity of these relationships constitutes the core of leadership in organizations. The nature of these relationships is changing significantly as organizations encompass more knowledge workers, move to flatter structures, and change the distribution of power.

### *Internal Relationships*

Leadership in an organization requires leaders and participants to play different but equal roles.[1] Leaders often generate or initiate critical factors such as vision, values, and change, or they create the environment for leaders and participants to generate these factors jointly. Consequently, leaders and participants in new-era organizations are involved in interpersonal relationships that go beyond traditional notions of boss-employee roles.

Leader–participant relationships necessitate tremendous mutual reliance and shared responsibility. Today's issues, people, information requirements, and problems are far too complex for one or a few individuals to fully comprehend and influence. In his book *On Leadership,* John Gardner commented:

> Most leadership today is an attempt to accomplish purposes through (or in spite of) large, intricately organized systems. There is no possibility that centralized authority can call all the shots in such systems, whether the system is a corporation or a nation. Individuals in all segments and at all levels must be prepared to exercise leaderlike initiative and responsibility, using their local knowledge to solve problems at their level.[2]

Beyond the appointed leadership positions throughout organizations, there are individuals without formal authority who *share leadership* tasks, by behaving responsibly with respect to the purpose of the group.[3] The challenge for new-era organizations is to create and sustain organizational settings that facilitate this form of leadership.

Robert Kelley describes leadership from the perspective of exemplary followers. He identifies several elements that contribute to strong leader–participant interactions and exceptional outcomes:

- Partnership—embracing exemplary followers as partners or cocreators;
- Cocreation of the vision and mission;
- Shared risks and rewards;
- Demonstrated value that leaders add to followers' productivity;
- Creation of environments where exemplary followers flourish; and
- Development of heroes among followers.

Ann Howard focuses on the role of *empowerment* in leadership. She contends that "empowerment fits a sleeker organization—one built for the speed, flexibility, quality, and service that are essential for global competition." The new organization demands that all participants take on more responsibility and authority. To prepare participants for these new responsibilities and support their accomplishments, the leader's role is transformed from its traditional focus on authority and control to delegator, visionary, change agent, inspirer, model of trust, supporter, champion, coach, team builder, facilitator, and partner.

Much of the new perspective on leader–participant relationships is embodied in the concept of organizational teams. Manz and Sims contend that bosses are becoming corporate dinosaurs. Teams have replaced the traditional roles of bosses by assuming responsibility and accountability through self-leadership. Team members complete whole projects, processes, and services by designing their own approaches and making their own decisions about how work is accomplished. This shift changes leader–participant interactions from a dependent relationship to one that is mutually reliant and interconnected.

The processes described by these authors require significant contributions from leaders and participants to be successful. Figure IV.1 identifies each party's contributions to vision, mission, values, power sharing, growth and development, enhancement of competence and self-esteem, trust, and credibility to attain exceptional outcomes for leaders, participants, and the organization.

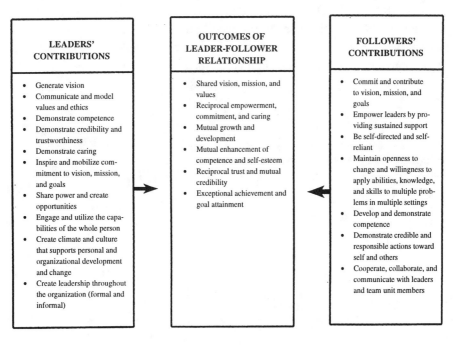

**Figure IV.1.** Leader-Follower Relationship in Organizations

### *External Relationships—Customers and Citizens*

The final two chapters in this section focus on leader–participant relationships with external participants—customers and citizens. These groups are the ultimate focus of organizational efforts and thus are important partners in the leadership process. Hammer and Champy explain that competition and an information-rich world have created tremendous choices of services and products for customers. Relationships between organizational participants and customers are not only more equalized, but they are also more individualized and personal. The customer's wants and needs are being incorporated into the organization's purposes, processes, and actions.

Public sector organizations have also adopted the language and practice of focusing on customers. Patricia Patterson cautions that citizens, as recipients of public services, are not equivalent to customers. She asserts that analogies to business and efforts toward reinvention "unnecessarily marginalize citizenship, followership, and citizens themselves." Because public leaders are not entrepreneurs and citizens cannot always take their business elsewhere, citizens may become resistant followers who act aggressively to gain attention to their needs. Patterson advises that public sector leaders might pay attention to the actions of such citizens and begin to harness their energies and engage their critical thinking to identify problems and develop solutions.

Given these internal and external relationships, leaders and participants are in an era of transition where leaders have to redefine themselves as visionaries, team builders, and coaches while participants become empowered, self-managed, and committed. The arrival of telecommuting, virtual organizations, and globalization has added to the complexity of these role changes and redefinitions. The major challenge for organizations is to determine how leaders and participants can develop and maintain the kinds of relationships that the authors in this section describe.

### *Notes*

1. See Robert Kelley, "In Praise of Followers," *Harvard Business Review,* 1988, Vol. 88, No. 6, pp. 142-148.
2. See John Gardner, *On Leadership* (New York: Free Press, 1990), p. xiii.
3. Ibid.

# 18

# Tyrannosaurus Rex

## The Boss as Corporate Dinosaur

CHARLES C. MANZ
HENRY P. SIMS, JR.

> In a hierarchical organization, bosses don't do much. . . . They just preside and take all the credit. It's criminal. A lot of good . . . people are buried down there, and their bosses are happy to keep them buried.[1]
>
> *Michael H. Walsh, CEO, Tenneco Corp.*

Down with bosses! Up with teams! is the new battle cry of many of the world's leading organizations in which the traditional role of the manager is under siege. Bosses limit, control, and too often waste the potential of employees; teams, in contrast, unleash it. This book is about how teams conduct business without bosses, a dramatic new revolution in which the traditional role of managers—bosses—is being redefined or even eliminated. We show how teams have replaced bosses in many leading companies and have been successful in producing a new competitiveness. Today's competitive environment de-mands intense improvement in productivity, quality, and response time. Teams can deliver this improvement. Bosses can't.

For years, bosses have been leading players in business around the world. They lead through a control system designed to limit employees' room for error. Bosses occupy central roles and are awarded powerful status. Bosses have been the kings and, more recently, queens of their workplace kingdoms. But just as dinosaurs once ruled the earth and later faded into extinction, the days of bosses may be numbered. They simply don't fit the current business environment of intense international competition, more demanding employees, and complex organizational environments.

*Business Without Bosses* examines the unique nature of the way teams have emerged over the past dozen years. Certainly teams can function quite well under the thumb of a strong-minded leader. We think of Mike Ditka, former coach of the Chicago Bears, as an example of a boss who demanded compliance and obedience from his players. By many standards, he was an effective leader, and his team did win a Super Bowl championship. But the way teams have emerged in the business sector is not like the Ditka teams. Teams have leaders but generally not bosses in the traditional sense.

Teams have evolved into a uniquely American style of participative management, but they can be successfully applied around the world. Teams don't need bosses, at least the old type of boss. They develop the capacity for managing and leading themselves. They furnish the initiative, the sense of responsibility, the creativity, and the problem solving from within. When they live up to these ideals, teams are uniquely self-reliant. They don't need a boss.

When we use the word *boss*, we typically mean an individual who influences subordinate employees through such leader behaviors as command, instruction, and top-down goal assignments, frequently accompanied by a healthy dose of reprimand and intimidation—A "do it my way or else!" approach. Bosses can generate compliance, especially in the short term. They have a tendency to create "yes persons" who are willing to comply but lack initiative and creativity. With a boss, the locus of innovation is always top down. Subordinate employees seldom venture forth with their own creative ideas. Their mental powers are centered on trying to say and do as the boss wishes.

In the new wave sweeping across the country, many bosses are being swept away or converted by this powerful force. In their place are teams of employees who serve as their own managers— their own bosses. This new organizational form goes by many labels: self-managing teams, self-directing teams, autonomous and semiautonomous work groups, empowered teams, and many others. We call the really effective ones self-managing

SuperTeams because they produce remarkable quality, productivity, innovation, and just plain good business, and they do it without bosses. In our previous book, *SuperLeadership,* we described SuperLeaders, who lead others to lead themselves to high performance. Empowerment, especially team empowerment, is central to creating effective self-leadership. We see effective self-managing teams as an integral part of the philosophy of SuperLeadership. Indeed we view them as SuperTeams.

Teams don't have bosses, but they do have leaders. No successful team is without leadership. Team leadership positions are sometimes emergent (elected) and sometimes appointed. They frequently have new names, like "coordinator," "facilitator," "coach," and even "team leader." This new form of leadership also demands a new set of behaviors, which we are only beginning to understand from the emerging research. For example, effective team leaders encourage their team to set their own goals and solve their own problems. Being a "boss" is not part of the behavioral repertoire.

If you are currently part of a company where management is resisting the trend and bosses refuse to stop bossing, consider this: Great, powerful, and apparently invulnerable dinosaurs once roamed the earth, seemingly invulnerable to extinction, but they did not evolve and now they no longer live and breathe. We believe the time has come when bosses need to evolve into something else. Our previous book called this "something else" a SuperLeader—one who leads others to lead themselves. SuperLeaders create SuperTeams where everyone on the team is important and makes a significant contribution. In this book, we provide a window to see how several organizations have created SuperTeams to pursue the tremendous competitive advantages of doing business without bosses. If the bosses of your organization don't make this evolution, your business, and with it your job, may be the next to go the way of the dinosaur.

### *Let's Get Realistic:*
### *Teams Are Not Always Super Teams!*

Although we are unabashed advocates, we hope we don't see the world of teams through rose-colored glasses. The stories in this book present a realistic view. Certainly we extol the virtues of teams, but we also bring forward the troubles, the problems, the issues, and the challenges that frequently accompany team implementation. In other words, we also describe the bumps and "warts." Our idealism and philosophy are tempered by a good dose of realism.

Thus, not all the teams described in this book are truly SuperTeams, those that control their own decision making, are generally self-managing, and are effective and successful. In fact, some of the teams examined in this book may seem ordinary or are struggling and experiencing frustration. But in the end, our aim and our hope is to provide a learning opportunity that draws on both success and failure so that readers will be further down the road toward creating their own SuperTeams.

### *What Is a Team? What Do Teams Do?*

Work designs based on self-management tend to give employees a high degree of autonomy and control over their immediate behavior. Teams are one type of the many forms of employee participation that have been developed in the United States. These include organizational approaches such as the following:

- Suggestion boxes
- Employee surveys
- Job enrichment
- Quality circles
- Gainsharing
- Self-managed teams
- Integrated high-involvement cultures

Clearly, there is considerable distance between a rather superficial participative approach like suggestion boxes and a completely integrated high-involvement culture that cuts across all levels of the organization. Self-managing teams fall near the sophisticated end of this continuum and, in fact, are a rather fundamental change from the traditional organization.

Typically, the employees organized into teams complete a whole or distinct part of a product or service. They make decisions on a wide range of issues, often including such traditional management prerogatives as who will perform which task, solving quality problems, settling conflicts between members on the team, and selecting team leaders. Following are some typical team responsibilities:

- Self-timekeeping
- Analyzing quality problems
- Assigning jobs
- Training team members
- Redesigning production processes
- Setting team goals
- Assessing internal performance
- Electing internal team leader
- Testing for competency
- Recording quality
- Maintaining in-process inventory control
- Solving technical problems
- Adjusting production schedules
- Resolving internal conflicts
- Preparing annual budgets
- Intrateam liaison
- Selecting team members

Team designs vary so much across companies that it's difficult to find one commonly accepted definition of the team approach. It seems to be more of an overall philosophy and approach to work design than a tightly defined set of rules. In fact, part of the essence of the team approach is to encourage each set of employees to find their own way, their own kind of self-managing team that best fits their own situation and team members. Most of all, the team approach is an attempt to utilize more fully the organization's human resources at all levels of the organization.

A typical objective of a work team is to improve productivity for the organization and the quality of working life for employees. Sometimes the dignity and freedom workers receive is especially publicized, but the drive toward productivity and competitiveness is always a constant theme.

Richard Hackman at Harvard University has described teams as having a distinct, recognizable task that workers can identify with (e.g., be able to service all of a mutual fund's customer's needs); members with a variety of skills related to the group task, discretion over issues such as how the work is done, scheduling the work, and assigning tasks; and compensation and performance feedback for the group as a whole.

The early days of the team system were heavily influenced by a concept known as sociotechnical systems (STS) theory, which emphasizes the need to optimize both the social and technical aspects of work. Typically, an STS analysis results in a shift to performing work in groups; technology and people are matched together in clusters, sometimes known as autonomous work groups (teams). The main rationale is that teams can more effectively apply resources to deal with the total variance (changes and unpredictable events) in work conditions than can individuals acting on their own. Today, the formal analysis techniques of STS are found less frequently, but the philosophy of matching the technical system and the social system remains and is an important part of successful team design.

## No, It's Not Japanese Management

The team concept we describe has emerged as a distinctly Western phenomenon (teams have been used in the United States, Canada, Europe, and Mexico), although it's frequently confused with so-called Japanese management. Both are often associated with the idea of participatory management, but each approach is targeted at a quite different population, with distinct cultural values. In our attempts to understand the team system, we have traveled to Japan and read extensively about Japanese management systems. Our main conclusion is that the West would be better served by attempting to learn from successful experiences with our own self-managing teams rather than looking to the Japanese for innovative organizational philosophies. The rationale and early successes with team designs originated in the United States and Europe and better fit Western cultures,

although they can be successfully applied around the world.

Most of all, the team concept is beginning to show proven worth for improving productivity, quality, and employee quality of work life, among other payoffs. It is an approach that is designed to take advantage of the strengths of Western culture and history. Teams in the United States, for example, take advantage of the individualism and diversity inherent in the culture.

## Why Teams?

We suspect that the notion of teams has reached the stage of the recurring management fads that occasionally sweep the United States. Therefore, some team applications are being undertaken simply because "it's the thing to do," with little thought given to how the approach fits a particular organization, a sure recipe for failure. Nevertheless, there are some solid reasons that teams make good sense:

Increased productivity

Improved quality

Enhanced employee quality of work life

Reduced costs

Reduced turnover and absenteeism

Reduced conflict

Increased innovation

Better organizational adaptability and flexibility

From a management viewpoint, productivity is typically the main reason to implement a team system. Teams are a way to undertake continuous improvement designed to increase productivity. Chapter 2 relates the story of a team-oriented battery plant that can produce its product at a 30 percent savings when compared with battery plants organized in the traditional manner.

Today, teams are often seen as a critical element to a total quality management (TQM) program. The story of the Texas Instruments Malaysia plant that uses teams as the capstone of a TQM program that has resulted in spectacular gains in quality over several years is the subject of Chapter 7.

Sometimes the implementation of teams is motivated by a humanistic ideology. That is, teams are seen as an important way for employees to find satisfaction and dignity in the work—in essence, an enhanced employee quality of work life. Chapter 4 presents evidence of substantially improved work satisfaction that is clearly linked to teams at IDS Financial Corporation.

Teams also typically been reduced conflict between management and labor. Frequently, the number of grievances is substantially reduced subsequent to a successful team implementation. Chapter 8 describes how an entire organization, AES Corporation, uses teams to enhance its adaptability and flexibility, and Chapter 6 tells the story of how W. L. Gore created an entire organizational concept that is directed toward fast-paced innovation.

All of these reasons are important, but as researchers and authors, we believe that issues of productivity and quality—the important elements of competitiveness—are the most important drivers. In the end, the team approach will be adopted only if teams really do work.

Recent years have brought many challenges for Western organizations. Intense international competition, a work force that demands more from work than simply a means for making a living, and the increasing complexity of technical knowledge and information flows have all pressured companies to explore innovative ways of using human resources more effectively. Among the more noteworthy and promising approaches is the concept of self-managing teams.

Traditional approaches to managing human resources have tended to emphasize control from above. Early work system designs tended to treat people as relatively fixed components of a large machine. The bureaucratic form of organization tends to treat people as interchangeable parts rather than unique human resources. Bureaucracy de-emphasizes the full use of human resources in favor of a maintenance of stability and status quo. Unfortunately, maintaining the status quo is incompatible with the innovation required for continuous improvement.

When international competition was not strong and when employees were less demanding of power and fulfillment, top-down control was sufficient for organizational success. Now, however, employees are asking that their work provide them with personal growth, fulfillment, and dignity from their work, and the emergence of the global marketplace has forced organizations to consider new ways of dealing with the competitive challenge.

Human resources are critical for the development and implementation of organizational strategy. Leadership has been elevated to a more significant status. Corporations are beginning to view people as an investment to be nurtured rather than a cost to be minimized. Teams have emerged as a prominent and pragmatic vehicle to enhance competitiveness through people.

### What Do Workers Want?

Each generation is different from previous ones.[2] The generation receiving most attention now is the large group born between the mid-1940s and the 1960s, who grew to maturity during a time of unprecedented prosperity and social turmoil and are variously called the "baby boomers," the "now generation," the "new breed," the "new values worker," and the "'60s kids." As they matured, campus unrest, the controversial Vietnam War, affluence, and societal conditions stimulated a revolution of changing values and mores in the United States. Baby boomers have a set of life and work values that are very different from that of their parents and grandparents. Most of all, they are less tolerant of bosses. They also have lower overall job satisfaction and less desire to lead or manage, move up the organizational hierarchy, and defer to authority. They believe that they are entitled to a "good" job, have a desire to control their own destiny, and have a low absenteeism threshold.[3] Additionally, they have a lower respect for authority and greater desire for self-expression, personal growth, and self-fulfillment. In other words, today's workers are not satisfied to report to work merely for the paycheck. They want something more—and teams can supply it. Teams foster a sense of dignity, self-worth, and greater commitment to achieving the performance that makes an organization competitive.

To complicate matters, an even newer set of workers, frequently described as the "baby busters," is now entering the work force. These employees carry yet another set of values and expectations that are significantly different from those of traditional organizations. They are slower to commit and less loyal to organizations. (It's also true that organizations are less loyal to employees.) They were recently described in this way: "They don't bow to any authority. Younger workers will not respect you just because you're the *boss*. They want to know why they're being asked to do things."[4] They were also described as competitive and as desiring an opportunity to learn and have fun at work.

These characteristics of the new employee generations, when coupled with rises in education and standards of living during this century, pose major challenges for organizations. The new workers' aspirations for self-fulfillment cannot be met by conventional approaches of the past. Teams have a special capacity to answer the needs of the new generation of employees.

This is not a new idea. Over ten years ago *Business Week* concluded that "U.S. industry must reorganize work and its incentives to appeal to new worker values, rather than try to retrofit people to work designs and an industrial relations system of 80 years ago."[5] The newer employees have an especially acute need to be treated as valuable and respected contributors and to be given the opportunity to learn, develop, and influence their work and their organizations. We believe self-managing work teams come closer to hitting the nail on the head in meeting these demands than any other tested work system alternative. They break down the traditional, hierarchical, boss-based system and provide employees with the freedom to grow and gain in respect and dignity. With teams, employees control and manage themselves and really make a difference. The message is simple: If you plan on staying in business into the next century, you had better consider teams. Otherwise, you will find yourself swimming upstream against the waves of change fueled by younger workers.

## Shifting Managerial Philosophy

One dilemma frequently encountered in changing to self-managing teams arises because of the transition needed in managerial thinking and philosophy. Empowering lower levels in the organization can be a very unnerving process for managers, who may perceive it as a threat to their own status and power. In addition, leading self-managing employees calls for new management and leadership perspectives and strategies that often do not seem to come naturally to bosses who cut their own teeth in a traditional hierarchical system. Indeed, the transition to employee self-management can be a troubling process for the managers of the self-managing.

## The Historical Emergence of Teams

Clearly, the notion of teams has had a different impact on the various sectors of our work society. The most extensive experience derives from the manufacturing sector, where this concept was introduced in the 1960s. In the manufacturing sector, it's no longer a question of whether or why to use teams but of fine-tuning to specific sites. The service sector has significantly lagged the manufacturing sector in adoption of teams, but experimentation is well under way. Competitiveness has started to become a hot issue in service, and we expect to see greater intolerance for poor-quality service. The IDS case we report in Chapter 4 is an example of the potential of teams in the service sector. While we still have much to learn, teams in the service sector are likely to be the most exciting applications of the 1990s.

The sector that has used the team approach least is the public/government sector. We do see a few sporadic examples (for example, see Tom Peters's program "Excellence in the Public Sector," shown on PBS). The U.S. Office of Personnel Management seems to be offering preliminary encouragement for experimentation with teams in government, but we expect to see only limited progress in the 1990s unless a major shift away from traditional bureaucratic thinking occurs.

In 1990, Edward Lawler, director of the Center for Organizational Effectiveness at the University of Southern California, estimated that about 7 percent of U.S. companies were currently using some form of self-managing teams.[6] Only a decade earlier, he had estimated in personal conversations to us that about 150 to 250 work sites were using teams. Clearly, the number of companies using teams has grown considerably. We believe that nearly every major U.S. company is currently trying or considering some form of empowered work teams somewhere in their organization. Our own informal estimate is that by the end of the decade, 40 to 50 percent of the U.S. work force may work in some kind of empowered teams. Hundreds of applications have taken place across industries in multiple settings including:

| | |
|---|---|
| pet food plant | coal mines |
| parts manufacturing | auto manufacturing |
| paint manufacturing | supply warehouse |
| paper mills | insurance offices |
| financial offices | government organizations |

The Procter & Gamble Company is generally considered an important U.S. pioneer in applying teams to their operations. Their work began in the early 1960s, although it was not publicized and virtually escaped media attention. P&G saw the team approach as a significant competitive advantage and through the 1980s attempted to deflect attention away from its efforts. The company thought of its knowledge about the team organization as a type of trade secret and required consultants and employees to sign nondisclosure statements. Nevertheless, Procter & Gamble's successes with teams received considerable off-the-record attention from a small group of consultants across the country who were inspired by the P&G success and learned techniques through an informal network. Many of them originally worked at P&G and were attracted away to other companies by lucrative job offers because of their unique knowledge and expertise.

Through the 1970s and 1980s, General Motors Corporation was also a locus of active experimentation with teams and was significantly less secretive than Procter & Gamble. Many of the GM team implementations have been very successful and have served as models for other changes around the country. These experiments ultimately led to the Saturn experiment, currently GM's most successful division.

GM remains an interesting enigma, however; it is a textbook case of how success with teams at one location does not necessarily transfer to another location within a huge corporation. (Further, teams are not the sole answer to the competitiveness challenge.) Diffusing the team concept throughout large corporations has proven to be a considerable challenge. Also, although specific GM manufacturing plants have been on the cutting edge of employee self-management, many analysts would suggest that the corporate level has maintained a more traditional top-down, control-based management mentality.

Other prominent companies have been active with teams, among them Gaines, Cummins Engine, Digital Equipment, Ford, Motorola, Tektronix, General Electric, Honeywell, LTV, Caterpillar, Boeing, Monsanto, AT&T, and Xerox.

We might also note, with some sadness and regret, that on our own turf (academia) the business and psychology professors are largely playing catch-up in their theoretical development and empirical investigations about teams. Companies such as Procter & Gamble and General Motors have been out there doing it, but, until recently, we have noted the absence of self-managing teams in business organizational behavior curricula. The notion of teams is starting to appear in management textbooks, but it seems to us a half-dozen years late. Clearly, we need more attention to teams in our educational institutions in both the research and teaching arenas.

Finally, at the beginning of the 1990s, the topic of teams had reached the front page. *Fortune* magazine featured a cover story, "Who Needs a Boss?"

about teams in the May 7, 1990, issue,[7] and *Business Week* also featured a cover story about teams in their July 10, 1989, issue.[8] Even Dan Rather speaks about "self-directed" teams. In a recent evening news segment he reported that about 7 percent of the major corporations in the United States and Canada are using empowered teams.

Although it's taken some time, teams have clearly reached the stage of becoming a popular "fad" with all the accompanying advantages and disadvantages, but we believe they will pass the test of time and prove to be enduring. We think that teams are here to stay, and that they constitute a fundamental change in the way we go about work. We suspect the label and approach will evolve and perhaps pass—like all so-called fads—but the fundamental ways that teams do business will remain with us for a long time, mainly because teams are effective. Teams may represent a whole new management paradigm. Perhaps they reflect a new business era as influential as the industrial revolution and are destined to revolutionize work for decades to come.

### The Bottom Line: Are Teams Effective?

Evidence that evaluates the effectiveness of self-managing teams can be divided into two categories: qualitative evidence, often reported in the popular press, and more rigorous scientific data, derived from well-designed quantitative research.[9]

*Business Week* claims that teams can increase productivity by 30 percent or more and can also substantially improve quality.[10] Other examples reported in the press include an Alcoa plant in Cleveland, where a production team came up with a method for making forged wheels for vans that increased output 5 percent and cut scrap in half. At Weyerhaeuser, the forest-products company, a team of legal employees significantly reduced the retrieval time for documents. At Federal Express, a thousand clerical workers, divided into teams of five to ten people, helped the company reduce service problems by 13 percent in 1989. At Rubbermaid, a multidisciplinary team from marketing, engineering, and design developed a new product

line in 1987; sales in the first year exceeded projections by 50 percent.[11]

Corning eliminated one management level at its corporate computer center, substituting a team adviser for three shift supervisors and producing $150,000 in annual savings and better service. Perceptions of autonomy and responsibility among workers increased because they felt they experienced more meaningful and productive work.[12] In an insurance firm, change to automation led to a shift from functional organizational design to self-managing teams, requiring redesigned contingencies to support organizational goals. A twenty-four-month follow-up found improved work structure, flows, and outcomes.[13]

Also, throughout this book we describe several organizations that have enjoyed impressive payoffs with teams in both the long and short term. In Chapter 2, for example, we tell the story of a mature General Motors automobile battery plant organized around teams in which company officials reported productivity savings of 30 to 40 percent when compared with traditionally organized plants. In Chapter 3 we tell how teams helped Lake Superior Paper Company enjoy possibly the most successful start-up in the history of the paper industry. In Chapter 1 we describe the very beginning adjustments of management to the team approach that a few short months later was credited with productivity improvements of 10 percent per year, cost savings of 10 to 20 percent of earnings, and customer service quality levels of over 99 percent.

Considerable data indicate the effectiveness of teams. Nevertheless, not all the evidence, especially from more rigorous academic research, is completely supportive. Perhaps the difficulty of evaluating the team concept in terms of any hard scientific data was best expressed by John Miner:

The results are often positive. It is hard to predict whether the outcomes will be greater output, better quality, less absenteeism, reduced turnover, fewer accidents, greater job satisfaction, or what, but the introduction of autonomous work groups is often associated with improvements. It is difficult to understand why a particular outcome such as increased productivity occurs in one study and not in another, and why, on some occasions, nothing improves. Furthermore, what actually causes the changes when they do occur is not known. The approach calls for making so many changes at once that it is almost impossible to judge the value of the individual variables. Increased pay, self-selection of work situations, multiskilling, with its resultant job enrichment and decreased contact with authority almost invariably occurs in autonomous work groups.[14]

In another report, researchers attempted a rigorously scientific review of the effectiveness of the team approach. Despite 1,100 studies conducted in actual organizations, they concluded that "there are not many well-designed studies that evaluate the impact of self-managed groups."[15]

Perhaps the most revealing scientific study of the bottom-line effect of teams is contained in a recent paper from Barry Macy and associates at the Texas Center for Productivity and Quality of Work Life.[16] Their analysis contrasted the success of various changes involving human resources, work structure, and technology—for example, training, reward systems, and work teams. Very strong effects, especially in terms of financial outcomes, were observed with team applications. The Macy study is one of the first rigorous scientific efforts that shows the clear financial effect of the team approach in dozens of organizations.

A vast body of experience lies unreported in the scientific literature. Those close to the self-management movement informally report substantial productivity gains and cost savings that typically range from 30 to 70 percent when compared with traditional systems. Self-managing teams have the potential to exert substantial effects on the bottom line. Perhaps the notion was captured best by Charles Eberle, a former vice-president at Procter & Gamble, who speaks with the advantage of years of practical experience.

At P&G there are well over two decades of comparisons of results—*side by side*—between enlightened work systems and those I call traditional. It is absolutely clear that the new work systems work better—*a lot better*—for example, with 30 to 50 percent lower manufacturing costs. Not only are the tangible, measurable, bottom line indicators such as cost, quality, customer service and reliability better, but also the harder-to-measure attributes such as quickness, deci-

siveness, toughness, and just plain resourcefulness of these organizations.[17]

## Resistance to Teams

A cover story in *Business Week* asked: "The gains in quality are substantial—so why isn't it spreading faster?" Why do companies and employees resist the change to more self-managing teams? There are several philosophical and practical barriers to the ready acceptance of the team concept. Many of these stem from discomfort with the unknown and general resistance to change. Some of the more notable resistances that frequently arise with a change to teams follow.[18]

### Emphasis on Individuality

In the United States, we have a strong political and personal tradition of individual freedom that at times runs counter to the collective nature of teamwork. For both managerial and nonmanagerial employees, an emphasis on team values threatens not only their traditional views of work but their approach to life. Many employees also have difficulty adjusting to the idea of working without a traditional boss or supervisor after so many years of dependence. We recently learned of a case where a large burly production worker, after learning about his company's move to self-managing teams, banged his fist on a table and demanded his right to have a boss to tell him what to do.

### Distrust

With a history of management-induced fads and poor management of industrial relations, some companies have no immediate credibility with first-line employees, especially unionized employees, to earn the trust needed to implement team processes. If management sees team development as an expense rather than an investment and employees see teams as another attempt to co-opt employees to management's views, an attempted shift to team values and work will likely fail. It is not surprising that many stories of successful team efforts have come from threatened companies or industries, where workers and management were forced to confront and discard traditional distrust in favor of teams.

## Lost Employment Opportunities for Middle Management

For managers, a shift to teams and to the corresponding flatter organizations reduces their opportunities for advancement in the traditional organizational hierarchy, if only because there is no longer much of a hierarchy. But certainly there are economic factors, not just a movement of teams, that have threatened the career prospects and aspirations of many managers. Downsizing and delayering will continue whether teams are used or not.

## Lack of Empathy and Understanding

The management of self-managing teams requires the ability to listen, to change views, to empathize, and to change basic behavior patterns. Without an adequate investment in the training and development of social work skills, team development will be retarded or even thwarted.

## Managerial Resistance

Managers who have been trained to manage in a forceful or threatening way may not readily accept the concept of teams. The change to a team approach results in a variety of disincentives to the traditional hard-charger manager.

## *A Preview of Business Without Bosses*

Our purpose in writing this book is to give you an insider's tour of several actual team experiences. Think of these stories as armchair site visits. Here's a preview of the stories we will tell.

Chapter 1, "On the Road to Teams: Overcoming the Middle Management Brick Wall," is about probably the biggest challenge to successful implementation of teams. Managers (especially first-line supervisors) are frequently the most threatened and resistant to the whole team concept. Their power and status as boss becomes vulnerable, and they may have difficulty learning a new organizational

role that is of central importance to team development. These managers in the middle risk the possibility that doing their job well may mean working themselves out of a job. Chapter 1 presents the struggles and transition of middle managers in a warehouse operation of Charrette Corporation as they prepare to lead workers into a team structure.

Chapter 2, "The Day-to-Day Team Experience: Roles, Behaviors, and Performance of Mature Self-Managed Teams," looks at a relatively mature team system at a General Motors plant that produces maintenance-free automobile batteries. The focus of the chapter is on the day-to-day behaviors, activities, and conversations of employees working in teams. It describes their necessary work and team skills and the system has become relatively stable. In addition, it reports on the leadership characteristics of team leaders and coordinators that enable the creation of business without bosses.

Chapter 3, "The Good and the Bad of Teams: A Practical Look at Successes and Challenges," provides a practical and balanced look at teams in a paper mill owned and operated by Lake Superior Paper Company. The teams examined in this chapter are still at the relatively early stage of their development. The story includes many significant successes, as well as many challenges that need to be resolved. This chapter is particularly useful for gaining a sense of the realities of the struggle to get a team system up and running.

Chapter 4, "The Early Implementation Phase: Getting Teams Started in the Office," examines the launch of a team system at IDS Financial Services. The story of the planning, prelaunch, and initial introduction of teams is related in detail, including the implementation decision, the involvement of the external consultant, and the formation of the primary committees and groups that have guided the transition. This chapter provides an understanding of what needs to be done to create business without bosses from the beginning and a sense of the relevance of teams for service organizations. It also contains a recent description of the organization and the benefits it has reaped from a team approach.

Chapter 5, "The Illusion of Self-Management: Using Teams to Disempower," looks at an application of self-managing teams as a mechanism to increase control of employees in an independent insurance firm. The story raises the caution that just because we use the word "self-management," it does not automatically follow that employees are empowered and that business without bosses is achieved. The champion of the introduction of self-managing teams in this company, the CEO, publicly espoused a strong commitment to the philosophy of employee empowerment, but, in reality, the system created only an illusion of self-management. After careful study, it became clear that the team system was actually used to *reduce* employee discretion and personal control.

Chapter 6, "Self-Management Without Formal Teams: The Organization as Team," describes an alternative way of establishing business without bosses and employee self-management without formally established teams. The approach of the very successful W. L. Gore corporation is examined in detail, revealing a fascinating system of self-developing teams that emerge only as needed. A system without bosses or managers but with lots of leaders is at the heart of this success story. The company has no "employees," only "associates" who team up directly with whomever they need to get the job done, without worrying about going through a chain of command. An inside view is provided of one of the most advanced self-leadership systems we have seen so far, where lots of teamwork takes place but teams are not formally defined by management. In fact, the term "unmanagement" (which implies the existence of "unbosses") is used to describe the Gore approach to business without bosses.

Chapter 7, "Teams and Total Quality Management: An International Application," looks at teams as part of an overall total quality management (TQM) effort. In this successful application at a Texas Instruments plant in Malaysia, teams are viewed as only one piece, albeit an important one, of an overall effort dedicated to total quality management. Also the plant employs a rich and culturally diverse work force. This story reveals a striking openness to combining good ideas originating from many sources to create an optimal team-based work system. Total quality management, cultural diversity, and striving to create an organizational hybrid from the best manufacturing ideas in the world are the main themes of this fascinating story.

Chapter 8, "The Strategy Team: Teams at the Top," emphasizes the importance of teamwork in developing corporate strategy. Many interlocking teams are used at AES Corporation to accomplish the "strategy-making" process. This chapter especially focuses on the importance of upper-level (executive) teams. Although teams and teamwork are a central part of the organization's culture and philosophy at all levels, a multilayered executive "onion" of overlapping committees provides the core of this impressive company, where strategy is driven by core values. This chapter represents an important reminder that teams are not just for lower-level employees but are appropriate at the top as well.

Chapter 9, "Business Without Bosses Through Teams: What Have We Learned? Where Are We Going?" identifies the primary lessons and challenges suggested by the team stories in this book. The book includes a diverse set of self-managing team systems across both manufacturing and service companies, representing a wide range of management philosophies. Yet there are some common prescriptions and cautions that flow from this fascinating set of stories. This final chapter outlines lessons and prescriptions that can serve as an important starting point for organizations considering or already grappling with the team approach. In particular, a beginning road map is provided for establishing very successful businesses without bosses. Overall, the stories reveal how in some very successful organizations the Boss has become an obsolete Corporate Tyrannosaurus Rex ready for a dinosaur graveyard. Now, prepare to begin your site visits to observe *Businesses Without Bosses.* We hope you find your journey interesting as well as informative.

## Notes

1. *New York Times,* January 18, 1993, p. D4.

2. This section is based in part on Charles C. Manz and Roger Grothe, "Is the Workforce Vanguard to the 21st Century a Quality of Work Life Deficient-Prone Generation?" *Journal of Business Research* 23 (1991): 67-82.

3. See, for example, Joseph A. Raelin, "60's Kids in the Corporation: More Than Just 'Daydream Believers,' " *Academy of Management Executive* 1 (1987): 21-30.

4. See "Baby Busters Enter the Work Force," in *Futurist* (May-June 1992): 53. The article is based on Lawrence J. Bradford and Claire Rains, with Jo Leda Martin, *Twenty Something: Managing and Motivating Today's New Work Force* (New York: Master Media Limited, 1992).

5. "The New Industrial Relations," *Business Week,* May 1981, pp. 84-88.

6. From a speech given at the International Conference on Self-Managed Teams, University of North Texas, Denton, Texas, 1990.

7. Brian Dumaine, "Who Needs a Boss?" *Fortune,* May 7, 1990, pp. 52-60.

8. John Horr, "The Payoff From Teamwork," *Business Week,* July 10, 1989, pp. 56-62.

9. This section borrows heavily from Henry P. Sims, Jr., and Peter Lorenzi, *The New Leadership Paradigm* (Newbury Park, CA: Sage, 1992).

10. Horr, "The Payoff From Teamwork."

11. Dumaine, "Who Needs a Boss?"

12. Madeline Weiss, "Human Factors: Team Spirit," *CIO* 2 (July 1989): 60-62.

13. Lee W. Frederiksen, Anne W. Riley, and John B. Myers, "Matching Technology and Organizational Structure: A Case in White Collar Productivity Improvement," *Journal of Organizational Behavior Management* 6 (Fall-Winter 1984): 59-80.

14. John B. Miner, *Theories of Organizational Structure and Process* (Hinsdale, IL: Dryden, 1982), pp. 110-111.

15. Paul S. Goodman, Rukmini Devadas, and Terri L. Griffith Hughson, "Groups and Productivity: Analyzing the Effectiveness of Self-Managing Teams," in *Productivity in Organizations* (San Francisco: Jossey-Bass, 1988).

16. Barry M. Macy, Paul D. Bliese, and Joseph J. Norton, "Organizational Change and Work Innovation: A Meta-Analysis of 131 North American Field Experiments—1961-1990," working paper (Texas Tech University, 1991).

17. Quoted by Kim Fisher, "Are You Serious About Self-Management?" (paper delivered at the International Conference on Self-Managed Work Teams, Dallas, October 1991).

18. This section is adapted from Sims and Lorenzi, *New Leadership Paradigm.*

*19*

# Leadership Secrets From Exemplary Followers

ROBERT E. KELLEY

## LEADERSHIP FROM THE EYE OF THE FOLLOWER

Based on my surveys, followers are very dissatisfied with the quality of business and government leadership in this country. From the followers' point of view:

- Two out of five bosses have questionable abilities to lead.
- Only one in seven leaders is someone that followers see as a potential role model to emulate.
- Less than half of the leaders are able to instill trust in subordinates.
- Nearly 40 percent have "ego" problems—are threatened by talented subordinates, have a need to act superior, do not share the limelight.

These statistics constitute a strong indictment by followers against the quality of leadership, and gives the lie to two current management gods: the god of "empowerment" and the god of "transformational" leadership, which supposedly remakes followers from a mindless mass into capable individuals. Whether the myth conjures up Gandhi mobilizing the masses or General Patton disciplining out-of-shape recruits into fighting soldiers, transformational leaders are lionized for bringing mightiness out of mediocrity. In this view, leaders are the active molders and followers are the passive clay. Influence runs in one direction only.

These statistics, however, tell a different story. Followers actively evaluate their leaders and find most of them wanting. Followers are insulted by the suggestion that they need empowering or transformation. They are not enslaved, waiting to be freed by benevolent masters. The major constraint upon their best performance is the stereotypes inside the leader's head.

SOURCE: From *The Power of Followership* by Robert E. Kelley. Copyright © 1992 by Consultants to Executives and Organizations, Ltd. Used by permission of Doubleday, a division of Bantam Doubleday Dell Publishing Group, Inc.

Followers can be likened to customers "buying" the quality of leadership. They compare what one leader has to offer with other alternatives. Then they make their purchase.

In one large consumer goods company, a new division leader instituted a new plan along with a set of autocratic procedures to back it up. Within three months, 25 percent of the division had initiated internal transfers to other parts of the company. Two hundred followers in all did not "buy" the leadership being offered them and voted with their feet. Followership implies a voluntary choice, not a contractual one. Like volunteers, followers decide where to invest their time and effort.

What is it, then, that followers look for in leaders that will make them want to volunteer their best effort? I asked followers to answer that question by specifying what the leader actually does, day to day, for and with them. When followers answered with an attribute such as "honest," I pushed for what the leader did to demonstrate honesty.

My research reveals that, given the opportunity, followers would design their "model" to:

- Embrace exemplary followers as partners or cocreators.
- Demonstrate the value they add to followers' productivity.

What follows is both a one-sided and a somewhat "ideal" model of leadership. It is one-sided because it derives only from the followers' perspective. It reveals what they want from leaders, recognizing that customers, stockholders, and the leader's own boss have equally valid claims on the leader. It is ideal because leaders like this don't exist . . . yet. Few leaders have seriously and continuously concerned themselves with the followers' perspective. Few role models exist. But they could, and if followers have their way, more will exist in the future.

## *Embrace Exemplary Followers as Partners or Cocreators*

Exemplary followers do not want leaders who decide their work or their fate for them. They want leaders who view them as partners in shaping the enterprise.

In true partnerships, competent people join together to achieve what they could not achieve alone. Drawing from its legal definition, partnership requires the partners to be individually and collectively accountable for the actions and liabilities of the firm. Unless explicitly negotiated otherwise, partners are viewed as equals. As equals, they decide how to work together, to share power, and to reward individual and joint contributions so that the partnership succeeds.

### Partnership Means Sharing Information

Because partners are accountable for each other's actions, they seek and share information. Too many leaders, however, hoard information—whether on budgets, key decisions, or financial returns. They view the dispensation of this information as a leader's prerogative. This approach generally breeds suspicion and resentment.

When Hugh Aaron's closely held plastics manufacturing company, called Customcolor, started losing money, he issued an austerity plan. Calling a company-wide meeting, he informed the employees that there would be no more overtime, bonuses, or new machinery. Wages were frozen. But the employees didn't believe the company was in trouble. They thought he was gouging them while keeping his own salary and perks.

To get the employees actively involved in turning the company around, Aaron reluctantly decided to show them the facts by opening up the books. Says Aaron, "Having built up my business through personal sacrifice and risk—from a money-losing operation into a prosperous, creditworthy enterprise—I found sharing its innermost secrets anathema, akin to revealing my sex life."

Although his accountant and business associates thought the idea was bizarre and dangerous, Aaron shut down the plant for an hour and held an all-employee meeting in the cafeteria. He went over the entire P&L statement, item by item. As it turned out, he had to hold several meetings to educate the employees in how to interpret the financial data. By sharing the bottom line and the details of expenses, however, he was also sharing the burden of having to take action.

The employees aggressively joined Aaron in reducing expenses. For example, not realizing that the company paid $16,000 each year for cleaning the workers' uniforms, they suggested that the company buy its own washer and dryer to shave expenses. The expense dropped to $4,000 per year—a savings equal to an office worker's annual wage. Likewise, they eliminated the Christmas party. Instead, they set aside and raffled off the accumulated earnings from the vending machines.

By sharing information, Aaron signaled that he wanted partners, not just employees. The employees responded in kind.

But sharing budget and financial performance data is only the first step in creating a partnership. Partners who are liable for each other's actions also share personal performance information. They touch base regularly to let each other know what and how they are doing, as well as to give feedback to each other.

For example, in a large computer company that I visited, managers held yearly performance evaluation meetings with their subordinates. The managers would discuss the subordinates' strengths and weaknesses along with goals for the next year. But they wouldn't reveal the actual 1 to 5 rating that they assigned to each employee or the person's rank compared with other employees. The company felt that the middle and lower performers would be demotivated if they knew this information. So the employees had to piece together cues from the manager's feedback. If they were told they were "solid and consistent," it meant they were a 3 or a 2, according to the employee grapevine.

The employees in this company did not know where they stood and they wasted much time trying to figure it out. In a partnership, people know where they stand. As equal adults, they don't need someone else to protect them from the reality of their own performance. Each is responsible for his or her own motivation.

While many performance evaluations focus on the subordinate's leadership skills, it is important to devote a section to followership and partnership skills, including the ability to shift easily between roles. Evaluations can come from peers, customers, subordinates, and the person himself or herself. Anyone who comes into regular contact with the person being evaluated can complete brief periodic questionnaires.

The sharing is also a two-way street. Followers should evaluate the leader's performance. Upward feedback, as it is coming to be known, is essential for a partnership. Most leaders get very little direct feedback on their performance—partly because they don't ask and partly because followers fear the boss will retaliate. Although subordinate feedback can be threatening to your ego, who can better tell you what kind of leader you are than your subordinates?

If you want to solicit this information, emphasize that it is meant to help you become a better leader and that no one will be hurt for giving their direct, candid view. If trust is low, make it anonymous.

Don't ask general and vague questions, like the overall quality of communications skills. Instead, be very specific about behaviors relevant to the follower and the leader: "Do I return phone calls quickly?" "Do I listen with an open mind?" "Are we in contact on a daily basis?" "Do I make sure you understand before moving on to a new topic?"

Then ask each subordinate to rate the boss on every behavior and to indicate how important that aspect is to the subordinates in doing their jobs. Have space for subordinates to write in specific comments and what they would need to see from the leader to give a higher rating.

The leader can then share the tabulated findings with the troops and tell them what she or he plans to do about weaknesses. This demonstrates to followers that they have been heard, allows them to help the leader interpret the findings, and enables them to contribute to the leader's development plan. It also gives them a chance to see if their individual appraisals of the leader match those of other followers.

Once performance data are shared, it opens the door to sharing an almost taboo topic—salary data. Many people are skeptical of sharing salary data. They believe it sets off a horse race, pitting co-worker against co-worker. But Ed Lawler's extensive research on open pay systems consistently shows higher morale and trust in organizations that share this information. In the absence of valid information, most people's fantasies will fill in the vacuum with erroneous beliefs about how they are being victimized.

It is for these reasons that Steve Jobs, the CEO of Next Computers and the cofounder of Apple, posts every employee's salary, including his own. In this way, all employees know how they are valued relative to every one else. As their contributions increase, they can see whether it is reflected in their salary standing.

## Partners Co-Create the Vision and Mission

Many leadership books tout the "visionary" role of leaders. Like Moses descending from the mountaintop, the leader unveils the new order. For their part in this scenario, dependent followers are supposed to stop wandering about aimlessly. Instead, they dutifully applaud, thank the leader profusely, and line up behind the leader's vision.

This scenario has little appeal to exemplary followers. They generally know where they are going. If not, they want to be part of the process that determines the end goal. This might be called "leadership by informed consent." As partners, followers want to forge the vision together to increase the probability of success.

To begin, the leader can present the first "straw model" so that followers can react, modify, and build upon it. For example, a CEO of a furniture company conducted twenty-six successive vision-building workshops with a different group of employees each weekend. The major purpose of each workshop was to build a cumulative vision for the company using the output of the previous session. Each successive group could challenge and change the previous output. The results of each session were published for everyone to see and comment on. At the end of the twenty-six weeks, a collective vision was established. Over the next six years, revenues soared from $6 million to over $70 million.

In contrast, when leaders develop a strategy without the help of followers, they are asking for trouble. A major money-center bank asked outside consultants to devise a new strategic plan. When top management unveiled to the bank's loan officers the new strategy of energy and Third World loans, these followers gave it a thumbs-down. These loan officers spend their entire careers analyzing strategic plans of companies seeking financing. They unanimously agreed that if their own bank asked for a loan on the basis of the new strategy, they would turn down the request. Rather than use this reaction to modify the strategy, top management shrugged off the criticism as due to the "Not Invented Here" syndrome and implemented the strategy. Consequently, many of the bank's top performers left rather than go down with what they called, and what eventually became, a sinking ship.

## Partners Share the Risks and the Rewards

Exemplary followers are willing to put themselves on the line, but they believe their leaders should do the same. As Admiral James Stockdale said, leaders should only issue orders that "the issuer is willing to carry out by him- or herself in order to set an example." When the work is done and if things go well, all should share the rewards equitably. If things go poorly, all should carry their fair share of the sacrifices.

Some leaders say one thing but do another. Out one side of the mouth comes, "People are our most important asset." Out the other side comes, "Downsize and lay off." As Ilene Gochman of the Opinion Research Corp. of Chicago observed after her firm surveyed 100,000 employees: "Employees have seen that if the company steams off on some new strategic tack and it doesn't work, employees lose their jobs, not management."

Followers particularly resent the leaders' profiting at the followers' expense. The fact that the average CEO now makes more than a hundred times the average worker's pay does not escape their attention. Many followers would agree with Bud Crystal, a compensation expert and a professor at Berkeley's Haas School of Business "[CEO pay] may be financed from the bodies of middle management. By having leaner, meaner organizations with fewer levels, the CEO—on the seventh day he rested—takes half the savings and puts it in his pocket."

Followers increasingly carry the downside burden and gain little of the upside benefits. When General Motors' profit slid 13 percent in 1989, CEO Roger Smith's annual bonus fell only 7 percent to $1.4 million. Profit sharing paid to hourly and lower-level salaried workers plunged 81 percent to $50 a person. Likewise, the CEO of Firestone received a $5.6 million bonus for improving the company's financial condition. To accomplish that feat, over 50 percent of the work force suffered serious job disruption as the work force shrank from 110,000 to 53,500.

Today the odds are greater that many followers will be hurt before any leader is. If the company goes belly up, most lower-level employees will have a much tougher time of it than a CEO with a golden parachute.

Exemplary followers prefer leaders who stand with them on the front line of adversity. Both Gandhi and Martin Luther King won follower support when they took the first blows from the police clubs. Jane Addams suffered severe social ridicule when she opened Hull House to help impoverished immigrants in 1889. The personal sacrifice of these leaders encouraged their followers to overcome fear and to extend themselves for the greater good. Likewise, when Alexander the Great's soldiers were dying of thirst and starvation as they marched across the Indian desert, he walked with them to share their suffering. Alexander's personal sacrifices encouraged his followers to overcome fear and extend themselves for the greater good.

It is difficult to find leaders who would follow in Alexander's footsteps, but some do exist. And followers love them for not deserting them.

One such leader is Ken Iverson at Nucor, a mini-mill steel company with $1.1 billion in sales. Iverson built the company on sharing risks and rewards. He established a lavish but simple employee incentive system: the more steel produced, the more money earned by employees. The work force produces almost twice as much steel per worker-hour as its larger competitors. In a good year, Nucor employees can double their annual salaries.

The employees, however, carry more risk than their large competitor counterparts. If sales or productivity is off, they forgo the extra income. But even then Iverson takes the lead. When the company faced tough times in 1988, Iverson took the first pay cut, and at 60 percent, also the deepest. The end result is a much admired boss and a very profitable company whose employees' rave ratings consistently put it on the best-run companies lists.

Partners not only know how much the others make, they share the same pay formula. If the leader gets a 25 percent bonus based on increased productivity or sales, then subordinates would receive the same. One of the biggest demotivators for exemplary followers is a discrepancy between how they and the leader are rewarded. Why should a subordinate try to reach the goal if only the boss gets rewarded? If everyone stands to gain or lose proportionately, then a unified effort is more likely.

One manager at a wholesale company told her subordinates exactly how she was paid: 50 percent base salary, 40 percent on meeting sales goals, and 10 percent on meeting cost goals. She stood to gain a 10 percent bonus increment for every 10 percent she exceeded her sales and cost goals. Her annual take could realistically range from her base salary to 150 percent with bonuses. Previously, her ten subordinates were paid only a salary. She invited them to revamp their pay scheme to match hers. By accepting more risks, they increased the upside potential. Even though the boss's total dollar take was greater due to the larger base salary, they could make considerably more than their current salary.

The more risk-averse shied away from the offer, but six employees jumped at the chance. With their fortunes rising and falling in tandem, they now had greater motivation to work together and with the boss to meet the goals. In addition, no one could complain that anyone profited at the other team members' expense. For four years in a row, this team has been the top producer in the company. Also, the previously risk-averse employees have signed on.

### Demonstrate the Value You Add to Followers' Productivity

Leaders traditionally believed that they added value to followers in two ways. First was being the export on the follower's job. The leader could look over the employee's shoulder, give advice, and make sure the job got done right. This was a supervision-cum-development function. Second was to give approval and distribute the rewards for good work. Current business literature also suggests that the leader provides the vision and does some "transformation and empowerment" intended to jump-start the organization.

From the exemplary followers' viewpoint, however, these functions are unnecessary. In many organizations, the followers know how to do their job better than the leader. This is especially true for technical fields where the actual job knowledge becomes obsolete quickly. The longer leaders are away from the technical job, the more dependent they become on the specialists working for them.

Likewise, exemplary followers look less to their bosses for approval. Bosses often do not have the expertise to determine the quality of the work itself. How could the boss give approval? Instead, these followers look to professional peers who can comment on the elegance and originality of their work. Also, as more workers get connected to either internal or external customers, they query those customers as to how happy they are with the work products. The boss, then, is simply left with deciding how much to pay or value the subordinates' work. But even that is being increasingly tied to concrete customer and profit targets on the front end.

The leader's vision, transformation, and empowerment roles also are superfluous for many exemplary followers. In fact, many would be insulted if leaders offered their vision as a fait accompli.

So what is a leader to do? What value can she or he add to exemplary followers? What will make an exemplary follower support one leader rather than sabotage or desert in favor of an alternative leader?

From the followers' viewpoint, leaders add value in two ways:

- Create environments where exemplary followers flourish.
- Be less a hero and more a hero maker.

## Create Environments Where Exemplary Followers Flourish

This may involve many different activities, depending on the particular work environment. For example, it can be as basic as successfully selling the group's ideas and obtaining the necessary resources so the group can accomplish its goals. This may require representing the group to larger organizational units, including government or society at large. Even CEOs, like Ken Olsen at Digital

Equipment and Paul Allaine at Xerox, are spending more time assisting in the sales of their products to key customers. They view this selling as a critical part of their job and as a way to help out their followers.

Leaders also should remove roadblocks to a follower's productivity. They can shield the followers from the bureaucracy—the "administrivia" and minutiae that interfere with getting real work done. It is not unusual for large organizations to require many employees to spend 20 to 30 percent of their time filling out paperwork and preparing various management reports. This large chunk of the day represents time not used performing the job they were hired to do. One organization hired engineers and economists to do fieldwork. Yet because of all the reports and revised reports that had to be filed after each field visit, these researchers spent only one-third of their time in the field and the other two-thirds filling out field reports.

Part of the role of the leader is to deflect as much of this administrative nonwork as possible. Leaders can create management systems that filter out the unnecessary and seemingly innocuous requests and demands that snowball into endless hours of work.

In one electronics company, the manager of R&D developed an extremely effective method of handling administrative requests. A simple request for information by the CEO often snowballed into hours of work for those on the lower rungs of the corporate ladder, especially if it required collecting or analyzing data outside the normal requirements. Every time this manager received such a request, she would calculate the cost in dollars, hours, and schedule setbacks on key R&D projects. Before she acted on the requests, she would send these calculations back up the chain, asking if she was still to proceed in light of the costs. The number of requests dropped drastically as she protected her staff from interruptions in their work.

At times, leaders may simply need to leave their followers alone. One of the greatest impediments to productivity is constant interruption. Several exemplary followers told me how they moved their offices to protect themselves from their bosses. When they were next door or across the hall, the boss would barge in or call over to them without any thought of the followers' work progress. They became on-call sounding boards for ideas or dumping grounds for delegation. Once they moved further away, they had longer periods to concentrate on their work.

Besides removing productivity roadblocks, leaders can encourage self-management in followers. For example, in an electronics firm, the followers design, schedule, and monitor the work in each semiautonomous work group. They hold weekly meetings with the department leader for briefings on progress and problems. They identify critical issues for the leader and suggest the steps to resolve them, especially if the issues involve other departments. This self-management allows the leader to attend to activities that are important at the division or company level or are best handled at the leader's administrative level.

These self-managed followers require fewer bosses, yielding a considerable payroll savings, and they often set higher productivity goals than management does. At one plant, the workers schedule, operate, and maintain the plant so well that no managers are even present during the night shift.

Another example of self-management relates to problem solving. People closest to the problem are given responsibility to solve it. They make the decision and have to live with it. Dean Ruwe, president of Copeland Corporation, a maker of refrigeration and air-conditioning products, discovered that "if you have 1,000 problem identifiers [followers] but only supervisors [leaders] can solve problems, you've got an overload in the system." Consequently, Copeland tells its workers to gather their own data so they can solve the problems themselves.

For example, a drill bit operator at Copeland collected data about two drill bits. The one the company wanted him to use cost $4.50. An alternative cost $9.00. He showed that the $9.00 bit produced three times as much at only twice the cost. Unlike the cheaper bit, it didn't break off in the product's deep holes, thus reducing damaged goods and downtime. He single-handedly sold the company on the more expensive bit. Not only did he receive company-wide recognition, but the story of his problem solving is now part of the company's folklore.

Just as exemplary followers want to manage themselves, they have no desire to actively monitor the leader's work progress. As partners, they want a relationship of equals who trust each other. Despite all the hubbub surrounding participative management, exemplary followers don't want to know the trivia of the leader's job. Nor do they want involvement in every decision. Instead, followers want involvement only in decisions which may affect them in direct and important ways.

While followers self-manage their individual work, leaders can help manage the "cracks" that fall between the technical work of different followers. As followers immerse themselves in their technical area, important interdependencies may get overlooked. By monitoring and integrating the work flow, the leader can make sure that the organization's efforts come together.

One manager I know posts a "picturegraph" in the coffee room illustrating the sequence and flow of work assignments. As individuals or teams complete their discrete tasks, they fill in the part of the picture that represents their contribution. As people get coffee, they can instantly learn the status of the department's work, which employees are on schedule, who might need some extra help, and what bottlenecks might occur.

Leaders can also serve as "synergy catalysts" who create and broker networks. Many major scientific breakthroughs are the result of some form of synergy or cross-fertilization from other fields. Individuals can experience individual breakthroughs as well as personal development by coming into contact with other creative, hardworking peers.

Leaders are in a position to see the big picture—all the various talents and projects that the subordinates are actively pursuing. If two followers are separated by organizational structure, time zones, cultural background, or fields of expertise, they may never know that their individual work has a bearing on the other's. Leaders can provide the network by means of which these talented people can put their heads together and come up with significant products or progress.

For example, the vice president of an aerospace company was very supportive of a personnel manager's development of innovative human-resource programs. He put the manager in touch with a manager in the engineering department who, as a result of her natural manner with people, had a high-productivity, high-morale work force. The vice president thought the pair would spark each other's creativity, resulting in higher quality people programs for the entire company. His expectations were met as the engineering department became the testing ground for many programs that, after their initial success, spread throughout the company.

Similarly, leaders can facilitate followers forming into a team. Many managers believe if you put people in the same room, a highly functioning team will result. Yet most football teams practice forty hours a week, executing plays together, identifying group mistakes, and talking over plans and strategies to prepare for a three-hour game on Sunday.

Few work groups engage in similar activities, even though they have to perform together forty hours per week instead of just three on Sunday. They do not review past actions. They rarely join together to learn from their mistakes, practice together, set new goals, or build up their team spirit. Any training workers do receive is individual in nature; one worker attends a seminar on a specific subject. This would be equivalent to a football team sending its quarterbacks to New York, its centers to Chicago, and its ends to Los Angeles to receive individualized instruction in their separate specialties. How could we expect them to perform as a team come opening game?

The leader can add value by using their interpersonal skills to get a team off the ground. Compare the team-building styles of two successive leaders. The government relations office of a major oil company was filled with dissatisfaction and dissension. The head of the office ran it in old-fashioned dictatorial style. She assigned the professional staff to relatively menial tasks while saving all meaningful lobbying work for herself. She seldom consulted the staff on strategy, yet she often unilaterally changed their work assignments and schedules. If she made a mistake, she found a convenient scapegoat to blame it on. In addition, having come up by the public affairs route, she treated the legal staff in the office as second-class

citizens. Since the legal staff reported to the general counsel back at headquarters and not to her, most staff members felt she went out of her way to provoke them. For instance, when one of her staff had a conflict with an attorney, rather than help the two people resolve it, she sided with her subordinate. Needless to say, her emotional bank account was overdrawn. Unfortunately for her, the office flubbed a major piece of legislation, and she was replaced.

The new boss took an entirely different approach. He got the entire staff—both public affairs and legal—involved in planning the office's strategy. He broke them into mixed teams, each of which would handle all aspects of one major piece of legislation, including lobbying. Each Monday and Friday they had staff meetings to brief each other on progress and contacts made. When conflicts arose within a team or between teams, he made it clear that it was their responsibility to work things out. If they needed his assistance, they must first present him with their proposal for resolving the conflict. He gave credit for success where it was due and made sure the entire office shared the limelight.

In summary, leaders do not create environments where exemplary followers flourish by simply decreeing that it will happen. This results in followership being no more than a pleasant conceit to which leaders can pay lip service but no dues. Instead, the best leaders build followership into the fabric of the organizational structure and culture by:

- Orientation programs that stress the importance of exemplary followership;
- Training programs that teach and hone the skills of exemplary followers;
- Performance evaluation systems that rate how the individual carries out the followership role;
- Reward systems that underscore the importance of exemplary followership;
- Rotational programs whereby people move back and forth between followership and leadership roles;
- Role modeling wherein the leader assumes the followership role and demonstrates exemplary followership skills; and

- Leadership activities that specifically encourage exemplary followership, such as team-building, removing roadblocks to a follower's productivity, or being a synergy catalyst.

### The Future of Leading

Leadership as defined by exemplary followers differs considerably from the myth espoused by leadership enthusiasts. Leaders are partners who simply do different things than followers. But both add value and both contributions are necessary for success. But one is not more important than the other.

Frequently, I encounter top technical people who desperately want to get promoted to a management job. They are lured into leadership positions by the power over decisions and people, visibility, higher pay, and inclusion in the inner circle. Many of these people are great followers and technical contributors.

I try to point out to them that most people who get promoted to the management ladder only advance one or two rungs. Rather than be stuck in a technical job they like, they are going to be stuck in a low-level management job they may dislike, earning slightly more money. Instead of spending twenty-five years in a technical job, they will spend twenty years as a first-level supervisor, with almost no real power. Is this really what they want?

What these followers don't realize is that they may not be suited to the actual work required of leaders. Their focus will become organizational issues, rather than technical.

In two informal surveys, I asked subordinates to rate their leaders on two questions: were they good at leading and did they like the job? In both surveys, only 25 percent of the leaders met both conditions.

In a companion survey, I asked the leaders how many would go back to their nonleader jobs if they could without a loss of face. Seventy-five percent said they would. One manager summarized her experience: "I traded in exciting professional work to spend 90 percent of my time deciding whether my people should have twelve- or fourteen-foot offices, what the vacation schedule should be, and who should get the 2 percent merit increase that isn't enough to motivate anyone anyway. I spend so much time on administrivia crises that I don't have time for people or managing."

While I do not know if the 75 percent who are unsuitable leaders are identical to the 75 percent who are dissatisfied, the statistics alone ensure that at least 50 percent of them are the same. Thus, many in leadership positions—at least one of every two in my surveys and perhaps as high as three out of four—should not be there and do not want to be there. The odds of their success are not very high, if they are mainly doing it for the extrinsic rewards, rather than the work itself.

Although there is no shortage of people who want to lead, there is a real shortage of people who can and want to do the actual work of leaders—I have watched even skilled managers return to their technical work because they found it less stressful and more gratifying.

Although the personal costs of leadership positions are glossed over by the leadership books and the executive recruiters, they are real nonetheless. As one executive put it, "I missed my kids' birthdays, ball games, and parent-teacher meetings. I was seldom there for the joy or the tears. When it came time to give away my children at their weddings, I realized I knew my business and my subordinates better than I knew my own kids."

More organizations are becoming like university departments, where faculty members have to be cajoled to be department heads. These faculty see very little personal gain from the experience and a huge drain on their time. In some universities, the faculty members rotate the position among themselves so that no one has to serve for too long. Each takes a turn in the spirit of organizational citizenship rather than professional interest.

# 20

# The Empowering Leader

## Unrealized Opportunities

ANN HOWARD

Empowerment forms the backbone of many approaches to organizational change, such as total quality management, reengineering, and self-managed teams. The concept is straightforward: Organizations push down decision-making responsibility to those close to internal and external customers, and employees take charge of their own jobs. The promise of empowerment is that associates will be motivated to higher and higher levels of performance and productivity.

Implementing the concept, however, has proved much more difficult than might be expected. Although organizations have reaped some rewards, empowerment so far has not lived up to its promise. I believed that one deterrent has been too much attention paid to the motivational properties of empowerment and too little to other important psychological mechanisms. This preoccupation with motivation may have grown out of the deep concerns in the 1960s and 1970s that work had

become so fragmented and deskilled that workers were overcome with boredom and apathy.

Empowerment *is* motivating, but that is not its only benefit. Research and theory that focus exclusively on the motivational properties of empowerment miss opportunities to explore its power. And real-world applications that focus exclusively on the motivational properties of empowerment mistake talk for action. A more robust treatment of the concept from a psychological perspective can be better researched scientifically and better applied practically.

### The Evolution of Empowerment

Empowerment can trace its roots to several sources (Howard, 1995b): (a) The company unions that flourished briefly in the industrial democracy movement after World War I; (b) Lewin's work on

SOURCE: From a paper prepared for the Kellogg Leadership Studies Project, September 1996. Portions of this chapter were presented at the meeting of the American Psychological Association, Toronto, Canada, August 1996. Reprinted with permission of the author.

group dynamics and its extension to participative management by writers such as Likert, McGregor, and others; (c) sociotechnical systems and self-managed teams explored by Trist, Emery, and other colleagues at the Tavistock Institute in England; and (d) attention to the motivating power of work content explicated by Herzberg and his colleagues. Yet the philosophy of empowerment today is even more extensive than any of these, because it calls for a level of top-to-bottom involvement and re-alignment of roles that demands extensive rethinking and restructuring.

"Empowerment" is not an entirely satisfactory term, for it implies giving away power by someone on high who could later take it away. Power should rest further out from the central coordination of the organization and should be taken back only as a last resort (Handy, 1994). Alternative terms, such as high involvement (Lawler, 1992) or subsidiarity (Handy, 1994), avoid this connotation but haven't had comparable appeal.

Mary Parker Follett understood the proper place of power in the 1920s; she believed that authority derives from the function or task and argued for "power with" rather than "power over" others (Follett, 1949). She is arguably empowerment's most explicit ancestor. An admirer of Gestalt psychology, Follett brought holistic thinking to such ideas as integrative unity, the law of the situation, and authority vested with knowledge and experience.

Follett's ideas were never fully implemented, but modern advances have made it not only possible but important for empowerment to take root. The possible is rendered by high technology, which enables decision making at frontline levels. The importance comes from two not unrelated sources: global competition, which pushes organizations to seek efficiencies in an uncertain environment, and the knowledge explosion, which is infusing the marketplace with complex, cognitive work.

These changed circumstances suggest that there finally may be synergy between the interests of employers and employees. The need for speed in a rapidly changing marketplace has led organizations to empower frontline workers to reason and make decisions on the spot. Reengineering inevitably leads to empowerment of individuals and self-directing teams because executing whole processes requires people to think, interact, use their judgment, and make decisions (Hammer & Champy, 1993). Total quality management also capitalizes on the knowledge and skills of frontline workers by empowering them to use their creativity to cut inefficiencies and waste. At the same time, associates gain autonomy, respect, and challenges that overcome boredom. "Organizations and workers have never needed each other more" (Howard, 1995a, p. 49).

## The Leadership Challenge

As frontline employees take on functions that used to be in the manager's domain, leaders might expect to find themselves with time on their hands. In fact, many resist empowerment in the interest of protecting their own jobs. But the assumption that their workload will be reduced is false. Associates cannot be expected to assume new functional responsibilities and authority without a great deal of guidance and support from their leaders. Moreover, the revolutionary change wrought by true empowerment gives leaders new responsibilities. They soon discover that empowerment requires not fewer leadership roles but more and vastly different ones.

### New Purposes

Traditional leadership inherited elements of the harsh practices of the turn-of-the-century drive system and the regimentation of scientific management, which were then overlaid with the hierarchical controls of midcentury bureaucracies. Traditional leaders maintain strong control over prescribed functions. They depend on rules to get work done and protect the organization and their own turf from outsiders.

As empowerment takes hold in an organization, these traditional approaches become dysfunctional. Empowerment fits a sleeker organization—one built for the speed, flexibility, quality, and service that are essential for global competition. Leaders must rely on an integrated and consistent system to get work done—the essence of Follett's

**Figure 20.1.** Empowering Leadership Roles

(1949) integrative unity. They must use order, not control, to accomplish the organization's objectives (Wheatley, 1992). Leaders must shape their organizations through concepts and feelings rather than through rules or structures (Howard, 1995c).

In an integrated organization, collaboration among employees and with external customers and suppliers becomes an essential mode of operating. Complex projects larger than one individual can handle have necessitated the use of teams and other collections of people as fundamental work units. This movement from individual to team unmasks both a new threat to workers, who may be uncomfortable with such codependency, and a hole in the psychological body of knowledge (Mohrman & Cohen, 1995).

Perhaps most important, the constantly shifting of priorities, technologies, and other aspects of work at a pace heated up by global competition has necessitated that all employees, especially those in frontline positions, take on more responsibility and authority. The leader's role is not just to permit them to take on more but to make sure that they are prepared to handle those responsibilities wisely.

## Empowering Leadership Roles

A new model of leadership to support the purposes of empowerment is illustrated in Figure 20.1. Because high involvement begins by enriching the responsibilities of lower-level employees, the role of delegator is taken as a prerequisite to empowering leadership—the platform (see Figure 20.1) from which other roles are launched. The *delegator* moves decision making to lower job levels and sees that responsibility and authority accompany job tasks.

An additional 10 empowering leadership roles are shown in Figure 20.1, arrayed by pairs under 5 key approaches. Each approach is associated with a different part of the body—head, mouth, heart, hand, or foot—that symbolizes how the approach is implemented.

*Discover the Way.* In traditional leadership the *controller* enforces a prescribed "one best way" of working. This is clearly unsuited to an environment of rapid change. Instead, the empowering leader constantly seeks new and better ways of accomplishing the work unit's mission. Symbolized by the head in Figure 20.1, discovering the way requires mental processes such as conceptualization, imagination, inquiry, and judgment. Roles that support this approach include: (a) The *visionary* visualizes a more perfect future and expresses potential achievements of the work unit consistent with the organization's vision, and (b) the *change agent* looks for better ways to perform work by challenging current paradigms and encouraging improvement ideas from direct reports and external stakeholders.

*Light the Way.* The traditional *commander* tells employees what to do and expects obedience. In contrast, the empowering leader illuminates and illustrates where the work group should be headed and the values that should guide goal accomplishment. The leader's goal is to inspire commitment, not demand compliance. Inspiring and influencing are hallmarks of lighting the way; hence its association with the mouth. Roles that light the way include: (a) The *inspirer* communicates the vision and inspires acceptance of and commitment to it, and (b) the *model of trust* personally illustrates priorities and values and is both trusting and trustworthy.

*Encourage the Way.* The traditional leader is a *judge* who sizes up employees' performance and metes out rewards and punishments. But if lower-level employees are to assume additional risks and responsibilities, the empowering leader must encourage them along the way by offering reassurance, applauding their accomplishments, and taking their interests to heart. The leader's objective is to boost direct reports' confidence rather than judge their incompetence. To encourage the way, leaders must assume the following roles: (a) The *supporter* constantly expresses confidence in direct reports' self-sufficiency and treats their mistakes as learning opportunities, and (b) the *champion* visibly celebrates accomplishments of direct reports and promotes their best ideas to higher management.

*Enable the Way.* The *ruler,* a traditional leader, harbors decision making as a management privilege. Contrarily, the empowering leader offers a helping hand so that direct reports can make their own decisions and manage their own responsibilities. It is not enough to simply delegate responsibility and decision making; the leader must play a direct role in enabling others to handle tasks. This is accomplished by the following tasks: (a) The *coach* helps others learn to be self-sufficient through personal development and arranging learning environments, and (b) the *team builder* establishes and supports teams that engage in self-managing activities.

*Smooth the Way.* The traditional leader is a *guard* of the home turf who protects resources from encroachment by other departments or sections of the organization. The empowering leader breaks away from such isolated protectionism and purposely seeks and attracts resources from outside the immediate group. Smoothing the way requires footwork. The leader must bring needed information and materials into the group and build mutually supportive relationships with outsiders. Roles that smooth the way include: (a) The *facilitator* provides resources (materials, information, etc.) for the work group and removes obstacles that impede the group's progress, and (b) the *partner* builds alliances with and communication bridges to other work units and external partners.

In many if not most respects these new roles contradict those of the traditional leader. Moreover, they require a broad repertory of actions, attitudes, and skills on the part of leaders that are complex and not well understood.

How does the foregoing model translate from theory into practice? Finding answers to this question was the primary goal of a study I undertook with Richard Wellins of leadership practices within 25 organizations—13 manufacturing and 12 service—in the United States and Canada (Howard & Wellins, 1994). Among the 1,332 participants were 61 senior managers, 323 mid- or first-level leaders, and 948 frontline or technical/professional associates.

Study participants evaluated the importance of items representing each of the 5 traditional leadership roles and the 11 empowering leadership roles just described (see italicized labels). Two of the traditional leadership roles, ruler and judge, were particularly unpopular, with average ratings well below the midpoint of 4 on the 7-point scale of importance. Only the commander was rated significantly above average in importance: leaders were still expected to "make sure employees comply with the leader's directions."

By contrast, all of the empowering leadership roles were rated above average in importance and most were rated around 6 on the 7-point scale. Even the champion, the lowest rated empowering role, averaged above 5. Thus, the study participants strongly favored the proposed model of empowering leadership roles. They judged modeling trust, represented by the item "be consistent in words and actions," as the most important role.

Yet when it came to the topic of empowerment, leaders were not consistent in words and action. Associates consistently reported that empowerment was promoted more extensively than it was implemented. In other words, there was more talk than action. As expressed by one associate,

> The "talk" is the only difference—the "walk" is the same. Though the leadership mentality has shifted from individual to group accomplishments, empowerment exists only as a figure of speech. Only the most minuscule decisions are permitted to be made by those not a member of the executive order.

Leaders also noticed this discrepancy. Said one, "Employees get frustrated because the promises do not match reality."

These comments suggest that the power of empowerment has only begun to be tapped. Certainly there was great hope and promise for empowerment in the eyes of senior management. When asked what they thought would be the impact on their organization if all barriers to empowerment were removed, almost half of the executives thought that empowering leadership would make their organizations "much better" and more than one fourth thought the impact would be "fantastic!" The "fantastic!" anchor point was so extreme that we expected almost no one to use it—the surprise was on us.

The senior executives had a strong vision of the potential gains from empowerment but they were not taking the bold actions that would guarantee its implementation. These actions require sharing, information, knowledge, power to act, and rewards throughout the workforce. In terms of Figure 20.1, the senior executives were relying too much on the upper part of the body—the head and the mouth. They were forgetting that delegation is the floor under the entire empowerment enterprise.

### *The Power of Empowerment*

Despite the rosy future anticipated by the senior executives, empowerment did not always have positive effects on the organization. Respondents reported that at times it encouraged excessive debate, generated false expectations, and produced chaos. Yet they also provided a great deal of evidence that the payoffs of empowering leadership far exceeded the negatives. These positive outcomes accrued to the newly empowered, to their leaders, and to the overall performance of their organizations.

### Benefits to the Empowered

*Motivation.* The classic psychological rationale for current treatises on empowerment (Byham, 1988; Lawler, 1992) is that it motivates the empowered. Other theorists have tied empowerment to constructs from expectancy theories of motivation (Conger & Kanungo, 1988; Thomas & Velthouse, 1990). Wall and Jackson (1995) made a similar point for psychological theories of job design. Both the job characteristics model, which focuses on individuals, and sociotechnical systems theory, which emphasizes group and organizational factors, have focused exclusively on enhancing motivation.

When leaders empower their followers they affect them in two ways. They can inspire them directly or facilitate their performance in a way that motivates them to do more. House (1995) ties the directly inspirational approach to neocharismatic theory, which includes transformational and charismatic leadership. For example, neocharismatic leaders strengthen feelings of self-efficacy and collective identification and arouse achievement-oriented behavior. House ties the enabling or facilitative mechanisms to his path-goal theory, which has much in common with expectancy theories of motivation. For example, leaders establish comprehensibility through path-goal clarification and empower interdependent action through interaction facilitation.

Regardless of the approaches leaders take, the underlying psychological impact on the empowered is presumed to be primarily motivational. The enabling role of leaders helps employees to feel that they can perform their work competently, and the inspirational role helps employees to believe that the work is worth doing well.

Our leadership study asked participants about their motivation and related it to the amount of empowerment provided by their leaders. Contrary to theoretical expectations, those reporting to more empowering leaders did not necessarily put more effort into their work. Most respondents thought they exerted considerable effort, and the similarity of their responses created little variance to correlate with leader behaviors (Howard & Wellins, 1994).

Motivation to work harder may not require the same level of concern in today's harried workplace that it evoked in earlier eras. A national study of nearly 3,400 workers found that 80 percent agreed or strongly agreed that their jobs require working very hard, and 42 percent indicated that they often or very often felt used up at the end of the work day (Galinsky, Bond, & Friedman, 1993). Schor (1991) found that the average American works about one month more per year compared to twenty years ago. In short, the economy's frantic pace, work demands, and anxiety about organizational failure and job security may have lit motivational fires under many employees that require little additional fuel.

Although empowerment may have limited influence on exertion of effort on an assigned task, it may still affect willingness to undertake new tasks and support the organization's efforts. Study participants who reported to more empowering leaders claimed to be more involved and more committed to the organization (Howard & Wellins, 1994). This suggests that motivation is still affected by empowerment although in somewhat different ways than traditionally expected.

*Learning.* Both the job characteristics model and sociotechnical systems theory arose in the era of concern that job simplification was destructive to employee attitudes and behavior. Wall and Jackson (1995) made a compelling case that psychologists need to supplement their emphasis on motivation in job design theory with a cognitive perspective, including knowledge based and learning processes. They argued that having control over one's job can affect not just willingness to work but ability to work. In other words, empowerment enables employees to work smarter, not harder.

Integrated manufacturing initiatives work best, according to Wall and Jackson, when they capital-ize on workers' experience and tacit knowledge. Workers with control can see the relationship between their actions and consequences, develop an understanding of the dynamic properties of systems, and thus anticipate, avoid, and prevent production difficulties. The authors' field experiments have demonstrated that empowered workers both apply existing knowledge more quickly and engage in more fault prevention over time. Our leadership research did not directly address learning, but participants who reported to more empowering leaders believed themselves to be more effective on the job (Howard & Wellins, 1994).

As Peter Vaill discusses elsewhere in this volume, empowerment initiates a learning process on the part of all involved. Expanding the psychological underpinnings of empowerment from motivation to learning has particular appeal for postindustrial work. If knowledge is the new resource for the emerging economy, then an important objective of working should be to increase knowledge (Howard, 1995a).

*Stress Tolerance.* The demand-control model from the job stress literature stipulates that in highly demanding situations, low worker control produces strain and symptoms whereas high control helps people avert or become more resistant to stress (Karasek & Theorell, 1990). Tight managerial control has also been related to emotional exhaustion (Saxton, Phillips, & Blakeney, 1991). A benefit to the empowered worker, then, should be greater ability to tolerate stress.

Our leadership study offered some evidence for this interpretation. Participants who reported to more empowering leaders testified to having less role strain than those who reported to less empowering leaders. Empowerment brought less role conflict, less ambiguity about what they were supposed to do, and less work overload. The latter was particularly true when leaders excelled as team builders and as facilitators who removed obstacles that hindered employees from doing their jobs (Howard & Wellins, 1994).

In sum, leaders who truly empower those who report to them are offering much more than motivation. They are giving their followers opportunities to learn and to protect themselves from the ravages of stress.

## Benefits to Leaders

Few researchers have concerned themselves with the impact of empowerment on leaders themselves. In fact, many leaders assume the impact will be negative—that they will suffer from less power and prestige, perhaps even lose their jobs. Our leadership study suggested to the contrary that leaders are themselves rewarded if they empower others (Howard & Wellins, 1994). This conclusion is based on correlations of leaders' descriptions of their own leadership behavior with their reactions to various aspects of their work. The more empowering leaders were shown to have:

1. Greater commitment to the organization. They were more loyal to the organization and cared what happened to it.
2. More job satisfaction. They liked their jobs more.
3. Less role ambiguity. They had more clarity about what they were supposed to do.
4. Less role overload. They found relief from routine work and decision making, particularly if they excelled in the roles of coach and facilitator.

A counterpart to reduced workload for leaders, however, was the need for more effort to perform four roles. Being a visionary and inspirer is intellectually and emotionally draining. Moreover, the roles of champion and partner require energy and skill to influence others outside the work unit.

These results suggest that empowerment does not make the leader's job any easier. Rather, it frees leaders from more routine, time-consuming duties while requiring them to take on more challenging responsibilities.

## Benefits to the Organization

Empowerment should benefit organizational flexibility. In manufacturing settings, for example, production uncertainty is best met by devolved decision making and higher employee discretion (Wall & Jackson, 1995). Moreover, as competition puts a premium on speed, organizations benefit directly if employees at the point of customer contact can make needed decisions and take appropriate actions. Organizations are constrained if individual workers lack the power to act.

Several results from our leadership study support this relationship (Howard & Wellins, 1994). Participants were asked to rate the impact of high-involvement leadership on seven organizational outcomes. On the average, organizations were made better by high-involvement leadership, and the more high involvement in the business unit, the greater the positive impact. Relevant to the flexibility issue, empowerment brought improvements in upward communication, speedier responses to requests and problems, and coordination across the organization.

Empowerment resulted in the greatest improvements in customer focus and the quality of products or services. These areas were most likely associated with particular organizational development programs, such as total quality management. Empowerment also brought rated improvements in organizational competitiveness and quality of work life.

In addition to these payoffs, there was simply more satisfaction with leaders who were empowering compared to those who were more traditional. In business units with considerable high involvement, people expressed much greater satisfaction with current leadership practices than did those in units where high involvement was limited.

## A Model for Research

The impact of empowering leadership on followers can be accounted for in a theoretical model such as that shown in Figure 20.2. Leader behaviors are shown in the ovals, and the desired outcomes for followers and the organization are in the circles.

*Leader Influences.* The model specifies that the inspirational and facilitative roles of leaders influence different psychological mechanisms, shown by the hexagons. When leaders focus on inspiring followers, they are influencing their perceptions of empowerment, which in turn influence motivation. When leaders perform their various facilitative

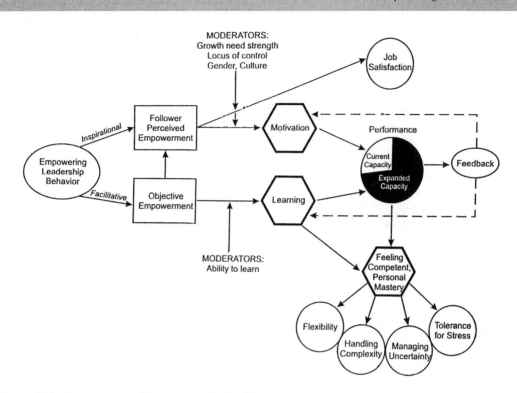

**Figure 20.2.** Consequences of Empowering Leadership

functions, they bring about objective empowerment. That is, they delegate responsibilities and authority, change the work itself, and assure that associates have the resources, opportunities, and smooth pathways to carry out their responsibilities. This objective change in the job and environment creates opportunities for associates to learn; thus learning is the primary psychological variable engaged.

Objective empowerment should naturally result in perceived empowerment. But the arrow points in only one direction; leaders can influence follower perceptions while doing little to provide objective empowerment. This, I suggest, is a primary cause of the failure of empowerment to line up to its promise.

*Moderators.* Individual differences moderate each process. As Lynn Offermann describes elsewhere in this volume, diversity in reactions to empowerment is inevitable and a challenging problem for leaders. Growth need strength is a proposed mod-

erator of motivation in the job characteristics model (Hackman & Oldham, 1976) and should serve a similar role here; people who genuinely want to develop will be most motivated by perceptions of empowerment. Coovert (1995) identified locus of control, gender, and culture as other possibilities. Ability to learn is a logical moderator of the learning side of the model.

*Performance.* Both motivation and learning have a positive impact on performance, but there is an important difference between them. Motivation affects performance within one's current capacity. People may try to work harder, but there is no guarantee that they will do anything differently. Learning, on the other hand, enhances capacity. Employees who learn from their empowered roles enhance their performance not by doing more of the same but by taking new and different approaches. The impact on performance should thus be more significant from learning than from motivation alone.

*Personal Mastery.* Learning and performing with expanded capacity lead to feelings of competency and personal mastery. Herein lies a major source of power for dealing with the demands of postindustrial life, from the increased complexity of information-age work to its uncertainty and stress (Howard, 1995a). In the demand-control model a key mechanism is learning: workers with control can learn to predict and avoid stressful situations, and their greater competence and feelings of mastery make them more resistant to the aversive demands that remain. Similarly, personal mastery and growing feelings of competence enable employees to provide the other organizational outcomes shown in the circles—handle complexity, manage uncertainty, and offer flexibility.

*Feedback.* An important linking mechanism across both the motivation and learning branches is feedback. This is represented in the model as an oval because of the leader's important role in providing information about performance. As Wall and Jackson (1995) noted, feedback in the job characteristics model is interpreted in motivational terms, yet another important purpose of feedback is to provide direction for learning. Both effects of feedback are shown in the model.

*Job Satisfaction.* Job satisfaction appears in the model as an outcome of perceived empowerment. This reflects the notion of job satisfaction as a pleasurable emotional state resulting from the perception that one's job allows for the fulfillment of important job values (Locke, 1976). These values should be based on the individual's needs, hence the influence of the moderators on job satisfaction. One of the frustrating anomalies in industrial organizational psychology is that work performance and job satisfaction are only weakly correlated despite the fact that most theory presumes that they have common determinants. This model suggests that there are two different causal paths to satisfaction and performance from the motivational and learning processes stimulated by empowerment.

*Learning.* While motivation may enhance performance to some degree, the most powerful impact of empowerment comes from the learning side of the equation. The leader must assure that the follower is objectively empowered; that is, there must be real responsibility and accountability and the follower must have the tools, resources, information, coaching, and other facilitators to make it work. Only when this happens does the follower learn. And only when the follower learns can organizations expect to reap the rewards of flexibility and management of complexity and uncertainty.

## Implementation of Empowerment

Our leadership study demonstrated some movement toward greater empowerment among the 25 organizations that participated (Howard & Wellins, 1994). Study respondents compared leaders in the same organization five years ago to those today using scales anchored at each end by 12 pairs of contrasting images (for example, tell vs. ask; promote stability vs. promote change). For all pairs, leaders five years ago were seen as closer to the traditional pole, while leaders today were viewed as more like the empowering pole.

Although progress was significant over the past five years, the leader images today typically ranged between 4 and 5 on the 7-point scale, a long way from the desirable range of 6 to 7. Thus, leaders are moving toward a more empowering style, but there is still much room for improvement. Their path is apparently strewn with obstacles and pitfalls.

### Barriers to Greater Empowerment in an Organization

Why isn't empowerment established more readily? One way we pursued answers to this question was to ask study participants to rate the extent to which 35 factors were barriers to high involvement in their organization. Evidence showed a number of significant obstacles:

*Senior Management Barriers.* Senior managers invested insufficient time and money in the change process. Moreover, they themselves often engaged in directive rather than empowering leadership practices, which did not set the proper expectations. As described earlier, they promoted the concept of high involvement more extensively than they implemented it.

*Systems Barriers.* Lack of appropriate rewards for high-involvement practices was the most prevalent systems barrier. In particular, both leaders and associates noted a lack of financial rewards for increasing knowledge and skills, although senior managers saw this as much less of a problem. Still, the senior managers confirmed that financial rewards were their least-used strategy in attempting to change their organizations during the past five years.

*Frontline Employee Barriers.* Employees and leaders considered mistrust and lack of self-motivation as frontline employees' most significant deterrents. These motives were rated much more important as barriers to high involvement than were frontline employees' skills. Senior managers, however, seriously underestimated associates' level of mistrust.

*Leader Barriers.* Leaders' skills, leaders' motives, and lack of joint action among managers were each important as barriers to high involvement. Associates cited motivational factors as their top three leader/manager barriers—managers' fear of losing status or power, rivalry and self-promotion, and distrust of employees. But in the eyes of the leaders and the senior managers, leaders' skills deficits— either a lack of coaching skills or lack of leader development—posed the biggest barriers to high involvement.

Other findings of the study helped pinpoint where leaders had difficulty mastering empowerment.

## Not Enough Heart

When leaders and associates were asked to describe how often their leaders performed empowering activities, they least often cited behavior that fell into the domain of "encourage the way." For example, leaders infrequently rewarded employee performance with symbols such as notes or public praise, and they typically blamed employees rather than circumstances for failures. By neglecting the

encouraging roles, leaders are missing feedback opportunities that can enhance their direct reports' motivation and direct their learning.

## Faulty Implementation

Another skill deficiency was leaders' failure to match the level of empowerment with the readiness of their direct reports to handle more responsibility. Direct reports alternately complained that their leaders offered too little, too much, or inconsistent levels of empowerment. As Mohrman and Cohen (1995) pointed out, managers have significantly different roles in a lateral organization compared to a line-and-box organization, and they need to strike an appropriate balance between exerting too much and too little authority.

Some leaders had problems letting go; for example, they told employees they could shut down the line but then forbade it when employees tried to do so. Other leaders did the opposite: they failed to provide enough direction and coordination to assure that their direct reports were comfortable with empowerment. Still other leaders had difficulty staying the course when faced with crises or plateaus. Commented an associate, "When we get really busy, everyone reverts to old habits: 'don't bother me with philosophy, I have too much work to do.' " Leaders who erred in either direction—too much, too little, or inconsistent—were not objectively empowering associates in ways that would ensure their learning.

## *Recommendations for Senior Managers*

Senior managers who want to go beyond talk to effective implementation of high-involvement leadership should consider the following.

### Get Closer to What's Happening

Transformational leaders need to be optimistic and enthusiastic; they must have a vision of how the organization can improve, and they must persuade others that the benefits associated with chance will outweigh the pitfalls. When top executives are overly optimistic about what has already taken place, however, they might become complacent about what remains to be done, which can be considerable. To plan appropriately for their next steps. executives should gather systematic, reliable information about the successes and problems associated with high-involvement leadership. Research studies, cultural surveys, focus groups, and "walking around" can go a long way toward providing such information.

## Get Trained

Leaders use their own leaders as role models. This was strongly suggested by the finding that leaders' ratings of how often they performed each empowering activity was highly related to how frequently their leaders did so. This implies that high-involvement leadership will flourish best if installed from the top to the bottom of the managerial hierarchy, because leaders will imitate behaviors of their own leaders.

Yet as reported earlier, executives tended to rely on directive leadership, which posed a significant barrier to greater empowerment. If leaders at the top can become pace-setting role models of empowering leadership, those lower in the organization will be both guided and rewarded. Training senior managers also might serve as an antidote to their rose-colored glasses. Executives who personally discover the challenges of high-involvement leadership might be more cautious about assuming that it will sweep effortlessly throughout the organization. They will be better able to realize the difference between objective empowerment and perceived empowerment.

## Get Other Managers Trained

Amount of training in empowering leadership was related to frequency of performing almost all leadership roles. One caveat about training, however, is that when leaders' self-descriptions were matched to those of their direct reports, those leaders with more extensive training were more likely to overstate how often they engaged in empowering behaviors. This suggests that leaders did not translate all they had learned into specific actions. Once again there is a substitution of perception for

action. Leaders must learn to change not only their mental images but their behaviors. This is best accomplished by development programs that emphasize practicing empowering leadership concepts in daily behaviors, receiving feedback, and practicing again.

## Focus on Individual Development Needs

Some leaders adapt more easily to empowerment than others. Leaders' behavior varied considerably, even in business units that were driving high-involvement practices. Given these inevitable individual differences, as well as the range of behaviors required by the many roles of empowering leadership, a single approach to development will not fit all needs. Leaders will benefit most from training if it is preceded by a powerful diagnostic process that can assess their strengths and uncover developmental requirements. Both assessment centers and multirater surveys can provide useful information in this regard.

## Reward High-Involvement Practices

Financial rewards were the least-used strategy to promote change in business units. They were seldom offered for team or group performance or for acquiring new skills or knowledge. Yet associates saw the lack of these rewards as a significant barrier to high involvement. This suggests that senior managers should align reward systems and gainsharing plans with the values of high involvement through new compensation schemes targeted to desired behaviors or outcomes. Senior managers who "put their money where their mouth is" will find themselves closer to actions that truly empower.

## *Conclusions*

The many challenges to implementing empowering leadership should not discourage organizations from undertaking this type of change. The compelling evidence of benefits to leaders, their direct reports, and to the organization suggests that mastering empowerment is definitely worth the effort. The challenge for organizations is to get beyond talk and to risk the organizational revolution implied by empowerment.

Stimulating organizations to action should be easier if the burden of proof of the benefits of empowerment is not confined to motivation alone. Motivating is too easily interpreted as influencing. It's a lot more difficult to claim that mere talk will get people to learn, handle complexity and uncertainty, physically tolerate stress, and create a more flexible organization.

## References

Byham, W. C. (1988). *Zapp! The human lightning of empowerment (and how to make it work for you)*. Pittsburgh: Development Dimensions International.

Conger, J. A., & Kanungo. R. N. (1988). The empowerment process: Integrating theory and practice. *Academy of Management Review, 13*, 471-482.

Coovert, M. D. (1995). Technological changes in office jobs: What we know and what we can expect. In A. Howard (Ed.), *The changing nature of work*. San Francisco: Jossey-Bass.

Follett, M. P. (1949). Freedom and co-ordination: Lectures in business organisation. London: Management Publications Trust, Ltd.

Galinsky, E., Bond, J. T., & Friedman, D. E. (1993). *The changing workforce* (1). Families and Work Institute.

Hackman, J. R., & Oldham, G. R. (1976). Motivation through the design of work: Test of a theory. *Organizational Behavior and Human Performance, 15*, 250-279.

Hammer, M., & Champy, J. (1993). *Reengineering the corporation: A manifesto for business revolution*. New York: HarperBusiness.

Handy, C. (1994). *The age of paradox*. Boston, MA: Harvard Business School Press.

House, R. J. (1995). Leadership in the twenty-first century: A speculative inquiry. In A. Howard (Ed.), *The changing nature of work* (pp. 411-450). San Francisco: Jossey-Bass.

Howard, A. (Ed.). (1995a). *The changing nature of work*. San Francisco: Jossey-Bass.

Howard, A. (1995b). A framework for work change. In A. Howard (Ed.), *The changing nature of work* (pp. 3-44). San Francisco: Jossey-Bass.

Howard, A. (1995c). Rethinking the psychology of work. In A. Howard (Ed.), *The changing nature of work* (pp. 513-555). San Francisco: Jossey-Bass.

Howard, A., & Wellins, R. S. (1994). *High-involvement leadership: Changing roles for changing times*. Development Dimensions International, Pittsburgh, PA.

Karasek, R., & Theorell, T. (1990). *Healthy work: Stress, productivity and the reconstruction of working life*. New York: Basic Books.

Lawler, E. E. I. (1992). *The ultimate advantage: Creating the high-involvement organization*. San Francisco: Jossey-Bass.

Locke, E. A. (1976). The nature and causes of job satisfaction. In M. D. Dunnette (Ed.), *Handbook of industrial and organizational psychology* (pp. 1297-1349). Chicago: Rand McNally.

Mohrman, S. A., & Cohen. S. G. (1995). When people get out of the box: New relationships, new systems. In A. Howard (Ed.), *The changing nature of work* (pp. 365-410). San Francisco: Jossey-Bass.

Saxton, M. J., Phillips, J. S., & Blakeney, R. N. (1991). Antecedents and consequences of emotional exhaustion in the airline reservations service sector. *Human Relations, 44*, 583-595.

Schor, J. B. (1991). *The overworked American*. New York: Basic Books.

Thomas, K. W., & Velthouse, B. A. (1990). Cognitive elements of empowerment: An "interpretive" model of intrinsic task motivation. *Academy of Management Review, 15*(4), 666-681.

Wall, T. D., & Jackson, P. R. (1995). New manufacturing initiatives and shopfloor job design. In A. Howard (Ed.), *The changing nature of work* (pp. 139-174). San Francisco: Jossey-Bass.

Wheatley, M. J. (1992). *Leadership and the new science: Learning about organization from an orderly universe*. San Francisco: Berrett-Koehler.

# 21

# Customers Take Charge

MICHAEL HAMMER
JAMES CHAMPY

Since the early 1980s, in the United States and other developed countries, the dominant force in the seller-customer relationship has shifted. Sellers no longer have the upper hand; customers do. Customers now tell suppliers what they want, when they want it, how they want it, and what they will pay. This new situation is unsettling to companies that have known life only in the mass market.

In reality, a mass market never existed, but for most of this century the *idea* of the mass market provided manufacturers and service providers—from Henry Ford's car company to Thomas Watson's computer company—with the useful fiction that their customers were more or less alike. If that were true, or if buyers behaved as if it were true, then companies could assume that a standard product or service—a black car or a big blue computer—would satisfy most of them. Even those that weren't satisfied would buy what was offered, because they had little choice. Mass market suppliers in the United States had relatively few competitors, most of which offered very similar products and services. In fact, most consumers weren't dissatisfied. They didn't know that anything better or different was available.

Now that they have choices, though, customers no longer behave as if they are all cast in the same mold. Customers—consumers and corporations alike—demand products and services designed for their unique and particular needs. There is no longer any such notion as *the* customer; there is only *this* customer, the one with whom a seller is dealing at the moment and who now has the capacity to indulge his or her own personal tastes. The mass market has broken into pieces, some as small as a single customer.

Individual customers—whether consumers or industrial firms—demand that they be treated individually. They expect products that are configured to their needs, delivery schedules that match their manufacturing plans or work hours, and payment terms that are convenient for them. Individually and in combination, a number of factors have contributed to shifting the balance of market power from producer to consumer.

---

Consumer expectations soared in the United States when competitors—many of them Japanese—burst upon the market with lower prices combined with higher-quality goods. Then the Japanese introduced new products that established American producers had not had time to bring to market—or maybe hadn't even thought of yet. What's more, the Japanese did it all with levels of service that traditional companies could not match. This was mass production *plus*—plus quality, price, selection, and service.

In the service sector, consumers expect and demand more, because they know they can *get* more. Technology, in the form of sophisticated, easily accessible databases, allows service providers and retailers of all kinds to track not only basic information about their customers but their preferences and requirements, thereby laying a new foundation for competitiveness.

In Houston, if a customer calls Pizza Hut to order a pepperoni and mushroom pie, the same kind of pizza that the customer ordered last week, the clerk asks if the caller would like to try a new combination. If the person says "yes," the clerk mails him or her discount coupons with offerings customized to that individual's tastes. When a consumer calls Whirlpool's service line, the call is automatically routed to the same service representative with whom the consumer spoke last time, creating a sense of personal relationship and intimacy in a world of 800 numbers. Mail-order retailers, which have the capability of collecting enormous amounts of data about their customers, have perfected an even higher targeted level of service. Once customers experience this superior service, they do not happily return to accepting less.

The incredible consolidation of customers in some markets—the growth of megadealers in the automobile business, the handful of fast-food franchises replacing thousands of independent eateries, and the mall-sized discounters that have emptied Main Street store fronts—has also profoundly changed the terms of the seller-customer relationship. If the sign out front now reads "Joe Smith's Oldsmobile, Nissan, Isuzu, Mercedes, Jeep, Honda, and Saturn," then Joe Smith, not General Motors, has the upper hand in their negotiations. With so many other brands available to

him, Joe needs General Motors less than GM needs him.

The threat of backward integration has also helped to shift power from producers to consumers. Often, customers now can do for themselves what suppliers used to do for them. Companies may not want to, but they can buy the same machines and hire the same people as their vendors. "Do it my way," they can say, "or I will do it myself." Inexpensive and easy-to-learn desktop publishing technology, for instance, gives companies the choice of doing for themselves jobs for which they used to rely on printers.

What holds true for industrial customers also holds true for consumers. When individual depositors realized that they could themselves purchase the same high-grade, short-term government securities and commercial paper that the banks were buying with their deposit money, many of them reduced their balances in those low-interest-bearing accounts, depriving the banks of an important source of revenue.

Customers have gained the upper hand in their relationships with sellers, in part, because customers now have easy access to enormously more data. The information-rich world made possible by new communications technologies doesn't even require the consumer to have a computer at home. Anyone can, for instance, pick up a daily newspaper and compare rates on CDs from banks all around the country. Publishers collect that data electronically and pass it on to readers, who now know positively if their local bank is offering a good deal and if not, who is. An auto dealer today has to assume that any customer has read the appropriate issue of *Consumer Reports* and is well aware of what the dealer paid the manufacturer for the car. This makes the negotiation process decidedly trickier for the dealer.

For companies that grew up with a mass market mentality, the hardest new reality to accept about customers is that *each one counts*. Lose a customer today and another doesn't just appear. For thirty years after World War II, consumer goods were in chronically short supply. Manufacturers could not produce enough of them at prices sufficiently low to satisfy every possible buyer. The effect of insatiable demand was to give producers the advantage over buyers. In a mass market, to paraphrase the movie, *Field of Dreams,* if you build it they will buy.

Consumer goods shortages no longer exist. On the supply side of the equation, more producers now operate around the world. On the demand side, developed countries now have lower population growths. Also, many product markets have matured. Almost everyone who wants one now owns a refrigerator, a videocassette recorder, and even a personal computer. Those industries are in a replacement mode. Consequently, consumers wield a great deal of power. They can, in other words, be very choosy.

In short, in place of the expanding mass markets of the 1950s, 1960s, and 1970s, companies today have customers—business customers and individual consumers—who know what they want, what they want to pay for it, and how to get it on the terms they demand. Customers such as these don't need to deal with companies that don't understand and appreciate this startling change in the customer-buyer relationship.

# 22

# *Strategic Customers or Strategic Citizens?*

## *Public Leadership and Resistant Followership*

PATRICIA M. PATTERSON

Metaphors matter. To say that one problem is like another is to prescribe similar treatments for both (Stone 1988: 118). In coming to grips with "America's crisis of confidence in government" at all levels (Osborne and Gaebler 1993: xxi), it is fashionable to infer a necessary parallel between government and market behavior. Public sector leaders are urged to find in facile analogies between democracy and capitalism both government's problems and their solutions. I argue an alternative view.

Because citizens are not customers and public leaders are not entrepreneurs, neither can necessarily take their "business" elsewhere (Lynch and Markusen 1994; Lynn 1994; Wilson 1994). And because citizens have a special status in a democracy, they cannot and should not be relied upon to follow like sheep. Instead, citizens must be encour-

aged to make active, collective choices, and to pursue them in the manner of Kelley's "effective followers" (Kelley 1995: 195). Alternatively, they must cope in sophisticated interactions with the public servants they are "stuck with," who are also stuck with them.

When public sector leaders accept market analogies uncritically, they undermine at their own peril the visibility and political legitimacy of citizen challenges to their leadership. In so doing, simplistic "reinvention" efforts unnecessarily marginalize citizenship, followership, and citizens themselves.

To analyze this problem, I explore the politics of street-level transactions in the public sector from the perspective of Kelley's sometimes effective, often alienated and reluctant followers. The answers to the leadership questions raised by this analysis are complex, but they do not lie in straight-forward adoption of private sector mechanisms. Nor will they be found it what Ciulla calls "bogus empowerment" (1996). The idea is not to make employees and citizens "feel empowered" so they will be happier, arguably the aim of "reinventions." Instead, effective public leadership will recognize the actual power of citizens, help them to recover it, and to expand its positive scope and significance. In the words of Cam Stivers, public administration professionals would promote this change by altering the way they see themselves: by valorizing the ability to interact with a broad spectrum of the public and coming to see "leadership as less a matter of being out in front of or on top of a bunch of followers, and more a matter of being at the center of a network of people engaged in a joint endeavor" (1991: 422).

## A Changing Environment of Public Sector Leadership

Today's public sector leaders are exhorted to adopt the practices inherent in the "government as business" metaphor. They are urged to reinvent government in the form of a private sector fantasy; if they lead well in this direction, government will be efficient, effective, and responsive, and its "customers" satisfied, just like in the private market.

But sound analogies rest on sturdy first premises, and on the appropriateness of the equivalence that has been asserted. The government/market analogy, and its implicit prescriptions, flounders first on its faulty premise that the market's customers really are more satisfied than the government's. Second, the analogy suffers from the unexamined assumption that conditions and services in markets are sufficiently like those in the public sector to benefit from similar fixes, and similar leadership.

Whether taken rhetorically or literally, the marketization of the public has important implications for public sector leadership, and for citizen followership. Following the metaphor, the citizen's role is simplified: citizens vote in elections, and cus-tomers vote with their feet. Though citizen customers may be dissatisfied, further participation is neither necessary nor invited. Citizens should merely follow, or take their "business" elsewhere. Overt political challenges by individuals to public leaders and to bureaucratic authority are inconceivable. And to the extent that market language obscures government's capacity to extract compliance, citizen resistance, whether covert or overt, goes unremarked.

With devolution and "reinvention" the context of bureaucratic discretion has changed (Vinzant and Crothers 1996), migrating downward. As more public workers are "empowered" with discretionary choices at street level, both public sector leaders and their would-be citizen followers must respond to new situations and to changes in process. Ironically, process issues, and the power of citizens to influence them, become less visible when an exaggerated focus on outcomes is imported into government enterprises.

This chapter examines the ways in which citizens covertly and overtly resist bureaucratic authority, in hopes of revealing the challenges to public leaders created by their reluctance to follow. It argues that, in the long run, false parallels between market and government obscure these political possibilities, depriving public leaders of important forms of feedback and support, and citizens of accessible means of expressing voice.

## Street Level: The Site of Bureaucratic Discretion

Despite the very real risk of "bogus empowerment" (Ciulla 1996), contemporary interest in public sector "customer empowerment" at least restores attention to individuals and provides renewed opportunities to look at micro-level transactions. Lipsky provided the seminal work on what he called bureaucrat-client relations at street level, occurring well below the typical radar of the public executive (1980). Lipsky's sympathetic view of bureaucrats at this interface shows them operating within the constraints of their work and resources, with uncertain, perhaps remote, leadership. These are bureaucrats whose routines, use of discretion and coping mechanisms become the policy itself (Lipsky 1980), and present challenges to public leaders and citizens alike.

Street-level bureaucrats have the power and responsibility to directly administer inducements and sanctions, rules, rights, information, and decision-making structures, and they do so with ample discretion. They would like citizens to follow their instructions. More exalted public leaders would enjoy this too, and most believers in democratic processes would fancy a bit of enthusiasm attached to this cooperation. Kelley's work on followership sheds light on these dynamics (1995).

By "followers," Kelley refers to the roles of participants in team efforts. Ideally, a participant in a given effort is independent in thought and enthusiastic in demeanor and action. The "effective follower" both thinks critically and takes action. He differentiates effective followers from "sheep," "yes people," and "alienated followers" by these criteria of thought and action.

If citizens resist and strategize in their dealings with street-level bureaucrats, this suggests they do not follow blindly. They are neither sheeplike nor yes people (though they may be mistaken for such, on grounds of strategy). Instead, they are inclined to the independent critical thinking Kelley admires. But citizens also know when they are being regulated, as even beneficiaries are. Their resistance implies that even though they have interests and needs, and are engaged in an active, not a passive relation, their actions are not always characterized by enthusiasm, competence, commitment and honesty. They may be disgruntled and acquiescent, "alienated" in Kelley's terms, but they have not turned off their brains.

In light of the regulatory properties of street-level interactions, citizens use a variety of strategies to cope and struggle with bureaucratic control. Adopting Kelley's terms, citizens may be as likely to be "alienated followers" as "effective followers," alienated or effective citizens, but either way, they are not passive "customers." How do people express dissatisfaction with the existence, form, and content of bureaucratic power? What do we observe as individuals cope with the power of

bureaucrats and bureaucracies in immediate power relations?

## *Citizens and Strategies at Street Level: A Continuum*

Through observation and attentiveness to the so-called powers of the weak (Janeway 1980) we can conceptualize a set of citizen strategies for coping with and struggling with bureaucracy in street-level relations.[1] These efforts preserve the dignity and agency of the individuals, even if they do not constitute a successful (or even advisable) challenge to bureaucratic power.

Such a set of strategies is presented in Figure 22.1, arrayed along a continuum. Neither the strategies nor the continuum are meant to offer the last word on this subject. The collection of strategies seems to involve an underlying dimension of increasing energy and engagement, and to range roughly from forms of exit to forms of voice (Hirschman 1971). Consequently, I present them in this order. For the attentive observer of citizen behavior, this may suggest more conspicuous opportunities. One has the sense that more energy and commitment, and more engagement with bureaucratic personnel, are required as one moves along the continuum.

According to Janeway, the powers of the weak "differ from those of the powerful, will often not be perceived as powers at all, and seldom be considered positive" (Janeway 1980: 157). Whether they will be considered positive or not no doubt depends on who is doing the considering, but the continuum is not a set of recommendations. Surely many of the strategies in Figure 22.1 are unwise, perhaps even unjust, in many circumstances. Depending on the situation, even the most disengaged strategy may invite reprimands or even death. Nor are they necessarily effective; serious consequences can flow from some of these strategies.

### A Continuum of Resistant Followership

Consider the endpoints of the continuum in Figure 22.1. At one end is complete disengagement,

1. Elude or avoid, physically (no entry)
2. Exit, after entry
3. Conform. (the anti-strategy)
4. Understand and conform
5. Adapt
6. Manipulate
7. Challenge, while conforming or appearing to conform
8. Elude or avoid, though physically present
9. Mount a direct challenge to try to make change
10. Challenge aggressively

**Figure 22.1.** A Continuum of Resistant Followership

even less involvement than Hirschman's "exit" (1971); at the other, the possibility of complete, and violent, engagement, well beyond his "voice." In between, is an array of other citizen strategies, including something akin to "loyalty."

To understand the details of the different strategies, I offer next an explanation of each strategy, along with manifestations and illustrations, interpretations and implications. No recommended responses are given for public leaders, as the idea is simply to consider the opportunities at citizens' disposal.

*Strategy 1. Elude or Avoid Bureaucracy*

The first strategy is one of pure avoidance, and it has several potential manifestations. For instance, one might decide not to respond or appear when summoned or otherwise obliged to do so, accepting (or avoiding!) the consequences. Or, one might conduct one's life in alternative ways, so as to avoid without having to "dodge," a particular bureaucracy or bureaucracies. One lowers one's bureaucratic profile as much as possible, even if it means forgoing benefits to which one is entitled.

Ample evidence of avoidance strategy is found among the homeless. For example, Louise, a homeless woman who refuses to apply for welfare, is "livid at the suggestion. 'I'm not eligible for public assistance,' she said. 'I'm employable. I've worked before and I can work now. Can't you understand that?' . . . In her head, her heart, her bones, she was a worker and wanted nothing to do with welfare" (Liebow 1993: 77).

Naturally, several interpretations are possible, including the ones to which market metaphors lead us. In the market, one who does not collect benefits to which she is entitled is a fool from whom profits are reaped.[2] but not a problem. Public leaders, on the other hand, might see avoidance as the consequence of ignorance, apathy or fatalism, but redouble outreach efforts to overcome those deficits.

Alternatively, this strategy can be seen as an active choice, a citizen's assertion of autonomy. How government should respond to such declarations is a separate question, but finding a way to see, recognize, and interpret a signal is analytically prior to responding to it. Even if that assertion of autonomy is misguided or less than optimal from another point of view, being attentive to it may offer a way to bring a needy citizen into an important relationship.

*Strategy 2. Exit, After Entry*

A second strategy on the continuum of those available to the individual citizen in a bureaucratic interaction is to exit. Exiting a regulatory frame is not the same, of course, as exiting the queue for benefits, and this difference needs to be taken into account. Nonetheless, one can exit an interaction, or at least attempt to do so.

One might go forward with or answer a claim, and then decide to exit for reasons having to do with service quality, personal preference, change of priority, and so forth. One might grow weary of a queue or waiting list, and then do without. Or one might develop a rationale for avoiding some legitimate responsibility.

Lipsky is quite humane in discussing the limited power of the poor to exercise the option to exit. Yet even the destitute do exit, as both Rossi's (1989) and Liebow's (1993) studies of the homeless also reveal. To withdraw with difficulty and suffering is still to withdraw.

At minimum, withdrawal results in labeling for the poor (Lipsky 1980: 56), but the consequences can be much more severe. In some cases, those who exit are both labeled and imperiled. Of 7,200 families in a Mississippi welfare experiment, 19% are reported to have lost their aid for failing to comply with work rules. Some failures to comply are no doubt inadvertent. Though one must be cautious in inferring resistance strategies, it bears noting that a Mississippi official was not himself reluctant to do so. In explaining his decision to administer consequences to roughly 1,400 people (women), he is reported to have said "[W]e're talking about people who are refusing to go to work to feed their children" (DeParle 1997: A11). One might quibble with his analysis and his attributions, but he plainly perceives resistance, and it is unlikely that it is organized.

If one is more advantaged, one might well be able to meet otherwise public needs or wants in the private sector, and in this instance, the customer metaphor seems to work. Similarly the more privileged person can use private sector participation as a rationale for exit when public obligation calls ("I gave at the office"; "I am a busy person.")

In speaking of Osborne and Gaebler, Lynch and Markusen say, "[The] authors, in embracing a slightly more liberal variant of public choice theory, favor 'exit' over 'voice' as a form of public accountability. The unhappy public service consumer, rather than voting, lobbying, or organizing politically to improve service performance, could jump ship and sign up elsewhere" (1994: 132). Well and good then to be a customer if one is well endowed and one takes no joy in making change.

### Strategy 3. Conform to the Bureaucrat's Expectations

A strategy of conformity requires one simply to do what is expected, with the least amount of effort possible. One gets by and doesn't think about it, though ultimately the interaction may affect one's self-image. Unless one makes an active decision to conform in the face of dissatisfaction, "to work to the rule," this is not a strategy. Perhaps this strategy leaves one in a position akin to Kelley's "sheep." Nevertheless, if there is a continuum, it is important to include this component.[3]

### Strategy 4. Understand and Conform

The fourth strategy requires the citizen to recognize and come to terms with the imperatives of a particular bureaucratic transaction. This more en-

ergetic approach to the citizen bureaucrat relation is not unlike Hirschman's "loyalty" (1971). It implies that the citizen, even when dissatisfied or internally resistant, makes an active effort to understand what is being done to or for her, and perhaps others in the system. In other words, this is not Skinnerian stimulus-response compliance, but rather the reasoned variety.

Including this point on the continuum acknowledges, rather than taking for granted, the citizen's effort to understand and accept public obligations. In the general case bureaucratic accountability processes, and not the personal suspicions of bureaucrats, require documents and proof. In an adequate civics curriculum, this fundamental type of citizen knowledge and competence can be taught. In the absence of it, the case for seeing the acquisition of such understanding as a way to negotiate bureaucracy, or even as an act of citizenship, is rather more persuasive.

Additionally, bureaucracies often call on citizens to make personal sacrifices for a political collectivity—to submit to conscription for example—even when they do not wish to do so. This situation is unlikely to arise in market transactions, and requires a context of political legitimacy.

### Strategy 5. Adapt to Bureaucracy

Adept citizens often adapt to bureaucratic demands by being equally bureaucratic. They rely on written communications (memos), follow procedures until they get satisfaction, know their rights and responsibilities, and treat bureaucrats as fellow professionals. They request names, phone numbers, and badge numbers, and use the hierarchy by asking to speak to supervisors, dropping names, and trying to get "backstage." Further, citizens who use a strategy of informed and adaptive compliance can often obtain clinical determinations, syndromes and authority to enhance their arguments (Stone 1993: 58). Poorer and less adept citizens often do not know how to or have the resources to adapt, finesse such situations, and get "backstage" (Sjoberg et al. 1966/1978).

It is fair to say that adapting to bureaucratic environments is not always an unqualified success for citizens, particularly if they are poor. Prottas

(1979) suggests that the type of assertion and knowledgeability such adaptation requires can result in a deficit for the seeker of social services. If bureaucratic competence conveys that the citizen is not needy after all, or is too knowledgeable of the system to be trusted, it works to the individual's detriment.

Calling adaptation a strategy, and recognizing its tactical character arises from the recognition that as pervasive as bureaucratic forms are, citizens often do not know which adaptations might meet their needs. Acquiring such political skills takes effort, and applying them suggests the assertion of one's rights and entitlements in a difficult or disadvantageous atmosphere.

### Strategy 6. Manipulate

Manipulative strategies are not unknown when citizens seek something from government,[4] and there are few more entertaining characters than those who are easily flattered or exploited. Although bureaucrats are as likely as anyone else to recognize flattery and ingratiation when they see it, some bureaucratic procedures are eased when citizens pursue this type of script (see Prottas 1979). More than merely "sucking up," this strategy may require the citizen to demonstrate sympathy, gratitude, or good humor to a bureaucrat. Another variant can be observed when the citizen acts more helpless than he is to assure himself of the public servant's maximum good will and assistance. The success of this strategy often hinges on how well a citizen's helplessness coheres with our socialized notions of what is plausible, decent, and proper to the "target population" (Ingraham and Schneider 1993) at hand. In essence, the strategy involves the citizen's finding the weaknesses and loopholes in the bureaucrat's position (or character), and exploiting them, and the bureaucrat's allowing this to occur.

Citizen's strategic manipulations also occur when it is government that seeks something. What citizen does not know that he can drag his feet? At minimum this gains him the benefits of delay, but it may also produce the satisfaction of additional assistance, the pleasure of gumming up the works, and the revenge of wasting the bureaucrat's time. This is not to say that such instrumental or expressive satisfactions are gained without penalty, but merely that the payoffs are sometimes worth the odds.

Citizens also manipulate bureaucrats by giving answers they believe people want to hear, and the most skilled among them seek the best structural arrangement to get the best outcome. For example, it is wise to do what one can to gain the most sympathetic judge (Lipsky 1980: 223, fn 18).

### Strategy 7. Mount a Challenge, While Appearing to Conform

On occasion, citizens quietly refuse to cooperate in the elements of transactions that they deem offensive or unwarranted, while cooperating most graciously with those elements of the interaction that seem reasonable. One can imagine such refusals at family planning clinics for instance, where government data gathering can be more explicit than some citizens find manageable. Similarly, one might feign ignorance, perhaps of jargon or even the language in its entirety, and allow a bureaucrat to confuse resistance with ignorance or incapacity. Or, one might participate in jury service, with no intention of deciding to convict (nullification).

Additionally, if one is privileged to have an intermediary, one can appear to conform while one's lawyer or advocate presents the bureaucrat with challenges. Or, one might mislabel a relationship to gain information (common enough in health bureaucracies, where bureaucratic discretion might result in the release of information to a "sister" but not to a friend). These are just a few of the ways in which citizens up the ante in their resistance, but in undeclared fashion. This is clearly Scott's domain of "infrapolitics" (1990).

### Strategy 8. Elude It, Though Physically Present

A second form of evasion of bureaucracy might be called the "ain't nobody here but us chickens" strategy. Unlike strategy number one, which involves absenting oneself completely, this measure involves absenting one's "authentic" self. In essence, it is a strategy of concealment and withholding of information, without the pretense of conformity. Through such devices as giving literal answers to questions one knows to be more sophisticated, truthful answers that do not fit, or answers that are otherwise ridiculous to questioners, the citizen both asserts her individuality and evades categorization and bureaucratic treatment.

A particularly vivid account of this type of behavior is provided in Rains's authoritative sociological treatment of unwed motherhood. She documents an interchange between municipal social worker and pregnant teen, from the teen's point of view. The teen recounts an interview where she answers the question "How did you get pregnant?" by taking it literally and responding "Shouldn't you know?" (Rains 1971: 136). The girls in the home parody the social worker, particularly when she asks "How did it feel?" which they deliberately take as an invitation to talk about sensations rather than self-esteem.[5] In defying the bureaucrat's definition of the situation, the teen resists being made a client or a case, and calls forth both her individuality and her membership in a sociopolitical group. While the girls take advantage of the health care offered by the municipal facility (Fraser 1990: 178), one by one they resist the clinical authority (Stone 1993) of the depoliticized therapeutic language game. Paradoxically, with it, they refuse the potential to become an organized clientele.

Strategy 8 may entail a slightly enhanced form of feigned ignorance than Strategy 7, and may prove particularly effective for individuals from populations whose intellects are devalued. Information control is particularly important to those with damaged identities, with the "stigmas" of which Goffman writes (1963: 92). The more one's status as a member of a "target population" provides a signal of policy benefits and burdens due (Ingraham and Schneider 1993), the more essential control over information and identity becomes.

Elusive strategies of this kind may work to the citizen's detriment if information is crucial. If information is withheld illegally, it may result in the equivalent of a finding of "contempt" (which may not be altogether inaccurate). On the other hand, it bears noting that bureaucrats themselves sometimes encourage or require this type of elision. If circumstances are unusual or bothersome, a citizen may be punished for honesty rather than subterfuge. For instance, Prottas (1979) claimed that Massachusetts welfare recipients were not expected to report small sums of outside income, as the paperwork and consequences of the reporting requirement were onerous for both worker and beneficiary. Similarly, a lesbian mother who does not refine an appearance of conforming with what is otherwise assumed, who does not observe the tacit practice of winking about her orientation, may soon find herself relieved of her children under law.

*Strategy 9. Declared Resistance—Mount a Direct Challenge to Change a Procedure or Outcome, or to Alter Its Effect on Oneself*

This strategy may involve an amplification of Strategy 5 (adaptation) above, with the added potential of changing outcomes for others in similar circumstances. Or it may involve a direct refusal or political action. A well-resourced citizen might complain to a legislator or pursue a legal strategy in a formal action designed to bring about change.

An openly resistant citizen taking action alone in a bureaucratic context might mount a visible protest, passively resist eviction, refuse to be drafted or to go to war, or otherwise stake an overt individual claim to an alternative policy vision or application. More subtly, but still directly and with the same potential consequences, a citizen might convert a bureaucratic transaction into an awkward social situation. Goffman discloses the potential impact of wearing a political button exposing what he refers to as a "spoiled identity" (1963: 100). One could easily imagine, for instance, the impact on a public servant of a citizen's claim to be HIV positive.

Neither the public servant nor the polis at large needs to be the audience for such a challenge. A case in point is provided by those victims of domestic violence who insist that recalcitrant police officers file reports. Even when they utterly lack the intention or confidence in the system required to follow through, such daring insistence strengthens dignity and sends an electric message to an important third party.

### Strategy 10. Challenge It Aggressively

Aggressive challenges may be expressive or instrumental in intent, covert or declared, and ethical or illegitimate. No moral equivalence among the following actions is implied, and though they differ in both degree and kind, they have aggressive, or at least energetic, features in common.

Groups like ACT-UP have used aggressive forms of humor and symbolism to both ridicule and draw attention to what they regard as fatal flaws in federal policy and administration. So too Tom Wolfe describes theatrical ritual exchanges between loosely aggregated citizens and bureaucratic "flakcatchers," mainly for expressive purposes (1970). Of course, these are the actions of groups, and not of citizens dealing with bureaucracies as individuals, but the strategy is also available for individual use. In the most extreme case, individual citizens destroy themselves, by immolation for instance, to send an aggressive symbolic and political message.

Not all aggressive acts are open and declared, and more disguised acts (Scott 1990) that "violate routine" (Edelman 1977: 124) are the safest province of individuals. Acts of vandalism, for instance, humorous or otherwise, are more easily and more often accomplished alone than in groups. The same is true of computer hacking and the introduction of viruses. It is a mistake to overlook the political impact and intent of such aggressive "uses of disorder" (Edelman 1977: 124). When citizens engage in such acts, important messages are being sent and a view of them as disgruntled customers adds little to our understanding of political structures or necessities.

Citizens in custody, perhaps for prior acts of aggression, do fight back, resist arrest, escape, and so forth. While many of such acts may be purely criminal and self-serving and thus outside the purview of this article, these clear challenges to individual bureaucrats and their authority often have a dimension of political resistance. Again, cautious interpretation is in order.

Finally, just as some groups make it their business to antagonize bureaucrats, MOVE or the Branch Davidians for instance, events in Oklahoma City suggest that such antagonism can also be expressed by individuals. Indications are that the bombing and attendant loss of life was the work of one or two individuals, not of an organized group, though the influence of an "offstage subculture" is in evidence, just as Scott (1990) would predict.

After such acts, or even lesser challenges to bureaucratic authority, we may wish to conclude that some citizens are paranoid, even evil, or no longer deserve to be regarded as citizens at all. But before such acts, attentiveness to resistant citizens is bound to lead us to a better understanding of their capacities, agonistic strivings (Honig 1993), and grievances. Before such extreme acts, careful recognition of the powers of the weak can highlight bureaucratic obligations, and the opportunities of a democratic political system.

## Strategic Customers or Strategic Citizens? Implications for Public Leaders

We can now recognize this range of strategies as an expression of the sometimes creative, sometimes dangerous exercises of individual citizens who are resistant followers, but not dissatisfied customers. In underlining rather than obscuring the public character of government regulations and services, patterns and opportunities for citizen participation and needs for effective leadership become visible. Whether "alienated" or "effective," citizens cope and struggle to be powerful, competent, and strategic in environments which do not easily accommodate their participation. This is considerably more complicated than buying ordinary goods.

Citizens are not necessarily sheep or yes people when they enter bureaucratic environments. They have great power and potential to put to use for public purposes, or even to create great harm, and public leaders do well to remember it. Public sector leaders are led astray when they are urged to pursue prescriptions embedded in faulty metaphors, as though formal leadership in public agencies is simply a question of providing quality commodities. The challenges of public service are much greater, as are their potential rewards.

It is important to note that this analysis does not suggest that public leaders are at fault or necessarily ought to accede to citizen demands. To the contrary, it suggests that where change is necessary, it might be arrived at by attention to all forms of feedback and through leadership and listening for more effective public discourse.

Public leaders might begin by using their attention to strategic citizens to identify problems and to develop the preferred solutions that lie within their discretion. With a new openness to observation, to noticing and interpreting even subtle forms of dissent, public leaders might begin to encourage more direct articulations of problems and dissatisfactions. Noticing subtle but pervasive dissatisfactions can allow public leaders to generate more informed changes in environments and practices and to address issues in ways that are publicly accountable.

Skilled observation of strategic citizen action can also help to differentiate those who do and do not have something to contribute to the creation of more democratic public agencies. Further distinctions are possible among citizens with something to contribute—among those who think for themselves but appear to acquiesce, those "survivors" (Kelley 1995) who do the best they can by surviving public sector interactions and change, and those who assert themselves resourcefully and effectively. Public leaders might accept the invitation to consider ways to convert the first two types of citizens into the last type, the alienated or tenacious into the more resourceful and competent. They might work at harnessing all of these types of energies to expand the possibilities for effective citizenship. And they might find, in consequence, a cadre of critical thinkers to be drawn into the leadership process and to community leadership and responsibility.

## Notes

1. This analysis does not equate power and authority; to do so would define these strategies out of existence.

2. And one who refuses to be regulated by government is often a hero.

3. This has the added virtue of bringing the number of strategies to ten, satisfying the need for symmetry that Paulōs (1995) finds so unnerving.

4. It bears repeating that this analysis does not refer to purely dishonest or criminal activity for personal gain.

5. Fraser calls this text and this passage to the reader's attention in her analysis of needs-talk (1990).

## References

Ciulla, Joanne B. "Leadership and the Problem of Bogus Empowerment." In J. B. Ciulla, *Ethics and Leadership: Working Papers.* College Park: Kellogg Leadership Studies Project, 1996: 43-63.

DeParle, Jason. "U.S. Welfare System Dies as State Programs Emerge." *New York Times,* Monday, June 30, 1997: pp. A1, A11, cols. 5-6.

Edelman, Murray. *Political Language: Words That Succeed and Policies That Fail.* New York: Academic Press, 1977.

Fraser, Nancy. "Talking About Needs: Interpretive Contests as Political Conflicts in Welfare State Societies." In Sunstein, Cass, ed., *Feminism and Political Theory.* Chicago: University of Chicago Press, 1990: 159-181.

Goffman, Erving. *Stigma: Notes on the Management of Spoiled Identity.* New York: Simon & Schuster, 1963.

Hirschman, Albert O. *Exit, Voice, and Loyalty.* Cambridge, MA: Harvard University Press, 1971.

Honig, Bonnie. *Political Theory and the Displacement of Politics.* Ithaca: Cornell University Press, 1993.

Ingraham, Helen and Anne Schneider. "Constructing Citizenship: The Subtle Messages of Policy Design." *Public Policy for Democracy.* Washington, DC: Brookings, 1993.

Janeway, Elizabeth. *Powers of the Weak.* New York: Knopf, 1980.

Kelley, Robert. "In Praise of Followers." In J. Thomas Wren, *The Leader's Companion: Insights on Leadership Through the Ages.* New York: Free Press, 1995: 193-204.

Liebow, Elliot. *Tell Them Who I Am: The Lives of Homeless Women.* New York: Penguin Books, 1993.

Lipsky, Michael. *Street Level Bureaucracy: Dilemmas of the Individual in Public Services.* New York: Russell Sage Foundation, 1980.

Lynch, Roberta and Ann Markusen. "Can Markets Govern?" *The American Prospect* 16 (Winter 1994): 124-134.

Lynn, Laurence E., Jr. "Government Lite." *The American Prospect* 16 (Winter 1994): 135-144.

Osborne, David, and Ted Gaebler. *Reinventing Government.* New York: Plume, 1993.

Paulōs, John Allen. *A Mathematician Reads the Newspaper.* New York: Basic Books, 1995.

Prottas, Jeffrey. *People Processing: The Street Level Bureaucrat in Public Service Agencies.* Lexington, MA: Lexington Books, 1979.

Rains, Prudence Mors. *Becoming an Unwed Mother.* Chicago: Aldine, 1971.

Rossi, Peter. *Down and Out in America: The Origins of Homelessness.* Chicago: University of Chicago Press, 1989.

Scott, James. *Domination and the Arts of Resistance: Hidden Transcripts.* New Haven: Yale University Press, 1990.

Sjoberg, Gideon. "Bureaucracy and the Lower Class" (1966), reprinted in *Bureaucratic Power in National Politics.* 3rd ed., pp. 40-53. Francis E. Rourke, ed., 1978.

Stivers, Camilla. "Some Tensions in the Notion of 'The Public as Citizen.' Rejoinder to Frederickson." *Administration and Society* 22 (February 1991): 418-423.

Stone, Deborah. *Policy Paradox and Political Reason.* New York: HarperCollins, 1988.

Stone, Deborah. "Clinical Authority in the Construction of Citizenship." *Public Policy for Democracy,* pp. 45-67. Washington, DC: Brookings, 1993.

Vinzant, Janet, and Lane Crothers. "Street Level Leadership: Rethinking the Role of Public Servants in Contemporary Governance." *American Review of Public Administration* 26 (4) (December 1996): 457-475.

Wilson, James Q. John Gaus Lecture, Annual Meeting of the American Political Science Association, New York, NY, September 1994.

Wilson, James Q. "Reinventing Public Administration." *PS* 27 (4) (December 1994): 667-677.

Wolfe, Thomas. *Radical Chic and Mau-Mauing the Flak Catchers.* New York: Bantam Books, 1970, 1971.

# V

# *The Impetus for Organizational Leadership*

## *Vision, Mission, and Goals*

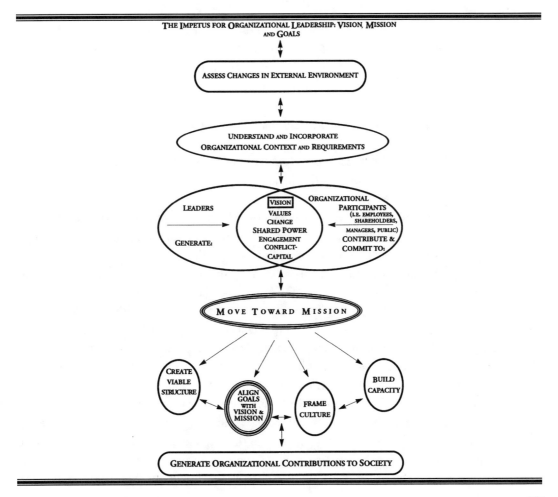

This segment emphasizes the importance of an organization's vision, mission, and goals and examines the interrelatedness among these factors. Vision is the fundamental inspiration for leadership. It is the driving force toward a future state that is so compelling it moves people to action. One expert commented that vision is a way of structuring the future—of embracing your most deeply held desires so completely that they become your experience.[1]

There are two issues that are of vital importance in the creation of vision—visionary leaders and the shared visions they help to create. Burt Nanus maintains that visionary leaders are captivated by their dreams. They are obsessed with the need to turn dreams into reality, infect others with enthusiasm and commitment, and use the vision to power great efforts and accomplishments.

Jay Conger warns of a "dark side" to visionary leadership. Just as effective visionary leadership can lead to extraordinary outcomes, misguided visionary leadership can lead to disaster. He cites many basic problems as the sources of failed vision:

- The leader projects his or her personal needs and beliefs onto constituents rather than considering the needs of constituents or the market;
- The leader seriously miscalculates the resources needed to achieve the vision;
- The leader has an unrealistic perception of the market or the vision is too far ahead of its time to be recognized; and
- The leader fails to redirect the vision based on recognized environmental changes.

Conger advises that organizations and educational institutions can play a crucial role in developing leaders in ways that enhance their potential for success and minimize negative qualities.

Conger's concerns lead to the second critical issue concerning vision—developing a *shared* vision. Many visionary leaders either fail to attain their dreams or become strongly autocratic because they are unable or unwilling to share their vision. Nanus states that the great leaders in history shared the dream so that it became a reality that inspired and motivated behavior. In this sense sharing the dream means that leaders and participants are able to align their aspirations, beliefs, and values with those manifested in the vision. They are attracted to the organization because of their personal alignment with the vision, or they are genuinely invited to participate in developing, enhancing, and implementing the vision as their own.

James Collins and Jerry Porras stress the importance of developing both organizational visions and visionary organizations. In visionary organizations, purpose and values live beyond the original founders or visionaries and become a way of life for organizational participants. They emphasize that "without vision, organizations have no chance of creating their future, they can only react to it." Visionary organizations embody a *guiding philosophy* combined with a *tangible image* that fully consider the organizations' expected *future environment*. They compel, excite, and inspire. Examples of such visions include

- Merck—We are in the business of preserving and improving human life. All of our actions must be measured by our success in achieving this;
- Patagonia—To serve as both a role model and a tool for social change;
- Telecare Corporation—To help people with mental impairments realize their full potential; and
- Apple—To contribute to the world by making tools for the mind that advance humankind.

Vision, mission, and goals are unequivocally linked. Gregory Dess and Alex Miller stress that a vision becomes tangible as a mission statement. The mission statement clearly defines an organization's primary purpose and reason for being. It answers the question, what business are we in? It describes what is unique or distinctive about the organization and establishes strategic direction and focus. The Merck Company describes its vision as preserving and improving human life. Its mission statement makes this vision more concrete by vowing to establish Merck as the preeminent drug maker worldwide, to commit to being the first drug maker with advanced research in every disease category, to conduct research as good as the science being done anywhere in the world, and so on.

Strategic goals are derived from the mission statement and identify specific end points that the organization wishes to meet. They often include factors such as financial and nonfinancial objectives, time dimensions for attaining outcomes, and indicators of measurable or observable achievements.

Finally, to place vision, mission, and goals in context, organizational leaders and participants must assess general trends continually in the external environment that may have significant impact on the organization's future. These important environmental factors include demographic, sociocultural, political and legal, technological, macroeconomic, and global developments. Understanding these environmental trends can help to identify new opportunities, discern indicators for change in mission or goals, and avoid some of the leadership pitfalls identified by Conger.

In his video *Vision 2000,* Shale Paul describes vision, mission, and goals as "successively more specific articulations of a single grand idea."[2] This grand idea provides the most powerful motivating force for leadership. Such forces bring into being new democracies, rectify social injustices, and create innovations that change the world.

### Notes

1. See Shale Paul, *Vision 2000,* Educational Video Network, 1995. (Educational Video Network, Inc., 1401 19th Street, Huntsville, TX 77340)
2. Ibid.

# 23

# Why Does Vision Matter?

BURT NANUS

Max DePree, CEO of the brilliantly successful Herman Miller Company, says, "The first responsibility of a leader is to define reality."[1] The reality of an organization has many dimensions:

- How it grew to its current size. The challenges it faced and overcame. The decisions that proved right and those that proved costly.

- Its character and culture. Its traditions and rituals. The way it conducts its business. Its organizational structure.

- The challenges and prospects facing it. Product obsolescence. Emerging opportunities. New production processes.

- Its competitive advantages and limitations. Its distinctive competence. Its resource base. Competitive threats.

- The skills and knowledge of its workers and managers. Its capacity for training and development.

- The trends in the outside world that affect it. New technologies. Possible government regulations. Changes in the needs and wants of customers.

All these factors converge to help an effective leader define a sense of direction or vision. A vision is "a realistic, credible, attractive future for the organization."[2] A vision is a beckoning symbol of all that is possible for the organization—a shining destination, a distinctive path that no other organization is likely to have, even one that may be in the very same business.

## Leaders and Visions

As the main person setting direction, the leader points the way. He or she champions a particular image of what is possible, desirable, and intended for the future of the enterprise. "Let's go this way," says the leader. "Together we'll be able to realize our own deepest desires for meaning, accomplishment, and self-fulfillment. Here's where the action is. Here's where we can make our unique contributions. On this path lie the glittering prizes. Follow me."

Such an image has great power. As deBono said, "The sense of direction urges action. The sense of direction shapes the action. The sense of direction allows the value of the action to be satisfied: has it got me nearer my goal? The sense of direction allows all judgments and decisions to be made more easily: does this help me toward my goal or hinder me?"[3]

Think of some of the great leaders of history: Jefferson, Lincoln, Gandhi, Henry Ford. We see them as great mainly because their unique visions powered great efforts and accomplishments. These leaders were captivated by their dreams. They were obsessed with the need to turn dreams into reality. They were able to infect others with enthusiasm and commitment to their visions. Eventually, a critical mass shared the dream, and the vision became a reality that motivated behavior. It became a target and plans were made for achieving it. Actions followed plans, and people were able to live the dream.

## The Power of a Vision

Why is vision so powerful? The key reason is that it grabs attention. It provides focus. Every organization has lots of ways to go. The outside world pulls it in every direction. Each has its own attractions. Yet, no organization can be all things to all people—not General Motors, not IBM, not even the United States of America. So amidst all the chaos and conflicting pressures, the vision compels an organization to remember what's really important and where it intends to go. With focus, other benefits follow:

- *Vision creates meaning for everyone in the organization.* It cuts through confusion and makes the world understandable. It helps explain why things are being done the way they are, why some things are considered good and rewarded while others are not. Once they see the big picture, people can see how their own jobs relate to it. They can look at their own skills and interests and see if there's a future for them in the organization.
- *Vision provides a worthwhile challenge.* It stretches people by showing them a joint accomplishment that they can be a part of. It generates pride in being part of a team with a useful goal. It makes people feel important. It goads them on to higher levels of commitment and performance.
- *Vision is energizing.* It provides something to believe in. It is exhilarating and exciting. Shared

aspirations lead to commitment, which energizes people. It provides the spark that ignites the engine of change. It encourages risk-taking, experimentation. It inspires new ways to think, behave, act, and learn.

- *Vision brings the future into the present.* When one imagines what can be and gives it a name, it becomes real right now. Real enough to become a beacon. Real enough to change perceptions and attitudes. Real enough to change today's decisions. Real enough to define what is essential and filter out distractions. Real enough to concentrate resources and decisions where they truly matter.
- *Vision creates a common identity.* People work together with a sense of common ownership and common destiny. A common identity fosters cooperation and promotes synergy. It aligns people's energies in a common direction.

In short, vision is the main tool leaders use to lead from the front. Effective leaders don't push or production their followers. They don't boss them around or manipulate them. They are out front showing the way. The vision allows leaders to inspire, attract, align, and energize their followers—to empower them by encouraging them to become part of a common enterprise dedicated to achieving the vision.

Contrast all this with organizations that lack vision (see Figure 23.1).

| | Organization Without Vision | Organizations With Shared Vision |
|---|---|---|
| Primary thrust | Problem-driven | Opportunity-driven |
| Worldview | Stability | Change |
| Information systems based on: | Past performance | Progress toward goals |
| Decision making | Tactical | Strategic |
| Performance measures | Short-term results | Long-term results |
| Control mechanism | Habit, fear | Peer group pressure |
| Planning style | Reactive | Proactive |

**Figure 23.1** Organizations With and Without Vision

If they're well managed, they may still operate reasonably well, at least in the short run. They may have a certain momentum. The products may get out the door on time. The bills get paid. Orders continue to come in. But there's no energy. No excitement. No sense of going somewhere. No sense of progress or renewal. None of the extra effort that people will invest only if they are committed to something challenging and worthwhile.

In the worst situations, organizations without a shared vision begin to stagnate. Managers can't agree on priorities. They are less willing to take risks. Forces for the status quo, always strong, may be unopposed. The initiative for innovation slowly erodes. Workers worry about their prospects for the future. Conflicts become difficult to resolve. Schedules begin to slip.

Eventually, the organization is less able to serve its customers or clients. Revenues erode. Staff may be laid off, further weakening morale and the ability to serve customers. The downward spiral may end up in total failure unless a new leader can be found who can give the organization a new sense of direction.

## Notes

1. Max DePree, *Leadership Is an Art.* (New York: Doubleday, 1989), 9.

2. B. Nanus, *Visionary Leadership.* (San Francisco: Jossey-Bass, 1992), 8.

3. Leonard deBono, *Tactics—The Art and Science of Success.* (Boston: Little, Brown, 1984), 4.

# 24

# Organizational Vision and Visionary Organizations

JAMES C. COLLINS
JERRY I. PORRAS

> The basic question is, what vision do you aspire to?
> —*Abraham Maslow*[1]

The few truly great companies have known for years—in some cases, for over a hundred years—the importance of having a vision. Recently, a wider range of companies (those who want to attain greatness) have come to believe in the importance of this elusive, yet vitally important, component of corporate success. One factor driving this new-found interest is that an increasing number of companies have become decentralized: they have pushed decisions out of corporate headquarters into divisions, out of divisions into departments, and so on down the line. In many cases, this flattening of organizations appears to have stimulated innovation, accelerated decision making, and increased the sense of responsibility for providing total quality on the part of people at all levels. However, this also creates a problem: How can a company decentralize and at the same time have coherent, coordinated effort? How can people in the far reaches of these flatter organizations know where it is heading? The development of a shared organizational vision represents a crucial response to this problem.

The purpose of this chapter is to present a framework that defines organizational vision, that removes the "fuzziness" surrounding the topic yet at the same time preserves the magic—the spark—that is an essential quality of vision.

## The Need for a Framework

If we look at the literature on organizations and strategy, we find numerous terms for "vision" that sometimes are used synonymously, sometimes have partially overlapping meanings, and sometimes are intended to be totally distinct from each other. As one CEO told us: "I've come to believe that we need a vision to guide us, but I can't seem to get my hands on what 'vision' is. I've heard lots of terms like 'mission,' 'purpose,' 'values,' 'strategic intent,' but no one has given me a satisfactory way of looking at vision that will help me sort out this morass of words and set a coherent vision for my company. It's really frustrating!"

Most organizations respond to the need for vision by creating something they typically call a "mission statement." While this is a step in the right direction, most mission statements are terribly ineffective as a compelling, guiding force. In fact, most corporate statements we've encountered—be they called mission, vision, purpose, philosophy, credo, or the company way—are of little value. They don't have the intended effect. They don't grab people in the gut and motivate them to work toward a common end. They don't focus attention. They don't galvanize people to put forth their best efforts toward a compelling goal. They don't mean something to people all up and down the organization. In fact, they are usually nothing more than a boring stream of words. Following are some typical examples of statements from actual companies:

> The Corporation is committed to providing innovative engineering solutions to specialized problems where technology and close attention to customer service can differentiate it from a commodity of production of job shop operations.

> We provide customers with retail banking, real estate, finance, and corporate banking products which will meet their credit, investment, security, and liquidity needs.

> [The company] is in the business of applying microelectronics and computer technology in two general areas: computer-related hardware; and computer enhancing services, which include computation, information, education, and finance.[2]

What's wrong with these? They're not compelling, nor are they exciting. They're not clear, crisp, and gut-grabbing. Like many poor guiding statements, they're nothing more than a description—and a bland one at that—of the operation of the company.

Here's one that's better but still substantially misses the mark:

> [We] are the best in the business. We are made a unique company through employee involvement. We promote from within regardless of race, religion, creed, or educational background. Only through Attitude, Pride, Enthusiasm will both our employees and our company prosper and grow. We not only demand excellence of ourselves, we demand excellence of our employees as well. [Our] explosive growth is due to the partnership between employees and the company. [We] are committed to rewarding employees who "Make it happen!"

This statement is better because it contains some inspirational words, but it isn't coherent. Like all too many such statements, it's a riddled stew of values, goals, purposes, philosophies, beliefs, and descriptions. A primary reason for the development of ineffective statements like those described above is a lack of clear concepts and useful tools.

*Who Should Set the Vision.* Who has the responsibility for setting the organization's vision? Is vision setting only for CEOs? We don't think so. Vision setting should take place at all levels of an organization and each group should set its own vision—consistent, of course, with the overall vision of the corporation. And what if there is no overall vision from above that can be latched onto? All the more reason to do it! In fact, one of the benefits of middle managers setting a vision is that it often encourages upper management to initiate the same process. As one manager pointed out: "Thinking about vision at my level forces my peers, those who report to

the more attractive of these markets became dominated by focused competitors that the managers finally made the crucial strategic decision regarding which markets to pursue and which to ignore. This decision became the foundation of their mission statement.

In using the mission statement to identify boundaries and provide focus for the organization, managers must reach a difficult balance between being too restrictive and providing guidelines that are unclear. Managers refer to these shortcomings as writing a mission statement which is either too broad or too narrow. The ideal mission statement is relatively stable and seeks to identify the broader goals that are least likely to ever become inappropriate. However, this mission statement is also flexible enough so that the organization can be a dynamic entity capable of responding to changes as they occur. A classic example of this sort of balancing is the effort involved in defining what business is given organization is in. Consider the examples below illustrating the range of broad and narrow options.

| Broad Definition | Narrow Definition |
|---|---|
| Transportation | Intracity light delivery |
| Clothing | Casual fashions for teenage girls |
| Engine repair | In-shop repair of foreign cars |
| Furniture | Waterbeds |
| Health care | Physical therapy for the aged[6] |

Managers who carefully consider what business they are in often reach important new insights about their organization—insights that can change the strategic management of the firm. For instance, MCI was one of several telecommunications startups to enter the long-distance telephone market once the Bell system was dismantled. Although MCI managers saw themselves as being in the telephone business, they grew to realize that this perspective did not make them unique, nor did it help to explain the tremendous success the firm enjoyed. After all, there were several new startups

in the telephone business, and they were not all successful.

After closer inspection, managers observed that they spent a tremendous amount of time working with government regulators trying to change the telecommunications industry from a regulated monopoly to a less regulated and more competitive market. Much of their success was due to the excellence of this work, and managers came to think of MCI as being not just in the telephone business but in the government relations business as well. Based on this new understanding, government relations was given more consideration in the strategic planning process of the firm.[7]

*Mission Statements Establish Standards for Organizational Performance Along Multiple Dimensions*

Exhibit 26.1 lists eight dimensions of performance illustrating expectations found in mission statements. Note that profitability, though clearly important, is only one of these eight dimensions. Research on the details of sixty-one mission statements from Fortune 500 firms found that 90 per-

---

**EXHIBIT 26.1**  Eight Dimensions of Strategic Goals

*Market standing:* Desired market share and competitive niche

*Innovation:* Efforts toward development of new methods and new products

*Productivity:* Aiming at specific levels of production efficiency

*Physical and financial resources:* Capital and equipment required to meet other strategic goals

*Profitability:* The level of profit and other indicators of financial performance

*Managerial performance:* Rates and levels of managerial productivity and growth

*Worker performance and attitude:* Expected rates of workers' productivity and positive attitudes

*Public responsibility:* The company's responsibilities to its customers and society

SOURCE: Based on Drucker, P. F. (1954). *The practice of management* (pp. 65-83). New York: Harper & Row.

**EXHIBIT 26.2**  Recognition of Multiple Stakeholders in Mission Statements

| Company | Stakeholder Group | Relevant Portion of Mission |
|---|---|---|
| Du Pont | Stockholders | Each of our businesses must deliver financial results superior to those of its leading competitors . . . for we consider ourselves successful only if we return to our shareholders a long-term financial reward comparable to the better-performing, large industrial companies. |
| Reynolds | Customers | In our relationship with customers, our objectives are:<br><br>Offer our products for sale on the basis of competitive price, quality, service, and reliability.<br><br>Furnish dependable products through continuing emphasis on product design, product development, quality standards, and manufacturing performance.<br><br>Provide innovative leadership in product development and marketing. |
| Dow | Employees | Employees are the source of Dow's success. We treat them with respect, promote teamwork, and encourage personal freedom and growth. Excellence in performance is sought and rewarded. |
| 3M | Community at large | 3M management recognizes that 3M's business operations have broad societal impact. It will endeavor to be sensitive to public attitudes and social concerns in the workplace, the community, the environment, and within the different political and economic systems where 3M conducts business. It will strive to keep the public, employees, and investors well informed about 3M business operations. |

SOURCE: Author's correspondence with companies.

cent mention financial soundness, profitability, or growth of the firm.[8] Without profit, the business cannot support itself or continue to attract outside support. Without profit, it will eventually cease to exist, failing to meet all of its performance standards, financial and nonfinancial alike. In fact, research shows profitability to be a good predictor of a firm's ability to invest significant funds in social programs.[9] Because profit is so fundamental, its inclusion in a mission statement seldom helps distinguish what is unique about a particular firm. In other words, knowing that McDonald's and IBM are both interested in making a profit offers little insight about the unique mission of either organization. In order to discern what makes such organizations unique, we generally look at their nonfinancial standards of performance.

While the firm's standards for financial performance are likely to be stated in terms of obligations to its stockholders, nonfinancial dimensions of performance are more likely to be discussed in terms

of the firm's obligations to a number of diverse stakeholders.[10] These stakeholders can include any parties that have an interest in the success or performance of the firm. Obligations to the firm's stockholders are referred to as its *fiscal responsibility,* while obligations to its stakeholders are referred to as its *social responsibility.* The mission statement's consideration of social responsibility may include discussion of the firm's relationship with customers, employees, the community, society at large, and so forth. Examples of these obligations are given in Exhibit 26.2.

Describing the firm's relationship with a broad range of stakeholders helps legitimize concern for issues other than financial returns. Broad-based understanding of such ideals translated into more explicit action-shaping statements is the cornerstone upon which effective strategic management is build, a point emphasized by Charles E. Exley, Jr., former chairman and CEO of NCR Corporation, in Application 26.2.

**APPLICATION 26.2**

The following is excerpted from a statement entitled "Stressing Corporate Values" by Charles E. Exley, Jr., former chairman and CEO of NCR Corporation.

How big a role do corporate values play in the continuing success of a corporation? . . . I believe that the key to our survival and success during this long period has been our focus on enduring values. These enduring values are the quality of the people who are the company and the institutional beliefs which these people share.

. . . Among the most important of these beliefs is that the primary mission in any company should be to create value for its *stakeholders*—that is, *all* of the constituencies with a stake in the fortunes of the company. These include customers, NCR people, suppliers, communities, and investors.

A growing company dedicated to achieving superior results needs to ensure that its actions are aligned with the legitimate expectations of its stakeholders. It is necessary, therefore, to try to anticipate the needs of the various stakeholder groups, and determine a course that will enable the company to achieve its management objectives while fulfilling responsibilities to the stakeholders.

. . . NCR's present characterization of its mission simply gives expression to what we have been doing for some time—creating value for our stakeholders—and serves as a useful reminder of key principles which must be translated into actions fundamental to our success.

The argument has been made that with this approach shareholders receive diminished status as merely one of the stakeholder groups and that the corporation's only direct obligation is to corporate owners. Yet we see no conflict in making a commitment to build mutually beneficial relationships with all of the stakeholders of a company. While it may appear that the various stakeholders will always have conflicting demands, in practice, the points of conflict are few, and the points of common interest are many.

. . . We at NCR are convinced that in today's competitive environment, strong corporate values are the key to success. Although we take our obligation to shareholders very seriously, we feel that this group is in no way downgraded as a result of being identified as a primary part of a larger stakeholder group. Each constituency plays a critical role that should never be overshadowed or ignored.

SOURCE: Authors' correspondence with the firm.

*Mission Statements Suggest Standards for Individual Ethical Behavior*

Ethics are the principles concerning an individual's duty to do what is morally right.[11] These duties often go well beyond the minimal requirements for legal behavior set forth in laws.[12] Carrying out these duties often requires making difficult judgments requiring decisions on how to balance the needs of one stakeholder groups against those of other groups. Suppose you discover that your firm's sole supplier of a vital chemical ingredient has for years been improperly disposing of chemicals. You are not sure how extensive the problem is, but you suspect that some of the chemicals being dumped are capable of serious environmental damage. You are inclined to report what you know to the Environmental Protection Agency, but you realize that such an action could have serious ramifications. A multimillion dollar cleanup may force your supplier (who is, after all, one of your stakeholders) out of business. That would be bad, but even worse, your business would also be shut down since they key ingredient would no longer be supplied.

Clearly, forcing your business to halt operations (even if just temporarily until an alternative solution is found) would have serious negative implications for several other stakeholder groups: stockholders, customers, and employees, in particular. If top managers in your organization have not made clear their opinion on such matters, uncertainty regarding how they might respond to your actions further complicates your reasoning. What risk do

**EXHIBIT 26.3** Examples of Strategic Objectives

*Financial objectives*

*Reynolds Aluminum:* To be an industry leader in profitability and growth and to achieve an average return on equity of 20%.

*Boeing:* Profitability as measured against our ability to achieve and then maintain a 20% average annual return on stockholder's equity.

*Boeing:* Growth over the plan period as measured against a goal to achieve: greater than 5% average annual real sales growth from 1988 base.

*General Electric:* We will run only businesses that are number 1 or number 2 in their global markets.

*Nonfinancial objectives*

*Boeing:* Integrity, in the broadest sense, must pervade our actions in all relationships, including those with our customers, suppliers, and each other. This is a commitment to uncompromising values and conduct. It includes compliance with all laws and regulations.

*General Electric:* We will be a more contemporary, more accessible, more responsive company, in touch with our customers, firmly in control of our own destiny, driven by more fulfilled people in control of theirs.

SOURCE: Authors' correspondence with companies.

you have of being labeled a "whistle blower" by disapproving superiors? What duty do you have to serve one stakeholder group (the community being affected by the dumping) versus all the other stakeholder groups and yourself? The longer you wait to act, the longer you may be guilty of condoning something that is illegal. On the other hand, the issues involved do not lend themselves to making snap judgments.

Obviously, the worst time to start thinking about how to best respond to such a crisis is *after* its eruption. Your options and your duty would be much clearer, and your response to this growing problem could take place much faster, if you had a well-reasoned and clearly articulated statement of how individuals in your organization are expected to behave in such situations. The mission statement is an ideal means of providing just such guidelines. In Chapter 11, we will provide detailed discussion of the role that mission statements can play in establishing clear guidelines for shaping individual behavior *before* an ethical dilemma arises.

**Objectives**

As suggested from the examples given in Exhibit 26.2, most mission statements are more spe-

cific than anyone's visionary thinking, but they are still hardly concrete directions for action. Therefore, just as mission statements try to make a vision more specific, objectives are attempts to make mission statements more concrete. (Short-term targets, called *action plans,* are still more specific, but we need not consider their role until Chapter 9.) The strategic objectives identified by most organizations share several features, discussed in the following sections.

*They Address Both Financial and Nonfinancial Issues*

Given the diverse interests of the stakeholders mentioned in most mission statements, it should not be surprising that most organizations have objectives that are both financial and nonfinancial in nature. Exhibit 26.3 gives examples of both.

*They Can Be Reached With a Stretch*

The best objectives appear to be those which require that an organization "stretch" in order to reach them. As Edwin Land, founder of Polaroid, described it, the sorts of objectives which draw the greatest strengths out of people are those they see as "manifestly important and nearly impossible."[13] By constantly setting goals that demand more effort, an organization is more likely to reach its fullest potential. However, this is not meant to suggest that goals should be set arbitrarily high. Unrealistically high objectives can actually harm an organization; knowing that the objective cannot be attained, the organization ignores it and finds itself operating without the guidance an objective is meant to offer.

## They Incorporate the Dimension of Time

Virtually all objectives require consideration for the time dimension if they are to be useful. A business that has moved up from number 6 to number 2 in market share in 2 years faces a far greater challenge than a similar firm that allows itself 10 years. Measurement is usually next to meaningless without some time limitation.

## They Facilitate Reasoned Tradeoffs

Most businesses will have a range of objectives, as suggested by Exhibit 26.3, and often these can contradict each other. For instance, a firm may have low-cost leadership and low employee turnover as simultaneous objectives. When a recession occurs, managers are faced with a dilemma. With orders down, maintaining the work force will incur an expense that may destroy the firm's cost competitiveness. But laying off employees means the lives of loyal and valued workers will be thrown into turmoil. Management's task is to make the tradeoffs required in such situations, and carefully established objectives help with such difficult decisions.

## They Reduce Conflict

Clearly stated objectives reduce misunderstandings and rivalry among organizational members. Such internal competition is often a manifestation of uncertainty regarding the overall direction of the firm. Objectives form the basis for cooperative managerial behavior. Focusing on overall firm progress, not divisional or departmental success, can facilitate beneficial intraorganiza-

tional relationships, such as resource and information sharing.

## They Can Be Measured

Not every objective can be easily measured, but it is still important to monitor and measure progress toward the most important objectives. For many firms, improved quality is a strategically important objective. Yet, quality is a very difficult concept to measure. So instead, most firms use proxies for quality, such as warranty claims, defect rates, or customer satisfaction surveys. In groping with the issue of quantifying hard-to-measure objectives, many firms use a simple rule of thumb stated in the form of a question: "Using this measurement, will we know when we have reached our objective?"

## They Avoid Unintended Consequences

There is potential danger involved in setting objectives and establishing measurements without considering the ramifications of the behavior they might motivate. There is an axiom: "Organizations produce whatever is measured." This warns against setting objectives casually and without regard to what will happen if the organization aggressively pursues improving performance along the resulting measure. If managers are not careful, they will establish performance measures that generate far different behavior from that intended. The authors know of several manufacturing facilities that have fallen prey to such situations.

One such case is a foundry, a manufacturing process in which the smelting furnace (1) represents a huge portion of the total investment in the plant, (2) generates the largest single category of operating expenses, (3) is largely a fixed cost, and (4) acts as a production bottleneck which creates the limit on production capacity for the entire operation. In light of these facts, it is reasonable to identify minimizing furnace expenses per ton of output as an important goal for this plant. And if this is a legitimate goal, then why wouldn't tons of furnace output per week be a good measure of progress toward meeting this goal? The problems with this practice did not become apparent until well after the goal and measurement were established.

The plant manager, aware that his performance was being measured in large part by tons of furnace output per week, sought to maximize production volume. One of the means of maximizing output was to produce sheets of metal in only the largest possible dimensions. But not all orders required the largest sizes, so much of the output had to be cut down to size after leaving the foundry. This, of course, added additional costs to the finished goods, but this additional cost was not reflected in the tons of output-per-week measure. In fact, since the trimmings could be melted down more quickly than the original raw ore, having lots of trimmings to add to future production helped raise efficiency as measured by the tons of furnace output per week. In other words, while the goal was to improve efficiency, progress toward the goal was being measured to actually encourage waste. As one seasoned veteran at this foundry explained, "The biggest problem with some of our objectives is that we meet them!" Given measurements' ability to shape behavior, they require careful consideration as a critical part of establishing strategic goals and laying the foundation for the rest of the strategic management process.

**Summary**

Strategies consist of goals, policies, and plans. We can discuss strategies for the future, or intended strategies, and we can also identify historical strategic developments, called realized strategies. Strategic management involves strategic analysis, strategy formulation, and strategy implementation.

Strategic management is evolving to include a much broader mix of managers from throughout the organization. Historically, only managers at the top of the organization were involved in strategic decisions. However, only managers at the top of the organization were involved in strategic decisions. However, there is an obvious trend for today's organizations to draw upon and integrate the managerial resources in their middle- and lower-level managers as well. This means that those preparing to manage at any organizational level should be well versed in the fundamentals of strategic management.

Because strategic management is expanding to encompass managers at so many different levels, there is greater need today for an organization to have a unifying sense of common purpose. The formal strategic planning process is one way to communicate that purpose, but it is not enough by itself. Organizations do not (and cannot) strictly adhere to the details of formal plans. Rather, they move toward goals in a series of small steps, occasionally readjusting their direction.

To keep an organization on track, there must be a sense of constancy in its overall purpose. Constancy of purpose requires that managers have a common vision, an accepted mission, and clear objectives. Experience shows that to be most effective, the hierarchy of vision/mission/objectives must include both financial as well as nonfinancial considerations. The stakeholder perspective explicitly acknowledges the multiple contingencies which organizations must serve, and helps balance the needs of each against the others.

# THE GENERAL ENVIRONMENT

The general environment consists of factors external to the industry that may have a significant impact on the firm's strategies. A firm cannot typically control its general environment. Also, many developments in the general environment are difficult to predict with any degree of accuracy. For example, macroeconomic developments, such as interest rates, the rate of inflation, and exchange rates, are extremely difficult to predict on a medium- and long-term basis. However, some trends in the general environment, such as population distribution by age, ethnicity, and income levels, can be forecast with a high degree of accuracy.

The general environment consists if many diverse but interrelated parts. Here we will look at six

**EXHIBIT 26.4** Some Important Factors in the General Environment

Demographic environment
  Aging of the population
  Ethnic composition
  Maturing of the baby boom generation
  Regional changes in population growth and decline

Sociocultural environment
  Women in the work force
  Health and fitness awareness
  Erosion of educational standards
  Spread of addictive drugs
  Concern for the environment

Political/legal environment
  Deregulation
  Relaxed antitrust enforcement
  Environmental protection laws

Technological environment
  Biotechnology
  Consumer electronics
  Superconductivity
  High-definition television technology
  Process innovations (e.g., robotics and minimills)
  Industrial disasters

Macroeconomic environment
  Interest rates
  Exchange rates
  Inflation rates
  Savings rates
  Trade deficit/surplus
  Budget deficit/surplus

Global environment
  Similarity in consumer tastes and preferences
  Powerful economic alliances
  Opening of eastern bloc countries
  Third world debt problems

broad segments: *demographic, sociocultural, political/legal, technological, macroeconomic,* and *global.* Exhibit 26.4 lists some major issues in each segment. These issues often overlap and developments in one area may influence those in another. The development of high-definition television by Japanese and European companies, for example, has forced the U.S. government to reevaluate provisions of the antitrust laws that could prevent U.S. companies from engaging in collective research and development activities. In this case, a technological development prompted a change in the political/legal environment.

Developments in the general environment often provide a firm with opportunities for expansion in terms of both products and markets. For example, the emergence of Hispanics as an increasingly important consumer group provides many firms with an opportunity to cater to their specific needs. Changes and trends in the general environment may also pose serious threats to entire industries. For example, high interest rates always have a very detrimental effect on the demand for "big ticket" items such as homes and automobiles. The competitive environment, on the other hand, largely determines the nature of competition among firms within an industry. A firm's managers typically have more influence over the competitive environment. Developments and trends in the competitive environment can usually be predicted with a relatively high degree of accuracy. However, in industries characterized by extremely high rates of technological change, such as prescription drugs, predicting future developments is quite difficult.

General environmental changes may alter the boundaries of an industry, as has been the case with deregulation in the financial services, telecommunications, and airlines industries.[14] An environmental trend that presents new opportunities for one industry may have the opposite effect on another industry. Even within the same industry, an environmental development that one firm perceives as an opportunity, may seem to be a threat to another. For example, the predicted decrease in the population of 18-year-olds to 24-year-olds is a threat to colleges and universities that only see their traditional market diminishing. However, institutions have turned this threat into an opportunity by successfully offering programs such as adult continuing education classes and degree programs to older students.

**Demographic Changes**

As we approach the 21st century, dramatic changes are taking place in the demographic profile of the United States. Some of these major changes pose significant challenges for many businesses. These include the aging of the population, population shifts among regions, changes in ethnic composition, and continuing effects of the baby boom generation (i.e., individuals born between 1946 and 1962). Let's now look at each of these changes.

Over the past few decades, stagnant or declining birth rates combined with increasing life expectancy have led to an increase in the average age of the population. This has resulted in increased demand for services and facilities appropriate for the elderly, such as convalescent homes and health services. Estimates project a decline of 17 percent in the 18-year-old to 24-year-old age group by 1995.[15] This will further aggravate the labor shortages currently experienced in some sectors of the economy.

The geographic distribution of the U.S. population is also changing continuously. Over the past few decades, more people have migrated to the south and west than to the northeast and midwest.[16] This trend has influenced relocation decisions for many firms.

Changes in the ethnic composition of the United States provide many challenges and opportunities for U.S. firms. The Census Bureau reported that the Hispanic population has increased by roughly 30 percent from 1980 to 1987 (14.5 million to 18.5 million)—five times the growth rate of the non-Hispanic population. By the year 2000, it is estimated that 25.2 million Hispanics will live in the United States.[17] Some organizations have started specifically targeting Hispanics in their advertising campaigns.

By the late 1980s, roughly one-third of the U.S. population belonged to the baby boom generation. Baby boomers are now in their peak earning and consumption years and therefore represent a very important market segment for products and services such as automobiles, specialty foods, financial services, travel, and clothing. Recognizing the importance of this demographic trend, automobile manufacturers, such as Toyota, Nissan, Honda, and Mercedes Benz, have introduced medium-priced luxury cars in the $25,000 to $40,000 price range.

## Sociocultural Changes

Social attitudes and cultural values constantly evolve and can have a significant impact on U.S. businesses. Some of these, which we will briefly

discuss below, include more women in the work force, a greater concern about health and fitness, an erosion of U.S. secondary education standards relative to other developed countries, the pervasive influence of addictive drugs, and the increasing militancy of consumer activists.

Since the 1970s, increasing numbers of women have joined the work force at all levels; approximately 80 percent of women aged 20 to 30 are currently employed outside of the home.[18] This trend has led to greater disposable incomes for families with two working members, thus increasing demand for "big ticket" items such as cars, homes, and leisure travel. It has also led to increased demand for childcare services, convenience foods, restaurants, and other products and services for working couples.

The current fitness boom has been responsible for the success of a wide variety of firms in businesses such as athletic shoes and equipment, health foods, and fitness clubs and spas. Increasing numbers of restaurants and hotels are offering low-calorie menus and exercise facilities to attract health-conscious customers.

Several sociocultural changes may pose major threats to many businesses. According to recent estimates, approximately a quarter of the U.S. labor force—20 to 27 million adults—lack basic reading, writing, and math skills. Consequently, more than half of the Fortune 500 companies have assumed an important role in educating the work force.[19] Application 26.3 describes efforts of some U.S. corporations to address the problem of decreasing skill levels in the work force.

Loss of productivity as a result of drug and alcohol abuse and cigarette smoking continues to represent a major expense to businesses and U.S. society. During the late 1980s, the abuse of drugs and alcohol cost the United States more than $140 billion annually, including $100 billion in lost productivity.[20] Such lost productivity further erodes U.S. competitiveness in comparison to firms from relatively drug-free societies, such as Japan, and has forced many companies to institute drug education and testing programs to stem these productivity losses.

Finally, lobbying by consumer activist groups, along with the surgeon general's reports, have had

**APPLICATION 26.3**

Maintaining a skilled and trained work force is an increasingly difficult challenge for U.S. businesses. Thirty percent of all high school students drop out before graduation. Many who do graduate do not have basic problem-solving skills. The challenge of American business is intensified by the decreasing number of available new workers.

William Wiggenhorn, Motorola's director of training, dramatizes America's comparative educational standing vis-à-vis the Japanese. He calculates it costs U.S. businesses $200 (on average) to train a worker in statistical quality control versus $0.47 for a worker in Japan. Unless the educational system dramatically improves, U.S. companies may be fighting a losing battle to regain their competitive edge over their foreign rivals.

Many U.S. corporations are playing an active role in employee education, spending approximately $30 billion each year to upgrade employee skills. General Motors spends more than 15 percent of its $170 million job training budget for remedial education. American Express devotes $10 million a year to basic English and social skills for its entry-level employees. Since 1982, 8,500 of Ford's 106,000 blue-collar workers have enrolled in the company's fifty learning centers located in its U.S. plants.

Developing close alliances with the public school system has also been a common practice for U.S. corporations. Chemical Bank finds that it must interview forty high school students to find one who is capable of completing its training program. In response, the firm has become involved in many educational activities in two high schools and has formed a high school debating league. General Electric spends $50,000 per year to work with top students at the Manhattan Center for Science and Mathematics, a new public school in New York's Spanish Harlem, to prepare students for careers in science and engineering. In 2 years, 95 percent of the seniors have graduated. One thousand Dallas businesses have adopted the city's 200 public schools—providing volunteers, funds, and equipment.

SOURCES:
Perry, N. J. (1988, July 9). The education crisis: What business can do. *Fortune*, pp. 71-81.
Gorman, C. (1988, December 19). The literacy gap. *Time*, pp. 56-58.
Ehrlich, E. (1988, September 19). Business is becoming a substitute teacher. *Business Week*, pp. 134-135.
Reich, R. B. (1990, November). Metamorphosis of the American worker. *Business Month*, pp. 58-61, 64-66.
Farrell, C. (1990, December 17). Why we should invest in human capital. *Business Week*, pp. 88-90.

a very negative impact on tobacco companies. In response, many companies, such as Phillip Morris, have diversified into nontobacco businesses.

**The Political and Legal Environment**

Political and legal developments can expand or limit a company's freedom of action and make the environment more hostile or more supportive of its activities. Major developments in recent years include greater deregulation in some industries and a more lenient interpretation of antitrust laws, a greater environmental protection legislation, growing power of political action committees, and decreased spending for national defense. We will now

look at an example from each of these developments.

Deregulation in industries such as airlines, trucking, banking, and utilities has led to new entries and increased competitive intensity. Firms that realized the trend early were able to complete large mergers and acquisitions in the 1980s. For example, Phillip Morris acquired Kraft for $13 billion, Chevron bought Gulf Oil Corporation for $13.3 billion, and Kohlberg, Kravis, Roberts (KKR) acquired RJR Nabisco for $25 billion. The enormous size of these deals suggests that very few companies are invulnerable to takeover attempts. Currently, there appears to be a renewed appreciation for the role governments need to play even in

## APPLICATION 26.4

The 1974 amendments to the Campaign Reform Act restrict the amount of money individuals may contribute to a single candidate to a thousand dollars and to multiple candidates in a federal elections to $25,000 per year. Although companies, unions, or other organizations may not contribute *directly* to political campaigns, they may form and contribute to PACs, which give the money to politicians. A PAC cannot donate more than $10,000 to a single campaign, but it may contribute to as many different campaigns as it wishes.

Overall, total PAC contributions to political campaigns skyrocketed from $25 million during the 1980 elections to more than $80 million during the 1988 elections. Not surprisingly, firms and industries most heavily regulated or influenced by legislation form the wealthiest PACs:

- AT&T ranks first with a PAC fund of $1.45 million (as of 1987), which was used to support 398 congressional candidates.
- United Parcel Service gave $616,000 in 1988 to more than 300 members of Congress through its corporate PAC.

During the 1988 congressional elections, PACs *increased* the amount of funds directed toward incumbents by 29.4 percent, while the money spent on challengers was relatively constant. Overall, for every dollar spent on challengers, approximately $19 goes to incumbents. Some argue that PAC money may freeze the balance of power between the two parties, giving many incumbents what can amount to a lifetime appointment to Congress.

Two extreme positions have emerged: Do PACs merely ensure that interest groups are given a fair hearing in the corridors of power? Or is it the case, as Fred Wertheimer, president of Washington-based Common Cause, has argued: "House members are shielded by a wall of political money that makes them nearly invincible"?

SOURCES:
Harbrecht, D.A., & Fly, R. (1987, June 1). Is Congress ready to bite the hands that feed it? *Business Week*, pp. 102-103.
Gorman, C., (1988, October 31). The price of power. *Time*, pp. 44-45.
Bonfonte, J., Gory, H., & Woodbury, R. (1990, November 19). Keep the bums in. *Time*, pp. 32-34, 39-42.
Dwyer, P. (1990, August 20). The campaign reform bill was born to be vetoed. *Business Week*, p. 45.

free markets. Deregulation is often cited as the major cause of the collapse of the savings and loan industry in the late 1980s. The expected cost to the government is estimated to be between $140 billion and $500 billion.[21]

Sometimes, government regulation foster the development of new industries. The increasing number of government regulations and stronger penalties for illegally dumping toxic waste caused additional expenses to several industries. But this also created a large demand for the services of waste disposal firms. Clean Harbors, Inc., located in Braintree, Massachusetts, had revenues exceeding $100 million annually within 8 years of inception. Chemical Waste Management, located in Oakbrook, Illinois, saw a profit growth from $25 million in 1985 to over $100 million by the end of decade.[22]

There is a growing debate about the influence exerted by political action committees (PACs) in public policy making. PACs are formed by interest groups to influence public policy making to their advantage. This is very often done by raising and contributing large amounts of funds to candidates for political office who are in a position to promote or defeat legislation. Application 26.4 discusses the growth of PACs in response to federal regulations regarding campaign contributions.

A political development of far-reaching significance is the end of the cold war. This is expected to bring about fundamental changes in the defense spending of the United States. Some estimates suggest that defense spending will fall by 13.6 percent to $261 billion by 1995, and to perhaps $225 billion by the year 2000. This may lead to the reduction of as many as one million defense-related jobs between 1989 and 1995, including 830,000 in the private sector. This represents approximately 20 percent of all jobs in defense-related industries.[23]

## Technological Developments

Technological developments affect most products and services as well as the processes by which they are created and delivered. Such advantages create new products, shorten the life cycle of existing products, and change the level of capital investment and production costs of individual products.

Recent advances in biotechnology have created a variety of new products ranging from new life-saving drugs to corn that produces its own pesticides. Companies like Genentech and Biosource Genetics Corporation have been successful in bringing to the marketplace several products based on advances in biotechnology. In the area of consumer electronics, the development of high-definition television may have application in areas such as military surveillance, production of semiconductor chips, and medical diagnosis.[24] Another exciting technological development of recent years has been advances in superconductivity. This is expected to lead to more efficient power plants and underwater propulsion systems.

The history of compact disks (CDs) illustrates how technological developments can abruptly shorten the life cycle of an existing product. The introduction of CDs has led to a significant decline in demand for long-playing (LP) records. As of 1988, CDs outsold LP records by 3 to 1.[25] By 1990, CDs had established complete market dominance and were outselling LPs by 24 to 1.[26] Another example is the advent of fax machines, which rendered telex equipment obsolete.[27] Similarly, major process improvements, such as minimill technology in steel manufacturing and the use of robotics in automobile assembly plants, have radically changed the economics of production. Mini-

mills require only a fraction of the capital necessary to build an integrated steel mill. On the other hand, the use of robotics and other process changes have greatly increased the capital investment necessary for a modern automobile plant.

Although technological innovations play a key role in industrial growth, they may also lead to problems. Major industrial disasters such as Chernobyl and Three Mile Island in the nuclear power industry; the chemical leakage in the Union Carbide Plant in Bhopal, India; and controversies regarding the possible impact of pesticides in the food chain have raised major concerns about the potential damage that technological developments can do to the environment. Policy makers need to consider issues such as the depletion of the ozone layer, acid rain, and the overall deterioration of the environment when assessing the full impact of technology.

## The Macroeconomic Environment

The overall state of the economy greatly influences the strategies and performance of various industries and competitors within each industry. Some of the more prominent indicators by which the health of an economy can be judged are growth in GNP, interest rates, inflation rates, savings rates, and trade and budget deficits/surpluses.

These indicators are highly interrelated. The GNP represents the dollar measure of the value of all goods and services produced within an economy. As such, an increase in the GNP is generally associated with higher levels of consumer and industrial demand for products and services. Demand for many goods and services, such as automobiles and entertainment, rises and falls according to fluctuations in interest rates; the higher the interest rate, the lower the demand. The cost of capital also goes up during periods of higher interest rates, thus depressing capital investment. Because interest rates are such an important factor in decisions involving major expenditures for plant and equipment, managers need to monitor them closely.

The fluctuating price of oil was a major cause of changes in inflation rates during most of the 1980s. Early in the decade, soaring oil prices fueled inflation to double-digit levels. When prices fell in the mid-1980s, the inflation rate dropped to below 2 percent. There is widespread concern about the low savings rate in the United States compared to other industrialized countries such as Japan, because the level of savings represents a pool of capital that can be used for industrial expansion.

Two important issues that continue to play a major role in the macroeconomic environment are the trade and budget deficits. The annual trade deficit during the latter half of the 1980s has ranged between $100 and $150 billion. Oil imports alone have fluctuated from a high of $80 billion early in the decade to a low of $35 billion in 1986.[28] Trade deficits are ultimately financed by increasing debt or by the sale of national assets. The continuing federal budget deficit during the late 1980s has been a cause for alarm since it negatively affects national savings. In other words, it diminishes U.S. capacity to make domestic and foreign investments. Further, debt servicing begins to claim a large part of the national budgets, diverting funds from investment in much needed areas such as infrastructure and education. From its earlier position as the world's biggest creditor nation, the United States has become a major debtor nation. Some of the major factors that contributed to substantial deficits include the aggressive export growth strategies pursued by many newly industrialized countries such as Korea and Taiwan, a gradual decline in the competitiveness of U.S. manufacturers, and the propensity of the U.S. consumer to save less and spend more. From a deficit of around $50 billion a year in the early 1980s, the deficit reached a peak of $170 billion by 1987, and then declined to approximately $125 billion per year for the rest of the 1980s.[29]

## The Global Environment

Today, most successful large business organizations have expanded the scope of their operations into the international arena. Both production and marketing efforts of large corporations have become increasingly globalized. This trend has been accelerated by factors such as cheaper and faster means of transportation, more powerful communi-

cation, and more similarity in tastes and consumption patterns across nations. Also, worldwide markets have made it easier for companies to recoup large investments in new technologies. In global markets, managers must be aware of potential competition from national and international competitors. Let's look at some of the trends that might affect organizations in the international arena.

One trend that has influenced the world economy is the emergence of powerful economic alliances among countries. Some of these are the European Community (EC), Organization of Petroleum Exporting Countries (OPEC), Organization of American States (OAS), and Association of South East Asian Nations (ASEAN). The creation of a "truly common market" in Europe by 1992, which greatly diminishes trade barriers among the twelve-member countries, presents major opportunities and threats.[30] For example, U.S. auto makers already present in Europe would greatly benefit from the common manufacturing standards that are being implemented. On the other hand, the rise of giant European corporations through the consolidation of several firms in member countries would pose a greater competitive threat to U.S. companies doing business in Europe.

In recent years, strategic alliances have become increasingly popular among multinational companies as a means to gain access to markets in other countries as well as to acquire state-of-the-art technologies.[31] Prominent examples of alliances include Texas Instruments and Kobe Steel to make logic semiconductors in Japan; Boeing and Fuji, Mitsubishi, and Kawasaki to produce the new Boeing 777; and Corning and Ciba-Geigy to produce a variety of medical equipment. However, not all alliances are successful. For example, AT&T's joint venture with Olivetti of Italy was a failure. The marriage between AT&T's communications equipment and Olivetti's personal computing equipment failed because of the problems in merging the two technologies. Further, cultural differences between the two companies also contributed to the failure.

Developments in the global environment may have both positive and negative implications for today's managers. Industries such as automobiles,

**EXHIBIT 26.5**  Interrelationships Among Different Segments of the General Environment

*Example 1: High-definition television (HDTV)*

The development of HDTV by Japanese electronics firms is indicative of Japan's supremacy in consumer electronics (global and technological). This could worsen the U.S. trade deficit with Japan (macroeconomic). U.S. electronics firms are trying to persuade the U.S. government to change antitrust laws in order to allow joint research and development (political/legal).

*Example 2: The U.S. trade deficit*

The persistence of large U.S. trade deficits (macroeconomic) has led to greater demand for protectionist measures,, such as trade barriers and quotas (political/legal). These measures lead to higher prices for U.S. consumers and fuel inflation (macroeconomic). Also,, in the long run,, the protected U.S. industry may become less competitive internationally (global).

*Example 3: Erosion of U.S. educational standards*

As U.S. educational standards decline,, American industry is confronted with the problem of a less-skilled work force (sociocultural). Such declining skill levels may especially have negative consequences for the high-technology sector of the U.S. economy (technological). This may lead to a decline in U.S. productivity (macroeconomic) and render U.S. industries less competitive in global markets (global).

NOTE: This exhibit does not attempt to represent all cause-and-effect relationships. Our intent is to illustrate some of the probable interrelationships among various environmental segments.

ship building, and personal computers are faced with a new competitor in Hyundai of South Korea. On the other hand, the large populations of the U.S.S.R., Eastern Europe, and China provide a lucrative market for many consumer goods firms. Companies such as Coca-Cola, Pepsi, and McDonald's have been among the first to make use of the opportunities provided by the move toward economic liberalization in these countries. Similarly, a united and prosperous Germany could prove to be a lucrative market for a variety consumer goods. The reunification of Germany is expected to result in the creation of an economic superpower with a combined population of 78 million. Some experts estimate that the rate of GNP growth of a united Germany will be 50 percent higher than what the West German growth rate would have been without unification.[32]

A problem that could have serious consequences for a variety of U.S. businesses is the international debt crisis. The inability on the part of many debtor nations to meet their credit obligations severely restricts capital inflows into these countries, which stifles their industrial development and purchasing power. It also threatens financial institutions in creditor nations since any default by debtors could seriously jeopardize their creditors' liquidity and solvency.

## Interrelationships Among Segments of the General Environment

As we have already noted, events and trends in any one segment of the general environment will often influence other segments as well. Managers must recognize that the segments do not operate independently of each other.

Exhibit 26.5 provides three examples of interrelationships among segments of the general environment: high-definition television, the U.S. trade deficit, and the erosion of U.S. educational standards.

## The Impact of the General Environment on Industries

The systematic analysis of the external environment should lead to the identification of major trends in various segments. This information becomes useful only if the firm also evaluates the impact of each of the trends on its future profitability and growth, and responds appropriately. Exhibit 26.6 provides several examples of how an environmental trend can influence various industries in very different ways.

There are three important issues to consider when assessing the impact of an environmental trend.

**EXHIBIT 26.6**  Impact of General Environmental Trends on Different Industries

| Segment/Trend | Industry | Very Positive | Somewhat Positive | Neither Positive nor Negative | Somewhat Negative | Very Negative |
|---|---|---|---|---|---|---|
| *Demographic* | | | | | | |
| Aging population | Medical services | ✓ | | | | |
| | Colleges and universities | | | | ✓ | |
| Increased purchasing power of baby boomers | Luxury automobiles | ✓ | | | | |
| | Financial services | | ✓ | | | |
| *Sociocultural* | | | | | | |
| More women in the work force | Convenience foods | ✓ | | | | |
| | Clothing | | ✓ | | | |
| Greater health and fitness awareness | Exercise equipment | ✓ | | | | |
| | Meat products | | | | | ✓ |
| *Political/legal* | | | | | | |
| Deregulation | Banking | | | | ✓ | |
| | Airline[a] | ✓ | | | | |
| Increased environmental legislation | Waste management | ✓ | | | | |
| | Automobile | | | | ✓ | |
| *Technological* | | | | | | |
| Advances in laser technology | Compact disc | ✓ | | | | |
| | Long-playing records | | | | | ✓ |
| Progress in biotechnology | Ethical drugs | ✓ | | | | |
| | Breakfast cereal | | | ✓ | | |
| *Macroeconomic* | | | | | | |
| Declining interest rates | Housing construction | ✓ | | | | |
| | Prescription drugs | | | ✓ | | |
| *Global* | | | | | | |
| Growing competitive strength of newly indus-trialized countries (NICs) | Domestic shoe manufacturing | | | | | 3 |
| | Book publishing | | | ✓ | | |
| Opening of communist countries | Fast food | | ✓ | | | |
| | Defense | | | | | ✓ |

a.  In general, airline deregulation has had a negative effect on the established airlines and a positive effect on the new entrants.

1. *The same environmental trend may have very different effects on various industries.* For example, growing awareness about health and fitness has greatly helped industries such as exercise equipment, athletic shoes, and frozen yogurt. However, fast foods as well as dairy and meat products have suffered as a result of this trend. For example, between 1987 and 1989, per capita consumption of beef declined 6.5 percent to 68.6 pounds while that of poultry—recognized as a healthier food—increased 8 percent to 84 pounds.[33]

2. *The impact of an environmental trend often differs significantly for different firms within the same industry.* For example, deregulation in the airline industry has brought on increased competition. As a result, many of the older, established airlines

have experienced declines in profitability. However, many smaller airlines, as well as newer entrants, were able to aggressively enter new markets.

3. *All environmental trends may not necessarily have much impact on a specific industry.* For example, even though advances in biotechnology have had a significant impact on the pharmaceutical industry, they are unlikely to have any serious impact on industries such as breakfast cereals and infant formulas in the near future.

## Notes

1. Want, J. H. (1986, August). Corporate mission: The intangible contributor to performance. *Management Review,* pp. 50-54.

2. For additional guidelines in preparing mission statements, see Pearce, J. A., II, & David, F. (1987). Corporate mission statements: The bottom line. *Academy of Management Executive, 1,* 109-115.

3. In general, nonprofit organizations appeared to have considered these particular issues more thoroughly than profit firms. See discussion in Drucker, P. F. (1989, July-August). What business can learn from non-profits. *Harvard Business Review, 67,* 88-93.

4. See McGinnis, V. (1981, July). The mission statement: A key step in strategic planning. *Business,* pp. 39-45; Nash, L. (1988, March-April). Mission statements: Mirrors and windows. *Harvard Business Review, 66,* 155-156; and Want, J. H. (1988, July). Corporate mission. *Management Review,* pp. 46-50.

5. Levitt, T. (1975, September-October). Marketing myopia. *Harvard Business Review,* p. 26.

6. Richman, T. (1983, August). What business are you really in? *Inc.,* pp. 77-86; Abell, D. F. (1980 *Defining the business: The starting point of strategic planning.* Englewood Cliffs, NJ: Prentice Hall.

7. McGowan, W. G. (1986, Fall). What business are we really in? The question revisited. *Sloan Management Review,* pp. 59-62.

8. Pearce & David (Ref. 2), loc. cit.

9. McGuire, J. B., Sundgren, A., & Schneeweis, T. (1988). Corporate social responsibility and firm financial performance. *Academy of Management Journal, 31,* 854-872.

10. For a discussion of the critical importance of these nonfinancial considerations, see Griesinger, D. W. (1990). The human side of economic organization. *Academy of Management Review, 15,* 478-499.

11. To learn more about how this general definition is stated more specifically in practice, see Nel, D., Pitt, L., & Watson, R. (1989). Business ethics: Defining the twilight zone. *Journal of Business Ethics, 8,* 781-791; and The business roundtable. (1988, February). *Corporate ethics: A prime business asset.*

12. Laws generally reflect society's belief in what is morally right and wrong. However, an issue's legality usually does *not* reflect the totality of its perceived morality. This distinction suggests that the letter of the law (a matter of what is legal) is not always the same as the spirit of the law (a matter of what is ethical). See Raiborn, C. A., & Payne, D. (1990). Corporate codes of conduct: A collective conscience and continuum. *Journal of Business Ethics, 9,* 879-889.

13. Peters, T. (1987). *Thriving on chaos* (p. 402). New York: Knopf.

14. Narayanan, V. K. (1989). How a broader environment can shape industry events. In Liam Fahey (Ed.), *Strategic planning management reader* (pp. 47-51). Englewood Cliffs, NJ: Prentice Hall.

15. Reich, R. B. (1990, November). Metamorphosis of the American worker. *Business Month,* pp. 58-61, 64-66.

16. Dodge, R. (1988, July 14). Stats show U.S. shrinking as it ages. *Dallas Morning News,* p. 1D.

17. For interesting perspectives on the impact of the growing Hispanic population on U.S. business, refer to Garcia, C. E. (1988, January 4). Hispanic market is accessible if research is designed correctly. *Marketing News,* pp. 46-47; de Cordoba, J. (1988, February 19). More firms court Hispanic customers—but find them a though market to market. *Wall Street Journal,* p. 25; Schwartz, J. (1988, January). Hispanics in the eighties. *American Demographics,* pp. 43-45.

18. The changing nature of the work force: An interview with John Elkins. (1987). *Journal of Business Strategy, 8*(2), 5-8; and Castro, J. (1990, Fall). Get set: Here they come. *Time,* pp. 50-52.

19. Gorman, C. (1988, December 19). The literacy gap. *Time,* p. 56.

20. Wrich, J. T. (1988). Beyond testing: Coping with drugs at work. *Harvard Business Review, 66*(1), 120-130.

21. Farnham, A. (1990, November 5). The S&L felons. *Fortune,* pp. 90, 94, 96-102, 104, 106, 108; Hector, G. (1990, September 10). S&Ls: Where did all those billions go? *Fortune,* pp. 84-85, 88. For an interesting historical perspective on the savings and loan crisis, see Mayer, M. (1990). *The greatest-ever bank robbery: The collapse of the savings and loan industry.* New York: Scribner's.

22. Hammer, J. (1988, October 3). The big haul in toxic waste. *Newsweek,* pp. 38-29.

23. Ellis, J. E., Schine, E., Griffiths, D., & Carlson, B. W. (1990, July 2). Who pays for peace? *Business Week,* pp. 64-67. 69-70.

24. Andrews, E. L. (1990, June). Translated, HDTV means "Beat Japan." *Business Month,* pp. 67-68.

25. Koretz, G. (1989, April 3). Higher oil prices are casting an ominous shadow. *Business Week,* p. 24.

26. Zachary, G. P. (1991, May 9). many record fans say vinyl LPs are groovier than CDs. *Wall Street Journal,* p. 1.

27. Lewin, R., & Sookdoo, R. (1991, January 17). The most fascinating ideas for 1991. *Fortune,* p. 32.

28. Koretz (Ref. 12), loc. cit.

29. The issue of the U.S. trade deficit and the associated policy alternatives are discussed in Lawrence, R. Z., & Litan, R. E. (1987). Why protectionism doesn't pay. *Harvard Business Review, 65,* 60-67; Magnusson, P. (1989, February 27). Will we

ever close the trade gap? *Business Week,* pp. 86-88; Baig, E. C. (1988, July 18). 50 leading U.S. exporters. *Fortune,* pp 70-71; Holstein, W. J. (1990, May 14). The stateless corporation. *Business Week,* 89-115.

30. See, for example, Kirkland, R. I., Jr. (1988, October 24). Outsider's guide to Europe in 1992. *Fortune,* pp 121-127; Demaree, A. T. (1990, December 3). The new Germany's glowing future. *Fortune,* p. 147; and Weihrich, H. (1991). Europe 1992 and a United Germany: Opportunities and threats for United States firms. *Academy of Management Executive, 5*(1), 93-96.

31. The following examples are based on Wysocki, B., Jr. (1990, March 26). Cross-border alliances become favorite way to crack new markets. *Wall Street Journal,* pp. A1, A5; Main, Jeremy. (1990, December 17). Making global alliances work. *Fortune,* pp. 121-124, 126.

32. Demaree, A. T. (1990, December 3). The new Germany's glowing future. *Fortune,* pp. 146-148, 150, 152, 154.

33. Whitaker, D. R. (1990 Meat and poultry products. *1990 U.S. industrial outlook* (pp. 34-2 to 34-7). Washington, DC: U.S. Government Printing Office.

# VI

# The Implementation of Organizational Leadership

## Structure and Organizational Design

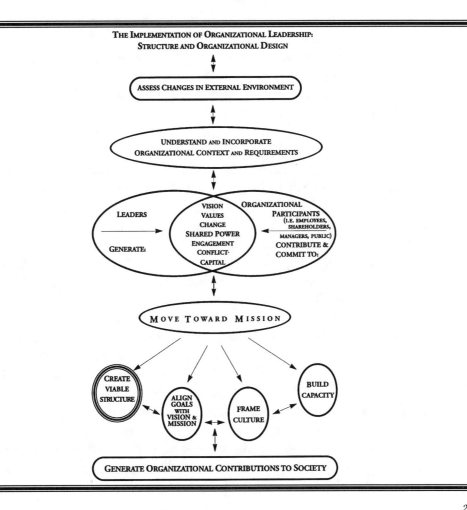

THE IMPLEMENTATION OF ORGANIZATIONAL LEADERSHIP:
STRUCTURE AND ORGANIZATIONAL DESIGN

ASSESS CHANGES IN EXTERNAL ENVIRONMENT

UNDERSTAND AND INCORPORATE
ORGANIZATIONAL CONTEXT AND REQUIREMENTS

LEADERS

GENERATE:

VISION
VALUES
CHANGE
SHARED POWER
ENGAGEMENT
CONFLICT-
CAPITAL

ORGANIZATIONAL
PARTICIPANTS
(I.E. EMPLOYEES,
SHAREHOLDERS,
MANAGERS, PUBLIC)
CONTRIBUTE &
COMMIT TO:

MOVE TOWARD MISSION

CREATE
VIABLE
STRUCTURE

ALIGN
GOALS
WITH
VISION &
MISSION

FRAME
CULTURE

BUILD
CAPACITY

GENERATE ORGANIZATIONAL CONTRIBUTIONS TO SOCIETY

This section explores the kinds of designs and structures that help leaders and participants achieve their ultimate purpose in new-era organizations. Often one of the first and most disrupting actions taken by a new leader is to restructure the organization without connecting its structure to the organization's vision, mission, and values. Instead leaders and participants need to ask, What design or structure do we need to accomplish our mutual purpose? Organizational structures must be designed to fit human processes and work relationships, not the reverse.

Gareth Morgan indicates that traditional rigid bureaucracies are being reshaped to meet human needs and the challenges of a rapidly changing environment. He describes a continuum of organizational forms—beginning with the rigidly organized bureaucracy, the bureaucracy run by a senior executive group, the bureaucracy that has created cross-departmental teams, the matrix organization, the project-based organization, and finally the loosely coupled organic network. The three latter forms are organic in nature and function more like a network than a bureaucracy.

Because the rigid bureaucracy was created to function in a very stable environment, leaders and participants in the competitive context of today's environment seek designs that provide flexibility and responsiveness. Morgan points out that organizations that begin as rigid bureaucracies may evolve over time and modify their structures. However, adoption of the project-based organization or loosely coupled organic network would likely require a major revolution due to the constraints of ingrained organization culture and politics.

Network and team structures are two forms of organization design that have gained prominence in this new era. Nitin Nohria indicates that the "new competition" has compelled organizational participants to create network structures as an adaptive response to changing business and technological conditions. Network organizations are distinguished by factors such as their dense horizontal linkages across formal organizational boundaries, reciprocal relationships between small firms in a regional economy, or interlocking relationships among economic institutions. This design allows linkages among and between individuals and groups to facilitate cooperation and swift action without the impediments of formal regulations and levels of authority.

Team structures provide another option for organizations in an era of rapid change and new technologies. Kimball Fisher indicates that organizational leaders have found that unleashing human potential is the answer to dealing with the changing environment. Self-directed work teams empower their members by granting authority and accountability to the team and providing essential resources and information. They bring together individuals with multiple skills and expertise who are capable of achieving their purpose and maintaining a total organization focus.

Some organizations use teams as their primary structure. Kenneth Smith and Henry Sims highlight an organization that uses a three-layer approach to their team structure.

The inner layer consists of the core vision team whose responsibility is to initiate, extend, enhance, and communicate the vision. The middle layer is charged with leadership of the planning team and is responsible for scanning the environment for ideas for new ventures. The outer-layer team leaders are charged with the responsibility for opening and starting up a new project location.

Structures for new-era organizations must allow people to share ideas and expertise in an interconnected framework. Far from the rigid bureaucracy of more stable times, organizations require wholly new designs that will transform with the needs of their participants and the changes in the environment. The key criteria are flexibility and fit, which mean that organizational participants can use an array of designs from bureaucracies to custom made arrangements to accomplish their purposes. Structures are no longer considered constraints, they are facilitators of human interaction.

# 27

# From Bureaucracies to Networks

## The Emergence of New Organizational Forms

GARETH MORGAN

Most of us are familiar with the bureaucratic organization that is specified in almost every detail and run in a tightly controlled way by the executive at the top. Many government organizations with their rigid departmental divisions and clearly defined roles and rules, mobilized through a hierarchical chain of command, provide obvious examples.

While this kind of organization once dominated many aspects of society, most bureaucracies are in the process of being reshaped along with the changing demands and challenges of the world around them. Sometimes the changes are quite marginal. Many organizations often resist fundamental change—because people, for one reason or another, wish to cling to a hierarchical model. But in some cases, significant transformations in orga-

nization can be achieved. The following pages explore some of these changes, and how the bureaucratic approach to management is being challenged and replaced by newer forms of organization that are much more like networks than hierarchical structures. Conceptually, the range of organizational forms to be discussed can be represented by a continuum ranging from the rigid bureaucracy on the one hand (model 1) to the loosely coupled network, or organic form of organization (model 6), on the other. The aim of the discussion is twofold:

(a) to illustrate how a bureaucracy can, in principle, begin to transform itself over time from one form of organization into another (but probably not all the way from model 1 to models 5 and 6); and

**EXHIBIT 27.1**

| Model 1 | Model 2 | Model 3 | Model 4 | Model 5 | Model 6 |
|---------|---------|---------|---------|---------|---------|
| The rigidly organized bureaucracy | The bureaucracy run by a senior executives' group | The bureaucracy that has created cross-departmental teams and task forces | The matrix organization | The project-based organization | The loosely coupled organic network |

◄──────────────────────────────────────────────────────────────────►

*MECHANISTIC/BUREAUCRATIC*
Organized for stability

*ORGANIC NETWORK*
Organized for flexibility and change

(b) to contrast the principles that underpin organizations at different ends of the continuum.

The purpose of the discussion is to provide a series of images and general principles against which you can identify the organizations with which you are familiar. A visual illustration of each model is presented in Exhibit 27.2.

**EXHIBIT 27.2**   Schematic Illustration of the Six Models

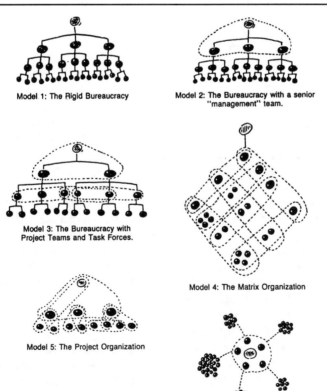

Model 1: The Rigid Bureaucracy

Model 2: The Bureaucracy with a senior "management" team.

Model 3: The Bureaucracy with Project Teams and Task Forces.

Model 4: The Matrix Organization

Model 5: The Project Organization

Model 6: The Loosely-coupled Organic Network

## Model 1

This is Weber's classical bureaucracy described in the opening paragraph (and in Resource 22). It represents the traditional organizational pyramid under the strict control of the chief executive. The organization has tried to codify all important operational principles, and is run in accordance with those principles. Meetings are viewed as a waste of time, and are rarely necessary, because almost every contingency is well understood: The organization is operating in an ultrastable environment.

## Model 2

This organization is finding that the environment is generating novel problems, issues, and concerns on an ongoing basis. It is impossible to codify all appropriate responses. The chief executive has thus decided to create a "management team," comprising himself and the heads of principal departments, which meets on a weekly basis. This team makes all policy decisions, and settles the problems that cannot be handled through the organization's normal routines. Each department head exercises clearly defined authority in relation to his or her area of influence. Managerial styles vary from department to department, being shaped by the personality of the department head and the kind of task being performed. Some departments are highly authoritarian; others are more participative.

## Model 3

This organization has found that the senior management team cannot handle all the issues that require an interdepartmental perspective and has created a number of project teams and task forces involving staff at lower levels of the organization. The departmental structure and sense of organizational hierarchy, however, are very strong. The members of the teams and task forces tend to see their primary loyalty as being to their department head rather than to the team to which they belong. They realize that promotion is largely a departmental affair. They sit in team meetings as representatives of their department. They tend to give the "departmental line" on issues, and report back to their departmental head on what happens. When real problems arise, they are thus usually "delegated upward" for resolution by the senior management team. Team leaders feel that they have relatively little power and find it difficult to develop commitment and momentum in relation to the activities that they're charged with managing. The organization *looks* as if it is moving toward a "matrix" or project team structure, but in reality it operates like a loosely structured bureaucratic organization where information is passed up the hierarchy, and decisions down.

## Model 4

This organization has decided to organize itself in a matrix form. Its special character rests in the fact that it has decided to give more or less equal priority to functional departments such as finance, administration, marketing, sales, production and R&D, and to various business or product areas. Thus people working in the various product or business teams that cut across the functional areas have to work with two perspectives in mind: functional and end product. This dual focus, under ideal conditions, allows the various operating teams to combine functional skills and resources with an orientation driven by the key tasks and challenges from the organization's environment—such as those relating to the need to fine-tune products for specific market segments or the needs of specific geographic areas.

## Model 5

This organization has decided to tackle most of its core activities through project teams. Notionally, there may be functional departments—but they only play a supporting role. Key specialists belong to teams and make their main contributions through their team. The organization recognizes that its future lies in the dynamism and innovativeness of these teams, and it tries to give them a free rein within the parameters and values that senior managers have used to define the strategic direction of the organization. The organization is much more like a network of interaction than a bureaucratic structure. The teams are powerful, exciting, and dynamic entities. Coordination is informal. There is frequent cross-fertilization of ideas, and a regular exchange of information, especially between team leaders and the senior management group. Much effort is devoted to creating shared appreciations and understandings of the nature and identity of the organization and its mission, but always within a context that encourages a learning-oriented approach. The organization is constantly trying to find and create the new initiatives, ideas, systems, and processes that will contribute to its success.

## *Model 6*

This organization has decided to become, and stay, a loosely coupled network. Rather than employ large numbers of people, it has decided to operate in a subcontracting mode. It has a small core of staff who set a strategic direction and provide the operational support necessary to sustain the network, but it contracts other individuals and organizations to perform key operational activities. Its network at any given time operational-izes the "ideas" that the central group wishes to develop. For example, the organization may be in the fashion industry. It has created a name and image—its "label"—but contracts out market surveys, product design, production, distribution, and so on. In the public eye, the firm has a clear identity. But in reality, it is a network of firms held together by the product of the day. It changes from month to month as different ideas and products come on line, and as the core organization experiments with different partners. The firm is really a system of firms—an open-ended system of ideas and activities, rather than an entity with a clear structure and definable boundary.

Models 1 through 6 are really different "species" of organizations. A firm beginning as model 1 may over time evolve into model 2, 3, perhaps even 4. And if it is prepared to engage in a major "revolution," it may develop the features of models 5 and 6. But in reality, the transformation process from one end of the continuum to the other is extremely difficult to make, and the required change is more than structural—it is cultural and political as well. The culture and politics of many organizations constrain the degree of change and transformation in which they can successfully engage, even though such change may be highly desirable for meeting the challenges and demands of the wider environment.

# 28

# *Is a Network Perspective a Useful Way of Studying Organizations?*

NITIN NOHRIA

The term "network" has become the vogue in describing contemporary organizations. From large multinationals to small entrepreneurial firms, from manufacturing to service firms, from emerging industries such as biotechnology to traditional industries such as automobiles, from regional districts such as Silicon Valley and Italy's Prato district to national economies such as those of Japan and Korea, more and more organizations are being described as networks.[1] Typically, the term "network" is used to describe the observed pattern of organization. But just as often it is used normatively: to advocate what organizations must become if they are to be competitive in today's business environment.

The concept of networking has also become a popular theme at the individual level of analysis:

Individuals are alerted to the importance of their so-called connections in getting things done or moving ahead in life and are therefore urged to network more—to build relationships that they can use to their advantage.[2] A growing number of networking organizations that help people make all sorts of contacts—from finding dates to finding a venture partner—have sprung up to capitalize on the interests in networks. Many firms (aided by willing consultants) have also joined the bandwagon, offering in-house training programs that help their employees learn about the importance of networks and how to go about funding and using them.[3]

What accounts for this enormous contemporary interest in networks? After all, the idea itself is not new. At least since the 1950s, the concept of networks has occupied a prominent place in such diverse fields as anthropology, psychology, sociology, mental health, and molecular biology. In the field of organizational behavior, the concept dates back even further. As early as the 1930s, Roethlisberger and Dickson (1939) described and emphasized the importance of informal networks of relations in organizations.

I believe that there are three major reasons for the increased interest in the concept of networks among those interested in organizational phenomena. The first is the emergence over the last two decades of what Best (1990) has labeled "the New Competition." This is the competitive rise over the last two decades of small entrepreneurial firms, of regional districts such as Silicon Valley in California and Prato and Modena in Italy, of new industries such as computers and biotechnology, and of Asian economies such as those of Japan, Korea, and Taiwan. This New Competition has been contrasted with the old in one important way. If the old model of organization was the large hierarchical firm, the model of organization that is considered characteristic of the New Competition is a network, of lateral and horizontal interlinkages within and among firms.

The competitive success of the New Competition has thus led to an increased interest in networks, particularly as the old seeks to become more like the new. Established firms are trying to restructure their internal organizations along the line of networks.[4] They are also trying to redefine their relationships with vendors, customers, and even competitors; instead of arm's-length, competitive relations, they are seeking more collaborative relations that will bind them together into a network.[5] Several regions have launched initiatives to grow their own version of the entrepreneurial network district.[6] Even at the level of national economic and legislative policy, we hear discussions about the feasibility of adopting Japanese kieretsu-type network structures and about relaxing traditional antitrust policies that forbid collaboration among the firms in an industry.[7]

In addition to the interest in the New Competition, a second reason for the increased interest in networks has to do with recent technological developments. New information technologies have made possible an entirely new set of more disaggregated, distributed, and flexible production arrangements, as well as new ways for firms to organize their internal operations and their ties to firms with which they transact. The rise of such manufacturing and telecommunications networks has led to a concomitant interest in the organizational networks that these new technological developments may spawn.[8]

The maturing of network analysis as an academic discipline over the same period is a third reason for the increased trend toward viewing organizations as networks. Network analysis has grown from the esoteric interest of a few mathematically inclined sociologists to a legitimate mainstream perspective. This development was spearheaded in the 1970s by Harrison White and his affiliates, who developed a formal apparatus for thinking about and analyzing social structure as networks.[9] White's work attracted and spurred several other scholars to produce a richer network approach to studying social structure, including theoretical and methodological tools that could be applied to several substantive areas.[10] It also led to the founding of a new journal on social networks, the publication of several edited volumes and books on network and structural analysis, and the network perspective's adoption and dissemination through articles in leading journals of sociology and organizational behavior.[11] Today, interest in the concept of networks is no longer restricted to a small group of sociologists. It has expanded to include students of organizations in such applied, interdisciplinary settings as business schools.[12]

As a consequence, the network concept "has indeed become fashionable and trendy," which, according to Sarason and Lorentz (1979:3) "of course is a mixed blessing." For those who have been advocates of a network perspective, this period may well be their day in the sun. On the other hand, the faddish popularity of the network concept has created a situation where an observation made by Barnes in 1972, and reiterated a decade later by Burt (1982), is more probably more on target than ever: Anyone reading through what purports to be network literature will readily perceive the analogy between it and a "terminological jungle in which any newcomer may plant a tree."

This indiscriminate proliferation of the network concept threatens to relegate it to the status of an evocative metaphor, applied so loosely that it ceases to mean anything.

If this were to happen, it would be most unfortunate, because there is a great deal to learn about organizations (and how to act in them) from a properly applied network perspective. It was in the hope of preventing the network concept from becoming another tired metaphor (as the concept of culture became some time ago), that Bob Eccles and I organized this conference and edited this volume. Our hope was that by bringing together scholars who were in various ways using a network perspective and showing how it could be applied to study organizational phenomena, we would be able to provide some focus and coherence to this mode of enquiry.

My purpose in this introduction, therefore, is to outline the main precepts of a network perspective for the study of organizations and to illustrate some of the main advantages of adopting such a perspective. Fritz Roethlisberger (1977) believed that organizations and behavior in them were such "elusive phenomena" that one could never hope for a definitive theory in the field. All that one could expect was the benefit of a perspective or a framework that could be used like a "walking stick" to support and navigate one's inquiry through the treacherous terrain of organizations. Sustaining Roethlisberger's metaphor, let me suggest that a network perspective is a particularly sturdy walking stick that is likely to hold up well in our intellectual inquiry of organizations. Of course, individuals are likely to have their own trusted walking sticks that they are loathe to relinquish in favor of the network perspective. To persuade them to try is the aim of this introduction and this book.

First, though, a word about the primary audience for whom this book is written: academics who are interested in organizations and organizational behavior. For those already familiar with a network perspective, this book provides a collection of some of the leading-edge ideas and research in this area. For those unfamiliar with this perspective, this book is an invitation to adopt a network perspective. By focusing on organizations and organizational behavior, this book differentiates itself from books that have been written to show how a network perspective may be employed to study social structures in general and from books that have elaborated on network methodology.[13] Though we focus on organizations, this book deals with an extremely broad range of organizational issues from a theoretical as well as an empirical standpoint. It is thereby intended to appeal to a wide audience in the field of organization studies.

Let me also say a word about the audience for whom this book has not been written. Though the concept of networks has certainly been taken up with considerable vigor by managers and other practitioners in organizational settings, this book is not directly written for them. The papers in this volume, as almost all the practitioners who attended our colloquium gently told us, belong to the genre of academics writing for other academics. But the intrepid practitioner who is willing to struggle through obtuse references, dense prose, and statistical analyses may well find several nuggets of genuine insight, as did some of the practitioners who attended our colloquium.

This is not to say that we are not interested in the relevance of the network perspective for practice. Since the majority of the contributors to this book are professors at business schools (and often consultants to organizations), the applicability of these ideas to the practical concerns of managers is of considerable import and something that we will inevitably have to address. In order to do that effectively, though, it is important first to build a coherent academic platform on the basis of which a network perspective can be applied usefully to study organizational phenomena.

Therefore let me now turn to the issue of what it means to study organizations from a network perspective.

### Studying Organizations From a Network Perspective

At the risk of imposing a greater unity of perspective than might be reflected in the subsequent chapters of this book, let me suggest that five basic premises underlie a network perspective on organizations.

1. *All organizations are in important respects social networks and need to be addressed and analyzed as such.* A social network, following Laumann et al. (1978:458) can be defined as "a set of nodes (e.g., persons, organizations) linked by a set of social relationships (e.g., friendship, transfer of funds, overlapping membership) of a specified type." As Lincoln (1982:26) points out, "To assert that an organization is not a network is to strip of it that quality in terms of which it is best defined: the pattern of recurring linkages among its parts." The premise that organizations are networks of recurring relationships applies to organizations at any level of analysis—small and large groups, subunits of organizations, entire organizations, regions, industries, national economies, and even the organization of the world system.

Equally important to note is that formal or prescribed relations (such as those that show up on organizational charts or on input-output tables) do not entirely capture the network of relationships that shape an organization. Informal or "emergent" relationships, to use a phrase suggested by Ibarra (Chapter 6, this volume), are just as important in understanding networks in organizations. These relations can be of many different types. Among other things, they may be based on friendship, advice, or conversational relationships within and across an organization's formal boundaries.[14] Identifying and analyzing these "hidden" networks can be of great significance in understanding organizations.

From a network perspective, then, the structure of any organization must be understood and analyzed in terms of the multiple networks of relationships in the organization (both prescribed and emergent) and how they are patterned, singly and in various combinations.

2. *An organization's environment is properly seen as a network of other organizations.* Ever since organizations were recognized as open systems, the critical significance that an organization's environment plays in shaping its activities has been a principal tenet in organization theory. But just as organization theorists have accused other social scientists (particularly economists) of treating the organization like a black box, they can be accused of treating the environment as a black box surrounding the organization. While organizational theorists talk a great deal about an organization's environment in such terms as the degree of uncertainty or resource scarcity it presents for the organization, they have tended to be vague about the source of these pressures.[15]

Building on the work of such earlier organizational theorists as Dill (1958), Evan (1966), and Warren (1967), proponents of a network perspective argue that the most significant elements of an organization's environment are the other organizations with which it must transact. Moreover, mere identification of those other organizations is insufficient; it is equally important to know the pattern of relationships among them. As Barley et al. (Chapter 12, this volume) so graphically put it, "Not only are organizations suspended in multiple, complex, and overlapping webs of relationships, the webs are likely to exhibit structural patterns that are invisible from the standpoint of a single organization caught in the tangle. To detect overarching structures, one has to rise above the individual firm and analyze the system as a whole."

From a network perspective, then, the environment consists of a field of relationships that bind organizations together. Also called an "interorganizational field" (DiMaggio and Powell 1983:148), these organizations include "key suppliers, resource and product consumers, regulatory agencies, and other organizations that produce similar services or products."

To those familiar with Michael Porter's (1980) framework for analyzing industries, this conception of the environment might appear remarkably similar. In many respects it is, except that greater attention is paid in the network perspective to the overall pattern of relationships among the firms in the industry, an issue that receives short shrift in Porter's framework.

In sum, a network perspective on organization-environment relations pushes beyond abstract notions of environmental uncertainty, resource dependencies, and institutional pressures. It seeks to locate the precise source of these environmental forces by analyzing the pattern of relationships among the organizations that make up the environment.

3. *The actions (attitudes and behaviors) of actors in organizations can be best explained in terms of their position in networks of relationships.* From a network perspective, variations in the actions of actors (and the success or failure of these actions) can be better explained by knowing the position of actors relative to others in various networks of relationships, than by knowing how their attributes differ from one another. For instance, knowing attributes like the relative size and technological capabilities of an organization may be less predictive of its conduct and performance than knowing the structural autonomy it enjoys in its transaction networks.[16]

To borrow a sorting scheme proposed by Ronald Burt, network analysts typically use five different principles—cohesion, equivalence, prominence, range, and brokerage—to analyze an actor's network position and to explain how it influences the actor's actions. Cohesion and equivalence are principles for sorting actors into common groups. Cohesion models group actors together if they share strong common relationships with one another; equivalence models group actors together if they have similar relations with other actors in the organization (even though they may not be directly linked to each other). Both cohesion and equivalence models are used to explain similarities in the attitudes and behaviors of the actors in an organization. Similarities by cohesion are argued to arise from actors discussing opinions in strong, socializing relations, whereas similarities by equivalence are argued to arise from actors playing similar roles with regard to others in the organization and so coming to a shared opinion.[17]

Prominence, range, and brokerage models are used to explain the extent to which an actor is advantageously positioned relative to others in an organization. Prominence models differentiate individuals according to who is in more or less demand. An actor's prominence increases as the actor is the object of relations from many others who are in turn the object of many relations. Actors can use their prominence to push others into doing things that further their own interests.[18]

Range and brokerage models tap a different action potential. They measure the extent to which actors can get away with pursuing their own inter-

ests. The simplest range measure is network size, a sum of an actor's relations—the more you have, the more access you have to social resources. More sophisticated range models highlight the importance of the bridging ties that an actor has.[19] Finally, brokerage models are based on the principle that actors are freer to pursue their own interests to the extent that their relations connect them with others who are disorganized and so can be played off against one another. The causal mechanism here is contact with disorganized others.[20]

While network analysts favor explanations based on an actor's location in various networks, they do, of course, recognize that actors also belong to categories based on similarities in their attributes (e.g., ethnicity, gender, etc.). While some, such as Burt (Chapter 2, this volume), argue that categories can be translated into network positions and are hence largely relevant to explanations, others (and I'm in this camp) don't take such an extreme position. As Blau (1982) concludes, an actor's network position and attributes offer complementary insights that taken together offer a fuller explanation of the actor's actions.

4. *Networks constrain actions, and in turn are shaped by them.* While a network perspective, as I have indicated, emphasizes how the network positions of actors constrain or enable their actions, it does not rule out the possibility that actors can change their network positions. Networks are constantly being socially constructed, reproduced, and altered as the result of the actions of actors. While network analysts would maintain that the patterns of relationships in any organization are to a large extent fairly stable and recurring, they recognize that new network ties are being constantly formed and that over time these new ties can change old network patterns in quite dramatic ways.

Thus actors in network models are not seen as atoms locked in a crystalline grid, their every action determined by their structural location. They are, as Harrison White suggests, active, purposeful agents who are constantly trying to wrest control for themselves or blocking others from taking control. This dynamic of actors wrestling for control and seeking advantage is, as White notes, "constantly throwing up fresh hunks of network" (Chapter 3, this volume). Therefore networks are as much process as they are structure, being continually shaped and reshaped by the actions of actors who are in turn constrained by the structural positions in which they find themselves.

5. *The comparative analysis of organizations must take into account their network characteristics.* Traditionally, as Nelson complains (1986:75), most comparative research "does not deal directly with the networks of relationships which make up organization structure. Rather researchers establish variables that are generalizations about these relationships. . . . The major problem with such variables is that they do not reveal the actual configurations of relations which comprise structure."

Centralization, for instance, in comparative studies such as those conducted by the Aston group (Pugh et al. 1968), is usually measured as the average degree of asymmetry in relationships in the organization and by the extent to which decision rights are concentrated among few individuals. What such a measure does not tell us is who the elites or dominant coalitions are in each of the organizations being compared, and what the precise structure of their relationship is with the other groups of actors in the organization. By not capturing the actual configuration of relations, traditional measures of centralization can tell us little about whether the dominant coalition in one organization is more vulnerable than that in another or if there is another group of actors in the organization that is really making the key decisions, the dominant coalition merely being a puppet coalition. By focusing directly on the patterns of relationships through such analytic techniques as graph analysis or block modeling, a network perspective offers a much sharper set of tools to address such questions in comparative analyses.[21]

To take another case, the structure of competition in markets is typically compared using a variable such as concentration ratios; but as White (1981) has shown in his analysis of various forms of markets, such a measure misses the very stuff of competition in markets, which can be understood only by directly modeling the pattern of interaction among market players.

A network perspective, therefore, pushes for comparisons in terms of variables and measures that reflect the overall structure of relationships in the organization, eschewing variables and measures that are generalizations of the pattern of dyadic interactions in the organization.

Taken together, the five basic premises described here define the core features of a network perspective on organizations. It should be readily apparent from the preceding discussion that adopting a network perspective is not merely adopting a new metaphysical image of organizations or bolting a few network variables onto traditional analytical perspectives. If we are to take a network perspective seriously, it means adopting a different intellectual lens and discipline, gathering different kinds of data, learning new analytical and methodological techniques, and seeking explanations that are quite different from conventional ones. This is a tall order and must therefore answer the skeptic's favorite questions—"Why bother?" and "Is it worth it?"

## *What Is to Be Gained by Adopting a Network Perspective?*

To fully appreciate the advantages of adopting a network perspective, one must read this entire book. It is hard to do adequate justice to any substantive theme within the space constraints of a brief introduction. But in an attempt to demonstrate that it would be worthwhile to read the rest of the book—and thus motivate the reader to do so—I shall briefly discuss four substantive themes that are dealt with more fully in several of the chapters. These four themes span several levels of analysis and have been the subject of considerable attention in organizational literature.

1. What explains differences in the power and influence of individuals in organizational settings? Or put differently, where does power come from?

2. What explains the recruitment patterns that result from different organizing efforts, such as the effort to create a new organization or to mobilize change in an existing organization?

3. What explains the strategic conduct of firms, in particular their choice to enter into strategic alli-

ances? Are these alliances viable long-term organizational arrangements?

4. What distinguishes the organizational characteristics of the so-called New Competition from that of the old? Does the mode of "network" organization characteristic of the New Competition represent the new model of the organization?

## 1. Power and Influence in Organizations

Questions about what accounts for the distribution of power in organizations have long occupied a central place in organizational theory. Explanations for what gives an individual power in an organization have usually focused, among other things, on the individual's personal characteristics (such as charisma and expertise); socioeconomic profile (including things like gender, race, educational attainments, and social class); formal position in the organization (including place in both the horizontal and vertical differentiation of labor); attitudes and values (such as the extent to which the individual exemplifies the norms and culture of the organization); control over critical resources (including capital, social approval and other rewards, and information); and control over critical contingencies (including task interdependencies and gatekeeping functions).[22]

These explanations have not been fruitless—much of what we currently know about the distribution of power and influence in organizations is based on these ideas. However, it has always been recognized that these factors are not sufficient from an explanatory standpoint and that an individual's position in various networks of relationships can be a source of power quite independent of other factors. We have long known, for instance, that being central in communication networks is a source of power.[23] What the network perspective provides is a more systematic way of understanding this classic intuition.

As Brass and Burkhardt (Chapter 7, this volume) contend, there are many different ways in which one can be central in a network. One can be central in the sense of degree (being the object of many relations), betweenness (being in the middle of paths that connect others), or closeness (having immediate access to others who are connected).

Each provides a different basis of power. To fully understand an individual's power, it is just as important to know which of the various kinds of organizational networks (e.g., advice, work flow, friendship) she is central in, as it is to know the relevant network boundaries within which she is more or less central (e.g., the network demarcated by the immediate subunit, the department in which the subunit is located, the entire organization, or the dominant coalition).

Moreover, as Burt (Chapter 2 this volume) argues, centrality in networks is not the only (or necessarily the most important) source of an individual's power. He suggests that the extent to which individuals can surround themselves with "structural holes" (i.e., sit in the middle of disorganized contacts), the more autonomy and power they are likely to have. Indeed, he would argue that this is a more important indicator of power and influence than centrality is.

As these chapters demonstrate, adopting a network perspective offers some very rich and interesting insights on where power comes from.[24] A network perspective can also shed light on what strategies individuals should employ to try to gain power or seize control, an issue on which the traditional literature is relatively silent. As Harrison White (Chapter 3, this volume) and Herminia Ibarra (Chapter 6, this volume) elaborate, there are some fairly specific propositions that can be derived from a network perspective on the strategies and actions that individuals should take under different situations to increase their power and be able to pursue their own interests.

## 2. Organizing Efforts

Organizational theorists have always been interested in explaining the factors that facilitate or impede organizing efforts leading to the creation of a new venture or those that involve mobilizing collective action, such as a unionization drive. Their explanations have typically hinged on the role and function of entrepreneurs or leaders—individuals with unusual organizing skills who can mobilize action by sheer dint of persuasion and an unyielding drive. Thus they have devoted considerable effort to understanding the psychological attributes of entrepreneurs and leaders and the conditions that are most conducive for them to flourish. Individual attributes such as achievement orientation and risk-taking propensity, and contextual conditions such as autonomy and slack resources have all been seen to facilitate organizing efforts.[25]

It is also recognized that organizing efforts involve identifying, persuading, and recruiting others to contribute to the objectives the organizing agents have in mind, and that the outcomes (in terms of who joins and who does not) can have a critical bearing on the success of the organizing effort. Organizational theorists such as Kanter (1983) have explicitly directed attention to the importance of the network of relations in which the organizing agents are embedded.

Several of the papers in this volume show more clearly just how critical these networks of relationships can be in shaping the outcomes of organizing efforts. Paul DiMaggio (Chapter 4, this volume), for instance, describes how the founders of New York's Museum of Modern Art (MOMA) used their networks of relationships to recruit key individuals to commit resources to fund the museum and how they recruited others to manage the museum and confer it with legitimacy. As DiMaggio shows, the success of the museum—a very risky idea at the time—could in large part be attributed to the pattern of recruitment that resulted from the way the founders tapped their networks.

David Krackhardt (Chapter 8, this volume) shows how, in contrast to the success of the MOMA organizers, the recruitment strategy of the organizers of a unionization drive led to the eventual failure of their effort. In this case, the organizers did not pay enough attention to an individual who was very central in the firm's friendship network and instead concentrated their recruitment efforts on those individuals who were central in the more visible work-flow networks of the firm. This proved to be their undoing, because in the final analysis the ambivalence of the individual who was central in the friendship network swayed his friends into not supporting the certification drive.

In another chapter, Nohria (Chapter 9, this volume) shows how crucial networks of relations (especially bridging ties) are to the entrepreneur's search for information in the creation of new ventures. Based on this analysis, he suggests that to understand the contextual conditions that facilitate entrepreneurial organizing efforts, one must pay careful attention to the pattern of relationships that exist in a social system, because it is these relations that serve as the pathways for information flows that not only facilitate search but also enable the production of trust and the governability of the system.[26]

## 3. Strategic Alliances

Organizational theorists typically have explained the strategic conduct of organizational actors, such as the creation of alliances among them as being strategic responses to mitigate and manage competitive uncertain ties and resource interdependencies.[27] Those who take a more transaction cost perspective explain alliances as an effective response to conditions where transactions cannot be easily conducted through market contracts, but the transaction costs involved are not so high as to mandate internal organization.[28] These explanations pay scant attention to how these alliances interconnect to bind the firms into a network of relationships. They also ignore how the network of relationships that emerges over time as a result of alliances between firms shapes and constrains the strategic conduct of firms involved in them.

As the chapters in this volume that analyze the pattern of strategic alliances among firms in the biotechnology industry argue, it is insufficient (and probably erroneous) to explain the strategic behavior of firms in this industry without paying explicit attention to the network of relationships among them. As Barley et al. (Chapter 12, this volume) show, firms in the industry can be partitioned into different niches based on commonalities in their alliancing strategy. These niches also reflect the participation of the firm in different market segments. While the causal direction of this link between alliance and market segmentation strategies is hard to establish, it is clear that the actions of firms are shaped by their position in the overall network.[29]

Moreover, as Kogut et al. (Chapter 13, this volume) demonstrate, the particular alliances that firms establish over time are a function of their position in the network of relationships in previous periods. Thus the decision to cooperate is shaped by, and in turn shapes, the network of relationships in the industry.

Finally, Powell and Brantley (Chapter 14, this volume), raise the interesting possibility that the overall network defines a stable ecology that operates as a learning system; hence the conduct of firms in the biotechnology industry must be understood within this framework.

While the authors in this volume have focused on a particular form of strategic conduct—strategic alliances—other scholars have shown how a network perspective can explain differences in firm conduct on issues such as pricing, philanthropy, and political contributions, and can also predict outcomes such as firm profitability and return on investments.[30]

## 4. The New Competition

The emergence of the New Competition is often seen by organizational theorists as an adaptive response to changing business and technological conditions that require and enable more "open" and "network" forms of organization. The same logic offered by Burns and Stalker (1961) to explain why firms that were successful in more dynamic environments had an "organic" character, is used to explain the success of new organizational forms such as small entrepreneurial firms, regional districts, and large network-like organizations such as the Japanese kieretsu. Because of historical circumstances, these firms are seen to have organizational characteristics that make them more like networks or organic organizations, and are hence better suited to the dynamic contemporary environment.[31]

It is here that the failure to adopt a coherent network perspective becomes most problematic. It is precisely the lack of a clear understanding of a network perspective that has led to the rampant and indiscriminate use of the network metaphor to describe these new organizational forms. In some cases, this tendency has gone even further and the network organization has been reified as a new ideal type of organization—one that will replace the bureaucracy as the basic model that all organi-

zations, in due course, will adopt if they are to survive and flourish.

From a network perspective, all organizations can be characterized as networks and indeed are properly understood only in these terms. So to say an organization has a network form is a tautology. Nevertheless, there are some proponents of a network perspective who have not rejected outright the idea that "it is meaningful to talk about networks as a distinct form of coordinating economic activity" (Powell 1990:301). The notion that it is meaningful to think of network organization as a distinct form should, in my view, be understood as a rhetorical strategy that is being employed by some theorists to get beyond the markets-and-hierarchies distinction that has become the dominant frame for the comparative analysis of organizations. The rhetoric of networks as a form of organization is an attempt to center attention fully on the distinctive "logic of collective action [in networks] that enables cooperation to be sustained over the long run" (Powell 1990:301).

By treating networks as a distinct form of organization, those who advocate this perspective deliberately direct attention to *particular network characteristics* that are to some degree relevant to any organization but are especially salient in so-called network organizations, such as dense horizontal linkages across formal organizational boundaries (e.g., Baker, Chapter 15, this volume), reciprocal relationships between small firms in a regional economy (e.g., Perrow, Chapter 17, this volume), or interlocking relationships among economic institutions in Asian economies (e.g., Biggart and Hamilton, Chapter 18, this volume; and Gerlach and Lincoln, Chapter 19, this volume). This rhetorical framing of network as form forces the analyst to attend to what it is that makes these new arrangements efficient, governable, and flexible compared with traditional modes of organizing. It pushes for analysis in network terms and directs attention to key features of these organizations that can be understood only from a network perspective, like the role of linking-pin institutions (such as the banks in the Japanese system and the "impannatore" in the regional districts of Prato and Modena) in the governance of these organizations, and the role of ties that create trust (such as shared ethnic, geographic, ideological, or professional background).

Adopting a network-as-form perspective forces us to understand these new organizations on their own terms (and in terms of those characteristics that best define them) instead of viewing them as merely the amorphous middle in the traditional markets-and-hierarchies continuum.[32]

## *An Agenda for Further Developing the Network Perspective*

The preceding discussion was designed to persuade skeptics that a network perspective can provide insights that other perspectives cannot. In this section, I offer some suggestions for those who already believe in the analytical power offered by the network perspective, by highlighting five fronts on which the network perspective must advance for it to flourish as a way of studying organizations:

### 1. A Theory of Action

Network analysts share a model of action that treats actors as purposeful, intentional agents. Most would agree with Granovetter (Chapter 1, this volume) that it is important to avoid both undersocialized and over socialized models of action, and recognize that actors have social as well as economic motives and that their actions are influenced by the networks of relationships in which they are embedded.

Beyond that, though, there are several points of divergence. Some such as Burt (1982) (Chapter 2, this volume) emphasize the rational, utility-maximizing side of actors, even though their actions are highly con strained by their structural positions. Others, such as DiMaggio (Chapter 4, this volume) emphasize the everyday practical considerations that shape the actions of actors, such as their boundedly rational, institutionally guided cognitive orientations. I will not even pretend to try to resolve this debate. It is one that has persistently dogged the social sciences. Instead, let me further muddy the waters by offering yet another model of action that in my view warrants careful consider-

ation. The motor of action in this model is the actor's pursuit of identity.

This model builds on the work of philosophers such as Arendt (1958) and has been taken up in the social sciences by such sociologists as White (forthcoming) and economists such as Sen (1985:348), who offers a succinct summary: Action is motivated by the

identity of a person, that is, how the person sees himself or herself. We all have many identities, and being "just me" is not the only way we see ourselves. Community, nationality, class, race, sex, union membership, the fellowship of oligopolists, revolutionary solidarity, and so on, can all provide identities that can be, depending on the context, crucial to our view of ourselves, and thus to the way we view our welfare, goals, or behavioral obligations. A person's concept of his or her own welfare may go well beyond "sympathizing" with them. Similarly, in arriving at goals, a person's sense of identity may be quite central. And, the pursuit of private goals may well be compromised by the consideration of the goals of others in the group with whom the person has some sense of identity.

### 2. Different Types of Ties and Their Implications

Organizations are composed of ties of a myriad nature. Ties can differ according to whether they are based on friendship, advice, or work; whether what flows through them is resources, information, or affection; whether they are strong or weak ties, unitary or multiplex ties, face-to-face or electronic ties; and so on. Though the complex nature of ties is recognized by everyone who takes a network perspective, there has been, as Wellman (1988:25) has observed, a tendency to "concentrate on the form of network patterns rather than their content . . . a Simmelian sensibility that similar patterns of ties may have similar behavioral consequences, no matter what the substantive context. Pushed to its extreme, [the] argument has been that the pattern of relationships is substantially the same as the content."

As several of the papers in this book reveal, the substance and type of ties in a network can have important implications for action. While there is a growing recognition about the importance of different types of network ties, we are nowhere near having a systematic framework or theory for predicting what kinds of ties matter under what kinds of circumstances in what ways. This is an area that must be given considerable attention in order for the network perspective to make more substantive progress.

### 3. The Etiology and Dynamics of Networks

Most network analysts treat the network of relations in any organization as a given. The question of what leads to the formation of different network patterns has bedeviled the network perspective for some time now. Competing theories abound. Some have tried to explain the formation of networks on the basis of exchange theory; others have focused on homophily and balance theory, with its emphasis on triad closure; still others have argued that networks are shaped by the control processes of agency, delegation, and specialization.[33] Resolving these debates by pitting them against one another in substantive settings is essential if we are to ever resolve this crucial issue.

In addition to theories of how networks are formed, we need better theories of how networks evolve and change over time. The dynamics of networks are beginning to receive considerable attention, and the findings of these studies will be of considerable interest.[34]

### 4. Methodological Advances

Though tools for the analysis of networks are now quite freely available, there has continued to be insufficient concern for the methodological limitations of network analysis, particularly in terms of the demanding data requirements to comprehensively analyze even a single organization, let alone being able to conduct large sample comparative studies of organizations. Advances in sampling technologies as well as collaborative large scale data-gathering projects are necessary for progress on this front.[35]

### 5. Problem-Centered Research Relevant to Practitioners

There has been a healthy trend in the network literature towards more applied, substantively oriented research. I believe that trend should be pushed with greater vigor so that the network perspective can be employed to address issues that are of direct concern to practitioners. This will require not only a continuing emphasis on problem-centered research but also a conscious effort to make the language and discourse of the network perspective more accessible to managers. As Kanter and Eccles (Chapter 20, this volume) conclude, network research can provide practitioners with the means to define and classify the properties of networks, assess outcomes associated with particular types of networks, and describe the dynamics of network formation and evolution. In this way, a network perspective can help practitioners identify the importance of networks to organizational activities and outcomes, diagnose their current state, and proactively change networks to improve their own performance and the effectiveness of their organizations.

If the network perspective makes rapid progress along the five fronts I have outlined here, I believe that it can have a greater impact than it has had on our understanding of organizations. A decade ago, in a review of the state of organization theory, Pfeffer (1982:276-277) offered the following assessment of the network perspective:

Social network analysis remains more of a paradigm and framework than a theory, and more promise than fulfilled potential. . . . But the importance of the findings of the network studies performed to date and the fundamentally structural nature of organizations argue for the additional development of theories and research on organizations using network properties both in hypotheses describing and explaining the development of networks and in relating network characteristics to other organizational properties.

While I firmly believe that this book demonstrates that the network perspective has made important strides in fulfilling the potential that Pfeffer saw a decade ago, there is still much to be done. Moreover, as Paul DiMaggio remarked at our conference, "The moment for those who come from a network perspective to be the head priests of organizational analysis is now." More than anything else, this book is a call to seize the moment and capitalize on this opportunity.

## Notes

1. For a discussion of multinationals as networks, see Bartlett and Ghoshal (1989) and Nohria and Ghoshal (1991); for entrepreneurial firms, see Gilder (1989) and Sengenberger et al. (1990); for manufacturing, see Jaikumar (1986) and Hayes et al. (1988); for professional services, see Eccles and Crane (1988); for biotechnology, see Kenney (1986); for automobiles, see Nohria and Garcia-Pont (1991); for regional districts, see Saxenian (1990) and Piore and Sabel (1984); and for the economies of Japan, Korea, and Taiwan, see Hamilton and Biggart (1988).

2. See, for instance, Maguire (1983), Lipnack and Stamps (1982), and Sarason and Lorentz (1979).

3. See, for instance, Mueller (1986).

4. See, for instance, Mills (1990) for several examples of large firms undergoing such a transformation.

5. See, for instance, Cash and Konsynski (1985), Miles and Snow (1986), and Powell (1987).

6. See Miller and Cote (1985).

7. See Gerlach (1991) and Kotz (1978) for a more detailed comparison of the Japanese and U.S. systems, and several papers in Hirst and Zeitlin (1989) for a discussion of how the adoption of network structures can potentially stem industrial decline.

8. See, for instance, Applegate, Cash, and Mills (1988); Child (1987); Drucker (1988, 1990); Malone and Rockart (1991); Nolan, Pollock, and Ware (1988, 1989); and Hiltz and Torhoff (1978).

9. See White (1970); Lorrain and White (1971); White, Boorman, and Breiger (1976); and Boorman and White (1976) for some of the seminal papers of this period.

10. See Alba (1981), and Burt (1980b, 1982) for comprehensive reviews of the work done in the 1970s.

11. The evolution of the field of network analysis is in detail by Wellman (1988).

12. This volume is testimony to this increasingly broad interest in networks.

13. For a collection of essays that deal with the applicability of network analysis to studying social structures generally, see Marsden and Lin (1982) and Wellman and Berkowitz (1988). For more methodologically oriented collections, see Burt and Minor (1983) and a review by Marsden (1990).

14. For discussion of the various types of network relations, see Mitchell (1969, 1974) and Tichy (1981).

15. See Scott (1987) for a detailed discussion of different ways in which organization-environment relations have been conceptualized by organizational theorists.

16. See, for example, Burt (1980a, 1983).

17. See Burt (1980a and b, 1982, 1987) for the distinctions and relative merits of studying similarities by cohesion and equivalence. In organizational behavior, Nelson (1989) provides a good example of how similarities develop by cohesion and how they can be the basis for intergroup conflict. Walker (1985), on the other hand, shows how similarities in attitudes can be based on equivalence.

18. See, for example, Coleman (1988), Bonacich (1987), and Marsden (1983) for prominence-based models of power and social influence.

19. See Granovetter (1973, 1982) and Lin et al. (1981) for examples of models of influence based on range.

20. See Freeman (1977), Cook and Emerson (1978), and Burt (1980a, 1983, and Chapter 2, this volume) for examples of models of power based on brokerage.

21. See Barney (1985) for a good example of a network perspective applied to the comparative analysis of organizations.

22. See Pfeffer (1980, 1992) for an exhaustive review of the literature on power in organizations.

23. See, for example, the early work of Guetzkow and Simon (1955) on the impact of an actor's position in various types of communication networks.

24. Also see Bonacich (1987) and Krackhardt (1990).

25. See, for example, Zaltman et al. (1973), Drucker (1985), and Stevenson and Gumpert (1985).

26. The importance of networks in mobilizing efforts has been brilliantly documented by Faulkner (1983) for the music industry, and by Jenkins (1983) for social movements.

27. See, for example, Pfeffer (1972) and Pfeffer and Nowak (1976).

28. See, for example, Williamson (1985, 1991).

29. Similar results are shown for the automobile industry by Nohria and Garcia-Pont (1991).

30. See, for example, Baker (1984), Burt (1983), and Mizruchi (1989a, 1989b).

31. See Miles and Snow (1986), who exemplify this argument.

32. See Thorelli (1996) and Powell (1987) for earlier framings in which networks were viewed as hybrid arrangements between markets and hierarchies, and Powell (1990) for the revised framing in which networks are seen as a distinctive form of organization.

33. For the exchange theoretic arguments, see Cook (1987); for the triad closure argument, see Leinhardt (1977); and for the control and identity argument, see White (forthcoming).

34. See, for example, Delany (1988) and Levine and Spadaro (1988) for dynamic models of labor market mobility.

35. See Marsden (1990) for a more exhaustive review of the state of network methodology.

# References

Alba, Richard D. 1981. "Taking Stock of Network Analysis: A Decade's Results." In S. Bacharach, ed., *Perspectives in Organizational Research.* Greenwich, CT: JAI Press, pp. 39-74.

Arendt, Hannah. 1958. *The Human Condition.* Chicago: University of Chicago Press.

Baker, Wayne. 1984. "The Social Structure of a National Securities Market." *American Journal of Sociology* 89:775-811.

Barnes, J. A. 1972. *Social Networks.* Reading, MA: Addison-Wesley.

Barney, Jay. 1985. "Dimensions of Informal Social Network Structure." *Social Networks* 7:1-46.

Bartlett, Christopher A., and Sumantra Ghoshal. 1989. *Managing Across Borders: The Transnational Solution.* Boston: Harvard Business School Press.

Best, Michael. 1990. *The New Competition.* Cambridge, MA: Harvard University Press.

Blau, Peter M. 1982. "Structural Sociology and Network Analysis: An Overview." In Peter V. Marsden and Nan Lin, eds., *Social Structure and Network Analysis.* Beverly Hills, CA: Sage, pp. 273-280.

Bonacich, Philip. 1987. "Power and Centrality: A Family of Measures." *American Journal of Sociology* 92:1170-1182.

Burns, Tom, and Gerald M. Stalker. 1961. *The Management of Innovation.* London: Tavistock.

Burt, Ronald S. 1980a. "Autonomy in a Social Topology." *American Journal of Sociology* 85:892-925.

———. 1980b. "Models of Network Structure." *Annual Review of Sociology* 6:79-141.

———. 1982. *Toward a Structural Theory of Action.* New York: Academic Press.

———. 1983. *Corporate Profits and Cooptation: Networks of Market Constraint and Directorate Ties in the American Economy.* New York: Academic Press.

———. 1987. "Social Contagion and Innovation: Cohesion Versus Structural Equivalence." *American Journal of Sociology* 92:1287-1335.

Burt, Ronald S., and Michael J. Minor, eds. 1983. *Applied Network Analysis.* Beverly Hills, CA: Sage.

Cash, James I., and Benn R. Konsynski. 1985. "IS Redraws Competitive Boundaries." *Harvard Business Review* 63(2) (Mar./Apr.): 134-142.

Child, John. 1987. "Information Technology, Organization, and the Response to Strategic Challenges." *California Management Review* (Fall): 33-50.

Coleman, James S. 1988. "Social Capital in the Creation of Human Capital." *American Journal of Sociology* 94:S95-S120.

Cook, Karen S., ed. 1987. *Social Exchange Theory.* Beverly Hills, CA: Sage.

Cook, Karen S., and Richard M. Emerson. 1978. "Power, Equity, and Commitment in Exchange Networks." *American Sociological Review* 43:721-739.

Delany, John. 1988. "Social Networks and Efficient Resource Allocation: Computer Models of Job Vacancy Allocation Through Contacts." In Barry Wellman and S.D. Berkowitz, eds., *Social Structures: A Network Approach.* New York: Cambridge University Press, pp. 430-451.

Dill, William, R. 1958. "Environment as an Influence on Managerial Autonomy." *Administrative Science Quarterly* 2 (Mar.): 409-443.

DiMaggio, Paul, and Walter W. Powell. 1983. "The Iron Cage Revisited: Institutional Isomorphism and Collective Rationality in Organizational Fields." *American Sociological Review* 48:147-160.

Drucker, Peter F. 1985. *Innovation and Entrepreneurship: Practice and Principles.* New York: Harper & Row.

———. 1988. "The Coming of the New Organization." *Harvard Business Review* 66 (Jan.-Feb.): 35-53.

———. 1990. *The New Realities.* New York: Harper & Row.

Eccles, Robert G., and Dwight B. Crane. 1988. *Doing Deals: Investment Banks at Work.* Boston: Harvard Business School Press.

Evan, William M. 1966. "The Organization-set: Toward a Theory of Interorganizational Relations." In James D. Thompson, ed., *Approaches to Organizational Design.* Pittsburgh: University of Pittsburgh Press, pp. 173-188.

Faulkner, Robert R. 1983. *Music on Demand.* New Brunswick, NJ: Transaction.

Freeman, Linton C. 1977. "A Set of Measures of Centrality Based on Betweenness." *Sociometry* 40:35-41.

Gerlach, Michael L. 1991. *Alliance Capitalism: The Social Organization of Japanese Business.* Berkeley: University of California Press.

Gilder, George. 1989. *Microcosm: The Quantum Revolution in Economics and Technology.* New York: Simon & Schuster.

Granovetter, Mark S. 1973. "The Strength of Weak Ties." *American Journal of Sociology* 78:1360-1380.

———. 1982. "The Strength of Weak Ties: A Network Theory Revisited." In P. V. Marsden and N. Lin, eds., *Social Structure and Network Analysis.* Beverly Hills, CA: Sage, pp. 105-130.

Guetzkow, Harold, and Herbert A. Simon. 1955. "The Impact of Certain Communication Nets Upon Organization and Performance in Certain Task-Oriented Groups." *Management Science* 1 (Apr.-July): 233-250.

Hamilton, Gary G., and Nicole W. Biggart. 1988. "Market, Culture, and Authority: A Comparative Analysis of Management and Organization in the Far East." *American Journal of Sociology* 94 (supplement): S52-S94.

Hayes, Robert H., Steven C. Wheelwright, and Kim B. Clark. 1988. *Dynamic Manufacturing: Creating the Learning Organization.* New York: Free Press.

Hiltz, Roxanne S., and Murray Torhoff. 1978. *Network Nation: Human Communication Via Computers.* Reading, MA: Addison-Wesley.

Hirst, Paul, and Jonathan Zeitlin, eds., 1989. *Reversing Industrial Decline.* New York: St. Martin's Press.

Jaikumar, Ramachandran. 1986. "Post-Industrial Manufacturing." *Harvard Business Review* 64(6) (Nov.-Dec.): 69-76.

Jenkins, Craig J. 1983. "Resource Mobilization and the Study of Social Movements." *Annual Review of Sociology* 9:527-553.

Kanter, Rosabeth M. 1983. *The Change Masters.* New York: Simon & Schuster.

Kenney, Martin. 1986. *Biotechnology: The University-Industrial Complex.* New Haven: Yale University Press.

Kotz, David M. 1978. *Bank Control of Large Corporations in the United States.* Berkeley: University of California Press.

Krackhardt, David. 1990. "Assessing the Political Landscape: Structure, Cognition, and Power in Networks," *Administrative Science Quarterly* 35(2):342-369.

Laumann, Edward O., L. Galskeiwicz, and P. V. Marsden. 1978. "Community Structure as Interorganizational Linkages." *Annual Review of Sociology* 4:455-484.

Leinhardt, S., ed., 1977. *Social Networks: A Developing Paradigm.* New York: Academic Press.

Levine, Joel H., and John Spadaro. 1988. "Occupational Mobility: A Structural Model." In Barry Wellman and S. D. Berkowitz, eds., *Social Structure: A Network Approach.* New York: Cambridge University Press, pp. 452-476.

Lin, Nan, Walter M. Ensel, and John C. Vaughn. 1981. "Social Resources and Strength of Ties." *American Sociological Review* 37:202-212.

Lincoln, James R. 1982. "Intra- (and Inter-) Organizational Networks." In Samuel B. Bacharach, ed., *Research in the Sociology of Organizations,* Vol. 1. Greenwich, CT: JAI Press.

Lipnack, Jessica, and Jeffrey Stamps. 1982. *Networking: The First Report and Directory.* Garden City: Doubleday.

Lorrain, Francois P., and Harrison C. White. 1971. "Structural Equivalence of Individuals in Social Networks." *Journal of Mathematical Sociology* 1:49-80.

Maguire, Lambert. 1983. *Understanding Social Networks.* Beverly Hills, CA: Sage.

Malone, Thomas W., and John F. Rockart. 1991. "Computers, Networks, and the Corporation." *Scientific American* 265(3):128-137.

Marsden, Peter V. 1983. "Restricted Access in Networks and Models of Power." *American Journal of Sociology* 88:686-717.

———. 1990. "Network Data and Measurement." *Annual Review of Sociology* 16:435-463.

Marsden, Peter V., and Nan Lin, eds. 1982. *Social Structure and Network Analysis.* Beverly Hills, CA: Sage.

Miles, Raymond E., and Charles C. Snow. 1986. "Network Organizations: New Concepts for New Forms." *California Management Review* 28:62-73.

Miller, Roger, and Marcel Cote. 1985. "Growing the Next Silicon Valley." *Harvard Business Review* 63(4) (July-Aug.): 114-123.

Mills, Quinn. 1990. *The Rebirth of the Corporation.* New York: Wiley.

Mitchell, J. C. 1969. "The Concept and Use of Social Networks." In J. C. Mitchell, ed., *Social Networks in Urban Situations.* Manchester, U.K.: Manchester University Press, pp. 1-50.

———. 1974. "Social Networks." *Annual Review of Anthropology* 3:279-299.

Mizruchi, Mark S. 1989a. "Similarity of Political Behavior Among Large American Corporations." *American Journal of Sociology* 95(2):401-424.

———. 1989b. "Cohesion, Structural Equivalence, and Similarity of Behavior: An Approach to the Study of Corporate Political Power." Working paper, Center for the Social Sciences at Columbia University.

Mueller, Robert K. 1986. *Corporate Networking: Building Channels for Information and Influence.* New York: Free Press.

Nelson, Reed E. 1986. "The Use of Blockmodeling in the Study of Organization Structure: A Methodological Proposal." *Organization Studies* 7(1):75-85.

———. 1989. "The Strength of Strong Ties: Social Networks and Intergroup Conflict in Organizations." *Academy of Management Journal* 32:377-401.

Nohria, Nitin, and Carlos Garcia-Pont. 1991. "Global Strategic Linkages and Industry Structure." *Strategic Management Journal* 12:105-124.

Nohria, Nitin, and Sumantra Ghoshal. 1991. "Distributed Innovation in the 'Differentiated Network' Multinational." Working paper, Harvard Business School.

Nolan, Richard L., Alex J. Pollock, and James P. Ware. 1988. "Creating the 21st Century Organization." *Stage-by-Stage* 8(4):1-11.

———. 1989. "Toward the Design of the Network Organization." *Stage-by-Stage* 9(1):1-12.

Pfeffer, Jeffrey. 1972. "Merger as a Response to Organizational Interdependence." *Administrative Science Quarterly* 17:218-28.

———. 1980. *Power in Organizations.* Boston: Pitman.

———. 1982. *Organizations and Organization Theory.* Boston: Pitman.

———. 1992. *Managing With Power.* Boston: Harvard Business School Press.

Pfeffer, Jeffrey, and Phillip Nowak. 1976. "Joint Ventures and Interorganizational Dependence." *Administrative Science Quarterly* 21:398-418.

Piore, Michael J., and Charles F. Sabel. 1984. *The Second Industrial Divide.* New York: Basic Books.

Porter, Michael. 1980. *Competitive Strategy.* New York: Free Press.

Powell, Walter W. 1987. "Hybrid Organizational Arrangements." *California Management Review* 30:67-87.

———. 1990. "Neither Market Nor Hierarchy: Network Forms of Organization." In B. Staw, ed., *Research in Organizational Behavior* Vol. 12. Greenwich, CT: JAI Press, pp. 295-336.

Pugh, D. S., D. J. Dickson, C. R. Hinings, and C. Turner. 1968. "Dimensions of Organization Structure." *Administrative Science Quarterly* 13:65-91.

Roethlisberger, Fritz J. 1977. *The Elusive Phenomena.* Boston: Harvard Business School Press.

Roethlisberger, Fritz J., and W. J. Dickson. 1939. *Management and the Worker.* Cambridge, MA: Harvard University Press.

Sarason, Seymour B., and Elizabeth Lorentz. 1979. *The Challenge of the Resource Exchange Network.* San Francisco: Jossey-Bass.

Saxenian, AnnaLee. 1990. "Regional Networks and the Resurgence of Silicon Valley." *California Management Review* 33(l):89-112.

Scott, Richard M. 1987. *Organizations: Rational, Natural, and Open Systems* 2d ed. Englewood Cliffs, NJ: Prentice Hall.

Sen, Amartya. 1985. "Goals, Commitment, and Identity." *Journal of Law, Economics, and Organization* 1(2):341-355.

Sengenberger, Werner, Gary Loveman, and Michael Piore, eds. 1990. *The Reemergence of Small Enterprise: Industrial Restructuring in Industrialized Economies.* Geneva, Switzerland: International Labor Organization.

Stevenson, Howard H., and David E. Gumpert. 1985. "The Heart of Entrepreneurship." *Harvard Business Review* 63(2) (Mar.-Apr.): 85-94.

Thorelli, Hans B. 1996. "Networks: Between Markets and Hierarchies." *Strategic Management Journal* 7:37-51.

Tichy, Noel. 1981. "Networks in Organizations." In P. C. Nystrom and W. G. Starbuck, eds., *Handbook of Organization Design,* Vol. 2. New York: Oxford University Press, pp. 225-248.

Walker, Gordon. 1985. "Network Position and Cognition in a Computer Software Firm." *Administrative Science Quarterly* 30:103-130.

Warren, Roland L. 1967. "The Interorganizational Field as a Focus for Investigation." *Administrative Science Quarterly* 12:396-419.

Wellman, Barry. 1988. "Structural Analysis: From Method and Metaphor to Theory and Substance." In Barry Wellman and S. D. Berkowitz, eds., *Social Structures: A Network Approach.* New York: Cambridge University Press, pp. 19-61.

Wellman, Barry, and S. D. Berkowitz, eds. 1988. *Social Structures: A Network Approach.* New York: Cambridge University Press.

White, Harrison C. 1970. *Chains of Opportunity.* Cambridge: Harvard University Press.

———. 1981. "Where Do Markets Come From?" *American Journal of Sociology* 87:517-547.

———. (forthcoming). *Identity and Control.* Princeton: Princeton University Press.

White, Harrison C., Scott A. Boorman, and Ronald L. Brieger. 1976. "Social Structures from Multiple Networks I: Blockmodels of Roles and Positions." *American Journal of Sociology* 81:730-780.

Williamson, Oliver. 1985. *The Economic Institutions of Capitalism.* New York: Free Press.

———. 1991. "Comparative Economic Organization: The Analysis of Discrete Structural Alternatives." *Administrative Science Quarterly* 36(2):269-296.

Zaltman, G., R. Duncan, and J. Holbek. 1973. *Innovation and Organization.* New York: Wiley.

# Self-Directed Work Teams

## What Are They and Where Did They Come From?

KIMBALL FISHER

> The great revolution of modern times has been the revolution of equality. The idea that all people should be equal in their condition has undermined the old structures of authority, hierarchy and deference. . . . But when rights are given to every citizen and the sovereignty of all is established, the problem of leadership takes a new form, becomes more exacting than ever before. It is easy to issue commands and enforce them by the rope and the stake, the concentration camp and the gulag. It is much harder to use argument and achievement to overcome opposition and win consent.[1]
>
> —*Arthur M. Schlesinger, Jr., historian and former advisor to Presidents Kennedy and Johnson*

Organizational rules are changing. Classic hierarchical work cultures, which functioned efficiently through the 60s and 70s, often became uncompetitive in the 1980s and 1990s, in the wake of increasing global competition which was quicker, more flexible, and more innovative.

Many cherished techniques of management instituted to organize and coordinate the work force became ineffective, if not counterproductive, in the rapidly changing work environment. Says John Stepp, undersecretary of the U.S. Department of Labor, about these lumbering organizations:

There are too many rigidities that have slowed us down and hampered our effectiveness. We see top-down decision making. We see overly prescribed tasks and narrow job definitions. We see long, drawn-out labor contracts and negotiations that more closely resemble cease-fire agreements among combatants than a rational agreement for organizing work and work relationships. Our industrial relations system is hampered by too many restrictions; too many inhibiting work practices, work rules, and personnel policies.[2]

## *Why Are Organizations Changing?*

Organizationally speaking, the decades of the 1980s and 1990s have been the best of times and the worst of times. The worst of times because it has become painfully clear that a lot of traditional work practices have slowed down many organizations and made them too inflexible to compete in the modern work environment. This includes the public sector as well. In the early nineties government agencies have come under especially heated attack for waste and inefficiencies caused by what many frustrated citizens believe is bureaucracy at its worst. The rapid infusion of new technologies, new worker expectations, and new customer demands of the last few years have not fit well with the restrictive job boxes, status-laden levels of hierarchy, and narrowly focused functions of traditional organizational thinking. Many organizations, including some of the mammoths that dominated the lesser mammals for years in the private and public sectors, just weren't working anymore.

But in some ways it has been the best of times, because we have been forced (sometimes painfully) to seek solutions that make us better. Unfettered by rigid organizational bureaucracies, some companies have demonstrated that they can effectively challenge anyone through speed, quality, and agility.

So what? There is an ancient Latin proverb that goes, *Tempora mutantur, nos et mutamur in illis.* Roughly translated it means, "The times are changed and we are changed with them." To paraphrase Bob Dylan (a more current philosopher),

"The times, they were a changing." For many organizations, the times demanded that they redesign themselves into new forms.

## *How Are Organizations Changing?*

A number of companies began to change. Some took desperate measures, closing down operations and laying off thousands of white and blue collar workers in an attempt to staunch the blood-colored ink on their income statements. Survivors in these operations found themselves in so-called lean and mean organizations with decreased resources and increased responsibilities.

Other organizations began to move in a more measured manner to alternative practices, which promised more flexibility and responsiveness to the turbulent business environment. Many large corporations, for example, started incorporating just-in-time inventory reduction processes to eliminate various forms of waste, and concurrent engineering practices to reduce the time required to get a new product idea to the marketplace. Some bet the farm on new whiz-bang technologies and product designs. Service organizations recommitted themselves to scrutinizing cost effectiveness and refocusing their operations on providing service excellence. Fortunately, almost everybody began incorporating total quality management perspectives into their operations with an emphasis placed on customer focus and continuous improvement.

## *People Are the Competitive Advantage*

But the bottom line of all of this activity didn't surprise anyone. We learned that people, not programs, are the answer to increased competitiveness in the changing work environment. Reports Norman F. Garrity, Executive Vice President of Corning, Inc., "We found that if you don't pay attention to the people aspects, such as empowering workers to make decisions, you could only get 50 percent of the potential benefits of restructuring."[3] And in companies like Corning who have the active support of leaders Garrity and Houghton, the CEO, the new work culture change appears to be working. Says Robert A. Hubble, a production worker in the Corning plant in Blacksburg, Virginia, "Everybody that works here is competitive. We're willing to work long hours. We want to be multiskilled and learn how we can make the product better so we can be the best in quality and service to the customer. And if we do that, this plant will be around a long time."[4] These skills and attitudes pay off. Blacksburg turned a $2 million profit in its first eight months of production, instead of losing $2.3 million as projected for the startup.[5]

Empowerment is also paying off in service organizations who are reforming themselves into nontraditional, empowered operations. "It's no longer coming to work and slugging data into a terminal," says Mary Vandehay, a member of an insurance rep team at Aid Association for Lutherans. "We have to work with each other. We can't pass problems up the line to managers. We have to be honest and up-front with our co-workers."[6]

The kind of attitude expressed by team members like Hubble and Vandehay may be the difference between the winners and the losers in the competitive marketplace. Tools, technologies, and projects are necessary but insufficient; they don't matter if people don't want to use them to full advantage. And almost everybody has access to the same tooling, technology, and funding nowadays. Competitive advantage comes from fully utilizing the discretionary effort of the work force, not from buying the latest gadget or using the latest management fad. Voluntary effort comes from employee commitment, and commitment comes from empowerment. It is simple human nature. Why? In the words of Weyerhaeuser Human Resources manager Doug King, "It's hard to resist your own ideas."

It is becoming increasingly clear that organizational responses like new product and service development, cross-functional projects, technology deployment, and initiatives like total quality management (TQM) require a flexible and empowered work force. Put more succinctly, without significant levels of empowerment, projects and programs won't deliver the promised results. Speed, quality, productivity, and new products and services come from people not programs. And the stakes are high. In a competitive work environment, only the winners survive.

## *Defining Empowerment*

What is empowerment? It is a function of four important variables: authority, resources, information, and accountability. You might remember these variables by using the memory word ARIA, which is composed of the first letter of each variable. The beauty of the opera solo of the same name depends on whether the music is written, performed, and accompanied well. Similarly, the empowerment melody works only when all the variables are in complete harmony. To feel empowered, people need formal authority and all the resources (like the budget, equipment, time, and training) necessary to do something with the new authority. They also need timely, accurate information to make good decisions. And they need a personal sense of accountability for the work. This definition of empowerment can be expressed as follows:

Empowerment = $f$(**A**uthority, **R**esources, **I**nformation, **A**ccountability)

Empowerment = **0** if **A**uthority or **R**esources or **I**nformation or **A**ccountability = **0**

In this formula we can see that empowerment is a function of the four variables and that if any of the variables in this equation go to zero then there is no empowerment. This explains why some empowerment initiatives are a sham. Authority without information and resources, for example, is only permission. Telling team members that they should go ahead and make decisions or solve problems without providing them access to accurate business information and without providing them the skills training, budget, and time to accomplish the task is a prescription for volatile failure. Not sharing accountability is paternalistic and condescending. It sends the message that the empowerment isn't real. Only when all four elements are present do people feel responsible and act responsibly.

## Defining Self-Directed Work Teams

Empowerment gives people greater control over their own destiny. And there are varying degrees of empowerment. It is not something you either have or you don't have. Visualize empowerment as a continuum of employee involvement with lower empowerment techniques like selected employee input on projects on one end, ongoing employee task forces and quality circles in the middle, and higher empowerment processes like SDWTs on the other end (see Figure 29.1).[7]

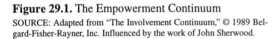

Empowerment

**Figure 29.1.** The Empowerment Continuum
SOURCE: Adapted from "The Involvement Continuum," © 1989 Belgard-Fisher-Rayner, Inc. Influenced by the work of John Sherwood.

Self-directed teams are the most advanced form of empowerment. Whether it is called employee involvement, a sociotechnical system, a high-performance system, partnership, semiautonomous work teams, or any of the multitude of names referring to organizations based on SDWT concepts, parts of companies like Corning, Procter & Gamble, Esso, Rockwell, TRW, Aid Association for Lutherans, Monsanto, Martin Marietta, Digital Equipment Corporation, Sherwin-Williams, Honeywell, Weyerhaeuser, Shell, and a host of others have been using them aggressively.

What are self-directed teams? Let's use a slightly modified version of the definition used by The Association for Quality and Participation for their study on the subject:

*Self-directed team* (noun): A group of employees who have day-to-day responsibility for managing themselves and the work they do with a minimum of direct supervision. Members of self-directed teams typi-

cally handle job assignments, plan and schedule work, make production and/or service related decisions, and take action on problems.

Where traditional work groups are typically organized into separate specialized jobs with rather narrow responsibilities, these teams are made up of members who are jointly responsible for whole work processes, with each individual performing multiple tasks. Whereas a traditional organization might be divided into groups of functional specialists, for example, SDWTs are usually responsible for delivery of an entire service or product, or they might be responsible for a geographic or customer base. This is done to create (wherever possible) small self-sustaining businesses that can be jointly managed by the organizational membership. At P&G Lima, for example, we were divided into product organizations. The team members made decisions about who would perform which task rather than having each individual separated into jobs like operators, mechanics, and trades people. Everyone had the same title, "technician," and everyone had shared responsibility for the success of the team. These are common elements of SDWTs. For other key differences between self-directed work teams and traditional organizations, see Table 29.1.

**TABLE 29.1** SDWTs vs. Traditional Organizations

| Self-Directed Work Teams | Traditional Organizations |
|---|---|
| Customer-driven | Management-driven |
| Multiskilled work force | Work force of isolated specialists |
| Few job descriptions | Many job descriptions |
| Information shared widely | Information limited |
| Few levels of management | Many levels of management |
| Whole business focus | Function/department focus |
| Shared goals | Segregated goals |
| Seemingly chaotic | Seemingly organized |
| Purpose achievement emphasis | Problem-solving emphasis |
| High worker commitment | High management commitment |
| Continuous improvements | Incremental improvements |
| Self-controlled | Management controlled |
| Values/principle based | Policy/procedure based |

## SDWT Watchouts

A caveat is in order when defining SDWTs. It is critically important that we recognize an enormous trap associated with overemphasizing the structure (self-directed work teams) more than the process of empowerment. For the sake of clarity and simplicity, this book, for example, spends a lot of time and attention on SDWTs as the unit of discussion. Inappropriate focus on the teams in the workplace, however, can cause serious problems.

Two problems in particular result from focusing too much on the teams themselves. First, we can begin to believe that the teams are the end instead of the means to an end. SDWTs are a method of improving results, not a substitution for them. This all too common means/ends inversion has caused some organizations to lose sight of their organizational purpose and to focus instead on the care and feeding of structures. ("Sorry, our poor customer service is caused by the fact that everyone is in a team meeting right now.") This is obviously a bad mistake.

Second, overemphasizing the "self-directedness" of the teams can lead people down the wrong path. In fact, the name "self-directed work team" itself can be misleading. Some believe that it connotes an absence of management personnel (which is inaccurate). SDWTs means a change in the role of management, not an elimination of supervisors and managers. Others assume that the name implies that the team has complete latitude to do whatever it wants (which is equally inaccurate). All teams operate within appropriate boundary conditions. Probably a more accurate term is the one favored by my colleague Bill Beigard: *work centered teams*. Simply stated, these operations are ones in which skilled, well-informed people take direction from the work itself rather than from management. More on this later in the book.

## SDWTs Outperform Traditional Operations

Whatever you call them, if all else is equal these work cultures are often credited with outperform-

ing their traditional counterparts. At a conference about these unique workplaces, Charles Eberle, a former vice president of Procter & Gamble, said:

> At P&G there are well over two decades of comparisons of results—*side by side*—between enlightened work systems and those I call traditional. It is absolutely clear that the new work systems work better—*a lot better*—for example, with 30 to 50 percent lower manufacturing costs. Not only are the tangible, measurable, bottom line indicators such as cost, quality, customer service and reliability better, but also the harder-to-measure attributes such as quickness, decisiveness, toughness, and just plain resourcefulness of these organizations. Importantly, the people in these organizations are far more self-reliant and less dependent upon hierarchy and control systems than in the traditional organizations.[8]

The excitement caused by these kinds of reports has accelerated the development of self-directed work teams. To better understand this emerging role of the team leader and to determine whether self-directed teams are here to stay, let's briefly consider the history of these unique work cultures.

## The Origin of Self-Directed Work Teams

Most attribute the origins of self-directed work team concepts to the early work of an Englishman named Eric Trist. In the 1950s Trist coauthored a paper in which the term "socio-technical system" first appeared.[9] In this and other papers that were to follow, Trist challenged many of the fundamental assumptions of "scientific management," an idea developed by Frederick Taylor at the turn of the century and perfected by Henry Ford in the U.S. automobile factories of the 1930s. At that time, scientific management appeared to be the answer to the problems in rapidly growing industries caused by their dependence on a largely unskilled and ill-educated work force. By breaking down job responsibilities into small specialized increments, the workers could become proficient more rapidly and a sense of order and predictability could be imposed on the emerging chaos of industrialization. This, coupled with having decision making and problem solving become the sole provenance of foremen and supervisors, facilitated the movement away from the little shops of independent craftsmen that characterized industry of the period and toward mass production and standardized factory work.

## Scientific Management: Strengths and Weaknesses

Scientific management brought with it a number of advantages that current critics often fail to remember, including improvements in the quality and efficiency of work processes. It helped workers with little experience and education become fairly productive quickly. In fact, it often actually improved the work life of the employee who had previously been subjected to deathtrap mining operations, exploitative sweatshops, and capricious shop owner management. Although it facilitated industrialization, scientific management also had some very serious negative side effects. It separated the workers from the results of their work. It stripped them of an opportunity to understand the whole work process, participate in a variety of tasks, and do the planning, evaluating, and improving of work processes. Perhaps most detrimentally, it prevented them from understanding the customers who used their workers' products and services. These were all normal aspects of working in a small workshop or family farm. Consequently, workers became focused over time on their own jobs and job rights which were often, ironically, counterproductive to both the good of the enterprise and the individual.

## Sociotechnical Systems

After discovering a remarkably productive coal mining team in postwar England, Trist suggested an alternative to scientific management. He said that by forming work teams that had complete responsibility for an entire operation, the interface between people (the social system) and their tools (the technical system) could be more fully optimized. This, he further postulated, would lead to

job performance that was more rewarding and productive for the increasingly experienced work force.

About a decade later, these ideas took root in the United States. In the 1960s and early 1970s, experiments with what were called "semiautonomous work teams" or "technician" operations started in Procter & Gamble plants in Ohio and Georgia, a Cummins Engine facility in Jamestown, New York, and a General Foods plant in Topeka, Kansas. In these organizations academicians joined ranks with practitioners to create self-directed work teams, which demonstrated remarkable competitive and social advantages over scientific management. Since that time numerous other organizations have followed suit by creating or redesigning workplaces in which teams of employees get involved in operational decisions and in many of the traditional supervisory responsibilities of managing the day-to-day business. In these organizations the traditional barriers to maximum employee contribution, such as narrow job descriptions, restrictive functional distinctions, lack of ongoing business information, and hierarchically geared compensation and status systems, are minimized.

## From Manufacturing to Service SDWTs

What started in a few manufacturing plants has also spread into the service sector in organizations like Shenandoah Life Insurance Company and American Transtech, a company broken off from the AT&T monolith during the divestiture. These teams have even spilled over into public organizations, and utilities like the financial arm of Seattle Metro, schools like those in the Dade County, Florida "school-based management" program, into hospital and research organizations like the Mayo Clinic, and into tourist and recreation facilities like the San Diego Zoo.

Is worker empowerment another of the countless flavor-of-the-month business fads we see from time to time? No. For reasons to be discussed in the next chapter, empowered work systems like the SDWT are the next inevitable step on the ladder of workplace evolution.

## Summary

Once-cherished rules for the organizing and managing of people are becoming obsolete in today's rapidly changing world. Numerous organizations in a wide array of industry and service sectors have started using SDWTs in an attempt to respond to the demand for increased flexibility and responsiveness. Some operations have made mistakes by not understanding that empowerment requires authority, resources, information, and accountability $[E = f(A,R,I,A)]$. Others have misapplied SDWTs by focusing too much attention on the structure and not enough on the purpose of the operation. But overall, those who have used SDWTs have been rewarded with significant organizational improvements. The first published writing about these remarkable workplaces is generally attributed to Eric Trist and other members of the Tavistock Group in postwar England. These unique workplaces have changed fundamentally the role of the supervisor at every level of the organization. And it looks like SDWTs—a commonsense idea that probably has been practiced by some people since the beginning of organizational history—are here to stay. A question asked by many team members and team leaders alike is, "What took so long?"

## Notes

1. Arthur Schlesinger, "On Leadership," in Roger Burns, *Abraham Lincoln* (Broomall, Penn. Chelsea House Publishers, 1986), p. 9. Used by permission.

2. John Stepp, from a speech presented at the *Ecology of Work Conference* sponsored by the Organization Development (O.D) Network and NTL, June 24-26, 1987, Washington D.C.

3. John Hoerr, "Sharpening Minds for a Competitive Edge," *Business Week* (December 17, 1990), p. 78. Used by permission.

4. Hoerr, p. 72. Used by permission.

5. Hoerr, p. 72. Used by permission.

6. Hoerr, p. 78. Used by permission.

7. Jack Sherwood, a prominent STS consultant, introduced this idea to us at Tektronix in 1983. We found it a simple and effective way to describe empowerment choices to people.

8. Charles Eberle, "Competitiveness, Commitment and Leadership," a speech delivered at the *Ecology of Work Conference,* 1987.

9. Eric Trist, "The Relations of Social and Technical Systems in Coal Mining," paper presented to the *British Psychological Society,* Industrial Section, 1950.

# 30

# The Strategy Team

## Teams at the Top—The Operating Committee: The Core of the Strategy Team

KENNETH A. SMITH
HENRY P. SIMS, JR.

This chapter examines how teamwork at the top can be used for organizational strategy making. The focus is on a network of teams that have emerged throughout the company and how this network interacts to determine and implement business strategy for a growing entrepreneurial organization. For this company, the dominant importance of shared values is a critical element in strategy making. These core values are to act with integrity, to be fair, to have fun, and to be socially responsible. Strategy is created through a bottom-up process that occurs on an annual cycle. Teamwork is also enhanced through annual executive visits to plants where they "stand in" for a wide variety of employees and through teams at the plant. Most of all, the chapter shows how individual psychological ownership can be a critical element in doing business without bosses.

* * *

This is a story of how teamwork is used as a critical element in framing and carrying out business strategy. In contrast to previous chapters, this one focuses on a network of teams that have emerged throughout a company because of the commitment of the team at the top—the executive team. Teams and teamwork are an important part of this story, although the company does not routinely use the term "team" in connection with strategy making. Nevertheless, relationships and com-

EDITOR'S NOTE: A portion of the original chapter appears as Chapter 34 in this volume.

munication both within and between teams clearly are important parts of strategy making. This bottom-up strategy making is an important element that helps the company to conduct business without bosses.

This company emphasizes the importance of shared values, which both define the company's culture and contribute to the teamlike atmosphere. We have also observed that shared values are major drivers of strategy making in this company.

As we begin, let us clarify what we mean by the phrase "strategy team." In reality, there is no single group at AES to which we might attach this label. Rather, the strategy team is a network of individuals and teams who collectively define strategy.

## AES Corporation: The Company

AES Corporation, formerly called Applied Energy Services, Inc., is an independent power producer; it develops, owns, and operates electric power plants and sells electricity to utility companies. All of its current plants are cogeneration facilities, a power generation technology in which two or more useful forms of energy, such as electricity and steam, are created from a single fuel source, such as coal or natural gas.

AES was cofounded as a privately held corporation in 1981 by Roger W. Sant (chairman of the board and chief executive officer) and Dennis W. Bakke (president and chief operating officer). Previously, Sant was assistant administrator of the Federal Energy Administration (FEA) for energy conservation and the environment from 1974 to 1976 and then director of the Energy Productivity Center, an energy research organization affiliated with the Mellon Institute at Carnegie-Mellon University, from 1977 to 1981. Bakke served with Sant as deputy assistant administrator of the FEA and as deputy director of the Energy Productivity Center.

AES was formed in response to certain legislative and business environment changes in the regulated utility industry. In response to the energy crisis of the 1970s, Congress passed the Public Utility Regulatory Policies Act (PURPA). As a result, a significant market for electric power produced by independent power generators developed in the United States. AES was an early entrant to this market and today is one of the largest independent power producers.

AES's stated mission is to help meet the need for electricity by offering a supply of clean, safe, and reliable power. It has pursued this objective by creating a portfolio of independent power plants, all of which use cogeneration technologies. Prior to obtaining financing for its first power plant, most of AES's revenue came from providing consulting services focused on least-cost energy planning for utilities, governmental agencies, and others interested in energy markets. AES still provides these services, although they no longer represent a significant portion of revenues. According to Roger Naill (vice-president), consulting serves as a way to stay on the cutting edge of economic and technological developments.

Since 1983, the company has developed, constructed, and is now operating five plants, with two more facilities under construction, and is pursuing additional projects in the United States and overseas. The combined capacity of the five plants is approximately 860 megawatts of electricity and approximately 400,000 pounds per hour of process steam. The combined total assets of these five plants and related facilities were approximately $1.4 billion at the end of 1991. The two plants under construction have a combined capacity of approximately 430 megawatts and 280,000 pounds per hour of process steam.

Pursuing a strategy of operating excellence, AES has established high standards of operation and has been a leader in environmental matters associated with independent power production. All of the solid fuel projects it owns and operates employ the very best "clean coal" technologies available, such as scrubbers or circulating fluidized-bed boilers. During 1991, AES facilities' emissions were recorded at levels considerably below those allowed under environmental permits, thereby exceeding the federal performance standards mandated for such plants under the Clean Air Act. AES has also offset carbon dioxide emissions by funding projects, such as the planting of trees in Guatemala and the preservation of forest land in Paraguay.

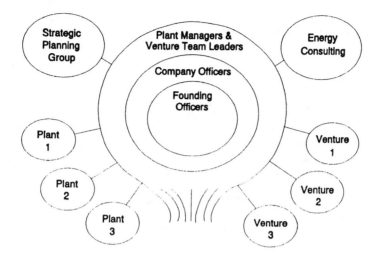

**Figure 30.1.** Operating Committee at AES

AES has established a better-than-average safety record for the electricity-generating industry. Further, its plants averaged 92 percent "availability" during 1990 and 90 percent during 1991, an above-average measure of plant reliability.

By December 1990, AES was generating $190 million in revenues on approximately $1.12 billion in total assets. It employed approximately 430 people in its plants and at its home office in Arlington, Virginia. In July 1991, it went public, selling approximately 10 percent of the company in an initial public offering. In the same year, the company generated $333 million in revenues on $1.44 billion in assets. By mid-1992, its market value reached $1.7 billion. In October, AES was ranked 58 on *Fortune*'s list of America's 100 fastest-growing companies. Clearly, the market evaluates AES as a substantial success.

### The Operating Committee: The Core of The Strategy Team

AES's Operating Committee is the core organizational unit through which strategy is developed. Think of the committee as an onion with three layers (Figure 30.1). The inner layer consists of the three founding officers: Sant, Bakke, and Bob Hemphill, the executive vice-president. This is the *core vision team*—the group that provided the initial guiding vision of the company and is still most actively involved in the extension, enhancement, and communication of that vision. This core vision team is also "first among equals." That is, although all members of the Operating Committee have equal access to and opportunity in the strategy process, in practice, Sant, Bakke, and Hemphill are generally seen as having more influence than the others, and typically they are more engaged in managing the core values of the company.

The middle layer of the "onion" consists of company officers who are not founders: Ken Woodcock and Tom Tribone (senior vice-presidents) and Mark Fitzpatrick, Roger Naill, and Barry Sharp (vice-presidents). They have been with AES for several years and carry out important policy and operating roles. This middle layer also has one important external linkage, Roger Naill, charged with leadership of the planning team, which has responsibility for scanning the environment for ideas for new ventures. The planning team also serves as a technology assessment unit that evaluates the potential of new and alternative technologies.

The outer layer of the onion generally contains two groups: the plant managers and the team leaders of new-venture teams. The plant managers carry out the operations of the current energy-

## BOX 30.1.
## Executive Plant Visits: We Have Met "They" and "They" Are Us

An important process through which AES has become a whole unified team has been annual visits of the plants by the corporation's top executives. Dennis Bakke, president:

> Every officer has to go once a year to one plant for a week. Partly symbolic, partly it's a tremendous time to get to know some of the folks. It lets them give us a bad time. They love it, to see us dirty, or whatever—make fools of ourselves. And partly it's a chance for them to tell us what things are right or wrong. While I was out there, I started to realize, "These people are no different. I don't understand. They have the same motivations, the same concerns, and they like to care about things and about people and about the company. What's different about them? Why are we treating them differently? Why are they being managed in a different way from what we do in Arlington?" I started asking a lot of questions about that. "Why are we doing it differently? Why are the maintenance people all here in their own group and office people in another? And here are operators, and the operators can't do any of this? Maintenance people have to come and do these kinds of things?" It's the old union thing, where you hold the plug and I'll plug it in. I said, "Why do we do that?"
>
> One guy was complaining, "Well, you know, maintenance guys never do this. They never get it done. I put the work order in, and it never gets done. And they wouldn't let us do that. And they . . ." I started saying, "Well, who in the world is 'They'? What do you mean by 'They'? "Well, uh . . . the guys in Arlington," or "the people in the administration building," or "the plant manager." They very seldom could tell you who "they" was, but it was somebody out there. Somebody other than themselves was responsible for their job and making them helpless. We heard all kinds of comments like that. And that bothered us a lot.
>
> Bob Hemphill came up with an idea for a major Anti-They campaign. Everyone had a great time with it. Anti-They. The big international symbol: "They" with a line through it. Everyone gets caught saying "they." Everybody. Even I do. A guy in the control room would say, "Well, they won't. They don't care. They don't want to do this." We'd say, "Who's they?" Now they do it to each other. Trying to get people to say "we." In fact, a reporter came out to do a report one time on one of our plants, and that was his headline on the article . . . "Everybody Says We."

The campaign against "they" is but one outgrowth of the annual visitations of senior executives to operating plants. Each executive voluntarily spends at least one week at a specific operating plant—not to review or receive briefings but to participate in the everyday activities of the plant by carrying out the work assigned to a specific job. In essence, each executive takes on at least one job per day, and some of these jobs can be fairly rough or dirty. Bob Hemphill recollects: "Since it was my big idea, I got to go first. It actually turned out that Dennis went the same week I did, in August. We both spent a week doing whatever they told us, basically. And since we had no skills, it meant we got to do whatever was hot, or wet, or dirty, or usually hot *and* wet *and* dirty. And although these are highly automated plants, there's still a bunch of lugging, toting, hauling, lifting and shoving. And it was very, very interesting."

These visits have two positive results. First, it is an opportunity for executives to listen and learn from direct experience on the firing line. More important, it is an extraordinarily vivid symbolic message to each employee. In keeping with the company's core values, it conveys the notion that each job is important, and no one is too good to work at any job—no matter how rough or dirty it is. More recently, company executives have begun a program of reciprocal visits; groups of employees from each location make periodic visits to the company home office at Arlington.

All of these exchanges evoke a strong sense of loyalty, commitment, and sense of ownership throughout the company. In addition to membership in their immediate work team, each employee feels a part of the larger organizational team.

generating projects. They work at operating locations geographically distant from the home offices in Arlington.

The team leaders are charged with the responsibility of opening and starting up a new project location. These members of the outer layer also serve as important linkages to the other parts of the organization. The plant managers are the primary links to each operating location, and the team leaders are the primary links to the new-venture teams.

Although distinctions between the three layers can be observed in terms of function, the distinctions do not represent rigid separation; the boundary between layers is very porous. The involvement and influence of individuals in the strategy process are largely dependent on personality and interest rather than organizational structure. On some decisions, according to Naill, "A project development leader might be more influential than some officers, just on the basis of their insights and gifts."

The Operating Committee serves as the core infrastructure through which the strategy process is carried out. In essence, the committee is a network of teams, of which the core vision team is the most central.

## *The Strategy-Making Process*

The strategic management literature distinguishes between the processes of strategy formulation—defining a strategy—and strategy implementation—putting the strategy to work. While this distinction makes theoretical sense, in practice, the line between the two processes is often unclear. This is certainly the case at AES, where issues of formulation and implementation are addressed in an integrated and continuous fashion. In our description, we combine formulation and implementation and call the process strategy making.

Roger Naill states, "We're always changing our strategy. It's changed at least once a year and maybe twice a year every year that I've been here. We never have the same strategy." Indeed, strategic flexibility has been characteristic of AES from the start. In describing the founding of the company, Roger Sant remembers, "We had a whole bunch of notions that were inaccurate. The data were identi-

fying an opportunity of one kind, and the market was identifying an opportunity of another kind. So, as we went along, we adapted to the opportunities and quickly decided that the cogeneration side of the business was the only one worth pursuing."

### An Annual Process

AES engages in an annual strategic planning process that is bottom-up in approach (Figure 30.2). The strategic planning group prepares and distributes a book of planning data to all participants in the process. Then one-day strategic planning meetings are held at each plant every September. At these meetings the plant personnel come together to address the strategic direction of their own plant and the company as a whole over the next five years. These one-day meetings are also attended by a senior member of the strategic planning group (Roger Naill or Sheryl Sturges) and, typically, two other officers—one of the core vision team (office of the CEO: Sant, Bakke, Hemphill) and one of the other vice-presidents.

The meeting is led by the plant manager. The agenda is somewhat structured but discussion fairly loose, designed to get people to talk openly about their ideas and their responses to the discussion materials. The corporate officers serve as resources, share information (sometimes through presentations on issues), and carry the results of the meeting back to the home office. Summaries of each meeting are prepared and distributed to members of the Operating Committee.

For the purpose of strategic planning, the corporate home office is treated as a plant. Participants there include the corporate officers and the team leaders of the new-venture groups. The meeting is structured similarly to the plant meetings, but it provides a forum for addressing the unique needs and concerns of the new-venture teams rather than those of plant operations.

The one-day meetings are, in effect, mini-strategy meetings for the plants. Although corporate strategy is discussed, most decisions at this level are focused on plant- or site-specific issues.

Later in September, all senior management (officers, plant managers, heads of new-venture teams), plus a number of additional representatives

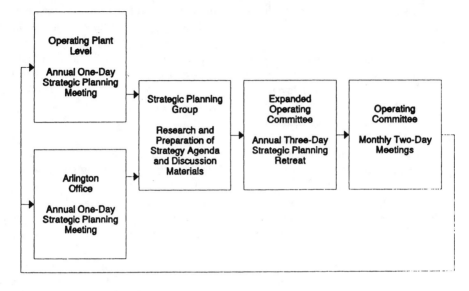

**Figure 30.2.** AES's Strategy-Making Process

from across the company (sometimes chosen at random), meet at a Washington-area retreat center. Attendees at the three-day session, the primary corporate strategy vehicle, are provided with a briefing document (about 200 pages) containing the current strategy statement and reviewing the current market situation, competitors, technologies, and potential customers. This briefing document serves as a basis for brainstorming important issues and decisions facing the company—for example, Should we go public? Should supervisors be elected? Can and should we create a partnership with our plant construction supplier? How should we open our plants? Why aren't we signing more contracts? What changes should we make?

All of the attendees will have attended one or more of the one-day plant meetings, and all have responsibility for initiating issues raised and reflecting opinions voiced at these earlier sessions. As in the one-day sessions, a summary document is prepared and distributed.

### A Continuous Process

Strategy making does not end with these annual meetings; rather, the process is much more fluid than the previous description implies. Strategic issues are often dealt with outside the annual planning structure, in a process that is virtually continuous. According to Roger Naill, "We start dealing with issues outside of this structure, as well as in it. What we end up talking about in September ends up sort of being whatever's current in September. Something else will come up in December and we'll deal with that one, and something else will come up in January or March, and we'll deal with that one. We're always changing our strategy."

By "always changing our strategy," Naill means in an incremental fashion: "You don't really change 'strategies' every few months. Strategic *issues* arise naturally outside the formal cycle, that could lead to a major change in strategy. It doesn't happen often, and mostly, because so much effort is spent thinking strategically during the annual cycle, *strategy* is changed annually."

Issues raised outside the annual planning structure become topics for discussion and action by the Operating Committee and its various subcomponents. In support of the committee's role in the strategy process, the planning group prepares short, focused reports and briefing documents on selected issues that arise throughout the year. For example, one report contained a market analysis that listed all the utilities in the United States and ranked them according to their attractiveness as potential customers.

The Operating Committee meets for two days each month. On the first day, primary attention is given to implementation issues. The manager of each project, from those in the earliest stages of development to plants in operation, gives a short presentation, bringing before the group issues that require brainstorming or decisions. He or she usually identifies several alternatives for action, including the alternative the manager thinks is most appropriate. The discussion following the presentation is likely to address whether the proposed alternative is in accordance with AES's values, as well as the technical and financial aspects of the specific situation. The final decision remains the manager's, but he or she has the resources of the Operating Committee to draw upon.

On the second day, attention turns to more general management issues. Committee members can place any item on the agenda and are encouraged to raise issues that pertain to the values of the company. Topics for discussion may relate to strategy formulation or implementation. One example of a formulation issue related to the core value of social responsibility was, says Bakke, "Should we continue our project in Poland? We face huge problems of poor environment to work in, currency issues, AES people working there, uncertainty about privatization by the government, etc. However, there is great potential for making a positive contribution to air and society." An example of an implementation issue also related to social responsibility was, "Should we build schools for strapped counties around [a U.S.] plant in lieu of taxes that state law exempts us from?" Because the committee addresses both strategy formulation and implementation issues as they arise, the formulation and implementation processes are truly integrated and continuous.

## Integrating the Whole

Various groups within the company play different, though overlapping, roles in the strategy process. The corporate officers and especially the core vision team have primary responsibility for defining the core values of the company.

Roger Naill and the strategic planning group provide a unique contribution to strategy making. They do not directly make strategy but serve as the primary information and analysis source from which strategy emerges. Thus, the function of the strategic planning group is not to provide the strategic plan, but, rather, to provide the information necessary for the company to act as "informed opportunists." Naill looks at the role for the strategic planning process as providing information: "It's not to provide a plan. My role is to provide information to the planners, which turn out to be as broad-based a group as we can get in the company. We're actually trying to involve everybody."

The planning group focuses its attention on many strategic issues. Should we be in the coal business or the gas business? Should we be building coal plants or gas plants? What is the Clean Air Act going to do to our business? If the Clean Air Act Amendment passes, should we build fluidized-bed coal plants, or should we build standard boilers with scrubbers? What kind of technology should we be involved in? Analyses of these and other issues result in the briefing documents prepared by the planning group for the annual and monthly meetings.

Members of the new-venture teams, especially the team leaders, also have a unique influence on the direction of the company, sometimes through their own interests and personal objectives. AES is committed to the development of its high-caliber personnel and encourages accomplished new-venture developers to seek out and define their own opportunities. AES became involved in international activities primarily as the result of the interests of several experienced new-venture developers seeking more responsibility and broader opportunities.

Finally, plant personnel, especially the plant managers, contribute to the strategy process as it more closely relates to the core business: the co-generation of electricity and steam. Input from the plants precipitated the strategic concern with operating excellence and continues to define and refine this concept through implementation.

Despite the expected contributions made by each of these groups to strategic management, it is clear that AES expects all participants in the process to be concerned about and take ownership and responsibility for all aspects of the company. Plant managers are encouraged to challenge corporate officers on issues relating to values, new-venture team leaders are expected to provide market information, and the planning group contributes to discussions of operating efficiency.

## The Team Structure

The term "team" is not widely used in everyday vocabulary at AES. Nevertheless, a sense of "teamness" pervades the company. Roger Naill articulated it best: "I don't think 'team' is an AES word, in the sense that we don't go around calling ourselves teams. But the concept is clear. For example, Project Honeycomb (see Box 30.2) is very clearly a team-oriented exercise. Work teams at the plant call themselves 'families.' Our strategic planning group is a 'group.'"

The essence of teams is synergy; that is, what is accomplished by the team is more than could be accomplished by a collection of individuals. By way of analogy, the best basketball teams are those whose members work well together to achieve a common objective. Although individual skills are important, it is their refined combination that maximizes performance. That is why the All-Star games, in which the teams are composed of highly skilled individuals who are not used to playing together, are less elegant than championship games. All-Star teams typically lack the capacity to come together into the well-oiled machines we often see in championship teams.

For synergy to be achieved, a combination of specialization, interchangeability, and trust is required. Individual team members can contribute to the team effort if they can develop some level of unique skills, but specialization is complemented by a basic understanding and skill level in all of the functions of the team. Thus, to use the basketball analogy again, play makers can take open shots, shooters can rebound, and rebounders can initiate plays. To make the rapid and continuous switching between specialization and generalization within the context of a fast and competitive game, each player needs to be able to trust that teammates can and will make the right play at the right time. Trust

provides the confidence to extend oneself to the limit.

Given this definition of a team, AES obviously exhibits team characteristics in numerous ways and at many levels.

The core vision team, each energy-generating plant, the new-venture groups, the strategic planning group, and the Operating Committee all act like teams. They provide a unique stimulus to enhance the motivation, initiative, and self-responsibility of employees throughout the company. Indeed, the word "ownership" best describes how teams influence the psychological perspective of employees. Employees feel ownership in the company and, especially, in their own jobs. Ownership leads to strong motivation and sometimes exceptional effort to perform well (see Box 30.3). Thus, individual ownership contributes to organizational competitiveness.

In addition, the use of teams leads to a highly adaptive, nonrigid organizational structure. Job assignments and roles are not engraved in granite, and they sometimes change significantly as the situation demands. The phrase "that's not my job" would be highly incompatible with the team system at AES.

Contrary to most other companies, AES deliberately avoids drawing and publishing a formal organization chart. The use of teams provides an adaptive structure that can change quickly to meet the demands of an emerging situation or a shift in strategic implementation.

The team structure strengthens AES's ability to scan its environment and identify strategic opportunities very early. Although the strategic planning group is specifically charged with environmental scanning activities, the new-venture teams—with their external contacts in the market, financial, and regulatory communities—and the plant personnel—with their expertise in operating plants—also provide insight into environmental opportunities and threats.

Teams also contribute to strategic flexibility. Rapid communication among and between teams provides a process for revising strategic implementation without undertaking a whole new formal planning process. In fact, the annual strategic planning cycle is seen mainly as a starting place; often, significant strategic changes are undertaken with short notice.

## BOX 30.2.
## Teams at the Plants: Operation Honeycomb

AES attempts to evoke employee psychological ownership through the use of teams at the generating plants. As outsiders, we would call these structures "self-managing teams" or "employee involvement teams," but AES uses the term "Honeycomb." Dennis Bakke describes the evolution of Operation Honeycomb:

> Our plants were running wonderfully when we said, "This isn't really consistent with our values and the way we want people to operate and relate to each other. We need to make huge changes in the way we do operations if we're going to be consistent with our values." We did this massive change that came to be known as Operation Honeycomb. We changed how our plants are organized and how people relate to each other. It's based on the premise that people will take responsibility and can be trusted. We didn't want arbitrary rules, detailed procedures manuals and handbooks, punch clocks, etc. We wanted a "learning organization," where people close to the action were constantly creating and recreating and where these people were making the decisions—strategy, financial, and capital allocations. For example, I went down and asked, "What if you didn't have shift supervisors? What if you didn't have this manual that tells you everything to do?" Two months later, they totally revolutionized the place. We discovered these people are no different from the managers. They have the same motivations, the same concerns, and they like to care about people and about the company. Why were we treating them differently? Why were they being managed in a different way?
>
> We outlined several elementary principles to be used in a Honeycomb structure. Cut the number of supervisor levels to improve communication, and get out of people's way. And then one of the plant people came up with, "Why don't we just divide up into teams?" The next thing I knew, the plant manager called me and said, "We got this all done. We've implemented it." They said, "We're going to call this stuff 'Honeycomb,' " and they had worked out all this symbolism regarding beehives and how all the bees were working together.
>
> Of course, the supervisors had to change. Some have adapted extremely well and are real stars. Others moved to special jobs that don't require them to supervise. A few have had to leave completely. So, it's all over the map.
>
> Now, the plants do their own capital allocations. The plant managers decided to change the order of criteria for hiring. First, how well does this person fit with our shared values; then, technical skill. They make almost every decision. They have the responsibility and authority to make every single decision in that plant. There are no exceptions that I know of.

Today, all AES generating plants are organized according to some form of self-managing teams. Since the process of change essentially is implemented bottom-up (although mandated top-down), the specific forms, labels, and language vary considerably from plant to plant. Further, the path leading to self-management has been quite different among the plants. Some were "changeover" of existing nonunion plants; one was a changeover of a union plant; finally, others have been implemented from the beginning.

This variety of implementation and form has given AES a tremendous diversity of experience while adapting to the specific condition unique to each plant. Nevertheless, the conversion to "honeycomb"-like teams has always been inspired and guided by the core values of the organization and always features a bottom-up process that displays great confidence that the employees have a special capability to work out the details of implementation that will suit them best.

Today, the Honeycomb principle is an important part of AES's strategic philosophy. The company believes that operating excellence is a distinctive competence that provides a special competitive advantage. In turn, a critical factor in achieving operating excellence is the responsibility, pride, and sense of ownership that stems from the Honeycomb operating philosophy. "Most important," says Bakke, "is that Honeycomb provides an environment where the 'fun' value can best work itself out for each AES person."

---

**BOX 30.3.**
## Individual Ownership: A Team Member Takes Initiative

One of the results of AES's team structure has been a high level of psychological ownership of the company on the part of workers at every level. Such ownership has been an objective of the core vision team since the company's inception. From the beginning, says Sant, the core vision team wanted "something that really makes people feel that they own us. Our instincts were that everybody likes to feel important. We did. We'd been in jobs where we were constantly told that we probably weren't important, and we thought that probably wasn't the way to turn young people on."

AES has been extremely successful in attaining the goal of ownership. Dennis Bakke provides this powerful example:

> Let me give you one example of what happened, the kind of thing I think we've had example after example of. We had a guy who, after this Honeycomb process, went Saturday shopping with his wife at one of the discount stores. He was waiting around, waiting for her to get done, and he noticed that they had fans on sale. He looked at the fans, and he realized that they were almost the same kind of fans that we were using at the plant in the process of making gypsum at the back end of our plant. We use a lot of them; they end up wearing out because there's a pretty dirty atmosphere, and so they burn out real fast. He looked and saw that they were selling them for something like $24 apiece, and he remembered that we were spending $75 from the original manufacturer who supplied them at first, and we kept going back to the same guy, at $75. Once or twice a month, we were paying to get new fans. So he immediately took his credit card and bought the entire stock in the store, period. Just bought it.
>
> Now that is the kind of action we're talking about. This is a nonsupervisor, just a regular guy in the plant. What had to be the situation for him? First of all, he had to understand what the technology was, that it was the same kind. He was aware that this was the same kind of fan, or very similar to it, and it would do the same thing in the plant. Second, he had to know all the cost numbers. Third, he had to know that he had authority to do it, that it was safe. And if he was wrong, it would be okay. If he really feared for his job in doing this or that he would have to pay for these hundreds of dollars of fans he had just bought, for a normal guy . . . he knew he would be backed up on it.
>
> That is the epitome of Honeycomb. That responsibility taking. We've had guys who have done that and been wrong. A guy did a whole bundle on an air heater and got it all done, and it was totally wrong—spent, I don't know, $10,000. But no one went back and said, "That's terrible, and you're getting your salary docked." We want to encourage that kind of thing. But that's the epitome of the Honeycomb story. We're trying to publicize it and be happy to have more people do it, every day. That kind of wraps it up.

---

Finally, teams contribute to high productivity and competitiveness. Bottom-line results speak for themselves. AES's energy-generating plants significantly exceed industry standards of availability—that is, the proportion of time that energy generation is on line. AES plants typically operate at less than 50 percent of allowable emissions. Voluntary turnover of people is under 1 percent. Accident rates, especially severe accidents, run far below the industry average, and the real cost per kilowatt-hour of electricity produced has been falling for three years. Finally, the company as a whole has maintained high profitability over the years. Before-tax return on sales was 10 percent in 1990 and 16 percent in 1991. Before-tax return on investment averaged 46 percent over the same two-year period.

"We think it's too early to draw long-term conclusions concerning our 'experiment' with regard to these traditional measures of excellence," Bakke

---

**BOX 30.4.**
**Key Lessons for Creating Business Without Bosses**

1. Teams at the top can be driven by a set of core values that pervade the total organization. At AES, these core values are to act with integrity, to be fair, to have fun, and to be socially responsible.

2. Organizational strategies may change in response to a changing environment or new opportunities. In contrast, core values are meant to be enduring, changing little over a longer period of time.

3. Strategy can be formulated and enacted by a bottom-up process that involves the entire organization. At AES, this process flows according to an annual cycle. The key ingredient is a network of interlocking teams, each feeding the strategy-making process.

4. Teamwork is enhanced by intentional contact between top executives and employees at all levels. This contact is expressed by a program of annual executive visits to plants, where top executives "stand in" for employees in a wide variety of jobs throughout the plant.

5. Teams at the top become a model for teams throughout the organization. Teams are not for professional employees alone. Teamwork is apparent at AES from the executive offices to the shop floor.

---

is quick to point out. "We are fairly bullish, however, regarding adherence to the values, especially the fun environment that has been created by the decentralized teams and other aspects of the corporate approach."

### *Summary: A Network of Teams as the Strategy Team*

We found the interlocking dynamics between the de facto teams and strategy making at AES unique and provocative. First, strategy making is consistent with a clearly articulated and differentiated set of core values. The philosophy represented by these core values is pervasive and affects strategy making in a profound way. Second, we found that teams were not only useful for the day-to-day issues and operations, as typically found in other companies, but were an essential element in the total strategy-making process. Both within-team and between-team elements provide the crucial structure and process for essential communication that makes broadly based strategy making at AES possible.

Strategy making essentially begins as a bottom-up process. However, the between-team processes, as represented by the annual strategy meeting and the monthly Operating Committee meetings, are the mechanisms that foster aggregation and integration from the diverse parts of the company. Moreover, the bottom-up approach to strategy making provides the means by which the integration of goals, objectives, and ways to achieve them, across all parts of the company, becomes possible.

We suspect that Lawler would call AES a "high involvement" organization, and Manz and Sims would certainly classify AES as a Super-Leadership type of culture.[1] AES emphasizes the importance of teams and teamwork throughout the entire organization. Its executives certainly do not see themselves as bosses, and they clearly have attempted to design a total organization that represents the essence of business without bosses. Whatever the label, AES has found a way to make teamwork an essential ingredient of strategy making through a network of teams. They have defined an exceedingly sophisticated form of the strategy team.

### Acknowledgments

Most of the quotations in this chapter are from on-site interviews conducted from 1990 to 1992.

We are especially thankful to Dennis Bakke, who facilitated the project, and to the special cooperation of AES employees. Other material is excerpted from AES's June 1991 prospectus and the 1991 annual report.

## Note

1. Edward E. Lawler III, *High Involvement Management* (San Francisco: Jossey-Bass, 1986); Charles C. Manz and Henry P. Sims, Jr., *SuperLeadership: Leading Others to Lead Themselves* (New York: Berkley, 1990).

# VII

# *Leadership Authenticity*

## *Organization Culture*

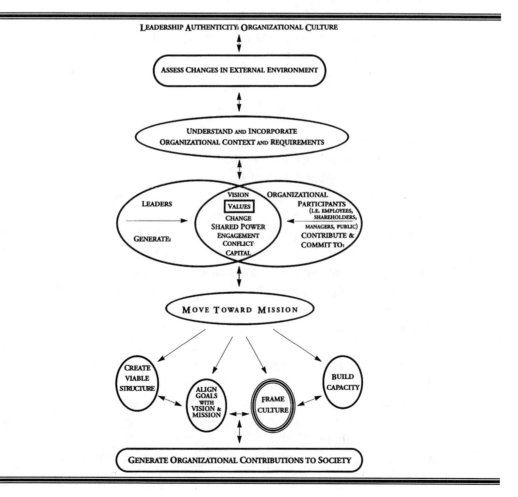

## *Culture*

Part VII looks at the essential responsibilities of leadership for framing the culture of an organization. Culture reflects the core values, ethics, and practices of daily life within an organization. It is the test for determining leadership authenticity, that is, determining whether leaders and participants base their actions on the values and ethics they purport to believe.

"In culture there is strength." Terrence Deal and Allan Kennedy assert that this statement represents the new law of organizational life. They define a strong organizational culture as "a system of informal rules that spells out how people are to behave most of the time." Culture is determined by several factors:

- The *business environment,* (product or service) market in which the organization operates;
- The *values* that comprise the organization's belief system;
- The *heroes* who represent tangible models of these beliefs in action;
- *Ritual* including ceremonies and celebrations of individuals and groups that exemplify the organization's values; and
- The *cultural network,* which is the carrier of the organization's informal communication system.

These cultural factors create meaning for the organization's participants and strongly contribute to its ultimate success or decline.

Research conducted by John Kotter and James Heskett indicates that the existence of a strong organizational culture alone does not assure success. Strong cultures in some large mature organizations may contribute to a lack of adaptiveness and produce moderate or unsatisfactory performance. Kotter and Heskett found that leadership makes a significant difference in creating performance-enhancing or adaptive cultures. In start-up organizations, entrepreneurial leadership can generate performance-enhancing cultures by combining a fitting business strategy with a sound philosophy based on enduring core values and adaptive practices.

Mature organizations present greater challenges. Their entrenched cultures often resist change, even when change is in their best interest. According to Kotter and Heskett, successful creation of performance-enhancing cultures in mature organizations requires leadership that establishes a sense of crisis or need for change, challenges the status quo, and creates a new direction or vision. Leaders of performance-enhancing cultures communicate their vision and strategy broadly and become the living embodiment of the new culture. They motivate and empower large numbers of managers to assume leadership roles in creating change, and they recognize and reward their successes.

## *Values and Ethics*

One of the critical assumptions identified at the beginning of this text is that organizations can become better and more responsive by basing their actions on a foundation of values and ethics. These concepts are central to an examination of organizational culture. *Core values* provide a centering mechanism for the organization and become the bases for aligning the actions and decisions of organizational leaders and participants. Kenneth Smith and Henry Sims provide an example of how one organization uses its core values to guide its business strategies and behaviors. They identified four values that are articulated and shared among its participants—integrity, fairness, fun, and social responsibility. These values are considered worthwhile goals in themselves and are used consistently to determine whether to pursue potential projects or affiliate with particular partners. Furthermore, managers are rated annually on how they perform in relation to the four shared values.

Aligning and acting on values are by no means simple tasks. Ronald Heifetz asserts that the role of leadership in organizations and in other contexts is to engage people in the "adaptive work" of learning. This adaptive work is required to address conflicts in the values they hold. Shared values are reached not by declaring them common beliefs but by shaping and refining them through their application to real problems. Adaptive work entails getting people to clarify what matters to them and orchestrating among competing value perspectives in the face of real opportunities and challenges.

The challenges involved in establishing values in an organization are intricately related to the issue of *ethics*. Al Gini proclaims that ethics is about the assessment and evaluation of values, because all of life is value laden, including work life. Ethics in organizations, as in other areas of life, compels leaders and participants to take into account the impact of their actions in relation to others. Gini contends that leaders and participants are required to ask the question, "What ought to be done in regard to the others we work with and serve?" Thus, ethics in organizations is about how customers and employees are treated. Without ethics, the organization's culture might ingrain self-serving values to clone its own rather than sustain moral agents who engage in critical reflection.

Like Heifetz, Gini believes that judgments must be made in regard to competing points of view.[1] The responsibility of leaders and participants is to continuously raise the important questions, engage in the assessment of how decisions and actions may affect self and others, and consider the potential consequences of alternative courses of action. Most important, leaders need to model moral behavior and create an organizational culture where ethical behavior permeates the entire organization.

How do leaders and participants model moral behavior and solve problems ethically in "real world" organizations—the world where issues are shades of gray? Joanne Ciulla suggests that we are capable of creating ethical solutions to real-world situations through the use of moral imagination. Moral imagination involves "inventing ways to live up to moral prescriptions, given the practical constraints of the world." It requires leaders and participants to see in innovative ways and to create new possibilities, rather than accept ethically inappropriate situations as givens. It entails generating a third possibility when two unacceptable ones are presented. The moral imagination and creative actions of leaders and participants can change the way that organizations function and interact in society. Leaders must establish organizational cultures where the use of moral imagination is encouraged, cultivated, and practiced as a common response to ethical problems that organizations face.

### *Diversity and Work-Family Issues*

Along with the values and ethical character of an organization's culture, the specific components of its culture are also critical factors for leaders and participants. Deal and Kennedy contend that when individuals choose an organization, they choose a way of life. A number of organizations pride themselves on building organizational cultures that strongly emphasize factors such as trust, learning, families, and diversity. These cultural characteristics serve as motivators for attracting individuals to the organization and retaining them over a substantial period of time. Work-family life and diversity have become two of the primary focuses in the culture of new-era organizations. The popular media even identify lists of the most "family friendly" or "diversity friendly" organizations in which to work.

Organizations are experiencing an influx of large numbers of women with young children and an accompanying increase in dual-career and single-parent families. Simultaneously, organizations are becoming flatter, more technologically driven, participatory oriented, flexible, productive, and competitive. The convergence of these events provides an impetus for new-era organizations to create cultures based on assumptions of diversity rather than uniformity. Lotte Bailyn points out, "In a diverse work force employees will differ in their needs, their values, their assumptions about the role of work and career in their lives, and their approaches to work." Different employees will have diverse commitments at varying points in their lives depending on their career progression, quantity of required work time, and family commitments.

In practical terms, these changes mean that organizations are providing new options for employees such as flexible work hours, working at home via computer linkages, job sharing, on-site child care, elder care benefits, and parental leave. In this new environment, employees and employers negotiate tasks, rewards, and appraisal procedures in relationship to their work-family needs and level of organizational commitment. An organizational culture that supports such diversity incorporates new assumptions about trust, motivation of employees, where and how work takes place, and the way in which work is assessed (output evaluation). The role of leadership in this environment is to serve as the culture change initiator by integrating these changes in a holistic manner.

Bailyn explains that such systemic change cannot be dealt with in a piecemeal fashion. Work-family issues and other diverse work needs of employees must be accepted as an integral part of organizational life.

Lynn Offermann concurs that diversity in its broadest sense is a primary issue that is critical to understanding the dynamics of leadership and followership in new-era organizations. She explains that diversity encompasses the traditional areas of gender, ethnicity, culture, and race as well as individual variations in "temperaments, age, personal preferences, knowledge, national origin, life experiences, capabilities, and worldviews." What is needed in this environment is leadership of unassimilated diversity. Empowerment offers one means of incorporating diverse leadership and followership in organizations. In organizations, empowerment ranges from increased worker participation in decisions concerning their job tasks and content to self-management of job content and context. Implemented successfully, empowerment allows for greater diversity of participants, contributions, skills, perspectives, and preferences. Offermann cautions that movement from tightly controlled bureaucracies to such empowerment requires time, trust, and training on the part of organizational leaders and participants.

John Fernandez believes successful inclusion of diversity in organizations requires simultaneous change in organizational structure, processes, and policies. He recommends several critical steps to help bring about changes in the culture and functioning of the organization:

- Commitment and support from executive level leadership;
- Establishing a clear linkage between organizational goals and team goals;
- Purposeful structuring of teams to include diversity;
- Time and training to become a functional team; and
- Change in policies, procedures, and reward systems.

Looking at constituents inside and outside the organization, Fernandez points out that the domestic and international environments of organizations in the United States are becoming increasingly more diverse with regard to ethnicity, race, language, gender, and so on. He maintains that success with increasingly diverse customers and service recipients requires that organizations have a diverse workforce that can understand changing customers and markets. Diversity is both a demographic reality domestically and a competitive advantage in a global environment.

New-era organizations require cultures where skilled participants from all races and genders are fully used and empowered to make creative decisions. Leadership in such organizations creates work structures and cultures that help their participants understand, value, and appreciate diverse people. To this end, Fernandez introduces the concept of *constituent capitalization*—a business strategy where the broad spectrum of diverse people's skills, perspectives, and styles are recognized, appreciated, valued, respected, and integrated into a postbureaucratic organizational structure and into new organizational operating practices to maximize marketplace options throughout the world.

Contemporary organizational structures such as teams that are intended to build trust, value differing contributions, and address diverse stakeholders provide the best opportunity for capitalizing on the new internal and external constituencies of organizations. Using a six-step model, Fernandez explains how organizations can position themselves to attain maximum success in today's environment.

Together, the readings in this section demonstrate how vitally important and complex leadership is in generating and sustaining the culture of new-era organizations. The test of "good" leadership lies in the extent to which the organization's leadership philosophy and behavior are experienced by participants, customers, service recipients, and other stakeholders as authentic in the everyday life and functioning of the institution.

### Note

1. See Heifetz in Chapter 33 of this volume.

# 31

# Strong Cultures

## The New "Old Rule" for Business Success

TERRENCE E. DEAL
ALLAN A. KENNEDY

S. C. Allyn, a retired chairman of the board, likes to tell a story about his company—the National Cash Register Corporation. It was August 1945, and Allyn was among the first allied civilians to enter Germany at the end of the war. He had gone to find out what had happened to an NCR factory built just before the war but promptly confiscated by the German military command and put to work on the war effort. He arrived via military plane and traveled through burned-out buildings, rubble, and utter desolation until he reached what was left of the factory. Picking his way through bricks, cement, and old timbers, Allyn came upon two NCR employees whom he hadn't seen in six years. Their clothes were torn and their faces grimy and blackened by smoke, but they were busy clearing out the rubble. As he came closer, one of the men looked up and said, "We knew you would come!" Allyn joined them in their work and together the three men began cleaning out the debris and rebuilding the factory from the devastation of war. The company had even survived the ravages of a world war.

A few days later, as the cleaning continued, Allyn and his co-workers were startled as an American tank rumbled up to the site. A grinning GI was at its helm. "Hi," he said, "I'm NCR Omaha. Did you guys make your quota this month?" Allyn and the GI embraced each other. The war may have devastated everything around them, but NCR's hard-driving, sales-orientated culture was still intact.

This story may sound unbelievable, but there are hundreds like it at NCR and every other company. Together they make up the myths and legends of American business. What do they mean? To us these stories mean that businesses are human institutions, not plush buildings, bottom lines, strategic analysis, or five-year plans. NCR was never just a factory to the three men who dug it out of the rubble. Nor was it to others like them. Rather it was a living organization. The company's real existence lay in the hearts and minds of its employees. NCR was, and still is, a corporate culture, a cohesion of values, myths, heroes, and symbols

SOURCE: T. E. Deal/A. A. Kennedy, *Corporate Cultures* (pages 3-19). © 1982 by Addison-Wesley Publishing Company, Inc. Reprinted by permission of Addison Wesley Longman, Inc.

that has come to mean a great deal to the people who work there.

Culture, as *Webster's New Collegiate Dictionary* defines it, is "the integrated pattern of human behavior that includes thought, speech, action, and artifacts and depends on man's capacity for learning, and transmitting knowledge to succeeding generations." Marvin Bower, for years managing director of McKinsey & Company and author of *The Will to Manage,* offered a more informal definition—he described the informal cultural elements of a business as "the way we do things around here."

Every business—in fact every organization—has a culture. Sometimes it is fragmented and difficult to read from the outside—some people are loyal to their bosses, others are loyal to the union, still others care only about their colleagues who work in the sales territories of the Northeast. If you ask employees why they work, they will answer "because we need the money." On the other hand, sometimes the culture of an organization is very strong and cohesive; everyone knows the goals of the corporation, and they are working for them. Whether weak or strong, culture has a powerful influence throughout an organization: it affects practically everything—from who gets promoted and what decisions are made to how employees dress and what sports they play. Because of this impact, we think that culture also has a major effect on the success of the business.

Today, everyone seems to complain about the decline in American productivity. The examples of industries in trouble are numerous and depressing. Books proclaim that Japanese management practices are the solution to America's industrial malaise. But we disagree. We don't think the answer is to mimic the Japanese. Nor do we think the solution lies with the tools of "scientific" management: MBAs' analyses, portfolio theories, cost curves, or econometric models. Instead we think the answer is as American as apple pie. American business needs to return to the original concepts and ideas that made institutions like NCR, General Electric, International Business Machines (IBM), Procter & Gamble, 3M, and others great. We need to remember that people make businesses work. And we need to relearn old lessons about how culture ties

people together and gives meaning and purpose to their day-to-day lives.

The early leaders of American business such as Thomas Watson of IBM, Harley Procter of Procter & Gamble, and General Johnson of Johnson & Johnson believed that strong culture brought success. They believed that the lives and productivity of their employees were shaped by where they worked. These builders saw their role as creating an environment—in effect, a culture—in their companies in which employees could be secure and thereby do the work necessary to make the business a success. They had no magic formulas. In fact, they discovered how to shape their company's culture by trial and error. But all along the way, they paid almost fanatical attention to the culture of their companies. The lessons of these early leaders have been passed down in their own companies from generation to generation of managers; the cultures they were so careful to build and nourish have sustained their organizations through both fat and lean times. Today, these corporations still have strong cultures and still are leaders in the marketplace.

We think that anyone in business can learn a lot from these examples. A major reason the Japanese have been so successful, we think, is their continuing ability to maintain a very strong and cohesive culture throughout the entire country. Not only do individual businesses have strong cultures, but the links among business, the banking industry, and the government are also cultural and also very powerful. Japan, Inc., is actually an expansion of the corporate culture idea on a national scale. Although this homogenization of values would not fit American culture on a national scale, we do think that it has been very effective for individual companies. In fact, a strong culture has almost always been the driving force behind continuing success in American business.

We came to this conclusion through our work and study—Kennedy at McKinsey & Company and Deal at Harvard's Graduate School of Education. The idea has several origins. One was at a meeting at Stanford. A group of sociologists was puzzling over absence of relationships among variables that organizational theory said should be related. If the structure of an organization doesn't control work activities, what does it do? These questions led to new theories and views: structure and strategy may be more symbolic that substantive. The other was a McKinsey meeting. We were talking about the problems of organizations, and someone asked, "What makes for consistently outstanding company performance?" Another person offered the hypothesis that the companies that did best over the long haul were those that believed in something. The example was, "IBM means service." Others chimed in, and soon the table was full of examples:

**GE:** "Progress is our most important product."

**DuPont:** "Better things for better living through chemistry."

**Chubb Insurance:** "Excellence in underwriting."

While the focus at that point was on slogan-like evidence of a paramount belief—which we later called a "superordinate goal"—we were struck by the fact that each of the companies named had an impressive track record in the marketplace.

Intrigued by this initial evidence of support for our somewhat unconventional hypothesis, we conducted an informal survey over the next several months by interviewing McKinsey consultants about companies or organizations[1] they knew on a firsthand basis. The questions we asked were:

- Does Company *X* have one or more visible beliefs?
- If so, what are they?
- Do people in the organization know these beliefs? If so, who? And how many?
- How do these beliefs affect day-to-day business?
- How are the beliefs communicated to the organization?
- Are the beliefs reinforced—by formal personnel processes, recognition, rewards?
- How would you characterize the performance of the company?

In total, over a period of about six months, we developed profiles of nearly eighty companies. Here's what we found out:

- Of all the companies surveyed, only about one third (twenty-five to be precise) had clearly articulated beliefs.
- Of this third, a surprising two-thirds had qualitative beliefs, or values, such as "IBM means service." The other third had financially orientated goals that were widely understood.
- Of the eighteen companies with qualitative beliefs, all were uniformly outstanding performers; we could find no correlations of any relevance among the other companies—some did okay, some poorly, most had their ups and downs. We characterized the consistently high performers as strong culture companies.[2]

These strong culture companies, we thought, were on to something. And so were we. Although this was far from a scientific survey, we did have evidence that the impact of values and beliefs on company performance was indeed real. We decided to follow up this "finding" by trying to figure out how these values got there and how they were transmitted throughout the corporation. We wanted to see what made America's great companies not merely organizations, but successful human institutions.

Here we stumbled onto a gold mine of evidence. Biographies, speeches, and documents from such giants of business as Thomas Watson of IBM, John Patterson (the founder of NCR), Will Durant of General Motors, William Kellogg of Kellogg's, and a host of others show a remarkable intuitive understanding of the importance of a strong culture in the affairs of their companies.

We read about Edwin Land, who built Polaroid into a successful $1 billion company (before losing control and having the company fall on hard times) and who developed a whole theory for Polaroid's culture: he called it "Semi-Topia" after the theories of Utopia. We also learned about Alfred Sloan, the manager who built General Motors into a monolith, who spent three full days every quarter reviewing person-by-person the career progression of his top 1,000 managers. And about Charles Steinmetz, the crippled Austrian dwarf who brought alternating current into electrical systems of the world while at GE, but also adopted his lab assistant and the man's entire family. These, and many other stories, led us to one unmistakable conclusion: the people who built the companies for which America is famous all worked obsessively to create strong cultures within their organizations.

In our own research and consulting, we also found that many of the exciting, new, high-tech businesses springing up around Route 128 in Boston and Silicon Valley in California seemed obsessed with culture. Consider the case of Tandem.

## The Business of Culture

The Tandem Corporation, one of Silicon Valley's most highly publicized companies, is a company whose president deliberately manages the "informal," human side of the business. Founded by four former Hewlett-Packard employees, Tandem has built a highly successful company by solving a simple problem: the tendency of computers to break down. By yoking two computers together in one mainframe, Tandem offers customers the assurance that they will always have computer power available. If one of the processors breaks down, the other will carry on.

"Tandem is saying something about the product and people working together. Everything here works together. People with people, product with product, even processor with processor, within the product. Everything works together to keep us where we are." The quotation is not from Jim Treybig, Tandem's chief executive officer. It came from one of Tandem's managers, and the same sentiment is echoed through the ranks of the employees:

"I feel like putting a lot of time in. There is a real kind of loyalty here. We are all putting in this together—working a process together. I'm not a workaholic—it's just the place. I love the place."

"I don't want anything in the world that would hurt Tandem. I feel totally divorced from my old company, but not Tandem."

These employees seem to be describing an ideal corporation, one most managers would give their eye teeth to create. And by most standards, Tandem is enormously successful. It is growing at the rate of 25 percent per quarter, with annual revenues over $100 million. The turnover rate is nearly three times below the national average for the computer industry. Tandem's loyal employees like their jobs and the company's product. They are led by a talented group of experienced managers, a group which so far has been able to handle the phenomenal growth of the company.

Only time will tell whether Tandem can maintain its pattern of high performance. While it is easy to attribute the success of the company to fast growth and lack of competition, other things at work internally at Tandem suggest an interesting rival explanation—that the strong culture of Tandem produces its success. Here is how.

*A Widely Shared Philosophy.* Tandem is founded on a well-ordered set of management beliefs and practices. The philosophy of the company emphasizes the importance of people: "that's Tandem's greatest resource—its people, creative action, and fun." This ethic is widely shared and exemplified by slogans that everyone knows and believes in:

"It's so nice, it's so nice, we do it twice."
"It takes two to Tandem."
"Get the job done no matter what it takes."
"Tandemize it—means make it work."

The slogans are broadcast by T-shirts, bulletin boards, and word of mouth.

Top management spends about half of its time in training and in communicating the management philosophy and the essence of the company. Work is under way on a book that will codify the philosophy for future generations of workers at Tandem. "The philosophy is our future," one senior manager notes:

It mostly tell the "whats" and "hows" for selecting people and growing managers. Even though everything else around here changes. I don't want what we believe in and what we want to change.

At Tandem the management philosophy is not an afterthought. It's a principle preoccupation.

*The Importance of People.* Tandem has no formal organizational chart and few formal rules. Its meetings and memos are almost nonexistent. Jobs are flexible in terms of duties and hours. The absence of name tags and reserved parking spaces suggests a less well-defined hierarchy than is typical in the corporate world. Despite this, the organization works and people get their jobs done.

What keeps employees off each other's toes and working in the same direction? One possibility is the unwritten rules and shared understandings. As one person put it: "There are a lot of unwritten rules. But there is also a lot of freedom to make a jerk out of yourself. Most of the rules are philosophical rules." Another is dispersed authority:

"The open door policy gives me access to anyone—even the president."

"Everyone here, managers, vice-presidents, even janitors, communicates on the same level. No one feels better than anyone else."

Tandem seems to maintain a balance between autonomy and control without relying heavily on centralized or formalized procedures or rigid status hierarchies.

*Heroes: The President and the Product.* Jim Treybig is a hero at Tandem, and his employees confirm it:

"Jimmy is really a symbol here. He's a sign that every person here is a human being. He tries to make you feel part of the organization from the first day you are here. That's something people talk about."

"The one thing you have to understand about the company—Treybig's bigger than life."

Treybig shares the hero's limelight with the Tandem Continuous 10 Computer—the backbone product of the company. The computer design is the company's logo and provides the metaphor for the "working together" philosophy.

"The product is phenomenal, everyone is proud to be a part of it."

"When a big order was shipped, everyone at the plant was taking pictures. There were 'oh's' and 'ah's.' People were applauding. Can you believe it? For a computer."

Treybig and the computer share the main spotlight. But there are countless other heroes at Tandem—people whose achievements are regularly recognized on bulletin boards as "Our Latest Greatest."

*Ritual and Ceremony.* Tandem is renowned for its Friday afternoon "beer busts" which everyone attends. But the ritual does more than help people wind down after a busy work week. It serves as an important vehicle for informal communication and mingling across groups.

Tandem's emphasis on ritual, ceremony, and play is not confined to beer busts, however. There is a golf course, exercise room, and swimming pool. Company-wide celebrations are staged on important holidays. These provide opportunities for employees to develop a spirit of "oneness" and symbolize that Tandem cares about employees.

Tandem's attention to ritual ceremony begins in its personnel selection interviews. During the hiring process, potential employees are called back two or three times for interviews and must accept the position before salary negotiations take place. The interviews have been likened to an "inquisition." The message conveyed to prospective employees is "we take longer, and take care of people we hire—because we really care." The impact of this process is significant.

"They had me here for four interviews. That's about four hours, for a position of stock clerk. It was clear that they were choosy about the people they hired. That said something good about what they thought I was. They thought I was good."

Treybig personally appears at each orientation to welcome new employees and to explain the company's motivation and commitment philosophy. His appearance reinforces the honor of being accepted to work at Tandem. It's no surprise that people at Tandem feel special—they were made to feel that way before they were hired. Moreover, they feel special because the company and its product are special. And their feelings are expressed in an unusual display of loyalty and commitment to the company.

> "My goals follow the company's. It's the company and I. I think that's pretty true of everyone. We all want to see it work. You have to have it all or don't have any of it."

Employees see their work as linked to Tandem's success:

> "My job is important, and if I don't do it, Tandem doesn't make a buck."

Tandem is a unique company. And much of its success appears as intimately tied to its culture as to its product and marketplace position. The company has explicit values and beliefs which its employees share. It has heroes. It has storytellers and stories. It has rituals and ceremonies on key occasions. Tandem appears to have a strong culture which creates a bond between the company and employees, and inspires levels of productivity unlike most other corporations. Established heroes, values, and rituals are crucial to a culture's continued strength, and Tandem has kept them. The trick is in sustaining the culture so that it in turn drives the company.

Will Tandem's culture last? Although Tandem is neither big enough nor old enough to judge whether or not it will ultimately take a place in the annals of great American business, we think it is off to a good start. Indeed, other companies like IBM and P&G have already succeeded in sustaining and evolving culture over generations. These strong culture companies truly are the giants of American industry. Yet, their cultures began taking shape in a way that was very similar to Tandem.

### The Elements of Culture

What is it about Tandem's organization that exerts such a grip on its employees? Why do other strong culture companies seem to inspire such loyalty? As we continued our research, we delved into the organizational literature to understand better the elements that make up a strong culture. What is it that determines the kind of culture a company will have in the first place? And how will that culture work in the day-to-day life of a company? Although we examine each in depth later in the book, let's summarize the elements now:

*Business Environment.* Each company faces a different reality in the marketplace depending on its products, competitors, customers, technologies, government influences, and so on. To succeed in its marketplace, each company must carry out certain kinds of activities very well. In some markets that means selling; in others, invention; in still others, management of costs. In short, the environment in which a company operates determines what it must do to be a success. This business environment is the single greatest influence in shaping a corporate culture. Thus, companies that depend for success on their ability to sell an undifferentiated product tend to develop one type of culture—what we call a work hard/play hard culture—that keeps its sales force selling. Companies that spend a great deal of research and development money before they even know if the final product will be successful or not tend to develop a different culture—one that we call a better-your-company culture—designed to make sure decisions are thought through before actions are taken.

*Values.* These are the basic concepts and beliefs of an organization; as such they form the heart of the corporate culture. Values define "success" in concrete terms for employees—"if you do this, you too will be a success"—and establish standards of achievement within the organization. The strong culture companies that we investigated all had a rich and complex system of values that were shared by the employees. Managers in these companies talked about these beliefs openly and without embarrassment and they didn't tolerate deviance from the company standards.

*Heroes.* These people personify the culture's values and as such provide tangible role models for employees to follow. Some heroes are born—the visionary institution builders of American business—and some are "made" by memorable moments that occur in day-to-day corporate life. Smart companies take a direct hand in choosing people to play these heroic roles, knowing full well that others will try to emulate their behavior. Strong culture companies have many heroes. At General Electric, for instance, the heroes include Thomas Edison, the inventor; Charles Steinmetz, the compleat engineer; Gerald Swope, and now Jack Welch, the CEO entrepreneurs; and a legion of lesser-known but equally important internal figures: the inventor of the high-torque motor that powered the electric toothbrush; the chief engineer of the turbine works; the export salesman who survived two overseas revolutions; the international manager who had ghosts exorcised from a factory in Singapore; and many others. These achievements are known to virtually every employee with more than a few months' tenure in the company. And they show every employee "here's what you have to do to succeed around here."

*The Rites and Rituals.* These are the systematic and programmed routines of day-to-day life in the company. In their mundane manifestations—which we call rituals—they show employees the kind of behavior that is expected of them. In their extravaganzas—which we call ceremonies—they provide visible and potent examples of what the company stands for. Strong culture companies go to the trouble of spelling out, often in copious detail, the routine behavioral rituals they expect their employees to follow.

*The Cultural Network.* As the primary (but informal) means of communication within an organization, the cultural network is the "carrier" of the corporate values and heroic mythology. Storytellers, spies, priests, cabals, and whisperers form a hidden hierarchy of power within the company. Working the network effectively is the only way to get things done or to understand what's really going on.

## The Importance of Understanding Culture

Companies that have cultivated their individual identities by shaping values, making heroes, spelling out rites and rituals, and acknowledging the cultural network have an edge. These corporations have values and beliefs to pass along—not just products. They have stories to tell—not just profits to make. They have heroes whom managers and workers can emulate—not just faceless bureaucrats. In short, they are human institutions that provide practical meaning for people, both on and off the job.

We think that people are a company's greatest resource, and the way to manage them is not directly by computer reports, but by the subtle cues of a culture. A strong culture is a powerful lever for guiding behavior; it helps employees do their jobs a little better, especially in two ways:

*A strong culture is a system of informal rules that spells out how people are to behave most of the time.* By knowing what exactly is expected of them, employees will waste little time in deciding how to act in a given situation. In a weak culture, on the other hand, employees waste a good deal of time just trying to figure out what they should do and how they should do it. The impact of a strong culture on productivity is amazing. In the extreme, we estimate that a company can gain as much as one or two hours of productive work per employee per day.

*A strong culture enables people to feel better about what they do, so they are more likely to work harder.* When a sales representative can say "I'm with IBM," rather than "I peddle typewriters for a living," he will probably hear in response "Oh, IBM is a great company, isn't it?" He quickly figures out that he belongs to an outstanding company with a strong identity. For most people, that means a great deal. The next time they have the choice of working an extra half hour or sloughing off, they'll probably work. Overall, this has an impact on productivity too.

Unlike workers ten or twenty years ago, employees today are confused. According to psychologist Frederick Herzberg, they feel cheated by their jobs; they allow special interests to take up their time; their life values are uncertain; they are blameful and cynical; they confuse morality with ethics. Uncertainty is the core of it all. Yet strong culture companies remove a great degree of that uncertainty because they provide structure and standards and a value system in which to operate. In fact, corporations may be among the last institutions in America that can effectively take on the role of shaping values. We think that workers, managers, and chief executive officers should recognize this and act on it.

People at all stages of their careers need to understand culture and how it works, because it will likely have a powerful effect on their work lives. People just starting their careers may think a job is just a job. But when they choose a company, they often choose a way of life. The culture shapes their response in a strong, but subtle way. Culture can make them fast or slow workers, tough or friendly managers, team players or individuals. By the time they've worked for several years, they may be so well conditioned by the culture they may not even recognize it. But when they change jobs, they may be in for a big surprise.

Take an up-and-coming executive at General Electric who is being wooed by Xerox—more money, a bigger office, greater responsibility. If his first reaction is to grab it, he's probably going to be disappointed. Xerox has a totally different culture than GE. Success (and even survival) at Xerox is closely tied to an ability to maintain a near frenetic pace, the ability to work and play hard, Xerox-style.

By contrast, GE has a more thoughtful and slow-moving culture. The GE culture treats each business activity seriously—almost as though each activity will have an enormous impact on the company. Success at GE is a function of being able to take work seriously, a strong sense of peer group respect, considerable deference for authority, and a sense of deliberateness. A person of proven success at GE will bring these values to Xerox because past experience in GE's culture has reinforced them. But these same values may not be held in high esteem elsewhere.

Bright young comers at GE could, for example, quickly fizzle out at Xerox—and may not even understand why. They'll be doing exactly what they did to succeed at GE—maybe even working harder at it—but their deliberate approach to issues large and small will be seen by insiders at Xerox as a sign that they "lack smarts." Their loss of confidence, self-esteem, and ability will be confusing to them and could significantly derail their careers. For Xerox, the loss of productivity could be appreciable.

This is no imaginary scenario. It happens again and again at Xerox, General Electric, and many other companies when managers ignore the influence of culture on individual approaches to work. Culture shock may be one of the major reasons why people supposedly "fail," when they leave one organization for another. Where they fail, however, is not necessarily in doing the job, but in not reading the culture correctly.

People who want to get ahead within their own companies also need to understand—at least intuitively—what makes their culture tick. If product quality is the guiding value of your company, then you'd better be thinking about getting into manufacturing where you can contribute to the work on quality control teams. If you're a marketing whiz in a company where all of the heroes are number crunchers, then you may have a problem. You can start taking accounting courses, or you can start trying to find a more compatible environment. Unless the culture itself is in a state of change—shifting, say, from a financial emphasis to a marketing orientation—then the chances are very slim for any single person who is out of step with the culture to make it to the very top.

Aside from considerations of personal success, managers must understand very clearly how the culture works if they want to accomplish what they set out to do. If you're trying to institute a competitive, tough approach to marketing in a company that is full of hail-fellow-well-met salesmen, then you have your work cut out for you. Even if everyone agrees with what you want to do, you must know how to manage the culture—for instance, create new role model heroes—in order to teach your legion of easy-going salesmen the new rules of the game.

Finally, senior executives and especially chief executive officers may be missing out on one of the key ingredients for their companies' eventual success by ignoring either the influence of culture on corporate success of their own central role in shaping it. Their culture may be rich with lore or starved for shared values and stories. It may be coherent and cohesive, or fragmented and poorly understood. It may create meaning or contribute to blind confusion. It may be rich, fiery, focused, and strong; or weak, cold, and diffuse. Understanding the culture can help senior executives pinpoint why their company is succeeding or failing. Understanding how to build and manage the culture can help the same executives make a mark on their company that lasts for decades.

Can every company have a strong culture? We think it can. But to do that, top management first has to recognize what kind of culture the company already has, even if it is weak. The ultimate success of a chief executive officer depends to a large degree on an accurate reading of the corporate culture and the ability to hone it and shape it to fit the shifting needs of the marketplace.

In reading this book, we can imagine that many managers will ask themselves, is culture too "soft"? Can serious managers actually take the time to deal with it? Indeed, we believe that managers must. Management scientists sometimes argue that corporations are so complex and vulnerable to diverse external and internal forces that managers' freedom to act and lead is limited. Their argument is plausible, but our experience does not support it. By and large, the most successful managers we know are precisely those who strive to make a mark through creating a guiding vision, shaping shared values, and otherwise providing leadership for the people with whom they work.

It all comes down to understanding the importance of working with people in any organization. The institution builders of old knew the value of a strong culture and they worked hard at it. They saw themselves as symbolic players-actors in their corporations. They knew how to orchestrate, even dramatize events to drive their lessons home. They understood how corporations shape personal lives and were not shy about suggesting the standards that people should live by. If we are to have such great institutions tomorrow, the managers of today will have to take up this challenge again.

Our goal in this book is to provide business leaders with a primer on cultural management. In showing how several excellent companies[3] manage their cultures, this book is meant to be suggestive only, not hard and fast or prescriptive. Our aim is to heighten the awareness of our readers, to jog them into thinking about the workplace in its role as a mediator of behavior, and to show the positive effects of culture building. Along the way, we hope to instill in our readers a new law of business life: In Culture There Is Strength.

## *Notes*

1. Our survey covered both profit-making companies and a few nonprofit organizations we found particularly intriguing. For simplicity we refer in the text to all of these as "companies."

2. These were: Caterpillar Tractor, General Electric, Du-Pont, Chubb Insurance, Price, Waterhouse & Co., 3M, Jefferson-Smurfit, The Training Services Administration Agency of the British government, Digital Equipment Corporations, International Business Machines, Dana Corporation, Procter & Gamble, Hewlett-Packard, Leo Burnett Advertising Agency, Johnson & Johnson, Tandem Computer, Continental Bank, and the Rouse Corporation.

3. You may see several companies—such as General Electric—and several individuals—such as Thomas Watson—named again and again throughout the book. This is because we consider them the absolutely best examples we could find to illustrate our ideas. Managers could do worse than to emulate these examples.

# 32

# On the Role of Top Management

JOHN P. KOTTER
JAMES L. HESKETT

Culture represents an interdependent set of values and ways of behaving that are common in a community and that tend to perpetuate themselves, sometimes over long periods of time. This continuity is the product of a variety of social forces that are frequently subtle, bordering on invisible, through which people learn a group's norms and values, are rewarded when they accept them, and are ostracized when they do not. The importance of this phenomenon has been recognized for decades. The research reported in this book demonstrates the specific power of culture in one setting: inside companies. Our studies clearly show that certain kinds of corporate cultures help, while others undermine, long-term economic performance.

Although it is widely believed today that strong cultures create excellent performance, we have found that the recent experiences of nearly two hundred firms do not support that theory. In firms with strong corporate cultures, managers tend to march energetically in the same direction in a well-coordinated fashion. That alignment, motivation, organization, and control can help performance, but only if the resulting actions fit an intelligent business strategy for the specific environment in which a firm operates. Performance will not be enhanced if the common behaviors and methods of doing business do not fit the needs of a firm's product or service market, financial market, and labor market. Strong cultures with practices that do not fit a company's context can actually lead intelligent people to behave in ways that are destructive—that systematically undermine an organization's ability to survive and prosper.

Furthermore, our research shows that even contextually or strategically appropriate cultures will not promote excellent performance over long periods unless they contain norms and values that can help firms adapt to a changing environment. We

SOURCE: Adapted/reprinted with the permission of The Free Press, a Division of Simon & Schuster from *Corporate Culture and Performance* by John P. Kotter and James L. Heskett. Copyright © 1992 by Kotter Associates, Inc. and James L. Heskett.

**EXHIBIT 32.1**   Adaptive vs. Unadaptive Corporate Cultures

|  | *Adaptive Corporate Cultures* | *Unadaptive Corporate Cultures* |
|---|---|---|
| Core values | Most managers care deeply about customers, stockholders, and employees. They also strongly value people and processes that can create useful change (e.g., leadership up and down the management hierarchy) | Most managers care mainly about themselves, their immediate work group, or some product (or technology) associated with that work group. They value the orderly and risk-reducing management process much more highly than leadership initiatives |
| Common behavior | Managers pay close attention to all their constituencies, especially customers, and initiate change when needed to serve their legitimate interests, even if that entails taking some risks | Managers tend to behave somewhat insularly, politically, and bureaucratically. As a result, they do not change their strategies quickly to adjust to or take advantage of changes in their business environments |

have found a number of prominent companies that performed adequately from strong market positions in slowly changing environments during the 1940s, 1950s, and 1960s, but that have not done well in the past ten to twenty years when the business world became more competitive and faster moving. In each of these cases, we have also found change-resistant cultures.

Cultures that are not adaptive take many forms. In large corporations, they are often characterized by some arrogance, insularity, and bureaucratic centralization, all supported by a value system that cares more about self-interest than about customers, stockholders, employees, or good leadership. In such cultures, managers tend to ignore relevant contextual changes and to cling to outmoded strategies and ossified practices. They make it difficult for anyone else, especially those below them in the hierarchy, to implement new and better strategies and practices. And they tend to turn people off—particularly those individuals whose personal values include an emphasis on integrity, trust, and caring for other human beings.

In corporate cultures that promote useful change, managers pay close attention to relevant changes in a firm's context and then initiate incremental changes in strategies and practices to keep firms and cultures in line with environmental realities. These behavioral norms seem to be driven by a value system that stresses meeting the legitimate needs of all the key constituencies whose cooperation is essential to business performance—especially customers, employees, and stockholders.

These values also emphasize the importance of people and processes that can create change—especially competent leadership throughout the management hierarchy. Such a value system, when expressed in written form, often sounds either hopelessly idealistic, or vague to the point of uselessness, or even inappropriately religious (e.g., "Treat others as you would have them treat you"). Yet that very value system is the key to excellent performance nowadays because it tends to energize managers and get them to do what is needed to help firms adapt to a changing competitive environment (see Exhibit 32.1).

Many companies today say that they care about customers, stockholders, and employees. More and more organizations nowadays say they believe in the importance of competent leadership at multiple levels in their hierarchies. But few really do, at least in a cultural sense—where who gets promoted says more about real values than any mission statement or credo. On average, those few that do seem to be outperforming most others by a considerable margin.

\*   \*   \*

When performance-enhancing cultures emerge in start-up situations, at least two elements seem to be critical: (1) an entrepreneur who has (or develops) a business philosophy that is similar to what we have found at the core of adaptive cultures and (2) a business strategy that fits the specific situation and that produces sufficient success to make the entrepreneur (and his or her philosophy) highly credible to the employees. We suspect these elements are not unusual in highly successful young companies, mostly because they are necessary for success in a competitive business environment. But we also have evidence that performance-enhancing cultures often erode over time, either because they are not effectively passed on to the hoards of new managers needed in a growing business or because time and success and other factors blur people's memories about why they were successful in the first place (see Exhibit 32.2).

We have considerable data on the creation of performance enhancing cultures in mature organizations that lacked such cultures. In general, this seems to happen infrequently and with great difficulty. In mature firms, even modestly unadaptive cultures can resist change with great intensity. Overcoming this tendency requires a specific combination of personal attributes and actions—a combination that appears to be all too rare today.

In the cases of successful change that we have studied, we have always found one or two unusually capable leaders on top. These individuals had track records for producing dramatic results. They also combined the "outsider's" objective view of their firms with the credibility and power base usually associated with insiders.

These leaders began the process of creating change soon after their appointment as president, chairman, or division general manager. They did so first by establishing a sense of crisis or need for change, and then by creating a new direction for their firms based on a constituencies-are-king philosophy and contextually appropriate business strategies. They challenged the status quo with very basic questions: Is this what customers really need and want? Is this the most efficient or productive way to deliver those products and services? They gathered or led others to gather all the information necessary to answer those questions, including data from outsiders and people lower in the organization. They were decisive—making choices about direction and acting on those choices.

To produce needed change, these leaders then communicated their visions and strategies broadly in order to obtain understanding and commitment from a wide range of people. They used every possible opportunity to repeat key messages again and again. They made the communication as simple and easy to understand as possible. They allowed people to challenge the messages—thereby establishing healthy dialogue to replace static, one-way monologue. And they kept their own actions consistent with the communication in order to bolster the message's credibility; in most cases, they became living embodiments of the new cultures they desired. By aligning people to an appropriate vision and business strategy, these leaders helped empower like-minded managers who wanted to introduce needed changes but were being blocked by others.

These leaders then motivated a large number of their middle managers to play a similar kind of leadership role in creating change for their own divisions, departments, and groups. To make this happen, top executives stressed those parts of their visions that appealed to the values of their managers. They gave those managers as much autonomy as possible to enable the needed leadership. They actively encouraged attempts to provide that leadership. They recognized and rewarded as many successes as possible.

As a result, a great deal changed. New business strategies began to emerge that made sense in light of competitive conditions. New structures were implemented, usually with fewer hierarchical layers and less complexity. People began paying more attention to customers and costs and excellence. Performance improved.

When these leaders began their work, only a small number of people typically understood and agreed with what they were doing. But as their efforts produced positive results, their coalitions grew and grew over time. As these coalitions expanded, so did the new cultures, ones that better fit the firms' contexts and were better able to adapt to change (see Exhibit 32.3). In very large settings, the total time required for all this was significant: on the order of five to fifteen years.

The performance improvements that accompanied these cases of cultural change ranged from good to extraordinary. More important, people well acquainted with these cases seem to agree almost

**EXHIBIT 32.2** The Origins of Unhealthy Corporate Cultures

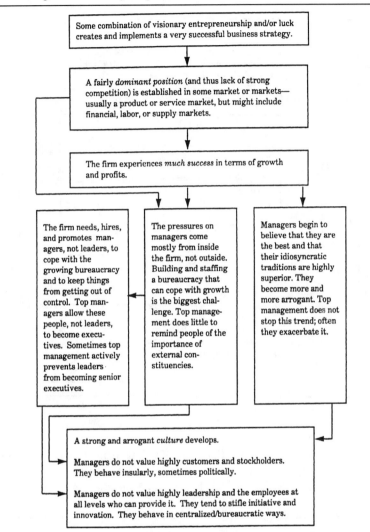

Some combination of visionary entrepreneurship and/or luck creates and implements a very successful business strategy.

A fairly *dominant position* (and thus lack of strong competition) is established in some market or markets—usually a product or service market, but might include financial, labor, or supply markets.

The firm experiences *much success* in terms of growth and profits.

The firm needs, hires, and promotes managers, not leaders, to cope with the growing bureaucracy and to keep things from getting out of control. Top managers allow these people, not leaders, to become executives. Sometimes top management actively prevents leaders from becoming senior executives.

The pressures on managers come mostly from inside the firm, not outside. Building and staffing a bureaucracy that can cope with growth is the biggest challenge. Top management does little to remind people of the importance of external constituencies.

Managers begin to believe that they are the best and that their idiosyncratic traditions are highly superior. They become more and more arrogant. Top management does not stop this trend; often they exacerbate it.

A strong and arrogant *culture* develops.

Managers do not value highly customers and stockholders. They behave insularly, sometimes politically.

Managers do not value highly leadership and the employees at all levels who can provide it. They tend to stifle initiative and innovation. They behave in centralized/bureaucratic ways.

---

universally that the firms involved were left better positioned for the future.

\* \* \*

The challenge for top management is different once a good culture has taken hold, but it is no less important.[1] Our research suggests that executives then need to cope with certain tensions and dilemmas. In a sense, the challenge is to orchestrate a difficult balancing act, the consequences of which determine whether a performance-enhancing culture is preserved or not.

Holding onto a good culture requires being both inflexible with regard to core adaptive values and yet flexible with regard to most practices and other values. It requires pushing hard to win, but not allowing the pride that comes with success to develop into arrogance. And it requires providing strong leadership, yet not strangling or smothering delicate leadership initiatives from below.

**EXHIBIT 32.3**  The Creation of a Performance-Enhancing Culture

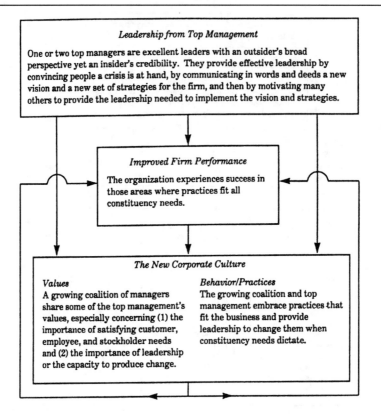

*Leadership from Top Management*

One or two top managers are excellent leaders with an outsider's broad perspective yet an insider's credibility. They provide effective leadership by convincing people a crisis is at hand, by communicating in words and deeds a new vision and a new set of strategies for the firm, and then by motivating many others to provide the leadership needed to implement the vision and strategies.

*Improved Firm Performance*

The organization experiences success in those areas where practices fit all constituency needs.

*The New Corporate Culture*

*Values*
A growing coalition of managers share some of the top management's values, especially concerning (1) the importance of satisfying customer, employee, and stockholder needs and (2) the importance of leadership or the capacity to produce change.

*Behavior/Practices*
The growing coalition and top management embrace practices that fit the business and provide leadership to change them when constituency needs dictate.

Our research suggests that two sets of actions can probably help with these dilemmas. In the first, executives need to differentiate basic values and behaviors that aid adaptation from the more specific practices needed to perform well today. This distinction needs to be made explicit when talking about culture. It also needs to be carefully noted in all written statements about culture and in all internal training courses. And it needs to be reflected and reinforced by specific actions. Without this distinction, practices of no long-term significance can easily become important forces in a culture. Such practices can evolve into "sacred" traditions that ossify, resist change, and eventually undermine economic performance.

Second, although executives need to foster pride among employees, they also must be as intolerant as possible of arrogance in others and in themselves. They need to confront, and make others confront, as many of their failings as is practical. They need to create events where everyone in management is forced to listen to dissatisfied customers, angry stockholders, and alienated employees—not to embarrass or punish their managers, but to keep them informed and to help them realistically assess their strengths and weaknesses. And this must be done on an ongoing basis.

Both of these sets of actions, if taken to an extreme, will create serious problems. An emphasis only on adaptive values and behaviors can make it difficult to implement successfully today's strategies and tactics. Too much intolerance of arrogance coupled with a constant focus on problems can be depressing and, ultimately, disempowering. The challenge is gaining the correct balance.

These actions are obviously not easy, but our research suggests they are both needed and feasible (see Exhibit 32.4).

**EXHIBIT 32.4**  Preserving Performance-Enhancing Cultures

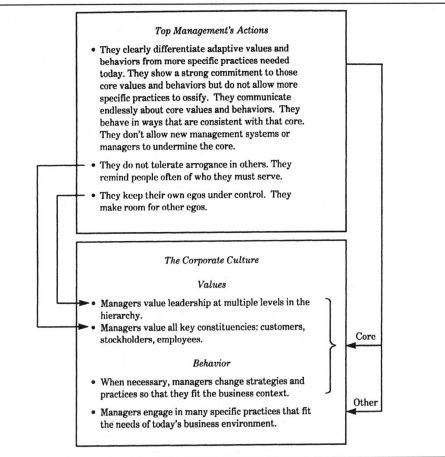

*Top Management's Actions*

- They clearly differentiate adaptive values and behaviors from more specific practices needed today. They show a strong commitment to those core values and behaviors but do not allow more specific practices to ossify. They communicate endlessly about core values and behaviors. They behave in ways that are consistent with that core. They don't allow new management systems or managers to undermine the core.
- They do not tolerate arrogance in others. They remind people often of who they must serve.
- They keep their own egos under control. They make room for other egos.

*The Corporate Culture*

*Values*

- Managers value leadership at multiple levels in the hierarchy.
- Managers value all key constituencies: customers, stockholders, employees.

*Behavior*

- When necessary, managers change strategies and practices so that they fit the business context.
- Managers engage in many specific practices that fit the needs of today's business environment.

Core

Other

\* \* \*

Ultimately, dozens, hundreds, or even thousands of managers became involved in important ways in the successful cultural change efforts that we studied—not only at the top, but at the middle and lower levels too. Without all this help, some of which typically came before a new CEO started providing strong leadership, and some of which may have influenced the CEO succession process, major cultural change would have been impossible. Nevertheless, excellent leadership from the top seems to be the essential ingredient in the cases we studied—leadership usually provided by a very small group of people. This leadership empowers other managers and employees who see the need

for change but have been constrained by the old culture. It also helps win over the hearts and minds of others who have not yet recognized the necessity of major change. In many organizations today, providing this kind of leadership is surely the number one challenge for top management.

By our calculations, the vast majority of firms currently do not have cultures that are sufficiently adaptive to produce excellent long-term economic performance in an increasingly competitive and changing business environment. To create those cultures, our research strongly suggests that top managers need to do more than manage well. Excellent management, by its very nature, is somewhat conservative, methodically incremental, and short-term oriented. As a result, the very best man-

**EXHIBIT 32.5**  Environmental Stability and World Competition: Indices of the Need for Adaptive Corporate Cultures

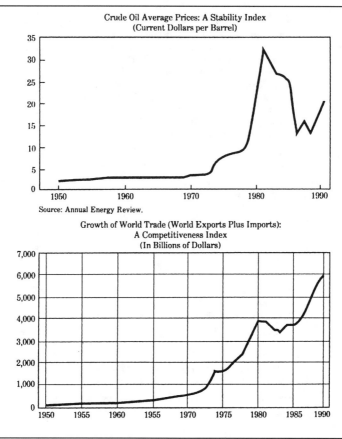

Crude Oil Average Prices: A Stability Index
(Current Dollars per Barrel)

Source: Annual Energy Review.

Growth of World Trade (World Exports Plus Imports):
A Competitiveness Index
(In Billions of Dollars)

SOURCE: International Monetary Fund

agement simply cannot produce major change. Only with leadership does one get the boldness, the vision, and the energy needed to create large and difficult changes and cultural change certainly tends to be large and difficult.

Until the late 1970s and early 1980s, there was enough stability in a world of moderated competition (see Exhibit 32.5) to allow firms with relatively unadaptive corporate cultures and managerially oriented corporate officers to survive and prosper. This is no longer the case. And all the evidence we see suggests an ever more unstable and competitive future, at least for the next decade.

The implications here are powerful—especially for those involved in executive staffing decisions and for aspiring executives everywhere. If our economic organizations are going to live up to their potential, we must find, develop, and encourage more people to lead in the service of others. Without leadership, firms cannot adapt to a fast-moving world. But if leaders do not have the hearts of servants, there is only the potential for tyranny.

## *Note*

1. Wilkins has reported cases that show how fragile a good culture can be if top managers do not pay attention to it and don't do what is needed to preserve it. See his *Developing Corporate Character.*

# 33

# *Values in Leadership*

RONALD A. HEIFETZ

Leadership arouses passion. The exercise and even the study of leadership stirs feeling because leadership engages our values. Indeed, the term itself is value-laden. When we call for leadership in our organizations and politics, we call for something we prize. If one asks: "Would you rather be known as a leader or a manager? A follower or a leader?" the response is usually "a leader." The term *leadership* involves our self-images and moral codes.

Yet the way we talk about leadership betrays confusion. On one hand, we use the word to denote people and actions of merit. During an election year, we want "a leader" for president, rather than "another politician." In our organizations, we evaluate managers for their "leadership," by which we mean a particular constellation of valued abilities. When we look abroad, we fasten the term to people like Gorbachev, Walesa, De Klerk, or Mandela, people we admire for their values, courage, commitment, and skill. On the other hand, we insist that the word leadership is value-free. We say that Pablo Escobar, head of the Medellin drug cartel, was a "leader," even if we detested his values, because he motivated followers to realize his vision.[1] Our media routinely use the term leader to denote people in authority or people who have a following. We talk about the leader of the gang, the mob, the organization—the person who is given informal or formal authority by others—regardless of the values they represent or the product they play a key part in producing.

We cannot continue to have it both ways. We may like to use the word *leadership* as if it were value-free, particularly in an age of science and mathematics, so that we can describe far-ranging phenomena and people with consistency. Yet when we do so, we ignore the other half of ourselves that in the next breath speaks of leadership as something we desperately need more of. We cannot talk about a crisis in leadership and then say leadership is value-free. Do we merely mean that we have too few people in our midst who can gather a following? Surely, we are not asking for more messiahs of Waco and Jonestown who meet people's needs by offering tempting visions of rapture and sacrifice.[2] The contradiction in our common under-

SOURCE: Reprinted by permission of the publisher from *Leadership Without Easy Answers* by Ronald A. Heifetz, Cambridge, Mass.: Harvard University Press, Copyright © 1994 by the President and Fellows of Harvard College.

standing clouds not only the clarity of our thinking and scholarship; it shapes the quality of leadership we praise, teach, and get.[3]

Understandably, scholars who have studied "leadership" have tended to side with the value-free connotation of the term because it lends itself more easily to analytic reasoning and empirical examination.[4] But this will not do for them any more than it will do for practitioners of leadership who intervene in organizations and communities everyday. Rigor in social science does not require that we ignore values; it simply requires being explicit about the values we study. There is no neutral ground from which to construct notions and theories of leadership because leadership terms, loaded with emotional content, carry with them implicit norms and values. For example, when we equate leadership with holding high office or exerting great influence, we reinforce a tendency to value station and power. We are not simply studying or using power; we unwittingly communicate that power has intrinsic worth.

We have to take sides. When we teach, write about, and model the exercise of leadership, we inevitably support or challenge people's conceptions of themselves, their roles, and most importantly their ideas about how social systems make progress on problems. Leadership is a normative concept because implicit in people's notions of leadership are images of a social contract. Imagine the differences in behavior when people operate with the idea that "leadership means influencing the community to follow the leader's vision" versus "leadership means influencing the community to face its problems." In the first instance, influence is the mark of leadership; a leader gets people to accept his vision, and communities address problems by looking to him. If something goes wrong, the fault lies with the leader.[5] In the second, progress on problems is the measure of leadership; leaders mobilize people to face problems, and communities make progress on problems because leaders challenge and help them do so. If something goes wrong, the fault lies with both leaders and the community.

This second image of leadership—mobilizing people to tackle tough problems—is the image at the heart of this book. This conception builds upon, yet differs from, the culturally dominant views. For example, in popular conceptions of politics, leadership generally refers to the exercise of influence: the leader stands out in front—usually in high office—influencing others. The person may also be the most influential member of a popular movement operating with little if any formal authority, such as Lech Walesa or the Ayotollah Khomeini (before they took political office).

In business, we see an evolution of the concept of leadership. For decades, the term leadership referred to the people who hold top management positions and the functions they serve. In our common usage, it still does. Recently, however, business people have drawn a distinction between leadership and management, and exercising leadership has also come to mean providing a vision and influencing others to realize it through noncoercive means.[6]

In the military, the term leadership commonly refers to people in positions of command, who show the way. Perhaps because warfare has played a central role historically in the development of our conceptions of leadership and authority, it is not surprising that the ancient linguistic root of the word "to lead" means "to go forth, die."[7] In our time, leadership in the military aims to draw forth a person's highest qualities, by influence more than coercion. "Be all that you can be" implies preparation based on the potential that resides in the enlistees when they enter. In the final test, however, the troops achieve the goals prescribed by the leaders in command.[8]

In biology, leadership is the activity of flying at the front of a flock of geese, or maintaining order in social relations and food gathering among primates. The leader has a particular set of physical attributes (big, colorful, fast, assertive). The leader functions as a focal point of attention by which the rest of the group instinctively organizes itself. Leadership is equated with prominence and dominance.

In horse racing, a field some would say bears a resemblance to politics, leading simply means being out in front. The jockey of the lead horse is leading nobody, except perhaps unintentionally to the extent that other jockeys set strategy and strive harder to overtake him.

There seem to be two common denominators of these various views: station and influence. Hence, many scholarly approaches to the study of leadership during the last two hundred years focus on the phenomena of prominent and influential people.[9] Theorists ask the following important questions: How and why do particular individuals gain power in an organization or society? What are their personal characteristics? What functions do they serve? How do they realize their vision? How do they move history, or does history move them? What motivates them and how do they motivate others?[10]

## Hidden Values in Theories of Leadership

Perhaps the first theory of leadership—and the one that continues to be entrenched in American culture—emerged from the nineteenth-century notion that history is the story of great men and their impact on society. (Women were not even considered candidates for greatness.) Thomas Carlyle crystallized this view in his 1841 volume *On Heroes, Hero-Worship, and the Heroic in History.* Although various scientific studies discount the idea, this *trait approach* continues to set the terms of popular debate.[11] Indeed, it saw a revival during the 1980s.[12] Based on this view, trait theorists since Carlyle have examined the personality characteristics of "great men," positing that the rise to power is rooted in a "heroic" set of personal talents, skills, or physical characteristics. As Sidney Hook described in *The Hero in History* (1943), some men are eventful, while others are eventmaking.[13]

In reaction to the great-man theory of history, *situationalists* argued that history is much more than the effects of these men on their time. Indeed, social theorists like Herbert Spencer (1884) suggested that the times produce the person and not the other way around. In a sense, situationalists were not interested in leadership per se. "Historymakers" were interesting because they stood at the vortex of powerful political and social forces, which themselves were of interest. Thus, the more or less contemporaneous emergence of the United States' first great leaders—Jefferson, Washington, Adams, Madison. Hamilton, Monroe, Benjamin Franklin—is attributed not to a demographic fluke but to the extraordinary times in which these men lived. Instead of asserting that all of them shared a common set of traits, situationalists suggest that the times called forth an assortment of men with various talents and leadership styles. Indeed, many of them performed marvelously in some jobs but quite poorly in other.[14] Thus, "What an individual actually *does* when acting as a leader is in large part dependent upon characteristics of the situation in which he functions."[15]

Beginning in the 1950s, theorists began (not surprisingly) to synthesize the trait approach with the situationalist view. Empirical studies had begun to show that no single constellation of traits was associated with leadership. Although this finding did not negate the idea that individuals "make" history, it did suggest that different situations demand different personalities and call for different behaviors. Primary among these synthetic approaches is *contingency theory,* which posits that the appropriate style of leadership is contingent on the requirements of the particular situation. For example, some situations require controlling autocratic behavior and others participative or democratic behavior.[16]

The field of inquiry soon expanded into the specific interactions between leaders and followers—the *transactions* by which an individual gains influence and sustains it over time.[17] The process is based on reciprocity. Leaders not only influence followers but are under their influence as well.[18] A leader earns influence by adjusting to the expectations of followers. In one variant of the transactional approach, the leader reaps the benefits of status and influence in exchange for reducing uncertainty and providing followers with a basis for action.[19] In another variant, bargaining and persuasion are the essence of political power, requiring a keen understanding of the interests of various stakeholders, both professional and public.[20]

Each of these theories is generally considered to be value-free, but in fact their values are simply hidden. The great-man or trait approach places value on the historymaker, the person with extraordinary influence. Although the approach does not specify in what direction influence must be wielded to constitute leadership, the very suggestion that the mark of a great man is his historical impact on society gives us a particular perspective on greatness. Placing Hitler in the same general category as Gandhi or Lincoln does not render the theory value-free. On the contrary, it simply leaves its central value—influence—implicit.[21]

The situational approach, ironically, does something similar. It departs radically from the great-man view by suggesting that certain people emerge to prominence because the times and social forces call them forth. Yet leaders are still assumed to be those people who gain prominence in society. The people that a trait theorist would select to study from history, the situational theorist would select as well.

Contingency theory, synthesizing the great-man and situational approaches, also began with a value-free image of itself. It examines which decisionmaking style fits which situational contingency in order for the decisionmaker to maintain control of the process. Sometimes a directive, task-oriented style is the most effective, and at other times a participative, relationship-oriented style is required. Yet even in this more specific rendition of the traditional view, the mark of leadership is still influence, or control.[22]

Advocates of transactional approaches, focusing on how influence is gained and maintained, also see themselves as value-neutral. Although they describe elegantly the relational dynamics of influence, they do not evaluate the purpose to which influence is put or the way purposes are derived. By stating that the mark of leadership is influence over outcomes, these theorists unwittingly enter the value realm. Leadership-as-influence implicitly promotes influence as an orienting value, perpetuating a confusion between means and ends.[23]

These four general approaches attempt to define leadership objectively, without making value judgments. When defining leadership in terms of prominence, authority, and influence, however, these theories introduce value-biases implicitly without declaring their introduction and without arguing for the necessity of the values introduced.[24] From a research point of view, this presents no real problem. Indeed, it simplifies the analytic task. The problem emerges when we communicate and

model these descriptions as "leadership" because "leadership" in many cultures is a normative idea—it represents a set of orienting values, as do words like "hero" and "champion."[25] If we leave the value implications of our teaching and practice unaddressed, we encourage people, perhaps unwittingly, to aspire to great influence or high office, regardless of what they do there.[26] We would be on safer ground were we to discard the loaded term leadership altogether and simply describe the dynamics of prominence, power, influence, and historical causation.[27]

Although these theories were designed primarily for value-free description and analysis, they still shed light on how to think about practice. For example, the trait theorists encourage us to believe that individuals can indeed make a difference. No activist can operate without that assumption. Furthermore, the decades of scholarship devoted to sifting and analyzing generic skills provide us with some basis to define the goals of leadership education. The situational approach directs us toward examining how the activity of leadership differs depending on the context. Coupled with the contingency approach, it tells us that the task of contextual diagnosis is central to leadership. In addition, it provides a host of variables to consider in analyzing different situations and the style of leadership that might apply. This will be critical to those who lead. For example, contingency theory frames the key question: Which situations call for authoritarian behavior and which demand "democratic" processes?[28] The transactional theorists contribute the basic idea that authority consists of reciprocal relationships: people in authority influence constituents, but constituents also influence them. We forget this at our peril.

### *Toward a Prescriptive Concept of Leadership*

In this study I will use four criteria to develop a definition of leadership that takes values into account. First, the definition must sufficiently resemble current cultural assumptions so that, when feasible, one's normal understanding of what it means to lead will apply. Second, the definition should be practical, so that practitioners can make use of it. Third, it should point toward socially useful activities. Finally, the concept should offer a broad definition of social usefulness.

How might we go about defining the term leadership in a way that employs our current knowledge, and the values associated with it? Leadership, which has long been linked to the exercise of authority or influence, usually suggests playing a prominent and coordinating role in an organization or society. To capture these uses of the term in a definition, we can use the word "mobilize," which connotes motivating, organizing, orienting, and focusing attention.

Rather than define leadership either as a position of authority in a social structure or as a personal set of characteristics, we may find it a great deal more useful to define leadership as an *activity*.[29] This allows for leadership from multiple positions in a social structure. A president and a clerk can both lead. It also allows for the use of a variety of abilities depending on the demands of the culture and situation. Personal abilities are resources for leadership applied differently in different contexts. As we know, at times they are not applied at all. Many people never exercise leadership, even though they have the personal qualities we might commonly associate with it.[30] By unhinging leadership from personality traits, we permit observations of the many different ways in which people exercise plenty of leadership everyday without "being leaders."

The common personalistic orientation to the term leadership, with its assumption that "leaders are born and not made," is quite dangerous. It fosters both self-delusion and irresponsibility. For those who consider themselves "born leaders," free of an orienting philosophy and strategy of leadership, their grandiosity is a set-up for a rude awakening and for blindly doing damage. Minimally, they can waste the time and effort of a community on projects that go, if not over a cliff, then at least in circles.[31] Conversely, those who consider themselves "not leaders" escape responsibility for taking action, or for learning how to take action, when they see the need. In the face of critical problems, they say, "I'm not a leader, what can I do?"[32]

So, we ought to focus on leadership as an activity—the activity of a citizen from any walk of life mobilizing people to do something. But what is the socially useful something? What mode of leadership is likely to generate socially useful outcomes? Several approaches to these questions might work. We could imagine that a leader is more likely to produce socially useful outcomes by setting goals that meet the needs of both the leader and followers.[33] This has the benefit of distinguishing leadership from merely "getting people to do what you want them to do." Leadership is more than influence.

Even so, setting a goal to meet the needs of the community may give no definition of what those needs are. If a leader personally wants to turn away from the difficulty of problems, and so do his constituents, does he exercise leadership by coming up with a fake remedy?

To address this problem, the leadership theorist James MacGregor Burns suggested that socially useful goals not only have to meet the needs of followers, they also should elevate followers to a higher moral level. Calling this *transformational leadership,* he posits that people begin with the need for survival and security, and once those needs are met, concern themselves with "higher" needs like affection, belonging, the common good, or serving others.[34] This approach has the benefit of provoking discussion about how to construct a hierarchy of orienting values. However, a hierarchy that would apply across cultures and organizational settings risks either being so general as to be impractical or so specific as to be culturally imperialistic in its application.

We might also say that leadership has a higher probability of producing socially useful results when defined in terms of legitimate authority, with legitimacy based on a set of procedures by which power is conferred from the many to the few. This view is attractive because we might stop glorifying usurpations of power as leadership. But by restraining the exercise of leadership to legitimate authority, we also leave no room for leadership that challenges the legitimacy of authority or the system of authorization itself.[35] No doubt, there are risks to freeing leadership from its moorings of legitimate authority. To take one celebrated case, perhaps we risk encouraging committed zealots like Oliver North. Yet we also face an important possibility: social progress may require that someone push the system to its limit. Perhaps Andrei Sakharov served such a role in the democratization of the former Soviet Union. Hence, a person who leads may have to risk his moral state, and not just his health and job, to protect his moral state.[36] Defining leadership in terms of legitimate authority excludes those who faced moral doubt and deep regret by defying authority. Vaclav Havel, Lech Walesa, Aung San Suu Kyi, Martin Luther King, Jr., Margaret Sanger, and Mohandas Gandhi, to name a few, risked social disaster by unleashing uncontrollable social forces.

Business schools and schools of management commonly define leadership and its usefulness with respect to organizational effectiveness. Effectiveness means reaching viable decisions that implement the goals of the organization. This definition has the benefit of being generally applicable, but it provides no real guide to determine the nature or formation of those goals.[37] Which goals should we pursue? What constitutes effectiveness in addition to the ability to generate profits? From the perspective of a town official viewing a local corporation, effectiveness at implementation seems an insufficient criterion. A chemical plant may be quite effective at earning a profit while it dangerously pollutes the local water supply. We are left with the question: Effective at what?

This study examines the usefulness of viewing leadership in terms of adaptive work. Adaptive work consists of the learning required to address conflicts in the values people hold, or to diminish the gap between the values people stand for and the reality they face. Adaptive work requires a change in values, beliefs, or behavior. The exposure and orchestration of conflict—internal contradictions—within individuals and constituencies provide the leverage for mobilizing people to learn new ways.[38]

In this view, getting people to clarify what matters most, in what balance, with what trade-offs, becomes a central task. In the case of a local industry that pollutes the river, people want clean water, but they also want jobs. Community and company interests frequently overlap and clash,

with conflicts taking place not only among factions but also within the lives of individual citizens who themselves may have competing needs. Leadership requires orchestrating these conflicts among and within the interested parties, and not just between the members and formal shareholders of the organization. Who should play a part in the deliberations is not a given, but is itself a critical strategic question. Strategy begins with asking: Which stakeholders have to adjust their ways to make progress on this problem? How can one sequence the issues or strengthen the bonds that join the stakeholders together as a community of interests so that they withstand the stresses of problem solving?

To clarify a complex situation such as this requires multiple vantage points, each of which adds a piece to the puzzle. Just as clarifying a vision demands reality testing, reality testing is not a value-free process. Values are shaped and refined by rubbing against real problems, and people interpret their problems according to the values they hold. Different values shed light on the different opportunities and facets of a situation. The implication is important: *the inclusion of competing value perspectives may be essential to adaptive success.* In the long run, an industrial polluter will fail if it neglects the interests of its community. Given the spread of environmental values, it may not always be able to move across borders. Conversely, the community may lose its economic base if it neglects the interests of its industry.

The point here is to provide a guide to goal formation and strategy. In selecting adaptive work as a guide, one considers not only the values that the goal represents but also the goal's ability to mobilize people to face, rather than avoid, tough realities and conflicts. The hardest and most valuable task of leadership may be advancing goals and designing strategy that promote adaptive work.[39]

Does this forsake the image of leadership as a visionary activity? Not at all. It places emphasis on the act of giving clarity and articulation to a community's guiding values. Neither providing a map for the future that disregards value conflicts nor providing an easy way out that neglects the facts will suffice for leadership.[40] Guiding values are interpreted in the context of problems demanding definition and action.[41] People discover and respond to the future as much as they plan it. Those who lead have to learn from events and take advantage of the unplanned opportunities that events uncover.[42] They have to improvise. In the midst of the Great Depression, Franklin Roosevelt called for "bold, persistent experimentation." As he put it, "It is common sense to take a method and try it. If it fails, admit it frankly and try another. But above all, try something."[43]

As an example to compare these frames of reference, we can use the case of Roosevelt's adversary, Adolf Hitler. When influence alone defines leadership, Hitler qualifies as an authentic and successful leader: he mobilized a nation to follow his vision. Indeed, he inspired millions of people to organize their lives by his word. Even with the added criterion that goals have to meet the needs of both leader and follower, we would say that Hitler led. His many followers in Germany shared his goals. He was not simply forcing his sentiments and views on everyone. He reached office, in part, by articulating the pains and hopes of many people.

Furthermore, by the standard of organizational effectiveness, Hitler exercised formidable leadership. Within hundreds of specific decisionmaking instances, Hitler succeeded in developing the effectiveness of German organizations. He set the goal of restoring the German economy, and for a period of time he succeeded.

If we assume that leadership must not only meet the needs of followers but also must elevate them, we render a different judgment. Hitler wielded power, but he did not lead.[44] He played to people's basest needs and fears. If he inspired people toward the common good of Germany, it was the good of a truncated and exclusive society feeding off others. By the standard of legitimate authority, Hitler also does not qualify as a leader. Elected once by a plurality of Germans in 1933, he destroyed the nascent democratic political apparatus and maintained his political dominance through terror.

By the criterion of adaptive work used here, we would also say that Hitler failed to exercise leadership. Although dramatically mobilizing his society, both socially and economically, he did so primarily in the direction of avoiding tough realities. By providing illusions of grandeur, internal scape-goats, and external enemies, Hitler misdiagnosed Germany's ills and brought his nation to disaster.[45] He exercised leadership no more than a charlatan practices medicine when providing fake remedies.[46]

There are several advantages to viewing leadership in terms of adaptive work. First, it points to the pivotal importance of reality testing in producing socially useful outcomes—the process of weighing one interpretation of a problem and its sources of evidence against others. Without this process, problem definitions fail to model the situation causing distress.[47] Conceptions of leadership that do not value reality testing encourage people to realize their vision, however faulty their sight. Thus, Hitler's error was diagnostic as well as moral.[48] To produce adaptive work, a vision must track the contours of reality; it has to have accuracy, and not simply imagination and appeal.[49]

In addition, focusing on adaptive work allows us to evaluate leadership in process rather than wait until the outcome is clear. We could have spotted Hitler's faulty reality testing early on. He gave plenty of clues. His election in 1933 based on a platform of exaltation and scapegoating would have made us question the health of the problem-solving apparatus in the German society, notwithstanding the appearance of legitimate authority flowing from a democratic election. We would not have had to wait for the results of his efforts.

Furthermore, in using the criterion of adaptive work, we need not impose our own hierarchy of human needs on the genuinely expressed needs of Germany at the time. In analyzing a community's response to hard realities, we would ask the following questions: Are its members testing their views of the problem against competing views within the community or are they defensively sticking to a particular perspective and suppressing others? Are people testing seriously the relationship between means and ends? Are conflicts over values and the morality of various means open to examination? Are policies analyzed and evaluated to distinguish fact from fiction?

In Nazi Germany, Hitler suppressed the competition among German perspectives. He established a norm of conformity that excluded the views that could test his vision of Germany's problems.

Hence, Germany could not test the hypothetical relationship between current economic conditions and the citizenship of Jews.[50] How establishing a "land free of Jews" would restore Germany was not subject to open scrutiny, either as a technical or moral prescription. Even in military operations, German policymakers lost the flexibility to respond to changed conditions. The ideal of will produced decisions that disregarded complex circumstances.

Working within the society's own frame of reference becomes particularly important in cases less obvious than Nazi Germany. For example, an international development consultant might plan a series of interventions into a foreign culture. To assess that culture's objectives according to her own values may be dangerous. But she can help assess the quality of work without imposing her beliefs. She can evaluate the extent to which the culture fails to address the problems arising from the culture's own values and purposes. And perhaps more significantly if she has any leverage, she may be able to help or push the society to do the hard work of clarifying its competing values and purposes, and of facing the painful trade-offs and adjustments required to narrow the gap between current conditions and purposes. If the society bans certain parties, disenfranchises segments of the population, or uses torture and repression, what value perspective is obliterated among those being silenced? What aspects of reality that they see are being kept hidden? What might she do to encourage the factions of the culture to speed their own change of attitudes, habits, and beliefs?

Because leadership affects many lives, the concept we use must be spacious. It has to allow for the values of various cultures and organizations. It cannot be imperialistic. Yet we cannot beg the issue altogether by saying that leadership is value-free and define it simply in terms of its instruments (influence, formal powers, prominence) or personal resources (skills, bearing, temperament). Those who listen to us do more with what we say. They turn instruments and resources into values that orient their professional lives.

In this study, leadership is oriented by the task of doing adaptive work. As we shall see, influence and authority are primary factors in doing adaptive work, but they also bring constraints. They are instruments and not ends. Tackling tough problems—problems that often require an evolution of values—is the end of leadership; getting that work done is its essence.

Our societies and organizations clearly need leadership in the sense developed here. We are facing major adaptive challenges. We need a view of leadership that provides a practical orientation so that we can evaluate events and action in process, without waiting for outcomes. We also need a governor on our tendencies to become arrogant and grandiose in our visions, to flee from harsh realities and the dailyness of leadership. Terms like transformational leadership fuel such grandiosity. Furthermore, as we shall see, a strategy of leadership to accomplish adaptive work accounts for several conditions and values that are consonant with the demands of a democratic society. In addition to reality testing, these include respecting conflict, negotiation, and a diversity of views within a community; increasing community cohesion; developing norms of responsibility-taking, learning, and innovation; and keeping social distress within a bearable range.

Yet this concept of leadership has potential drawbacks that require investigation. The word adaptation too readily connotes coping, as if one must passively submit to an unbending reality. It may often be true that there are unbending realities that we should face rather than avoid, but since much of social reality is a product of social arrangements, and physical reality has become increasingly amenable to technological impact, there is obviously a great deal of plasticity to many of our realities, and we would do ourselves a disservice to adopt a coping relationship to them.[51] In addition, because adaptation is a metaphor from biology where the objective is survival leadership as "activity to mobilize adaptation" may connote an overemphasis on survival. Clearly, we have a host of quite precious values—liberty, equality, human welfare, justice, and community—for which we take risks, and a concept of adaptation applied to human organizations and societies must account for these squarely. With these concerns in mind, we turn to a deeper examination of adaptive work.

# *Notes*

1. Most of the 100 top executives in education, business, and politics with whom I worked through the Instituto FES de Liderazgo in Colombia, 1991-1992, insisted that Escobar was a "real leader," even though they reviled his behavior.

2. "After Waco, the Focus Shifts to Other Cults," *The Boston Globe,* April 30, 1993, p. Al; "Growing Up Under Koresh: Cult Children Tell of Abuses," *The New York Times,* May 4, 1993, p. Al.

3. As long as scholars allow the contradictions and confusion of common cultural assumptions to define how we conceive and study leadership, then our body of research will reflect the confusion rather than resolve it. Calder makes this point by suggesting that our scholarly research on leadership has been dominated by everyday assumptions, thereby failing to generate "higher-order" abstractions. Instead of examining common attributions about leadership as phenomena indicative of cultural patterns, scholars have limited their field of view by letting these attributions serve as the frame of reference. *"The paradox of leadership research is resolved by the realization that what has been attempted is not the development of scientific theory but the systematic and consistent use of everyday thought"* (Bobby J. Calder, "An Attribution Theory of Leadership," in Barry M. Staw and Gerald R. Salancik, eds., *New Directions in Organizational Behavior* [Chicago: St. Clair, 1977], p. 182, italics in the original).

4. Among the most prominent connotations: (1) Leadership is the process of influence between a leader and followers to attain organizational objectives. (2) Leadership is the ability to provide the managerial functions associated with positions of senior authority. (3) Leadership means having a vision and getting people to realize it. (4) Leadership is the ability to influence others, particularly by noncoercive means. See Joseph C. Rost, *Leadership for the Twenty-First Century* (New York: Praeger, 1991), pp. 38-44.

5. See Calder, "An Attribution Theory of Leadership," for a discussion of how people commonly attribute social causation to the personal capacities of individuals, and then call those capacities leadership. Wildavsky suggests that people routinely interpret their problems in a characteristic way: "for or against existing authority." See Aaron Wildavsky, "A Cultural Theory of Leadership," in Bryan D. Jones, ed., *Leadership and Politics: New Perspectives in Political Science* (Lawrence: University Press of Kansas, 1989), pp. 98-100.

6. For some examples, see Elliott Jaques, *Requisite Organization: The CEO's Guide to Creative Structure and Leadership* (Arlington, VA: Cason Hall, 1989), p. 121; and John P. Kotter, *The Leadership Factor* (New York: Free Press, 1988). Kotter goes farther than many business scholars in his view that vision is not only the product of the CEO alone, but the CEO's effort to identify and articulate the long-term interests of the parties involved. Like Jaques, he also provides a normative conception of process.

7. "Indo-European Roots," in William Morris, ed., *The American Heritage Dictionary of the English Language* (Boston: Houghton Mifflin, 1969), p. 1526.

8. See Howard T. Prince and Associates, eds., *Leadership in Organizations,* third edition (West Point, NY: United States Military Academy, 1985).

9. The following overview simplifies a rich and varied literature on leadership. The taxonomy is based on Edwin P. Hollander, "Leadership and Power," in Gordon Lindzey and Elliot Aronson, eds., *The Handbook of Social Psychology,* third edition (New York: Random House, 1985), pp. 485-537. For the reader interested in other surveys and typologies of the leadership literature, the following are helpful. For a view taken largely from social psychology and management studies, see Cecil A. Gibb, "Leadership," in Gardner Lindzey and Elliot Aronson, eds., *The Handbook of Social Psychology,* second edition (Reading, MA: Addison-Wesley, 1969), vol. 4, pp. 205-282; and Bernard M. Bass's survey of over 7,500 studies of leadership in *Bass and Stogdill's Handbook of Leadership,* third edition (New York: Free Press, 1990). For a political science view, see Glenn D. Paige, *The Scientific Study of Political Leadership* (New York: Free Press, 1977), chaps. 2-4. For normative views, see Robert Terry, *Authentic Leadership: Courage in Action* (San Francisco: Jossey-Bass, 1993); and Rost, *Leadership for the Twenty-First Century,* chaps. 1-4. For views from across a range of disciplines, see Barbara Kellerman, ed., *Leadership: Multidisciplinary Perspectives* (Englewood Cliffs, NJ: Prentice Hall, 1984).

10. For example, Barbara Kellerman in her edited volume *Political Leadership: A Source Book* (Pittsburgh: University of Pittsburgh Press, 1986), pp. ix-xi, organizes her selection of primary sources with the following questions: "Do leaders change history? Why do leaders lead? Why do followers follow? What are the types of leaders? How do leaders and followers relate? Is there a leadership for all seasons?" In the same vein, Jean Blondel asks, "What are the origins of [a leader's] power? What are the instruments by which this power is exercised? What difference do leaders make?" Jean Blondel, *Political Leadership: Towards a General Analysis* (Beverly Hills, CA: Sage, 1987), p. 4.

11. Most dictionaries define leadership as "the ability to lead," that is, as a set of personality traits. Following this cultural preference, research on leadership has focused at various times on identifying these traits. Yet the hypothesis that there are generic abilities to be identified or developed remains somewhat confused in the leadership literature because the frame of reference for leadership shifts in different studies. Conflicting definitional frames of reference are used to select whom to analyze. Attempts have even been made to lump together different trait studies to see which traits are found across a variety of them, yet the studies themselves often select for different things: position, informal following, and function. For example, if we select a group of CEOs to identify their common characteristics, we implicitly equate leadership with holding high positions of authority, or the ability to get them. If we define leadership in terms of a set of functions or the presence of an informal following, then the people we select to study will be different, and the characteristics we identify will differ. For an introduction to this methodological quandary and a review of the critical literature on *trait theory,* see Bass, *Bass*

*and Stogdill's Handbook of Leadership,* chaps. 4 and 5. For specific analyses, see Ralph M. Stogdlll, "Personal Factors Associated With Leadership: A Survey of the Literature," *Journal of Psychology,* vol. 25, 1948, pp. 35-71; Charles Bird, *Social Psychology* (New York: Appleton-Century, 1940), pp. 369-395; and William O. Jenkins, "A Review of Leadership Studies With Particular Reference to Military Problems," *Psychological Bulletin,* vol. 44, 1947, pp. 54-79.

12. For an analysis of these trends, see "Leadership Definitions: The 1980s," in Rost, *Leadership for the Twenty-First Century,* chap. 4.

13. See Thomas Carlyle, *On Heroes, Hero-Worship, and the Heroic in History,* written in 1841 (Boston: Houghton Mifflin, 1907); William James, "Great Men, Great Thoughts and Their Environment," *Atlantic Monthly,* vol. 46, October 1880, pp. 441-459; Frederick M. Thrasher, *The Gang: A Study of 1,313 Gangs in Chicago,* second revised edition (Chicago: University of Chicago Press, 1936); and Sidney Hook, *The Hero in History: A Study in Limitation and Possibility* (New York: John Day, 1943). James, Thrasher, and Hook, coming long after Carlyle, take serious account of situational variables as well as traits. For a critique of Hook's distinction, see Robert C. Tucker, *Politics as Leadership* (Columbia: University of Missouri Press, 1981), pp. 27-30, who argues that all actors give meaning to events, framing them according to their values. Different actors may give the same event different meanings and, as a result, engage with it differently, but all actors are responsive to events. For an illustrative study of characteristics believed to be associated with leadership, see W. H. Cowley, "The Traits of Face-to-Face Leaders," *Journal of Abnormal Psychology,* vol. 26, 1931, pp. 304-313. Early perspectives on a hereditary basis for leadership include: Frederick Adams Woods, M.D., *The Influence of Monarchs: Steps in a New Science of History* (New York: Macmillan, 1913); and Albert E. Wiggam, "The Biology of Leadership," in Henry C. Metcalf, ed., *Business Leadership* (New York: Pitman, 1931), pp. 13-32.

14. James Madison, for example, exercised leadership brilliantly as congressman and as key framer of the Constitution, but performed far less brilliantly, some say poorly, as president. John Quincy Adams, as diplomat and secretary of state, "must rank among the greatest this nation has produced, yet as president was a disappointment." Richard Ellis and Aaron Wildavsky, " 'Greatness' Revisited: Evaluating the Performance of Early American Presidents in Terms of Cultural Dilemmas," *Presidential Studies Quarterly,* vol. 21, winter 1991, p. 31.

15. John K. Hemphill, *Situational Factors in Leadership* (Columbus: Ohio State University Bureau of Educational Research, 1949), p. v, italics added. Also see Herbert Spencer, *The Study of Sociology* (New York: D. A. Appleton, 1884); Fillmore H. Sanford, *Authoritarianism and Leadership: A Study of the Follower's Orientation to Authority* (Philadelphia: Institute for Research in Human Relations, 1950); and Alvin W. Gouldner, ed., *Studies in Leadership* (New York: Harper and Brothers, 1950). A large body of work within political science investigates the institutional constraints on individual action. This tradition lies in dynamic tension with the biographical tradition, which

asserts that individual action impacts events and institutions significantly. Fred Greenstein seems to have found common ground by suggesting that "the impact of an individual's actions varies with (1) the degree to which the actions take place in an environment which admits of restructuring, (2) the location of the actor in that environment, and (3) the actor's peculiar strengths or weaknesses." Fred I. Greenstein, "The Impact of Personality on Politics: An Attempt to Clear Away Underbrush," *American Political Science Review,* vol. 61, 1967, pp. 633-634. For a review of these arguments, see Bryan D. Jones, ed., *Leadership and Politics: New Perspectives in Political Science* (Lawrence, KS: University Press of Kansas, 1989); Dankwart Rustow, "Introduction to the Issue 'Philosophers and Kings: Studies in Leadership,' " *Daedalus,* vol. 97, summer 1968, pp. 683-694; and Jameson W. Doig and Erwin C. Hargrove, " 'Leadership' and Political Analysis," in Jameson W. Doig and Erwin C. Hargrove, eds., *Leadership and Innovation: A Biographical Perspective on Entrepreneurs in Government* (Baltimore: Johns Hopkins University Press, 1987), chap. 1. Also see Tucker, *Politics as Leadership,* pp. 27-30; James Q. Wilson, "The Politics of Regulation," in James Q. Wilson, ed., *The Politics of Regulation* (New York: Basic, 1980), pp. 357-394; Blondel, *Political Leadership,* chap. 5; and Norman Frohlich, Joe A. Oppenheimer, and Oran R. Young, *Political Leadership and Collective Goods* (Princeton: Princeton University Press, 1971), pp. 3-11.

16. For the original study distinguishing autocratic and democratic styles of authority, see Kurt Lewin and Ronald Lippitt, "An Experimental Approach to the Study of Autocracy and Democracy: A Preliminary Note," *Sociometry,* vol. 1, 1938, pp. 292-300. Also see "Leadership as a Function of Regime," in Aaron Wildavsky, *The Nursing Father: Moses as a Political Leader* (Alabama: University of Alabama Press, 1984), pp. 182-216, for a framework of political development and the challenges of leadership appropriate to it. For other analyses of the mesh between leadership style and various situational contingencies, see Fred E. Fiedler, *A Theory of Leadership Effectiveness* (New York: McGraw-Hill, 1967); Victor Vroom and Philip W. Yetton, *Leadership and Decision-Making* (Pittsburgh: University of Pittsburgh Press, 1973); Paul Hersey and Kenneth Blanchard, *Management of Organizational Behavior: Utilizing Human Resources* (Englewood Cliffs, NJ: Prentice Hall, 1977); and Gary A. Yukl, *Leadership in Organizations,* second edition (Englewood Cliffs, NJ: Prentice Hall, 1989).

17. See Edward E. Jones, Kenneth J. Gergen, and Robert E. Jones, "Tactics of Ingratiation Among Leaders and Subordinates in a Status Hierarchy," *Psychological Monographs,* vol. 77, 1963, pp. 1-20; Edwin P. Hollander, *Leadership Dynamics: A Practical Guide to Effective Relationships* (New York: Free Press, 1978); and Morris P. Fiorina and Kenneth A. Shepsle, "Formal Theories of Leadership: Agents, Agenda Setters, and Entrepreneurs," in Jones, ed., *Leadership and Politics,* pp. 17-40.

18. This approach overlaps with the situational perspective, which places emphasis on the institutional forces that influence leadership behavior. The difference is perhaps a matter of balance. Are patterns of influence a matter of mutual trans-

action, or is influence primarily "in the hands" of institutions that determine the behavior of actors? See "The Nature of Leadership," in David B. Truman, *The Governmental Process* (New York: Knopf, 1951), pp. 188-193; "The Ambiguity of Leadership," in Robert A. Dahl, *Who Governs?* (New Haven: Yale University Press, 1961), pp. 89-103; and Bruce J. Crowe, Stephen Bochner, and Alfred W. Clark, "The Effects of Subordinates' Behavior on Managerial Style," *Human Relations,* vol. 25, July 1972, pp. 215-237. Cecil Gibb, who calls the transactional approach interaction theory, describes it this way: "Followers subordinate themselves not to an individual who is utterly different but to a member of their group who has superiority at this time and who is fundamentally the same as they are, and who at other times is prepared to be a follower just as they are. . . . The leader inevitably embodies many of the qualities of the followers. Any individual's personality at a given point in time reflects the field forces with which it is interacting" (Cecil A. Gibb, ed., *Leadership* [Middlesex, England: Penguin, 1969], p. 210).

19. Hollander, *Leadership Dynamics.*

20. Richard E. Neustadt, *Presidential Power and the Modern Presidents: The Politics of Leadership From Roosevelt to Reagan,* third edition (New York: Free Press, 1990), pp. 40-49.

21. Glenn Paige grapples with this problem explicitly in his comparison of Hitler and Gandhi along various dimensions. His eighteen dimensions of analysis (e.g., coercion, consensus, technicity, creativity, and morality) generate normative assessments and predictions. However, Paige joins with nearly all political scientists in *defining* leadership in "value-free" terms: the behavior of people in positions of political authority, and their competitors. Thus, both Gandhi and Hitler are considered leaders. See Glenn D. Paige, *The Scientific Study of Political Leadership* (New York: Free Press, 1977), pp. 1 and 139-149.

22. Fred E. Fiedler, *A Theory of Leadership Effectiveness* (New York: McGraw-Hill, 1967). Other major theorists of contingency theory, like Vroom and his collaborators, place value on "organizational effectiveness," and not simply the ability to maintain control or power. Organizational effectiveness means the accomplishment of organizational objectives. The hypothesis is that some situations call for autocratic decisionmaking while others call for various forms of consultation and participation. The decisionmaker should decide which mode of decisionmaking is most effective given the nature of the situation. For example, one should engage the participation of subordinates whenever one thinks their perspectives are necessary either to the decision itself, or to their commitment to the decision. See Victor Vroom and Philip W. Yetton, *Leadership and Decision-Making* (New York: Wiley, 1974); and Victor Vroom and Arthur Jago, *The New Leadership: Managing Participation in Organizations* (Englewood Cliffs, NJ: Prentice Hall, 1988).

23. One might ask: Could transactional and political theorists correct the problem of the consumption of their "value-free" theories as normative values by simply clarifying that they are speaking about means and not ends? In theory, perhaps. But in practice, I do not think people will internalize the distinction as long as the word leadership is used. The term, in my experi-

ence, is already firmly attached to the orienting values and self-images of young adults and working people. See Ronald A. Heifetz, Riley M. Sinder, Alice Jones, Lynn M. Hodge, and Keith A. Rowley, "Teaching and Assessing Leadership Courses at the John F. Kennedy School of Government," *Journal of Policy Analysis and Management,* vol. 8, summer 1989, pp. 536-562. Under the direction of Dr. Sharon Parks, the Lilly Endowment has sponsored a more full description and evaluation of these courses to determine, in part, their impact on the construction of values.

24. Operating in a descriptive tradition, many leadership scholars assume that the task of scholarship is to identify, describe, and analyze what leadership *is.* Yet, as others before me have suggested, this has been difficult because there are no clear cultural agreements defining the term. "The existing literatures do not 'add up' (Argyris, 1979) partly for the reason that diverse phenomena have been studied in the name of leadership" (Hosking and Morley [p. 89], cited in Rost [p. 61]. Consequently, scholars have studied a variety of things under the rubric of leadership, and, in addition, have frequently left the value dimensions implicit. In this regard, Joseph Rost stands out for his recent effort to define his terms and analyze why he chooses them. Yet even Rost seems to offer a normative definition of leadership in a classical mode when he complains that "leadership scholars still have no clear understanding of what leadership is" (p. 14), and then proceeds to offer his value-infused perspective in the spirit of a truth, as if it were the nature and essence of leadership. It seems to me that scholars might usefully consider that leadership is less an "is" than a "should be," and that our arguments might center not around who has most accurately described objective reality (or perhaps prevailing cultural assumptions) but around what image we can usefully offer to people who in part shape their self-images by our conceptions. That may be quite a hard task from the point of view of research methodology, but at least we will be wrestling with the problem before us. See Rost, *Leadership for the Twenty-First Century;* Dian-Marie Hosking and Ian E. Morley, "The Skills of Leadership," in James G. Hunt, B. Rajaram Baliga, H. Peter Dachler, and Chester A. Schriesheim, eds., *Emerging Leadership Vistas* (Lexington, MA: Lexington Books, 1988), pp. 89-106; and Chris Argyris, "How Normal Science Methodology Makes Leadership Research Less Additive and Less Applicable," in James G. Hunt and Lars L. Larson, eds., *Crosscurrents in Leadership* (Carbondale: Southern Illinois University Press, 1979).

25. I prefer the term "orienting values" over "end values" because I think "end values" function by orienting people's choices of instruments. They are "where people come from," and not where they are going, as the term "end" suggests. For example, in decisionmaking about one's children, one is oriented by the value love. Love serves not as an end or a goal, but as a source of daily orientation.

26. Political scientists have tended to conceive of politics using powers and influence as the units of analysis. Yet there is a school of political thought, going back at least as far as Plato, that uses the polity's direction and work as the frame of reference. See Tucker, *Politics as Leadership,* pp. 4-9. Carl Friedrich

put it this way, "To differentiate the leadership of a Luther from the leadership of a Hitler is crucial for a political science that is to 'make sense'; if a political science is incapable of that, it is pseudo-science, because the knowledge it imparts is corrupting and not guiding" (Carl J. Friedrich, "Political Leadership and the Problem of the Charismatic Power," *Journal of Politics,* vol. 24, February 1961, p. 19).

27. I owe this idea to Thomas C. Schelling.

28. As suggested, this idea is analyzed by Vroom, Yetton, and Jago. Their focus is on decisionmaking processes by authority figures within organizations rather than, as in this study, problem-defining and problem-solving processes in complex political environments, or leadership without authority. See Vroom and Yetton, *Leadership and Decision-Making;* and Vroom and Jago, *The New Leadership: Managing Participation in Organizations.*

29. Tucker makes this point from a purely analytic perspective: "In the final analysis, the strength of leadership as an influencing relation rests upon its effectiveness as activity" (Tucker, *Politics as Leadership,* p. 25). Preceding this perspective is a research approach established in the 1950s in social psychology and organizational behavior in which researchers began to examine behavior instead of personality. Specifically, they focused on two behaviors of people in positions of organizational authority: consideration for the satisfaction of subordinates and the initiation of structure (defining the task, initiating and organizing the work process, and maintaining standards). Most researchers have assumed that different situations will demand different balances between these two behaviors, and they have studied the contingencies distinguishing them. In contrast, some have advocated an all-seasons approach. In particular, Robert R. Blake and Jane S. Mouton, in *The Managerial Grid III* (Houston: Gulf Publishing Company, 1985), recommend both a high concern for people and a high concern for production as a generic approach to leadership. In general, these studies focus on the behavior of those with organizational authority. For the classic description of this work, see Ralph M. Stogdill and Alvin E. Coons, eds., *Leader Behavior: Its Description and Measurement* (Columbus: Ohio State University Bureau of Business Research, 1957). For a review, see "Consideration, Initiating Structure, and Related Factors for Describing the Behavior of Leaders," in Bass, Bass and Stogdill's *Handbook of Leadership,* chap. 24.

30. Many researchers and training organizations spend a great deal of time reinforcing the personalistic view of leadership by administering batteries of personality tests as a core element of leadership development. Although the tests may be of great use in generating reflection and insight among the people tested, which may be important skills of leadership, they are often unhinged from any clear operational conception of leadership. Lacking a basis in a conceptual framework of leadership strategy, they do not tell people enough about the effective use of their skills in the practice of leadership. For the pioneering efforts in this area of inquiry, see the various publications of the Center for Creative Leadership, Greensboro, North Carolina.

31. For a discussion of pathological personality structures and their mesh with institutional roles of authority, see Otto F. Kernberg, "Regression in Organizational Leadership," in Arthur D. Colman and Marvin H. Geller, eds., *Group Relations Reader 2* (Washington, DC: A. K. Rice Institute, 1985), pp. 96-106.

32. Pierre M. Turquet describes this dynamic in "Leadership: The Individual and the Group," in Colman and Geller, eds., *Group Relations Reader 2,* p. 85. There is little doubt in my mind that talented individuals have much to learn to lead effectively. To use an analogy, even the most gifted young violinist is ruined by poor training. To become a great violinist requires both talent and great training. Furthermore, quite average children with fine training make excellent musicians. All too often, terms like talent and character suggest something immutable after an early age. Indeed, following the influence of Freud's theory of human development, many scholars of leadership and politics make the assumption that inclinations and preferences are fixed in early childhood. In contrast, Dankwart Rustow stresses the importance of "conceiving of the leader's personality, not as fixed, but as changing; to consider, in turn, the character traits that he may display in long years of waiting for his opportunity, the new resources of personality that he brings to bear as he assumes his role as leader, and the decline which his personality may undergo as his historic task is accomplished." Rustow draws on Albert Hirschman's notion of "reform-mongering" in his study of economic development in Latin America to suggest that the reform-monger or the charismatic leader is likely to emerge as the teacher in such a process, but to teach others he must first learn himself" (Rustow, "Introduction," pp. 690 and 683-694.) Rustow is not being naive about adult learning capacity. Erik Erikson, Robert Kegan, Elliott Jaques, and others have studied and persuasively argued that people continue to learn and develop through adolescent and adult years beyond merely the acquisition of information, but in profound ways. See Erik Erikson, *Young Man Luther: A Study in Psychoanalysis and History* (New York: Norton, 1958); Robert Kegan, *The Evolving Self* (Cambridge: Harvard University Press, 1982); and "Cognitive Processes: How They Work and How They Mature," in Elliott Jaques, *Requisite Organization: The CEO's Guide to Creative Structure and Leadership* (Arlington, VA: Cason Hall, 1989), sect. 5.

33. See "The Power of Leadership," in James MacGregor Burns, *Leadership* (New York: Harper Colophon, 1978), chap. 1.

34. "The Structure of Moral Leadership," in Burns, *Leadership,* chap. 2. Other organizational and political theorists have modified and elaborated Burns's concept of transformational leadership by converting it into a nonnormative framework. See Bernard M. Bass, *Leadership and Performance Beyond Expectations;* and Erwin C. Hargrove, "Two Conceptions of Institutional Leadership," in Jones, ed., *Leadership and Politics,* pp. 57-83. Both conceive of transformation, not in Burns's sense of elevating the moral functioning of a polity but in the sense of inspiration, intellectual stimulation, and personal consideration (Bass), or altering the basic normative principles that guide an institution (Hargrove, p. 66).

35. See Tucker, *Politics as Leadership,* pp. 77-79, for his discussion of nonconstituted leaders.

36. See Max Weber, "Politics as a Vocation," in Gerth and Mills, eds., *From Max Weber,* pp. 77-128. Professor Michael O'Hare at the University of California, Berkeley, provided the articulation of this idea.

37. See Vroom and Jago, *The New Leadership: Managing Participation in Organizations.*

38. Burns, *Leadership,* pp. 42-43; and Tucker, *Politics as Leadership,* pp. 98-105. For a review of the leadership literature in regard to conflict, its sources and management, see "Conflict and Legitimacy in the Leadership Role," in Bass, *Bass and Stogdill's Handbook of Leadership,* chap. 15.

39. Robert C. Tucker follows a similar logic, although he stops short of a normative conception. By building on Cecil Gibb's statement that "leadership flourishes in a problem situation," Tucker orients leadership by the activities of problem definition, policy formulation, and policy implementation. His emphasis on problem definition points us in the direction of reality testing as a key instrumental value in leadership. See Tucker, *Politics as Leadership,* pp. 18-19; and Cecil A. Gibb, "The Principles and Traits of Leadership," in Gibb, ed., *Leadership,* p. 211.

40. Selznick provides an elegant analysis of the role of organizational leadership in shaping the orienting values of an institution, in Philip Selznick, *Leadership in Administration: A Sociological Interpretation* (New York: Harper & Row, 1957). Also Drath and Palus at the Center for Creative Leadership have been working on a conception of leadership (based on Robert Kegan's work) as "meaning making in collective experience," which points us toward the task of giving people a way to make sense of their situation. Wilfred Drath and Charles Palus, "Leadership as Meaning Making in Collective Experience" (Greensboro: Center for Creative Leadership, 1993).

41. Collins and Porras divide vision into two components: purpose (a statement of orienting values) and mission (a medium-term practical goal that accounts for current reality). See James C. Collins and Jerry I. Porras, "Organizational Vision and Visionary Organizations," *California Management Review,* vol. 34, fall 1991, pp. 30-52.

42. See Neustadt's analysis of Truman's mishandling of the Korean War in *Presidential Power,* pp. 103-122, in which he analyzes the president's role as teacher in taking events and giving them meaning. His analysis could be used to support Tucker's critique of Sidney Hook's distinction between eventful and event-making men, as described in note 13, above.

43. Quoted in Arthur M. Schlesinger Jr., "A Clinton Report Card, So Far," *The New York Times,* April 11, 1993, Section 4, p. 13. Schlesinger suggests, "Except for the part about admitting failure frankly, that was the story of Roosevelt's New Deal." For examples of improvisation in other contexts, see "War Is the Domain of Uncertainty," in Major General Baron Hugo von Freytag-Loringhoven, "The Power of Personality in War," *Roots of Strategy: 3 Military Classics,* Book 3 (Harrisburg, PA: Stackpole, 1991), chap. 4, pp. 252-289; Michael Cohen and James March, *Leadership and Ambiguity: The American Col-*

*lege President,* second edition (Boston: Harvard Business School Press, 1986); and Robert D. Behn, *Leadership Counts: Lessons for Public Managers* (Cambridge: Harvard University Press, 1991).

44. Burns, *Leadership,* chap. 1.

45. For a discussion of Hitler's faulty diagnoses, see Tucker, *Politics as Leadership,* pp. 89-96. For an analysis of the domestic causes of war, with implications for the genesis of World War II, see Jack S. Levy, "Domestic Politics and War," in Robert I. Rotberg and Theodore K. Rabb, eds., *The Origin and Prevention of Major Wars* (Cambridge: Cambridge University Press, 1989).

46. In the postwar years, Jasper Shannon wrote, "Perhaps a more realistic, not to say more scientific age will look upon our belief in leaders who can solve our social ills by political magic as absurd as we regard the divine power attributed to monarchs in the healing of bodily ills." "The Study of Political Leadership," in Jasper B. Shannon, ed., *The Study of Comparative Government* (New York: Greenwood, 1949); cited also in Paige, *The Scientific Study of Political Leadership,* p. 42.

47. In the U.S. system, reality testing takes both analytic and political forms as each political faction sends its own policy analysts to work, and where open deliberation about the differences among them is often the norm. See, for example, Charles E. Lindblom, *The Policy-Making Process* (Englewood Cliffs, NJ: Prentice Hall, 1968).

48. A diagnostic error, made consciously, is also immoral. Because a common tendency in human societies is to flee bad news, seek simplifying solutions, or cluster around old ones, we become vulnerable to charlatans who mislead us through misdiagnosis.

49. Other scholars have tackled this normative problem in a way somewhat similar to mine, yet with formulations that seem to me less useful to the practitioner. For example, ethicist Robert Terry, formerly director of the Reflective Leadership Center at the Hubert H. Humphrey School of Public Affairs, University of Minnesota, offers this definition: "Leadership is the courage to bring forth and let come forth authentic action in the commons." His use of "authentic action" is akin to what I mean by reality testing. See Terry, *Authentic Leadership.* Joseph Rost offers this definition: "Leadership is an influence relationship among leaders and followers who intend real changes that reflect their mutual purposes." By "real changes," Rost is again tracking the idea of adaptive work. See Rost, *Leadership for the Twenty-First Century,* p. 102.

50. For an analysis of conspiracy theories used historically by people to explain their predicaments, see Franz Neumann, "Anxiety and Politics," in *The Democratic and the Authoritarian State: Essays in Political and Legal Theory* (New York: Free Press of Glencoe, 1957), pp. 283-287. Neumann suggests that "just as the masses hope for their deliverance from distress through absolute oneness with a person [a charismatic figure], so they ascribe their distress to certain persons who brought this distress into the world through a conspiracy. . . . Hatred, resentment, dread, created by great upheavals, are concentrated on certain persons who are denounced as devilish conspirators" (p. 279); cited also in Robert C. Tucker, "The Theory of Char-

ismatic Leadership," *Daedalus,* vol. 97, summer 1968, p. 752. For a view of scapegoating from object relations theory, see Leonard Horwitz, "Projective Identification in Dyads and Groups," in Colman and Geller, eds., *Group Relations Reader 2,* pp. 28-30.

51. See Eric J. Miller, "Organizational Development and Industrial Democracy: A Current Case-Study," in Colman and Geller, eds., *Group Relations Reader 2,* p. 245.

# 34

# The Strategy Team

## Teams at the Top— Core Values as a Strategic Driver

KENNETH A. SMITH
HENRY P. SIMS, JR.

An important underlying framework for AES's strategy is its four core or "shared" values.

- To act with integrity
- To be fair
- To have fun
- To be socially responsible

These values emerged over time, mainly from the founders and officers, and have now been articulated to the degree that they are written and were published as a part of the prospectus for the initial stock offering of the company. Says Bakke, "The only thing that we hold tightly as to what has to be done are the four values." These values permeate AES and serve to unify the company as it pursues its objectives. They also foster a strong team spirit.

Bakke describes *integrity* as " . . . it fits together as a whole . . . wholeness, completeness." In practice, this means that the things that AES people say and do in all parts of the company should fit together with truth and consistency. "The main thing we do is ask the question, 'What did we commit?'" At AES, the senior representative at any meeting can commit the company, knowing that the team will back him or her up.

*Fairness* means treating its people, customers, suppliers, stockholders, governments, and the communities in which it operates fairly. Defining what is fair is often difficult, but the main point is

EDITOR'S NOTE: This chapter is excerpted from the material that appears as Chapter 30 of this volume and continues the focus on AES Corporation. For background information on AES, see Chapter 30.

that the company believes it is helpful to question routinely the relative fairness of alternative courses of action. This may mean that AES does not necessarily get the most out of each negotiation or transaction to the detriment of others. Bakke asks the question, "Would I feel as good on the other side of the table as I feel on this side of the table on the outcome of this meeting or this decision with my employee or supervisor or customer?"

Bakke also says, "If it isn't fun, we don't want it. . . . We either want to quit or change something that we're doing." Sant agrees: "It just isn't worth doing unless you're having a great time." Thus, *fun* is the third value. AES wants the people it employs and those with whom the company interacts to have fun in their work. Bakke elaborates: "By fun we don't mean party fun. We're talking about creating an environment where people can use their gifts and skills productively, to help meet a need in society, and thereby enjoy the time spent at AES."

The fourth value is *social responsibility.* "We see ourselves as a citizen of the world," says Bakke. This value presumes that AES has a responsibility to be involved in projects that provide social benefits, such as lower costs to customers, a high degree of safety and reliability, increased employment, and a cleaner environment. "We try to do things that you'd like your neighbor to do."

One might question whether a commitment to these shared values might be detrimental to profits or to the value to the shareholders. "We have specifically said that maximized profit is not our objective," says Bakke. In fact, the company's prospectus stated, "Earning a fair profit is an important result of providing a quality product to [our] customers. However, when a perceived conflict has arisen between these values and profits, the company has tried to adhere to its values—even though doing so might result in diminished profits or forgone opportunities. The company seeks to adhere to these values, not as a means to achieve economic success, but because adherence is a worthwhile goal in and of itself."

How are values at AES connected with strategy? Answering this question deserves careful consideration. Many, if not most, companies define their strategies in terms of profit potential, market share opportunities, or minimization of financial risk.

Although these elements are important to AES, the company considers them within a larger framework represented by the question: Does this strategy enhance or diminish our achievements when evaluated within the context of the four shared values? Roger Naill elaborates: "We have a business strategy that has certain goals—for example, the corporate goals in our strategic plan—and our values represent the rules that we play the business game by."

As an example, consider the element of risk. Most corporations seek to contain or minimize the financial risk of a potential strategy, and AES is no exception. For each new cogeneration project, the capitalization and legal entity is deliberately made distinct from the main AES corporation. The project must stand or fall on its own merits without directly threatening the financial integrity of AES as a whole.

Nevertheless, financial risk does not seem to generate the greatest debate and most careful consideration within the company. The issue of whether a potential project (strategy) threatens the shared values seems more prominent. For one project, the company was considering an investor partner for a proposed cogeneration venture. This partner owned a tobacco subsidiary. The so-called risk of this project was not considered predominantly in financial terms but in terms of whether the association with this particular financing partner would be consistent with the shared values of the company. Dennis Bakke provided another example: "When considering what to do about mitigating carbon dioxide emissions and their effect on global warming, the company decided on a strategy of planting and/or preserving trees, including the planting of 52 million trees in Guatemala. This strategic decision turned more on the company's social responsibility value rather than the fact that the cost of tree planting exceeded the company's net profit in the year the decision was made."

Bakke describes the relationship between strategy and values as follows: "There is both a strong linkage and no linkage at all. All strategy for meeting the electricity needs of the world is developed in the context of the shared values. But whether the strategy we choose and implement is successful in actually meeting the world's need for clean, reliable electricity has almost nothing to do with the shared values." Sant elaborates:

> The thing we made clear was that the values were not likely to change over time. Those were considered fundamental truths. There wasn't ambiguity about them. There might be ambiguity about what's fair or not fair, but there wasn't ambiguity that we really wanted to be fair, and it was not likely to change to wanting to be unfair, whereas strategy is going to change constantly. We may be doing something now that says coal plants are really a great strategy, but we ought to know that those things are going to change. We're not going to get locked into those or, if we do, we're in trouble. So we should be very clear that there are some things that we are tight on. In Bob Waterman's book, *In Search of Excellence,* he called those tight-loose. We're tight, very tight, on values; very loose on almost everything else. What is important, though, is that the strategy chosen not be inconsistent with the values.

AES's shared values contributed to the team spirit that pervades the company. The content of the values encourages AES personnel to think of themselves not as individuals but rather as members of the AES team. Integrity stresses the need for individuals to fulfill commitments—their own and those made by the company. Fairness generates sensitivity to the positions and perspectives of others, both in and outside the company. Fun, as defined at AES, results from using one's abilities to contribute to the effort of the whole. Social responsibility stresses being aware of and serving the needs of others. Together, these values build an outward-looking orientation in the minds of AES personnel and foster a desire to work with others.

The processes by which the values are implemented and evaluated contribute to AES's team orientation. For example, each manager is rated annually on "values performance"—that is, how he or she performs in relation to the four shared values. According to Bakke, "We rate each other, fifty-fifty, on the basis of technical performance and values performance." More broadly, all AES employees are encouraged to challenge any and all others on how strategic and operating decisions reflect the core values. This fosters an air of mutual accountability and serves as a constant reminder that all are members of the same team. Thus, the shared values contribute to a company-wide culture that is characterized by a teamlike atmosphere.

# 35

# Moral Leadership and Business Ethics

AL GINI

> Those who really deserve praise are the people who, while human enough to enjoy power nevertheless pay more attention to justice than they are compelled to do by their situation.
>
> *Thucydides*

Conventional wisdom has it that two of the most glaring examples of academic oxymorons are the terms "business ethics" and "moral leadership." Neither term carries credibility in popular culture and when conjoined constitutes a "null-set" rather than just a simple contradiction in terms. The reason for this is definitional, but only in part. More significant is that we have so few models of businesses and leaders operating on ethical principles. Simply put, the cliché persists because of the dearth of evidence to the contrary. At best, both these terms remain in the lexicon as wished-for ideals rather than actual states of being.

A *New York Times/CBS News Poll* conducted in 1985 revealed that 55% of the American public believe that the vast majority of corporate executives are dishonest, and 59% think that executive white-collar crime occurs on a regular basis. A 1987 *Wall Street Journal* article noted that one-fourth of the 671 executives surveyed by a leading research firm believed that ethics can impede a successful career, and that over one-half of all the executives they knew bent the rules to get ahead.[1] Most recently, a 1990 national survey published by Prentice Hall concluded that the standards of ethical practice and moral leadership of business leaders merit at best a C grade. Sixty-eight percent of those surveyed believed that the unethical behavior of executives is the primary cause of the decline in business standards, productivity, and success. The survey further suggested that because of the perceived low ethical standards of the executive class, workers feel justified in responding in kind—through absenteeism, petty theft, indifference, and a generally poor performance on the job. Many workers openly admitted that they spend more than 20% (eight hours a week) of their time at work totally goofing off. Almost half of those surveyed admitted to chronic malingering on a regular basis. One in six of the workers surveyed said that he or she drank or used drugs on the job. Three out of four workers reported that their primary reason for working was "to keep the wolf from the door"; only one in four claimed to give his or her "best effort" to the job. The survey concluded that the standard equation of the American workplace is a simple one: American workers are as ethical/dutiful in doing their jobs as their bosses and companies are perceived to be ethical/dutiful in leading and directing them.[2]

Sadly, ample evidence suggests that this mutually reinforcing thesis often starts long before one enters the confines of the workplace. Recently one of the teacher/coaches in the Chicago public school system not only encouraged his high school students to cheat in the city-wide Academic Decathlon contest, he fed them the answers. According to the 18-year-old student captain of the team: "The coach gave us the answer key. . . . He told us everybody cheats, that's the way the world works and we were fools to just play by the rules."[3] Unfortunately, just as workers often mirror the standards set by their bosses, these students followed the guidance of their teacher.

As a student of business ethics, I am convinced that without the continuous commitment, enforcement, and modeling of leadership, standards of business ethics cannot and will not be achieved in any organization. The ethics of leadership—whether they be good or bad, positive or negative—affect the ethos of the workplace and thereby help to form the ethical choices and decisions of the workers in the workplace. Leaders help to set the tone, develop the vision, and shape the behavior of

all those involved in organizational life. The critical point to understand here is that, like it or not, business and politics serve as the metronome for our society. And the meter and behavior established by leaders set the patterns and establish the models for our behavior as individuals and as a group. Although the terms "business ethics" and "moral leadership" are technically distinguishable, in fact, they are inseparable components in the life of every organization.

The fundamental principle that underlies my thesis regarding leadership and ethical conduct is age old. In his *Nichomachean Ethics,* Aristotle suggested that morality cannot be learned simply by reading a treatise on virtue. The spirit of morality, said Aristotle, is awakened in the individual only through the witness and conduct of a moral person. The principle of the "witness of another," or what we now refer to as "patterning," "role modeling," or "mentoring," is predicated on a four-step process, three of which follow: (1) As communal creatures, we learn to conduct ourselves primarily through the actions of significant others; (2) when the behavior of others is repeated often enough and proves to be peer-group positive, we emulate these actions; (3) if and when our actions are in turn reinforced by others, they become acquired characteristics or behavioral habits.

According to B. F. Skinner, the process is now complete. In affecting the actions of individuals through modeling and reinforcement, the mentor in question (in Skinnerean terms, "the controller of the environmental stimuli") has succeeded in reproducing the type of behavior sought after or desired. For Skinner the primary goal of the process need not take into consideration either the value or worth of the action or the interests or intent of the reinforced or operant-conditioned actor. From Skinner's psychological perspective, the bottom line is simply the response evoked.[4] From a philosophical perspective, however, even role modeling that produces a positive or beneficial action does not fulfill the basic requirements of the ethical enterprise at either the descriptive or normative level. Modeling, emulation, habit, results—whether positive or negative—are neither the sufficient nor the final goal. The fourth and final step in the process must include reflection, evaluation, choice, and conscious intent on the part of the actor, because ethics is always "an inside-out proposition" involving free will.[5]

John Dewey argued that at the precritical, prerational, preautonomous level, morality starts as a set of culturally defined goals and rules which are external to the individual and are imposed or inculcated as habits. But real ethical thinking, said Dewey, begins at the evaluative period of our lives, when, as independent agents, we freely decide to accept, embrace, modify, or deny these rules. Dewey maintained that every serious ethical system rejects the notion that one's standard of conduct should simply and uncritically be an acceptance of the rules of the culture we happen to live in. Even when custom, habit, convention, public opinion, or law are correct in their mandates, to embrace them without critical reflection does not constitute a complete and formal ethical act and might be better labeled "ethical happenstance" or "ethics by virtue of circumstantial accident." According to Dewey, ethics is essentially "reflective conduct," and he believed that the distinction between custom and reflective morality is clearly marked. The former places the standard and rules of conduct solely on habit; the latter appeals to reason and choice. The distinction is as important as it is definite, for it shifts the center of gravity in morality. For Dewey, ethics is a two-part process: it is never enough simply to do the right thing.[6]

In claiming that workers/followers derive their models for ethical conduct from the witness of leaders, I am in no way denying that workers/ followers share responsibility for the overall conduct and culture of an organization. The burden of this chapter is not to exonerate the culpability of workers, but rather to explain the process involved: the witness of leaders both communicates the ethics of our institutions and establishes the desired standards and expectations leaders want and often demand from their fellow workers and followers. Although it would be naive to assert that employees simply and unreflectively absorb the manners and mores of the workplace, it would be equally naive to suggest that they are unaffected by the modeling and standards of their respective places of employment. Work is how we spend our lives, and the lessons we learn there, good or bad, play a part in the development of our moral perspective and the manner in which we formulate and adjudicate ethical choices. As a business ethicist I believe that without the active intervention of effective moral leadership, we are doomed to forever wage a rearguard action. Students of organizational development are never really surprised when poorly managed, badly led businesses wind up doing unethical things.

## *Ethics and Business*

Jean-Paul Sartre argued that, like it or not, we are *by definition* moral creatures because our collective existence "condemns" us continuously to make choices about "what we ought to do" in regard to others.[7] Ethics is primarily a communal, collective enterprise, not a solitary one. It is the study of our web of relationships with others. When Robinson Crusoe found himself marooned and alone on a tiny Pacific atoll, all things were possible. But when Friday appeared and they discovered pirates burying treasure on the beach, Crusoe was then involved in the universe of others, an ethical universe. As a communal exercise, ethics is the attempt to work out the rights and obligations we have and share with others. What is mine? What do I owe you?

According to John Rawls, given the presence of others and our need of these others both to survive and to thrive, ethics is elementally the pursuit of justice, fair play, and equity. For Rawls, building on the cliché that "ethics is how we decide to behave when we decide we belong together," the study of ethics has to do with developing standards for judging the conduct of one party whose behavior affects another. Minimally, "good behavior" intends no harm and respects the rights of all affected, and "bad behavior" is willfully or negligently trampling on the rights and interests of others.[8] Ethics, then, tries to find a way to protect one person's individual rights and needs against and alongside the rights and needs of others. Of course, the paradox and central tension of ethics lie in the fact that while we are by nature communal and in need of others, at the same time we are by disposition more or less egocentric and self-serving.[9]

If ethics is a part of life, so too are work, labor, business. Work is not something detached from the rest of human life, but, rather, "man is born to labor, as a bird to fly."[10] What are work and business about? Earning a living? Yes. Producing a product or service? Sure. Making money or profit? Absolutely. In fact, most ethicists argue that business has a moral obligation to make a profit. But business is also about people—the people you work for and work with. Business is an interdependent, intertwined, symbiotic relationship. Life, labor, and business are all of a piece. They should not be seen as separate "games" played by different "rules." The enterprise of business is not distinct from the enterprise of life and living because they share the same bottom line—people. Therefore, as in the rest of life, business is required to ask the question, What ought to be done in regard to others?

While no one that I am aware of would argue seriously against the notion of ethics in our private lives, many would have it that ethics and business don't or can't mix. That is, many people believe that "business is business," and that the stakes and standards involved in business are simply different from, more important than and, perhaps, even antithetical to the principles and practices of ethics. Ethics is something we preach and practice at home in our private lives, but not at work. After all, it could cost us prestige, position, profits, and success.

Theologian Matthew Fox maintains that we lead schizophrenic lives because we either choose or are forced to abandon our personal beliefs and convictions "at the door" when we enter the workplace. The "destructive dualism" of the workplace, says Fox, separates our lives from our livelihood, our personal values from our work values, our personal needs from the needs of the community. Money becomes the sole reason for work, and success becomes the excuse we use to justify the immoral consequences of our behavior.[11] This "dualism" produces and perpetuates the kind of "occupational schizophrenia" recently articulated by nationally known jurist Alan Dershowitz: "I would never do many of the things in my personal life that I have to do as a lawyer."[12]

According to ethicist Norman E. Bowie, the disconnection between business and ethics and the dualism of the workplace stem from the competing paradigms of human nature of economists and ethicists. Economics is the study of the betterment of self. Most economists, says Bowie, have an egoistic theory of human nature. Their analyses focus on how an individual rationally pursues desired tastes, wants, or preferences. Within the economic model, individuals behave rationally when they seek to strengthen their own perceived best interests. Individuals need only take the interests of others into account when and if such considerations work to their advantage. Economics, Bowie claims, is singular and radically subjective in its orientation. It takes all taste, wants, and desires as simply given, and does not evaluate whether the economic actor's preferences are good or bad. The focus remains on how the individual can achieve his/her wants and desires.

Ethics, on the other hand, is nonegoistic or pluralistic in nature. Its primary paradigm of evaluation is always self in relation to others. The ethical point of view, says Bowie, requires that an actor take into account the impact of his/her action on others. If and when the interests of the actor and those affected by the action conflict, the actor should at least consider suspending or modifying his/her action, and by so doing recognize the interests of the other. In other words, ethics requires that on occasion we "ought to act" contrary to our own self-interest and that on occasion a person "ought to" act actively on behalf of the interests of another. Economists ask, What can I do to advance my best interests against others? Ethicists ask, In pursuing my best interests what must I do, what "ought" I do in regard to others? Whereas economics breeds competition, ethics encourages cooperation.[13]

For R. Edward Freeman, these competing paradigms are firmly entrenched in our collective psyches, and give rise to what he calls "The Problem of the Two Realms." One realm is the realm of business. It is the realm of hard, measurable facts: market studies, focus groups, longitudinal studies, production costs, managed inventory, stock value, research and development, profit and loss statements, quantitative analysis. The other realm is the realm of philosophy/ethics. This is the soft realm, says Freeman. This is the realm of the seemingly ineffable: myth, meaning, metaphor, purpose, quality, significance, rights, values. While the realm of business can be easily dissected, diagnosed, compared, and judged, the realm of philosophy is not open to precise interpretation, comparison, and evaluation. For Freeman, in a society that has absorbed and embraced the Marcusian adage "the goods of life are equal to the good life," these two realms are accorded separate but unequal status. Only in moments of desperation, disaster, or desire does the realm of business solicit the commentary and insights of the realm of ethics. Otherwise, the realm of business operates under the dictum of legal-moralism: Everything is allowed which is not strictly forbidden.

For Freeman the assertion that "business is business" and that ethics is what we try to do in our private lives simply does not hold up to close scrutiny. Business is a human institution, a basic part of the communal fabric of life. Just as governments come to be out of the human need for order, security, and fulfillment, so too does business. The goal of all business, labor, and work is to make life more secure, more stable, more equitable. Business exists to serve more than just itself. No business can view itself as an isolated entity, unaffected by the demands of individuals and society. As such, business is required to ask the question, What ought to be done in regard to the others we work with and serve? For Freeman, business ethics, rather than being an oxymoron, a contradiction in terms, is really a pleonasm, a redundancy in terms.[14] As Henry Ford, Sr. once said: "For a long time people believed that the only purpose of industry is to make a profit. They are wrong. Its purpose is to serve the general welfare."[15]

What business ethics advocates is that people apply in the workplace those commonsensical rules and standards learned at home, from the lectern, and from the pulpit. The moral issues facing a person are age old, and these are essentially the same issues facing a business—only writ in large script.[16] According to Freeman, ethics is "how we treat each other, every day, person to person. If you want to know about a company's ethics, look at how it treats people—customers, suppliers, and employees. Business is about people. And business

ethics is about how customers and employees are treated."[17]

What is being asked of the business community is neither extraordinary nor excessive: a decent product at a fair price; honesty in advertisements; fair treatment of employees, customers, suppliers, and competitors; a strong sense of responsibility to the communities it inhabits and serves; and a reasonable profit for the financial risk-taking of its stockholders and owners. In the words of General Robert Wood Johnson, founder of Johnson & Johnson:

> The day has passed when business was a private matter—if it even really was. In a business society, every act of business has social consequences and may arouse public interest. Every time business hires, builds, sells or buys, it is acting for the . . . people as well as for itself, and it must be prepared to accept full responsibility.[18]

## *Leadership*

According to Georges Enderle, business leadership would be relatively simple if corporations only had to produce a product or service, without being concerned about employees; management only had to deal with concepts, structures, and strategies, without worrying about human relations; businesses just had to resolve their own problems, without being obligated to take the interests of individuals or society into consideration.[19] But such is not the case. Leadership is always about self and others. Like ethics, labor and business leadership is a symbiotic, communal relationship. It's about leaders, followers-constituencies, and all stakeholders involved. And, like ethics, labor and business leadership seems to be an intrinsic part of the human experience. Charles DeGaulle once observed that men can no longer survive without direction than they can without eating, drinking, or sleeping. Putting aside the obvious fact that DeGaulle was a proponent of "the great-person theory" of leadership, his point is a basic one. Leadership is a necessary requirement of communal existence. Minimally, it tries to offer perspective, focus, appropriate behavior, guidance, and a plan by which to handle the seemingly random and arbitrary events of life. Depending on the type of leadership/followership involved, it can be achieved by consensus, fiat, or cooperative orchestration. But whatever techniques are employed, leadership is always, at bottom, about stewardship—"a person(s) who manages or directs the affairs of others . . . as the agent or representative of others." To paraphrase the words of St. Augustine, regardless of the outcome, the first and final job of leadership is the attempt to serve the needs and the well-being of the people led.

What is leadership? Although the phenomenon of leadership can and must be distinguishable and definable separately from our understanding of what and who leaders are, I am convinced that leadership can only be known and evaluated in the particular instantiation of a leader doing a job. In other words, while the terms "leadership" and "leader" are not strictly synonymous, the reality of leadership cannot be separated from the person of the leader and the job of leadership. Given this caveat, and leaning heavily on the research and insights of Joseph C. Rost,[20] we can define leadership as follows: Leadership is a power- and value-laden relationship between leaders and followers/constituents who intend real changes that reflect their mutual purposes and goals. For our purposes, the critical elements of this definition that need to be examined are, in order of importance: followership, values, mutual purposes, and goals.

## Followership

As Joseph Rost has pointed out, perhaps the single most important thesis developed in leadership studies in the last 20 years has been the evolution and now *almost* universal consensus regarding the role of followers in the leadership equation. Pulitzer prize-winning historian Garry Wills argues that we have long had a list of the leader's requisites—determination, focus, a clear goal, a sense of priorities, and so on. But until recently we overlooked or forgot the first and all-encompassing need. "The leader most needs followers. When those are lacking, the best ideas, the strongest will, the most wonderful smile have no effect."[21] Fol-

lowers set the terms of acceptance for leadership. Leadership is a "mutually determinative" activity on the part of the leader and the followers. Sometimes it's cooperative, sometimes it's a struggle and often it's a feud, but it's always collective. Although "the leader is one who mobilizes others toward a goal shared by leaders and followers," leaders are powerless to act without followers. In effect, Wills argues, successful leaders need to understand their followers far more than followers need to understand leaders.[22]

Leadership, like labor and ethics, is always plural; it always occurs in the context of others. E. P. Hollander has argued that while the leader is the central and often the most vital part of the leadership phenomenon, followers are important and necessary factors in the equation.[23] All leadership is interactive, and all leadership should be collaborative. In fact, except for the negative connotation sometimes associated with the term, perhaps the word "collaborator" is a more precise term than either "follower" or "constituent" to explain the leadership process.[24] But whichever term is used, as James MacGregor Burns wrote, one thing is clear, "leaders and followers are engaged in a common enterprise; they are dependent on each other, their fortunes rise and fall together."[25]

From an ethical perspective, the argument for the stewardship responsibilities of leadership is dependent upon the recognition of the roles and rights of followers. Followership argues against the claim of Louis XIV, *"L'état c'est moi!"* The principle of followership denies the Machiavellian assertions that "politics and ethics don't mix" and that the sole aim of any leader is "the acquisition of personal power." Followership requires that leaders recognize their true role within the commonwealth. The choices and actions of leaders must take into consideration the rights and needs of followers. Leaders are not independent agents simply pursuing personal aggrandizement and career options. Like the "Guardians" of Socrates' *Republic,* leaders must see their office as a social responsibility, a trust, a duty, and not as a symbol of their personal identify, prestige, and lofty status.[26] In more contemporary terms, James O'Toole and Lynn Sharp-Paine have separately argued that the central ethical issue in business is the rights of stakeholders and the obligation of business leaders to manage with due consideration for the rights of all stakeholders involved.[27]

In his cult classic *The Fifth Discipline,* management guru Peter Senge has stated that of all the jobs of leadership, being a steward is the most basic. Being a steward means recognizing that the ultimate purpose of one's work is others and not self; that leaders "do what they do" for something larger than themselves; that their "life's work" may be the "ability to lead"; but that the final goal of this talent or craft is "other directed."[28] If the real "business of business" is not just to produce a product/service and a profit but to help "produce" people, then the same claim/demand can be made of leadership. Given the reality of the "presence of others," leadership, like ethics, must by definition confront the question, What ought to be done with regard to others?

## *Values*

Ethics is about the assessment and evaluation of values, because all of life is value-laden. As Samuel Blumenfeld emphatically pointed out, "You have to be dead to be value-neutral."[29] Values are the ideas and beliefs that influence and direct our choices and actions. Whether they are right or wrong, good or bad, values, both consciously and unconsciously, mobilize and guide how we make decisions and the kinds of decisions we make. Reportedly, Eleanor Roosevelt once said, "If you want to know what people value, check their checkbooks!"

I believe that Tom Peters and Bob Waterman were correct when they asserted, "The real role of leadership is to manage the values of an organization."[30] All leadership is value-laden. And all leadership, whether good or bad, is moral leadership at the descriptive if not the normative level. To put it more accurately, all leadership is ideologically driven or motivated by a certain philosophical perspective, which upon analysis and judgment may or may not prove to be morally acceptable in the colloquial sense. All leaders have an agenda, a series of beliefs, proposals, values, ideas, and issues that they wish to "put on the table." In fact, as Burns has suggested, leadership only asserts itself, and followers only become evident, when there is something at stake—ideas to be clarified, issues to be determined, values to be adjudicated.[31] In the words of Eleanor's husband, Franklin D. Roosevelt:

> The Presidency is . . . preeminently a place of moral leadership. All our great Presidents were leaders of thought at times when certain historic ideas in the life of the nation had to be clarified.[32]

Although we would prefer to study the moral leadership of Lincoln, Churchill, Gandhi, and Mother Teresa, like it or not we must also evaluate Hitler, Stalin, Saddam Hussein, and David Koresh within a moral context.

All ethical judgments are in some sense a "values vs. values" or "rights vs. rights" confrontation. Unfortunately, the question of "what we ought to do" in relation to the values and rights of others cannot be reduced to the analog of a simple litmus-paper test. In fact, I believe that all of ethics is based on what William James called the "will to believe." That is, we choose to believe, despite the ideas, arguments, and reasoning to the contrary, that individuals possess certain basic rights that cannot and should not be willfully disregarded or overridden by others. In "choosing to believe," said James, we establish this belief as a factual baseline of our thought process for all considerations in regard to others. Without this "reasoned choice," says James, the ethical enterprise loses its "vitality" in human interactions.[33]

If ethical behavior intends no harm and respects the rights of all affected, and unethical behavior willfully or negligently tramples on the rights and interests of others, then leaders cannot deny or disregard the rights of others. The leader's worldview cannot be totally solipsistic. The leader's agenda should not be purely self-serving. Leaders should not see followers as potential adversaries to be bested, but rather as fellow travelers with similar aspirations and rights to be reckoned with.

How do we judge the ethics of a leader? Clearly, we cannot expect every decision and action of a leader to be perfect. As John Gardner has pointed out, particular consequences are never a reliable assessment of leadership.[34] The quality and worth of leadership can only be measured in terms of what a leader intends, values, believes in, or stands for—in other words, character. In *Character: America's Search for Leadership,* Gail Sheehy argues, as did Aristotle before her, that character is the most crucial and most elusive element of leadership. The root of the word "character" comes from the Greek word for engraving. As applied to human beings, it refers to the enduring marks or etched-in factors in our personality, which include our inborn talents as well as the learned and acquired traits imposed upon us by life and experience. These engravings define us, set us apart, and motivate behavior.

In regard to leadership, says Sheehy, character is fundamental and prophetic. The "issues [of leadership] are today and will change in time. Character is what was yesterday and will be tomorrow."[35] Character establishes both our day-to-day demeanor and our destiny. Therefore, it is not only useful but essential to examine the character of those who desire to lead us. As a journalist and longtime observer of the political scene, Sheehy contends that the Watergate affair of the early 1970s serves as a perfect example of the links between character and leadership. As Richard Nixon demonstrated so well, says Sheehy, "The Presidency is not the place to work out one's personal pathology."[36] Leaders rule us, run things, wield power. Therefore, says Sheehy, we must be careful about whom we choose to lead, because whom we choose is what we shall be. If, as Heraclitus wrote, "character is fate," the fate our leaders reap will also be our own.

Putting aside the particular players and the politics of the episode, Watergate has come to symbolize the failings and failures of the people in high places. Watergate now serves as a watershed, a turning point, in our nation's concern for integrity, honesty, and fair play from all kinds of leaders. It is not a mere coincidence that the birth of business ethics as an independent, academic discipline can be dated from the Watergate affair and the trials that came out of it. No matter what our failings as individuals, Watergate sensitized us to the importance of ethical standards and conduct from those who direct the course of our political and public

lives. What society is now demanding, and what business ethics is advocating, is that our business leaders and public servants should be held accountable to an even higher standard of behavior than we might demand and expect of ourselves.

## *Mutual Purposes and Goals*

The character, goals, and aspirations of a leader are not developed in a vacuum. Leadership, even in the hands of a strong, confident, charismatic leader remains, at bottom, relational. Leaders, good or bad, great or small, arise out of the needs and opportunities of a specific time and place. Leaders require causes, issues and, most important, a hungry and willing constituency. Leaders may devise plans, establish an agenda, bring new and often radical ideas to the table, but all of them are a response to the milieu and membership of which they are a part. If leadership is an active and ongoing relationship between leaders and followers, then a central requirement of the leadership process is for leaders to evoke and elicit consensus in their constituencies, and conversely for followers to inform and influence their leaders. This is done through the uses of power and education.

The term "power" comes from the Latin *posse:* to do, to be able, to change, to influence or effect. To have power is to possess the capacity to control or direct change. All forms of leadership must make use of power. The central issue of power in leadership is not will it be used, but rather will it be used wisely and well. According to James MacGregor Burns, leadership is not just about directed results; it is also about offering followers a choice among real alternatives. Hence, leadership assumes competition, conflict, and debate, whereas brute power denies it.[37] "Leadership mobilizes," said Burns, "naked power coerces."[38] But power need not be dictatorial or punitive to be effective. Power can also be used in a noncoercive manner to orchestrate, direct, and guide members of an organization in the pursuit of a goal or series of objectives. Leaders must engage followers, not merely direct them. Leaders must serve as models and mentors, not martinets. Or to paraphrase novelist James Baldwin, power without morality is no longer power.

For Peter Senge, teaching is one of the primary jobs of leadership.[39] The "task of leader as teacher" is to empower people with information, offer insights, new knowledge, alternative perspectives on reality. The "leader as teacher" is not just about "teaching" people how "to achieve their vision." Rather, it is about fostering learning, offering choices, and building consensus.[40] Effective leadership recognizes that in order to build and achieve community, followers must become reciprocally coresponsible in the pursuit of a common enterprise. Through their conduct and teaching, leaders must try to make their fellow constituents aware that they are all stakeholders in a conjoint activity that cannot succeed without their involvement and commitment. Successful leadership believes in and communicates some version of the now famous Hewlett-Packard motto: "The achievements of an organization are the results of the combined efforts of each individual." In the end, says Abraham Zaleznik, "leadership is based on a compact that binds those who lead with those who follow into the same moral, intellectual and emotional commitment."[41] However, as both Burns and Rost warn us, the nature of this "compact" is inherently unequal because the influence patterns existing between leaders and followers are not equal. Responsive and responsible leadership requires, as a minimum, that democratic mechanisms be put in place which recognize the right of followers to have adequate knowledge of alternative options, goals, and programs, as well as the capacity to choose among them. "In leadership writ large, mutually agreed upon purposes help people achieve consensus, assume responsibility, work for the common good, and build community."[42]

## *Structural Restraints*

There is, unfortunately, a dark side to the theory of the "witness of others." Howard S. Schwartz, in his radical but underappreciated managerial text *Narcissistic Process and Corporate Decay,*[43] argues that corporations are not bastions of benign, other-directed ethical reasoning; nor can corpora-

tions, because of the demands and requirements of business, be models and exemplars of moral behavior. The rule of business, says Schwartz, remains the "law of the jungle," "the survival of the fittest," and the goal of survival engenders a combative "us-against-them mentality" which condones the moral imperative of getting ahead by any means necessary. Schwartz calls this phenomenon "organizational totalitarianism": Organizations and the people who manage them create for themselves a self-contained, self-serving worldview, which rationalizes anything done on their behalf and which does not require justification on any grounds outside of themselves.[44] The psychodynamics of this narcissistic perspective, says Schwartz, impose Draconian requirements on all participants in organizational life: do your work; achieve oral goals; obey and exhibit loyalty to your superiors; disregard personal values and beliefs; obey the law when necessary, obfuscate it whenever possible; and deny internal or external discrepant information at odds with the stated organizational worldview. Within such a "totalitarian logic," neither leaders nor followers, rank nor file, operate as independent agents. To "maintain their place," to "get ahead," all must conform. The agenda of "organizational totalitarianism" is always the preservation of the status quo. Within such a logic, like begets like, and change is rarely possible. Except for extreme situations in which "systemic ineffectiveness" begins to breed "organization decay," transformation is never an option.

In *Moral Mazes,* Robert Jackall parallels much of Schwartz's analysis of organizational behavior, but from a sociological rather than a psychological perspective. According to critic and commentator Thomas W. Norton, both Jackall and Schwartz seek to understand why and how organizational ethics and behavior are so often reduced to either dumb loyalty or the simple adulation and mimicry of one's superiors. While Schwartz argues that individuals are captives of the impersonal structural logic of "organizational totalitarianism," Jackall contends that "organizational actors become personally loyal to their superiors, always seeking their approval and are committed to them as persons rather than as representatives of the abstractions of organizational authority." But in either case, both authors maintain that organizational operatives are prisoners of the systems they serve.[45]

For Jackall, all American business organizations are examples of "patrimonial bureaucracies" wherein "fealty relations of personal loyalty" are the rule and the glue of organizational life. Jackall argues that all corporations are like fiefdoms of the Middle Ages, wherein the lord of the manor (CEO, president) offers protection, prestige, and status to his vassals (managers) and serfs (workers) in return for homage (commitment) and service (work). In such a system, advancement and promotion are predicated on loyalty, trust, politics, and personality as much as, if not more than, on experience, education, ability, and actual accomplishments. The central concern of the worker/minion is to be known as a "can-do-guy," a "team player," being at the right place at the right time and master of all the social rules. That is why in the corporate world, asserts Jackall, 1,000 "atta-boys" are wiped away with one "oh, shit!"

Jackall maintains that, as in the model of a feudal system, employees of a corporation are expected to become functionaries of the system and supporters of the status quo. Their loyalty is to the powers that be, their duty is to perpetuate performance and profit, and their values can be none other than those sanctioned by the organization. Jackall contends that the logic of every organization (place of business) and the collective personality of the workplace conspire to override the wants, desires, and aspirations of the individual worker. No matter what a person believes off the job, said Jackall, on the job all of us to a greater or lesser extent are required to suspend, bracket, or only selectively manifest our personal convictions.

> What is right in the corporation is not what is right in a man's home or his church. What is right in the corporation is what the guy above you wants from you . . .[46]

For Jackall the primary imperative of every organization is to succeed. This logic of performance, what he refers to as "institutional logic," leads to the creation of a private moral universe; a moral universe that, by definition, is totalitarian (self-sustained), solipsistic (self-defined), and nar-

cissistic (self-centered). Within such a milieu truth is socially defined and moral behavior is determined solely by organizational needs. The key virtues, for all alike, become the virtues of the organization: goal preoccupation, problem solving, survival/success, and, most important, playing by the house rules. In time, says Jackall, those initiated and invested in the system come to believe that they live in a self-contained world which is above and independent of outside critique and evaluation.

For both Schwartz and Jackall, the logic of organizational life is rigid and unchanging. Corporations perpetuate themselves, both in their strengths and weakness, because corporate cultures clone their own. Even given the scenario of a benign organizational structure which produces positive behavior and beneficial results, the etiology of the problem and the opportunity for abuse that it offers represent the negative possibilities and inherent dangers of the "witness of others" as applied to leadership theory. Within the scope of Schwartz's and Jackall's allied analyses, "normative" moral leadership may not be possible. The model offered is both absolute and inflexible, and only "regular company guys" make it to the top. The maverick, the radical, the reformer are not long tolerated. The "institutional logic" of the system does not permit disruption, deviance, or default.

The term "moral leadership" often conjures up images of sternly robed priests, waspishly severe nuns, carelessly bearded philosophers, forbiddingly strict parents, and something ambiguously labeled the "moral majority." These people are seen as confining and dictatorial. They make us do what we should do, not what we want to do. They encourage following the "superego" and not the "id." A moral leader is someone who supposedly tells people the difference between right and wrong from on high. But there is much more to moral leadership than merely telling others what to do.

The vision and values of leadership must have their origins and resolutions in the community of followers, of whom they are a part, and whom they wish to serve. Leaders can drive, lead, orchestrate, and cajole, but they cannot force, dictate, or demand. Leaders can be the catalyst for morally sound behavior, but they are not, by themselves, a sufficient condition. By means of their demeanor and message, leaders must be able to convince, not just tell others, that collaboration serves the conjoint interest and well-being of all involved. Leaders may offer a vision, but followers must buy into it. Leaders may organize a plan, but followers must decide to take it on. Leaders may demonstrate conviction and willpower, but followers, in the new paradigm of leadership, should not allow the leader's will to replace their own.[47]

Joseph C. Rost has argued, both publicly and privately, that the ethical aspects of leadership remain thorny. How, exactly, do leaders and collaborators in an influence relationship make a collective decision about the ethics of a change that they want to implement in an organization or society? Some will say, "option A is ethical," while others will say, "option B is ethical." How are leaders and followers to decide? As I have suggested, ethics is what "ought to be done" as the preferred mode of action in a "right vs. right," "values vs. values" confrontation. Ethics is an evaluative enterprise. Judgments must be made in regard to competing points of view. Even in the absence of a belief in the existence of a single universal, absolute set of ethical rules, basic questions can still be asked: How does it affect the self and others? What are the consequences involved? Is it harmful? Is it fair? Is it equitable? Perhaps the best, but by no means most definitive, method suited to the general needs of the ethical enterprise is a modified version of the scientific method: (a) *observation,* the recognition of a problem or conflict; (b) *inquiry,* a critical consideration of facts and issues involved; (c) *hypothesis,* the formulation of a decision or plan of action consistent with the known facts; (d) *experimentation and evaluation,* the implementation of the decision or plan in order to see if it leads to the resolution of the problem. There are, of course, no perfect answers in ethics or life. The quality of our ethical choices cannot be measured solely in terms of achievements. Ultimately and ethically, intention, commitment, and concerted effort are as important as outcome: What/why did leader/followers try to do? How did they try to do it?

Leadership is hard to define, and moral leadership is even harder. Perhaps, like pornography, we only recognize moral leadership when we see it.

The problem is, we so rarely see it. Nevertheless, I an convinced that without the "witness" of moral leadership, standards of ethics in business and organizational life will neither emerge nor be sustained. Leadership, even when defined as a collaborative experience, is still about the influence of individual character and the impact of personal mentoring. Behavior does not always beget like behavior in a one-to-one ratio, but it does establish tone, set the stage, and offer options. Although to achieve ethical behavior an entire organization, from top to bottom, must make a commitment to it, the model for that commitment has to originate from the top.[48] Labor Secretary Robert Reich recently stated, "The most eloquent moral appeal will be no match for the dispassionate edict of the market."[49] Perhaps the "witness" of moral leadership can prove to be more effective.

## Notes

1. Maynard M. Dolecheck and Carolyn C. Dolecheck, "Ethics: Take It From the Top," *Business* (Jan.-March 1989): 13.

2. James Patterson and Peter Kim, *The Day America Told the Truth* (New York: Prentice Hall Press, 1991), 1, 20, 21, 22.

3. "Quotable Quotes," *Chicago Tribune Magazine,* January 1, 1996, 17.

4. B. F. Skinner, *Beyond Freedom and Dignity* (New York: Alfred A. Knopf, 1971), 107, 108, 150, 214, 215.

5. Stephen R. Covey, *The Seven Habits of Highly Effective People* (New York: A Fireside Book, 1990), 42, 43.

6. John Dewey. *Theory of the Moral Life* (New York: Holt, Rinehart and Winston, 1960), 3-28.

7. Jean-Paul Sartre, *Existentialism and Human Emotions* (New York: The Wisdom Library, n.d.), 23, 24, 32, 33, 39, 40, 43, 44.

8. John Rawls, "Justice as Fairness: Political not Metaphysical," *Philosophy and Public Affairs* 14 (1985): 223-251.

9. The academic issue of which system of ethics best answers the question "what we ought to do" is a moot point and may in fact be an artificial one. However, the reality is, whichever way one decides to answer the question, "what we ought to do" is an endemic requirement of the human condition.

10. Pope Pius XI, *Quadragesimo Anno (On Reconstructing the Social Order)* in David M. Byers, ed. *Justice in the Marketplace: A Collection of the Vatican and U.S. Catholic Bishops on Economic Policy, 1981-1984* (Washington, D.C.: United States Catholic Conference, 1985), 61.

11. Matthew Fox, *The Reinvention of Work* (San Francisco: Harper San Francisco, 1994), 298, 299.

12. "Tempo" section, *Chicago Tribune,* Feb. 1, 1995, 2.

13. Norman E. Bowie, "Challenging the Egoistic Paradigm," *Business Ethics Quarterly,* vol. 1, no. 1 (1991): 1-21.

14. R. Edward Freeman, "The Problem of the Two Realms," Speech, Loyola University Chicago, The Center for Ethics, Spring, 1992.

15. Henry Ford, Sr., quoted by Thomas Donaldson, *Corporations and Morality* (New Jersey: Prentice Hall, 1982), 57.

16. Ibid., 14.

17. Freeman, "The Problem of the Two Realms."

18. General Robert Wood Johnson, quoted by Frederick G. Harmon and Gary Jacobs, "Company Personality: The Heart of the Matter," *Management Review* (Oct. 1985): 10, 38, 74.

19. Georges Enderle, "Some Perspectives of Managerial Ethical Leadership," *Journal of Business Ethics,* 6 (1987): 657.

20. Joseph C. Rost, *Leadership for the Twenty-First Century* (Westport, CT: Praeger, 1993).

21. Garry Wills, *Certain Trumpets* (New York: Simon & Schuster, 1994), 13.

22. Ibid., 17.

23. E. P. Hollander, *Leadership Dynamics* (New York: Free Press, 1978), 4, 5, 6, 12.

24. In a recent article Joseph Rost made a change in his use of the word *followers:* "I now use *collaborators* when I write about leadership in the postindustrial paradigm. This is a change from *Leadership in the Twenty-First Century,* in which I use the word *followers* all the time. The reason for the change is the unanimous feedback I received from numerous professionals throughout the nation.... After trying several alternative words, I settled on the word *collaborators* because it seemed to have the right denotative and connotative meanings. In other words, *collaborators* as a concept fits the language and values of the postindustrial paradigm of leadership." See Rost, "Leadership Development in the New Millennium," *The Journal of Leadership Studies,* vol. 1., no. 1 (1993): 109, 110.

25. James MacGregor Burns, *Leadership* (New York: Harper Torchbooks, 1979), 426.

26. Al Gini, "Moral Leadership: An Overview," *Journal of Business Ethics* (1996): to be published.

27. James O'Toole, *Leading Change* (San Francisco: Jossey-Bass, 1994); Lynn Sharp-Paine, "Managing for Organizational Integrity," *Harvard Business Review* (March-April 1994): 106-117.

28. Peter M. Senge, *The Fifth Discipline* (New York: Double/Currency Books, 1990), 345-352.

29. Christina Hoff Sommers, "Teaching the Virtues," *Chicago Tribune Magazine,* September 12, 1993, 16.

30. Thomas J. Peters and Robert H. Waterman, Jr., *In Search of Excellence* (New York: Harper & Row, 1982), 245.

31. Burns, chapters 2, 5.

32. Ibid., xi.

33. William James, *The Will to Believe* (New York: Dover Publications, 1956), 1-31, 184-215.

34. John W. Gardner, *On Leadership* (New York: Free Press, 1990), 8.

35. Gail Sheehy, *Character: America's Search for Leadership* (New York: Bantam Books, 1990), 311.

36. Ibid., 66.

37. Burns, 66.

38. Ibid., 439.

39. For Senge the three primary tasks of leadership include: leader as designer; leader as steward; leader as teacher.

40. Senge, 353.

41. Abraham Zaleznik, "The Leadership Gap," *Academy of Management Executives,* vol. 4., no. 1 (1990): 12.

42. Joseph C. Rost, *Leadership for the Twenty-First Century,* p. 124.

43. Howard S. Schwartz, *Narcissistic Project and Corporate Decay* (New York: New York University Press, 1990).

44. Howard S. Schwartz, "Narcissistic Project and Corporate Decay: The Case of General Motors," *Business Ethics Quarterly,* vol. 1., no. 3: 250.

45. Thomas W. Norton, "The Narcissism and Moral Mazes of Corporate Life: A Commentary on the Writings of H. Schwartz and R. Jackall," *Business Ethics Quarterly,* vol. 2, no. 1: 76.

46. Robert Jackall, *Moral Mazes* (New York: Oxford University Press, 1988), 6.

47. Wills, 13.

48. Dolecheck and Dolecheck, 14.

49. William Pfaff, "It's Time for a Change in Corporate Values," *Chicago Tribune,* Jan. 16, 1996, 17.

# 36

# Business Ethics as Moral Imagination

JOANNE B. CIULLA

Business ethics would be a dull subject if ethics came in two off-the-rack colors, black and white. Most of us aren't lucky enough to have such simple ethical tastes. We're stuck with designer ethics, the decorator variety of moral puzzles that come in gray or spectacularly mixed tones of competing claims and conflicting duties. Gray is the color that thoughtful people often see when they initially confront an ethical problem. And gray problems seldom surrender to lily-white solutions. Sometimes we aren't quite sure we did the morally right thing. So, business ethics embraces much more than simply cultivating the ability to "Just say no" or "Just say yes" to clear-cut alternatives. It includes the discovering, anticipating, encountering, and constructing of moral problems, some of which are bona fide dilemmas, and the creating of workable solutions.

This requires what Ezra Bowen calls cultural or civic literacy and ethical literacy, or the ability to use moral language effectively.[1] But it's not what literacy is but what literacy does that is important. By opening up other possible worlds of business and morality, literacy stimulates imagination and gives us a new way of seeing. Traditions can be assessed and reapplied and moral language can be woven into contexts and situations in ways that actually transform them. Business ethics shouldn't just add a chapter to the book of business education—it should rewrite it. We can do more than just heighten moral awareness or produce obedient employees—we can develop moral imagination in our students. By exploring the moral grays of business life, students must be inspired to use their creativity and technical know-how to produce workable multicolored solutions.

Ethical behavior can be seen to encompass prescriptive and creative functions. The prescriptive side says, "Do no harm" or "Thou shalt not" or "You ought to always do X" (i.e., always tell the truth) or "Promote the good." It is explicit and seeks to put certain limits on human behavior. The

SOURCE: From *Business Ethics: The State of the Art,* edited by R. Edward Freeman. Copyright © 1991 by Oxford University Press, Inc. Used by permission of Oxford University Press, Inc.

creative involves inventing ways to live up to moral prescriptions, given the practical constraints of the world. A student once asked me, "Does acting ethically mean that if I work in the loan department of a bank and a poor person can't make his mortgage payment, I shouldn't foreclose on it because it would put him out on the street? You can't run a bank that way." Some people would just do their job and foreclose on the mortgage, others would try to come up with creative financing, and a few would invent a system for humanely dealing with such problems. Educators should ask themselves, "Which response do we want our graduates to have?" Moral commitment comes in many hues, some of which demand that we go out of our way to make the world better. This takes imagination, vision, maturity, and technical know-how. While teaching business ethics to undergraduates generally requires more emphasis on the prescriptive side of ethics, teaching it to adults requires a greater emphasis on the creative side. The study of ethics should lead them to think about new possibilities for business. In this respect a course in business ethics overlaps with courses on leadership and innovation.

## The Superiority of the Real World

As essayist C. K. Chesterton points out in his essay on ethics and imagination, the businessman prides himself on pragmatism not idealism.

> When the businessman rebukes the idealism of his office-boy, it is commonly in some such speech as this: "Ah, yes, when one is young, one has these ideals in the abstract and these castles in the air; but in middle age they all break up like clouds, and one comes down to a belief in practical politics, to using the machinery one has and getting on with the world as it is."[2]

One of the first things you hear upon entering a business school is references to something called the "real world." This "real world" consists of concrete, contingent things, current business practices, rules of the market, black-letter laws, and statistics. It dictates what you can and can't do.

Some students enter business school infatuated with this world. They want to live in it and don't want it to change in any fundamental way. It smacks of certainty and promise and appeals to those who pride themselves on having their feet planted squarely on the ground. Neither immoral nor amoral, the real world does not preclude morality—it just has a hard time making it fit in.[3]

Because of this reverence for the "real world," the most damning indictment of business ethics is that it's not practical. Here one needs to look critically at a variety of business assumptions concerning economics and consumer behavior. As Chesterton goes on to point out in his essay, he never gave up his childlike ideals, but he did give up his childlike faith in practical politics. You can't teach ethics to business students without first forcing them to confront their childlike faith in things like the rules of the market. This may sound a bit harsh, but as anyone who has taught business students knows, if you don't come to class armed with some pretty good reasons and counterexamples to show why the market alone is not a sufficient force for punishing and regulating the behavior of people, you will have a pretty hard time getting them to appreciate what Kant has to say. I'm not saying that students have to reject everything that they have learned—on the contrary. Rather they have to dampen their enthusiasm for the certainty of these presuppositions. One has to learn to think critically before one can think creatively.

## Moral Language

Business students have a basic understanding of right and wrong and general agreement on the merits of honesty. They possess the right moral concepts or linguistic tools but have not mastered them in the environment of business and the culture of particular organizations. If we take the view that thought is embodied in language and language is embedded in a shared form of life, then it makes perfect sense to say that experience can enrich our concept of, say, "honesty," while the concept itself remains the same.[4] On this theory of language, understanding is not reduced to definition, but expanded by experience.

The use of moral concepts by individual speakers over time is grounded in an increasingly diversified capacity for participation in a variety of social practices.[5] It takes time to understand the practices of a new culture or community. Hence, someone who is competent at solving ethical problems in his or her personal life is not necessarily good at solving ethical problems in corporate life. Ethical and cultural literacy are lifelong projects. Mastery of moral language not only reveals new possible worlds but allows us to create them.

### Fairy Tales and Real-Life Stories

Imagination does not have to lead to fantasy, but fantasy can stir imagination. Case studies are about real situations, but they can nonetheless be taught in a way that challenges students to come up with creative solutions. The only limitation is that the solutions be workable. Imaginative problem solving operates between two broad and expandable assumptions. The first is a critical one: just because business is a certain way does not mean that it necessarily has to be that way. I don't know how many times I have heard managers rebuke me, like Chesterton's office boy, with what they consider a prudent rule of business, "If it ain't broke, don't fix it." This phrase is symbolic of both competitive and moral mediocrity—the idea that we only confront problems when we are forced to. Hence we only worry about making better cars after the Japanese do, and we only worry about our accounting practices after we are convicted of fraud.

The second assumption, borrowed from Kant, is a practical one. It rests on the old adage "Ought implies can," or, you are only morally obliged to do that which is possible for you to do (or you are free to do). This assumption needs to be critically explored and constantly expanded. Students often think that taking a moral or socially responsible stand requires either individual or corporate martyrdom—that is, you lost your job or your market share. They feel powerless and sometimes prefer to mortgage their ethics until they are the CEO of a company because they think that only those at the top can effectively take a moral stand. However, the really creative part of business ethics is discovering

ways to do what is morally right and socially responsible without ruining your career and company. Sometimes such creativity requires being like the cartoon mouse who outsmarts the cat.

Perhaps it wouldn't be a bad idea for people to go back and read fairy tales. In his book, *The Uses of Enchantment,* Bruno Bettelheim says that the main message of fairy tales is that the struggle against severe difficulties is a fundamental part of life, but "if one does not shy away, but steadfastly meets unexpected and often unjust hardships, one masters the obstacles and emerges victorious." He stresses the fact that fairy tales impress because they are not about everyday life. They "leave to the child's fantasizing whether and how to apply to himself what the story reveals about life and human nature."[6]

Fairy tales teach children an inspiring lesson—they can use their wits to resolve insurmountable problems. Take, for example, "The Genie and the Bottle." In it, a poor fisherman casts his net three times and brings up a dead jackass, a pitcher full of sand and mud, potsherds and broken glass. On the fourth try, he brings up a copper jar. When he opens it, out comes a giant genie. The genie threatens to kill the fisherman and the fisherman begs for mercy. Then, using his wits, the fisherman taunts the genie by doubting the ability of such a large genie to fit into such a small jar. The genie goes back into the jar to prove the fisherman wrong. The fisherman closes the lid, casts the jar into the ocean and lives happily ever after.[7]

Now this may not be the best case for your business ethics class. Getting students to talk about literature that doesn't refer directly to business can be an uphill battle. Yet, just as most adults remember their fairy tales, students tend to remember the unreal literary cases long after they have forgotten the real ones.[8] I've found that some of the stories my students tell about their work experience pack the same punch as "The Genie and the Bottle."

In a class on international business ethics, an Indian student explained that, before enrolling at Wharton, he had worked for a steel company in India. His company bid on and won the contract for a $20 million project in Venezuela (the first of its kind for an Indian steelmaker). However, the transaction could not proceed until the Indian government approved the deal. When the government official met with the student the official indicated that all would go well if a $2,000 bribe were paid. The student halted his story there and the rest of the class then discussed what they would have done in this predicament. A majority of students felt the bribe request posed an insurmountable barrier to closing the deal. They saw two incompatible possibilities—either you paid the bribe and got the contract, or you didn't pay the bribe and lost the contract. Arguments for paying the bribe rested on commonality of bribes in various parts of the world, the size of the transaction, its benefits to India, and the relatively small size of the agent's request.

As the discussion heated up, some students got frustrated and said, "Ethics is one thing, but this is the real world." They then asked the Indian student if he had gotten the contract and he said, "Yes." Satisfaction fell over the room. Order had been restored to their real world. Morality hadn't interfered with business. The class, half of which consisted of foreign students, assumed that the bribe was paid. But then the Indian student said, "Now, let me tell you what I did. That day, I just happened to have my Walkman in my pocket. I switched it on and put it on the table. Then I said to the government official, I'm sorry, but I forgot to tell you that we tape all of our official conversations with government officials and send them to the appropriate supervisors." Like the quick-witted fisherman, the Indian had tricked the evil genie back into his bottle. He avoided doing evil and won the contract. Unlike his classmates, he saw more than two ways to solve the problem.

Most important, morality entered the real world and altered it. The student's behavior, based on rejection of bribery as wrong, offered a novel solution to a common and serious problem. At this point, a clever moralist might raise the questions, "Is it right to lie to a briber? Is blackmailing a briber like breaking a promise to a terrorist? Do two wrongs make a right?" But for a businessperson this story might prompt thinking about how a company can protect itself in such situations—perhaps taping transactions is a good policy. Sometimes the act of an individual opens up a new repertoire of action for others in like circumstances.

According to Bettelheim, some stories demonstrate why self-interest must be integrated into a broader notion of the good in order for people to effectively cope with reality. For example, the Brothers Grimm story, "The Queen Bee," tells the tale of a king's three sons. The two smart sons go off to seek adventure and lead a wild and self-centered existence. Simpleton, the youngest and least intelligent son, sets out to find his brothers and bring them home. The three brothers finally meet up and travel through the world. When they come to an anthill, the two older ones want to destroy it just to enjoy the ants' terror. But Simpleton will now allow it—later, he also forbids his brothers to kill a group of ducks or set fire to a tree in order to get honey from a bee's nest. Finally the trio comes to a castle where a little gray man tells the oldest brother that if he doesn't perform three tasks in a day, he'll be turned into stone. The first and second brothers fail at the three tasks. Then Simpleton is put to the test. The tasks—gathering 1,000 pearls hidden in the moss in the forest, fetching from the lake a key that opens the bedchamber of the king's daughters, and selecting the youngest and most lovable princess from a room full of identical sleeping sisters—are impossible. Simpleton sits down despondently and cries. At that point the animals that he saved come and help him. The ants find the pearls, the ducks volunteer to find the key, and the Queen Bee settles on the lips of the youngest princess. The spell is broken, Simpleton's brothers are brought back to life, and Simpleton marries the Princess and gains a kingdom.[9]

"The Queen Bee" might well be the child's version of stakeholder analysis. It highlights the interdependence and reciprocal relationships between individuals and groups. Most important, it shows that, contrary to some economic assumptions, decisions based on the self-interest, and not the interest of others, may not be the most profitable way to meet the challenges of life.

Our view of what is possible in the business world comes from personal experience and the media. We are bombarded with reports of unethical behavior. These reports create both outrage and cynicism. It is, however, interesting to note how the business community responds to morally responsible behavior that bucks conventional wisdom.

Think for a moment about the impression that Johnson and Johnson made when it recalled Tylenol because someone had put poison in some of the bottles. It took morally responsible action at a high cost for something that wasn't the company's fault. Johnson and Johnson was later rewarded by the market for its responsible behavior. This story offered the business community a new paradigm for responding to a problem. It was a real-life story of what we had hoped to be true in fairy tales. Doing the morally right thing may be difficult and costly, but in the end, you win back the kingdom. People have always needed to believe that ethical behavior will bring about some good even if the good is simply self-respect and peace of mind.

## Moral Dilemmas

There are, however, a variety of moral conflicts that don't seem to bring about the good. Moral dilemmas are situations in which two equally important obligations conflict. You morally ought to do A and morally ought to do B, but can't do both because B is just not doing A, or some contingent feature of the world prevents you from doing both. Tragedy and drama sometimes focus on such conflicts. Often cited is the conflict in Sophocles' play *Antigone.* Antigone wants to bury her brother but Creon won't let her, because her brother was a traitor and his burial could stir up unrest in the city. Her obligation to the State conflicts with her obligations to her family and the gods. Antigone is in a fix. She's damned if she buries her brother and damned if she doesn't. With real moral dilemmas we never feel quite happy with our decision. Some students mistakenly believe that all moral conflicts are unsolvable and draw the conclusion that there are no answers to ethical problems, only opinions.

Recently there has been a lively debate over whether moral dilemmas exist. Many philosophers have denied that bona fide dilemmas exist (lest they be put out of business). Kant, Ross, and Hare offer levels of analysis and hierarchies of duties that serve as tiebreakers in what at first glance appear to be moral conflicts, but turn out to be sloppy or inadequate descriptions and analysis. Hare, for ex-

ample, approvingly quotes a message posted on a sign outside of a Yorkshire church. It said, "If you have conflicting duties, one of them isn't your duty."[10]

Bernard Williams argues that moral conflicts are more like conflicts of desire than conflicts of belief about facts. If, for example, you believe that Camden is in Pennsylvania, and you believe that Camden is in New Jersey, unless there is something to explain how both of these beliefs can be true, you must give up one belief in favor of the other. So by accepting belief B, it is logically necessary for you to reject belief A. Williams says that we respond much differently to conflicting desires. For example, the desire of a man to be a loyal husband may conflict with his desire to have an affair with another woman. When it comes to strong conflicting desires, we usually try to imagine ways to satisfy both. Often this isn't possible. Yet, choosing to act on one desire does not logically eliminate the second desire in the same way that choosing one fact necessarily eliminates another. The husband may choose to act on his desire to remain loyal to his wife, but still desire to have an affair with the other woman. Williams says, in this kind of case, a person may believe that he "acted for the best" but the case is not closed as it is in a factual dispute. What is left, or the "remainder" of the conflict, Williams calls "regret," or the "What if?" question.[11]

While I wouldn't draw a relativist conclusion from Williams's argument, I think he has put his finger on an extremely important point of moral psychology. We feel different when we reject a moral claim than we do when we reject a factual one. In serious moral conflicts, our desire, like the desire of the married man, is to satisfy both. Ambivalent feelings about a particular moral decision do not necessarily mean that it is a bad one. Regret is the emotion we try to minimize when we construct solutions to moral problems. We do this by imagining how we will feel about different possible outcomes. In serious dilemmas, both outcomes may appear equally attractive or unattractive, just as conflicting moral obligations may carry equal weight. The hallmark of this peculiar species of moral problem—the true dilemma—is that regret is built into the problem.

## Conclusion

Philosophers throughout the ages have offered tiebreakers or means for resolving conflicts. Their insights offer a window on the rich complexity of moral reasoning. Snappy case studies and engaging stories are a key part of teaching business ethics, but equally important are the powerful ways of seeing provided by the legacy of moral philosophy. People who think morality is black and white and believe that all we have to do is teach values in our schools may not like the idea of imaginative ethics. As I have tried to show, it isn't theories or values alone that will change business, but rather the critical perspective and creative actions of our students. Companies that want ethical employees but business as usual are bound to be disappointed.

## Notes

1. Ezra Bowen. "Literacy—Ethics and Profits (The Centrality of Language)," Ruffin Lectures, 1988.

2. C. K. Chesterton. "The Ethics of Elfland," *Collected Works,* Vol. I (San Francisco: Ignatius Press, 1986), p. 249.

3. Business schools still suffer from the legacy of positivism, which stipulated that facts are subject to truth conditions while values are not. Hence, facts are objective things that happen in the real world and values are subjective actions guiding things. By cleaning up language for science, the fact/value distinction muddied the waters for ethics. We were left with the problem of building a bridge between distinct categories—fact/value and theory/practice. It's no surprise that with the emergence of applied ethics there is a renewed interest in ethical realism and virtue theory. Both of these approaches offer an integrated picture of facts and values, which allows us to study what people and institutions do, because values are embedded in practices and traditions. For business ethics this theoretical approach makes the study of ethics inseparable from the study of business practice.

4. Ludwig Wittgenstein, *Philosophical Investigations,* 3rd ed. trans. G. E. M. Anscomb (New York: Macmillan, 1986), pts. 18-21 and 241.

5. Sabina Lovibond, *Realism and Imagination in Ethics* (Minneapolis: University of Minnesota Press, 1983), p. 32.

6. Bruno Bettelheim, *The Uses of Enchantment* (New York: Vintage, 1983), p. 8.

7. Ibid., p. 28.

8. See Robert Coles, "Storyteller Ethics," *Harvard Business Review* (April-May 1987).

9. Bettelheim, *Enchantment,* pp. 76-77.

10. R. M. Hare, *Moral Theory* (New York: Oxford University Press, 1981), p. 26.

11. Bernard Williams, *Problems of the Self: Philosophical Papers, 1956-72* (Cambridge: Cambridge University Press, 1973), pp. 166-186.

# 37

# Changing the Conditions of Work

## Responding to Increasing Work Force Diversity and New Family Patterns

LOTTE BAILYN

That the work force is changing, and that the distribution of family types in the United States is dramatically different from what it has been—these are by now familiar facts. More than half of all mothers with children under one are now in the paid labor force (Hayes, Palmer, and Zaslow, 1990); 45 percent of all paid workers are women (Johnston and Packer, 1987). And 28 percent of all households are female-headed households (U.S. Department of Commerce, 1989). Further, at present, 60 percent of men in the labor force are married to wives who also hold jobs (U.S. Department of Labor, 1988b). It is not surprising, therefore, that a study by the Bank Street Work and Family Life staff has found that between two and

three of every five employees are having problems managing the often conflicting demands of jobs and family life (Galinsky, 1988). Yet the structure of the workplace is still geared to the assumption that workers can commit all their energy and time to their employment.

Today, less than 10 percent of families follow the pattern of a husband at work and a wife at home caring for the children (U.S. Department of Labor, 1988a). Nor is this likely to be a transient phenomenon, as happened with the influx of women into the work force during World War II. On the contrary, these changes will be even more dramatic by the end of the century (Fullerton, 1989). These trends—combined with an increasingly aging

SOURCE: From *Transforming Organizations,* edited by Thomas A. Kochan and Michael Useem. Copyright © 1992 by Sloan School of Management. Used by permission of Oxford University Press, Inc.

population, an expected shortage of labor (particularly of well-educated, skilled men and women), and an increasing disparity between rich and poor, between employment in "good" companies (usually large, with many benefits) and smaller companies without benefits—these new patterns of work and family suggest a potential national crisis.

Its proportions are most evident in the decreasing welfare of the nation's children (Hayes et al., 1990), who are, after all, the future's workers, consumers, and citizens. But it affects, also, the care of other dependents (e.g., the elderly) and the fueling of the "thousand points of light," which, according to the present administration, are to substitute for government involvement. Almost alone among industrialized countries, the United States has no national family policy that can respond to the massive movement of women into the labor force.

Perhaps the best way to highlight the underlying presuppositions that govern the U.S. approach to work-family issues is to consider the situation in Sweden, which represents an entirely different picture. Swedish policy in this area is based on the following critical set of beliefs (Galinsky, 1989):

1. A basic commitment to gender equality: "Women and men are to have the same rights, obligations, and opportunities in all of the main fields of life" (Ministry of Labor Report on Equality Between Men and Women in Sweden, 1988). This premise was already stated in a report of the Swedish government to the United Nations on the Status of Women in Sweden (1971), though its implementation has only recently begun.

2. A basic commitment to economic self-sufficiency: "Every individual should have a job paid sufficiently to enable her or him to earn a living" (Ministry of Labor Report on Equality Between Men and Women in Sweden, 1988). This premise was also stated in the 1971 report, though, again, its actual implementation is a more recent phenomenon.

Together, these two commitments imply a strong belief that women should have jobs and that fathers should be involved in the care of their children.

3. The care of families, particularly children, lies within the responsibilities of the state, and is very much in its interest. Children are seen as a public good, and their proper care is necessary for the continuing success of the society.

And so the government has mandated a comprehensive set of family policies to enable these goals to be met. They are anchored in the economic reality of a long-standing labor shortage, and they are enhanced by a recent push by government to change social attitudes in the direction of valuing balance between work and family for both women and men (Galinsky, 1989).

Contrast these assumptions with those of the United States (Auerbach, 1988):

1. Families/children are in the private domain. The decision to have children is entirely personal and should neither be encouraged or discouraged. Hence any kind of government help in this area is seen as a stigma, a sign of personal failure.

2. Nurturance (children/elder care) is rightfully the province of women, either because they do it better or because it is somehow their specific job.

3. In an individualistic, achieving society, balance in life between work and personal life is not seen as a high-priority goal. Career and work success are more important.

It is important to recognize that these contrasting sets of assumptions represent different visions of the world (Dowd, 1989a) and do not necessarily reflect entirely different realities. In neither country has there yet been much change in the structure of the workplace. Nonetheless, these assumptions have differentially influenced developments in the two countries. Progress in the United States has come from allowing women to meet male work demands. But there has been little attempt to redefine gender roles. In contrast, Sweden has made a serious effort to change gender roles, primarily by urging men to be more involved in the family (Rapoport and Moss, 1990). As a result, Swedish women have a much easier time combining the conflicting demands of work and family and have few of the feelings of conflict and guilt that are so prevalent in the United States (Galinsky, 1989).

But they are even more likely than American women to have unequal work roles (Dowd, 1989a).

It is the mixture of considering family a private, individual concern and yet having to respond to the new demography of the workplace that has shaped the U.S. response to these issues. The response, as of now, has mainly come in the form of new employer-based benefits: parental leave; employee assistance programs (EAPs), originally geared to substance abuse and now more often involved in work-family issues; help of various kinds with dependent care, including flexible spending accounts; alternative work schedules; flexible benefits or cafeteria plans (Bureau of National Affairs, 1986; Employee Benefit Research Institute, 1987).

IBM, for example, recently added to its already generous family services (e.g., child and elder care referral services, EAPS, adoption assistance) two new initiatives: a personal leave program of three years during which time employees receive company-paid benefits and are assured of a job on returning; and expanded flextime, where employees have the option of starting work up to an hour before or after the normal starting time. The first initiative—personal leave—is accompanied by the option of part-time work during the first year, with the requirement that employees be available for part-time work during the second and third years if their services are needed. IBM is also starting a pilot program that will allow employees on personal leave to work at home, as long as the tasks they are assigned are amenable to this arrangement and they agree to come to their workplace location at least four consecutive hours during the week. And a new labor contract at AT&T includes a family care package consisting of a fund for the development of community child care centers and services for the elderly, grants for adoption, and parental and family illness leaves up to one year with continuation of basic benefits and a guaranteed job at the end.

Neither IBM nor AT&T, however, is representative of all U.S. employers—certainly not of small firms, or of those with fewer skill requirements or less benevolent attitudes, though similar arrangements on an *individual* basis are often possible for valued[1] employees in those cases. But since these more enlightened benefits are gener-

ally seen as a model for the U.S. response to work-family issues, it is important to subject them to analysis.

## Corporate Response

The responses of these leading American corporations fall into two general categories, which have different consequences for other organizational concerns. First are benefits provided by employers—in the form of services or financial and information aid in obtaining these services—that allow employees with family responsibilities more easily to meet the requirements of work as currently defined. Such responses are meant, as much as possible, to help employees in different family situations and with different needs to fit the procedures originally designed for a more homogeneous work force, one where 100 percent commitment to work and organization could be presumed because an employee either was single or had family support at home. Hospitals, for example, badly in need of primarily female nursing help, often at irregular hours, frequently provide on-site child care arrangements. And at least two law firms, one in Washington and one in Boston, recently made provision for employees' children when they are sick or when normal arrangements break down. Second are policies that create flexibility in location and time as well as varying arrangements for personal leave. The aim here is to provide employees with sufficient control and discretion over the conditions of work to respond themselves to the needs of their families.

Both sets of responses have begun to meet the needs of the current work force. But without attention to how they fit into existing organizational procedures, both may have unintended negative consequences: the first by actually exacerbating the very conditions the benefits were designed to alleviate; the second by creating—or reinforcing—a two-tier structure of employment. It is the thesis of this chapter that the introduction of family benefits must take these negative consequences into consideration and that an effective resolution of such competing concerns will not be possible without restructuring of the conditions of work (cf. Dowd, 1989b).

## Exacerbating Family/Work Pressures

During much of this century the pressures on the conditions of employment have served to *reduce* the amount of time people spent in the workplace, but recently that trend has been reversed. Over the last fifteen years or so, work time in the United States has increased 15 percent (Gordon, 1989); among managers the increase is estimated as almost 20 percent over the last decade (Fowler, 1989). And though most European countries provide longer periods of paid time away from work than does the United States, the example of competitors in the Far East has led a number of analysts to conclude that longer working hours are necessary to bring the United States back to its previous competitive position (e.g., Subotnik, 1989; Weigand, 1986).

In particular, it is the example of Japan that is held up to support this conclusion.[2] And it is Japan, also, that serves as a model for the more participative and committed form of organization that is now recommended to increase U.S. productivity (Dertouzos, Lester, and Solow, 1989; Kanter, 1989; Lawler, 1986). Such recommendations seem to ignore the Japanese institutional norms that underlie that system, such as the role of women as family support and the economic/financial framework that exchanges employment security for total commitment in the core work force (Dore, Chapter 2, this volume). But neither of these conditions exists in the United States, and it is unlikely that either could be made congruent with contemporary American values. Yet productivity pressures, combined with globalization and increased international competition, have resulted in longer work hours, just when increased family demands are also putting greater pressure on employee time. Family benefits of the first kind, which either provide or allow workers to buy family services, do not make U.S. employees less time poor. And because the availability and quality of the services thus provided are still not adequate, such responses may actually increase the work-family concerns now facing American workers.

Much of what we read about the need for organizational change in U.S. companies reflects a concern about productivity. More participation, flatter organizations, more responsibility and authority at lower levels—all of these demand increased commitment from employees, a commitment that tends, according to current rules, to translate into more time and involvement with work. But if the demographic changes over the past few decades have left the family, children in particular, as vulnerable as many now fear, then the answer is not to ensure that employees can give more time to work, but rather to find ways to make possible more time devoted to family needs. And that is the goal of the second set of benefits which the most enlightened employers are now introducing.

## Creating (Reinforcing) a Two-Tier Structure of Employment

In essence, these benefits—flextime and flexplace, part-time and job-sharing opportunities, personal leaves of various kinds—are geared to freeing time for employees to attend to family needs. As such, they make legitimate a different, more accommodating set of workplace requirements. But trouble arises if other organizational procedures remain unchanged. As long as organizations continue to reward the full commitment of their employees, gauged by the amount of time spent at work, flexibility, even when available, will not be popular with core employees. Yet dependents will continue to need care. And even though the solution that evolved at the Industrial Revolution—a specialization of labor between bread winning and care taking—is no longer seen as optimal, either economically or psychologically, women still seem to be primarily responsible for care. Thus, at the present time, flexible options are more likely to be used by women than by men. And as long as such a differential pattern of use exists, it can only *increase* the disadvantages that women already face in the workplace through the feminization of poverty, the wage gap, the glass ceiling. By itself, flexibility superimposed on existing assumptions about the conditions of employment is not likely to change these basic facts. It needs to be accompanied by a reevaluation of the meaning of employment in contemporary American society—one that can provide equity and fairness along with the productive use of the nation's talents and skills. Even IBM's response, important as it is, fails to meet this challenge. And the same is true of most other examples of organizational responses to employees' family needs (see, e.g., Bureau of National Affairs, 1986; Rodgers and Rodgers, 1989).

By law, U.S. policy in these matters has been "gender-neutral." Pregnancy leave is generally subsumed under disability provisions; custody decisions in divorce cases now go as often to fathers as to mothers. But is such mandated equality equitable? Can it overcome the effect of a wage-labor system premised on an ideal worker with no family responsibilities (Williams, 1989)? Can it be equitable in the face of a deeply held cultural assumption that caring is the province of women? Does it not force everyone (both women and men) to choose between economic success without family responsibilities and economic marginalization combined with family care? And does it not, therefore, contribute to the economic vulnerability of women—as has been shown recently by the differential consequences of divorce for men and women in a "gender-neutral" world (Arendell, 1987; Weitzman, 1985)?

These are the issues involved in this second set of benefits, which provide needed leeway, under current conditions, to employees with families. But as long as women are the primary beneficiaries, these benefits may also entail a cost. As already stated for the previous category, what is needed is a reexamination of the assumptions underlying the structure of work.

### Conditions of Employment

If it is true that American industry will require the full utilization of all talent—male and female— in order to stay globally competitive, and if we want to achieve this goal within the constraints of our notions of equity and of the needs of future generations, then a critical analysis of the premises underlying current employment practices is in order. And, just possibly, the rapidly changing demography in this country may provide the catalyst

for this endeavor (cf. Briggs, 1987). But for reasons already discussed, organizations will have to do more than provide family benefits to be used primarily by women. Schwartz (1989), in her famous or infamous article in the *Harvard Business Review,* has made companies aware that family concerns must be taken into account in the conditions of employment for women. What she did not make clear is that these considerations may soon generalize to male employees, since they also, more and more frequently, do not fit the model of an employee totally committed to work with no other significant responsibilities. In this there is another compelling decision to reevaluate the basic assumptions underlying employment.

One critical issue centers on location and time (Bailyn, 1988). Too often the amount of time spent at work is seen as a prime indicator of commitment and, indirectly, of productivity; visibility is seen as a prerequisite for advancement. But long hours and a heavy workload, particularly when rigidly prescribed, are key elements in the inability to meet conflicting responsibilities. Witness the comments of a young male assistant professor: "[The university's] expectations about one's commitment to individual career—to the exclusion of spouses' career and family—make it virtually impossible to live a life in which personal goals can be considered (much less accomplished) apart from work." At that same university, two out of five young faculty parents report that they have seriously considered leaving because of conflict between family and work.

Nor is it clear that time at work is always positively related to productivity. On the contrary, some research indicates that part-time work and job sharing increase productivity per hour worked (Cohen and Gadon, 1978; Ronen, 1984). It seems important to ask, therefore, whether it is really necessary to work long hours in order to perform effectively, or whether this requirement is simply part of the traditional way to manage careers. Might long hours not be a sign of *inefficiency* rather than of commitment and motivation? Similarly, is continuous presence at an office really required in an age of knowledge-intensive work with the aid of technology for information and communication? In a California pilot project, for example, state employees who work at home were "3 to 5 percent more productive than they would be if they spent full time in the office" (*Work in America,* August 1989, p. 8). Perhaps visibility is another proxy signal used by organizations to control employees' careers, a control that is anchored in outdated ways of managing (cf. Drucker, 1989; Dumaine, 1989; Houghton, 1989).

A second key issue, therefore, centers on new ways of managing people, a transformation that is difficult because it goes against the received wisdom about how to manage. Management by walking around, by overseeing the way subordinates work, would no longer be possible. A basic trust (in both competence and effort) would have to take its place (Perin, 1991), and managers would have to shift their emphasis away from input and concentrate on output instead. It would bring us back, perhaps, to McGregor's Theory Y—a set of assumptions that people not only enjoy their work but are willing to take responsibility for it. It has been said, for example, that the reason Sweden does not worry about employees misusing the sixty days each year they are allowed to take off for illness of children (the actual average is between six and seven) is their sense of fairness and commitment.[3] So why do U.S. (and British) managers assume that if they don't see their subordinates working, they probably aren't?

In interviews exploring the possibility of using computers to work at home during the regular work week on tasks that require cognitive concentration, Perin (1991) heard again and again managers asking, "How do I know he's working if I don't see him?" And yet they had no answer to the responding question: "How do you know he's working when you *do* see him?" Their assumptions about control stem from a scientific management model of work—McGregor's Theory X. And whether such a view makes any sense in today's world is a real question. Thus a change in management practice may be a key to effecting the kind of organizational transformation that is required—not only for individuals trying to mesh work and family concerns, but more generally for easier organizational adaptation to a rapidly changing environment.

Technology can play a role in this process. It both enables and supports, under the right condi-

tions, changes in the organization of work that could help alleviate workplace constraints on accommodations between work and family. The ability to loosen constraints on location is a prime example of technology's potential for effecting change. So, for example, a comparison of systems developers working from home instead of being office-based shows that the former arrangement, though no substitute for child care, is associated with greater satisfaction with health and other personal concerns than is the traditional office-based pattern (Bailyn, 1989). But, as already indicated, it is difficult to convince supervisors that the arrangement is tenable (Cooperson, 1990), for it conflicts with basic cultural beliefs about time and the meaning of "office" and "home" in industrial society (Perin, 1991). Consider, however, the following example.

The task of writing a technical manual for a large consumer product manufacturer usually took about six months and required the efforts of people separated both geographically and functionally. Once an experimental network was introduced that connected these people electronically, the time to complete the task was cut to less than two months, with no change in quality. What was particularly interesting about this experiment was that one of the people involved quietly took his computer home. Other members of the group were not aware that he had changed his location, and it is interesting to speculate whether knowledge of this change would have affected the outcome.

Another example, from the same organization, relates to the introduction of computer-aided design (CAD) machines in an engineering design department. Engineering managers had been used in monitoring the work of their subordinates, seated around a large drafting table, by overseeing the process by which they arrived at their designs. But once these design engineers were huddled over individual computer screens, this control over process was no longer possible. The screen was too small for two people, and it contained more detail than could be seen as a whole. Thus supervision had to shift to the output—which appeared as a printout two floors below the design floor—and away from the input, the process by which the design was created.

The designer gained autonomy, and the supervisor had to be more trusting of the competence of his subordinates and also had to be clearer about the specifications of the final product.

What all of this indicates is that a basic change in the conditions of employment is needed for family-work issues to be usefully resolved in the context of other pressures on organizations to change. Without such systemic change, responses to family-work conflicts may lead to unintended negative consequences. To illustrate the process I would like to examine the career development system currently in use in most U.S. organizations, and to highlight the aspects of that system that would need to change.

## *Career Development*

Current career development procedures in organizations are based on the assumption that long-term planning for positions is not only possible but desirable. So effort is put into early identification of future potential with little concern for the long-range consequences of these decisions. Such a career system has linear continuity built into it. It assumes that the appropriate career direction is up and that what happens at the beginning is a strong determiner of the future. In one R&D lab, for example, there still is a significant positive correlation between current and starting salary twenty years into the career. And, as Rosenbaum (1984) has shown in his depiction of the tournament model, the probability of getting a promotion drops dramatically after a certain fairly clearly defined period of about seven to ten years. This procedure of early selection of high-potential employees (the fast track) ignores the possibility that the selection itself may determine the outcome—the self-fulfilling prophecy. And, most critically for the present concerns, it puts a premium on time and effort spent on work during years where family concerns are likely to make an employee particularly vulnerable.

The system is geared to matching an individual to a job that has been carefully specified independently of the person filling it. It is based on a desire to make career procedures as homogeneous as possible and to have them apply equally to all parts of the firm and to all people, whatever their individual situations. Such a system, by definition, cannot be responsive to individual needs. On the contrary, it is designed to minimize the probability of special treatment for certain groups and is supported by the legal system for just that purpose. But for a diverse work force, with employees in widely differing family situations, equality in procedures does not necessarily produce equal employment opportunity; it may produce the opposite.

Continuity, linearity, and homogeneity are already under pressure from concerns about efficiency and productivity. In particular, since the restructuring we have seen during the last decade in the United States has often been accompanied by massive displacement of workers, the assumption of continuity is really obsolete. Hence a new approach, one that would also help employees deal with family needs, may be in order. I think of such a system as "zero-based budgeting" in careers. It would involve planning for a particular career segment, perhaps of five to seven years, and then renegotiating the level of commitment, the tasks, the compensation and evaluation procedures de novo for the next segment. I have elsewhere discussed a similar idea in calling for negotiation of career procedures based on a personally defined extent of occupational commitment (Bailyn, 1984). Let employees decide, at different points in their lives, the extent to which they can commit themselves to their work, and then negotiate tasks, rewards, and appraisal procedures in line with this level of commitment. Such a system would not only fit better with the current organizational reality in this country, but it would also allow employees to better mesh the needs of their families with the requirements of work. As presently constituted the career development system is geared neither to a changing organizational environment nor to the work-family issues of employees.

But changes in deeply entrenched procedures are not easily accomplished. They are anchored in largely taken-for-granted assumptions (Schein, 1985), which may have been functional at an earlier time but now serve as constraints on change. These constraining assumptions are listed in Table 37.1, which also juxtaposes new assumptions, more relevant to current needs.

**TABLE 37.1** Need to Change Assumptions

| Old Assumptions (constraining) | New Assumptions (facilitating) |
| --- | --- |
| Commitment/loyalty = time Manage via input; before-the-fact approval | Discontinuity Accountability; after-the-fact review |
| Homogeneity in outlook and values | Building on diversity (self-design) |

The difficulties of measuring commitment and loyalty by time, particularly visible time, have already been discussed, as has the equally constraining tendency for managers to feel that they must monitor in detail the way their subordinates meet their work objectives. Together, these presumptions lead managers to walk around and to insist on the need for before-the-fact approval. Such a definition of managerial control resides in the principles of hierarchy, still firmly embedded in business organizations, and on the difficulties of specifying clearly the output goals of work. But it also represents a basic mistrust of the motivation of one's employees and of their willingness to be responsible for their work (cf. Perin, 1991). Consider, for example, the thorny question of whether employees are allowed to take time off to stay home with a sick child. In many cases no such provision is available and employees with a sick child either call in sick themselves—which some find very disagreeable—or have supervisors who are willing to accept family illness as a legitimate reason for absence. And even when organizations provide a certain number of personal days for family illness, the procedures for "applying" are sometimes so cumbersome that they are not used. Similarly, the rules for taking sick leave in some cases include a note from the doctor. (A regression to childhood where a note was necessary to excuse an absence?) If we can provide a certain number of paid work days to cover absences for personal reasons, why not leave the monitoring of their use to the employee? Why do we feel that employees will exploit this privilege? Why cannot we assume that they are mature adults, with a sense of responsibility about their work (cf. Gambetta, 1988)? In

the case of the home-based systems developers, for example, there was sufficient trust that time records were completely accepted by managers, and there was no evidence whatsoever of any misuse of this trust. And a study by the National Council of Jewish Women (1987) has shown that when employers are accommodating and flexible in their policies, pregnant women take *fewer* sick days, work *later* in their pregnancies, and are *more* likely to spend time doing things related to their jobs outside regular work hours without compensation. They are also more likely to return to their jobs after childbirth (NCJW Report, 1988).

Finally, there is the presumption, despite evidence to the contrary (cf. Schein, 1987), that all people in a given organizational position should be homogeneous in outlook and values. Firms try to select for this in their hiring practices, or they count on socialization to produce it. But this attempt, besides running the risk of not being successful with the current demographic reality, also may miss a valuable source of new ideas and change. In a diverse work force employees will differ in their needs, their values, their assumptions about the role of work and career in their lives, and their approaches to work and to the people around them. And though such differences cannot guarantee adaptive change, they may provide the necessary variety from which change emerges, and may result in a rethinking of organizational routines and the establishment of new and possibly more effective procedures (cf. Weick, 1979; Weick and Berlinger, 1989).

Career procedures based on this new set of assumptions would be quite different, I think, from those now prevalent in organizations. The essence of the current procedures is an independently defined job system into which people are selected or socialized to fit. "Misfits" are weeded out in the process, and with them the potential for new ideas and approaches. In contrast, a system based on this different set of assumptions would rest on individual negotiation based on discontinuity, which would force both the system and the people in it to construct their relationship in new and different ways. More innovation would be possible; more authority could be given to those with the necessary expertise and information. Care would have to be taken that individual negotiation would be truly individual and would not turn into assignments according to stereotyped expectations about people's abilities or circumstances. None of this would be easy, but it seems to be an approach that would make it possible to combine the productivity needs of organizations with the work-family issues now confronting the U.S. work force. The alternative, of dealing with demographic and family change in isolation by superimposing family policies on the current system, might not actually improve workers' work-family conflicts and might, in the absence of other changes, reinforce the already existing gender inequity in the workplace.

## *Potential for Change*

These are some of the key issues that need to be confronted if there is to be an easier accommodation between organizational needs and the work-family concerns of employees. And the question now remains, where can the leverage for change be found? For there are deeply held assumptions that constrain such change. So how does one get from here to there?

There are some who say that the change in demographics itself will provide the necessary impetus. But demographic trends, and national need, tend to go in cycles, and the question of how such changes can be institutionalized remains (Rapoport and Moss, 1990). Moreover, such institutionalization will have to occur in the procedures that govern all people, not only women or mothers. Felice Schwartz, in defense of her article in the *Harvard Business Review* (1989), claims that practicality mandates a change only for women, and that the generalization to all employees, regardless of sex, will follow. Auerbach (1988), in her analysis of employer practices regarding child care, is also cautiously optimistic. She feels that these efforts already point to the acceptance by American business that the workplace and the family have changed forever—that both men and women play roles in both arenas. There is no real evidence for Schwartz's optimism or for Auerbach's. In the end, it may be that only if men's roles and men's work-

place behavior change (cf. Pleck, 1989) will there be the requisite leverage to alter the underlying assumptions.

One way to guide such change is to amass information on what is currently happening. In particular, one would want to establish the family demographics of the work force, since most organizations have no notion of the families in which their employees live. The IBM data, for example, on marital status and presence of young children and elder dependents by sex, were an eye opener to management and a powerful impetus for introducing new policies. And a number of leading universities are currently engaged in similar exercises as they review their policies. The prime motivation here is the recruitment and retention of top talent. But more information than simply family demographics should be collected. Data on the problems people face in meeting current organizational requirements, indicated perhaps by absenteeism and turnover, are also required. Identification of the demographic groups that find these requirements most difficult, and the extent to which they are changing, would be a key indicator of where change is needed in order to help employees mesh their concerns with work and family.

But even more important is an assessment of the utilization and effects of new, as well as existing, procedures. Policy and practice do not always go together and it is important to know who actually takes advantage of existing policies, with what consequence for their future roles in the organization. A leading university, for example, which for fifteen years has had on its books the provision of personal leave for child care for its faculty (which would stop the tenure clock), has discovered that no woman who took such a leave has ever subsequently been awarded tenure (Rowe, personal communication). Here, however, a word of caution is in order. Such information can be used to effect change; it can also be used to justify the status quo. It is just this fear that has led to so much concern over Felice Schwartz's statement that women cost the corporation more than men do. To prevent such a "misuse" of data it is critical to surface the assumptions underlying current practices (cf. Martin, 1990). Otherwise, new procedures, no matter how well meant, may have unexpected and undesirable consequences (see, e.g., Bento and Ferreira, 1990).

The most important need is for the acceptance of work-family issues as an integral part of organizational life, as an important business concern (cf. Rodgers and Rodgers, 1990), and a realization that they cannot be dealt with in a piecemeal fashion but must be central to any consideration of systemic change. Though not an easy assignment, it is possible that a confluence of forces—demographic change, expected labor shortages, an emerging national concern, models from other parts of the world, and the new technologies—may make this a propitious time to proceed in this direction.

## Acknowledgments

I am grateful to the Ford Foundation (grant 890-3012) for support during the writing of this chapter. I also want to acknowledge the very helpful comments given by the following people on previous drafts: Regina Bento, Rae Goodell, Deborah Kolb, Nancy Lonstein, Rhona Rapoport, Amelie Ratliff, and John Thompson.

## *Notes*

1. That the perceived value of employees may itself be a function of an employee's gender and family position is analyzed by Martin (1990).

2. It is ironic that Japan is currently trying to induce its workers to take more vacation time and is putting in place a whole set of interrelated procedures in order to move to a five-day week ("Coming: The 5-Day Week for All," Editorial, *The Japan Times,* August 28, 1988, p. 18).

3. Overall, however, Sweden has a very high absentee rate, something in the order of 25 percent. One company, however, found that by increasing the control of their employees over the conditions of work they reduced their absentee rate from 30 percent to 5 percent (personal communication), evidence again that one cannot superimpose family benefits on existing conditions but must accompany them by structural change in these conditions.

## *References*

Arendell, T. J. 1987. "Women and the Economics of Divorce in the Contemporary United States." *Signs* 13: 121-135.

Auerbach, J. D. 1988. *In the Business of Child Care: Employer Initiatives and Working Women.* New York: Praeger.

Bailyn, L. 1984. "Issues of Work and Family in Organizations: Responding to Social Diversity." *In Working With Careers,* edited by M. B. Arthur, L. Bailyn, D. J. Levinson, and H. A. Shepard. New York: Center for Research in Career Development, Columbia University.

Bailyn, L. 1988. "Freeing Work from the Constraints of Location and Time." *New Technology, Work and Employment* 3: 143-152.

Bailyn, L. 1989. "Toward the Perfect Workplace? The Experience of Home-Based Systems Developers." *Communications of the ACM* 32: 460-471.

Bento, R. F., and L. D. Ferreira. 1990. "Incentive Pay and Organizational Culture." Paper presented at the Colloquium on Performance Measurement and Incentive Compensation, Harvard Business School, June 25-26, 1990.

Briggs, V. M., Jr. 1987. "The Growth and Composition of the U.S. Labor Force." *Science,* October 9, pp. 176-180.

Bureau of National Affairs. 1986. *Work and Family: A Changing Dynamic.* (BNA special report) Washington, D.C.

Cohen, A. R., and H. Gadon. 1978. *Alternative Work Schedules: Integrating Individual and Organizational Needs.* Reading, Mass.: Addison-Wesley.

Cooperson, D. A. 1990. Telecommuting: A Way to Ease Work/Family Conflicts Through Increased Employee Time Flexibility? MIT Sloan School of Management, unpublished term paper.

Dertouzos, M. L., R. K. Lester, and R. M. Solow. 1989. *Made in America: Regaining the Productive Edge.* Cambridge: MIT Press.

Dowd, N. E. 1989a. "Envisioning Work and Family: A Critical Perspective on International Models." *Harvard Journal on Legislation* 26: 311-348.

Dowd, N. E. 1989b. "Work and Family: The Gender Paradox and the Limitations of Discrimination Analysis in Restructuring the Workplace." *Harvard Civil Rights-Civil Liberties Law Review* 24: 79-172.

Drucker, P. 1989. "The Futures That Have Already Happened." *The Economist,* October 21, pp. 19ff.

Dumaine, B. 1989. "What the Leaders of Tomorrow See." *Fortune,* July 3, pp. 48ff.

Employee Benefit Research Institute. 1987. *Fundamentals of Employee Benefit Programs,* 3rd ed. Washington, D.C.

Fowler, E. M. 1989. "More Stress in the Workplace." *New York Times,* September 20, p. D22.

Fullerton, H. N., Jr. 1989. "New Labor Force Projections, Spanning 1988 to 2000." *Monthly Labor Review,* November, pp. 3-12.

Galinsky, E. 1988. "Child Care and Productivity." Paper prepared for the Child Care Action Campaign Conference, Child Care: The Bottom Line, New York. Quoted in E. Galinsky and P. Stein, "Balancing Careers and Families: Research Findings and Institutional Responses." In *Marriage, Family, and Scientific Careers: Institutional Policy Versus Research Findings,* edited by M. L. Matyas, L. Baker, and R. Goodell. Proceedings, Symposium of American

Association for the Advancement of Science, Annual Meeting, San Francisco, January 16, 1989.

Galinsky, E. 1989. "The Implementation of Flexible Time and Leave Policies: Observations From European Employers." Paper prepared for the Panel on Employer Policies and Working Families, Committee on Women's Employment and Related Social Issues, Commission on Behavioral and Social Sciences and Education, National Research Council, Washington, D.C.

Gambetta, D. 1988. "Can We Trust Trust?" In *Trust: Making and Breaking Cooperative Relations,* edited by D. Gambetta. New York: Basil Blackwell.

Gordon, S. 1989. "Work, Work, Work." *Boston Globe,* August 20, pp. 16ff.

Hayes, C. D., J. Palmer, and M. Zaslow. 1990. "Who Cares for America's Children: Child Care Policy for the 1990's," Report of the Panel on Child Care Policy, Committee on Child Development Research and Public Policy. Commission on Behavioral and Social Sciences and Education, National Research Council, Washington, D.C.

Houghton, J. R. 1989. "The Age of the Hierarchy Is Over." *New York Times,* September 24, Business Section, p. 3.

Johnston, W. B., and A. E. Packer., 1987. *Workforce 2000: Work and Workers for the Twenty-First Century.* Indianapolis: Hudson Institute.

Kanter, R. M. 1989. *When Giants Learn to Dance: Mastering the Challenges of Strategy, Management, and Careers in the 1990s.* New York: Simon & Schuster.

Lawler, E. E. 1986. *High Involvement Management: Participative Strategies for Improving Organizational Performance.* San Francisco: Jossey-Bass.

Martin, J. 1990. "Deconstructing Organizational Taboos: The Suppression of Gender Conflict in Organizations." *Organizational Science* 1: 339-359.

National Council of Jewish Women. 1987. "Accommodating Pregnancy in the Workplace." *NCJW Center for the Child Report.* New York: National Council of Jewish Women.

National Council of Jewish Women. 1988. "Employer Supports for Child Care." *NCJW Center for the Child Report.* New York: National Council of Jewish Women.

Perin, C. 1991. "The Moral Fabric of the Office: Panopticon Discourse and Schedule Flexibilities." In *Research in the Sociology of Organizations,* edited by S. Bacharach, S. R. Barley, and P. S. Tolbert. Greenwich, Conn.: JAI Press. (Volume on Organizations and Professions).

Pleck, J. H. 1989. "Family-Supportive Employer Policies and Men's Participation." Paper prepared for the Panel on Employer Policies and Working Families, Committee on Women's Employment and Related Social Issues, Commission on Behavioral and Social Sciences and Education, National Research Council, Washington, D.C.

Rapoport, R., and P. Moss. 1990. *Men and Women as Equals at Work: An Exploratory Study of Parental Leave in Sweden and Career Breaks in the UK.* London: Thomas Coram Research Unit.

Rodgers, F. S., and C. Rodgers. 1989. "Business and the Facts of Family Life." *Harvard Business Review,* November-December, pp. 121-129.

Ronen, S. 1984. *Alternative Work Schedules: Selecting . . . Implementing . . . and Evaluating.* Homewood, Ill.: Dow Jones-Irwin.

Rosenbaum, J. E. 1984. *Career Mobility in a Corporate Hierarchy.* New York: Academic Press.

Schein, E. H. 1985. *Organizational Culture and Leadership.* San Francisco: Jossey-Bass.

Schein, E. H. 1987. "Individuals and Careers." In *Handbook of Organizational Behavior,* edited by J. W. Lorsch. Englewood Cliffs, N.J.: Prentice Hall.

Schwartz, F. N. 1989. "Management Women and the New Facts of Life." *Harvard Business Review,* January-February, pp. 65-76.

Subotnik, D. 1989. "Productivity's Little Secret: Hard Work." *New York Times,* May 14, Business Section, p. 2.

U.S. Department of Commerce. 1989. *Current Population Reports* (Special Studies Series P-23, No. 159). Washington, D.C.: Bureau of the Census.

U.S. Department of Labor. 1988a. *Child Care: A Workforce Issue.* Report of the Secretary's Task Force. Washington, D.C.

U.S. Department of Labor. 1988b. *Employment and Earnings.* Washington, D.C.: Bureau of Labor Statistics.

Weick, K. E. 1979. *The Social Psychology of Organizing.* 2nd ed. Reading, Mass.: Addison-Wesley.

Weick, K. E., and L. R. Berlinger. 1989. "Career Improvisation in Self-Designing Organizations." In *Handbook of Career Theory,* edited by M. B. Arthur, D. T. Hall, and B. S. Lawrence. Cambridge: Cambridge University Press.

Weigand, R. E. 1986. "What's a Fair Day's Work?" *New York Times,* April 19, p. 27.

Weitzman, L. J. 1985. *The Divorce Revolution: The Unexpected Social and Economic Consequences for Women and Children in America.* New York: Free Press.

Williams, J. C. 1989. "Deconstructing Gender." *Michigan Law Review,* 87: 797-845.

---

## *Commentary by Derek Harvey*

Work and family issues are to the 1990s what comprehensive family medical coverage was to the 1950s. They are a necessary business expense, which includes the provision of services and policies that offer time flexibility. Time flexibility will initially include dependent care leave, flextime, and other similar tools that managers can offer their people.

In the long term, these policies will not be sufficient for dual-career employees and other heads of households. As the demand for family "care" grows so will the demand for much more substantial time flexibility. One key to achieving these changes is through management practices. Companies that appoint (or train) managers who have a value system that includes empowering employees, managing diversity, and practicing flexibility will build a climate that allows subordinates to manage their work and family lives. The manager of the nineties will be much more concerned with contribution and outcomes than the number of hours spent at the workplace.

This trend when seen alongside other trends toward flatter organizations, larger spans of managerial control, and the greater use of computer technology suggest that the workplace of the year 2000 will be radically different from today's.

Alongside these trends companies need to rethink their linear career paths and live with the reality that at different times in a career employees will give different levels of commitment.

# 38

# Going Beyond the Rhetoric of Race and Gender

JOHN P. FERNANDEZ

## A. Introduction

In this chapter we are going to present an overview of a holistic approach which is needed to go beyond the rhetoric of race and gender in corporate America. The changing demographics of the United States and the globalization of the economy have implications for both the marketplace and workforce in solving race and gender issues. In an environment in which customers are becoming increasingly diverse (regarding race, ethnicity, language, gender, etc.), a "one-size-fits-all" approach to the U.S. domestic marketplace can no longer be the business strategy of choice for successful organizations. Instead, successful organizations will create strategies that focus on creating new flexible diverse team-based organizations and segmenting the numerous markets and customizing products and services to appeal to diverse market segments. Corporations must recognize that when a "one-size-fits-all" approach is no longer applicable to the marketplace, it is also no longer applicable to

the workforce. Success with increasingly diverse customers will require that corporations have a diverse workforce that can understand changing markets.

Customers will not be serviced effectively unless corporations help their employees in understanding, valuing, and appreciating diverse people, especially based on race, culture, and gender. In addition, corporations must create an environment in which these skilled employees from all races and genders are fully utilized and empowered to make the creative decisions necessary to produce timely quality products and services. This environment can no longer be one in which bureaucracy, conformity, and uniformity of approach are the driving forces. Instead, the focus will shift to flexible, heterogeneous, team organizations with a variety of creative approaches to customers and employees. No matter where companies do business human interactions based on trust and respect relationships among the different races and genders are the critical success factors to having effective

SOURCE: Reprinted with permission of the author.

teams, customer and stakeholder relations. These interactions are key to the bottom line.

Let's look in more detail at the current situation in corporate America—in particular, what major changes are occurring in corporate America that complicate the understanding and development of solutions to the race and gender issues and that also make it more difficult to develop a global business and marketing strategy worldwide.

### B. The Complexities of the Issues: Race, Gender, Education, Economics, Bureaucracy, and Humans

The first major change is the "browning" of the United States. By the year 2000, California, which produces 24% of the U.S. GNP and is the eighth greatest economic power in the world, will have a majority people of color population, followed closely by New York state and Texas. Concurrent with this increasing diversity of the population in the United States is the issue that, for much of corporate America to survive and prosper, they must find new opportunities globally. Thus, many corporations' employees and customer bases are becoming more diverse through location of plants in foreign countries and through mergers and acquisitions.

While we have always had diversity among our labor force, few would argue with the observation that we have never had a more diverse and varied labor force than we do today, as seen in the statistics showing that both spouses work in more than half of married households, almost half of the labor force is comprised of women, a quarter of the labor force is comprised of people of color, and less than a tenth of new entrants to the labor force are white males. In addition increasing numbers of U.S. companies are recognizing that more than half their workforces are in other countries than the U.S. These foreign employees bring to the workplace in some cases vastly different cultures than U.S. corporations are used to dealing with. In short, these trends in the external characteristics of population groups are accompanied by changes in the values that people hold today about work and nonwork activities.

Another factor impacting U.S. corporations is the fact that the educational level of the work force is rising in huge part due to the demand for smarter, more highly skilled workers and, with this workforce, come rising aspirations to move up the corporate ladder, to obtain choice job assignments, and to be rewarded and compensated equitably and fairly for skills and contributions to the organization. Women play a key role in explaining this rise in education. Women have for over ten years received more master's, bachelor's, and associate's degrees than men. In addition they are obtaining degrees in the "business areas." An example, in 1971 women received only 9% of the degrees in business administration; in 1995 they received 48%. These women are entering the work force on a permanent, full-time basis. In addition, these groups are creating a much larger pool of talent. Not only women but more people of color are completing college and earning these types of degrees. This educational phenomenon is occurring not only in the United States but also on a global basis as new economic realities require more educated people. Regardless of the country more educated people are more demanding.

In the United States, the worker of today displays a marked difference in attitudes about work and careers than that of a generation or more ago. For example, in our training sessions with employees representing the spectrum of age cohorts in the labor force, we are hearing the difference between the thirty-year veteran of the company and the thirty-month employee. Each acknowledges this difference in attitudes described variously as those reflecting work ethic, loyalty, or expectations. Whatever the anticipation, we hear that young people today want more flexibility from their employer and want to be recognized for the value they add to the organization now, as opposed to paying their dues or waiting their turn. Because these younger workers have seen the downsizing of the corporate work force, they are less likely to put their jobs before their other interests; that is, they are more loyal to themselves and their well-being than they are to the corporation.

The values people hold as workers and customers reflect other changes as well. Today's consumers demand more quality at a "fair" cost from the businesses that provide them products and ser-vices. While workers as consumers are more de-manding of others, they are also less willing to devote themselves entirely to their jobs, to their employer, or to consumerism. Against the back-drop of massive layoffs through restructuring, the reality of multiple careers over the life of a worker, and the changed mores of society regarding achievement, success, and consumption, people, especially in the U.S., are saying very strongly through their behaviors that there is more to their lives than their jobs and consumption. A recent Bozell Worldwide 1996 survey supports this obser-vation, finding that the three factors most fre-quently cited throughout the world as the top priorities in a person's life are family life, spir-itual life, and good health. Material possessions were among the factors cited the least as top pri-orities.

As corporations try to adjust to global compe-tition—through acquisitions, mergers, "new" or-ganizational structures, re-engineering, selling off or closing unprofitable operations, generally cut-ting its work force and leveling the organization—the level of frustration among workers world-wide is increasing, and for ample reason. Ewart Wooldridge notes:

> As we put our organizations through processes of downsizing, delayering and derecognition, the simul-taneous exhortations for teamwork, empowerment, partnership and vision come across as somewhat hypocritical. What was actually happening for so many employees was a widening gap between the rhetoric of empowerment and the increasingly inse-cure and unrewarding reality of work.[1]

In the United States at a time when large num-bers of baby boomers, many very well educated, are coming of age the number of opportunities at the middle and top of corporate America is decreas-ing relative to the numbers aspiring to achieve those levels. These factors have naturally created not only significant moral issues in corporate America in terms of who gets promotions and opportunities but also a sense of both frustration and uncertainty for the employees. Along with ineffective management of human resources, these

factors are translated increasingly in the minds of employees that they are not getting their well-deserved opportunities because of their race and/or gender and other subjective criteria, rather than to the simple increase in the numbers of competent, qualified people. This situation is intensified by corporate America's inability to recognize and ad-mit that, regardless of race and or gender, it does a poor job in selecting and equipping managers with skills to manage people effectively. It is also diffi-cult for them to admit that they do not have the resources to reward all who are deserving or who believe they are deserving.

As alluded to earlier, there are two other factors that have created the problems of integrating peo-ple of color, women, and different ethnic groups into the workplace and to expand effectively the ability of organizations to attract and retain diverse customers. First is the basic characteristics of bu-reaucracies, and second is the fact that we as human beings have some natural programing that can be either a plus or a minus in being effective in the new competitive diverse environment. In addition, to varying degrees we have our own subjectivity and, at times, unhealthy psychological issues to address.

In its heyday, for most of the early and mid-twentieth century, the bureaucratic, hierarchical structure was a significant improvement over the old nepotistic and feudal, federal systems. One could argue that were it not for the bureaucratic organizational structure, the Industrial Revolution would not have occurred.

The ideal bureaucracy was a hierarchical struc-ture with a rational division of labor or activities, all governed or ruled by a set of general policies and procedures, administered by objectively evalu-ated, recruited, and promoted (not elected) people who were loyal to the organization and who had a clear understanding of both their limited, specific role and organizational values and culture. These roles held that bureaucratic authority resided in the office, not the person, and that a strict separation should exist between professional and personal life. This supposedly led to the smooth functioning of the organization.

In the more highly educated, competitive, di-verse work environment that must form high-performance teams based on trust and respect in order to create timely, quality products and services for increasingly diverse and demanding customers, the old hierarchical bureaucratic structure is not the most effective organizational form. Our data indicate, in general, the old bureaucratic structure pits people against one another competitively and eventually condemns all but a few to failure. This structure discourages cooperation and risk taking and nurtures empire building, self-centeredness, inertia, and conformity. It breeds fear, distrust, dishonesty, and intolerance of different race and gender groups. It is slow, inefficient, and generally reacts too slowly to the changing needs of customers. This structure is much more internally focused than externally focused.

Put another way, most bureaucracies, in general, employ people in the service of their own needs and not the customer's needs. They are inherently unfair. Despite their promise to reward equitably all those who are deserving, bureaucracies have too few advancement opportunities, limited resources, out-of-date and/or inflexible reward systems, and too many ineffective managers to keep this promise to all employees. As noted earlier, this problem of rewarding employees will increase greatly in the next two decades as millions of baby boomers compete for limited opportunities, the work force becomes increasingly diverse, and downsizing and flattening the organization continues. In addition, as U.S. companies become more global, developing reward and recognition systems which are culturally specific is not one of the old bureaucratic values. In these structures, the individual manager is more concerned about his/her operations and his/her successes, rather than the organization as a whole and the success of the organization in meeting the desires and needs of customers.

Tied into the inherent shortcomings of bureaucracies are the shortcomings we have as human beings. Part of the problems of racism, sexism, ethnocentrism, and other human problems in organizations is that we, as human beings, have over tens of thousands of years developed certain brain functions and thought processes that served us well in the Stone Age but are very limiting in modern civilization. For example, in order to have survived in the Stone Age our minds developed a way of thinking which allowed us to make decisions in milliseconds in order to sense danger. As our civilization emerged, our minds still make decisions in milliseconds about all things, whether they are dangerous to us or not. In milliseconds we make decisions on whether we feel positive or negative about something. Thus, in the context of people, our minds make evaluative decisions about someone in milliseconds and many of these decision are based on our feeling on stereotypes about a person's race and gender. Most of us would deny this, but the realities are that, consciously or subconsciously, our mind does this to us.

Another factor that has emerged in our brain is that we as humans can't process all the millions of pieces of information in a timely, effective manner without stereotyping; that is, grouping information into some "logical" manner—stereotyping—is as natural as sleeping. Throughout the history of humankind various groups of people have developed stereotypes about one another which greatly hindered the trust and respect necessary to be truly competitive in the global economy.

Neither of these mind functions is dangerous as long as we understand not only how our mind works but also that we have capabilities to combat our tendencies to make snap judgments based on stereotypes.

While the previous comments apply to all humans, the following comments are related to us as individuals. Each of us has his or her own unique programing and personality that, in most cases, has been influenced, to some extent by socialization, by families, by societal institutions. Each of us through his or her own genetic makeup and socialization develops some human shortcomings, more specifically, despite the conviction that we are, on the whole, rational, objective people, we must acknowledge that human beings, as a species, are not objective or rational all the time. On the contrary, the operative question is, "To what degree, as individuals and groups, are we aware of our subjectivity and irrationality?" People who recognize their issues and work on them are healthier than the majority who have never taken a hard look at themselves. People who recognize their shortcomings and work on them are much more likely to operate effectively working with different races and genders and dealing with diverse markets. Managing relationships is a tough job because it demands high levels of intellectual and emotional development. Every relationship—personal, business, and otherwise—involves interpersonal problems where there is a mismatch between our expectations and the behavior and feelings of those we are interacting with. Interpersonal problems are part of the intrinsic nature of relationships. Problems arise in relationships all the time; if they didn't, our jobs would be simple—or simply unnecessary. In the past 34 years, many of the interpersonal problems between people of different races and/or genders have been attributed to these differences whether or not they are the cause of the problem.

The picture isn't very good, as alluded to earlier, as our studies over the past twenty-five years have painted a negative picture of corporate America for many of its employees. Overall these employees believe it to be unimaginative and authoritarian, characterized by untrustworthy leadership that create a debilitating environment not conducive to risk taking, plagued by a plethora of politicking and insufficient opportunities, and lacking in proper recognition and rewards. In an increasingly diverse domestic and international work environment, because of the previously discussed views and attitudes, these employees perceive a great deal of discrimination based on subjective factors such a race, gender, and ethnicity. Employees who feel the way these employees feel will have a very difficult time building trust and respect, especially with people who are different than they are, which is the crucial ingredient in forming high-performance teams and long-term effective customer and stakeholders relations.

Over the past twenty-five years of our research in the United States, when employees responded to questions about career planning, performance appraisal, reward and recognition, being valued, supervisors, teams, leadership, and perceptions of the company, there have been few significant differences by race and gender; however, there are many differences by level in the organization or the particular department in which one works. When it comes to questions about affirmative action and equal employment opportunity and the treatment of women, people of color, white males, gays and lesbians, and people with disabilities in the company and/or organization, there are key significant differences by race/gender or the other key relevant demographic variables. This reinforces our view that a holistic approach must be taken to solve the issue of racism and sexism in corporations—it is intricately tied to many other factors and processes in corporations. There is not one solution but multiple solutions. The biggest conundrum for corporate America is to determine what the real issues are with regard to snail-paced progress by employees of color at the middle and upper ranks of corporate America and white women's decent progress at lower and middle but not so decent progress at the upper and top levels. What are the real issues for corporate America's failures and inabilities to penetrate and capitalize on diverse markets especially those based on race and gender?

## C. The Holistic Approach: The Only Solution to Race and Gender Issues

We believe the term diversity should be replaced. One word cannot describe a strategic, ongoing business strategy. As a word and conceptually, diversity is very "loaded" just like affirmative action. It compels a variety of reactions and it means many different things to different people. The term itself has grown beyond its original meaning, and it is very difficult to talk about a concept which currently has no clear definition.

Let's start with our working definition of *constituent capitalization:*

Constituency capitalization is a business strategy where the broad spectrum of diverse people's skills, perspectives and styles are recognized, appreciated, valued, respected and integrated into a post-bureaucratic organizational structure and into new organizational operating practices in order to maximize marketplace options throughout the world.

We advocate the model of constituent capitalization, which takes account of the importance of results, how those results are achieved, and who and what influence these results. At the same time, it more clearly describes the organizational structures and environments necessary for organizational successes. Let's look at a step approach to becoming the best employer and the best place to do business.

*Step 6*. A post-bureaucratic organization where the environment is based on trust and respect. Where diverse employees are valued and integrated into all aspects of an organization's work. Work is enhanced by rethinking tasks and redefining missions, strategies, business practices, culture, markets, and products to address the needs of increasingly diverse customers and stakeholders.

*Step 5*. Redefine the organizational culture by creating operating practices that enable the integration of a broad range of viewpoints leading to the redefinition of how work gets done and how diverse markets are approached.

*Step 4*. Understand that diversity is a business imperative and a continuous learning process.

*Step 3*. Identify current corporate culture and how the culture enables changes and creates barriers.

*Step 2*. Define and implement affirmative actions that enhance compliance with EEO laws.

*Step 1*. Comply with EEO laws.

Notice that the above steps are focused on not only changing structure but also behavior. Implementing each of these steps will enable organizations to incorporate (to unite with another body, forming a new unit) rather than to try and assimilate (to bring to conformity or agreement with something else, to digest, to absorb and convert into a homogeneous part of the absorbing agent—complete adoption) by retrofitting diverse people's perspectives and styles into old bureaucratic structures. What we are suggesting is that both the structure and the environment must be changed in order to utilize fully all employees and to be competitive in the new global environment by promoting value-based services to diverse customers and

stakeholders. In the past, the assimilation process in the United States was easier because there was a workforce that was much more similar in age, race, gender, and education. In addition, there were mass markets and mass production. It is no wonder that assimilation became the norm. Today, mass markets and mass production have been replaced with diverse, international markets that require products to meet the needs of diverse cultures, and also with niche markets and niche production lines. It is through the efforts of harnessing the hearts, minds, competencies, and commitment of all employees, domestically and internationally, that the competitive advantage will be achieved in domestic and international markets.

Specifically, constituent capitalization is an organizational strategy tied to the business strategy for managing organizational change, improving productivity, and increasing market share. Constituent capitalization is a crucial strategy that has direct linkage with team building and quality efforts. The establishment of trust and respect among team members is critical to this strategy. Trust and respect also needs to be established among other constituencies, including customers and those who have been traditionally defined as stakeholders. This latter group includes, but is not limited to, government regulators, public agencies, shareholders, and residents of communities in which an organization is located or upon which it has some impact. In short, stakeholders—in the broadest sense and as used in our model—include any individual or group affected by, and impacting upon, an organization. At the core of this strategy is the belief that understanding, appreciating, respecting, and valuing differences of employees, customers, and stakeholders will lead to more varied ways of looking at corporate problems, more creative ways of solving these problems, more flexibility in responding to change, stronger commitment as well as better cooperation within heterogeneous work teams, and better-quality products and services.

Constituent capitalization recognizes the importance of an organization's constituency base to its future successes. This base includes employees, customers, and those individuals and groups traditionally labeled stakeholders. However, recognizing that all of the individuals and groups with which an organization deals are stakeholders, our focus broadens as our model does not predispose us to addressing singularly the needs of the workforce.

Furthermore, fundamental to the constituent capitalization model is the notion that employees, customers, and stakeholders are groups that are not mutually exclusive. For example, we may be employees of an organization and customers of it as well. We, too, are stakeholders and frequently customers. So, as the groups of employee, customer, and stakeholder are not always comprised of clearly identifiable pieces (as membership boundaries in these groups overlap), it is critical that we view all individuals that have an impact on our business as stakeholders.

As a result a successful business strategy will recognize the interrelatedness of these groups and will seek to ensure the success of the totality. The successful strategy will, for example, seek to improve an organization's bottom line; better serve its customers; enrich, reward, and motivate its employees; and better meet the needs of its various stakeholders.

It is important to note that this strategy is sequential. In other words, the organization must begin by focusing on its relations within and among the workforce. Success in this area is the necessary building block to success with customers and other stakeholders. If organizations cannot build trust and respect based on understanding, valuing, and appreciating the differences among employees, they will be unable to build trust and respect among their customers and stakeholders who mirror these same differences.

The constituent capitalization model emphasizes the importance of both output and results in ways that diversity does not. At the same time, this model emphasizes that the way we try to achieve those results—the process that we use—is equally important. In recognition of this, this book will focus on how and why we do things as much as it focuses on what we want to achieve.

We will, however, continue to use the word diversity in its original meaning, outside of the context of the constituent capitalization model, throughout this book. The term diversity has a very rich meaning and remains recognizable to a good many of us, and so we will utilize it in its literal sense to mean something characterized by variety and heterogeneity.

## D. Conclusion

In order for corporate America to go beyond the rhetoric of race and gender, it must face several key realities. It must face the reality that racism and sexism still exist and develop strategies to deal with them. These strategies must be holistic and focus on employees, customers, and stakeholders. In the remaining chapters of this book, we will outline our strategy and explore, in detail, each of its components.

### Note

1. Wooldridge, Ewart. "Time to stand Maslow's research on its head?" *People Management,* December 21, 1995, p. 17.

# 39

# Leading and Empowering Diverse Followers

LYNN R. OFFERMANN

In examining recurrent themes and challenges for leadership research and practice in the years ahead, our study group, along with the other Kellogg study groups, has consistently identified diversity issues as critical to understanding the dynamics of leadership and followership. As organizations change and become more demographically and internationally diverse, and as relationships between individuals within and across organizations become ever more critical in the realization of organizational success, diversity of followership becomes increasingly important as a leadership issue. Although it has always been naive to assume that followers are a monolithic block of people with similar needs and expectations, that assumption is becoming increasingly foolhardy. Perhaps now that organizations are faced with the obvious challenge of managing diversity—diversity that is visible, undeniable, and increasing—the importance of considering follower perspectives in the study of leadership will receive greater attention. This chapter will examine the challenges of fol-

lower diversity for the process of leadership, and in keeping with our theme of empowerment, particularly focus on the challenge of empowering a diverse workforce.

**What Hasn't Worked**

It's interesting that organizations that never really mastered affirmative action and equal opportunity are now scrambling to "manage diversity." In the U.S., despite the protestations of those working in the field, the term "managing diversity" has often been associated with concerns about women and major minority groups—traditionally African-Americans, Hispanics, Asians, and native Americans. This focus not only limits consideration of diversity to particular groups but obscures the reality that differences within any categorical group often exceed differences between groups. In this chapter, my comments were designed to be interpreted in the larger context of individual differences, diversity that certainly includes differences

---

SOURCE: From a paper prepared for the Kellogg Leadership Studies Project. Reprinted with permission of the author.

in all of those categories just mentioned but extends beyond to encompass the wide individual variations in temperaments, age, personal preferences, knowledge, national origins, life experiences, capabilities, and worldviews.

Prior attempts to force diverse groups to meld into a homogeneous organization were never totally successful, because they assumed that individuals wanted to meld into the traditional mainstream (and thereby risk losing previous identifications) and that melding was the most desirable end-point. More recently, an awareness of the desire of people to maintain ties with their origins and with themselves as unique individuals, and the virtues of bringing different perspectives to the table in terms of productivity, has questioned these assumptions. For example, numerous studies examining a variety of forms of diversity (including differences in personality, attitudes, and gender), have now supported the conclusion that diversity in teams improves performance in terms of decision quality (see Jackson, May, & Whitney, 1995, for a review). Why push for homogeneity when heterogeneity offers greater organizational promise?

Unfortunately, U.S. companies that have actively recruited women and minorities in the recent past have often been discouraged to find that those hired have not progressed as far in the organization as was hoped. For example, both Corning and Digital Equipment have found it easier to recruit minorities and women than it is to keep them (Dreyfuss, 1990). According to Thomas (1990), many companies faced with this pattern blamed selection strategies for failing to bring in the "right" people, and proceeded to try again—again searching for women and minorities to bring into the pipeline, only to fail again. What they failed to realize is that diverse recruitment alone is not enough to achieve diversity at all levels in an organization. One suspects that given this difficulty in diversifying in even these obviously observable ways, that other less visible forms of diversity are likewise being underrepresented at many levels. What is needed is a radical reassessment of how to change organizations to make them more hospitable to the variety of individuals who populate them.

The stakes involved in effectively managing diversity are high: recent work has shown that organizations receiving awards for exemplary affirmative action programs (one indicator of attempts at good diversity management) have had significant positive changes in their stock prices associated with award announcement, whereas announcements of admission of discriminatory practices were related to significant negative changes in organizational stock prices (Wright, Ferris, Hiller, & Kroll, 1995). In order to realize the promise of diversity, the goal can no longer be assimilation but the leadership and affirmation of unassimilated diversity. Achieving this goal will require the skill, support, and implementation of those in leadership roles.

## Examining Leadership With a Diverse Followership

Most existing models of leadership have been developed and validated with white, male U.S. managers working with white, male U.S. followers. What is needed is a closer examination of what happens to the process of leadership in the more diverse environments that typify today's organizations, and which will even more strongly typify tomorrow's. While work on diversity in the leadership ranks through studies of women and minority managers has been ongoing for some years now, less attention has been paid to the impact of diversification in the follower ranks on the process of leadership. Yet work by Tsui and O'Reilly (1989) suggests that the demographic composition of superior subordinate dyads does affect important outcome variables. Specifically, these authors found that increasing disparity between superior-subordinate demographic characteristics was associated with lower superior ratings of subordinate effectiveness, less attraction toward subordinates, and the experience of greater role ambiguity by subordinates. These findings suggest that leaders may need to make concerted efforts to overcome tendencies to work more effectively with demographically similar subordinates, and to learn to utilize the talents of individuals from dissimilar backgrounds more effectively.

## Empowering a Diverse Followership

In keeping with the empowerment theme running through the papers in this volume, the following comments focus on concerns about empowerment strategies in diverse, multicultural organizational environments. It should be acknowledged up front that research in the area of empowerment has been hampered by the lack of an agreed definition of what empowerment really entails. In work organizations, the term empowerment incorporates strategies ranging from increasing worker participation in decisions surrounding their immediate job tasks (job content) up to and including full self-management both of job content and job context (Ford & Fottler, 1995).

Although there are many possible forms of empowerment, all essentially involve the passing of some degree of responsibility from those traditionally called "leaders" to those traditionally called "followers." In a very real sense, full empowerment distributes leadership throughout the organization, although those in different positions will be accountable for different leadership functions. Leaders need not fear for loss of work in an empowered system, but rather their work will be vastly different—and, I believe, far more challenging. For any organization, the "best" empowerment strategy will depend on the particular situation, with one of the determining factors being the readiness of staff for empowerment. Diversity in followership is likely to be one important factor in determining readiness.

## Cultural Influence on Readiness for Empowerment

The desire of many U.S. workers for greater challenge and autonomy can be fulfilled through leader behavior empowering followers to participate more actively in making decisions. Even among U.S. workers, however, there are some people—leaders and followers alike—who resist the change to greater empowerment. According to Byhan (see Kinni, 1994), about 20% of the workforce have been waiting anxiously for empowerment, most of the rest will move slowly into that opportunity when offered, and 5% will be completely unable to make the transition to an empowered system. Although the precise accuracy of these numbers may be questioned, many managers have been surprised and stymied by the reluctance of large numbers of staff to take more responsibility when offered. This reluctance suggests that even in the U.S. most staff perceive the introduction of empowerment with at least initial skepticism.

If there is skepticism in the U.S. workforce to the move to empowerment, consider the difficulties others from different backgrounds may face. The U.S. at least has a cultural tradition that is consistent in many ways with empowerment. Using Hofstede's (1980) classic dimensions of culture, the U.S. is low in power distance, where power distance is defined as the extent to which it is accepted by both those low and high in power that power should be distributed unequally. Unlike the U.S., high power distance societies accept unequal distribution of power as the norm, and subordinates expect to be told what to do more than those in lower power distance societies. For both leaders and followers from high power distance societies, empowering followers to perform functions traditionally associated with leadership is at best strange and at worst unfathomable.

In a similar vein, the U.S. is low on the cultural dimension of uncertainty avoidance, where uncertainty avoidance is defined as the extent to which people feel threatened by ambiguous situations and seek clear rules, norms, and procedures to guide them. The low uncertainty avoidance typified by the U.S. is compatible with a greater willingness to take initiative and tolerate risks, both of which are consistent with the philosophy underlying empowerment. Even the high U.S. value on individualism may be of value in embracing empowerment, in that empowerment can increase freedom and challenge in jobs, encourage individual initiative, and self-leadership. However, in situations where the chosen empowerment strategy takes the form of promoting the use of teams, as is often the case, strong U.S. individualism may also be a detriment.

Based on these cultural value differences, there needs to be an awareness that some cultures have different expectations that may impede attempts at follower empowerment. Some multinational corporations are finding that an employee empowerment strategy that works in one country may not work in another. For example, Alpander (1991) found within a single multinational corporation that a similar amount of control over work and the work environment fulfilled Japanese workers more than their Australian and German counterparts. Just as there are different types of empowerment strategies, there will be different responses to any given strategy in different follower groups.

Cultural views of what is "good leadership" may also vary (Bass, 1990). By cultural tradition, some followers expect leader authoritarianism, and see attempts at empowerment as a dereliction of leader duty and responsibility, or a sign of weak leadership. One can gain some appreciation of this with the realization that the English word "leader" does not translate directly into such languages as French, Spanish, or German, where available words such as *le meneur, el jefe,* or *der Führer* tend to connote only leadership that is directive (Graumann, 1986). Small wonder that individuals from authoritarian cultures may view the delegation of responsibility typically advocated as empowering with great skepticism. Such attitudes need to be respected and carefully managed. Only when the leader is viewed with trust are such attitudes likely to be overcome, and trust itself may not come easily when cultural differences are large.

Although research in the area is scarce, there is some evidence that the leader's own background may influence his or her willingness to be empowering as well. Offermann and Hellmann (1995) present evidence from a multinational organization using Hofstede's cultural dimensions that leaders from high uncertainty avoidance societies were viewed by their subordinates as controlling more and delegating less, two behaviors that are clearly related to many empowerment efforts. In addition, such leaders were also rated as less approachable by their staffs, which might make communication and support to followers transitioning to more empowered work more difficult. As cultural differences express themselves in leadership behavior as was found, they likely will also relate to leader reactions to empowering others. Based on our work, we would predict that regardless of their origin, leaders with individual values reflecting high power distance and high uncertainty avoid-

ance will be most resistant to sharing power through workplace empowerment initiatives.

## Empowerment Through Participation

One of the most common ways organizations attempt to empower staff is through increasing worker participation, particularly in decision making. Yet taken in broad international context, cultural background may well affect the acceptability of participation as an organizational norm. Participation as a concept is not value free. Erez and Earley (1993) argue that from a political perspective, encouraging broad worker participation serves to increase workers' control over production and convey the belief that participatory democracy is a social value. They note that it was ideological differences between the U.S. and Europe that drove U.S. organizations to voluntarily adopt more participative approaches, while in Europe compulsory participation was advocated through legislation. Clearly, other countries with less democratic traditions may have far greater difficulty with the concept of worker participation in any form or by any means.

In addition to political considerations, the methods used to enhance empowerment through participation may themselves be culturally insensitive. For example, the technique of brainstorming, where individuals are encouraged to throw out all sorts of ideas without evaluation or consideration of quality and feasibility, makes some people uncomfortable. For some, concerns about evaluation in a public forum may be insurmountable, in these cases, electronic brainstorming may be helpful to reduce evaluation apprehension (Gallupe, Bastianutti, & Cooper, 1991) and to allow individuals to raise issues privately and anonymously. Although a fairly new technique, electronic brainstorming has now been used in a variety of cross-cultural situations. For example, the World Bank has successfully used these methods in both Malawi and Zimbabwe to reach out and bring diverse individuals from throughout society at large (including representatives from the clergy, trade unions, nongovernmental organizations, and tribal groups) into the dialogue surrounding country development priorities.

Other, more reserved, people may simply need time for quiet reflection about issues before being able to participate actively. The manager who distributes a clear agenda well in advance of meetings, with topics for discussion listed, can help such people to join the discussion process—and possibly help improve the quality and thoughtfulness of the discussion at the same time.

## Overcoming Follower Resistance to Empowerment Via Three "T"s: Time, Trust, and Training

How can a leader empower staff with different styles, temperaments, and backgrounds? I would like to propose three "T"s to answer this question: time, trust, and training.

First, be willing to spend the *time*. Expect initial skepticism from most staff. Many experienced staff will assume that empowerment is now the "flavor of the month" and will fade over time. Only the lasting leadership commitment to developing leadership in followers will convince people that empowerment is now a regular on the menu. Viewing empowerment as a perceptual frame of mind rather than a technique (Russ, 1995) may help differentiate it from the numerous other organizational initiatives to which staff have been exposed. This frame of mind represents nothing less than a fundamental shift in attitudes toward how work should be accomplished.

Movement toward empowerment can be gradual, allowing both managers and staff to develop greater comfort with shared decision making, and allowing staff to develop greater skills in participating in areas which were previously not open to them. Changing a lifetime belief in the appropriateness of more directive models of leader-follower interaction requires time for exploration of new behaviors and their consequences. In Ford and Fottler's (1995) model, this might take the form of beginning by increasing worker involvement first in the decisions surrounding how they do the work given them by others, then into more autonomous work groups with some responsibility for both determining what work should be done as well as how to do it, and finally into full self-management of both the work itself and the work context.

Although a progressive sequence toward full empowerment can be identified, there can be no set time frame to accomplish this transition, if indeed the full sequence is desired. Potential gains from employee empowerment are thought to be most notable in organizational environments where employees have high needs for growth, social needs, and good interpersonal skills, and where the nature of the business is such that customized service is desirable, relationships are long term, technology is complex, and the environment is unpredictable (Ford & Fottler, 1995). Motivational gains may begin to be realized from the first steps toward empowerment, and these gains can then be used to develop empowerment further. Where the effort begins and ends, as well as how long it takes, will vary tremendously from organization to organization, and even between departments or units within any given organization.

Incremental empowerment also helps in the development of my second "T": *trust*. In addition to the initial skepticism discussed above centering around management commitment to true empowerment is the very real fear of the accountability that comes with greater decision-making responsibility. People need to learn through new experiences that they work in an environment that supports them—*all* of them—as they take new risks and expand their domain of influence. The role of organizational leaders is critical, in the development of this trust. Failure of leaders in this process to assume their own new roles of coach, facilitator, external coordinator, and vision developer/communicator will quickly doom the process. Individual follower differences will require flexible leadership to reach out to people in different ways, as each requires.

Kouzes and Posner (1995) argue that the leader's behavior is more than that of anyone else in determining the level of trust that exists within a group and that when leaders do not show trust in followers—by monitoring them too closely, or failing to delegate significant work, for example—followers will not trust them either. Lack of follower trust in a leader in turn can have important ramifications. For example, a classic study by Likert and Willits (1940) showed that the primary difference between high- and low-performing salespeople was the degree of trust they had in their immediate supervisor. If leaders want to reap the benefits of empowered staff, they must be willing to trust in their staff to get the job done. This can be difficult for leaders when the leaders perceive that their own job success will be measured by the success of others over whom they have little control. To develop a sound trust in staff, leaders must actively help develop staff capabilities to the point that the leader can delegate with comfort.

Which brings me to my final "T," *training.* It is totally unreasonable to expect leaders or followers to make the transition to an empowered workforce without extensive training support. Much has been made in the literature about the so-called learning organization (e.g., Senge, 1990), but beyond the fad and folderol, the truth remains that without continuous access to self-development empowerment will flounder. In his contribution to this volume, my colleague Peter Vaill discusses the major learning challenges for leaders in empowered systems. Learning for empowerment is a challenge for everyone, leaders and led, and training is one method to provide a context in which to learn. Such training needs to go beyond areas of technical expertise to emphasize the development of strong interpersonal and communication skills, including teaming, problem solving, and decision making.

Training may also be needed to explore with staff the changing nature of the psychological contract between today's employers and employees (e.g., Rousseau, 1995), contracts which tend to place increasing responsibility on individual staff to develop themselves and see themselves more proactively as independent contractors rather than indentured servants. These changing contracts put leader-follower relationships in a totally new light and encourage a shift from employee dependence on formal leaders as authority structures to employee empowerment as organizationally coordinated independent contributors. Again, these changes may be more acceptable to some than to others. For staff with high security needs, low risk tolerance, or strong economic dependency on their job, coupled with low confidence of fungibility, these changes may be highly unpalatable. For those accustomed to viewing organizations and their leaders as parental figures who should take care of

staff in return for staff effort and cooperation, these "new deals" may be perceived as very bad deals indeed. Leaders must find ways to extend basic security to staff through the development of transferable, cutting-edge skill sets that keep an employee employable.

The time factor enters here as well. The common training areas to support empowerment mentioned above are not areas amenable to a quick fix. All too often employee training is provided up front in the initiation of changes toward empowerment, but follow-up support is scant. Yet for changes to become firmly enmeshed in the organization, staff at all levels need continuing access to assistance in their learning process. All are learning to assume different leadership roles and relationships. This assistance may be more concentrated at first, and then scheduled at just-in-time intervals determined by the work program itself. This support may include formal training courses, but should ideally extend into the less formal but often more powerful learning experience provided by mentoring, coaching, and process facilitation. Here, too, developmental experiences should be offered in a variety of formats to accommodate individual differences in learning styles.

### Conclusion

Future leadership models need to be able to incorporate diversity in both leaders and the led if we are to understand leadership dynamics into the next century. The needs of a diverse followership demand attention in the enactment of leadership. In the case of the movement toward an empowered followership, cultural traditions may influence success. Looking ahead, it may be critical to entertain the question as to whether the entire idea of empowerment is too distinctly Western to be successful in diverse environments, or, if not, what issues and implications need to be considered in implementing empowerment with diverse followers. Some suggested considerations have been raised here, and await research validation and expansion.

The successful implementation of empowerment throughout the fabric of an organization is nothing less than the development of leadership throughout the organization at all levels. To the extent that some people have stronger expectations that leadership rests at some organizational levels and not others, the change to empowered systems will be more difficult. Some of the more basic, core management functions of task and method selection will continue to move downward to front-line employees, who will need time and training to discharge their new responsibilities effectively. Increasingly as empowerment takes hold, other functions, including recruitment and evaluation of team members will follow, until full self-management is evident. In the process, the successful organization will be developing the kind of trust among employees that truly frees people to give their best.

And what work is left for the most senior leaders in this empowered landscape? Nothing short of determining the long-term direction, strategy, and vision for the organization and ensuring that the values which the organization maintains are driven down and throughout the organization. In this manner, everyone in the organization knows the criteria against which decisions will be measured, and the standards under which all are expected to labor.

## References

Alpander, G. G. (1991). Developing managers' ability to empower employees. *Journal of Management Development, 10,* 13-24.

Bass, B. M. (1990). *Bass and Stogdill's handbook of leadership: Theory, research, and managerial application* (3rd ed.). New York: Free Press.

Dreyfuss, J. (1990). Get ready for the new workforce. *Fortune, 121,* 165-181.

Erez, M., & Earley, P. C. (1993). *Culture, self-identity and work.* New York: Oxford University Press.

Ford, R. C., & Fottler, M. D. (1995). Empowerment: A matter of degree. *Academy of Management Executive, 9,* 21-29.

Gallupe, R. B., Bastianutti, L., & Cooper, W. H. (1991). Unblocking brainstorms. *Journal of Applied Psychology, 76,* 137-142.

Graumann, C. F. (1986). Changing conceptions of leadership: An introduction. In C. F. Graumann & F. Moscovici (Eds.), *Changing conceptions of leadership.* New York: Springer-Verlag.

Hofstede, G. (1980). *Culture's consequences: International differences in work-related values.* Beverly Hills, CA: Sage.

Jackson, S. E., May, K. E., & Whitney, K. (1995). Understanding the dynamics of diversity in decisionmaking teams. In R. Guzzo & E. Salas (Eds.), *Team effectiveness and decisionmaking in organizations* (pp 204-261). San Francisco: Jossey-Bass.

Kinni, T. B. (1994, September 19). The empowered workforce. *Industry Week,* pp. 37-41.

Kouzes, J. M., & Posner, B. M. (1995). *The leadership challenge: How to keep getting extraordinary things done in organizations.* San Francisco: Jossey-Bass.

Likert, R., & Willits, J. M. (1940). *Morale and agency management.* Hartford, CT: Life Insurance Agency Management Association.

Offermann, L. R., & Hellmann, P. S. (1995, May). *Culture's consequences for leadership behavior: National values in action.* Paper presented at the meeting of the Society for Industrial and Organizational Psychology, Orlando, FL.

Rousseau, D. M. (1995). *Psychological contracts in organizations: Understanding written and unwritten agreements.* Thousand Oaks, CA: Sage.

Russ, D. (1995). Executive commentary. *Academy of Management Executive, 9,* 29-30.

Senge, P. M. (1990). *The fifth discipline: The art and practice of the learning organization.* New York: Doubleday.

Thomas, R. R., Jr. (1990, March-April). From affirmative action to affirming diversity. *Harvard Business Review,* pp. 107-117.

Tsui, A. S., & O'Reilly, C. A., III (1989). Beyond simple demographic effects: The importance of relational demography in superior-subordinate dyads. *Academy of Management Journal, 32,* 402-423.

Wright, P., Ferris, S. P., Hiller, J. S., & Kroll, M. (1995). Competitiveness through management of diversity: Effects on stock price valuation. *Academy of Management Journal, 38,* 272-287.

# *VIII*

# *Leadership and Capacity Building in Organizations*

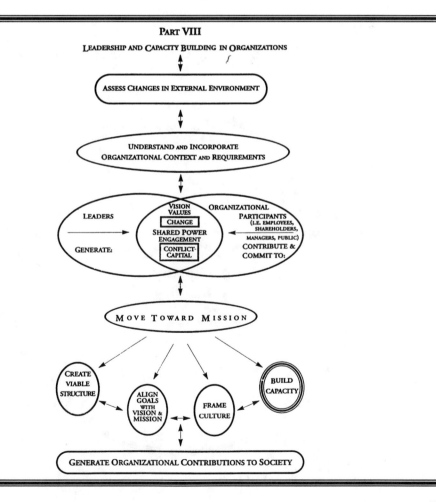

**PART VIII**

**LEADERSHIP AND CAPACITY BUILDING IN ORGANIZATIONS**

**ASSESS CHANGES IN EXTERNAL ENVIRONMENT**

**UNDERSTAND AND INCORPORATE ORGANIZATIONAL CONTEXT AND REQUIREMENTS**

**LEADERS**

**GENERATE:**

**VISION VALUES**

**CHANGE**

**SHARED POWER ENGAGEMENT**

**CONFLICT-CAPITAL**

**ORGANIZATIONAL PARTICIPANTS** (I.E. EMPLOYEES, SHAREHOLDERS, MANAGERS, PUBLIC) **CONTRIBUTE & COMMIT TO:**

**MOVE TOWARD MISSION**

**CREATE VIABLE STRUCTURE**

**ALIGN GOALS WITH VISION & MISSION**

**FRAME CULTURE**

**BUILD CAPACITY**

**GENERATE ORGANIZATIONAL CONTRIBUTIONS TO SOCIETY**

Part VIII focuses on individual and organizational capacity building through development of personal mastery, organizational change, conflict capital, and recognition of contributions. Individual capacity building involves assisting organizational participants to development or enhance self-knowledge, self-esteem, physical and emotional wellness, and professional or job competencies and skills. Organizational capacity building entails team learning, development of integrative and holistic thinking, engagement in organizational change, innovation, and renewal. Both individual and organizational capacity building are critical contributors to the development of new era organizations.

Figure VIII.1 illustrates the interrelatedness among essential elements in the development of human capacity in organizations. The chapters in this section contribute to the understanding of each of the linked components.

## CAPACITY BUILDING IN ORGANIZATIONS

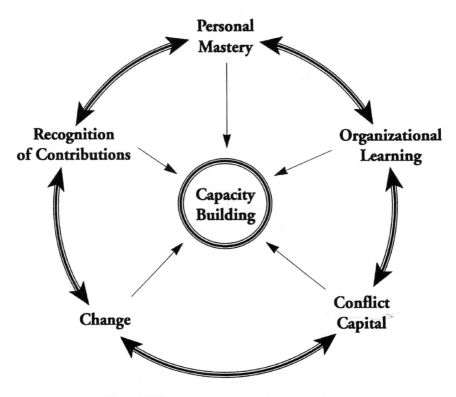

**Figure VIII.1.** Capacity Building in Organizations

## Building Individual Capacity

Peter Senge indicates that individuals build their capacity through *personal mastery*. He defines personal mastery as "approaching one's life as a creative work, living life from a creative as opposed to reactive viewpoint." It engages individuals in a continual process of clarifying what is important to them and learning how to see current reality more clearly. This process and practice facilitates lifelong generative learning that expands our ability to produce the results that we want in life. Personal mastery entails developing personal vision, holding creative tension (the gap between vision and current reality), committing to truth telling in dealing with structural conflict, and using the subconscious through focused visioning. The responsibility of leadership in organizations is to create and sustain an environment that encourages personal mastery and to model the practice.

Affirming Senge's assertion that organizational learning can only occur through individuals who learn, Gouillart and Kelly advocate the development of individual learning as a means of concurrently unleashing individual potential and organizational vitality. They advise that architects of the organization need to assume responsibility for fostering individual learning through

- Committing to the development of the individual;
- Creating mentor-guided, life-forming projects for high-caliber individuals;
- Identifying critical skills and designing an education strategy; and
- Balancing the supply of and demand for skills inside the corporation.

## Building Organizational Capacity

Change is an inherent component of capacity building in organizations and is a fundamental component of the organization's larger environment. John Kotter's examination of successful organizational change revealed that the most important components are, first, using a multistep process that creates power and motivation and, second, effectively employing high-quality leadership. His research revealed an eight-stage process for successful change: (a) establishing a sense of urgency, (b) creating the guiding coalition, (c) developing a vision and strategy, (d) communicating the change vision, (e) empowering broad-based action, (f) generating short-term wins, (g) consolidating gains and producing more change, and (h) anchoring new approaches in the culture. In this change process, leadership helps organizational participants to define what the future should look like, aligns people with that vision and inspires them to make it happen.

Inevitably, the attainment of learning and change in organizations depends on the ability of leaders and participants to effectively use the conflict that arises from differences. The beneficial outcome of such processes can be termed conflict capital—a substantially enhanced outcome that results from the effort to bring about change among leaders and participants with diverse perspectives.[1] Barbara Gray believes that *collaboration* is an effective process for bringing together all the stakeholders in a process that involves conflict. Collaboration is defined as "a process through which parties who see different aspects of a problem can constructively explore their differences and search for solutions that go beyond their own limited vision of what is possible." The opportunity for collaboration is present when the stakeholders recognize the potential advantages of working together for a mutual purpose. Like organizational learning and change, collaboration is advanced through the creation of shared vision. It is also enhanced by heightening the stakeholders' awareness of their interdependence, respecting and dealing constructively with differences, and assuming joint ownership of decisions and joint responsibility for future interactions.

The development of leadership competencies and processes that generate conflict capital is a necessity in new-era organizations. Old approaches such as win-lose and compromise are often inadequate to build the sustained relationships that are needed to address complex change and challenges in organizations. Capacity building in today's organizations requires the ability to develop conflict capital from the processes of collaboration and constructive conflict resolution within new structures and among diverse participants.

The issues of change and conflict are handled most effectively in the context of a learning organization. Senge's second article in this section describes the need for building learning organizations as the leader's new work. Learning organizations focus on "generative" learning (creating) as well as adaptive learning (coping). Such organizations require leaders who are designers, teachers, and stewards. Leaders in learning organizations build shared vision, challenge prevailing mental models, foster systemic thinking, and are continually expanding the capabilities of participants to shape the organization's future.

### *Recognizing Contributions*

The final component of this section involves recognizing contributions, behaviors, and accomplishments that support efforts to build or change the capacity of organizations. In the previous section on organizational culture, Deal and Kennedy indicated that organizations with strong cultures recognize and celebrate heroes or role models that exemplify the kinds of accomplishments that are most valued. Recognition of such accomplishments sends a clear message of support for those who contribute to successes such as attaining the goals of self-directed teams, practicing self-mastery, contributing to organizational learning or leading collaborative processes. James Kouzes and Barry Posner maintain that "this kind of feedback helps to ensure that learning takes place so that people acquire the competence that comes with experience." Successful leadership involves having high expectations about what leaders and participants can accomplish and rewarding large and small achievements. Determining the kind of recognition and rewards that are most appropriate in an organization requires knowing and understanding the individuals and teams in the organization and involving those who have a stake in the outcome in the creation and development of their rewards and recognition system.

## *Note*

1. The editor originated this definition.

# 40

# *Personal Mastery*

PETER M. SENGE

## *The Spirit of the Learning Organization*

Organizations learn only through individuals who learn. Individual learning does not guarantee organizational learning. But without it no organizational learning occurs.

A small number of organizational leaders are recognizing the radical rethinking of corporate philosophy which a commitment to individual learning requires. Kazuo Inamori, founder and president of Kyocera (a world leader in advanced ceramics technology used in electronic components, medical materials, and its own line of office automation and communications equipment), says this:

> Whether it is research and development, company management, or any other aspect of business, the active force is "people." And people have their own will, their own mind, and their own way of thinking. If the employees themselves are not sufficiently motivated to challenge the goals of growth and technological development . . . there will simply be no growth, no gain in productivity, and no technological development.[1]

Tapping the potential of people, Inamori believes, will require new understanding of the "sub-conscious mind," "willpower," and "action of the heart . . . sincere desire to serve the world." He teaches Kyocera employees to look inward as they continually strive for "perfection," guided by the corporate motto, "Respect Heaven and Love People." In turn, he believes that his duty as a manager starts with "providing for both the material good and spiritual welfare of my employees."

Half a world away in a totally different industry, Bill O'Brien, president of Hanover Insurance, strives for

> . . . organizational models that are more congruent with human nature. When the industrial age began, people worked 6 days a week to earn enough for food and shelter. Today, most of us have these handled by Tuesday afternoon. Our traditional hierarchical organizations are not designed to provide for people's higher order needs, self-respect and self-actualization. The ferment in management will continue until organizations begin to address these needs, for all employees.

Also like Inamori, O'Brien argues that managers must redefine their job. They must give up "the old dogma of planning, organizing and controlling," and realize "the almost sacredness of their responsibility for the lives of so many people." Managers' fundamental task, according to O'Brien, is "providing the enabling conditions for people to lead the most enriching lives they can."

Lest these sentiments seem overly romantic for building a business, let me point out that Kyocera has gone from startup to $2 billion in sales in thirty years, borrowing almost no money and achieving profit levels that are the envy of even Japanese firms. Hanover was at the rock bottom of the property and liability industry in 1969 when O'Brien's predecessor, Jack Adam, began its reconstruction around a core set of values and beliefs about people. Today, the company stands consistently in the upper quarter of its industry in profits and has grown 50 percent faster than the industry over the past ten years.

No less a source of business acumen than Henry Ford observed,

> The smallest indivisible reality is, to my mind, intelligent and is waiting there to be used by human spirits if we reach out and call them in. We rush too much with nervous hands and worried minds. We are impatient for results. What we need . . . is reinforcement of the soul by the invisible power waiting to be used. . . . I know there are reservoirs of spiritual strength from which we human beings thoughtlessly cut ourselves off . . . I believe we shall someday be able to know enough about the source of power, and the realm of the spirit to create something ourselves . . .
>
> I firmly believe that mankind was once wiser about spiritual things than we are today. What we now only believe, they knew.[2]

"Personal mastery" is the phrase my colleagues and I use for the discipline of personal growth and learning. People with high levels of personal mastery are continually expanding their ability to create the results in life they truly seek. From their quest for continual learning comes the spirit of the learning organization.

## *The Discipline of Personal Mastery*

The way to begin developing a sense of personal mastery is to approach it as a *discipline,* as a series of practices and principles that must be applied to be useful. Just as one becomes a master artist by continual practice, so the following principles and practices lay the groundwork for continually expanding personal mastery.

### Personal Vision

Personal vision comes from within. Several years ago I was talking with a young woman about her vision for the planet. She said many lovely things about peace and harmony, about living in balance with nature. As beautiful as these ideas were, she spoke about them unemotionally, as if these were things that she *should* want. I asked her if there was anything else. After a pause, she said, "I want to live on a green planet," and started to cry. As far as I know, she had never said this before. The words just leaped from her, almost with a will of their own. Yet, the image they conveyed clearly had deep meaning to her—perhaps even levels of meaning that she didn't understand.

Most adults have little sense of real vision. We have goals and objectives, but these are not visions. When asked what they want, many adults will say what they want to get rid of. They'd like a better job—that is, they'd like to get rid of the boring job they have. They'd like to live in a better neighborhood, or not have to worry about crime, or about putting their kids through school. They'd like it if their mother-in-law returned to her own house, or if their back stopped hurting. Such litanies of "negative visions" are sadly commonplace, even among very successful people. They are the byproduct of a lifetime of fitting in, of coping, of problem solving. As a teenager in one of our programs once said, "We shouldn't call them 'grown ups' we should call them 'given ups.' "

A subtler form of diminished vision is "focusing on the means not the result." Many senior executives, for example, choose "high market share" as part of their vision. But why? "Because I want our company to be profitable." Now, you might think that high profits is an intrinsic result in and of itself, and indeed it is for some. But for surprisingly many other leaders, profits too are a means toward a still more important result. Why choose high annual profits? "Because I want us to remain an independent company, to keep from being taken over."

Why do you want that? "Because I want to keep our integrity and our capacity to be true to our purpose in starting the organization." While all the goals mentioned are legitimate, the last—being true to our purpose—has the greatest intrinsic significance to this executive. All the rest are means to the end, means which might change in particular circumstances. *The ability to focus on ultimate intrinsic desires, not only on secondary goals, is a cornerstone of personal mastery.*

Real vision cannot be understood in isolation from the idea of purpose. By purpose, I mean an individual's sense of why he is alive. No one could prove or disprove the statement that human beings have purpose. It would be fruitless even to engage in the debate. But as a working premise, the idea has great power. One implication is that happiness may be most directly a result of living consistently with your purpose. George Bernard Shaw expressed the idea pointedly when he said:

> This is the true joy in life, the being used for a purpose recognized by yourself as a mighty one . . . the being a force of nature instead of a feverish, selfish little clod of ailments and grievances complaining that the world will not devote itself to making you happy.[3]

This same principle has been expressed in some organizations as "genuine caring." In places where people felt uncomfortable talking about personal purpose, they felt perfectly at ease talking about genuine caring. When people genuinely care, they are naturally committed. They are doing what they truly want to do. They are full of energy and enthusiasm. They persevere, even in the face of frustration and setbacks, because what they are doing is what they must do. It is *their work.*

Everyone has had experiences when work flows fluidly; when he feels in tune with a task and works with a true economy of means. Someone whose vision calls him to a foreign country, for example, may find himself learning a new language far more rapidly than he ever could before. You can often recognize your personal vision because it creates such moments; it is the goal pulling you forward that makes all the work worthwhile.

But vision is different from purpose. Purpose is similar to a direction, a general heading. Vision is a specific destination, a picture of a desired future. Purpose is abstract. Vision is concrete. Purpose is "advancing man's capability to explore the heavens." Vision is "a man on the moon by the end of the 1960s." Purpose is "being the best I can be," "excellence." Vision is breaking four minutes in the mile.

It can truly be said that nothing happens until there is vision. But it is equally true that a vision with no underlying sense of purpose, no calling, is just a good idea—all "sound and fury, signifying nothing."

Conversely, purpose without vision has no sense of appropriate scale. As O'Brien says, "You and I may be tennis fans and enjoy talking about ground strokes, our backhands, the thrill of chasing down a corner shot, of hitting a winner. We may have a great conversation, but then we find out that I am gearing up to play at my local country club and you are preparing for Wimbledon. We share the same enthusiasm and love of the game, but at totally different scales of proficiency. Until we establish the scales we have in mind, we might think we are communicating when we're not."

Vision often gets confused with competition. You might say "My vision is to beat the other team." And indeed, competition can be a useful way of calibrating a vision, of setting scale. To beat the number-ten player at the tennis club is different from beating the number one. But to be number one of a mediocre lot may not fulfill my sense of purpose. Moreover, what is my vision after I reach number one?

Ultimately, vision is intrinsic not relative. It's something you desire for its intrinsic value, not because of where it stands you relative to another. Relative visions may be appropriate in the interim, but they will rarely lead to greatness. Nor is there anything wrong with competition. Competition is one of the best structures yet invented by humankind to allow each of us to bring out the best in each other. But after the competition is over, after the vision has (or has not) been achieved, it is one's sense of purpose that draws you further, that compels you to set a new vision. *This, again, is why personal mastery must be a discipline. It is a process of continually focusing and refocusing on what one truly wants, on one's visions.*

Vision is multifaceted. There are material facets of our visions, such as where we want to live and how much money we want to have in the bank. There are personal facets, such as health, freedom, and being true to ourselves. There are service facets, such as helping others or contributing to the state of knowledge in a field. All are part of what we truly want. Modern society tends to direct our attention to the material aspects, and simultaneously foster guilt for our material desires. Society places some emphasis on our personal desires—for example, it is almost a fetish in some circles to look trim and fit—and relatively little on our desires to serve. In fact, it is easy to feel naive or foolish by expressing a desire to make a contribution. Be that as it may, it is clear from working with thousands of people that personal visions span all these dimensions and more. It is also clear that it takes courage to hold visions that are not in the social mainstream.

But it is exactly that courage to take a stand for one's vision that distinguishes people with high levels of personal mastery. Or, as the Japanese say of the master's stand, "When there is no break, not even the thickness of a hair comes between a man's vision and his action."[4]

In some ways, clarifying vision is one of the easier aspects of personal mastery. A more difficult challenge, for many, comes in facing current reality.

### Holding Creative Tension

People often have great difficulty talking about their visions, even when the visions are clear. Why? Because we are acutely aware of the gaps between our vision and reality. "I would like to start my own company," but "I don't have the capital." Or, "I would like to pursue the profession that I really love," but "I've got to make a living." These gaps can make a vision seem unrealistic or fanciful. They can discourage us or make us feel hopeless. But the gap between vision and current reality is also a source of energy. If there was no gap, there would be no need for any action to move toward the vision. Indeed, the gap is *the* source of creative energy. We call this gap *creative tension*.

VISION

CURRENT REALITY

**Figure 40.1.**

Imagine a rubber band, stretched between your vision and current reality. When stretched, the rubber band creates tension, representing the tension between vision and current reality. What does tension seek? Resolution or release. There are only two possible ways for the tension to resolve itself: pull reality toward the vision or pull the vision toward reality. Which occurs will depend on whether we hold steady to the vision.

The principle of creative tension is the central principle of personal mastery, integrating all elements of the discipline. Yet, it is widely misunderstood. For example, the very term "tension" suggests anxiety or stress. But creative tension doesn't feel any particular way. It is the force that comes into play at the moment when we acknowledge a vision that is at odds with current reality.

Still, creative tension often leads to feelings or emotions associated with anxiety, such as sadness, discouragement, hopelessness, or worry. This happens so often that people easily confuse these emotions with creative tension. People come to think that the creative process *is all about being in a state of anxiety.* But it is important to realize that these "negative" emotions that may arise where there is creative tension are not creative tension itself. These emotions are what we call *emotional tension.*

If we fail to distinguish emotional tension from creative tension, we predispose ourselves to lowering our vision. If we feel deeply discouraged about a vision that is not happening, we may have a strong urge to lighten the load of that discouragement. There is one immediate remedy: lower the vision! "Well, it wasn't really that important to shoot seventy-five. I'm having a great time shooting in the eighties."

Or, "I don't really care about being able to play in recital. I'll have to make money as a music teacher in any case; I'll just concentrate there." The dynamics of relieving emotional tension are insidious because they can operate unnoticed. Emotional tension can always be relieved by adjusting the one pole of the creative tension that is completely under our control at all times—the vision. The feelings that we dislike go away because the creative tension that was their source is reduced. Our goals are now much closer to our current reality. Escaping emotional tension is easy—the only price we pay is abandoning what we truly want, our vision.

The dynamics of emotional tension deeply resemble the dynamics of eroding goals that so troubled WonderTech and People Express, in Chapters 7 and 8. The interaction of creative tension and emotional tension is a shifting the burden dynamic, similar to that of eroding goals, represented in Figure 40.2.

When we hold a vision that differs from current reality, a gap exists (the creative tension) which can be resolved in two ways. The lower balancing process represents the "fundamental solution": taking actions to bring reality into line with the vision. But changing reality takes time. This is what leads to the frustration and emotional tension in the upper balancing process, the "symptomatic solution" of lowering the vision to bring it into line with current reality.

But a onetime reduction in the vision usually isn't the end of the story. Sooner or later new pressures pulling reality away from the (new, lowered) vision arise, leading to still more pressures to lower the vision. The classic "shifting the burden" dynamic ensues, a subtle reinforcing spiral of failure to meet goals, frustration, lowered vision, temporary relief, and pressure anew to lower the vision still further. Gradually, the "burden" is shifting increasingly to lowering the vision.

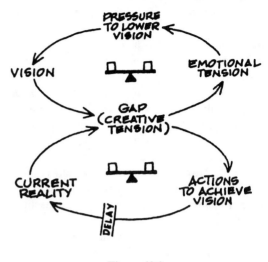

**Figure 40.2.**

At WonderTech and People Express relieving emotional tension took the form of decline in key operating standards that seemed impossible to meet—standards for delivery performance and for service quality. The decline was especially difficult to see because it was gradual. During each crisis at WonderTech delivery standards eroded just a bit relative to where they had settled after the last crisis. Likewise, managers at People Express didn't wake up one morning and declare, "We've solved our problems keeping pace with growth, we'll lower our service standards." Rather, service standards eroded quietly during repeated crises and with turnover among key leaders. So, too, do eroding personal goals go unrecognized, as we gradually surrender our dreams for the relationships we want to have, the work we want to do, and the type of world we want to live in.

In organizations, goals erode because of low tolerance for emotional tension. Nobody wants to be the messenger with bad news. The easiest path is to just pretend there is no bad news, or better yet, "declare victory"—to redefine the bad news as not so bad by lowering the standard against which it is judged.

The dynamics of emotional tension exist at all levels of human activity. They are the dynamics of compromise, the path of mediocrity. As Somerset Maugham said, "Only mediocre people are always at their best."

We allow our goals to erode when we are unwilling to live with emotional tension. On the other hand, when we understand creative tension and allow it to operate by not lowering our vision, vision becomes an active force. Robert Fritz says, "It's not what the vision is, it's what the vision does." Truly creative people use the gap between vision and current reality to generate energy for change.

For example, Alan Kay, who directed the research at Xerox Palo Alto Research Center (PARC) that led to many key features of the personal computer, actually had a vision for a different machine, which he called the "dynabook." This would be a book that was interactive. A child could test out his understanding, play games, and creatively rearrange the static presentation of ideas offered by the traditional book. Kay failed, in a sense, because the "dynabook" never became a reality. But the vision reshaped the computer industry. The prototype machines developed at PARC achieved the functionality—windows, pull-down menus, mouse control, iconic displays (images rather than words)—that was introduced commercially ten years later in the Macintosh.

Bill Russell, the legendary center for the Boston Celtics basketball team, used to keep his own personal scorecard. He graded himself after every game on a scale from one to one hundred. In his career he never achieved more than sixty-five. Now, given the way most of us are taught to think about goals, we would regard Russell as an abject failure. The poor soul played in over twelve hundred basketball games and never achieved his standard! Yet, it was the striving for that standard that made him arguably the best basketball player ever.[5]

It's not what the vision is, it's what the vision does.

Mastery of creative tension transforms the way one views "failure." Failure is, simply, a shortfall, evidence of the gap between vision and current reality. Failure is an opportunity for learning about inaccurate pictures of current reality, about strategies that didn't work as expected, about the clarity of the vision. Failures are not about our unworthiness or powerlessness. Ed Land, founder and president of Polaroid for decades and inventor of instant photography, had one plaque on his wall. It read:

A mistake is an event, the full benefit of which has not yet been turned to your advantage.

Mastery of creative tension brings out a capacity for perseverance and patience. A Japanese executive in one of our seminars once told me how, in his view, Japanese and Americans have quite different attitudes toward time. He said that "U.S. businessmen in Japan to negotiate business deals often find the Japanese evasive and reticent to 'get down to business.' The American arrives in Japan on a tight, carefully planned five-day schedule and immediately wants to get to work. Instead, the Japanese greet them with a polite, formal tea ceremony, never getting down to nuts and bolts. As the days go by, the Japanese keep their slow pace, while the Americans become antsier and antsier. For the American," the executive said, "time is the enemy. For the Japanese, time is an ally."

More broadly, current reality itself is, for many of us, the enemy. We fight against what is. We are not so much drawn to what we want to create as we are repelled by what we have, from our current reality. By this logic, the deeper the fear, the more we abhor what is, the more "motivated" we are to change. "Things must get bad enough, or people will not change in any fundamental way."

This leads to the mistaken belief that fundamental change *requires* a threat to survival. This crisis theory of change is remarkably widespread. Yet, it is also a dangerous oversimplification. Often in workshops or presentations, I will ask, "How many of you believe people and organizations only change, fundamentally, when there is a crisis?" Reliably, 75 to 90 percent of the hands go up. Then I ask people to consider a life where everything is exactly the way they would like—there are absolutely no problems of any sort in work, personally, professionally, in their relationships, or their community. Then I ask, "What is the first thing you would seek if you had a life of absolutely no problems?" The answer, overwhelmingly, is "change—to create something new." So human beings are more complex than we often assume. We both fear and seek change. Or, as one seasoned organization change consultant once put it, "People don't resist change. They resist being changed."

Mastery of creative tension leads to a fundamental shift in our whole posture toward reality. Current reality becomes the ally not the enemy. *An accurate, insightful view of current reality is as important as a clear vision.* Unfortunately, most of us are in the habit of imposing biases on our perceptions of current reality, a subject we will return to in depth in the following chapter on mental models. "We learn to rely on our concepts of reality more than on our observations," writes Robert Fritz. "It is more convenient to assume that reality is similar to our preconceived ideas than to freshly observe what we have before our eyes."[6] If the first choice in pursuing personal mastery is to be true to your own vision, the second fundamental choice in support of personal mastery is commitment to the truth.

Both are equally vital to generating creative tension. Or, as Fritz puts it, "The truly creative person knows that all creating is achieved through working with constraints. Without constraints there is no creating."

## "Structural Conflict":
## The Power of Your Powerlessness

Many people, even highly successful people, harbor deep beliefs contrary to their personal mastery. Very often, these beliefs are below the level of conscious awareness. To see what I mean, try the following experiment. Say out loud the following sentence: "I can create my life exactly the way I want it, in all dimensions—work, family, relationships, community, and larger world." Notice your internal reaction to this assertion, the "little voice" in the back of your head. "Who's he kidding?" "He doesn't really believe that." "Personally and in work, sure—but, not 'community' and 'the larger world.'" "What do I care about the 'larger world' anyhow?" All of these reactions are evidence of deep-seated beliefs.

Robert Fritz, who has worked with literally tens of thousands of people to develop their creative capacities, has concluded that practically all of us have a "dominant belief that we are not able to fulfill our desires." Where does this belief come from? Fritz argues that it is an almost inevitable by-product of growing up:

As children we learn what our limitations are. Children are rightfully taught limitations essential to their survival. But too often this learning is generalized. We are constantly told we can't have or can't do certain things, and we may come to assume that we have an inability to have what we want.[7]

Most of us hold one of two contradictory beliefs that limit our ability to create what we really want. The more common is belief in our powerlessness—our inability to bring into being all the things we really care about. The other belief centers on unworthiness—that we do not deserve to have what we truly desire. Fritz claims that he has met only a handful of individuals who do not seem to have one or the other of these underlying beliefs. Such an assertion is difficult to prove rigorously because it is difficult to measure deep beliefs. But if we accept it as a working premise, it illuminates systemic forces that can work powerfully against creating what we really want.

Fritz uses a metaphor to describe how contradictory underlying beliefs work as a system, counter to achieving our goals. Imagine, as you move toward your goal, there is a rubber band, symbolizing creative tension, pulling you in the desired direction. But imagine also a second rubber band, anchored to the belief of powerlessness or unworthiness. Just as the first rubber band tries to pull you toward your goal, the second pulls you back toward the underlying belief that you can't (or don't deserve to) have your goal. Fritz calls the system involving both the tension pulling us toward our goal and the tension anchoring us to our underlying belief "structural conflict," because it is a structure of conflicting forces: pulling us simultaneously toward and away from what we want.

Thus, the closer we come to achieving our vision, the more the second rubber band pulls us away from our vision. This force can manifest itself in many ways. We might lose our energy. We might question whether we really wanted the vision. "Finishing the job" might become increasingly difficult. Unexpected obstacles develop in our path. People let us down. All this happens even though we are unaware of the structural conflict system, because it originates in deep beliefs of which we are largely unaware—in fact, our un-

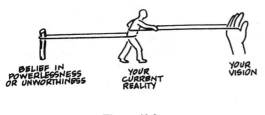

BELIEF IN
POWERLESSNESS
OR UNWORTHINESS          YOUR              YOUR
                        CURRENT           VISION
                        REALITY

**Figure 40.3.**

awareness contributes to the power of structural conflict.

Given beliefs in our powerlessness or unworthiness, structural conflict implies that systemic forces come into play to keep us from succeeding *whenever* we seek a vision. Yet, we *do* succeed sometimes, and in fact many of us have become adept at identifying and achieving goals, at least in some areas of our lives. How do we overcome the forces of structural conflict?

Fritz has identified three generic "strategies" for coping with the forces of structural conflict, each of which has its limitations.[8] Letting our vision erode is one such coping strategy. The second is "conflict manipulation," in which we try to manipulate ourselves into greater effort toward what we want by creating artificial conflict, such as through focusing on avoiding what we don't want. Conflict manipulation is the favored strategy of people who incessantly worry about failure, managers who excel at "motivational chats" that point out the highly unpleasant consequences if the company's goals are *not* achieved, and of social movements that attempt to mobilize people through fear. In fact, sadly, most social movements operate through conflict manipulation or "negative vision," focusing on getting away from what we don't want, rather than on creating what we do want: antidrugs, antinuclear arms, antinuclear power, antismoking, anti-abortion, or antigovernment corruption.

But many ask, "What's wrong with a little worry or fear if it helps us achieve our goals?" The response of those who seek personal mastery is the simple question: "Do you really want to live your life in a state of fear of failure?" The tragedy is that many people who get hooked on conflict manipulation come to believe that *only* through being in a

state of continual anxiety and fear can they be successful. These are the people who, rather than shunning emotional tension, actually come to glorify it. For them, there is little joy in life. Even when they achieve their goals, they immediately begin worrying about losing what they have gained.

Fritz's third generic strategy is the strategy of "willpower," where we simply "psych ourselves up" to overpower all forms of resistance to achieving our goals. Lying behind willpower strategies, he suggests, is the simple assumption that we "motivate ourselves through heightened volition." Willpower is so common among highly successful people that many see its characteristics as synonymous with success: a maniacal focus on goals, willingness to "pay the price," ability to defeat any opposition and surmount any obstacle.

The problems with "willpower" are many, but they may hardly be noticed by the person focused narrowly on "success." First, there is little economy of means; in systems thinking terms, we act without leverage. We attain our goals, but the effort is enormous and we may find ourselves exhausted and wondering if "it was worth it" when we have succeeded. Ironically, people hooked on willpower may actually look for obstacles to overcome, dragons to slay, and enemies to vanquish—to remind themselves and others of their own prowess. Second, there are often considerable unintended consequences. Despite great success at work, the master of "willpower" will often find that he or she has gone through two marriages and has terrible relationships with his or her children. Somehow, the same dogged determination and goal orientation that "works" at work doesn't quite turn the trick at home.

Worse still, just as with all of the coping strategies, "willpower" leaves the underlying system of structural conflict unaltered. In particular, the underlying belief in powerlessness has not really changed. Despite significant accomplishments, many "highly successful people" still feel a deep, usually unspoken, sense of powerlessness in critical areas of their lives—such as in their personal and family relationships, or in their ability to achieve a sense of peace and spiritual fulfillment.

These coping strategies are, to a certain extent, unavoidable. They are deeply habitual and cannot be changed overnight. We all tend to have a favorite strategy—mine has long been "willpower," as those close to me can attest.

Where then is the leverage in dealing with structural conflict? If structural conflict arises from deep underlying beliefs, then it can be changed only by changing the beliefs. But psychologists are virtually unanimous that fundamental beliefs such as powerlessness or unworthiness cannot be changed readily. They are developed early in life (remember all those "can'ts" and "don'ts" that started when you were two?). For most of us, beliefs change gradually as we accumulate new experiences—as we develop our personal mastery. But if mastery will not develop so long as we hold unempowering beliefs, and the beliefs will change only as we experience our mastery, how may we begin to alter the deeper structures of our lives?

**Commitment to the Truth**

We may begin with a disarmingly simple yet profound strategy for dealing with structural conflict: telling the truth.

Commitment to the truth often seems to people an inadequate strategy. "What do I need to do to change my behavior?" "How do I change my underlying belief?" People often want a formula, a technique, something tangible that they can apply to solve the problem of structural conflict. But, in fact, being committed to the truth is far more powerful than any technique.

Commitment to the truth does not mean seeking the "Truth," the absolute final word or ultimate cause. Rather, it means a relentless willingness to root out the ways we limit or deceive ourselves from seeing what is, and to continually challenge our theories of why things are the way they are. It means continually broadening our awareness, just as the great athlete with extraordinary peripheral vision keeps trying to "see more of the playing field." It also means continually deepening our understanding of the structures underlying current events. Specifically, people with high levels of personal mastery see more of the structural conflicts underlying their own behavior.

Thus, the first critical task in dealing with structural conflicts is to recognize them, *and* the result-

ing behavior, when they are operating. It can be very difficult to recognize these coping strategies while we are playing them out, especially because of tensions and pressures that often accompany them. It helps to develop internal warning signals, such as when we find ourselves blaming something or somebody for our problems: "The reason I'm giving up is nobody appreciates me," or "The reason I'm so worried is that they'll fire me if I don't get the job done."

In my life, for example, I often felt that people let me down at critical junctures in major projects. When this happened, I would "bulldoze" through, overcoming the obstacle of their disloyalty or incompetence. It took many years before I recognized this as a recurring pattern, my own special form of the "willpower" strategy, rooted in a deep feeling of being powerless to change the way others let me down. Invariably, I ended up feeling as if "I've got to do it all myself."

Once I recognized this pattern, I began to act differently when a colleague let me down. I became angry less often. Rather, there was a twinge of recognition—"Oh, there goes my pattern." I looked more deeply at how my own actions were part of the outcome, either by creating tasks that were impossible to accomplish, or by undermining or demotivating the other person. Further, I worked to develop skills to discuss such situations with the people involved without producing defensiveness.

I would never have developed those skills or known how to put them into practice without a shift of mind. So long as I saw the problem in terms of events, I was convinced that my problems were externally caused—"*they* let me down." Once I saw the problem as structurally caused, I began to look at what I could do, rather than at what "they had done."

Structures of which we are unaware hold us prisoner. Once we can see them and name them, they no longer have the same hold on us. This is as much true for individuals as it is for organizations. In fact, an entire field is evolving, structural family therapy, based on the assumption that individual psychological difficulties can be understood and changed only by understanding the structures of interdependencies within families and close personal relationships. Once these structures are recognized, in the words of David Kantor, a pioneer in the field, "It becomes possible to begin to alter structures to free people from previously mysterious forces that dictated their behavior."[9]

Discovering structures at play is the stock and trade of people with high levels of personal mastery. Sometimes these structures can be readily changed. Sometimes, as with structural conflict, they change only gradually. Then the need is to work more creatively within them while acknowledging their origin, rather than fighting the structures. Either way, once an operating structure is recognized, the structure itself becomes part of "current reality." The more my commitment to the truth, the more creative tension comes into play because current reality is seen more for what it really is. In the context of creative tension, commitment to the truth becomes a generative force, just as vision becomes a generative force.

## *Personal Mastery and the Fifth Discipline*

As individuals practice the discipline of personal mastery, several changes gradually take place within them. Many of these are quite subtle and often go unnoticed. In addition to clarifying the "structures" that characterize personal mastery as a discipline (such as creative tension, emotional tension, and structural conflict), the systems perspective also illuminates subtler aspects of personal mastery—especially integrating reason and intuition; continually seeing more of our connectedness to the world; compassion; and commitment to the whole.

### Integrating Reason and Intuition

According to an ancient Sufi story, a blind man wandering lost in a forest tripped and fell. As the blind man rummaged about the forest floor he discovered that he had fallen over a cripple. The blind man and the cripple struck up a conversation, commiserating on their fate. The blind man said, "I have been wandering in this forest for as long as I can remember, and I cannot see to find my way

out." The cripple said, "I have been lying on the forest floor for as long as I can remember, and I cannot get up to walk out." As they sat there talking, suddenly the cripple cried out. "I've got it," he said. "You hoist me up onto your shoulders and I will tell you where to walk. Together we can find our way out of the forest." According to the ancient storyteller, the blind man symbolized rationality. The cripple symbolized intuition. We will not find our way out of the forest until we learn how to integrate the two.

Intuition in management has recently received increasing attention and acceptance, after many decades of being officially ignored. Now numerous studies show that experienced managers and leaders rely heavily on intuition—that they do not figure out complex problems entirely rationally. They rely on hunches, recognize patterns, and draw intuitive analogies and parallels to other seemingly disparate situations.[10] There are even courses in management schools on intuition and creative problem solving. But we have a very long way to go, in our organizations and in society, toward reintegrating intuition and rationality.

People with high levels of personal mastery do not set out to integrate reason and intuition. Rather, they achieve it naturally—as a by-product of their commitment to use all resources at their disposal. They cannot afford to choose between reason and intuition, or head and heart, any more than they would choose to walk on one leg or see with one eye.

Bilateralism is a design principle underlying the evolution of advanced organisms. Nature seems to have learned to design in pairs; it not only builds in redundancy but achieves capabilities not possible otherwise. Two legs are critical for rapid, flexible locomotion. Two arms and hands are vital for climbing, lifting, and manipulating objects. Two eyes give us stereoscopic vision, and along with two ears, depth perception. Is it not possible that, following the same design principle, reason and intuition are designed to work in harmony for us to achieve our potential intelligence?

Systems thinking may hold a key to integrating reason and intuition. Intuition eludes the grasp of linear thinking, with its exclusive emphasis on cause and effect that are close in time and space.

The result is that most of our intuitions don't make "sense"—that is, they can't be explained in terms of linear logic.

Very often, experienced managers have rich intuitions about complex systems, which they cannot explain. Their intuitions tell them that cause and effect are not close in time and space, that obvious solutions will produce more harm than good, and that short-term fixes produce long-term problems. But they cannot explain their ideas in simple linear cause—effect language. They end up saying, "Just do it this way. It will work."

For example, many managers sense the dangers of eroding goals or standards but cannot fully explain how they create a reinforcing tendency to underinvest and a self-fulfilling prophecy of under-realized market growth. Or, managers may feel that they are focusing on tangible, easily measured indicators of performance and masking deeper problems, and even exacerbating these problems. But they cannot explain convincingly why these are the wrong performance indicators or how alternatives might produce improved results. Both of these intuitions can be explained when the underlying systemic structures are understood.[11]

The conflict between intuition and linear, nonsystemic thinking has planted the seed that *rationality* itself is opposed to intuition. This view is demonstrably false if we consider the synergy of reason and intuition that characterizes virtually all great thinkers. Einstein said, "I never discovered anything with my rational mind." He once described how he discovered the principle of relativity by imagining himself traveling on a light beam. Yet, he could take brilliant intuitions and convert them into succinct, rationally testable propositions.

As managers gain facility with systems thinking as an alternative language, they find that many of their intuitions become explicable. Eventually, reintegrating reason and intuition may prove to be one of the primary contributions of systems thinking.

### Seeing Our Connectedness to the World

My six-week-old son Ian does not yet seem to know his hands and feet. I suspect that he is aware of them, but he is clearly not aware that they are *his*

hands and feet, or that he controls their actions. The other day, he got caught in a terrible reinforcing feedback loop. He had taken hold of his ear with his left hand. It was clearly agitating him, as you could tell from his pained expression and increasing flagellations. But, as a result of being agitated, he pulled harder. This increased his discomfort, which led him to get more agitated and pull still harder. The poor little guy might still be pulling if I hadn't detached his hand and quieted him down.

Not knowing that his hand was actually within his control, he perceived the source of his discomfort as an external force. Sound familiar? Ian's plight was really no different from the beer game players of Chapter 3, who reacted to suppliers' delivery times as if they were external forces, or the arms race participants in Chapter 5 ("A Shift of Mind") who reacted to each other's arms buildups as if they had no power to change them.

As I thought about Ian, I began to think that a neglected dimension of personal growth lies in "closing the loops"—in continually discovering how apparent external forces are actually interrelated with our own actions. Fairly soon, Ian will recognize his feet and hands and learn he can control their motions. Then he will discover that he can control his body position—if it is unpleasant on his back, he can roll over. Then will come internal states such as temperature, and the realization that they can be influenced by moving closer or further from a heat source such as Mommy or Daddy. Eventually comes Mommy and Daddy themselves, and the realization that their actions and emotions are subject to his influence. At each stage in this progression, there will be corresponding adjustments in his internal pictures of reality, which will steadily change to incorporate more of the feedback from his actions to the conditions in his life.

But for most of us, sometime early in life this process of closing the loops is arrested. As we get older, our rate of discovery slows down; we see fewer and fewer new links between our actions and external forces. We become locked into ways of looking at the world that are, fundamentally, no different from little Ian's.

The learning process of the young child provides a beautiful metaphor for the learning challenge faced by us all: to continually expand our awareness and understanding, to see more and more of the interdependencies between actions and our reality, to see more and more of our connectedness to the world around us. We will probably never perceive fully the multiple ways in which we influence our reality. But simply being open to the possibility is enough to free our thinking.

Einstein expressed the learning challenge when he said:

> [The human being] experiences himself, his thoughts and feelings as something separated from the rest—a kind of optical delusion of our consciousness. This delusion is a kind of prison for us, restricting us to our personal desires and to affection for a few persons nearest to us. Our task must be to free ourselves from this prison by widening our circle of compassion to embrace all living creatures and the whole of nature in its beauty.

The experience of increasing connectedness which Einstein describes is one of the subtlest aspects of personal mastery, one that derives most directly from the systems perspective. His "widening . . . circle of compassion" is another.

### Compassion

The discipline of seeing interrelationships gradually undermines older attitudes of blame and guilt. We begin to see that *all of us* are trapped in structures, structures embedded both in our ways of thinking and in the interpersonal and social milieus in which we live. Our knee-jerk tendencies to find fault with one another gradually fade, leaving a much deeper appreciation of the forces within which we all operate.

This does not imply that people are simply victims of systems that dictate their behavior. Often, the structures are of our own creation. But this has little meaning until those structures are seen. For most of us, the structures within which we operate are invisible. We are neither victims nor culprits but human beings controlled by forces we have not yet learned how to perceive.

We are used to thinking of compassion as an emotional state, based on our concern for one another. But it is also grounded in a level of awareness. In my experience, as people see more of the systems within which they operate, and as they understand more clearly the pressures influencing one another, they naturally develop more compassion and empathy.

### Commitment to the Whole

"Genuine commitment," according to Bill O'Brien, "is always to something larger than ourselves." Inamori talks about "action of our heart," when we are guided by "sincere desire to serve the world." Such action, he says, "is a very important issue since it has great power."

The sense of connectedness and compassion characteristic of individuals with high levels of personal mastery naturally leads to a broader vision. Without it, all the subconscious visualizing in the world is deeply self-centered—simply a way to get what I want.

Individuals committed to a vision beyond their self-interest find they have energy not available when pursuing narrower goals, as will organizations that tap this level of commitment. "I do not believe there has been a single person who has made a worthwhile discovery or invention," Inamori states, "who has not experienced a spiritual power." He describes the will of a person committed to a larger purpose as "a cry from the soul which has been shaken and awakened."

### *Fostering Personal Mastery in an Organization*

It must always be remembered that embarking on any path of personal growth is a matter of choice. No one can be forced to develop his or her personal mastery. It is guaranteed to backfire. Organizations can get into considerable difficulty if they become too aggressive in promoting personal mastery for their members.

Still many have attempted to do just that by creating compulsory internal personal growth training programs. However well intentioned, such programs are probably the most sure-fire way to impede the genuine spread of commitment to personal mastery in an organization. Compulsory training, or "elective" programs that people feel expected to attend if they want to advance their careers, conflict directly with freedom of choice.

For example, there have been numerous instances in recent years of overzealous managers requiring employees to participate in personal development training, which the employees regarded as contradictory to their own religious beliefs. Several of these have resulted in legal action against the organization.[12]

What, then, can leaders intent on fostering personal mastery do?

They can work relentlessly to foster a climate in which the principles of personal mastery are practiced in daily life. That means building an organization where it is safe for people to create visions, where inquiry and commitment to the truth are the norm, and where challenging the status quo is expected—especially when the status quo includes obscuring aspects of current reality that people seek to avoid.

Such an organizational climate will strengthen personal mastery in two ways. First, it will continually reinforce the idea that personal growth is truly valued in the organization. Second, to the extent that individuals respond to what is offered, it will provide an "on the job training" that is vital to developing personal mastery. As with any discipline, developing personal mastery must become a continual, ongoing process. There is nothing more important to an individual committed to his or her own growth than a supportive environment. An organization committed to personal mastery can provide that environment by continually encouraging personal vision, commitment to the truth, and a willingness to face honestly the gaps between the two.

Many of the practices most conducive to developing one's own personal mastery—developing a more systemic worldview, learning how to reflect on tacit assumptions, expressing one's vision and listening to others' visions, and joint inquiry into different people's views of current reality—are embedded in the disciplines for building learning organizations. So, in many ways, the most positive actions that an organization can take to foster personal mastery involve working to develop all five learning disciplines in concert.

The core leadership strategy is simple: be a model. Commit yourself to your own personal mastery. Talking about personal mastery may open people's minds somewhat, but actions always speak louder than words. There's nothing more powerful you can do to encourage others in their quest for personal mastery than to be serious in your own quest.

## Notes

1. K. Inamori, "The Perfect Company: Goal for Productivity," Speech given at Case Western Reserve University, June 5, 1985.

2. H. Ford, *Detroit News,* February 7, 1926.

3. George Bernard Shaw, *Man and Superman,* Preface (Penguin, 1950).

4. Peter Wack, "Scenarios: Uncharted Ahead," *Harvard Business Review* (September/October 1985): 73-89.

5. Bill Russell and Taylor Branch, *Second Wind: The Memoirs of an Opinionated Man* (New York: Random House), 1979.

6. R. Fritz, in *The Path of Least Resistance* (New York: Fawcett-Columbine), 1989, delves into the reasons behind this habit.

7. Ibid.

8. Ibid.

9. David Kantor and William Lehr, *Inside the Family: Toward a Theory of Family Process* (San Francisco: Jossey-Bass), 1975.

10. Weston Agor, *Intuitive Management: Integrating Left and Right Brain Management Skills* (Englewood Cliffs, NJ: Prentice Hall), 1984; Henry Mintzberg, "Planning on the Left Side and Managing on the Right," *Harvard Business Review* (July/August 1976), 49-58; Daniel Isenberg, "How Top Managers Think," *Harvard Business Review* (July/August 1976), 49.

11. The cases described in the "Microworlds" chapter illustrate developing systemic explanations to explain previously inexplicable intuitions.

12. Karen Cook, "Scenario for a New Age: Can American Industry Find Renewal in Management Theories Born of Counterculture?" *New York Times Magazine,* September 25, 1988; Robert Lindsey, "Gurus Hired to Motivate Workers Are Raising Fears of Mind Control," *New York Times,* April 17, 1987.

# 41

# *Building Individual Learning*

FRANCIS J. GOUILLART
JAMES N. KELLY

The New England Aquarium in Boston presents daily sea lion shows in which children and adults watch with delight as the sea lions toss balls, clap their fins, jump over hurdles and through rings, and splash the front row on cue. With every trick, the crowd roars and the animals are rewarded with fish. Through their trainers, they have made the association: No trick, no fish. Conversely, they know their just due and protest loudly, to the further delight of the crowd, if a nice jump doesn't immediately win a fishy prize. The system works well, and several generations of sea lions have proven quite reliable in front of an audience. The system has a limit, however: No sea lion has yet been known to develop new tricks spontaneously.

To a significant extent, most corporate rewards systems are based on a similar Pavlovian model. And to that extent, they constitute the weakest form of renewal. Money, banners, trophies, and other symbols are held out as carrots to stimulate motivation in the pursuit of specifically defined objectives. Employees and managers learn to expect certain returns for certain behaviors, each of them operating in their assigned slot. The model remains predominantly paternal, authoritarian, and reactive in that top management "provides" and the firm's personnel receive the various forms of compensation made available. The problem is that the clearly defined rewards produce expected results, not the creative, unexpected, and dramatic outcomes that comprise the very heart of renewal.

Individual learning represents a more advanced stage of renewal. It builds the individual's sense of self-esteem by enhancing his or her store of knowledge, thus promoting an increased level of competence and efficacy in approaching work-related problems. More importantly, it creates the opportunity for people to experience perhaps the most fulfilling of all rewards, a sense of *self-actualization*—the pride of recognizing the output of one's mind in the external reality of the workplace, and the sense of purpose, productivity, and participation that comes with such achievement as part of a collective quest.

By promoting individual learning, the corporation recognizes the individual's responsibility for

SOURCE: From *Transforming the Organization,* by F. J. Gouillart and J. N. Kelly. New York: McGraw-Hill. Copyright 1995. Reproduced with permission of The McGraw-Hill Companies.

his or her own personal and professional development, while accepting its responsibility to create an environment of opportunity in which all can thrive. As greater numbers of high-self-esteem individuals unleash their creativity, they reshape the contours of the firm. The corporation comes alive as employees continuously adapt and improve the way they do their work, and constantly redefine their roles and interactions. Rather than dealing with a machine-like firm, leaders become conductors of the biocorporate symphony, orchestrating the organic growth of the firm as the cells and organs of the corporate body adapt, change, and reproduce.

Too often, corporate leaders lose the perspective of seeing employees as a collection of individual human beings, each one with unlimited potential. In an organization that fosters individual learning, these individuals shine forth as a living resource, by far the corporation's most valued and irreplaceable assets. The formerly inert organization comes alive—constantly learning and adapting—defined by human wills and passions. Squashing these wills and passions through rigid organizational principles is a terrible waste, both to the organization and of the individual human spirit.

Instead of matching an organizational chart with a description of each employee's skills, the new leader now deals with a rapidly accumulating set of capabilities, planting seeds of innovation and creativity by moving key people and teams to points of need inside the corporation, animating the organization with an eagerness to discover new horizons. Rather than dealing with the cold facts of each employee's track record and skills, the leader uses the energy of the individual to pursue key objectives. Heptagon and rhomboid designs replace round pegs and square holes. Palpitating hearts displace industrial motors and pumps. The CEO observes the genesis of new cells within the corporate body, watching the cells divide and grow as people define their own jobs to serve the purposes of the body as a whole. The respective definitions of *job* and *project* become blurred. As a result, the boundaries of skills and innovation in the corporation themselves expand, allowing the firm to conquer new spaces.

There are four genes associated with the chromosome of individual learning, implying four cor-

responding tasks for the genetic architects of the organization:

1. *Committing to the development of the individual.* The value created by a firm resides in the accumulated knowledge of the people within it, expressed in the form of products and services sold. A firm succeeds by building capabilities in its people first. Only then do capabilities begin to translate into more efficient operations, more satisfied customers, and higher levels of financial performance.

Advocating a commitment to individual development is the responsibility of the corporate leader. In many corporations, individual development is entrusted to a disempowered human resource function, displaced from the focus and attention of leaders. Perhaps the best way for the CEO to communicate and demonstrate this commitment is to urge executive leaders to participate directly in development activities as a natural extension of their line responsibilities.

2. *Creating mentor-guided, life-forming projects for high-caliber individuals.* People learn best on the job, especially in the execution of ad hoc projects, often self-defined by individuals with a passion for a particular area. Authorizing and helping to design jobs and projects for high-potential individuals is therefore a key responsibility of the leadership team. It allows individuals who can make a difference to develop new skills and achieve higher levels of personal and professional fulfillment, thus enhancing the individual's life, while also injecting new life into the biological corporation.

The selection of the proper mentors for each high-caliber individual is another vital responsibility of the leadership team. Mentors are senior executives with the flair and patience for developing less experienced executives, and they are tasked with providing guidance and directing learning throughout the project experience.

3. *Identifying critical skills and designing an education strategy.* The principal sin committed in most training programs occurs when they become disconnected from the core business, taking on a life of their own. To be effective, such programs need to be rooted in a model of individual and organizational skills that need nurturing. Skills

modeling is a complex exercise, requiring the selection of a few key capabilities directly tied to the transformation agenda of the company. Once key skills have been identified, high-performance corporations often find it advisable to develop their own educational facility, with programs focused on "real-life" problem solving in their business.

The role of the corporation's leadership is to emphasize the role of education in individual development and to personally utilize the education strategy as a vehicle of transformation.

4. *Balancing the supply of and demand for skills inside the corporation.* Company leaders have long recognized the business inefficiency and the ethical quandary involved in laying off large pools of qualified people in some areas, while aggressively hiring and training large numbers of new specialists in other areas. In some countries, particularly in Europe, the ethical problem has been translated into labor legislation that all but prohibits companies from using layoffs as a cost-cutting tool. Consequently, large companies throughout the world are experimenting with new ways to enrich the learning experience and to deploy people to match skills to business needs.

The behavioral and psychological dimensions of changing jobs are proving to be the greatest obstacle to the success of redeploying people. In some cases, technology provides the critical link allowing people to identify their learning requirements, gain access to the knowledge they need, and connect themselves and their skills to emerging opportunities in the corporation.

The role of the leadership team is to experiment with new ways to enhance learning and to match individuals and their skills to the needs of the organization; to pilot new programs that open doors to individual opportunity, while reshaping the corporation's skills portfolio.

## Committing to the Development of the Individual

The value of a firm consists first and foremost of the knowledge possessed by the individuals that comprise it. When we buy software from Microsoft, we buy the collective knowledge of the people at Microsoft who developed it. We don't buy their headquarters in Redmond, Washington, or their sales and distribution network, or their patents. We purchase the collective ability of a group of several thousand people, expressed as a software program.

Misguided by traditional accounting practices, companies have long measured their value in terms of the auction price of their underlying "hard" assets, almost completely discounting from their financial decisions knowledge, and the people who hold it. Witness how bankers insist on collateralizing only hard assets, arguing that land, buildings, and machines cannot walk away at night, whereas employees can. It is true that people's attachment to a firm can be fleeting. That doesn't imply, however, that only the inanimate can retain its value over time. Assets may be more permanent, but that is also their downfall: They become obsolete proportional to the rate of innovation, and therefore proportionally irrelevant to the value of a firm. Conversely, people are the source of innovation, and they can grow and adapt with it. The company that can attract, develop, and retain high-caliber individuals guarantees the continuous replenishment of its knowledge base, ensuring a continuous increase in the firm's valuing capacity and, therefore, its performance.

Consider how great sports teams sustain their enterprises. Every sport on any continent has teams that waste their considerable resources and teams that do much more with much lesser means. In French soccer, the Olympique de Marseille has long had a history of acquiring internationally renowned star players at extraordinary premiums. Every few years they rush to the top of the French, and more recently, the European championships. Those spasmodic rushes to the top, however, are interspersed with periods of nearly complete oblivion—the team often doesn't even play in the major French league anymore. All in all, the club has never managed to balance its finances through these huge peaks and valleys, relying on municipal subsidies to survive.

Conversely, for the last several years the A.J. Auxerre soccer club has consistently ranked in the top four or five clubs in France, and has qualified for the various European cups nearly every year for the last 15 years. Auxerre is a midsized town, one that doesn't have anywhere near the stadium attendance of Marseilles at its peak. The key to Auxerre's success? Its soccer school and development program. The club spends considerable time identifying young, promising players all over the country, offers them scholarships in its junior teams, and develops them into competitive professional players. Auxerre often finds it difficult to hang on to its players once they have achieved greater fame, but the team gets compensated for those transfers, and the club considers watching its best players achieve greater wealth in richer European clubs a natural outcome of its commitment to player development.

The same is true for corporations. But how many corporations have Auxerre's commitment to the development of individuals inside the firm? When we think of fostering the growth of individuals, we immediately think of recruiting, training, career path building, succession planning, and other related processes. Too often we tend to aggregate all of those critical processes into one big lump: human resource management. Making it all the job of HR seems a tidy solution, and allows us to return to our somnolence.

This attitude is but another outgrowth of a perverted logic that has permeated our thinking for many years. If one thinks back to the four sets of goals in the Balanced Scorecard—financial, customer, operations, learning and innovation—we erroneously assume that the flow goes from setting financial goals, to creating customer goals, then establishing operational goals, and finally developing the learning and innovation capabilities in the back room to support the rest of the strategy. As a consequence, we believe that learning and innovation come last, after the corporation has defined the other three elements.

This assumption mistakes the chronology of conceptual development for the chronology of implementation. In thinking about what the firm should do, it does indeed help to follow a sequence that starts with financial goals and customer needs and then works back to the skills and capabilities required to meet these needs. In actually meeting them, however, the firm needs to start by building capabilities, and then watch as capable people produce results that ripple through operations, touch the customer, and produce the expected financial

results. Like the Auxerre soccer club, sustaining performance requires building competences in the back room *first*. Individual development is the lead indicator, with customers and financial achievements lagging behind the building of capabilities.

Putting HR in charge of fostering the development of individuals involves the same mistake companies have made when they put a strategic planning function in charge of strategy, or quality czars in charge of quality. The only difference is that strategy and quality have managed to escape their functional ghetto, whereas human resource functions to a large degree have not.

Consider the sad situation most firms are in. For many firms, recruiting remains a lonely HR function, tasked by management "to find good people." Such recruiting departments are full of young college graduates eagerly trying to excite campus candidates and more seasoned applicants about the prospect of being with the firm. There's only one problem: They are human resources specialists without real field experience. Their only real experience with the firm relates to compensation grids and benefits packages. It rapidly becomes clear to potential recruits that they are merely going through "an HR screen," with the result that no goodwill gets generated in the discussion, particularly if a competitor's interview was conducted by senior line executives.

Too often, training is in the hands of midlevel managers. Their expertise often is limited to facilitation and behavioral techniques, without any real content knowledge of the business. Every year the training manager runs a survey that gets sent to all managers of the firm, asking them "what skills and capabilities they want people to be trained in." Responses, when they come, are superficial, for line managers aren't always the best judges of skills required, nor do they really trust that the training department can provide them with what they need anyway. Consequently, such courses are by and large misaligned with the needs of the business. Regardless of the firm's explicit training policy, the people of the firm regard training as predominantly optional, and last-minute cancellations are frequent. Dutifully, the training department surveys those who do attend, usually amid the mild euphoria that sets in at the end of the session, and typically the survey shows favorable ratings. A few weeks later, however, the relevance of the training has eroded to virtually nothing. Consequently, the training budget is often the first to get cut at crunch time.

In such firms, career path and succession planning are little more than bureaucratic exercises. Individuals develop confidence in their firm's ability to help them along only when they see professionals committed to their own success, not when they see paperwork being exchanged between their managers and headquarters. In itself, building lists of high-potential people and formally planning the succession of key individuals is of little help, unless successful people inside the firm get involved, thereby leading the next generation of high-potential people to believe that there is a true support mechanism at play. Absent such involvement, no career path management or succession planning effort can be successful.

The situation is perhaps not *quite* as bleak as we are painting it here. Many corporations are awakening to the importance of developing people. Increasingly, the human resource function is coming out of its torpor, and some directors of HR actually play the role of second-in-command behind the CEO. Many have discovered that success lies in transcending functional boundaries, and in getting line managers to involve everyone in the firm in learning and people development. In some cases, human resources directors have earned the right to influence the strategy dramatically, spearheading the development of new capabilities for the firm.

*Professor Karl, or the Birth*
*of a Teaching Vocation*

Karl, the Woodbridge scheduler, thought he had seen it all. As it turns out, he hasn't. He's about to lead a discussion with new employees about the ongoing transformation project. *"Me, a teacher? They gotta be kidding! Why not make me wear a clown's nose or a tutu while they're at it?"*

Well, here he is, waiting in the wings, coached by the training manager. He's brought about 200 slides with him, because he's afraid he'll run out of things to say. For a two-hour slot, that ought to do. *Yeah, yeah, she wants it to be interactive. Well, I'll*

*ask them whether they have any questions, and if they do, it will be interactive. How many folks are there in here?* About 20, from all parts of the firm, she tells him, trying to get him pumped up.

Karl doesn't even know where to stand as she's introducing him. *Gosh, they look so young! The fellow in the front row looks downright prepubescent. And it says on his name tag that he's with sales.* Karl sure wouldn't buy any paper from a kid that young. The new-hires are observing him eagerly, as if he were a polar bear at the zoo.

Clearing his voice, he nervously gets started. His early transparencies describe how the project came about, how the order fulfillment process needed to be shortened, and how they organized themselves to achieve that. Karl feels tense, mumbling at the screen, trying hard to forget that there's a group watching him. Only 20 minutes have gone by, but he knows he's very boring, as confirmed by the yawns he sees from some of young recruits. The training manager is attacking her nails in the back of the room, trying to smile encouragingly whenever her eyes meet his, hoping it will get better.

Mercifully, a young woman has a question. "How is paper made?" she asks with disarming innocence.

For 10 seconds, Karl looks at her, mouth open, completely aghast. He's been discussing the subtleties of scheduling and order fulfillment, but he suddenly realizes that these young folks have no clue what he's talking about. He looks at the remaining 170 transparencies, wondering how he can use them without further deepening the hole he's dug for himself. Then, inspiration strikes like a lightning bolt.

"Why don't we go across the street?" he asks. "I'll show you the plant and how we make paper. I can pretty much cover what I wanted to right by the machine."

The training manager in the back of the room looks up, thanking the powers-that-be for divine intervention. She jumps up, waving everybody to follow Karl.

Transplanted into his natural habitat, the self-absorbed, stooped silhouette that was Karl in the training center is gone, replaced by an enthusiastic manager with a confident smile and shining eyes. He gathers everybody close to him and they listen intently, in spite of the bustle surrounding them. Taking in Karl's safety instructions, they all look a little intimidated and feel a little self-conscious wearing the unfamiliar safety glasses and hard hats.

Karl leads them through the process. First, they go over to the huge pulp vats and the tossing of the magic brew with its secret additives and coloring agents. Then to the giant paper machine with its fast moving bed of pulp that dries rapidly into paper. In the heater section, the new recruits' glasses fog up instantaneously, and they have to cock their heads back to see, to the boisterous amusement of the operators who had been waiting for the moment. Then to the wind-up section, where giant master rolls are moved away by huge cranes and placed with the semi-finished inventory. Finally to the finishing section, with its huge scissors cutting the master rolls to the desired width and length.

All of a sudden, lights start to flash in the finishing section, and the whirring sound of the alarm overrides any other noise in the plant. A swarm of workers rushes to the paper machine. To the unsuspecting recruits, it looks like a scene out of *Rescue 911.*

"Don't worry, folks," Karl says reassuringly, "there's no danger. It's what we call a break. Look right in front of you, and you'll see that the paper has ripped right down the middle. What they'll now do is clear this through the machine, then start a new run."

Some excited, some scared, the new recruits move nervously, trying to stay out of the way of the workers who are trying to solve the problem. They have a million questions. What produces a break? How much does it cost? How can it be prevented?

Even as things quiet down, the rolling fire of questions continues, most of them quite naive. But it doesn't matter. Karl knows all the answers, no matter how much they push him. He never knew he was this good. There's something happening inside him, something he likes, even though he can't quite put his finger on it. He's growing fond of these bright, eager minds, looking for knowledge. It feels as if he's taking them by the hand and showing them the world for the first time, the same kind of thing he felt when he helped his daughter get through middle-school math. Much to his sur-

prise, he finds himself—the legendary grump and misanthrope—being patient. There's pride involved as well. Suddenly, he wants to give these young folks a favorable first impression of the place they've just committed their future to.

He's getting downright pedagogical, although he couldn't spell the word if they asked him to. Back in the training class after the tour, he asks them to sketch out the production process as they remember it. It's amazing, but as he walks around the room he sees that some of them can do a pretty good job of it. He also asks them to describe what to do during a break. There again, they've evidently learned a bunch. Had he known what they could do, he really could have used a few of these bright kids on his project.

When the training manager tells him that his time is up, he feels sorry. He had so much more to say, and he can tell that his students also would have liked more time. But at least he knows some of their names, and he'll be able to greet them whenever he runs into them day-to-day. He also knows that they'll now be able to call him if they have any questions about the production process. The training manager, in the enthusiasm of the moment, gets him to promise to come back for the other entering classes for the rest of the year. It's a big commitment, but he finds himself agreeing to it, not so much because he feels it's important, but because it's fun.

On the way back to his office, he finds himself whistling a tune from *Snow White,* one of his daughters' favorite Disney movies.

### Creating Mentor-Guided, Life-Forming Projects for High-Caliber Individuals

Great organizations rely on more than just an elite few to manage themselves. They know how to use the people and capabilities they have to the fullest extent, creating second and third opportunities for those who have not quite made it the first time but whose values and intentions are in the right place. Betting everything on the assumption that one has hired only the "qualified" is simply unrealistic, if not naive. What distinguishes great corporations from others is their ability to inject learning into, and therefore extract more value out of, their middle- and lower-rank performers.

Of all the forms of personal development, none is more effective than learning on the job under the guidance of a mentor. Although there are many advantages to more formal training and development programs, they are usually poor substitutes for learning by doing. Many new training designs blur the distinction between formal training and real problem solving, and most programs disconnect people from their work, inducing a sense that it's not quite "the real thing." Therefore, assigning high-caliber individuals to mentor-guided, life-forming projects remains the most effective way of accelerating individual development.

Life-forming projects are those that enrich the experience and knowledge base of the individuals working on them, while also carrying the potential to inject new energy and growth into the corporation. The major attraction of project work is that it doesn't distinguish between doing one's job and learning new things. The individual's official responsibility may be to deliver against a "line" commitment, but a clever design of the job or project ensures that the only way the individual can succeed is by acquiring new knowledge and skills.

The ability to design such ad hoc projects is one of the most valuable talents a leader can have. Few are great at it. It isn't taught in books, nor is it recognized as a discipline. Consequently, many leaders limit themselves by picking up on loosely defined, but often fashionable, themes, such as reengineering or total quality management, and designing equally vague projects around them. Great leaders focus on more specific themes, often linking the development of a new capability for the firm with a defined performance goal. Inspiration for such ad hoc programs often is provided by enterprising individuals who have a passion for something a little bit off the beaten path. Allowing people to express and act upon their passions in projects of this type can yield enormous payoffs, and the growth of many firms can be traced back to such roots.

Astute leaders recognize that the success of these projects depends on the people driving them, and therefore they start to pick talent early. After designing the project, they search for up-and-coming young individuals, able to spearhead the project independently of the constraints of the line organization. Obviously, the people who suggest the projects are the likely candidates to lead them, because their passion will carry them farther than those who have been randomly assigned. Once selected, the team leader is assigned a *mentor,* an executive with experience, authority, and the will to teach, who will provide air cover in times of trouble, and who will serve as a learning resource to the individual.

Although mentors can be among an organization's most valuable resources, most companies treat mentoring more like a hobby than a legitimate leadership role. Few career management programs list mentoring as an explicit objective, yet successful managers almost always credit one or two mentors for their success.

Mentors lead from behind. Their counsel is discreet, the antithesis of micromanagement. Often, they're warm in day-to-day contact, but they're tough when they have to be. Because they enjoy great credibility in the organization, they often act as back-channel providers of information, helping line managers understand how the project is progressing and, if necessary, suggesting what should be done to change it. The best mentors often are managers in the twilight of their careers, men and women who identify with the less experienced and younger individuals they are coaching.

Like a good parent, the good mentor allows the person they are coaching to make mistakes, recognizing that the best learning often occurs from making errors. This can be extremely difficult at times, for it's difficult for an executive to willingly see something go wrong in an organization and among people he or she cares for. The idea is to exert subtle influence, such that the damage caused by the error is minimal, while the learning from it is great. This sort of creative *error management* is an integral part of a well thought-out development process.

## John, the CIGNA Accountant, Spreads His Wings

"We used to be the know-it-alls, the sharp-pencils," John Downham confesses. "We were the superstaff, not really part of the business, but checkers in charge of interpreting for corporate what was going on inside the division."

John Downham is describing the financial staff of CIGNA P&C as it existed before Gerry Isom's arrival. Downham is a friendly accountant with a keen sense of metaphor, who today carries the title of Transformation Officer for one of the three main divisions of CIGNA P&C, Commercial Insurance Services (CIS). Until Isom's arrival he worked in the controller's area, doing expense management and budgeting, worrying about receivables and cashflow.

Downham, although he has become a leader in the transformation effort, refuses to indulge in simple black-and-white characterizations of the past and present. "Today, it's easy to dump on the old regime," he states. "But I respected my boss. He was a man of conviction who believed that insurance was a financial business that had to be run by financial people. Perhaps that was his blind spot. He wore that belief on his sleeve, and he alienated some people. But he was a man of integrity, and I often regret he's not with us anymore."

Clearly, it's hard for Downham to put the entire episode of his boss's departure behind him.

"My boss left a week after I'd signed on to become a full-time member of Isom's transformation team," he continues. "I had a sense of a terrible loss. I'm not afraid to say it, I was in tears when I said my good-byes to Howard. I first felt mad, then let down."

Slowly, Downham worked his way out of his depression, and became involved in the whirlwind of activities created by project OAR (Organization Alignment Review), the second phase of Isom's transformation effort, in the fall of 1993.

"Now, I had an open field," he recalls. "I had no sense of defending anything. I didn't have to be my boss's emissary anymore; I could use my own judgment. At the same time, that was scary. It took me a while to work out that philosophical difference."

Downham remembers the first three months of project OAR as mostly frustrating. "In this phase of work, we were mostly highlighting existing organizational problems," he says. "We also supported the discovery process with financial infor-

mation. I knew it all by heart, and had to educate lots of people on the numbers. We were also running survey after survey on cultural issues, and I thought it was nonsense. One year later, I now recognize that culture is everything in a successful company."

Like Ward Jungers, he remembers the dinner the transformation team had with Gerry Isom shortly before Christmas 1993. The diagnostic phase of project OAR was now over, and Isom was trying to encourage the team to pursue the task they had initiated some three months earlier. "I was in a lousy mood," he remembers. "All 10 of us, full-time team members, were burned out. I had a sense of impending failure. It was as if we'd seen the promised land, but were unsure we could bring the rest of the organization with us."

Downham had been assigned to the "support alignment team," which had perhaps the toughest job in the effort, spearheading a dramatic personnel reduction in the home office support functions. "No more studying, it was time for action," he recalls. "It was a brand-new ball game. I started with the financial organization, since I knew it well. I was moderately successful overall, quite successful with some of my colleagues, less so with others. In that position, I rapidly learned the power of leadership. When you're dealing with leaders, you get results. When you don't, you might as well forget it."

A few frustrating experiences remain vivid in Downham's mind. "At one point, I launched a blitzkrieg of natural work teams in a number of areas, but all it left me was Magic Marker on my hands. We got locked out of at least two departments that I can remember. But it didn't matter."

In the heat of the battle, Downham remembers losing a sense of perspective. "In early October 1994, our team wanted to write our own obituary," he states. "We assembled our team and produced a long list of reasons we thought the transformation had been unsuccessful. We got pessimistic, nearly morbid. Based on that, we generated a report and sent it to senior management."

Finally, at the beginning of the new year, Gerry Isom invited the group to a session. Much to the group's surprise, the tone was decidedly upbeat. "Gerry Isom is the one who pointed out that we'd been quite successful," Downham remembers. "He showed us things we were too close to even notice. Perhaps our stream of work was not as spectacularly successful as some others, like underwriting, but we'd had an indirect impact on the whole business. Jim Engel, the head of claims, for example, had decided to align his big organization more closely with the businesses, and even though we hadn't worked with him directly day-to-day, he credited our work with having helped him think through the issues."

Downham remembers finding himself once again at a crossroads in late 1994. He had a choice between returning to his old job in finance or continuing in a transformation role.

"That boost from Isom got us pumped," he beams. "We started talking about what would be needed to continue the fight. It wasn't done for personal reasons. We simply wanted to make sure that we kept the flame alive. We talked ourselves right into those positions. First I felt a little like Woody Allen: 'These jobs are too important to give them to the likes of me.' Then I thought I'd learned a few things over the last year, and maybe I could help move the company."

Dick Wratten, the head of Commercial Insurance Services (CIS), offered Downham the job of transformation officer within CIS. It was a brief conversation, in which Wratten simply told him he'd like to have him as part of the team.

"I accepted on the spot," Downham recalls. "Then I went back to my old boss and told him what I was going to do. He asked me a bunch of questions, such as "Who are you going to report to?" and "What will your level be?" Somewhat embarrassed, I told him I didn't know. It hadn't dawned on me that those things could be important. I went back to Wratten and asked him whom I would report to. 'Me, of course,' was his answer. The point is, I knew what I was doing was important, and that's all that really mattered to me."

In spite of his early misgivings, Downham feels the year just elapsed [1994] has been the most important in his professional career. "I can't imagine a scenario in my old job where I could have had the same impact," he says. What I've been through has been so unique, I can't really explain it. Sometimes people who knew me look at me as if I have three heads. I talk differently, I think differently. Yet deep inside, I know I'm just a simple accountant, trying to do this transformation thing."

## *Identifying Critical Skills and Designing an Education Strategy*

Project assignments and mentoring are the most effective ways to foster individual learning, but they can reach only a limited number of individuals. The next best thing is an education strategy involving less customization but more employees.

What distinguishes good educational programs from bad ones is not so much the level of resources committed or the quality of the facilities, but their relevance to the business. Most training dollars spent today are wasted on the ill-focused development of generic skills, usually triggered by some functional manager's personal hobby, or in response to a proposal made by a third-party training or consulting company.

The design of an education strategy cannot occur in a vacuum. A skills or competency model needs to be defined *first;* only then can skill and competency training be focused and meaningful. Building a skills model involves striking a balance between two extremes. On the one hand, having no skills model is clearly not the answer. At the opposite extreme, building the world's most *thorough* model is equally dangerous.

We vividly remember the case of a firm that developed a skills model so comprehensive and complex that it took on a life of its own. Millions of consulting dollars were spent on developing it to such absurd levels of detail as "tries to engage colleagues in friendly, interpersonal manner most of the time, while exhibiting the necessary firmness in emergency periods." How would you like to be tested on such an ability? Now imagine this dimension to be one of 35 attributes, pertaining to one group of individuals among 68 groups of "key individuals." And imagine the puzzlement of the head of human resources or the CEO, trying to find the high-stakes skills he or she should invest in within this 68 by 35 matrix in which every coordinate is conceivably a development area.

Efficiency dictates that the skills model should focus on high-payoff skills. Experience shows that such skills usually are associated with the key processes and learning loops of the firm. Once again, the intertwining of the biocorporate systems prevents us from neatly isolating pockets of skills that can be individually nurtured. Skills development is all integral part of transformation, and it cannot be dissociated from the mapping of key interrelationships within the firm. Yet few firms carry their change aspirations all the way to an educational agenda, and few human resource departments have the capability to trace the firm's skill development needs all the way back to the firm's transformation path.

All educational programs run the risk of losing relevance to the core business. Even the highly regarded grandfather of all corporate education programs—the Crotonville executive training program of General Electric—once lost its relevance, in the 1970s, when it started to benchmark itself too much against other schools rather than remain focused on the specific needs of GE. It's easy for training centers to fall in love with themselves and their prestigious teaching staffs and to start overinvesting in their bricks and mortar.

Aligning an education program to a results measurement system is the best way to prevent training centers from becoming irrelevant to the corporation. Ideally, one should be able to track the skills developed through educational programs to bottom-line results. For example, Allstate Insurance and Federal Express have been able to link an increase in customer service skills among their customer-facing employees to objective increases in customer loyalty and even revenues.

## Unipart U

In Chaps. 2 and 10, we saw how Unipart, a U.K. automotive parts manufacturer and distributor led by CEO John Neill, achieved exceptional performance through its constituency-based mission and values. In particular, we looked at the firm's explicit commitment to what it calls *shared destiny relationships* with customers, suppliers, and throughout the supply chain. In Chap. 10 we delved more deeply into Unipart's external relationships,

examining how it aligns measures and rewards with its "demand chain partners," as Neill might put it. Unipart is equally remarkable in its commitment to employee learning. It is so committed, in fact, that it has established its own university, modeled to a significant extent after Motorola's University, which Neill admires.

In September of 1993, Unipart U, the company university formed by Unipart, was formally opened by John Patten, British Secretary of State for Education. "The U has a clear mission," says Neill, "that derives logically from the group's mission: to build an enduring, upper-quartile performing company in which our stakeholders are keen to participate."

"The U reflects our intention to train and inspire people to achieve world-class performance, both within the Unipart Group and among its stakeholders," he continues. "There is a good commercial argument for the U: it's a support route to commercial advantage, and it enhances shareholder value by helping to prevent us from becoming obsolete."

Unipart's vision for the U is "to help us create the world's best lean enterprise," says Neill. "It is by working with all our stakeholders in long-term shared-destiny relationships, and by using the best learning, that we can eliminate waste and improve quality and customer service. Learning and training are fundamentally and inextricably linked with the very being of our company."

"We have therefore created our *deans' group,* consisting of the divisional managing directors. They have their own *faculties,* responsible for defining the critical success factors of their businesses and ensuring that high-quality training courses are available to meet them," he explains with pride. One envisions busy executives hastily throwing professorial robes over their three-piece suits in the backseat of a car on their way to a lecture.

"So now, our managing directors have two roles: first, as managers of their businesses, and, second, as deans of their faculties and full members of the deans' group," Neill explains. "It's through this that we share the best available learning with our colleagues. Each dean writes and presents training courses in the U, and we've all been schooled in how to teach—not only the deans, but managers and employees at all levels teach other in the U. We're transforming our managers into coaches."

Unipart U has 10 faculties, all directly traceable to its business:

1. Commercial
2. Communications
3. Core
4. Finance
5. Industries
6. IT
7. Marketing
8. Outlets
9. Sales
10. Warehousing and distribution

The deans' group is chaired by Professor Dan Jones of Cardiff Business School, a world-recognized motor industry expert and coauthor of the book, *The Machine That Changed the World.* Professor Jones acts as the business philosopher and mentor of Unipart U, and lectures two days a month on "lean thinking."

There is nothing "virtual" about Unipart U. It boasts state-of-the-art facilities, 14 training rooms, a lecture theater with remote-control auto-cues and touch-sensitive controls for projection equipment. The U's library, called The Learning Curve, contains books, audio and video cassettes, reference works, maps, periodicals, newspapers, and librarians who can get anything you want through an interlibrary loan system. Laptop computers can be checked out for weekend or overnight use. The library is connected to various on-line information services. Not bad for a $1 billion automotive parts company, operating in a traditionally low-margin business!

Attached to the U is The Leading Edge, a showroom and classroom for computer hardware and software where employees can learn at their own pace, starting basic computing skills and moving right through to the most sophisticated software. The latest software releases are on display, available for employees to test. The Leading Edge has glass walls and is deliberately placed next to the entrance and reception area of Unipart's Oxford headquarters. Neill wants everyone—existing and prospective stakeholders, tradesmen, visitors, or passersby—to understand Unipart's commitment to harnessing information technology in preparing for the future, as well as to think about how they might harness it in working with Unipart.

Neill believes that many of the ideas incorporated in the U could be of value to industry as a whole. "We're building physical infrastructure, a new platform to use. We've got to build it here, because it will safely see us into the next century."

He says people are still intimidated by IT, but insists that everyone must be computer literate. "We have to seduce people through the pain barrier, and we need a place for that."

Neill says the major strategic idea behind Unipart U is to make line managers responsible for training. Their time is costed at an appropriate rate, not including their opportunity cost, and programs are costed too. It takes 10 days, for example, to teach Ten-to-zero, Unipart's quality philosophy, at the U, and the course begins with a lecture on the philosophies underlying it, delivered by Neill himself.

Neill believes that many of the ideas incorporated in the U could be of value to the industry as a whole. "The U is a platform from which we will be able to see future possibilities in a way which might not otherwise have been possible," he says. "It has a fundamental role to play in inspiring the learning that will be essential to getting us safely into the next century."

### *Balancing the Supply of and Demand for Skills Inside the Corporation*

It has long been the dream of socially minded CEOs and government officials alike that people displaced by restructuring at one end of the firm could be redeployed, often after retraining, in another end of the same firm. This generous thinking is born both of human compassion and of the belief that most firms display inefficiencies in their internal labor market. Without a doubt these inefficiencies do exist, especially in large, established corporations that are simultaneously involved in the restructuring of more mature businesses and the development of others.

The telecommunication industry perhaps best illustrates this phenomenon, with the dramatic restructuring occurring in the regulated telephone business, simultaneous with the explosive growth in deregulated markets such as cellular phones, yellow pages, and many other facets of the future "electronic superhighway."

The challenge, of course, has proven to be a practical one. Companies and governments have discovered that skills, even after making a generous provision for "reskilling," are not infinitely fungible. It isn't easy to take shop floor foremen and transform them into automation specialists, nor is it a cinch to turn repair and maintenance personnel into customer service representatives inside telephone companies. Some people *will* adapt more readily than others. Some people *can* adapt more readily than others. Unfortunately, the objective realities are bound to create obstacles for even the most generous and well intended redeployment programs.

The major obstacle, however, is psychological, and the major limitation has proven to be behavioral. Most of us carry a picture of displaced employees as rational beings who, given the chance, would welcome an opportunity to be redeployed. It is seldom that way, and the choices are seldom that clear. Many people who know that their positions are going to be eliminated can't get past their feelings of anger and betrayal. Those who have survived previous bad times may feel that their job could survive after all, so why move before they are forced to? Often the redeployment alternative is equally ill defined, frequently amounting to a vague promise of a hypothetical future, for an undetermined compensation level, supported by an unproven program. Only now are companies beginning to understand the psychology of the displaced within the context of restructurings.

Individuals undergo a personal trauma in the transition. Self-esteem drops. Denial, anger, and depression may become factors. Employees become confused, defensive, and sometimes irrational, in turn producing frustration for the leadership team, whose members can't fathom why threatened employees don't spontaneously reach out for the hand that has been extended to them. "If I were in their place," they think, "I'd jump at the opportunity in a minute." But the threatened employee doesn't have as clear a view of his or her choices as the leadership team does, nor can he or she look at the situation dispassionately.

To add economic motivation to good intentions, many countries, primarily in Europe, have built up a high social cost around layoffs and other displacements of full-time employees. This has provided an added incentive for corporations to look for alternate solutions, encouraging internal retraining schemes and producing a flurry of experiments vis-à-vis within company redeployment.

The results to date have been mixed at best, but a few companies are getting good at it. The key to success is the creation of the internal equivalent of market processes to match supply and demand. The companies that have done the best offer a strong behavioral support infrastructure, while simultaneously opening pathways for individual exploration of opportunities throughout the firm. They help displaced employees deal with the psychological trauma, while providing a process through which they can take action toward finding their next job.

Technology has entered the equation, sometimes with great success. Critical to the success of an internal labor exchange is a forum that can link "many to many." In corporations with tens of thousands of employees—where the potential inefficiencies are greatest due to the size of the pool involved—the simple logistics of communicating job availability can be enormous. Technology can provide that forum, and in addition can become the platform for individuals to devise skill-building and career path planning within a corporatewide framework of opportunities.

Barclays Bank in the United Kingdom has developed such a technology. A few years ago, Barclays made the commitment that it would not lay off its large group of MIS specialists, whose skills had been built around the now obsolete COBOL programming language for mainframes. Rather than fire them and hire new employees with the requisite "modern skills," the firm invested in the development of a large-scale IT application designed initially to help the MIS people, but eventually to allow every employee in the firm to acquire new skills to ensure themselves a place within the organization in the future.

Designed for delivery through desktop systems, the program starts with a multimedia module, in which the CEO communicates the general strategy of the bank and the implications of the strategy in terms of new skills requirements for the MIS department. The program then itemizes what the new jobs are likely to be over a period of a few years, and what skills will comprise each job. Employees then are prompted into an interactive session designed to characterize their current jobs and associated skills, and to explore potential paths leading them from their current skills to the required new skills. At any point a human resources counselor may be invited to step in electronically, to offer advice or to validate the self-assessment. As an incentive for employees to log on, the program also lists all available jobs within the bank at any given time. Employees also know that their superiors look upon use of the program as an indication of a commitment to learn and grow with Barclays.

*AT&T Resource Link®*

Among the many experiments conducted in the area of intracompany employee redeployment, the one established by AT&T in October 1991 is one of the most successful. AT&T Resource Link® is an in-house, temporary-services unit that supplies general management and technical professionals to AT&T divisions and helps satisfy the ever-changing work-force requirements across the firm's business.

The idea was to improve the responsiveness and flexibility of the firm's internal labor market, so that talented managers, who might otherwise have left the company as a result of its restructuring activities, could be retained and developed. It is now AT&T policy that all business units and divisions must consider AT&T Resource Link® before resorting to agency temps or other contractors to fill management needs. Though assignments are temporary, "associates" retain their status as regular AT&T employees.

Since its formation, AT&T Resource Link® has developed into a vigorous, self-confident supplier of internal know-how to help AT&T manage its fluctuating skills needs, and it has acquired a clear idea of its mission and its customers.

The unit commends its services to its customers—the rest of the company—in precisely the same way as an external temp agency would. In effect, their market positioning is: "In today's competitive environment, leaders must constantly seek new and creative ways to achieve business objectives. AT&T Resource Link® can provide you with flexibility to perform short-term project work, to temporarily back-fill a vacant position, or to support temporary peaks in workload. Our associates offer customers a variety of technical and managerial expertise and, in contrast to outside temps, are familiar with AT&T products, services, and infrastructure. In addition to minimizing 'on-boarding' costs, associates offer knowledge and experience gained in other parts of the AT&T group, offering clients the opportunity to extend their networks and enhance their collaborative efforts."

The unit is aware of the potentially negative perception of being the home for the victims of AT&T's restructuring. The basic operating premise, however, is that there's nothing intrinsically wrong with employees who have been displaced by restructurings; they just happen to have skills that were no longer needed at that particular place and time. AT&T Resource Link® screens its associates and assesses their skills, knowledge, and adaptability. Given the proper direction, they can represent a tremendous resource for other parts of the business. As of March 1994, the unit had over 400 people on contract with more than 25 different business units and divisions throughout AT&T.

In March 1994, about a third of the unit's associates were on technical assignments, and the demand for nontechnical skills was increasing. Most assignments were from 3 to 12 months, some much longer, and most assignments are extended. As a result, once a displaced employee signs up with Resource Link®, he or she spends on average less than 2 percent of his or her time between jobs, a remarkable result by the standard of the temporary services industry.

Customer satisfaction surveys give high scores (90 percent and above) on quality, ease of use, and readiness to use AT&T Resource Link® again. Associates also value the unit's responsiveness and its ability to match skills to work requirements. The following two testimonials from associates illustrate how the system is being used:

> Working for AT&T Resource Link® has been one of the most rewarding and challenging experiences of my AT&T career. It enabled me to acquire new skills and gain exposure to other areas of the company, both of which led directly to my promotion into NSD Human Resources.

> [AT&T Resource Link®] offers me the ability to increase my overall market value by giving me the opportunity to continue to develop myself and my skills set, to work within many new and existing business units, to gain a better understanding of where the BUs are headed, and to be a part of the overall growth of AT&T.

Perhaps the most remarkable feature of the whole program is the way in which an initiative that was designed to salve the wounds of restructuring and to give tangible substance to AT&T's Common Bond philosophy, is producing a new career option and a new kind of AT&T manager. A significant number of associates end up in permanent positions, and at least 15 percent of those placements are promotions. Even more encouragingly, many people have turned down permanent offers, preferring to take advantage of the variety of assignments AT&T Resource Link® offers. AT&T Resource Link® has become a legitimate career path in itself.

Over 50 percent of associates choose Resource Link® as a career move, because they see, in the peripatetic nature of the work, an opportunity to expand their knowledge of the group, enhance their skills, raise their profiles, and expand their network. These are not traumatized victims of restructuring; they are high-fliers, cruising around the group, picking up contracts, establishing credibility, and searching for the most exciting areas or the most promising routes to the top.

### Reskilling at France Telecom

France Telecom faces the massive redeployment challenge of major telecommunication companies, with a double twist. First, it operates in a country whose social legislation is among the most comprehensive and restrictive, essentially barring France Telecom from using the type of restructuring chosen by its American and British counterparts. Second, its work force is strongly unionized, further restricting its freedom to adjust its workforce level to its perceived needs.

This in itself would not be of major consequence if France Telecom could continue to compete as a regional player, protected by a set of local regulations. But this isn't the case. To survive, France Telecom has no choice but to participate in the global telecommunications race, which means achieving status as a global competitor as quickly as possible. To do that, France Telecom has undertaken a massive transformation in the last few years, and today it bears little resemblance to the sleepy monopoly the French people once loved to make fun of. The company, since 1991, has a new status, partly government- and partly public-owned. It also has formed a major alliance with its German equivalent, Deutsche Telekom, to develop a global service offering. No more Gallic isolationism—the global war is on.

The need for the massive transformation of France Telecom is triggering an equally massive shift of skills requirements, resulting in potentially large displacements of individuals. For example, in a complete redesign of its order-activation process—the process of making a phone line available to anyone who requests it as quickly and efficiently as possible—the company has found that it can reduce manpower by a considerable margin in this area. Given the social context, however, France Telecom was puzzled as to where to go next.

The Toulouse regional district was put in charge of piloting the new order-activation process as well as of proposing solutions to the arduous social questions involved. Of the 80 full-time-equivalent people working in service activation—close to 180 people actually were involved, many on a part-time basis—it found that 14 could be made redundant (the job could be eliminated) in the new process.

Painstakingly, the managers of the Toulouse regional district proceeded to search elsewhere in the firm for employment opportunities for the 14 employees. They found needs across numerous functions, in areas as diverse as complaint management, agency-based customer service, field service, new cable offering for large buildings, and relationship management with municipalities and developers.

With great care, they organized in-depth interviews with all 14 employees, working with them on matching their skills and interests with the available options. In addition, they jointly determined which skills the displaced employees would have to acquire. In the end, each of the 14 employees was successfully redeployed, each in customized fashion. Remarkably, the unions, traditionally perceived as fairly antagonistic, supported the program throughout.

Finding a solution to the fate of 14 people in the Toulouse region may not look like much in light of the fact that France Telecom has 168,000 employees in all! But the approach that was created sent a wonderful signal to the organization as a whole. For the first time, something concrete had been done about helping along the individual renewal of people whose future was threatened by the company's transformation. As one of the 14 testified recently with great gratitude: "It's wonderful when our bosses worry about implementation at this level of detail. Because that's where my future is, in this detail."

# 42

# The Leader's New Work

## Building Learning Organizations

PETER M. SENGE

Over the past two years, business academics and senior managers have begun talking about the notion of the learning organization. Ray Stata of Analog Devices put the idea succinctly in these pages last spring: "The rate at which organizations learn may become the only sustainable source of competitive advantage." And in late May of this year, at an MIT-sponsored conference entitled "Transforming Organizations," two questions arose again and again: *How can we build organizations in which continuous learning occurs?* and, *What kind of person can best lead the learning organization?* This chapter, based on Senge's recently published book, *The Fifth Discipline: The Art and Practice of the Learning Organization,* begins to chart this new territory, describing new roles, skills, and tools for leaders who wish to develop learning organizations.

Human beings are designed for learning. No one has to teach an infant to walk, or talk, or master the spatial relationships needed to stack eight building blocks that don't topple. Children come fully equipped with an insatiable drive to explore and experiment. Unfortunately, the primary institutions of our society are oriented predominantly toward continuing rather than learning, rewarding individuals for performing for others rather than for cultivating their natural curiosity and impulse to learn. The young child entering school discovers quickly that the name of the game is getting the right answer and avoiding mistakes—a mandate no less compelling to the aspiring manager.

"Our prevailing system of management has destroyed our people," writes W. Edwards Deming, leader in the quality movement.[1] "People are born with intrinsic motivation, self-esteem, dignity, curiosity to learn, joy in learning. The forces of destruction begin with toddlers—a prize for the best Halloween costume, grades in school, gold stars, and on up through the university. On the job, people, teams, divisions are ranked—reward for the one at the top, punishment at the bottom. MBO, quotas, incentive pay, business plans, put together separately, division by division, cause further loss, unknown and unknowable."

Ironically, by focusing on performing for someone else's approval, corporations create the very conditions that predestine them to mediocre performance. Over the long run, superior performance depends on superior learning. A Shell study showed that, according to former planning director Arie de Geus, "a full one-third of the Fortune '500' industrials listed in 1970 had vanished by 1983."[2] Today, the average lifetime of the largest industrial enterprises is probably less than *half* the average lifetime of a person in an industrial society. On the other hand, de Geus and his colleagues at Shell also found a small number of companies that survived for seventy-five years or longer. Interestingly, the key to their survival was the ability to run "experiments in the margin," to continually explore new business and organizational opportunities that create potential new sources of growth.

If anything, the need for understanding how organizations learn and accelerating that learning is greater today than ever before. The old days when a Henry Ford, Alfred Sloan, or Tom Watson *learned for the organization* are gone. In an increasingly dynamic, interdependent, and unpredictable world, it is simply no longer possible for anyone to "figure it all out at the top." The old model, "the top thinks and the local acts," must now give way to integrating thinking and acting at all levels. While the challenge is great, so is the potential payoff. "The person who figures out how to harness the collective genius of the people in his or her organization," according to former Citibank CEO Walter Wriston, "is going to blow the competition away."

## Adaptive Learning and Generative Learning

The prevailing view of learning organizations emphasizes increased adaptability. Given the accelerating pace of change, or so the standard view goes, "the most successful corporation of the 1990s," according to *Fortune* magazine, "will be something called a learning organization, a con-summately adaptive enterprise."[3] As the Shell study shows, examples of traditional authoritarian bureaucracies that responded too slowly to survive in changing business environments are legion.

But increasing adaptiveness is only the first stage in moving toward learning organizations. The impulse to learn in children goes deeper than desires to respond and adapt more effectively to environmental change. The impulse to learn, at its heart, is an impulse to be generative, to expand our capability. This is why leading corporations are focusing on *generative* learning, which is about creating, as well as *adaptive* learning, which is about coping.[4]

The total quality movement in Japan illustrates the evolution from adaptive to generative learning. With its emphasis on continuous experimentation and feedback, the total quality movement has been the first wave in budding learning organizations. But Japanese firms' view of serving the customer has evolved. In the early years of total quality, the focus was on "fitness to standard" making a product reliably so that it would do what its designers intended it to do and what the firm told its customers it would do. Then came a focus on "fitness to need," understanding better what the customer wanted and then providing products that reliably met those needs. Today, leading edge firms seek to understand and meet the "latent need" of the customer—what customers might truly value but have never experienced or would never think to ask for. As one Detroit executive commented recently, "You could never produce the Mazda Miata solely from market research. It required a leap of imagination to see what the customer *might* want.[5]

Generative learning, unlike adaptive learning, requires new ways of looking at the world, whether in understanding customers or in understanding how to better manage a business. For years, U.S. manufacturers sought competitive advantage in aggressive controls on inventories, incentives against overproduction, and rigid adherence to production forecasts. Despite these incentives, their performance was eventually eclipsed by Japanese firms who saw the challenges of manufacturing differently. They realized that eliminating delays in the production process was the key to reducing instability and improving cost, productivity, and service. They worked to build networks of relationships with trusted suppliers and to redesign physical production processes so as to reduce delays in materials procurement, production set up, and in-process inventory—a much higher-leverage approach to improving both cost and customer loyalty.

As Boston Consulting Group's George Stalk has observed, the Japanese saw the significance of delays because they saw the process of order entry, production scheduling, materials procurement, production, and distribution *as an integrated system.* "What distorts the system so badly is time," observed Stalk—the multiple delays between events and responses. "These distortions reverberate throughout the system, producing disruptions, waste, and inefficiency."[6] Generative learning requires seeing the systems that control events. When we fail to grasp the systemic source of problems, we are left to "push on" symptoms rather than eliminate underlying causes. The best we can ever do is adaptive learning.

### The Leader's New Work

"I talk with people all over the country about learning organizations, and the response is always very positive," says William O'Brien, CEO of the Hanover Insurance Companies. "If this type of organization is so widely preferred, why don't people create such organizations? I think the answer is leadership. People have no real comprehension of the type of commitment it requires to build such an organization."[7]

Our traditional view of leaders—as special people who set the direction, make the key decisions, and energize the troops—is deeply rooted in an individualistic and nonsystemic worldview. Especially in the West, leaders are *heroes*—great men (and occasionally, women) who rise to the fore in times of crisis. So long as such myths prevail, they reinforce a focus on short-term events and charismatic heroes rather than on systemic forces and collective learning.

Leadership in learning organizations centers on subtler and ultimately more important work. In a learning organization, leaders' roles differ dramatically from that of the charismatic decision maker.

Leaders are designers, teachers, and stewards. These roles require new skills: the ability to build shared vision, to bring to the surface and challenge prevailing mental modes and to foster more systemic patterns of thinking. In short, leaders in learning organizations are responsible for *building organizations* where people are continually expanding their capabilities to shape their future—that is, leaders are responsible for learning.

### *Creative Tension: The Integrating Principle*

Leadership in a learning organization starts with the principle of creative tension.[8] Creative tension comes from seeing clearly where we want to be, our "vision," and telling the truth about where we are, our "current reality." The gap between the two generates a natural tension (see Figure 42.1).

Creative tension can be resolved in two basic ways: by raising current reality toward the vision, or by lowering the vision toward current reality. Individuals, groups, and organizations who learn how to work with creative tension learn how to use the energy it generates to move reality more reliably toward their visions.

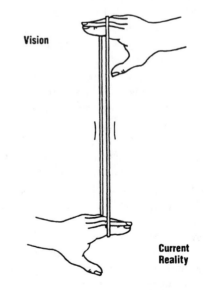

**Figure 42.1.** The Principle of Creative Tension

The principle of creative tension has long been recognized by leaders. Martin Luther King, Jr., once said, "Just as Socrates felt that it was necessary to create a tension in the mind, so that individuals could rise from the bondage of myths and half truths . . . so must we . . . create the kind of tension in society that will help men rise from the dark depths of prejudice and racism."[9]

Without vision there is no creative tension. Creative tension cannot be generated from current reality alone. All the analysis in the world will never generate a vision. Many who are otherwise qualified to lead fail to do so because they try to substitute analysis for vision. They believe that, if only people understood current reality, they would surely feel the motivation to change. They are then disappointed to discover that people "resist" the personal and organizational changes that must be made to alter reality. What they never grasp is that the natural energy for changing reality comes from holding a picture of what might be that is more important to people than what is.

But creative tension cannot be generated from vision alone; it demands an accurate picture of current reality as well. Just as King had a dream, so too did he continually strive to "dramatize the shameful conditions" of racism and prejudice so that they could no longer be ignored. Vision without an understanding of current reality will more likely foster cynicism than creativity. The principle of creative tension teaches that *an accurate picture of current reality is just as important as a compelling picture of a desired future.*

Leading through creative tension is different than solving problems. In problem solving, the energy for change comes from attempting to get away from an aspect of current reality that is undesirable. With creative tension, the energy for change comes from the vision, from what we want to create, juxtaposed with current reality. While the distinction may seem small, the consequences are not. Many people and organizations find themselves motivated to change only when their problems are bad enough to cause them to change. This works for a while, but the change process runs out of steam as soon as the problems driving the change become less pressing. With problem solving, the motivation for change is extrinsic. With creative tension, the motivation is intrinsic. This distinction mirrors the distinction between adaptive and generative learning.

## New Roles

The traditional authoritarian image of the leader as "the boss calling the shots" has been recognized as oversimplified and inadequate for some time. According to Edgar Schein, "Leadership is intertwined with culture formation." Building an organization's culture and shaping its evolution is the "unique and essential function of leadership."[10] In a learning organization, the critical roles of leadership—designer, teacher. and steward—have antecedents in the ways leaders have contributed to budding organizations in the past. But each role takes on new meaning in the learning organization and, as will be seen in the following sections, demands new skills and tools.

### Leader as Designer

Imagine that your organization is an ocean liner and that you are "the leader." What is your role?

I have asked this question of groups of managers many times. The most common answer, not surprisingly, is "the captain." Others say, "The navigator, setting the direction." Still others say, "The helmsman, actually controlling the direction," or, "The engineer down there stoking the fire, providing energy," or, "The social director, making sure everybody's enrolled, involved, and communicating." While these are legitimate leadership roles, there is another which, in many ways, eclipses them all in importance. Yet rarely does anyone mention it.

The neglected leadership role is the *designer* of the ship. No one has a more sweeping influence than the designer. What good does it do for the captain to say, "Turn starboard 30 degrees," when the designer has built a rudder that will only turn to port, or which takes six hours to turn to starboard? It's fruitless to be the leader in an organization that is poorly designed.

The functions of design, or what some have called "social architecture," are rarely visible; they take place behind the scenes. The consequences that appear today are the result of work done long in the past, and work today will show its benefits far in the future. Those who aspire to lead out of a desire to control, or gain fame, or simply to be at the center of the action, will find little to attract them to the quiet design work of leadership.

But what, specifically, is involved in organizational design? "Organization design is widely misconstrued as moving around boxes and lines," says Hanover's O'Brien. "The first task of organization design concerns designing the governing ideas of purpose, vision, and core values by which people will live." Few acts of leadership have a more enduring impact on an organization than building a foundation of purpose and core values.

In 1982, Johnson & Johnson found itself facing a corporate nightmare when bottles of its best-selling Tylenol were tampered with, resulting in several deaths. The corporation's immediate response was to pull all Tylenol off the shelves of retail outlets. Thirty-one million capsules were destroyed, even though they were tested and found safe. Although the immediate cost was significant, no other action was possible given the firm's credo. Authored almost forty years earlier by president Robert Wood Johnson, Johnson & Johnson's credo states that permanent success is possible only when modern industry realizes that

- Service to its customers comes first;
- Service to its employees and management comes second;
- Service to the community comes third; and
- Service to its stockholders, last.

Such statements might seem like motherhood and apple pie to those who have not seen the way a clear sense of purpose and values can affect key business decisions. Johnson & Johnson's crisis management in this case was based on that credo. It was simple, it was right, and it worked.

If governing ideas constitute the first design task of leadership, the second design task involves the policies, strategies, and structures that translate guiding ideas into business decisions. Leadership theorist Philip Selznick calls policy and structure the "institutional embodiment of purpose."[11] "Policy making (the rules that guide decisions) ought to be separated from decision making," says Jay Forrester.[12] "Otherwise, short-term pressures will usurp time from policy creation."

Traditionally, writers like Selznick and Forrester have tended to see policy making and implementation as the work of a small number of senior managers. But that view is changing. Both the dynamic business environment and the mandate of the learning organization to engage people at all levels now make it clear that this second design task is more subtle. Henry Mintzberg has argued that strategy is less a rational plan arrived at in the abstract and implemented throughout the organization than an "emergent phenomenon." Successful organizations "craft strategy" according to Mintzberg, as they continually learn about shifting business conditions and balance what is desired and what is possible.[13] The key is not getting the right strategy but fostering strategic thinking. "The choice of individual action is only part of . . . the policymaker's need," according to Mason and Mitroff.[14] "More important is the need to achieve insight into the nature of the complexity and to formulate concepts and world views for coping with it."

Behind appropriate policies, strategies, and structures are effective learning processes; their creation is the third key design responsibility in learning organizations. This does not absolve senior managers of their strategic responsibilities. Actually, it deepens and extends those responsibilities. Now, they are not only responsible for ensuring that an organization has well-developed strategies and policies, but also for ensuring that processes exist whereby these are continually improved.

In the early 1970s, Shell was the weakest of the big seven oil companies. Today, Shell and Exxon are arguably the strongest, both in size and financial health. Shell's ascendance began with frustration. Around 1971 members of Shell's "Group Planning" in London began to foresee dramatic change and unpredictability in world oil markets. However, it proved impossible to persuade managers that the stable world of steady growth in oil demand and supply they had known for twenty years was about to change. Despite brilliant analysis and artful presentation, Shell's planners realized, in the words of Pierre Wack, that they "had failed to change behavior in much of the Shell organization."[15] Progress would probably have ended there, had the frustration not given way to a radically new view of corporate planning.

As they pondered this failure, the planners' view of their basic task shifted: "We no longer saw our task as producing a documented view of the future business environment five or ten years ahead. Our real target was the microcosm (the 'mental model') of our decision makers." Only when the planners reconceptualized their basic task as fostering learning rather than devising plans did their insights begin to have an impact. The initial tool used was "scenario analysis," through which planners encouraged operating managers to think through how they would manage in the future under different possible scenarios. It mattered not that the managers believed the planned scenarios absolutely, only that they became engaged in ferreting out the implications. In this way, Shell's planners conditioned managers to be mentally prepared for a shift from low prices to high prices and from stability to instability. The results were significant. When OPEC became a reality, Shell quickly responded by increasing local operating company control (to enhance maneuverability in the new political environment), building buffer stocks, and accelerating development of non-OPEC sources—actions that its competitors took much more slowly or not at all.

Somewhat inadvertently, Shell planners had discovered the leverage of designing institutional learning processes, whereby, in the words of former planning director de Geus, "Management teams change their shared mental models of their company, their markets, and their competitors."[16] Since then, "planning as learning" has become a byword at Shell and Group Planning has continually sought out new learning tools that can be integrated into planning process. Some of these are described below.

## Leader as Teacher

"The first responsibility of a leader," writes retired Herman Miller CEO Max DePree, "is to define reality."[17] Much of the leverage leaders can actually exert lies in helping people achieve more accurate, more insightful, and more *empowering* views of reality.

Leader as teacher does *not* mean leader as authoritarian expert whose job it is to teach people the "correct" view of reality. Rather, it is about helping everyone in the organization, oneself included, to gain more insightful views of current reality. This is in line with a popular emerging view of leaders as coaches, guides, or facilitators.[18] In learning organizations, this teaching role is developed further by virtue of explicit attention to people's mental models and by the influence of the perspective.

The role of leader as teacher starts with bringing to the surface people's mental models of important issues. No one carries an organization, a market, or a state of technology in his or her head. What we carry in our heads are assumptions. These mental pictures of how the world works have a significant influence on how we perceive problems and opportunities, identify courses of action, and make choices.

One reason that mental models are so deeply entrenched is that they are largely tacit. Ian Mitroff, in his study of General Motors, argues that an assumption that prevailed for years was that, in the United States, "Cars are status symbols. Styling is therefore more important than quality."[19] The Detroit automakers didn't say, "We have a *mental model* that all people care about is styling." Few actual managers would even say publicly that all people care about is styling. So long as the view remained unexpressed, there was little possibility of challenging its validity or forming more accurate assumptions.

But working with mental models goes beyond revealing hidden assumptions. "Reality," as perceived by most people in most organizations, means pressures that must be borne, crises that must be reacted to, and limitations that must be accepted. Leaders as teachers help people *restructure their views of reality* to see beyond the superficial conditions and events into the underlying causes of problems and therefore to see new possibilities for shaping the future.

Specifically, leaders can influence people to view reality at three distinct levels: events, patterns of behavior, and systemic structure.

Systemic Structure
(Generative)

↓

Patterns of Behavior
(Responsive)

↓

Events
(Reactive)

The key question becomes *where do leaders predominantly focus their own and their organization's attention?*

Contemporary society focuses predominantly on events. The media reinforces this perspective, with almost exclusive attention to short-term, dramatic events. This focus leads naturally to explaining what happens in terms of those events: "The Dow Jones average went up sixteen points because high fourth-quarter profits were announced yesterday."

Pattern-of-behavior explanations are rarer, in contemporary culture, than event explanations, but they do occur. "Trend analysis" is an example of seeing patterns of behavior. A good editorial that interprets a set of current events in the context of long-term historical changes is another example. Systemic, structural explanations go even further by addressing the question, "What causes the patterns of behavior?"

In some sense, all three levels of explanation are equally true. But their usefulness is quite different. Event explanations—who did what to whom—doom their holders to a reactive stance toward change. Pattern-of-behavior explanations focus on identifying long-term trends and assessing their implications. They at least suggest how, over time, we can respond to shifting conditions. Structural explanations are the most powerful. Only they address the underlying causes of behavior at a level such that patterns of behavior can be changed.

By and large, leaders of our current institutions focus their attention on events and patterns of behavior, and, under their influence, their organizations do likewise. That is why contemporary organizations are predominantly reactive, or at best responsive—rarely generative. On the other hand, leaders in learning organizations pay attention to all three levels, but focus especially on systemic structure; largely by example, they teach people throughout the organization to do likewise.

**Leader as Steward**

This is the subtlest role of leadership. Unlike the roles of designer and teacher, it is almost solely a matter of attitude. It is an attitude critical to learning organizations.

While stewardship has long been recognized as an aspect of leadership, its source is still not widely understood. I believe Robert Greenleaf came closest to explaining real stewardship, in his seminal book *Servant Leadership.*[20] There, Greenleaf argues that "The servant leader *is* servant first. . . . It begins with the natural feeling that one wants to serve, to serve *first*. This conscious choice brings one to aspire to lead. That person is sharply different from one who is leader first, perhaps because of the need to assuage an unusual power drive or to acquire material possessions."

Leaders' sense of stewardship operates on two levels: stewardship for the people they lead and stewardship for the larger purpose or mission that underlies the enterprise. The first type arises from a keen appreciation of the impact one's leadership can have on others. People can suffer economically, emotionally, and spiritually under inept leadership. If anything, people in a learning organization are more vulnerable because of their commitment and sense of shared ownership. Appreciating this naturally instills a sense of responsibility in leaders. The second type of stewardship arises from a leader's sense of personal purpose and commitment to the organization's larger mission. People's natural impulse to learn is unleashed when they are engaged in an endeavor they consider worthy of their fullest commitment. Or, as Lawrence Miller puts it, "Achieving return on equity does not, as a goal, mobilize the most noble forces of our soul."[21]

Leaders engaged in building learning organizations naturally feel part of a larger purpose that goes beyond their organization. They are part of changing the way businesses operate, not from a vague philanthropic urge, but from a conviction that their efforts will produce more productive organizations, capable of achieving higher levels of organizational success and personal satisfaction than more traditional organizations. Their sense of stewardship was succinctly captured by George Bernard Shaw when he said,

This is the true joy in life, the being used for a purpose you consider a mighty one, the being a force of nature rather than a feverish, selfish clod of ailments and grievances complaining that the world will not devote itself to making you happy.

### New Skills

New leadership roles require new leadership skills. These skills can only be developed, in my judgment, through a lifelong commitment. It is not enough for one or two individuals to develop these skills. They must be distributed widely throughout the organization. This is one reason that understanding the *disciplines* of a learning organization is so important. These disciplines embody the principles and practices that can widely foster leadership development.

Three critical areas of skills (discipline) are building shared vision, surfacing and challenging mental models, and engaging in systems thinking.[22]

#### Building Shared Vision

How do individual visions come together to create shared visions? A useful metaphor is the hologram, the three-dimensional image created by interacting light sources.

If you cut a photograph in half, each half shows only part of the whole image. But if you divide a hologram, each part, no matter how small, shows the whole image intact. Likewise, when a group of people come to share a vision for an organization, each person sees an individual picture of the organization at its best. Each shares responsibility for the whole, not just for one piece. But the component pieces of the hologram are not identical. Each represents the whole image from a different point of view. It's something like poking holes in a window shade; each hole offers a unique angle for viewing the whole image. So, too, is each individual's vision unique.

When you add up the pieces of a hologram, something interesting happens. The image becomes more intense, more lifelike. When more people come to share a vision, the vision becomes more real in the sense of a mental reality that people can truly imagine achieving. They now have partners, cocreators; the vision no longer rests on their shoulders alone. Early on, when they are nurturing an individual vision, people may say it is "my vision." But, as the shared vision develops, it becomes both "my vision" and "our vision."

The skills involved in building shared vision include the following:

- *Encouraging personal vision.* Shared visions emerge from personal visions. It is not that people only care about their own self-interest—in fact, people's values usually include dimensions that concern family, organization, community, and even the world. Rather, it is that people's capacity for caring is *personal.*

- *Communicating and asking for support.* Leaders must be willing to continually share their own vision, rather than being the official representative of the corporate vision. They also must be prepared to ask, "Is this vision worthy of your commitment?" This can be difficult for a person used to setting goals and presuming compliance.

- *Visioning as an ongoing process.* Building shared vision is a never-ending process. At any one point there will be a particular image of the future that is predominant, but that image will evolve. Today, too many managers want to dispense with the "vision business" by going off and writing the Official Vision Statement. Such statements almost always lack the vitality, freshness, and excitement of a genuine vision that comes from people asking, "What do we really want to achieve?"

• *Blending extrinsic and intrinsic visions.* Many energizing visions are extrinsic—that is, they focus on achieving something relative to an outsider, such as a competitor. But a goal that is limited to defeating an opponent can, once the vision is achieved, easily become a defensive posture. In contrast, intrinsic goals like creating a new type of product, taking an established product to a new level, or setting a new standard for customer satisfaction can call forth a new level of creativity and innovation. Intrinsic and extrinsic visions need to coexist; a vision solely predicated on defeating an adversary will eventually weaken an organization.

• *Distinguishing positive from negative visions.* Many organizations only truly pull together when their survival is threatened. Similarly, most social movements aim at eliminating what people don't want: for example, antidrugs, antismoking, or anti-nuclear arms movements. Negative visions carry a subtle message of powerlessness: people will pull together when there is sufficient threat. Negative visions also tend to be short term. Two fundamental sources of energy can motivate organizations:fear and aspiration. Fear, the energy source behind negative visions, can produce extraordinary changes in short periods, but aspiration endures as a continuing source of learning and growth.

## Surfacing and Testing Mental Models

Many of the best ideas in organizations never get put into practice. One reason is that new insights and initiatives often conflict with established mental models. The leadership task of challenging assumptions without invoking defensiveness requires reflection and inquiry skills possessed by few leaders in traditional controlling organizations.[23]

• *Seeing leaps of abstraction.* Our minds literally move at lightning speed. Ironically, this often slows our learning, because we leap to generalizations so quickly that we never think to test them. We then confuse our generalizations with the observable data upon which they are based, treating generalizations *as if they were data*. The frustrated

sales rep reports to the home office that "customers don't really care about quality, price is what matters," when what actually happened was that three consecutive large customers refused to place an order unless a larger discount was offered. The sales rep treats her generalization, "customers care only about price," as if it were absolute fact rather than assumption (very likely an assumption reflecting her own views of customers and the market). This thwarts future learning because she starts to focus on how to offer attractive discounts rather than probing behind the customers' statements. For example, the customers may have been so disgruntled with the firm's delivery that they are unwilling to purchase again without larger discounts.

• *Balancing inquiry and advocacy.* Most managers are skilled at articulating their views and presenting them persuasively. While important, advocacy skills can become counterproductive as managers rise in responsibility and confront increasingly complex issues that require collaborative learning among different, equally knowledgeable people. Leaders in learning organizations need to have both inquiry *and* advocacy skills.[24]

Specifically, when advocating a view, they need to be able to

- Explain the reasoning and data that led to their view;
- Encourage others to test their views (e.g., Do you see gaps in my reasoning? Do you disagree with the data upon which my view is based?); and
- Encourage others to provide different views (e.g., Do you have either different data, different conclusions, or both?)

When inquiring into another's views, they need to

- Actively seek to understand the other's view, rather than simply restating their own view and how it differs from the other's view; and
- Make their attributions about the other and the other's views explicit (e.g., Based on your statement that . . . ; I am assuming that you believe . . . ; Am I representing your views fairly?)

If they reach an impasse (others no longer appear open to inquiry), they need to

- Ask what data or logic might unfreeze the impasse, or if an experiment (or some other inquiry) might be designed to provide new information.

• *Distinguishing espoused theory from theory in use.* We all like to think that we hold certain views, but often our actions reveal deeper views. For example, I may proclaim that people are trustworthy, but never lend friends money and jealously guard my possessions. Obviously, my deeper mental model (my theory in use) differs from my espoused theory. Recognizing gaps between espoused views and theories in use (which often requires the help of others) can be pivotal to deeper learning.

• *Recognizing and defusing defensive routines.* As one CEO in our research program puts it, "Nobody ever talks about an issue at the 8:00 business meeting exactly the same way they talk about it at home that evening or over drinks at the end of the day." The reason is what Chris Argyris calls "defensive routines," entrenched habits used to protect ourselves from the embarrassment and threat that come with exposing our thinking. For most of us, such defenses began to build early in life in response to pressures to have the right answers in school or at home. Organizations add new levels of performance anxiety and thereby amplify and exacerbate this defensiveness. Ironically, this makes it even more difficult to expose hidden mental models, and thereby lessens learning.

The first challenge is to recognize defensive routines, then to inquire into their operation. Those who are best at revealing and defusing defensive routines operate with a high degree of self-disclosure regarding their own defensiveness (e.g., I notice that I am feeling uneasy about how this conversation is going. Perhaps I don't understand it or it is threatening to me in ways I don't yet see. Can you help me see this better?)

## Systems Thinking

We all know that leaders should help people see the big picture. But the actual skills whereby leaders are supposed to achieve this are not well understood. In my experience, successful leaders often *are* "systems thinkers" to a considerable extent. They focus less on day-to-day events and more on underlying trends and forces of change. But they do this almost completely intuitively. The consequence is that they are often unable to explain their intuitions to others and feel frustrated that others cannot see the world the way they do.

One of the most significant developments in management science today is the gradual coalescence of managerial systems thinking as a field of study and practice. This field suggests some key skills for future leaders:

• *Seeing interrelationships, not things, and processes, not snapshots.* Most of us have been conditioned throughout our lives to focus on things and to see the world in static images. This leads us to linear explanations of systemic phenomenon. For instance, in an arms race each party is convinced that the other is *the cause* of problems. They react to each new move as an isolated event, not as part of a process. So long as they fail to see the interrelationships of these actions, they are trapped.

• *Moving beyond blame.* We tend to blame each other or outside circumstances for our problems. But it is poorly designed systems, not incompetent or unmotivated individuals, that cause most organizational problems. Systems thinking shows us that there is no outside—that you and the cause of your problems are part of a single system.

• *Distinguishing detail complexity from dynamic complexity.* Some types of complexity are more important strategically than others. Detail complexity arises when there are many variables. Dynamic complexity arises when cause and effect are distant in time and space, and when the consequences over time of interventions are subtle and not obvious to many participants in the system. The leverage in most management situations lies in understanding dynamic complexity, not detail complexity.

• *Focusing on areas of high leverage.* Some have called systems thinking the "new dismal science" because it teaches that most obvious solutions don't work—at best, they improve matters in the short run, only to make things worse in the long run. But there is another side to the story. Systems thinking also shows that small, well-focused actions can produce significant, enduring improvements, if they are in the right place. Systems thinkers refer to this idea as the principle of "leverage." Tackling a difficult problem is often a matter of seeing where the high leverage lies, where a change—with a minimum of effort—would lead to lasting, significant improvement.

• *Avoiding symptomatic solutions.* The pressures to intervene in management systems going awry can be overwhelming. Unfortunately, given the linear thinking that predominates organizations, interventions usually focus on symptomatic fixes, not underlying causes. This results in only temporary relief, and it tends to create more pressures later on for further, low-leverage intervention. If leaders acquiesce to these pressures, they can be sucked into an endless spiral of increasing intervention. Sometimes the most difficult leadership acts are to refrain from intervening through popular quick fixes and to keep the pressure on everyone to identify more enduring solutions.

While leaders who can articulate systemic explanations are rare, those who *can* will leave their stamp on an organization. One person who had this gift was Bill Gore, the founder and long-time CEO of W.L. Gore and Associates (makers of Gore-Tex and other synthetic fiber products). Bill Gore was adept at telling stories that showed how the organization's core values of freedom and individual sensibility required particular operating policies. He was proud of his egalitarian organization, in which there were (and still are) no "employees," only "associates," all of whom own shares in the company and participate in its management. At one talk, he explained the company's policy of controlled growth: "Our limitation is not financial resources. Our limitation is the rate at which we can bring in new associates. Our experience has been that if we try to bring in more than a 25 percent per year increase, we begin to bog down. Twenty-five percent per year growth is a real limitation; you can do much better than that with an authoritarian organization." As Gore tells the story, one of the

associates, Esther Baum, went home after this talk and reported the limitation to her husband. As it happened, he was an astronomer and mathematician at Lowell Observatory. He said, "That's a very interesting figure." He took out a pencil and paper and calculated and said, "Do you realize that in only fifty-seven and a half years, everyone in the world will be working for Gore?"

Through this story, Gore explains the systemic rationale behind a key policy, limited growth rate—a policy that undoubtedly caused a lot of stress in the organization. He suggests that, at larger rates of growth, the adverse effects of attempting to integrate too many new people too rapidly would begin to dominate. (This is the "limits to growth" systems archetype explained below.) The story also reaffirms the organization's commitment to creating a unique environment for its associates and illustrates the types of sacrifices that the firm is prepared to make in order to remain true to its vision. The last part of the story shows that, despite the self-imposed limit, the company is still very much a growth company.

The consequences of leaders who lack systems thinking skills can be devastating. Many charismatic leaders manage almost exclusively at the level of events. They deal in visions and in crises, and little in between. Under their leadership, an organization hurtles from crisis to crisis. Eventually, the worldview of people in the organization becomes dominated by events and reactiveness. Many, especially those who are deeply committed, become burned out. Eventually, cynicism comes to pervade the organization. People have no control over their time, let alone their destiny.

Similar problems arise with the "visionary strategist," the leader with vision who sees both patterns of change and events. This leader is better prepared to manage change. He or she can explain strategies in terms of emerging trends, and thereby foster a climate that is less reactive. But such leaders still impart a responsive orientation rather than a generative one.

Many talented leaders have rich, highly systemic intuitions but cannot explain those intuitions to others. Ironically, they often end up being authoritarian leaders, even if they don't want to, because only they see the decisions that need to be made.

They are unable to conceptualize their strategic insights so that these can become public knowledge, open to challenge and further improvement.

## New Tools

Developing the skills described above requires new tools—tools that will enhance leaders' conceptual abilities and foster communication and collaborative inquiry. What follows is a sampling of tools starting to find use in learning organizations.

### Systems Archetypes

One of the insights of the budding, managerial systems-thinking field is that certain types of systemic structures recur again and again. Countless systems grow for a period, then encounter problems and cease to grow (or even collapse) well before they have reached intrinsic limits to growth. Many other systems get locked in runaway vicious spirals where every actor has to run faster and faster to stay in the same place. Still others lure individual actors into doing what seems right locally, yet which eventually causes suffering for all.[25]

Some of the system archetypes that have the broadest relevance include

- *Balancing process with delay.* In this archetype, decision makers fail to appreciate the time delays involved as they move toward a goal. As a result, they overshoot the goal and may even produce recurring cycles. Classic example: Real estate developers who keep starting new projects until the market has gone soft, by which time an eventual glut is guaranteed by the properties still under construction.
- *Limits to growth.* A reinforcing cycle of growth grinds to a halt, and may even reverse itself, as limits are approached. The limits can be resource constraints, or external or internal responses to growth. Classic examples: Product life cycles that peak prematurely due to poor quality or service, the growth and decline of communication in a management team, and the spread of a new movement.

- *Shifting the burden.* A short-term "solution" is used to correct a problem, with seemingly happy immediate results. As this correction is used more and more, fundamental long-term corrective measures are used less. Over time, the mechanisms of the fundamental solution may atrophy or become disabled, leading to even greater reliance on the symptomatic solution. Classic example: Using corporate human resource staff to solve local personnel problems, thereby keeping managers from developing their own interpersonal skills.
- *Eroding goals.* When all else fails, lower your standards. This is like "shifting the burden," except that the short-term solution involves letting a fundamental goal, such as quality standards or employee morale standards, atrophy. Classic example: A company that responds to delivery problems by continually upping its quoted delivery times.
- *Escalation.* Two people or two organizations, who each see their welfare as depending on a relative advantage over the other, continually react to the other's advances. Whenever one side gets ahead, the other is threatened, leading it to act more aggressively to reestablish its advantage, which threatens the first, and so on. Classic examples: Arms race, gang warfare, price wars.
- *Tragedy of the commons.*[26] Individuals keep intensifying their use of a commonly available but limited resource until all individuals start to experience severely diminishing returns. Classic examples: Sheepherders who keep increasing their flocks until they overgraze the common pasture; divisions in a firm that share a common salesforce and compete for the use of sales reps by upping their sales targets, until the salesforce burns out from overextension.
- *Growth and underinvestment.* Rapid growth approaches a limit that could be eliminated or pushed into the future, but only by aggressive investment in physical and human capacity. Eroding goals or standards cause investment that is too weak, or too slow, and customers get increasingly unhappy, slowing demand growth and thereby making the needed investment (apparently) unnecessary or impossible. Classic example: Countless once successful growth firms that

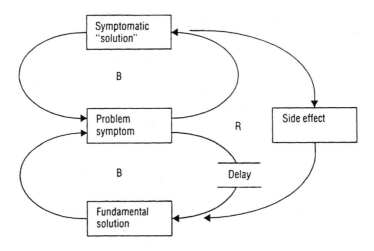

**Figure 42.2.** "Shifting the Burden" Archetype Template

NOTE: In the "shifting the burden" template, two balancing processes (B) compete for control of a problem symptom. Both solutions affect the symptom, but only the fundamental solution treats the cause. The symptomatic "solution" creates the additional side effect (R) of deferring the fundamental solution, making it harder and harder to achieve.

allowed product or service quality to erode and were unable to generate enough revenues to invest in remedies.

The Archetype template is a specific tool that is helping managers identify archetypes operating in their own strategic areas (see Figure 42.2).[27] The template shows the basic structural form of the archetype but lets managers fill in the variables of their own situation. For example, the shifting the burden template involves two balancing processes ("B") that compete for control of a problem symptom. The upper, symptomatic solution provides a short-term fix that will make the problem symptom go away for a while. The lower, fundamental solution provides a more enduring solution. The side effect feedback ("R") around the outside of the diagram identifies unintended exacerbating effects of the symptomatic solution, which, over time, make it more and more difficult to invoke the fundamental solution.

Several years ago, a team of managers from a leading consumer goods producer used the shifting the burden archetype in a revealing way. The problem they focused on was financial stress, which could be dealt with in two different ways: by running marketing promotions (the symptomatic solution) or by product innovation (the fundamental solution). Marketing promotions were fast. The company was expert in their design and implementation. The results were highly predictable. Product innovation was slow and much less predictable, and the company had a history over the past ten years of product-innovation mismanagement. Yet only through innovation could they retain a leadership position in their industry, which had slid over the past ten to twenty years. What the managers saw clearly was that the more skillful they became at promotions, the more they shifted the burden away from product innovation. But what really struck home was when one member identified the unintended side effect: the last three CEOs had all come from advertising function, which had become the politically dominant function in the corporation, thereby institutionalizing the symptomatic solution. Unless the political values shifted back toward product and process innovation, the managers realized, the firm's decline would accelerate—which is just the shift that has happened over the past several years.

### Charting Strategic Dilemmas

Management teams typically come unglued when confronted with core dilemmas. A classic example was the way U.S. manufacturers faced the low cost-high quality choice. For years, most assumed that it was necessary to choose between the two. Not surprisingly, given the short-term pressures perceived by most managements, the prevailing choice was low cost. Firms that chose high quality usually perceived themselves as aiming exclusively for a high-quality, high-price market niche. The consequences of this perceived either-or choice have been disastrous, even fatal, as U.S. manufacturers have encountered increasing international competition from firms that have chosen to consistently improve quality *and* cost.

In a recent book, Charles Hampden-Turner presented a variety of tools for helping management teams confront strategic dilemmas creatively.[28]

He summarizes the process in seven steps:

- *Eliciting the dilemmas.* Identifying the opposed values that form the "horns" of the dilemma, for example, cost as opposed to quality, or local initiative as opposed to central coordination and control. Hampden-Turner suggests that humor can be a distinct asset in this process since "the admission that dilemmas even exist tends to be difficult for some companies."

- *Mapping.* Locating the opposing values as two axes and helping managers identify where they see themselves, or their organization, along the axes.

- *Processing.* Getting rid of nouns to describe the axes of the dilemma. Present participles formed by adding "ing" convert rigid nouns into processes that imply movement. For example, central control versus local control becomes "strengthening national office" and "growing local initiatives." This loosens the bond of implied opposition between the two values. For example, it becomes possible to think of "strengthening national services from which local branches can benefit."

- *Framing/contextualizing.* Further softening the adversarial structure among different values by letting "each side in turn be the frame or context for the other." This shifting of the "figure-ground" relationship undermines any implicit attempts to hold one value as intrinsically superior to the other, and thereby to become

mentally closed to creative strategies for continuous improvement of both.

- *Sequencing.* Breaking the hold of static thinking. Very often, values like low cost and high quality appear to be in opposition because we think in terms of a point in time, not in terms of an ongoing process. For example, a strategy of investing in new process technology and developing a new production-floor culture of worker responsibility may take time and money in the near term, yet reap significant long-term financial rewards.

- *Waving/cycling.* Sometimes the strategic path toward improving both values involves cycles where both values will get "worse" for a time. Yet, at a deeper level, learning is occurring that will cause the next cycle to be at a higher plateau for both values.

- *Synergizing.* Achieving synergy where significant improvement is occurring along all axes of all relevant dilemmas. (This is the ultimate goal, of course.) Synergy, as Hampden-Turner points out, is a uniquely systemic notion, coming from the Greek *syn-ergo* or "work together."

## "The Left-Hand Column": Surfacing Mental Models

The idea that mental models can dominate business decisions and that these models are often tacit and even contradictory to what people espouse can be very threatening to managers who pride themselves on rationality and judicious decision making. It is important to have tools to help managers discover for themselves how their mental models operate to undermine their own intentions.

One tool that has worked consistently to help managers see their own mental models in action is the "left-handed column" exercise developed by Chris Argyris and his colleagues. This tool is especially helpful in showing how we leap from data to generalization without testing the validity of our generalizations.

When working with managers, I start this exercise by selecting a specific situation in which I am interacting with other people in a way that is not working, that is not producing the learning that is needed. I write out a sample of the exchange, with

---

**BOX 42.1**
## The Left-Hand Column: An Exercise

Imagine my exchange with a colleague, Bill, after he made a big presentation to our boss on a project we are doing together. I had to miss the presentation, but I've heard that it was poorly received.

**Me:**  How did the presentation go?
**Bill:**  Well, I don't know. It's really too early to say. Besides, we're breaking new ground here.
**Me:**  Well, what do you think we should do? I believe that the issues you were raising are important.
**Bill:**  I'm not so sure. Let's just wait and see what happens.
**Me:**  You may be right, but I think we may need to do more than just wait.

Now, here is what the exchange looks like with my "left-hand column":

| What I'm Thinking | What Is Said |
|---|---|
| Everyone says the presentation was a bomb. | **Me:** How did the presentation go? |
| Does he really not know how bad it was? Or is he not willing to face up to it? | **Bill:** Well, I don't know. It's really too early to say. Besides, we're breaking new ground here. |
| | **Me:** Well, what do you think we should do? I believe that the issues you were raising are important. |
| He really is afraid to see the truth. If he only had more confidence, he could probably learn from a situation like this. | **Bill:** I'm not so sure. Let's just wait and see what happens. |
| I can't believe he doesn't realize how disastrous that presentation was to our moving ahead. | **Me:** You may be right, but I think we may need to do more than just wait. |
| I've got to find some way to light a fire under the guy. | |

---

the script on the right-hand side of the page. On the left-hand side, I write what I am thinking but not saying at each stage in the exchange (see Box 42.1).

The left-hand column exercise not only brings hidden assumptions to the surface, it shows how they influence behavior. In the example, I make two key assumptions about Bill: he lacks confidence and he lacks initiative. Neither may be liter-ally true, but both are evident in my internal dia-logue, and both influence the way I handle the situation. Believing that he lacks confidence, I skirt the fact that I've heard the presentation was a bomb. I'm afraid that if I say it directly, he will lose what little confidence he has, or he would see me as unsupportive. So I bring up the subject of the presentation obliquely. When I ask Bill what we should do next, he gives no specific course of action. Believing he lacks initiative, I take this as evidence of his laziness; he is content to do nothing when action is definitely required. I conclude that I will have to manufacture some form of pressure to motivate him, or else I will simply have to take matters into my own hands.

The exercise reveals the elaborate webs of assumptions we weave, within which we become our own victims. Rather than dealing directly with my assumptions about Bill and the situation, we talk around the subject. The reasons for my avoidance are self-evident: I assume that if I raised my doubts, I would provoke a defensive reaction that would only make matters worse. But the price of avoiding the issue is high. Instead of determining how to move forward to resolve our problems, we end our exchange with no clear course of action. My assumptions about Bill's limitations have been reinforced. I resort to a manipulative strategy to move things forward.

The exercise not only reveals the need for skills in surfacing assumptions but that we are the ones most in need of help. There is no one right way to handle difficult situations like my exchange with Bill, but any productive strategy revolves around a high level of self-disclosure and willingness to have my views challenged. I need to recognize my own leaps of abstraction regarding Bill, share the events and reasoning that are leading to my concern over the project, and be open to Bill's views on both. The skills to carry on such conversations without invoking defensiveness take time to develop. But if both parties in a learning impasse start by doing their own left-hand column exercise and sharing them with each other, it is remarkable how quickly everyone recognizes their contribution to the impasse and progress starts to be made.

## Learning Laboratories: Practice Fields for Management Teams

One of the most promising new tools is the learning laboratory or "microworld": constructed microcosms of real-life settings in which management teams can learn how to learn together.

The rationale behind learning laboratories can best be explained by analogy. Although most man-

agement teams have great difficulty learning (enhancing their collective intelligence and capacity to create), in other domains team learning is the norm rather than the exception—team sports and the performing arts, for example. Great basketball teams do not start off great. They learn. But the process by which these teams learn is, by and large, absent from modern organizations. The process is a continual movement between practice and performance.

The vision guiding current research in management learning laboratories is to design and construct effective practice fields for management teams. Much remains to be done, but the broad outlines are emerging.

First, since team learning in organizations is an individual-to-individual and individual-to-system phenomenon, learning laboratories must combine meaningful business issues with meaningful interpersonal dynamics. Either alone is incomplete.

Second, the factors that thwart learning about complex business issues must be eliminated in the learning lab. Chief among these is the inability to experience the long-term, systemic consequences of key strategic decisions. We all learn best from experience, but we are unable to experience the consequences of many important organizational decisions. Learning laboratories remove this constraint through system dynamics simulation games that compress time and space.

Third, new learning skills must be developed. One constraint on learning is the inability of managers to reflect insightfully on their assumptions and to inquire effectively into each other's assumptions. Both skills can be enhanced in a learning laboratory, where people can practice surfacing assumptions in a low-risk setting. A note of caution: It is far easier to design an entertaining learning laboratory than it is to have an impact on real management practices and firm traditions outside the learning lab. Research on management simulation has shown that they often have greater entertainment value than educational value. One of the reasons appears to be that many simulations do not offer deep insights into systemic structures causing business problems. Another reason is that they do not foster new learning skills. Also, there is no connection between experiments in the learning

**BOX 42.2**
## Learning at Hanover Insurance

*Hanover Insurance has gone from the bottom of the property and liability industry to a position among the top 25 percent of U.S. insurance companies over the past twenty years, largely through the efforts of CEO William O'Brien and his predecessor, Jack Adam. The following comments were excerpted from a series of interviews Senge conducted with O'Brien as background for this book.*

**Senge:** Why do you think there is so much change occurring in management and organizations today? Is it primarily because of increased competitive pressure?
**O'Brien:** That's a factor, but not the most significant factor. The ferment in management will continue until we find models that are more congruent with human nature.

One of the great insights of modern psychology is the hierarchy of human needs. As Maslow expressed this idea, the most basic needs are food and shelter. Then comes belonging. Once these three basic needs are satisfied, people begin to aspire toward self-respect and esteem, and toward self-actualization—the fourth—and fifth-order needs.

Our traditional hierarchical organizations are designed to provide for the first three levels, but not the fourth and fifth. These first three levels are now widely available to members of industrial society, but our organizations do not offer people sufficient opportunities for growth.

**Senge:** How would you assess Hanover's progress to date?
**O'Brien:** We have been on a long journey away from a traditional hierarchical culture. The journey began with everyone understanding some guiding ideas about purpose, vision, and values as a basis for participative management. This is a better way to begin building a participative culture than by simply "letting people in on decision making." Before there can be meaningful participation, people must share certain values and pictures about where we are trying to go. We discovered that people have a real need to feel they're part of an ennobling mission. But developing shared visions and values is not the end, only the beginning.

Next we had to get beyond mechanical, linear thinking. The essence of our jobs as managers is to deal with "divergent" problems—problems that have no simple answer. "Convergent" problems—problems that have a "right" answer—should be solved locally. Yet we are deeply conditioned to see the world in terms of convergent problems. Most managers try to force-fit simplistic solutions and undermine the potential for learning when divergent problems arise. Since everyone handles the linear issues fairly well, companies that learn how to handle divergent issues will have a great advantage.

The next basic stage in our progression was coming to understand inquiry and advocacy. We learned that real openness is rooted in people's ability to continually inquire into their own thinking. This requires exposing yourself to being wrong—not something that most managers are rewarded for. But learning is very difficult if you cannot look for errors or incompleteness in your own ideas.

What all this builds to is the capability throughout an organization to manage mental models. In a locally controlled organization, you have the fundamental challenge of learning how to help people make good decisions without coercing them into making *particular* decisions. By managing mental models, we create "self-concluding" decisions—decisions that people come to themselves—which will result in deeper conviction, better implementation, and the ability to make better adjustments when the situation changes.

*(Continued)*

---

**BOX 42.2**

**(Continued)**

**Senge:** What concrete steps can top managers take to begin moving toward learning organizations?

**O'Brien:** Look at the signals you send through the organization. For example, one critical signal is how you spend your time. It's hard to build a learning organization if people are unable to take the time to think through important matters. I rarely set up an appointment for less than one hour. If the subject is not worth an hour, it shouldn't be on my calendar.

**Senge:** Why is this so hard for so many managers?

**O'Brien:** It comes back to what you believe about the nature of your work. The authoritarian manager has a "chain gang" mental model: "The speed of the boss is the speed of the gang. I've got to keep things moving fast, because I've got to keep people working." In a learning organization, the manager shoulders an almost sacred responsibility: to create conditions that enable people to have happy and productive lives. If you understand the effects the ideas we are discussing can have on the lives of people in your organization, you will take the time.

---

lab and real-life experiments. These are significant problems that research on learning laboratory design is now addressing.

### *Developing Leaders and Learning Organizations*

In a recently published retrospective on organization development in the 1980s, Marshall Sashkin and N. Warner Burke observe the return of an emphasis on developing leaders who can develop organizations.[29] They also note Schein's critique that most top executives are not qualified for the task of developing culture.[30] Learning organizations represent a potentially significant evolution of organizational culture. So it should come as no surprise that such organizations will remain a distant vision until the leadership capabilities they demand are developed. "The 1990s may be the period," suggest Sashkin and Burke, "during which organization development and (a new sort of) management development are reconnected."

I believe that this new sort of management development will focus on the roles, skills, and tools for leadership in learning organizations. Undoubtedly, the ideas offered above are only a rough proximation of this new territory. The sooner we begin seriously exploring the territory, the sooner the initial map can be improved—and the sooner we will recognize an age-old vision of leadership:

The wicked leader is he who the people despise.

The good leader is he who the people revere.

The great leader is he who the people say, "We did it ourselves."

—Lao Tsu

### *Notes*

1. P. Senge. *The Fifth Discipline: The Art and Practice of the Learning Organization* (New York: Doubleday/Currency, 1990).

2. P. de Geus, "Planning as Learning," *Harvard Business Review,* March-April 1988, pp. 70-74.

3. B. Domain, *Fortune,* 3 July 1989, pp. 48-62.

4. The distinction between adaptive and generative learning has its roots in the distinction between what Argyris and Schon have called their "single-loop" learning, in which individuals or groups adjust their behavior relative to fixed goals, norms, and assumptions, and "double-loop" learning, in which goals, norms, and assumptions, as well as behavior, are open to change (e.g., see C. Argyris and D. Schon, *Organizational Learning: A Theory-in-Action Perspective,* Reading, Massachusetts: Addison-Wesley, 1978).

5. All attributed quotes are from personal communications with the author.

6. G. Stalk, Jr., "Time: The Next Source of Competitive Advantage," *Harvard Business Review,* July-August 1988, pp. 41-51.

7. Senge (1990).

8. The principle of creative tension comes from Robert Fritz's work on creativity. See R. Fritz, *The Path of Least Resistance"* (New York: Ballantine, 1989) and *Creating* (New York: Ballantine, 1990).

9. M. L. King, Jr., "Letter from Birmingham Jail," *American Visions,* January-February 1986, pp. 52-59.

10. E. Skein, *Organizational Culture & Leadership,* (San Francisco: Jossey-Bass, 1985). Similar views have been expressed by many leadership theorists, For example, see P. Selznick, *Leadership in Administration* (New York: Harper & Row, 1957); W. Bennis and B. Nanus, *Leaders* (New York: Harper & Row, 1985); and N. M. Tichy and M. A. Devanna, *The Transformational Leader* (New York: Wiley, 1986).

11. Selznick (1957).

12. J. W. Forrester, "A New Corporate Design," *Sloan Management Review* (formerly *Industrial Management Review*), Fall 1965, pp. 5-17.

13. See, for example, H. Mintzberg, "Crafting Strategy," *Harvard Business Review,* July-August 1987, pp. 66-75.

14. R. Mason and I. Mitroff, *Challenging Strategic Planning Assumptions* (New York: Wiley, 1981), p. 16.

15. P. Wack, "Scenarios: Uncharted Waters Ahead," *Harvard Business Review,* September-October 1985, pp. 73-89.

16. de Geus (1988).

17. M. DePree, *Leadership Is an Art* (New York: Doubleday, 1989), p. 9.

18. For example, see T. Peters and N. Austin, *A Passion for Excellence* (New York: Random House, 1985) and J. M. Kouzes and B. Z. Posner, *The Leadership Challenge* (San Francisco: Jossey-Bass, 1987).

19. I. Mitroff, *Break-Away Thinking* (New York: Wiley, 1988), pp. 66-67.

20. R. K. Greenleaf, *Servant Leadership: A Journey Into the Nature of Legitimate Power and Greatness* (New York: Paulist Press, 1977).

21. L. Miller, *American Spirit: Visions of a New Corporate Culture* (New York: William Morrow, 1984), p. 15.

22. These points are condensed from the practices of the five disciplines examined in Senge (1990).

23. The ideas below are based to a considerable extent on the work of Chris Argyris, Donald Schon, and their Action Science colleagues. C. Argyris and D. Schon, *Organizational Learning: A Theory-in-Action Perspective* (Reading, Massachusetts: Addison-Wesley, 1978); C. Argyris, R. Putnam, and D. Smith, *Action Science* (San Francisco: Jossey-Bass, 1985); C. Argyris, *Strategy, Change, and Defensive Routines* (Boston: Pitman, 1985); and C. Argyris, *Overcoming Organizational Defenses* (Englewood Cliffs, New Jersey: Prentice Hall, 1990).

24. I am indebted to Diana Smith for the summary points below.

25. The system archetypes are one of several systems diagraming and communication tools. See D. H. Kim, "Toward Learning Organizations: Integrating Total Quality Control and Systems Thinking" (Cambridge, Massachusetts: MIT Sloan School of Management, Working Paper No. 3037-89-BPS, June 1989).

26. This archetype is closely associated with the work of ecologist Garrett Hardin, who coined its label: G. Hardin, "The Tragedy of the Commons,": *Science,* 13 December 1968.

27. These templates were originally developed by Jennifer Kemeny, Charles Kiefer, and Michael Goodman of Innovation Associates, Inc., Framingham, Massachusetts.

28. C. Hampden-Turner, *Charting the Corporate Mind* (New York: Free Press, 1990).

29. M. Sashkin and W. W. Burke, "Organization Development in the 1980s" and "An End-of-the-Eighties Retrospective," in *Advances in Organization Development,* ed. F. Massarik (Norwood, New Jersey: Ablex, 1990).

30. E. Schein (1995).

# 43

# Successful Change and the Force That Drives It

JOHN P. KOTTER

People who have been through difficult, painful, and not very successful change efforts often end up drawing both pessimistic and angry conclusions. They become suspicious of the motives of those pushing for transformation; they worry that major change is not possible without carnage; they fear that the boss is a monster or that much of the management is incompetent.

After watching dozens of efforts to enhance organizational performance via restructuring, re-engineering, quality programs, mergers and ac-quisitions, cultural renewal, downsizing, and stra-tegic redirection, I draw a different conclusion. Available evidence shows that most public and private organizations can be significantly im-proved, at an acceptable cost, but that we often make terrible mistakes when we try because his-tory has simply not prepared us for transforma-tional challenges.

## *The Globalization of Markets and Competition*

People of my generation or older did not grow up in an era when transformation was common. With less global competition and a slower-moving business environment, the norm back then was stability and the ruling motto was: "If it ain't broke, don't fix it." Change occurred incrementally and infrequently. If you had told a typical group of managers in 1960 that businesspeople today, over the course of eighteen to thirty-six months, would be trying to increase productivity by 20 to 50 percent, improve quality by 30 to 100 percent, and reduce new-product development times by 30 to 80 percent, they would have laughed at you. That magnitude of change in that short a period of time would have been too far removed from their per-sonal experience to be credible.

**EXHIBIT 43.1**   Economic and Social Forces Driving the Need for Major Change in Organizations

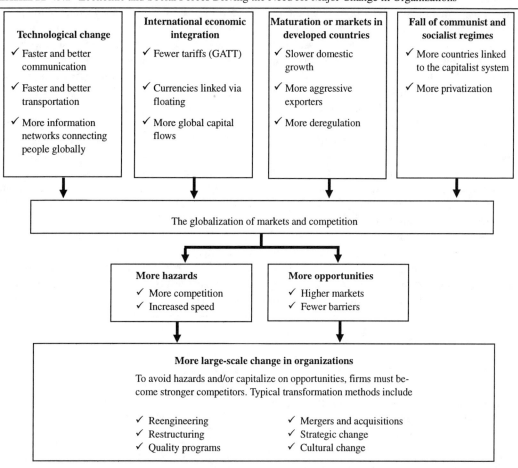

SOURCE: Adapted with the permission of The Free Press, a Division of Simon & Schuster from *The New Rules: How to Succeed in Today's Post-Corporate World* by John P. Kotter. Copyright © 1995 by John P. Kotter.

The challenges we now face are different. A globalized economy is creating both more hazards and more opportunities for everyone, forcing firms to make dramatic improvements not only to compete and prosper but also to merely survive. Globalization, in turn, is being driven by a broad and powerful set of forces associated with technological change, international economic integration, domestic market maturation within the more developed countries, and the collapse of worldwide communism. (See Exhibit 43.1.)

No one is immune to these forces. Even companies that sell only in small geographic regions can feel the impact of globalization. The influence route is sometimes indirect: Toyota beats GM, GM lays off employees, belt-tightening employees demand cheaper services from the corner dry cleaner. In a similar way, school systems, hospitals, charities, and government agencies are being forced to try to improve. The problem is that most managers have no history or legacy to guide them through all this.

Given the track record of many companies over the past two decades, some people have concluded that organizations are simply unable to change much and that we must learn to accept that fact. But this assessment cannot account for any of the dramatic transformation success stories from the recent past. Some organizations have discovered how to make new strategies, acquisitions, reengineering, quality programs, and restructuring work wonderfully well for them. They have minimized the change errors described in Chapter 1. In the process, they have been saved from bankruptcy, or gone from middle-of-the-pack players to industry leaders, or pulled farther out in front of their closest rivals.

An examination of these success stories reveals two important patterns. First, useful change tends to be associated with a multistep process that creates power and motivation sufficient to overwhelm all the sources of inertia. Second, this process is never employed effectively unless it is driven by high-quality leadership, not just excellent management—an important distinction that will come up repeatedly as we talk about instituting significant organizational change.

## The Eight-Stage Change Process

The methods used in successful transformations are all based on one fundamental insight: that major change will not happen easily for a long list of reasons. Even if an objective observer can clearly see that costs are too high, or products are not good enough, or shifting customer requirements are not being adequately addressed, needed change can still stall because of inwardly focused cultures, paralyzing bureaucracy, parochial politics, a low level of trust, lack of teamwork, arrogant attitudes, a lack of leadership in middle management, and the general human fear of the unknown. To be effective, a method designed to alter strategies, reengineer processes, or improve quality must address these barriers and address them well.

All diagrams tend to oversimplify reality. I therefore offer Exhibit 43.2 with some trepidation. It summarizes the steps producing successful change of any magnitude in organizations. The process has eight stages, each of which is associated with one of the eight fundamental errors that

undermine transformation efforts. The steps are: establishing a sense of urgency, creating the guiding coalition, developing a vision and strategy, communicating the change vision, empowering a broad base of people to take action, generating short-term wins, consolidating gains and producing even more change, and institutionalizing new approaches in the culture.

The first four steps in the transformation process help defrost a hardened status quo. If change were easy, you wouldn't need all that effort. Phases five to seven then introduce many new practices. The last stage grounds the changes in the corporate culture and helps make them stick.

People under pressure to show results will often try to skip phases—sometimes quite a few—in a major change effort. A smart and capable executive recently told me that his attempts to introduce a reorganization were being blocked by most of his management team. Our conversation, in short form, was this:

"Do your people believe the status quo is unacceptable?" I asked. "Do they really feel a sense of urgency?"

"Some do. But many probably do not."

"Who is pushing for this change?"

"I suppose it's mostly me," he acknowledged.

"Do you have a compelling vision of the future and strategies for getting there that help explain why this reorganization is necessary?"

"I think so," he said, "although I'm not sure how clear it is."

"Have you ever tried to write down the vision and strategies in summary form on a few pages of paper?"

"Not really."

"Do your managers understand and believe in that vision?"

"I think the three or four key players are on board," he said, then conceded, "but I wouldn't be surprised if many others either don't understand the concept or don't entirely believe in it."

In the language system of the model shown in Exhibit 43.2, this executive had jumped immediately to phase 5 in the transformation process with his idea of a reorganization. But because he mostly

**EXHIBIT 43.2**  The Eight-Stage Process of Creating Major Change

---

**1. Establishing a sense of urgency**

✓ Examining the market and competitive realities
✓ Identifying and discussing crises, potential crises, or major opportunities

↓

**2. Creating the guiding coalition**

✓ Putting together a group with enough power to lead the change
✓ Getting the group to work together like a team

↓

**3. Developing a vision and strategy**

✓ Creating a vision to help direct the change effort
✓ Developing strategies for achieving that vision

↓

**4. Communicating the change vision**

✓ Using every vehicle possible to constantly communicate the new vision and strategies
✓ Having the guided coalition role model the behavior expected of employees

↓

**5. Empowering broad-based action**

✓ Getting rid of obstacles
✓ Changing systems or structures that undermine the change vision
✓ Encouraging risk taking and nontraditional ideas, activities, and actions

↓

**6. Generating short-term wins**

✓ Planning for visible improvements in performance, or "wins"
✓ Creating those wins
✓ Visibly recognizing and rewarding people who made the wins possible

↓

**7. Consolidating gains and producing more change**

✓ Using increased credibility to change all systems, structures, and policies that don't fit together and don't fit the trans-formation vision
✓ Hiring, promoting, and developing people who can implement the change vision
✓ Reinvigorating the process with new projects, themes, and change agents

↓

**8. Anchoring new approaches in the culture**

✓ Creating better performance through customer- and productivity-oriented behavior, more and better leadership, and more effective management
✓ Articulating the connection between new behaviors and organizational success
✓ Developing means to ensure leadership development and succession

---

SOURCE: Reprinted by permission of *Harvard Business Review.* An exhibit from "Why Transformation Efforts Fail," by John P. Kotter, March–April 1995. Copyright © 1995 by the President and Fellows of Harvard College; all rights reserved.

skipped the earlier steps, he ran into a wall of resistance.

Had he crammed the new structure down people's throats, which he could have done, they would have found a million clever ways to undermine the kinds of behavioral changes he wanted. He knew this to be true, so he sat in a frustrated stalemate. His story is not unusual.

People often try to transform organizations by undertaking only steps 5, 6, and 7, especially if it appears that a single decision—to reorganize, make an acquisition, or lay people off—will produce most of the needed change. Or they race through steps without ever finishing the job. Or they fail to reinforce earlier stages as they move on, and as a result the sense of urgency dissipates or the guiding coalition breaks up. Truth is, when you neglect any of the warm-up, or defrosting, activities (steps 1 to 4), you rarely establish a solid enough base on which to proceed. And without the follow-through that takes place in step 8, you never get to the finish line and make the changes stick.

## *The Importance of Sequence*

Successful change of any magnitude goes through all eight stages, usually in the sequence shown in Exhibit 43.2. Although one normally operates in multiple phases at once, skipping even a single step or getting too far ahead without a solid base almost always creates problems.

I recently asked the top twelve officers in a division of a large manufacturing firm to assess where they were in their change process. They judged that they were about 80 percent finished with stage #1, 40 percent with #2, 70 percent with #3, 60 percent with #4, 40 percent with #5, 10 percent with #6, and 5 percent with #7 and #8. They also said that their progress, which had gone well for eighteen months, was now slowing down, leaving them increasingly frustrated. I asked what they thought the problem was. After much discussion, they kept coming back to "corporate headquarters." Key individuals at corporate, including the CEO, were not sufficiently a part of the guiding coalition, which is why the twelve division officers judged that only 40 percent of the work in #2 was

done. Because higher-order principles had not been decided, they found it nearly impossible to settle on the more detailed strategies in #3. Their communication of the vision (#4) was being undercut, they believed, by messages from corporate that employees interpreted as being inconsistent with their new direction. In a similar way, empowerment efforts (#5) were being sabotaged. Without a clearer vision, it was hard to target credible short-term wins (#6). By moving on and not sufficiently confronting the stage 2 problem, they made the illusion of progress for a while. But without the solid base, the whole effort eventually began to teeter.

Normally, people skip steps because they are feeling pressures to produce. They also invent new sequences because some seemingly reasonable logic dictates such a choice. After getting well into the urgency phase (#1), all change efforts end up operating in multiple stages at once, but initiating action in any order other than that shown in Exhibit 43.2 rarely works well. It doesn't build and develop in a natural way. It comes across as contrived, forced, or mechanistic. It doesn't create the momentum needed to overcome enormously powerful sources of inertia.

## *Projects Within Projects*

Most major change initiatives are made up of a number of smaller projects that also tend to go through the multistep process. So at any one time, you might be halfway through the overall effort, finished with a few of the smaller pieces, and just beginning other projects. The net effect is like wheels within wheels.

A typical example for a medium-to-large telecommunications company: The overall effort, designed to significantly increase the firm's competitive position, took six years. By the third year, the transformation was centered in steps 5, 6, and 7. One relatively small reengineering project was nearing the end of stage 8. A restructuring of corporate staff groups was just beginning, with most of the effort in steps 1 and 2. A quality program was moving along, but behind schedule, while a few small final initiatives hadn't been launched yet.

Early results were visible at six to twelve months, but the biggest payoff didn't come until near the end of the overall effort.

When an organization is in a crisis, the first change project within a larger change process is often the save-the-ship or turn-around effort. For six to twenty-four months, people take decisive actions to stop negative cash flow and keep the organization alive. The second change project might be associated with a new strategy or reengineering. That could be followed by major structural and cultural change. Each of these efforts goes through all eight steps in the change sequence, and each plays a role in the overall transformation.

Because we are talking about multiple steps and multiple projects, the end result is often complex, dynamic, messy, and scary. At the beginning, those who attempt to create major change with simple, linear, analytical processes almost always fail. The point is not that analysis is unhelpful. Careful thinking is always essential, but there is a lot more involved here than (a) gathering data, (b) identifying options, (c) analyzing, and (d) choosing.

Q:　So why would an intelligent person rely too much on simple, linear, analytical processes?

A:　Because he or she has been taught to manage but not to lead.

### Management Versus Leadership

Management is a set of processes that can keep a complicated system of people and technology running smoothly. The most important aspects of management include planning, budgeting, organizing, staffing, controlling, and problem solving. Leadership is a set of processes that creates organizations in the first place or adapts them to significantly changing circumstances. Leadership defines what the future should look like, aligns people with that vision, and inspires them to make it happen despite the obstacles (see Exhibit 43.3).

This distinction is absolutely crucial for our purposes here: A close look at Exhibits 43.2 and 43.3 shows that successful transformation is 70 to 90 percent leadership and only 10 to 30 percent management. Yet for historical reasons, many or-

ganizations today don't have much leadership. And almost everyone thinks about the problem here as one of *managing* change.

For most of this century, as we created thousands and thousands of large organizations for the first time in human history, we didn't have enough good managers to keep all those bureaucracies functioning. So many companies and universities developed management programs, and hundreds and thousands of people were encouraged to learn management on the job. And they did. But people were taught little about leadership. To some degree, management was emphasized because it's easier to teach than leadership. But even more so, management was the main item on the twentieth-century agenda because that's what was needed. For every entrepreneur or business builder who was a leader, we needed hundreds of managers to run their ever-growing enterprises.

Unfortunately for us today, this emphasis on management has often been institutionalized in corporate cultures that discourage employees from learning how to lead. Ironically, past success is usually the key ingredient in producing this outcome. The syndrome, as I have observed it on many occasions, goes like this: Success creates some degree of market dominance, which in turn produces much growth. After a while, keeping the ever-larger organization under control becomes the primary challenge. So attention turns inward, and managerial competencies are nurtured. With a strong emphasis on management but not leadership, bureaucracy and an inward focus take over. But with continued success, the result mostly of market dominance, the problem often goes unaddressed and an unhealthy arrogance begins to evolve.

All of these characteristics then make any transformation effort much more difficult. (See Exhibit 43.4.) Arrogant managers can overevaluate their current performance and competitive position, listen poorly, and learn slowly. Inwardly focused employees can have difficulty seeing the very forces that present threats and opportunities. Bureaucratic cultures can smother those who want to respond to shifting conditions. And the lack of leadership leaves no force inside these organizations to break out of the morass.

**EXHIBIT 43.3**  Management Versus Leadership

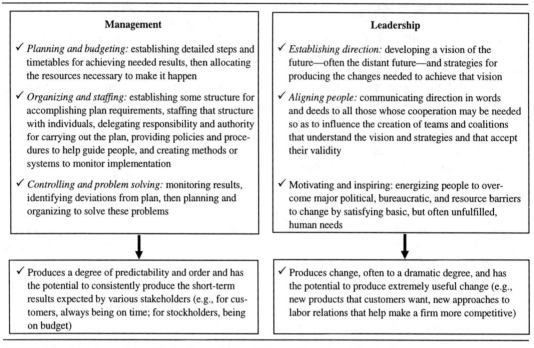

| Management | Leadership |
|---|---|
| ✓ *Planning and budgeting:* establishing detailed steps and timetables for achieving needed results, then allocating the resources necessary to make it happen | ✓ *Establishing direction:* developing a vision of the future—often the distant future—and strategies for producing the changes needed to achieve that vision |
| ✓ *Organizing and staffing:* establishing some structure for accomplishing plan requirements, staffing that structure with individuals, delegating responsibility and authority for carrying out the plan, providing policies and procedures to help guide people, and creating methods or systems to monitor implementation | ✓ *Aligning people:* communicating direction in words and deeds to all those whose cooperation may be needed so as to influence the creation of teams and coalitions that understand the vision and strategies and that accept their validity |
| ✓ *Controlling and problem solving:* monitoring results, identifying deviations from plan, then planning and organizing to solve these problems | ✓ Motivating and inspiring: energizing people to overcome major political, bureaucratic, and resource barriers to change by satisfying basic, but often unfulfilled, human needs |

| | |
|---|---|
| ✓ Produces a degree of predictability and order and has the potential to consistently produce the short-term results expected by various stakeholders (e.g., for customers, always being on time; for stockholders, being on budget) | ✓ Produces change, often to a dramatic degree, and has the potential to produce extremely useful change (e.g., new products that customers want, new approaches to labor relations that help make a firm more competitive) |

SOURCE: Adapted with the permission of The Free Press, a Division of Simon & Schuster from *A Force for Change: How Leadership Differs From Management* by John P. Kotter. Copyright © 1990 by John P. Kotter.

The combination of cultures that resist change and managers who have not been taught how to create change is lethal. The errors described in chapter 1 are almost inevitable under these conditions. Sources of complacency are rarely attacked adequately because urgency is not an issue for people who have been asked all their lives merely to maintain the current system like a softly humming Swiss watch. A powerful enough guiding coalition with sufficient leadership is not created by people who have been taught to think in terms of hierarchy and management. Visions and strategies are not formulated by individuals who have learned only to deal with plans and budgets. Sufficient time and energy are never invested in communicating a new sense of direction to enough people—not surprising in light of a history of simply handing direct reports the latest plan. Structures, systems, lack of training, or supervisors are allowed to disempower employees who want to help implement the vision—predictable, given

how little most managers have learned about empowerment. Victory is declared much too soon by people who have been instructed to think in terms of system cycle times: hours, days, or weeks, not years. And new approaches are seldom anchored in the organization's culture by people who have been taught to think in terms of formal structure, not culture. As a result, expensive acquisitions produce none of the hoped-for synergies, dramatic downsizings fail to get costs under control, huge reengineering projects take too long and provide too little benefit, and bold new strategies are never implemented well.

Employees in large, older firms often have difficulty getting a transformation process started because of the lack of leadership coupled with arrogance, insularity, and bureaucracy. In those organizations, where a change program is likely to be overmanaged and underled, there is a lot more pushing than pulling. Someone puts together a plan, hands it to people, and then tries to hold

**EXHIBIT 43.4**  The Creation of an Overmanaged, Underled Corporate Culture

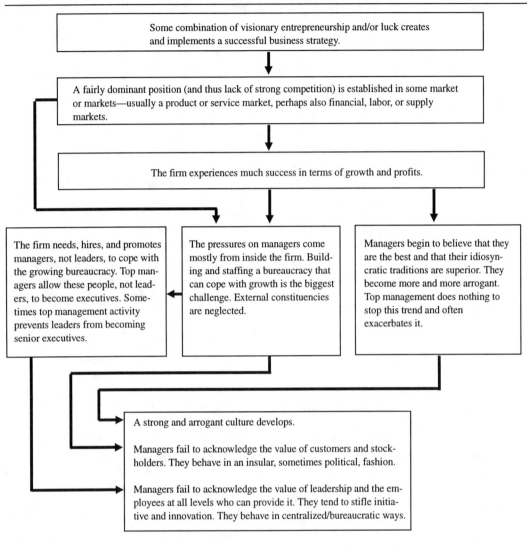

SOURCE: Adapted/reprinted with the permission of The Free Press, a Division of Simon & Schuster from *Corporate Culture and Performance* by John P. Kotter and James L. Heskett. Copyright © 1992 by Kotter Associates, Inc. and James L. Heskett.

them accountable. Or someone makes a decision and demands that others accept it. The problem with this approach is that it is enormously difficult to enact by sheer force the big changes often needed today to make organizations perform better. Transformation requires sacrifice, dedication, and creativity, none of which usually comes with coercion.

Efforts to effect change that are overmanaged and underled also tend to try to eliminate the inherent messiness of transformations. Eight stages are reduced to three. Seven projects are consolidated into two. Instead of involving hundreds or thousands of people, the initiative is handled mostly by a small group. The net result is almost always very disappointing.

Managing change is important. Without competent management, the transformation process can get out of control. But for most organizations, the much bigger challenge is leading change. Only leadership can blast through the many sources of corporate inertia. Only leadership can motivate the actions needed to alter behavior in any significant way. Only leadership can get change to stick by anchoring it in the very culture of an organization.

This leadership often begins with just one or two people. But in anything but the very smallest of organizations, that number needs to grow and grow over time. The solution to the change problem is not one larger-than-life individual who charms thousands into being obedient followers. Modern organizations are far too complex to be transformed by a single giant. Many people need to help with the leadership task, not by attempting to imitate the likes of Winston Churchill or Martin Luther King, Jr., but by modestly assisting with the leadership agenda in their spheres of activity.

### The Future

The change problem inside organizations would become less worrisome if the business environment would soon stabilize or at least slow down. But most credible evidence suggests the opposite: that the rate of environmental movement will increase and that the pressures on organizations to transform themselves will grow over the next few decades. If that's the case, the only rational solution is to learn more about what creates successful change and to pass that knowledge on to increasingly larger groups of people.

From what I have seen over the past two decades, helping individuals to better understand transformation has two components, both of which will be addressed in some detail in the remainder of this book. The first relates to the various steps in the multistage process. Most of us still have plenty to learn about what works, what doesn't, what is the natural sequence of events, and where even very capable people have difficulties. The second component is associated with the driving force behind the process: leadership, leadership, and still more leadership.

If you sincerely think that you and other relevant people in your organization already know most of what is necessary to produce needed change and, therefore, are quite logically wondering why you should take the time to read the rest of this book, let me suggest that you consider the following. What do you think we would find if we searched all the documents produced in your organization in the last twelve months while looking for two phrases: "managing change" and "leading change"? We would look at memos, meeting summaries, newsletters, annual reports, project reports, formal plans, etc. Then we would turn the numbers into percentages—X percent of the references are to "managing change" and Y percent to "leading change."

Of course the findings from this exercise could be nothing more than meaningless semantics. But then again, maybe they would accurately reflect the way your organization thinks about change. And maybe that has something to do with how quickly you improve the quality of products or services, increase productivity, lower costs, and innovate.

*44*

# Collaboration

## The Constructive Management of Differences

BARBARA GRAY

The world must be kept safe for differences.
—*Clyde Kuckholn*

### The Need to Manage Differences

Our society is at a critical juncture. Constructive approaches for confronting difficult societal problems are essential to managing our global future. The pace at which new problems are generated is rapid, and individual organizations are hard-pressed to make effective or timely responses. As a result, problems are piling up; new problems are cropping up daily, while yesterday's problems often go unsolved. Problems range in scope from local (such as allocating water rights for local development) to global (such as preventing deterioration of the ozone layer, which shields our planet from ultraviolet radiation).

This pileup of problems and the inability of organizations to contend with them reflects the turbulence of our environment. Under turbulent conditions organizations become highly interdependent with others in indirect but consequential ways (Emery and Trist, 1965, 1972; Trist, 1977). Under these circumstances it is difficult for individual organizations to act unilaterally to solve problems without creating unwanted consequences for other parties and without encountering constraints imposed by others. Because of this interdependence, the range of interests associated with any particular problem is wide and usually controversial.

Consider the situation in Franklin Township, rural community adjacent to a growing Midwestern university town.

In 1970 Franklin Township was a thriving farming community comprising many large family farms. Over the next fifteen years Franklin Township's population increased from 759 to 975 residents as a few scattered tracts of farmland were sold for development. By the mid-1980s, developers began eyeing the township as a potential bedroom community. When an eighty-acre tract of farmland was sold to a local farmer whose family had lived in the area since 1830, township residents breathed a sigh of relief. Development had been coming too fast, creating traffic and excessive demands on the local water system operated by the township's water company.

Local residents were shocked a few months later when the farmer submitted plans to the township supervisors for a development of eighty one-acre lots. The community mobilized quickly, and fifty-seven people showed up at the supervisors' meeting to protest the development. Many residents expressed concerns about overtaxing an already inadequate water supply. They carried a petition demanding the supervisors oppose the development and threatened to sue the water company and the township if they did not. The previous summer these residents had gone without water on several occasions during dry spells, and they feared the situation would worsen when eighty additional faucets were turned on.

A second group of residents, dubbed the "horse people," complained that the development would block their access to the riding trails in the state game lands that abutted the proposed development. These residents requested an easement for public access to the game lands. Objections also came from the residents whose private road was to become the gateway to the new homes and from the fruit farmer whose irrigation system depended on private wells close to the proposed development.

Franklin Township is a simple illustration of a situation in which the interests of multiple parties have become intertwined. The parties in the Franklin Township scenario include a neighbor-turned-developer, part-time township supervisors, local interest groups such as the "horse people," water company authorities, a local commercial farmer, and ordinary citizens concerned about taxes, traffic, and so forth. From many of their perspectives, the solution to the problem seems black-and-white—either support or oppose the development. Yet, for the township supervisors, the problem is more complex. They are faced with several questions: How should the township supervisors handle the developer's request for permits? How should they respond to the opposition from homeowners? What is the developer's responsibility to the community? Are the residents' concerns legitimate? Is it prudent to expect the water system to accommodate the new level of demand? What if other farmers followed suit and similar developments were proposed?

The township supervisors have several options. One is the "ostrich approach." They can postpone making a decision for as long as possible and hope the problem will go away. That outcome is, of course, unlikely since township ordinances usually mandate a specific response period. A second option is to take sides with one or more of the parties. There are several possible consequences of this choice, including escalation of the conflict, as township supervisors in North Salem, New York, recently discovered (Foderaro, 1988). In North Salem a developer sued the supervisors, charging that a new zoning ordinance was exclusionary. Dissension among the supervisors over development also caused one to resign and another to lose a bid for reelection.

Other options are available to the supervisors in Franklin Township. They can adopt a "hands off, let the experts decide" approach in which they rely on legal or engineering advisers to make the decisions for them. A fourth option, the traditional approach, involves holding public hearings in which interested parties can vent their concerns. These, however, frequently churn up issues and raise community expectations, often well beyond what responsible public officials can reasonably deliver. Though well intended, both of these options also often lead to less than satisfactory solutions.

One reason the solutions are unsatisfactory is that they are often not accepted by the public. For highly controversial issues, it is likely at least some of the public will not accept the decision of public officials, even when these officials decide only after conscientiously gathering and weighing information from all interested parties. Often, these officials must spend countless future hours justifying their decision after the fact. This problem occurs because parties who gave input do not know if or how their interests were considered during decision making (Delbecq, 1974; Wondolleck, 1985). Because parties are not privy to the process by which their interests and those of others are evaluated, those who gave input initially often feel betrayed when the final solution does not satisfy their requests (Carpenter and Kennedy, 1988). The problem of acceptance increases if the decision threatens basic values or creates a situation of high perceived risks for some stakeholders (Klein, 1976).

Seasoned public officials often become thick skinned, shrugging off the conflict with the adage "you can't please everyone." Unfortunately, heated issues do not die easily and often reemerge in an escalated form.

Additionally, there is growing evidence that for complex problems of this type, individual and collective efforts to solve them are often suboptimal because even well-intended decision makers do not really understand the interests they are trying to reconcile (Fisher and Ury, 1981; Wondolleck, 1985; Lax and Sebenius, 1986). Research has shown, for example, that it is often possible to improve on an agreement through a procedure called postsettlement settlement (Raiffa, 1985). In this procedure, parties reach a preliminary agreement and then invite a third party to review it and recommend improvements that benefit all of the parties. Often these opportunities for joint gains lie in trade-offs that the parties were unable to recognize for themselves (Lax and Sebenius, 1986). Procedures that encourage parties to search for

these joint gains have the potential to produce better agreements and to prevent escalation.

In light of this, consider a fifth option available to the Franklin Township supervisors. They can assemble a representative sample of the stakeholders (those with a stake in the problem) and let them work out an agreement among themselves. The stakeholders in this case include the developer, the commercial fruit farmer, the township supervisors, the "horse people," the water company board, the homeowners concerned about water, and the homeowners concerned about traffic. This option has the advantage of dealing with interrelated issues in the same forum, since the township supervisors do not have jurisdiction over the water company but do have authority to approve or disapprove the rest of the development plan. Getting all the stakeholders together to explore their concerns in a constructive way allows them to search for a solution they can all accept and averts the potential for escalation of the conflict. Additionally, the supervisors do not abdicate their responsibility, because they must agree to any decision that is reached. This approach is called collaboration.

## Collaboration as an Alternative

Collaboration is a process through which parties who see different aspects of a problem can constructively explore their differences and search for solutions that go beyond their own limited vision of what is possible. Collaboration is based on the simple adages that "two heads are better than one" and that one by itself is simply not good enough! Those parties with an interest in the problem are termed stakeholders. Stakeholders include all individuals, groups, or organizations that are directly influenced by actions others take to solve the problem. Each stakeholder has a unique appreciation of the problem. The objective of collaboration is to create a richer, more comprehensive appreciation of the problem among the stakeholders than any one of them could construct alone. The term *problem domain* will be used here to refer to the way a problem is conceptualized by the stakeholders (Trist, 1983).

A kaleidoscope is a useful image to envision what joint appreciation of a domain is all about. As the kaleidoscope is rotated, different configurations of the same collection of colored shapes appear. Collaboration involves building a common understanding of how these images appear from their respective points of view. This understanding forms the basis for choosing a collective course of action.

Collaboration is not really a new concept. It is not unlike the town meeting concept, which is a cornerstone of the democratic process. Town meetings turn on the principles of local participation and ownership of decisions. Collaboration reflects a resurgence of interest in those fundamental principles. Any one of the stakeholders in Franklin Township could suggest that they try collaboration. Because of their responsibility for rendering a permit decision, however, the township supervisors are in the best position to initiate a collaborative dialogue. Their role in such a process would be to help the parties articulate their interests and to facilitate a reconciliation.

Questions like those facing the supervisors and residents of Franklin Township are being asked in communities around the world. In some, like Franklin Township, the issues are controversial. In other cases, such as those concerning the cleanup of toxic dumps or the destruction of the ozone layer, the issues are scientifically and politically complex, involve many interested parties, and are often hotly contested.

Not all occasions for collaboration are conflict induced. In some cases, parties may have a shared interest in solving a problem that none of them alone can address. The opportunity for collaborating arises because stakeholders recognize the potential advantages of working together. They may need each other to execute a vision that they all share. Managing a joint business venture is a good example. Addressing the problem of illiteracy in a community is another. Parties come together because each needs the others to advance their individual interests. Opportunities for collaborating are arising in countless arenas in which business, government, labor, and communities are finding their actions interconnected with those of other stakeholders. In the next section, several public- and private-sector opportunities for constructive collaboration are considered.

## *Opportunities for Collaborating*

Situations that provide opportunities for collaborating are many and varied. They include joint ventures among selected businesses, settlement of local neighborhood or environmental disputes, revitalization of economically depressed cities, and resolution of major international problems. These opportunities can be classified into two general categories: resolving conflicts and advancing shared visions.

### Resolving Conflict

Collaboration can be used effectively to settle disputes between the parties in multiparty conflict. Collaboration transforms adversarial interaction into a mutual search for information and for solutions that allow all those participating to insure that their interests are represented. Often, parties in conflict are motivated to try collaboration only as a last-ditch effort when other approaches have reached impasse or have produced less than acceptable outcomes. Parties will try collaboration only if they believe they have something to gain from it. In protracted stalemates, for example, the cost to all parties of inaction may be a sufficient incentive to induce collaboration.

Collaboration has been used to settle hundreds of site-specific environmental disputes (Bingham, 1986), important product liability cases, intergovernmental disputes, and many other community controversies involving transportation, housing, and mortgage lending. Within the environmental area, Bingham (1986) has identified six broad categories within which collaborative solutions to disputes have been sought: land use, natural resource management and public land use, water resources, energy, air quality, and toxics.

The potential for collaboration in international affairs also appears promising. Within the last year a number of major political conflicts have moved from stalemate to early dialogue, signaling a growing potential to search for alternatives to violence. In addition, the list of major global issues in which the interests of several nation-states, nongovernmental organizations (NGOs), and multinational corporations intersect continues to grow. Salient issues include a variety of property rights issues related to the use of the seas and exploration in Antarctica, global environmental issues such as the future of rain forests and control of acid rain, and transnational technology issues such as the management of international telecommunications. For problems of this scope, international collaboration is essential for finding solutions.

The chlorofluorocarbons treaty reached in Montreal in March 1987 provides one model of successful international collaboration. The treaty is historical because it is the first international agreement designed to avert a global disaster (Benedick, 1988). The treaty restricts the production of chemicals (chlorofluorocarbons and others) that erode the stratospheric ozone layer, which protects the earth from the sun's damaging ultraviolet rays. Stakeholders included chlorofluorocarbon producers in several countries, NGOs such as environmental groups and the United Nations Environment Program, members of the scientific community, and governments from the North and the South. Forty-eight countries have signed the treaty, and it is awaiting formal ratification by the countries involved. In addition to the freeze on production, the treaty paves the way for discussions of longer-term strategies to preserve the ozone layer.

## Advancing Shared Visions

Collaborations induced by shared visions are intended to advance the collective good of the stakeholders involved. Some are designed to address socioeconomic issues such as illiteracy, youth unemployment, housing, or homelessness, which cut across public- and private-sector interests. Collaborating is also becoming increasingly crucial to successful business management, as companies see advantages in sharing research and development costs (Dimancescu and Botkin, 1986)

and exploring new markets through joint ventures (Perlmutter and Heenan, 1986). The proliferation of joint ventures in the auto industry alone has surprised analysts, who a decade ago were predicting a major shakeout in that industry would force many automakers to go out of business (Holusha, 1988).

Public-private partnerships that have sprung up to address deteriorating conditions in U.S. cities are illustrative of collaborative efforts across sectors to advance shared visions. In these partnerships, public and private interests pool their resources and undertake joint planning to tackle economic redevelopment, education, housing, and other protracted problems that have plagued their communities. In the area of education, for example, representatives of industry, labor, and schools have teamed up to deal with youth unemployment and juvenile crime (Elsman and the National Institute for Work and Learning, 1981). These and other partnerships such as the Boston Compact, the Greater Baltimore Committee, the Newark Collaboration, and the Whittier Alliance in Minneapolis began with stakeholders articulating a desirable future they collectively wanted to pursue.

Successfully advancing a shared vision, whether in the public or the private sector, requires identification and coordination of a diverse set of stakeholders, each of whom holds some but not all of the necessary resources. To be successful, coordination must be accomplished laterally without the hierarchical authority to which most managers are accustomed. These circumstances require a radically different approach to organizing and managing, especially for international joint ventures.

> The challenge of managing these coalitions is staggering, given the complexity of the stakeholder network that often involves at least two foreign governments. As a result, interorganizational relations must be carefully worked through in order to gain the advantages of such a union. (Heenan and Perlmutter, 1979, p. 82)

Even when parties agree initially on a shared vision, collaboration among them is not necessarily free of conflict. Conflicts inevitably ensue over plans for how the vision should be carried out. And further problems typically arise when stakeholders try to implement their agreements. Overcoming the barriers created by different institutional cultures is frequently a formidable task. Getting the business community and a major urban school district to work together on problems of youth employment, for example, requires considerable adaptation on the part of each. Similar obstacles must be overcome by Japanese and American managers who are trying to implement a management system for a new joint venture (Holusha, 1988).

## Nature of Collaborative Problems

It should be clear by now that there is no shortage of problems for which collaboration offers a decided advantage over other methods of decision making. The characteristics of these problems can be described generally as follows:

- The problems are ill defined, or there is disagreement about how they should be defined.
- Several stakeholders have a vested interest in the problems and are interdependent.
- These stakeholders are not necessarily identified a priori or organized in any systematic way.
- There may be a disparity of power and/or resources for dealing with the problems among the stakeholders.
- Stakeholders may have different levels of expertise and different access to information about the problems.
- The problems are often characterized by technical complexity and scientific uncertainty.
- Differing perspectives on the problems often lead to adversarial relationships among the stakeholders.
- Incremental or unilateral efforts to deal with the problems typically produce less than satisfactory solutions.
- Existing processes for addressing the problems have proved insufficient and may even exacerbate them.

Problems with these characteristics have been dubbed "messes" (Ackoff, 1981) or metaproblems

(Chevalier, 1966). What is needed to deal constructively with problems of this type is an alternative model of how to organize to solve them. This book proposes a model of organizing based on collaboration among the parties rather than on competition, hierarchy, or incremental planning (Trist, 1977). This book offers a comprehensive treatment of collaborative dynamics in the hope that potential parties will appreciate how they can use collaboration to successfully address multiparty problems. Let us turn now to an in-depth look at what collaborating entails.

## *Dynamics of Collaboration*

Collaboration involves a process of joint decision making among key stakeholders of a problem domain about the future of that domain. Five features are critical to the process: (1) the stakeholders are interdependent, (2) solutions emerge by dealing constructively with differences, (3) joint ownership of decisions is involved, (4) stakeholders assume collective responsibility for the future direction of the domain, and (5) collaboration is an emergent process.

### Collaboration Implies Interdependence

Collaboration establishes a give and take among the stakeholders that is designed to produce solutions that none of them working independently could achieve. Therefore, an important ingredient of collaboration is interdependence among the stakeholders. Initially, the extent of interdependence may not be fully appreciated by all the parties. Therefore, the initial phase of any collaboration usually involves calling attention to the ways in which the stakeholders' concerns are intertwined and the reasons why they need each other to solve the problem. Parties in conflict especially lose sight of their underlying interdependence. Heightening parties' awareness of their interdependence often kindles renewed willingness to search for trade-offs that could produce a mutually beneficial solution. In the collaborations investigated in this book, external events often propel reexamination of taken-for-granted interdependencies.

## Solutions Emerge by Dealing Constructively With Differences

Respect for differences is an easy virtue to champion verbally and a much more difficult one to put into practice in our day-to-day affairs. Yet differences are often the source of immense creative potential. Learning to harness that potential is what collaboration is all about.

Consider the parable of the elephant and the blind men. Several blind men walking through the jungle come upon an elephant. Each approaches the elephant from a different angle and comes into contact with a different part of the elephant's anatomy. The blind man who contacts the elephant's leg declares, "Oh, an elephant is like a tree trunk." Another, who apprehends the elephant's tail, objects to the first's description, exclaiming, "Oh, no, the elephant is like a rope." A third, grasping the elephant's large, floppy ear, insists, "You are both wrong; the elephant is like a fan." Clearly, each man, from his vantage point, has apprehended something important and genuine about the elephant. Each one's perception of the elephant is accurate, albeit limited. None of the blind men, through his own inquiries, has a comprehensive understanding of the phenomenon called "elephant." Together, however, they have a much richer and more complete perspective.

Like the blind men, most of us routinely make a number of assumptions that limit our ability to capitalize on this creative potential. One assumption that we frequently make is that our way of viewing a problem is the best. Best to us may mean the most rational, the fairest, the most intelligent, or even the only way. No matter what the basis, we arrive at the conclusion that our way is superior to any other. Thus we lose sight of the possibility that multiple approaches to the elephant yield multiple perceptions about what is possible and what is desirable.

Even if we grant that multiple perceptions are possible, we can easily fall prey to another common assumption; that is, we conclude that different interpretations are, by definition, opposing interpretations. But here we need to distinguish between interpretations that differ from each other and those that are truly opposed. As Fisher and Ury have aptly pointed out, "Agreement is possible precisely because interests differ" (1981, p. 44). Without differing interests, the range of possible exchanges between parties would be nonexistent. Because parties' interests do vary, as do the resources and skills they have to solve a problem, they are able to arrange trade-offs and to forge mutually beneficial alliances.

It is also frequently the case that as we strive to articulate our differences, we discover that our underlying concerns are fundamentally the same. These shared concerns may have been masked by the different ways we described or framed the problem or may have been obscured by strong emotions that deafened us to the messages coming from the other parties. Parties in conflict are known to engage in selective listening and to pay more attention to information that confirms their preconceived stereotypes of their opponents. Stereotypes cause us to discount the legitimacy of the other's point of view and cause both sides to ignore data that disconfirm their stereotypes (Sherif, 1958). Stereotypes also restrict the flow of information between the parties. Without this exchange of information, the parties cannot discover clues about their shared or differing interests that may contain the seeds of an agreement.

Stereotyping figures prominently in the type of complex multiparty disputes addressed in this book. Frequently the parties have had a long history of interaction, fighting out their differences in legislative and judicial arenas. Working on opposite sides in these arenas allows the parties to continually reconfirm their stereotypic impressions with hard evidence (about the other side's motives, values, and willingness to reach accommodation). Collaboration operates on the premise that the assumptions that disputants have about the other side and about the nature of the issues themselves are worth testing. The premise is that testing these assumptions and allowing a constructive confrontation of differences may unlock heretofore disguised creative potential. Through such exploration stakeholders may discover new options that permit constructive mergers of interests previously unimagined or judged infeasible.

## Collaboration Involves Joint Ownership of Decisions

*Joint ownership* means that the participants in a collaboration are directly responsible for reaching agreement on a solution. Unlike litigation or regulation, in which intermediaries (courts, regulatory agencies, legislators) devise solutions that are imposed on the stakeholders, in collaborative agreements the parties impose decisions on themselves. They set the agenda; they decide what issues will be addressed; they decide what the terms will be. Any agreements that are reached may be freestanding contracts, or they may serve as input to a legal or a public policy process that ratifies, codifies, or in some other way incorporates the agreements. Clearly where matters of public policy are under consideration, collaboration cannot serve as a substitute for constitutional decision-making processes. However, it can "provide a sense of direction, smooth social conflict, and speed formal processes" (Dunlop, 1986, p. 24).

When collaboration occurs, the various stakeholders bring their idiosyncratic perceptions of the problem to the negotiations. Each holds assumptions, beliefs, and viewpoints that are consistent with their independent efforts to confront the problem. Through collaboration these multiple perspectives are aired and debated, and gradually a more complete appreciation of the complexity of the problem is constructed. This more complete appreciation forms the basis for envisioning new alternatives that take into account the stakeholders' multiple interests. Thus, the outcome of collaboration is a weaving together of multiple and diverse viewpoints into a mosaic replete with new insights and directions for action agreed on by all the stakeholders. Three key steps in reaching a joint decision include (1) the joint search for information about the problem, (2) the invention of a mutually agreed upon solution about the pattern of future exchanges between stakeholders, and (3) ratification of the agreement and plans for implementing it.

## Stakeholders Assume Collective Responsibility for Future Direction of the Domain

One outcome of collaboration is a set of agreements governing future interactions among the stakeholders. Trist (1983) refers to this as self-regulation of the domain. During collaboration a new set of relationships among the stakeholders is negotiated as they address the problem at hand. The process of collaborating essentially restructures the socially accepted rules for dealing with problems of this type. The negotiations may also restructure the rules governing how stakeholders will interact with respect to the problem in the future. That is, formal or informal contracts about the nature of subsequent exchanges among the stakeholders are forged during collaboration. Collaboration may lead to increased coordination among the stakeholders, although that is not a necessary outcome of the process.

## Collaboration Is an Emergent Process

Collaboration is essentially an emergent process rather than a prescribed state of organization. By viewing collaboration as a process, it becomes possible to describe its origins and development as well as how its organization changes over time. Hence, collaboration can be thought of as a temporary and evolving forum for addressing a problem. Typically, collaborations progress from "underorganized systems" in which individual stakeholders act independently, if at all, with respect to the problem (Brown, 1980) to more tightly organized relationships characterized by concerted decision making among the stakeholders.

Collaboration as it is defined here should be distinguished from the terms *cooperation* and *coordination* as used by Mulford and Rogers (1982). They use these terms to classify static patterns of interorganizational relations. Coordination refers to formal institutionalized relationships among existing networks of organizations, while cooperation is "characterized by informal trade-offs and by attempts to establish reciprocity in the absence of rules" (Mulford and Rogers, 1982, p. 13). While these distinctions may be useful for distinguishing formal and informal relationships, they do not capture the dynamic evolutionary character of the phenomenon described in this book. To presume that the parties in a collaborative effort are already part of an organized relationship underrepresents the developmental character of the process and ignores the delicate prenegotiations that are often necessary to bring stakeholders together initially.

Both cooperation and coordination often occur as part of the process of collaborating. The process by which reciprocity is established informally in the absence of rules is as important to collaboration as the formal coordination agreements that eventually emerge. Skillful management of early interactions is often crucial to continued collaboration, since these informal interactions lay the groundwork for subsequent formal interactions.

Once initiated, collaboration creates a temporary forum within which consensus about the problem can be sought, mutually agreeable solutions can be invented, and collective actions to implement the solutions can be taken. Understanding how this process unfolds is critical to successfully managing the kinds of multiparty and multiorganizational relations described earlier in the chapter.

Envisioning interorganizational relations as processes rather than as outcomes in which stakeholders assume decision making responsibility for their collective future permits investigation of how innovation and change in currently unsatisfactory exchange relationships can occur. If collaboration is successful, new solutions emerge that no single party could have envisioned or enacted. A successful example can best illustrate the dynamics of collaboration.

## *Successful Collaboration*

Pernicious stereotypes and misinformation precipitated a major conflict between government agencies and citizens in the community surrounding Three Mile Island Nuclear Reactor. The conflict surfaced over plans for cleanup of the reactor, which was badly damaged during a catastrophic accident in 1979. Through an unprecedented intervention, called the Citizens' Radiation Monitoring Program, local residents and the federal and state governments collaboratively generated credible information to assuage residents' fears about radiation exposure during the initial phase of the cleanup (see Gricar and Baratta [1983] for a more detailed description).

## Citizens' Radiation Monitoring Program

The accident at Three Mile Island (TMI) in March 1979 released small but significant levels of radioactivity into the atmosphere, exposing residents of the area surrounding TMI to a maximum radiation dosage twice that of average yearly background levels. Despite reports of no immediate or long-term health effects from the accident, many residents were concerned about the risks associated with radiation exposure. These concerns were heightened when Metropolitan Edison (the operator of Three Mile Island) proposed releasing low levels of radioactive krypton gas into the atmosphere as the first step in the proposed cleanup of the reactor. The full extent of damage to the reactor could not be determined until the gas it contained was removed. The staff of the Nuclear Regulatory Commission (NRC) had determined that the purge would not endanger the health and safety of the public (TMI Support Staff, 1980).

At the time public trust in Met Ed and the NRC was seriously eroded because of the widespread belief that these agencies had deliberately misled the public about radiation levels during the accident. The NRC's own special inquiry into the accident attributed what it called "public misconceptions about risks" to "a failure to convey credible information regarding the actual risks in an understandable fashion to the public" (Rogovin, 1980). This mistrust prompted several communities to appeal to the governor and to the president for independent sources of information about radiation levels. Concern about the risks grew to extreme proportions in March 1980 during public meetings on the environmental impact of the purge. Public opposition to the proposed purge was so fierce that it drowned out the NRC's announcement that a community monitoring program was under way.

In February, the U.S. Department of Energy (DOE) assembled a team of representatives (called the Technical Working Group) from the Environmental Protection Agency, the Pennsylvania Department of Environmental Resources (DER), the Pennsylvania State University, and EG&G Idaho (a technical consultant to Met Ed) to design and implement the Citizens' Radiation Monitoring Program. The program's purpose was to ensure that citizens in the vicinity of TMI received accurate and credible information about radiation levels during the purge. The program was based on the premise that citizens were more likely to believe information generated by themselves or by their neighbors than by government officials, whose credibility they considered questionable. Through the program, local citizens conducted routine monitoring of radiation levels using equipment provided by the Department of Energy.

The Technical Working Group (TWG) sought input on the design of the program from officials of three counties and twelve municipalities that fell within a five-mile radius of TMI. Each community nominated four citizens to serve as monitors. The monitors included teachers, secretaries, engineers, housewives, police officers, and retirees. They ranged in age from early twenties to senior citizens. Their political persuasions about nuclear power ran the gamut from pro- to antinuclear. The monitors were given an intensive "crash course" on radiation and its effects and detection methods and were given hands-on training so that they could operate the monitoring equipment and interpret the measurements for their fellow citizens.

Each participating community drew up its own monitoring schedule and selected the locations for its monitoring equipment. The citizen monitors posted daily results of the monitoring in the townships, and the TWG disseminated the results to the local media and to the participating agencies.

The Citizens' Radiation Monitoring Program represents a dramatic departure from typical government efforts to communicate with the public. In this case, traditional efforts by government agencies to disseminate public information were grossly ineffective and only increased public mistrust of the agencies. Following months of technical review of Met Ed's proposal for the purge,

the NRC tried at public meetings to present a rational argument in support of the purge. Both the meetings and the environmental assessment itself focused exclusively on the technical aspects of reactor decontamination. Rational arguments, however, meant little to citizens whose calculation of the risks involved was much more personal. The accident clearly had left social and psychological scars on the community (Scranton, 1980; Kemeny, 1979; Brunn, Johnson, and Ziegler, 1979) and had created widespread uncertainty about safety. Because of general unfamiliarity with radiation and its effects, the lack of credible information, and the imperceptible nature of radiation itself, the public had little basis for judging either the level of danger or its seriousness. With no precedents to consider, it is not surprising that public fears about potential risks were running high.

Perceptions by public officials that those who resisted were troublemakers or fanatics only fueled the controversy. By underestimating the degree to which emotional concerns for safety shaped public attitudes, these officials reduced their own credibility and further escalated public mistrust.

Collaboration in this case occurred among the Department of Energy, the other agencies involved in the Technical Working Group, and the local municipalities and counties.

Let us examine this case with respect to the five features of collaboration described above. First, how were the stakeholders interdependent? The stakeholders in this case were interdependent because neither Met Ed nor the community could afford not to begin cleanup of the reactor. Leaving the krypton gas inside the reactor posed an unknown risk to the public and prevented Met Ed from determining the extent of damage from the accident. Thus safe but timely decontamination of the reactor was critical.

Second, how were differences handled? Initially in this case there were very different perceptions about safety and about the credibility of those agencies disseminating safety information. Prior to the monitoring program, Met Ed and the government agencies had relied on a rational, technocratic approach to educate the public and had dismissed the citizens' concerns as irrational. The monitoring program was an acknowledgment that these differing perceptions of risk needed to be addressed, not ignored. Enlisting local citizens as monitors was a novel and unprecedented step by these agencies, which typically relied on narrow, technically oriented solutions.

Third, were the stakeholders jointly involved in decision making? The initial proposal for citizen monitoring came from the mayor of one of the affected communities. Exploratory meetings involved several, but not all, stakeholder groups. Once the DOE made the decision to go ahead, decision making was shared among several agencies in the TWG, and, to a lesser extent, the local communities and their citizen monitors participated in making decisions about the execution of the program. Met Ed, a key stakeholder, was purposely excluded from the group because its participation would likely have damaged the credibility of the entire effort. Thus, this process did not provide for full participation by all the stakeholders, but it did incorporate widespread representation in the overall planning.

Fourth, who assumed responsibility for the future direction of the domain? This case graphically illustrates how responsibility for ensuring that credible information about radiation levels was available to the communities surrounding TMI was shared among the stakeholders. The DOE supplied the financial resources; EG&G Idaho, the EPA, and the DER contributed technical expertise and staff; the university designed the equipment and provided training and organizational expertise; and the citizens donated their time and talent to carry out the monitoring.

Finally, to what extent was the collaboration emergent? The process of collaborating grew out of a major public controversy. At the outset, mechanisms for managing the differing interests and coordinating a viable plan of action were underdeveloped. The Citizens' Radiation Monitoring Program emerged through a series of steps. It began with the citizens' opposition to the venting and their plea for credible information. This was followed by the formation of the TWG, involvement of the communities, creation of the training program, and, finally, the monitoring itself. Because of the urgency

of the situation, the entire collaborative process lasted only five months.

The consequences of this collaborative effort are summarized below:

- Met Ed was allowed to execute a critical first step in the reactor cleanup process.
- Residents in the community received information they could trust to judge their own levels of radiation exposure. A survey conducted before and after the training indicated a significant increase in the monitors' belief that they could get accurate information about radiation levels and that they had sufficient information to make a judgment about their own safety (Gricar and Baratta, 1983).
- Residents who participated as monitors gained a deeper appreciation for the technical issues associated with nuclear power and engaged in rational dialogue and debate with each other on contested topics during the training program.

In addition to the above outcomes, the Citizens' Radiation Monitoring Program demonstrated that government, communities, and the private sector often hold very different perceptions about a problem. Without a frank and open dialogue characterized by reason and respect, these perceptions cannot be examined. Had the NRC proceeded with the purge without community guarantees about credible information, the conflict would only have escalated, probably to the level of violence.

## Benefits of Collaborating

When collaboration is used to address multiparty problems, several benefits are possible (see Table 44.1).

First, collaboration increases the quality of solutions considered by the parties because solutions are based on a broad, comprehensive analysis of the problem. The collective capacity to respond to the problem is also increased as stakeholders apply a variety of complementary resources to solving it. Collaboration also offers a way to reopen negotiations when impasse imperils more traditional processes. More important, use of collaboration early

**TABLE 44.1**  The Benefits of Collaboration

---

- Broad comprehensive analysis of the problem domain improves the quality of solutions.
- Response capability is more diversified.
- It is useful for reopening deadlocked negotiations.
- The risk of impasse is minimized.
- The process ensures that each stakeholder's interests are considered in any agreement.
- Parties retain ownership of the solution.
- Parties most familiar with the problem, not their agents, invent the solutions.
- Participation enhances acceptance of solution and willingness to implement it.
- The potential to discover novel, innovative solutions is enhanced.
- Relations between the stakeholders improve.
- Costs associated with other methods are avoided.
- Mechanisms for coordinating future actions among the stakeholders can be established.

---

in a multiparty conflict can minimize the possibility that impasse will occur.

The process of collaborating builds in certain guarantees that each party's interests will be protected. It does so by continually remanding ownership of the process and any decisions reached to the parties themselves. Parties often assume that by collaborating they will lose any individual leverage they have over the problem. This concern about loss of control is deceptive, however. It is rare in any multiparty conflict that any party satisfies 100 percent of their interests and incurs no costs while the other parties gain nothing. Collaborative processes protect each party's interests by guaranteeing that they are heard and understood. In addition, the processes are structured to ensure that ownership of the solution remains with the participants since ratification hinges on their reaching agreement among themselves.

Instead of trying to restrict participation, a common tactic, the professional manager gains more control over the situation by ensuring that all the necessary parties are there at the table, recognizing that parties in a dispute often engage in adversarial behavior

because no other approach is available to protect their interests. (Carpenter and Kennedy, 1988, p. 261)

Parties retain control during collaboration precisely because *they* must be the ones to adopt or reject the final agreement.

Ownership of the process and of the outcomes generates two additional benefits. The parties themselves, who are most familiar with the problem, not their agents, fashion the solution. Additionally, commitment to the solution is generally high as a result of collaboration. Investment in a process of building a comprehensive appreciation of the problem and designing a solution jointly enhances the parties' acceptance of the solution and their commitment to carry it out (Delbecq, 1974).

By focusing on interests and encouraging the exploration of differences, the potential to discover novel, innovative solutions like the Citizens' Radiation Monitoring Program is enhanced. Even when parties are unable to reach closure through collaboration, some benefits from collaborating are still possible. Collaborating usually leaves parties with a clearer understanding of their differences and an improved working relationship. These outcomes permit the parties to amicably "agree to disagree" or to accept a decision imposed by a traditional dispute resolution forum in lieu of reaching a collaborative agreement. Sometimes parties reach agreement on all but one or two areas and turn to a judicial or administrative agency to resolve the remaining disagreements.

Collaboration also has the potential to reduce the costs parties incur from acting alone or the costs associated with protracted conflict among the stakeholders. Although it is difficult to make reliable comparisons (of the cost of collaborating versus not doing so), it is reasonable to assume that collaboration can reduce the cost of hiring intermediaries (such as attorneys in legal disputes), the cost of research and development (R&D) expenditures for partners in R&D consortia, and a myriad of social costs stemming from protracted inaction on critical social and international problems.

Finally, through collaboration stakeholders can develop mechanisms to coordinate their future interactions. Through this coordination, stakeholders take concerted rather than disconnected actions to manage the problem domain, and interdependencies become more predictable.

## *Realities of Collaborating*

Just as it is important to articulate the benefits of collaborating, it is equally important to dispel the notion that collaboration is a cure for all evils. There are many circumstances in which stakeholders are unable or unwilling to engage each other in this way. Collaboration is not always an appropriate alternative. For example, when one party has unchallenged power to influence a domain, collaboration does not make sense.

Nor is collaboration an idealistic panacea. Realistically, collaboration involves difficult issues that have often eluded simple solutions in the past. Many multiparty problems are political in nature because they involve "distributional" issues. In distributional disputes the stakeholders are concerned about the allocation of funds, the setting of standards, or the siting of facilities. Groups in distributional disputes are contesting "a specific allocation of gains and losses" (Susskind and Cruikshank, 1987, p. 19). Allocating gains and losses, however, involves the allocation of risks that, as the Three Mile Island case illustrated, are perceived very differently by different stakeholders. Moreover, perceptions of risk often have deep psychological and emotional roots. Dealing with these emotional attachments is a tricky business. Success depends as much on the process of legitimizing parties' interests as on the substantive outcomes. The design of meetings between stakeholders is crucial to success. Many well-intended efforts to involve the public in government decisions, for example, are exercises in frustration and often exacerbate rather than improve the situation because careful attention to the process of managing differences is neglected (Wondolleck, 1985; Carpenter and Kennedy, 1988).

Thus, solving complex multiparty problems requires more than sound economic policies and technological breakthroughs. It also demands careful attention to the process of making decisions. Successful collaborations are not achieved without considerable effort on the part of the participating stakeholders and usually not without the skill and forbearance of a convening organization and/or a skilled third party. Often parties perceive real risks to collaborating, if only because the process is unfamiliar and the outcomes are uncertain. Unless issues like these and more serious ones such as concerns about co-optation or lack of fairness are dispelled up front, attempts at collaboration will not succeed. It is often the convener or third party who initially proposes the possibility of collaborating and who then shepherds the parties through a collaborative process. Hence, for collaboration to occur, someone must introduce a mind set, a vision, a belief in the creative potential of managing differences, and must couple this mind set with a constructive process for designing creative solutions to complex multiparty problems.

It is important to clarify how the terms *negotiation, consensus building,* and *mediation* are used. Negotiation is not used here to denote specific tactics of positional bargaining, which are often associated with collective bargaining or buyer-seller transactions. Instead, negotiation is used in the broader sociological sense used by Strauss (1978). Through their talk, stakeholders try to arrive at collective interpretations of how they see the world. These interpretations form the basis for actions. Negotiation, therefore, refers to conversational interactions among collaborating parties as they try to define a problem, agree on recommendations, or design action steps. In this way they create a negotiated order.

Not all collaborations lead to agreements for action, but when agreements are reached, they are arrived at by consensus. Consensus is achieved when each of the stakeholders agrees they can live with a proposed solution, even though it may not be their most preferred solution. Both consensus building and negotiation will be used to refer to the process of constructing agreements among the stakeholders.

Collaboration can occur with or without the assistance of a third party who serves as a mediator or facilitator. The task of the third party is not to render a decision (in the way that a judge does, for instance) but to help structure a dialogue within which the parties can work out their differences.

The term *mediator* will generally be used here to refer to this third-party role.

## References

Ackoff, R. L. *Creating the Corporate Future.* New York: Wiley, 1981.

Benedick, R. *An International Success Story: The Chlorofluoro-Carbon Treaty.* Presentation at the Fourth National Conference on Environmental Dispute Resolution, sponsored by the Conservation Foundation, Washington, D.C., June 2-3, 1988.

Bingham, G. *Resolving Environmental Disputes: A Decade of Experience.* Washington, D.C.: Conservation Foundation, 1986.

Brown, L. D. "Planned Change in Underorganized Systems." In T. G. Cummings (ed.), *Systems Theory for Organizational Development.* New York: Wiley, 1980.

Brunn, S. D., Johnson, J. H., and Ziegler, D. J. "Final Report on a Social Survey of Three Mile Island Area Residents." East Lansing: Department of Geography, Michigan State University, August 1979.

Carpenter, S. L., and Kennedy, W. J. D. *Managing Public Disputes: A Practical Guide to Handling Conflict and Reaching Agreements.* San Francisco: Jossey-Bass, 1988.

Chevalier, M. *A Wider Range of Perspectives in the Bureaucratic Structure.* Ottawa, Canada: Commission on Bilingualism and Biculturalism, 1966.

Delbecq, A. L. "Contextual Variables Affecting Decision-Making in Program Planning." *Journal of the American Institute for Decision Sciences,* 1974, *5* (4), 726-742.

Dimancescu, D., and Botkin, J. *The New Alliance: America's R&D Consortia.* Cambridge, Mass.: Ballinger, 1986.

Dunlop, J. T. "A Decade of National Experience." In J. M. Rosow (ed.), *Teamwork, Joint Labor Management Programs in America.* New York: Pergamon, 1986.

Elsman, M., and the National Institute for Work and Learning. *Industry-Education-Labor Collaboration: An Action Guide for Collaborative Councils.* Report prepared by the Industry-Education-Labor Collaboration Project of the Center for Education and Work. Washington, D.C.: National Institute for Work and Learning, 1981.

Emery, F. E., and Trist, E. L. "The Causal Texture of Organizational Environments." *Human Relations,* 1965, *18,* 21-32.

Emery, F. E., and Trist, E. L. *Towards a Social Ecology.* New York: Plenum, 1972.

Fisher, R., and Ury, W. *Getting to Yes: Negotiating Agreement Without Giving In.* Boston: Houghton Mifflin, 1981.

Foderaro, L. W. "When Development Becomes Divisive." *New York Times,* April 20, 1988, B1, B5.

Gricar, B. G., and Baratta, A. J. "Bridging the Information Gap: Radiation Monitoring by Citizens." *Journal of Applied Behavioral Science,* 1983, *19* (1), 35-41.

Heenan, D. A., and Perlmutter, H. V. *Multinational Organization Development.* Reading, Mass.: Addison-Wesley, 1979.

Holusha, J. "Mixing Cultures on the Assembly Line." *New York Times,* June 5, 1988, 1, 8.

Kemeny, J. G. *Report on the President's Commission on the Accident at Three Mile Island.* Washington, D.C.: U.S. Government Printing Office, October 31, 1979.

Klein, D. "Some Notes on the Dynamics of Resistance to Change: The Defender Role." In W. Bennis, K. D. Benne, R. Chin, and K. E. Cory (eds.), *The Planning of Change.* New York: Holt, Rinehart & Winston, 1976.

Lax, D. A., and Sebenius, J. K. *The Manager as Negotiator.* New York: Free Press, 1986.

Mulford, C. L., and Rogers, D. L. "Definitions and Models." In D. L. Rogers and D. A. Whetten (eds.), *Interorganizational Coordination.* Ames: Iowa State University Press, 1982.

Perlmutter, H. V., and Heenan, D. A. "Cooperate to Compete Globally." *Harvard Business Review,* March-April 1986, 136-152.

Raiffa, H. "Post-Settlement Settlements." *Negotiation Journal,* 1985, *1,* 9-12.

Rogovin, M. *Three Mile Island. Report to the Commissioners and to the Public.* Washington, D.C.: U.S. Nuclear Regulatory Commission Special Inquiry Group, January 24, 1980.

Scranton, W. W. *Report on the Governor's Commission on Three Mile Island.* Harrisburg: Commonwealth of Pennsylvania, February 26, 1980.

Sherif, M. "Superordinate Goals in the Reduction of Intergroup Conflicts." *American Journal of Sociology,* 1958, *63,* 349-358.

Strauss, A. *Negotiations: Varieties, Contexts, Processes, and Social Order.* San Francisco: Jossey-Bass, 1978.

Susskind, L. E., and Cruikshank, J. *Breaking the Impasse.* New York: Basic Books, 1987.

TMI Support Staff. *Environmental Assessment for Decontamination of the Three Mile Island, Unit 2 Reactor Building Atmosphere.* (NUREG-0662.) Washington, D.C.: Office of Nuclear Regulation, U.S. Nuclear Regulatory Commission, March 1980.

Trist, E. L. "A Concept of Organizational Ecology." *Australian Journal of Management,* 1977, *2,* 162-175.

Trist, E. L. "Referent Organizations and the Development of Interorganizational Domains." *Human Relations,* 1983, *36* (3), 247-268.

Wondolleck, J. "The Importance of Process in Resolving Environmental Disputes." *Environmental Impact Assessment Review,* 1985, *5,* 341-356.

# 45

# Recognize Contributions

## Linking Rewards With Performance

JAMES M. KOUZES
BARRY Z. POSNER

> People value being appreciated for their contributions. Recognition does not have to be elaborate, just genuine.
>
> —*Alfonso Rivera, Engineering Consultant*

"I was teaching math to sixth graders. We were working with students who had been 'low performers' and felt like they were already failures in math. Their attention spans seemed to be about two minutes long! The challenge was to increase their speed and accuracy in solving math problems." So begins Cheryl Breetwor's "personal best"—her story about a time when she accomplished something extraordinary as a leader. Breetwor, who went on to direct investor relations for Rolm Corporation before starting her own company (Share-Data), chose this experience as a sixth-grade teacher as one of her personal bests. Why?

"Because it's all about how you make work fun and rewarding. We wanted to show these kids they could win. If you can do that, you can get the best out of anybody," explains Breetwor. "And what's more, I knew we could do it!" Everyday, Breetwor handed out awards—awards primarily for "speed, skill, and accuracy," but also for persistence. Breetwor used these opportunities to recognize the small wins and milestones reached by the kids on their path toward mastering math fundamentals.

It's not unusual for people to work very intensely and for extraordinarily long hours during personal bests. To persist for months at such a pace, people

SOURCE: Kouzes, J. M., & Posner, B. Z. (1995). *The Leadership Challenge: How to Get Extraordinary Things Done in Organizations.* San Francisco: Jossey-Bass. Reprinted with permission.

need encouragement; they need the heart to continue with the journey. One important way that leaders give heart to others and keep them from giving up is by recognizing individual contributions. When participants in our workshops and seminars summarize the key leadership practices that make a difference in getting extraordinary things accomplished, recognizing people's contributions is on just about every list.

Likewise, when nonmanagers are polled regarding the skills their managers need in order to be more effective, at the top of the list is the ability to recognize and acknowledge the contributions of others.[1] Executives, too, need recognition, as indicated in a recent survey about why they leave their jobs: the number one reason given was limited praise and recognition.[2] To some people, praise and recognition may seem unimportant or inappropriate, even trivial. But assuming that constituents will know when their manager thinks they've done a good job doesn't work.

This assumption helped to account for the gap Paul Moran discovered between his perception of encouraging the heart and the views of his constituents (as measured by the Leadership Practices Inventory): "In the past, I usually neglected to celebrate my team's accomplishments (and my own accomplishments), because I never personally placed much importance on this aspect of the job for myself and I tended to forget about recognizing the accomplishments of others. Rather, I treated their accomplishments as part of their normal job, which required no unique recognition." To rectify this situation, when Moran was at Pacific Bell, he developed a specific outline of various recognition techniques to remind him of the importance of recognition and to make available a few simple techniques to recognize various types of accomplishments. When his team reached a key milestone in reengineering corporate accounting processes, he shook the hand of each member of the project team, took several key team members out to lunch, made telephone calls to all members thanking them personally for their efforts in the project, and invited them all to a small office party for cake and coffee. Upon further reflection, Moran felt that he should have done even more. The reason is found in an insight from Leonard (Swamp)

Marsh, COO and executive vice president of Medical Coaches Inc.: recognition "would have made folks more excited to get started on our next project," he noted, faulting his own personal-best leadership experience for inadequate recognition.

But there's much more at stake here than simply recognizing individuals for their contributions. Breetwor and the other leaders in our study practiced these *essentials* in their recognition of individuals:

- Building self-confidence through high expectations
- Connecting performance and rewards
- Using a variety of rewards
- Being positive and hopeful

By putting these four essentials into practice and recognizing contributions, leaders can stimulate and motivate the internal drives within each individual.

### *Building Self-Confidence Through High Expectations*

Successful leaders have high expectations, both of themselves and of their constituents. These expectations are powerful, because they're the frames into which people fit reality: we often wind up seeing what we expect rather than what's actually occurring. Social psychologists have referred to this as the self-fulfilling prophecy or the Pygmalion effect. In Greek mythology. the sculptor Pygmalion carved a statue of a beautiful woman, fell in love with the statue, and brought it to life by the strength of his perceptions. Leaders play Pygmalion-like roles in developing people. Research on the phenomenon of self-fulfilling prophecies provides ample evidence that other people act in ways that are consistent with our expectations of them.[3] If we expect others to fail, they probably will.

The self-fulfilling prophecy can be applied in a variety of situations. For example, Dov Eden, director of Israel's Institute of Business Research, Tel Aviv University, and his colleagues have shown that the rate of volunteering for special-forces military service can be increased by raising candidates' expectations about their ability to succeed. In a study he directed, the only difference between the experimental and control groups was that the recruiters stressed their own personal similarity to the experimental candidates (for example, "I've been where you are, and look where I am now").[4] In another study, the self-fulfilling prophecy was able to raise the productivity of an entire group, not just individuals (illustrating the fact that producing higher expectations for some doesn't require not raising expectations for others).[5]

Indeed, when we ask people to describe exemplary leaders, they consistently talk about people who have been able to bring out the best in them. This is one of the defining characteristics of a leader, one of the things that make constituents willing to be led: that person has our best interests at heart and wants us to be as successful as possible. Leading others requires that leaders have high expectations about what people can accomplish. Consequently, leaders treat people in ways that bolster their self-confidence, thereby making it possible for those people to achieve more than they may have initially believed possible. Leaders' belief in others creates a self-fulfilling prophecy: we do as we're expected to do. Leaders understand that feeling appreciated increases a person's sense of self-worth, which in turn precipitates success at school, home, and work.

It's also evident that the self-fulfilling prophecy is a reciprocal process; not only can leaders influence the expectations of others, but the expectations of constituents can influence the behaviors of their leaders. If constituents communicate high expectations of how good an individual could be as a leader, that potential leader may adjust his or her self-concept and self-expectation to be congruent with that of others. With this motivation for exemplary leadership behaviors, the constituents' prophecy is fulfilled.[6]

Nathaniel Branden, one of the pioneers in the field of self-esteem, has noted that "of all the judgments we pass in life, none is more important than the judgment we pass on ourselves. That judgment impacts every moment and every aspect of our existence. Our self-evaluation is the basic context in which we act and react, choose our values,

set our goals, meet the challenges that confront us. Our responses to events are shaped in part by whom and what we think we are."[7] Research and everyday experience confirm that men and women with high self-esteem—regardless of their age, level of education, and socioeconomic background—"feel unique, competent, secure, empowered, and connected to the people around them."[8]

To illustrate this point, social psychologists Robert Wood and Albert Bandura had working professionals manage a simulated organization. Participants had to match employee attributes to job requirements and master a complex set of decision rules in how best to guide and motivate their employees. Half the subjects were told that decision-making skills are developed through practice (and hence are acquired skills); the others were informed that decision-making skills reflect the basic cognitive capabilities that people possess (and hence are stable skills).

Throughout the simulation, the subjects rated the strength of their perceived self-efficacy in getting the group they were managing to perform at various productivity levels. Initially subjects in both groups expressed a moderately strong sense of managerial effectiveness. However, as they tried to fulfill the difficult production standard, those in the stable-skill condition displayed a progressive decline in perceived self-efficacy, while those in the acquired-skill condition maintained their sense of managerial efficacy. Those in the stable-skill group were quite uncharitable in their views of their employees, regarding them as incapable of being motivated, unworthy of supervision, and deserving of termination. In contrast, those in the acquired-skill condition set more challenging goals in subsequent trials and made more efficient use of analytical strategies, because from their perspective errors didn't imply a basic cognitive deficiency.[9]

Nancy Tivol, executive director of Sunnyvale Community Services (SCS), believes strongly in her own ability and in the capacity of every staff member and volunteer at SCS to contribute something valuable. When Tivol first arrived, in 1991, volunteers were working at SCS in a very limited capacity. Certain staff members insisted, for example, that volunteers couldn't run the front office because they wouldn't be able to handle client and corporate contact adequately. Tivol refused to share that view, however, and today SCS has volunteers doing things that only staff members did previously. Indeed, every department at SCS is run by a volunteer over seventy years of age. And SCS is the county's only emergency assistance agency that doesn't turn people away, having increased its funding for preventing evictions, utility disconnections, and hunger by 421 percent and having increased the number of families served by its monthly food program by 365 percent—even while funding for operations was cut back significantly.

By recognizing the valuable contributions that others make, we can help bring about the achievement of extraordinary things. Tivol demonstrated this not only through her belief in the volunteer staff but through her faith in another unexpected group of volunteers. Tivol recognized how desperately the agency needed to become computerized. With some donated computers but no money for computer training, Tivol entrusted her fifteen-year-old son with that responsibility. For his Eagle Scout project, he wrote a forty-one-page manual and trained ten Boy Scouts to teach agency staff and volunteers. Each Scout then "adopted" a staff member or volunteer and tutored that person in computer and software skills. Now everyone at SCS is computer-literate, and all office operations are computerized.

As Tivol demonstrated, leaders have a high degree of confidence in others and in themselves. To be sure, some people we surveyed were nervous or anxious on the eve of their personal bests, but each was also ready for the plunge. All were excited by and willing to accept the challenges they faced (either by circumstance or by choice). Without exception or hesitation, these people expressed confidence that they could work well with others and assemble a team to address whatever problems might lie ahead. The high expectations that leaders have of others are based in large part on their expectations of themselves. This is one reason why leaders model the way. What gives their expectations for others credibility is their own record of achievement and dedication, along with their daily demonstrations of what and how things need to be done.

Leaders' expectations have their strongest and most powerful influence in times of uncertainty and turbulence. When accepted ways of doing things aren't working well enough, leaders' strong expectations about the destination, the processes to follow, and the capabilities of the team serve to make dreams come true.

What's more, leaders tend not to give up on people, because doing so means giving up on themselves, their judgment, and their ability to get the best out of other people. Breetwor was convinced that she was a capable enough teacher to improve that group of sixth-graders' math skills. She never gave up on them; she never gave up on herself. Likewise, when Antonio Zárate turned Metalsa from a company with a 10 percent rejection rate and only a domestic market into an award-winning, world-class automotive metal stamping company with 40 percent exports, he did so using the same local Mexican workforce that had always staffed Metalsa. The difference was in what Zárate believed those workers could do. He believed that there are no poor-quality workers, only underled companies. He never gave up on his workers; he never gave up on himself.

## *Connecting Performance and Rewards*

The outcomes of our present actions play a major role in determining our future actions. People repeat behavior that's rewarded, avoid behavior that's punished, and drop or forget behavior that produces neither result.[10] If especially hard work and long hours on a project go unnoticed and unrewarded, people will soon minimize their efforts. That's why manufacturing support manager Russ Douglass used what he called "spot strokes" on his personal-best project—"instant payoffs like 'Have this lunch on me' or 'Take the afternoon off.' " As he said, "Sometimes we'd put on a party in the parking lot on a half-hour notice."

One of the oldest, most important, and strongest prescriptions for influencing motivation is to tie job-related outcomes (such as rewards and recognition) to job effort and/or performance.[11] If a concern for quality is desired, rewards should be given to those who consistently meet quality standards, and low-quality performers shouldn't be rewarded until they conform to this norm. Today we see performance-reward linkages everywhere.[12]

AT&T, General Mills, Continental Bank, and Nucor Steel, for example, have all instituted pay-for-performance systems or variable pay systems. Saloman Brothers, the New York investment firm, has found that linking performance and rewards works for brokers and traders with profit responsibility—and for staff and support groups as well. Under a system the organization calls Teamshare, as training and technology push costs down, back-office staffers (over 500 people in all) get to keep 10 percent of the savings.[13]

Another example of how specific performance-reward linkages affect behavior comes from U.S. Healthcare, a Pennsylvania-based health maintenance organization. U.S. Healthcare's quality-oriented compensation plan rewards primary-care providers for attaining certain quality-of-care standards as well as for controlling costs. Like most HMOs, U.S. Healthcare pays its physicians a monthly fee for each patient. However, unlike most HMOs, it also pays up to a 28 percent premium to physicians based upon a number of quality and customer service goals. Scheduling office hours at night, linking up with the HMO by computer, and attaining high immunization rates for children and mammography rates for women over age forty are all rewarded, for example, as are accepting and retaining new U.S. Healthcare patients. And while doctors whose patients spend fewer days in the hospital or see fewer specialists are rewarded, those whose referral rate seems *too* low can be penalized. In evaluating physician performance, U.S. Healthcare audits medical records and surveys its members, whose views and satisfaction ratings further influence each physician's compensation. Healthcare physicians receive monthly reports on their quality and customer service performance.

The success of the program is evident. As a result of the organization's quality emphasis, all six U.S. Healthcare HMOs received full three-year accreditation, the best performance of any U.S. managed-care company. In addition, despite the bonus system (which can result in primary-care physicians' receiving greater compensation for their U.S.

Healthcare patients than for traditional fee-for-service patients), U.S. Healthcare has been able to keep its premiums competitive with other HMOs and well below traditional health insurance premiums, while providing a healthy return to investors. Since 1988, U.S. Healthcare's stock has risen twelvefold.[14]

When integrating performance with rewards, leaders must

- Make certain that people know what's expected of them.
- Provide feedback about contributors' performance.
- Reward only those who meet the standards.[15]

It's not always easy to meet these criteria, yet their significance shouldn't be underestimated. They've been shown across a wide variety of organizational settings to improve the job performance of such diverse workgroups as clerks in a small grocery store, mountain beaver trappers, engineers, telephone service crews, truck drivers, and salespeople.[16]

Consider how Nolan Dishongh (profiled in Chapter Five) linked performance and rewards—and achieved extraordinary results. During his first day as construction trades instructor and education coordinator for at-risk students at Alice Johnson Junior High School, he saw no order, no plan. When he asked students what they were supposed to be working on, they said it didn't matter: the instructor who had just quit had let them do anything they wanted, including doing nothing. Not surprisingly, most of them were failing not just construction trades but their other classes also.

Dishongh began planning projects and events to increase interest. To participate, however, his students had to do more than merely show up. Taking his role as education coordinator seriously, Dishongh required all construction trades students to give him a report from each of their academic instructors regarding their academic performance (class attendance and homework completion) before they could participate in class activities each week. And Dishongh graded each of these reports. Reports revealing unexcused absences or incomplete homework received a 0 and the student was "benched"; reports showing completed homework and perfect attendance were given a mark of 100. Each Monday morning, the reports were reviewed openly during a group discussion, with Dishongh giving praise and encouragement and eliciting group involvement when a member wasn't keeping up his commitments. Dishongh made it clear that each student's weekly average of what he called the "zero-zeros" reports counted for a full third of the grade in construction trades—and that no one with a class average below 70 would be allowed to attend the end-of-the-year field trip he was organizing to a wildly interesting and otherwise inaccessible location: the local heavy-metal radio station.

As the year progressed, the group's grades began to improve—in all academic classes as well as construction trades. Dishongh is still amazed by the dramatic change in Weldon Creech: he went from a depressing academic record of 47 Fs to an astounding record of all As and Bs within one year. And Creech wasn't alone: Dishongh made it possible for all of his students to accomplish something significant and was rewarded by seeing the growth of their self-respect. Kenton Miles reflected the deep feelings of many of his classmates when he handed Dishongh a plaque inscribed, "Thanks for being my friend and showing me even I can make a difference in the world."[17]

Like Dishongh, successful leaders strive skillfully and diligently to see that the system works. Two additional notes about the significance of linking performance and rewards. First, feedback is the loop that provides learning, both to the individuals involved and to the organizational system. Experience without feedback is unlikely to build or enhance competence. Put another way, learning results when people can see the relationship between what they're doing and how their needs are (or aren't) being met, as was certainly the case with Dishongh's students. This assessment is possible only when people are able to measure their performance, of course, whether through satisfaction surveys or units sold or words typed per minute. The most powerful measurements are those that offer timely feedback and can be monitored by the individuals doing the work. No one could imagine designing a measurement system for driving in which only the police could determine one's speed. Instead, each automobile is equipped with a speed-ometer, always visible to the driver. Why, then, do many organizations design feedback systems in which only the inspectors and managers (the police) have the tools to monitor performance?

Second, although compensation plans include rewards as a critical element, these are just one part of a total strategy—along with communication, employee involvement, feedback, and financial justifications. As a result, the size of rewards is important but not critical.[18]

## Using a Variety of Rewards

Leaders use many types of rewards to recognize the efforts and contributions of their constituents. Indeed, the creative use of rewards is another defining characteristic of leaders. Leaders tend not to be dependent upon the organization's formal reward system (typically financial), which offers only a limited range of options. Breetwor, for example, relied on much more than grades to motivate students. In the business world, promotions and raises are scarce resources and can't be applied frequently. On the other hand, verbal or written praise, "spot strokes," buttons, and other informal and more personal rewards are almost unlimited resources.

Furthermore, relying upon an organization's formal reward system typically requires considerable effort and time. In one study, we found that the time lapse between performance and promotion is seldom less than six months. Similarly, most organizations' performance appraisal systems allow for raises or any other merit awards to be handed out only once per year.[19] Naturally enough, this delay limits people's ability to see the connection between their efforts, performance, and rewards and thereby diminishes motivation.

### Intrinsic Rewards

Instead of relying only (or even primarily) on formal rewards, leaders make tremendous use of *intrinsic* rewards—rewards that are built into the work itself. As Chapter Three emphasized, challenge is a powerful motivator. If work lacks challenge, no incentive system in the world can sustain long-term success. Other intrinsic rewards include a sense of accomplishment and the thrill of creation—rewards that are immediate outcomes of an individual's effort. Intrinsic rewards can also be as subtle as the leader's lending a helping hand and listening without interrupting. Other, more personal currencies include lunch with a key executive, a night out on the company, tickets for a ballgame or the theater, and the afternoon off.

Some people make the mistake of assuming that individuals respond only to money. Although salary increases and bonuses are certainly appreciated, individual needs for and appreciation of rewards extend much further. Verbal recognition of performance in front of one's peers and visible awards (such as certificates, plaques, and other tangible gifts), for example, are powerful rewards. Spontaneous and unexpected rewards are often more meaningful than the expected formal rewards. The motivational impact of Christmas bonuses, for example, is limited, because they're expected; the only unknown is what their amount will be. Many people consider these "entitlements" to be part of their annual salary expectations, not something extra for their efforts during a particular year. Thus annual bonuses are generally linked in workers' minds only to job level or even longevity, not performance.

Praise is a significant and underutilized form of recognition. Not enough people make adequate use of a very powerful and inexpensive two-word reward—"Thank you." Personal congratulations rank at the top of the most powerful nonfinancial motivators identified by employees.[20] There are few, if any, more basic needs than to be noticed, recognized, and appreciated for our efforts. That's as true for volunteers, teachers, doctors, priests, and politicians as it is for the maintenance staff and those in the executive suite. There's little wonder, then, that a greater volume of thank-yous is reported in highly innovative companies than in low-innovation firms.[21] Extraordinary achievements don't come easily and seldom bloom in barren and unappreciative settings.

Joan Carter, whose work was discussed in Chapter Six, discovered the powerful effect of publicly giving thanks when she was general manager and executive chef of the Faculty Club at Santa Clara

University. Following her extremely successful (but difficult) first year at the club, in which revenues increased by 20 percent and costs decreased by 5 percent (ending a period of deficits that had threatened the club's continued existence), she sent a letter to all club members, club staff members, and university departments. In this "Open Letter of Thanks," she not only described in glowing detail the party the club had thrown to celebrate its dramatic turnaround but took the opportunity to describe the contributions of individuals, both on her staff and within the university community, who had made that night, and the past year, so successful. As she recalls,

> So many people had come up to me during that party to thank me for the changes that had occurred at the club, and all I could think about was that it was my *staff* whose efforts and willingness to make changes had made us successful: they were the ones who needed to be thanked. So I wrote the letter. But as I wrote it, I realized that the list of people who needed to be thanked was endless, and I began feeling very humble. I needed to thank each staff member by name and contribution. I also needed to thank so many others on campus who helped every day—and our customers. I wanted them all to know that I knew we couldn't have done it without them.

The response, she recalls, was totally unexpected: "I received dozens of phone calls and personal notes echoing the mutual admiration that had grown between the club and the university during that year. Those notes were posted on the bulletin board in the kitchen for the staff and further reinforced the staff's commitment to their customers. It was incredible. I never dreamed saying thank you would make me feel so good or be so good for our business."

Certainly, you can't buy people's commitment—to get them to care, to stay late, or come in early—with just thank-you notes, stickers, or plaques. What makes these effective is the leader's genuine concern and respect for those who are doing the work. Being at our personal best as leaders requires acknowledgment that we can't do it alone and recognition that unless constituents feel appreciated by their leaders, they're not likely to put forth great effort. Social scientist Daniel

Yankelovich points out that overall organizational effectiveness and efficiency depend on employees' personal dedication and sense of responsibility. You get these intangibles, he says, "only when people are motivated to work hard, to give of themselves."[22] With this kind of motivation, leaders are able to help others get extraordinary things accomplished.

Consider the case of Albert "Smitty" Smith, room service captain for Marriott's Marquis in Atlanta. National Football League (NFL) teams playing in Atlanta had been staying with the Marriott for several years when a local competitor substantially reduced its rates. In response to that reduction, some of the teams began staying at that hotel instead. Smith was deeply disappointed. He loved football, and he wanted the NFL teams back at Marriott. Whenever a team was staying at the competing hotel, Smith would take the day off, contacting the coaches and team management to let them know that he was available to meet all of their special needs and reminding them that he understood those needs well after working with the teams for so many years. The teams were so impressed by Smith's one-person marketing effort that they all returned to the Atlanta Marriott the following year. At Marriott's International Marketing Meeting, Smith was featured as the guest speaker on salesmanship and received a special leadership trophy from J. Willard Marriott, Jr. Following his remarks, the group gave Smith the first standing ovation to be received at any of the organization's marketing meetings.[23]

Leaders are constantly on the lookout for ways to spread the psychological benefits of making people feel like winners, because winners contribute in important ways to the success of their projects. Leaders often serve as a mirror for the team, reflecting back to others what a job well done looks like and making certain not only that the members of the team know that they've done well but that others in the organization are aware of the group's effort and contributions.

Think about the impact of the "fabulous bragging sessions" held once per quarter at the corporate headquarters of Milliken & Company in Spartanburg, South Carolina. While attendance is voluntary, as many as 200 people participate in each Corporate Sharing Rally, as the sessions are called. Dozens of teams of workers from all areas of the company give crisp, five-minute reports in rapid-fire succession about improving product quality, describing their own programs and quantifying their impact. Everyone who attends receives an award signed by the president and framed on the spot. And everyone who attends is likely to go back to one of the company's sixty plants with a host of ideas—not demands that have been forced on them by top management but suggestions from their peers—about how all of them can be doing their jobs better and making the company more competitive and successful. These rallies are a wonderful example of providing recognition and celebrating people's accomplishments.

## The Blend of Intrinsic and Extrinsic Rewards

What happens if people are given both intrinsic and extrinsic rewards? Unfortunately, while the idea of an additive effect is intuitively appealing, it doesn't always occur. There's some evidence that intrinsic and extrinsic rewards are negatively related and may actually work against one another. For example, in a situation that's already intrinsically rewarding, the addition of extrinsic rewards may reduce the effectiveness of the intrinsic rewards.[24] On the other hand, some studies show that while achievement-oriented people do find success rewarding in and of itself, money and fame are also important rewards, serving as symbols of that success.[25] One executive referred to this combination as the "fun being in playing the game down on the field, while the results are posted on the scoreboard." What we found among leaders wasn't so much an either/or mentality as a both/and type of thinking. Leaders are remarkably skillful in using these two types of rewards in complementary ways.

The Hampton Inn hotel group offers an example of creatively incorporating a variety of rewards. Winning the quarterly President's Award as an employee of the hotel group is a big deal, and everyone knows it. It starts with a personal phone call of thanks and congratulations from Ray Schultz, president and CEO. The phone call is followed by two plaques (one for the employee to take home and one for the hotel to display); a check for $500; publication of the winner's photo and profile in the company's quarterly magazine—a profile that features the winner's "extra mile" example and his or her personal guest service philosophy, as well as both a guest comment and a co-worker comment about the recipient; and a trip to the company's annual conference for the Hampton Inn System Conference Awards Ceremony, where the current year's President's Award recipients take a prominent place in the ceremony's program.

Who wins these awards? Any employee—head housekeepers, guest service representatives, sales directors, maintenance workers, room attendants, and breakfast hostesses. The winners are the stars who "shine brightly in the Hampton Inn system" and who make its "100% Satisfaction Guarantee" a reality.

### *Being Positive and Hopeful*

By recognizing individual achievement, leaders give courage to their constituents. This courage enables people to maintain composure during anxiety-producing situations and to endure hardships. Courage to continue the quest and hope in a positive future were central elements of Don Quixote's legacy: "to dream the impossible dream."

Don Bennett's teenage daughter stayed by his side for over four hours during one particularly difficult stretch of his seemingly impossible dream of scaling Mount Rainier. With each new hop across the ice field, she told him, "You can do it, Dad. You're the best dad in the world. *You can do it, Dad.*" This spontaneous verbal encouragement kept Bennett going, strengthening his commitment to make it to the top. Bennett told us that there was no way he could have quit with his daughter voicing such words of love and encouragement.

Research points to the impact that positive feedback has on motivation and physical stamina. One study involved soldiers who had just finished several weeks of intensive training and were undergoing a forced march in competition for places in special units.[26] Motivation was extremely high

among the recruits—failure to maintain the pace during the forced march meant losing the chance to join the special units. The soldiers were divided into four groups, which were unable to communicate with one another. All the men marched twenty kilometers (about twelve and one-half miles) over the same terrain on the same day. The first group was told how far the soldiers were expected to go and was kept informed of its progress along the way. The second group was told only that "this is the long march you hear about." These soldiers received no information about the total distance they were expected to travel or how far they had marched. The third group was told to march fifteen kilometers, but when the soldiers had gone fourteen kilometers, they were told that they had to go six kilometers farther. Members of the fourth group were told that they had to march twenty-five kilometers, but when they reached the fourteen-kilometer mark, they were told that they had only six more kilometers to go.

The groups were assessed as to which had the best performance and which endured the most stress. The results indicated that the soldiers in the first group—those who knew exactly how far they had to go and where they were during the march—were much better off than the soldiers who didn't get this information. The next-best group was the soldiers who thought that they were marching only fifteen kilometers. Third-best was the group told to march a longer distance and then given the good news at the fourteen-kilometer mark. Those who performed worst were the soldiers who received neither information about the goal (total distance) nor feedback about the distance they had already traveled. Blood tests taken during the march and again twenty-four hours later showed similar patterns: blood levels of cortisol and prolactin (chemical substances whose levels rise as stress increases) were, as expected, highest for the group that knew the least about the march and lowest for those soldiers who knew exactly where they were and how much farther they were expected to go.

Even with highly motivated, achievement-oriented people, the type of leadership provided makes a definite difference in performance, in the levels of stress experienced, and in long-term health. Leaders provide people with a positive sense of direction that encourages them to reach inside and do their best. By having a positive outlook and being hopeful, leaders make the impossible a possibility and then motivate people in their drive to transform the possible into reality.

## Committing to the Challenge: Building Confidence and Courage

Leaders have high expectations of themselves and of their constituents. They create self-fulfilling prophecies about how ordinary people can produce extraordinary actions and results. They provide people with clear directions, substantial encouragement, personal appreciation, and a positive outlook. Along the way, they offer feedback in response to small wins, stimulating, rekindling, and focusing people's energies and drive.

Leaders make people winners, and winning people like to up the ante, raise the standards, and conquer the next mountain. They want to serve more people, raise more money, enlarge market share, lower costs, increase production, reduce reject rates, experiment with technologies and processes, and explore uncharted territory. Leaders recognize and reward what individuals do to contribute to vision and values. And leaders express their appreciation far beyond the limits of the organization's formal performance appraisal system. Leaders enjoy being spontaneous and creative in saying thank you, whether they send personal notes, hand out stickers and buttons, listen without interrupting, or try one of the myriad other forms of recognition.

In this commitment, we provide a variety of strategies that you can adapt to situation for help in using recognition as a leadership process.

*Commitment Number 9: Recognize Individual Contributions to the Success of Every Project*

- **Be creative about rewards and recognition and give them personally.**

People respond to all kinds of rewards other than promotions and raises. One of our university colleagues takes his highest-performing students each term out for lunch and bowling to show his appreciation for their hard work. A shop foreman we know presents employees who achieve their production objectives with a new chair for the workplace. The chairs are a good reward themselves, but a major part of the reward—the part that's even more pleasurable than comfortable seating to the employees—comes with the presentation. The employee being rewarded is called into the foreman's office, presented with the new chair, and then wheeled in the chair back to the work station by the foreman—amid the cheers of co-workers.

Make rewards and recognition tangible. By themselves, a meal, chair, check, or plaque won't significantly contribute to sustaining the value of the action rewarded. But tangibility does help sustain the memory and importance of the act and contributes positively to repetition of the behavior.

There's no limit—except your creativity—to creative rewards. Consider the following:

- "Super person of the month" awards
- Employee photographs with the president
- Verbal encouragement
- Spot strokes
- Pictures in annual reports and company newsletters
- Published thank-yous
- Contributions to employees' favorite charities
- Gift certificates and merchandise credits
- Embossed business cards
- Gifts for spouses and families
- Banners displayed in the cafeteria
- Symbolic stuffed animals
- Flextime

Place your emphasis on noticing and recognizing small wins—and do so personally. A sincere word of thanks from the right person at the right time can mean more to the recipient than fame, fortune, or a whole wall of certificates and plaques. It's well worth the effort.[27] Even movements in the right direction warrant your personal seal of appreciation and encouragement to continue the effort.

• **Make recognition public.**

You may be reluctant to recognize people in public, fearing that to do so might cause jealousy or resentment. But private rewards do little to set an example, and often the recipient, not wanting to brag or appear conceited, has no opportunity to share the story with others. So tell your workers and colleagues that they've done well as soon as you find out about it, and let other people know about the accomplishment too. When recognition is public, the individual's self-esteem is bolstered, the behavior being recognized serves as a model to others, and employees see that doing the right thing will be noticed and rewarded. While all recognition encourages others to continue their good work, public recognition portrays the recipient as a role model, conveying to all employees the message, "Here's someone just like you. You too can do this."

Recognition also helps to empower recipients by increasing their visibility. Military organizations, for example, make tremendous use of medals and insignias, which are almost always handed out at ceremonies. Awards serve the same purpose. Nolan Dishongh planned well in advance for a ceremony to reward and recognize his students. During the year, he entered his students' work in every contest he could find, collecting in a classroom display case the winning ribbons and trophies that would be awarded formally to their owners during the year-end banquet attended by parents and students. Public recognition also builds commitment, because it makes people's actions visible to their peers and therefore difficult to deny or revoke.

At Household Credit Services, extra effort by members of the young clerical staff is often rewarded with "casual dress" passes. For many staff members right out of high school, being able to wear their nice casual clothes (while their friends and co-workers have to wear business attire) provides public recognition. The passes are immediate (supervisors don't need higher-level approval to award them), inexpensive, and fun, and they're a very visible way to show appreciation for a job well done.

• **Design the reward and recognition system participatively.**

People are most excited about activities and events that they've had a hand in designing. In addition, when you involve others, you're more likely to design a system in which rewards are closely linked to performance norms. Because it's their system, people will feel more strongly that they can influence it directly through their efforts. For example, when the CEO of Alta Bates Hospital, in Berkeley, California, raved to food service staffers about the great job they were doing, expressing his pride in the creativity and conscientiousness of their attempt to make hospital food imaginative and tasty, they were pleased. But what they really wanted was to demonstrate just how good they were, to show that working in a hospital didn't mean that they were second-class restaurateurs and chefs.

After some discussion, food service personnel were given the chance to offer a Sunday buffet in the hospital cafeteria, open to the public and complemented by ice sculptures and a string quartet. During the buffet, crew members walked the line talking with customers (many of whom were on the hospital staff). The crew's pride in their food preparation and presentation created an atmosphere of sheer delight, increased their motivation, and generated more efficient operations overall.

• **Provide feedback en route.**

People produce best when they're given feedback about how they're progressing. Production may continue without feedback, but it will be less efficient and will exact a significant toll in the form of increased levels of stress and anxiety. Recognition signals successful accomplishment, reinforcing both the employee's "I can do it" attitude and the leader's expectations: "I knew you could do it."

A study of the winningest high school and college athletic coaches revealed that they pay great attention to providing real-time feedback on their players' performance and will, as appropriate, recognize and reward outstanding contributions. Players—regardless of fame or fortune—need to hear when they do well and when they don't. As the coaches explained, ongoing feedback "is a highly effective way to shape the behavior of the athletes so as to increase the team's ability to continue winning. Without immediate and precise feedback, the learning process ends and mediocrity is sure to emerge. Ongoing evaluation of the players' ability to play your game, to your expectations, is critical given the constant need to restock the team with younger athletes."[28] What's true of athletes also applies to those on the factory floor, behind the counter, in city hall, and in the corner office.

By giving feedback, leaders enable people to persevere in moments of hardship and times of uncertainty and turbulence. In fact, studies show that learning is severely hampered without feedback and that people's motivation (and subsequent performance) diminishes over time unless they know how they're doing.[29] Leaders use feedback to make sure that people acquire the competence that should come with experience.

- **Create Pygmalions.**

Be more conscious about realizing that your behavior toward people is based upon your expectations about them. Treating people in a friendly, pleasant, and positive fashion and being attentive to their needs—behavior that reflects your high expectations of them—produces increased performance because that behavior has a favorable effect on their motivation. Likewise, when you have high expectations of others, you tend to give them more input—suggestions, helpful hints, and responsive answers to their questions—and more feedback about the results of their efforts. Both of these factors enhance people's learning and increase the likelihood that they'll achieve competence and mastery rather than repeat mistakes or let ineffective habits become ingrained.

Finally, the standards of performance (or "output levels") that you set communicate what your expectations of others are, and these in turn affect others' levels of aspiration. Therefore, make sure that these standards are high and that they're linked directly to what's important to the success of your organization. Make sure, too, that your performance standards include what's important

to constituents as well as what's important to management, stockholders, or the larger organization.

Creating Pygmalions entails developing a winner's attitude, since only those who envision themselves as winners are likely to work hard, try new actions, and become leaders in their own right. This means paying considerable attention to your constituents' successes and, should those people stumble or fall, discussing this result with them as only a temporary lack of success. If criticism is necessary, comments should be restricted to behavior rather than character. Similarly, feedback—preferably extensive—should stress continuous progress in terms of past performance rather than comparisons with other people.[30] Leaders also make certain that constituents understand that (and how) goal achievement is the result of their own efforts.

- **Find people who are doing things right.**

Rewards are most effective when they're highly specific and in close proximity to the appropriate behavior. In order to provide such timely and specific feedback, you have to go out and find the behavior you want to foster. One of the most important results of being out and about as a leader is that you can personally observe people doing things right and then reward them either on the spot or at the next public meeting.

Consider initiating a system for collecting information from constituents and customers about people who are observed doing things right. Weekly breakfast meetings are perfect opportunities to ask for such incidents. Add to your agenda the question, "Who have you seen doing something special this week that's really helped our organization?"

Once you've selected people for recognition, be sure to tell them—and everyone else—why they've been chosen. Make the recognition effective. Tell the story of why the person is being recognized, and make it specific. Stories that describe valued actions are very powerful ways to communicate what behaviors are expected and will be rewarded. Walk employees through the specific actions that contributed to goal attainment and explain why they were consistent with the shared values.

You might say something along these lines: "Sue was selected as the employee of the month because she called five different stores to locate an item that a customer requested but that we didn't have in stock. And because the store couldn't deliver the item until the next week, she picked it up on her way home from work so that the customer could have it in time for an important event. That's the kind of behavior that makes us so highly valued by our customers. Thank you, Sue. We make this award to you in appreciation of your contribution to our organization's goal of delighting every customer."

This kind of positive example can be particularly useful to leaders trying to get people to understand the right things to do to achieve a high standard. It provides a behavioral map that people can store in their minds and rely on when a similar situation arises in the future.

To broaden the net for recognition, set up systems that make it possible for people to be recognized by their constituents—be they peers, customers, or suppliers—not just managers. This encourages everyone in the organization to be on the lookout for good behaviors—and to be mindful that others are observing their actions as well. The nursing home at St. Francis Hospital in Memphis, Tennessee, recognizes its staff with a simple pin that says, "Caught Caring." In an environment where the patients often can't say thank you, the pins mean a great deal to staff members: they announce that someone recognizes how much they give.[31]

- **Coach.**

Athletic coaches don't wait until the season is over to let their players know how they're doing, and neither should you. Coaching involves spending time with people on the job day by day, talking with them about game strategies, and providing them with feedback about their efforts and performance. Then, when the game is over, you need to get together with the players and analyze the results of your efforts. Where did we do well? Where do we need to improve our efforts? What will we have to do differently, better, or more of the next time? And then it's time for practice again and getting ready for the next game.

---

**BOX 45.1**
**Commitment Number 9**

*Recognize Individual Contributions to the Success of Every Project*

- Be creative about rewards and recognition and give them personally.
- Make recognition public.
- Design the reward and recognition system participatively.
- Provide feedback en route.
- Create Pygmalions.
- Find people who are doing things right.
- Coach.

SOURCE: *The Leadership Challenge* by James M. Kouzes and Barry Z. Posner. Copyright © 1995.

---

The best teams, whether in athletics, business, education, health care, government, or religion, always emphasize the fundamentals of their game. This means being clear about your vision and values, to which recognition and celebration should always be linked.

### Notes

1. T. E. Deal and W. A. Jenkins, *Managing the Hidden Organization: Strategies for Empowering Your Behind-the-Scenes Employees* (New York: Warner, 1994).

2. Survey by Robert Hall International, Inc. (Menlo Park, Calif.), 31 August 1994.

3. See, for example, E. C. Jones, "Interpreting Interpersonal Behavior: The Effects of Expectancies," *Science 234* (1986): 41-46; R. H. G. Field and D. A. Van Seters, "Management by Expectations (MBE): The Power of Positive Prophecy," *Journal of General Management 14* (2) (1988): 1-33; D. Eden, *Pygmalion in Management: Productivity as a Self-Fulfilling Prophecy* (New York: Lexington Books, 1990); and D. Eden, "Leadership and Expectations: Pygmalion Effects and Other Self-Fulfilling Prophecies in Organizations," *The Leadership Quarterly 3* (4) (1992): 271-305.

4. D. Eden and J. Kinnar, "Modeling Galatea: Boosting Self-Efficacy to Increase Volunteering," *Journal of Applied Psychology 76* (6) (1991): 770-780.

5. D. Eden, "Pygmalion Without Interpersonal Contrast Effects: Whole groups Gain From Raising Manager Expectations," *Journal of Applied Psychology 75* (4) (1990): 394-398.

6. D. Eden, "Pygmalion, Goal Setting, and Expectancy: Compatible Ways to Boost Productivity," *Academy of Management Executive 13* (4) (1988): 639-652.

7. N. Branden, *The Six Pillars of Self-Esteem* (New York: Bantam, 1994).

8. R. J. Blitzer, C. Peterson, and L. Rogers, "How to Build Self-Esteem," *Training and Development Journal,* February 1993, 59.

9. R. Wood and A. Bandura, "Impact of Conceptions of Ability on Self-Regulatory Mechanisms and Complex Decision Making," *Journal of Personality and Social Psychology 56* (3) (1989): 407-415.

10. A. R. Cohen, S. L. Fink, H. Gadon, and R. D. Willits, *Effective Behavior in Organizations,* 6th ed. (Homewood, Ill.: Irwin, 1994).

11. Cohen, Fink, Gadon, and Willits, *Effective Behavior in Organizations.*

12. J. L. McAdams and E. J. Hawke, *Executive Summary: Organizational Performance & Rewards* (Scottsdale, Ariz.: American Compensation Association, 1993), 35; see also C. Braddick, M. Pfefferle, and R. Gandossy, "How Malcolm Baldrige Winners Reward Employer Performance," *Journal of Compensation and Benefits 9* (3) (1993): 47-52.

13. S. Tully, "Your Paycheck Gets Exciting," *Fortune,* 1 November 1993, 98.

14. R. Winslow, "U.S. Healthcare Cuts Costs, Grows Rapidly, and Irks Some Doctors," *Wall Street Journal,* 6 September 1994, A1.

15. C. C. Pinder, *Work Motivation: Theory, issues, and Applications* (Glenview, Ill.: Scott, Foresman, 1984), 286-298; see also V. H. Vroom, *Work and Motivation* (San Francisco: Jossey-Bass, 1994).

16. Pinder, *Work Motivation,* 226.

17. K. Huber, "A Growing Desire to Learn," *Houston Chronicle,* 14 July 1994, C1; and discussion with Nolan Dishongh, August 1994.

18. McAdams and Hawke, *Executive Summary,* 12.

19. J. L. Hall, B. Z. Posner, and J. W. Harder, "Performance Appraisal Systems: Matching Theory With Practice," *Group and Management Studies 14* (1) (1989): 51-69.

20. G. Graham, "Going the Extra Mile: Motivating Your Workers Doesn't Always Involve Money," *San Jose Mercury News,* 7 January 1987, 4C.

21. R. M. Kanter, "The Change Masters," presentation to the Executive Seminar in Corporate Excellence, Santa Clara University, 13 March 1984.

22. M. VerMeulen, "When Employees Give Something Extra," *Parade,* 6 November 1983, 11.

23. R. J. Dow, "Keeping Employees Focused on Customer Service," presentation to the Executive Seminar in Corporate Excellence, Santa Clara University, 28 October 1986.

24. E. L. Deci, *Intrinsic Motivation* (New York: Plenum, 1975); E. L. Deci and R. M. Ryan, *Intrinsic Motivation and Self-Determination in Human Behavior* (New York: Plenum, 1985). For an intelligent critique of incentive systems and the potentially detrimental effect of reliance on rewards on long-term performance, see A. Kohn, *Punished by Rewards* (Boston: Houghton Mifflin, 1993).

25. D. C. McClelland, *The Achieving Society* (New York: Van Nostrand Reinhold, 1961).

26. S. Squires, "Clinging to Hope," *San Jose Mercury News,* 25 February 1984, 12C; see also S. Breznitz, "The Effect of Hope on Coping With Stress," in M. H. Appley and R. Trumbell (eds.), *Dynamics of Stress: Physiological, Psychological, and Social Perspectives* (New York: Plenum, 1986), 295-306; M. E. P. Seligman, *Learned Optimism* (New York: Knopf, 1990); and C. Peterson and L. M. Bossio, *Health and Optimism: New Research on the Relationship Between Positive Thinking and Physical Well-Being* (New York: Free Press, 1991).

27. For more ideas, see B. Nelson, *1001 Ways to Reward Employees* (New York: Workman, 1994); and B. Basso and J. Klosek, *This Job Should Be Fun!* (Holbrook, Mass.: Bob Adams, 1991).

28. A. E. Schnur and C. Butz, "The Best Finish First: Top Coaches Talk About Winning," Towers Perrin (San Francisco, 1994).

29. A. Bandura and D. Cevone, "Self-Evaluative and Self-Efficacy Mechanisms Governing the Motivational Effects of Goal Systems," *Journal of Personality and Social Psychology 45* (1983): 1017-1028.

30. Field and Van Seters, "Management by Expectations (MBE)."

31. S. Shepard, "Quality Buy: St. Francis Avoids Reinventing Wheel," *Memphis Business Journal 15* (14) (1993): 3; and phone conversation on 12 September 1994 with the vice president of quality management, St. Francis Hospital.

# IX

# Social Responsibility and Organizational Leadership

## The New Work of 21st-Century Organizations

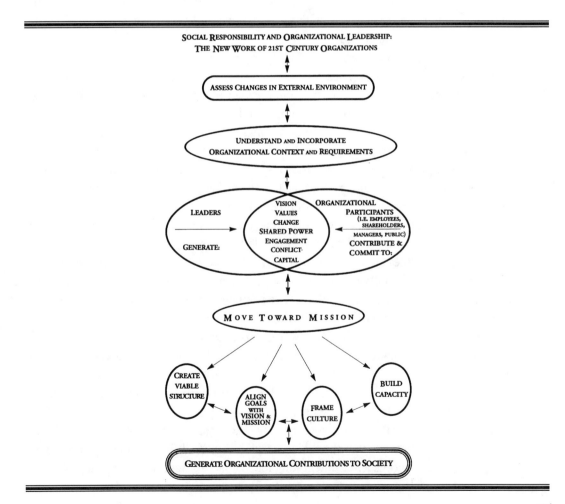

Organizations may be in the most advantageous position to facilitate unprecedented advances for society and resolve highly complex problems based on their capacity to mobilize resources and often to transcend political entities. Some pioneering organizational leaders and participants perceive that it will be difficult to sustain their own viability without also using a portion of their resources to engage in work for societal viability. A growing number of these organizational leaders and participants are incorporating societal issues as important components of their organizational vision and purpose.

James Liebig's research confirms this societal component in a study of 90 business leaders in 70 organizations from 14 countries. These leaders are concerned with local, internal and global issues including (a) enhancing social equity, (b) protecting our natural environment, (c) enabling human creativity, (d) seeking to serve higher purposes, (e) the ethical conduct of business, and (f) the need for personal transformation in business leadership. Their concern motivated them to implement programs or systems in their organizations to help deal with societal issues and, in some cases, transform the organization and its leadership.

L. Lawrence Embley focuses on several organizations that he describes as involved in *philanthropic economics*. These organizations purposefully and actively select social issues in which to engage the energy of their leaders and participants while carrying out the business mission of their organizations. Embley contends that in the future, "it may not be acceptable for any business to sit on the sidelines of this social trend shift."

In concurrence with Embley's contentions, Samuel Greengard and Charlene Solomon provide examples of corporate America's specific efforts to turn around harmful conditions in the nation's inner cities. Kathleen Dechant and Barbara Altman focus on organizational efforts to provide environmental leadership. They describe the practices of companies that have integrated environmentalism into their business planning and operations in ways that translate into profitable benefits.

Although Embley reports that early-entry companies in the social activism movement have been financially rewarded by the public and have attained increased prestige, Anne Murphy warns that "high-minded entrepreneurs" need to be aware that doing the right thing can be risky business. It is often difficult to attend to social issues and run the organization simultaneously. She warns: "You may succeed as a business and fail as a force for social change. But you cannot succeed as a reform movement while failing as a business."

In the past, social problems have been limited primarily to the domain of the public or nonprofit sectors. In the final chapter in this section, Peter Drucker broadens this domain beyond the efforts of any one entity. He describes a need for "social sector work." Drucker contends that the "joint work" of both public and private leaders and participants is to become a new integrating mechanism for resolving societal problems.

Together this public-private alliance forms the capacity that communities will need to tackle previously unmanageable problems.

If social activism is to occur in new-era organizations, leadership will need to become "transforming" in the sense that James MacGregor Burns intended originally when he applied this concept to the political and social movement context.[1] Burns indicated that leaders who aspire to be truly transforming must generate collective purpose and transforming processes that are ultimately linked to social change.[2]

The issues that all of the authors raise in this section go to the core of social activism on the part of organizations. Is it possible or desirable to pursue social activism in contemporary organizations, especially in profit-making organizations? If the new work of leadership in 21st-century organizations is to "do well while doing good" what do they need to do to assure economic viability? Can their efforts really make a difference?

## *Notes*

1. See James MacGregor Burns's chapter, "Transactional and Transforming Leadership," In Part III, Chapter 13, of this text.

2. See James MacGregor Burns, *Leadership* (New York: Harper & Row, 1978), p. 3.

# 46

# *The Merchants and Their Visions*

JAMES E. LIEBIG

It is an undeniable fact that today's world is in the midst of dramatic changes on many levels and within many categories of life. The same can be said of business. With major technological advances occurring, particularly in transnational communications and transportation, business competition and complexity have increased rapidly. The need to protect the environment from further degradation is repeatedly colliding with business-driven economic expansion. Among the world's peoples everywhere there are rising expectations of living a better life within increasingly democratic institutions.

At the same time, business has become the most pervasive and influential institution in world society. Certainly business does not stand alone nor apart from other institutions. What businesses do or do not do directly affects the conditions of other institutions. Because of this position of central importance, business now bears greater responsibility for the future of the world than ever before.

An increasing number of business leaders understand and agree with this assessment of the situation prevailing in the world today. They are grappling with issues regarding the appropriate response of business to new realities. Profiles of some of them, what they have been thinking about, what has inspired their thinking and visions of the future, and, in many cases, how they are proceeding, form the contents of this book.

What these leaders have envisioned are neither final nor perfect solutions to the dilemmas facing business today. They think systematically and, as "systemic thinkers," can readily see the connections between issues. These people are not easily categorized. This has provided me many challenges as an author. As a result, I have arranged the book so as to allow their wholistic thinking to explore issues related to, but going beyond, the boundaries of each chapter's central theme.

These progressive business men and women continually seek to reconcile their idealism with what they experience to be real in the world of commerce. Though they have personally enjoyed the challenges of business and been successful by traditional standards, they recognize that the business system has often not adequately served nor rewarded others. They know as well that the natural world is suffering under the strains of resource depletion and environmental damage. These leaders have acknowledged that changes in the agendas of business are inevitable and necessary.

Because each person profiled is unique and has experienced life in a different setting and under different circumstances, each has a valuable perspective to offer. Because of their uniqueness and the individuality of each reader, any given reader may find some profiles more valuable than others. The book is best read over a period of time, two or three profiles at any one sitting, to permit comparing and contrasting.

*Merchants of Vision* is a status report on an intricate system and some of its most thoughtful leaders, all of whom are simultaneously in transition. It is meant to encourage others to join in the discussion of why and how business must change to meet its new responsibilities, turning as many of them as possible into opportunities for the benefit of business and the world. This task is certainly not finished—perhaps it never will be. What is clear today is that the status quo is untenable.

Since late 1990, I have conducted empirical research by interviewing 90 business men and women, most at their places of work, in 70 organizations from 14 countries. The visionary observations and actions of approximately half of the people interviewed are included in this book.

Common threads run through their perspectives. These threads include their local and global concerns for (1) enhancing social equity, (2) protecting our natural environment, (3) enabling human creativity, and (4) seeking to serve higher purposes. Two other themes, prerequisite to the accomplishment of these four, occupy the attention of many of

the visionaries as well. They are (5) the ethical conduct of business and (6) the need for personal transformation in business leadership.

## Enhancing Social Equity

The leaders' thoughts on enhancing social equity range over concern for the growing disparity between rich and poor, both within and among nations; the acceptance of culturally and radically diverse people; the full enfranchisement of women in business; and recognition of the feminine perspective as a valuable and necessary corrective to traditional masculine domination. Several also address the extension of free enterprise into formerly communist economies as both an opportunity and a necessity to leaven living conditions and to enhance the people's ability to participate in the world economy.

## Protecting Our Natural Environment

In the area of our environment, the issues the leaders address include the necessity of business to proactively raise environmental protection standards, seek alternatives to natural resource depletion, engage in voluntary recycling of materials and products, and develop creative opportunities for business to improve the natural context within which all life is lived. To accomplish this, these innovators suggest a variety of systems changes which, though they maybe prototypical today, are the necessary first steps toward enabling greater business accountability for the future of the planet.

## Enabling Human Creativity

As examples of human creativity, several new venture approaches are presented that engage the imagination of their participants. Profiles of other visionaries emphasize the necessity of enabling all personnel within a company—regardless of sex, race, position, or level—to participate in all aspects of the organization. This approach, which is seen as essential for the mutual benefit of a company and its employees, leads to identifying new business opportunities, enhancing business effectiveness, fostering human growth and development, and satisfying the individual's need to contribute. For many leaders, a key ingredient in accomplishing this is the complete reorganization of business activity, particularly the hierarchical and bureaucratic structures, systems, and attitudes. This theme of creativity, which flows through the majority of profiles, is clearly one of the dominant concerns of these business leaders.

## Serving Higher Purposes

Many of those profiled recognize that business consciously serving higher purposes can inspire the people involved to achieve challenging objectives that fulfill the most significant needs, both their own and the needs of those whom they serve. These businesses can also provide models of a more inclusive community, recognizing that supportive social connectedness is essential to the growth of the human spirit. Such organizations also enable recognition of the universal "oneness" of life. Businesses serving higher purposes involve participants in building a better world, bringing the attributes of love and service into the processes of enterprise.

## Behaving Ethically

With business becoming the most influential institution in the world society, several leaders have stressed that it must continually model the highest levels of ethics. The attributes of ethical behavior they value include businesses honoring the traditional virtues and living by consciously developed principles of conduct; understanding clearly who they are and establishing what they wish to become; being mindful of the social impact of their operations, culture, and products; and assuming responsibility for all of their actions.

## Transforming Personally

Many leaders suggest that the emerging era of global connectedness and interdependence both enables and requires a new level of human consciousness. This new level of consciousness involves revising our view of the nature of reality, merging reason and scientific knowledge with the inspiration of practiced intuition. In short, they declare, it requires the transformation of each business leader before the organizations they lead, or the institution itself can be transformed. They relate a variety of experiences and observations in the accomplishment of this task.

To identify visionary business men and women, I relied heavily on contacts made through the World Business Academy (WBA), located in Burlingame, California, and of other progressive business sources. Members of the WBA are committed to creating a better world through business. They come together in chapter meetings and in conferences throughout the world to receive presentations and discuss what the changes occurring in society today imply for the conduct of business. The merchants of vision profiles here, however, include both members of the Academy and those who are not.

I was not particularly interested in identifying or interviewing business leaders who have already been broadly recognized for their progressive views or actions. The movement toward business transformation, while plodding torpidly over the past three decades, is now accelerating and widening beyond the efforts of the elite. I specifically wanted to demonstrate the pervasive character of this growing phenomenon. I sought and found visionary business women and men in a variety of international locations and various positions within organizations. Some have been surviving and even growing under oppressive local circumstances.

In the sense that it is used here, being visionary goes beyond being informed by the past. Abiding values, of course, need to be reaffirmed, but these visionary business men and women have come to realize that many traditional business forms and systems have stifled life, injuring both people and business in the process. As visionaries, they recognize that in the apparent turmoil of today's events, evolutionary forces are at work to move civilization to a new level.

They see macro movements furthering democracy, and demassing, decentralizing, and feminizing institutions while refocusing them on the value of human uniqueness and on the need to protect our natural environment.

As visionaries, they are open to the future. Their visions often rest on trust arising from intuitive sources, and on their faith that whatever will be necessary to achieve the visions will be present when needed. When their inspiring visions are shared, they can attract and empower the commitment and action of others. In this sense, visionary people become cocreators of the future.

The profiles that follow portray the thoughts and actions of exemplary business leaders who serve organizations composed of anywhere from one person to thousands. Their personal and business experiences and their natural and cultural environments have generated a rich variety of approaches to the issues facing business leadership today. Their perspectives are, of course, subject to change. What they said to me and what I have written about them is time-bound, shaped by their dispositions of the moment, my interpretations, and other prevailing circumstances.

Yet the evidence they present is unmistakable. Over a broad expanse of the world, visionary business women and men see similar things occurring regardless of local conditions. The globalization of society and of the world's economy, enabled by technological advances, provides a common backdrop. But, as influential as the products of science may be, the men and women profiled recognize that more profound dynamics, at once more fundamental and more transcendental, are at work here.

These merchants of vision do not live out their days removed from the realities of the world. Most attend innumerable meetings, spend hours on the phone, generate correspondence, pass memos back and forth, address a multitude of problems large and small, attempt to satisfy a growing number of stakeholders, sweat decisions, and live ordinary human lives striving to meet their financial obligations, return a profit, and still be able to achieve their corporate responsibilities.

To meet their corporate responsibilities, some have chosen the path of philanthropy. Others are redirecting the focus of their businesses to deal with issues increasingly impinging on society. Still others are involved in the process of completely transforming their organizations. In most cases, these men and women are themselves consciously engaged in the iterative process of personal transformation.

This book opens with several observers' interpretations of the major movements they see occurring in the world today. The profiles that follow are arranged according to a major theme emphasized in each profile. Again, this method of organization is not meant to categorize these visionaries in any way, but to present them in some orderly fashion. As systemic observers, thinkers, and doers, these exemplary merchants readily relate each concern to other interdependent issues that ultimately encompass the whole web of life. As fellow instruments of the evolution of humankind, you are invited to explore how some of your peers have chosen to aid in the birth of a new era.

# 47

# A New Wave

L. LAWRENCE EMBLEY

A new business phenomenon is under way. Businesses of all sizes are entering into partnerships with consumers by supporting dozens of socially relevant issues that affect all of us in direct and indirect ways—issues such as the environment, education, the homeless, children, and the elderly. The list of social issues being addressed by American business/consumer partnerships is increasing every day.

This new thrust of business activism has developed into a strategy that I call doing well while doing good, an outgrowth of a concept we have dubbed *philanthropic economics.* Firms large and small are embracing this strategy. We examine who these firms are and, just as important, what motivates their managements to undertake philanthropic economics. In profiling the results of these corporate strategies, the motivation of the American consumer will also be examined.

How is it that as consumers we have recently developed deep and broadening social concerns, ones about issues that in many cases may seem as if they don't affect our lives today, but they do? The great myth of the uniformly passive consumer will

soon be exposed. In 1988, then-presidential candidate George Bush spoke of a kinder, gentler nation and a vision of the "thousand points of light."

Little did I realize that four years later I would write on the very same topic, nor did I realize that this topic would alter the way I conduct my business. In fact, social activism led me to move my business into a direct partnership with child-related initiatives. I have experienced a form of enlightenment over the past several years, and sharing this experience is the purpose of this book. My understanding and motivation came through study and research into the entire phenomenon.

Some of the personal profiles of innovators who link their business mission with a social mission are very telling. These innovators are self-described as enlightened capitalists. They have turned around their business strategy by placing equal emphasis on social relevance first as well as company profits. This extremely inventive strategy is providing them with exciting ways of managing their business, ways that allow them the opportunity to make a contribution to society as well as to the shareholders.

SOURCE: From *Doing Well While Doing Good: The Marketing Link Between Business and Nonprofit Causes,* by L. Lawrence Embley. Copyright 1992. Reprinted with permission of Prentice Hall.

What kind of person can place values and personal commitments to do good alongside of conventional business logic? What happened to those businesses and their owners—did they fail? There is controversy surrounding this business strategy. Many believe that businesses bent on providing social characteristics would do less well economically than companies that chose a strict profitability profile. Quite the opposite is true. The following profiled companies are not your mainstream corporations, but they are some of the most passionate of the models of socially sensitive companies in the country. For many executives in the country, these enlightened companies will become the models of the future.

The following are some of these smaller enlightened companies:

- The Body Shop, founded by Anita Roddick, is an $800 million company that is helping thousands of people around the world through her environmental stance and her human rights activism.
- Ben & Jerry's Homemade, Inc. was founded by Ben Cohen and Jerry Greenfield. This dynamic duo has built an $80 million business in the town of Waterbury, Vermont, based on a business mission of helping local farmers by buying their milk/cream.
- Patagonia was founded by Yvon Chouinard and prospers as a privately held $117 million company creating clothes for a range of adventures such as climbing, skiing, sailing, fly-fishing, and kayaking. Adventure is a byword of Patagonia, which gives substantially to, and strongly supports, more than 300 environmental organizations.
- Matrix Essentials, Inc. was founded in 1980 by husband-and-wife team Arnold and Sydell Miller. Their haircare products are naturally effective and environmentally sound. Matrix joined Dick Clark productions to produce "What About Me? I'm Only Three," an environmental television special targeted toward the misuses that continue to deplete our world of its natural resources.
- Esprit de Corp, giants in the trendy clothes industry, has a department called the "Eco Desk," which coordinates environmental and community affairs encouraging individual volunteerism in a wide range of environmental activities.

- Aveda Corporation was founded by Horst Rechelbacher in Minneapolis, Minnesota. Aveda's number one concern is manufacturing green. They produce perfume, skincare, haircare, and household cleansers. Aveda compounds endeavor to naturally ensure personal and planetary preservation and rejuvenation.
- Stonyfield Farms was founded in 1983 with two goals: (1) to produce the purest, most natural and nutritious yogurts available, and (2) to encourage consumers' support of family farmers and local agriculture in the northeastern United States—objectives include "serving as a model that environmentally and socially responsible businesses can also be profitable."

These companies, and many others, are doing well while doing good. Larger companies are also responding to the growing awareness of community and world social issues. They are modifying corporate culture to incorporate social responsibility initiatives and philanthropic economics into their everyday business. Some of these companies are Colgate-Palmolive, Hershey Foods, Johnson SC & Sons, Kellogg Company, Procter & Gamble, Polaroid Corporation, and Quaker Oats. The programs of several of these companies, and others, will be profiled in later chapters.

The motivation or the motivator, which comes first? Why is it that as consumers we are moved by this way of doing business? In this book, we will examine how and why we as consumers have evolved into a socially sensitive society. We may be living in the most socially relevant time in U.S. history. This book will prove beyond a shadow of a doubt that there is life beyond profit for the truly enlightened capitalist. As a marketing strategist for major corporations and an entrepreneur, I see and hear about numerous business problems and, just as important, the steps taken toward proposed solutions. The problems these firms face are twofold:

1. Building their businesses with a strong belief in product, service, and quality
2. At the same time facing the social problems in their local communities—feeding the hungry; shelter-

ing the homeless; educating and protecting the children; defending and safeguarding the environment; dealing with substance abuse; providing health care for the elderly; and preserving the history, arts, and culture of the community.

The list of social needs can be overwhelming. The answer may lie in the new alliance of social activism and business involvement called *philanthropic economics*. By taking a highly visible and active position of social support, firms have altered forever the ways in which they will conduct business. To date, consumers have responded favorably.

## *The Enlightened Consumer*

The enlightened consumer is acutely aware and educated as to the current state of our society. They make their buying decisions more astutely as a result of that information. They will not support companies that are not socially responsible. They will know the difference between a company's socially relevant public relations campaign and its real business practice. They will favor companies that demonstrate principles and values in their workplace and in the products they develop, and will look at how the company behaves as a community citizen. The new consumer will influence and dictate the financial well-being of many companies.

In all fairness, the enlightened consumer is a paradigm that has of yet not fully emerged. At the rate in which they are growing, I believe it will be fair to say that in ten years the enlightened will outnumber the unaware.

### Economic Realignment Results in Consumer Realignment[1]

Consumers have been motivated essentially by two determinants:

1. Wants
2. Needs

Needs are basic, the definition of "basic" being relative: what is basic to one person may seem a fantasy to another. Business has played a role in finding ways to make basic *needs* fulfillment become basic *wants* fulfillment. *Want,* however, is beyond basic need and fulfills some other desire that the buyer may have. The conflicts between needs and wants are the battles that American businesses wage every day to fit their product or service into the appropriate target audience, to develop selling strategy, merchandising, distribution, packaging, advertising, and promotional tactics that move their business into the *minds of the consumer.*

A result of the last 25 years of various cultural, social, and world changes has developed a trend that clearly defines the emergence of the *sensible* or *intelligent* consumer. The sensible or intelligent consumer is much harder for business to define clearly outside of the pure wants versus needs methods of prior years. This growing number of intelligent consumers is the trend of the future; as a result, we will become more informed and therefore buy smarter. American businesses need to redefine themselves on how to appeal to the new consumer.

A society of our magnitude has hundreds, if not thousands, of different factions, groups within groups, communities within communities, families within families, and values. Some issues are defined only within the limits of a specific area or ethnic group, and of those, the general public unfortunately remains unaware or unconcerned. Then there are issues that affect a majority of us. Issues such as children, the environment, or the spread of AIDS are widely ranging core social issues.

The growth of the intelligent consumer will send a clear message to business. That message states: "If you want to sell products or services to us, you must be *responsible.*" The growth of nonprofit organizations over the trend period has acted in many ways as a barometer. For American business, it clearly points out what the consumer feels strongly about. This very basic fact is the reason some American businesses are beginning to take a socially responsible stance.

Consider, if you will, the basic fact that to some greater or lesser degree, every American citizen recognizes that we have an environmental and ecological problem—some 240 or so million people. If you are intending to conduct business with any of these 240 million people and you are environmentally irresponsible, you may have a real problem!

The tremendous growth of environmental and ecological groups, such as the Sierra Club, the World Wildlife Fund, the National Conservatory and the National Parks Foundation, over the last ten years is a clear signal that the American public is concerned. These organizations represent just a few of the better-known groups, and their members and subscribers total tens of millions of people. The numbers are very impressive—so much so that the numbers are now beginning to take on a dynamic of their own as they generate even greater numbers.

**Development Beyond Critical Mass**

When environmental and conservation issues begin to escalate, they do so at all ends of the socioeconomic scale. They infiltrate our basic educational settings and recreational time, including news media and entertainment media. They then begin to impact our buying decisions, which will ultimately alter our lifestyles and culture.

Awareness is the first step in a progressive chain toward the ultimate goal of *elective* or *selective change.* Change is what is required for ecological survival and environmental salvation, but awareness may be sufficient for another less volatile issue or cause. Awareness itself does not require change, but *getting the message out* is critically important.

Consumers are either driven by their own original concerns about the environment, or now that business has either joined or initiated the awareness campaign, it is a moot point. The fact is, environmental issues are important for the intelligent consumer. Businesses that want to attract the informed consumer will need to be more responsible to this group. Green marketing done with a slick public relations campaign will not match their buying criteria. These issues are now just as important to business that wants to attract intelligent consumers.

As the connection begins to emerge between social issues and business issues, the lines begin to blur. The messages are sometimes left to the consumers' interpretation. Today, more and more companies recognize that environmentally or socially conscious reflections in their advertisements and public relations campaigns are having a positive effect on sales and company image. The informed consumer can discriminate between fact and fiction. Unfortunately, the majority of consumers still can't. The questions that all consumers should be asking about a company are

1. Is the company using environmentally unsound components to manufacture its products?
2. Does the company require animal testing in its research and developments?
3. Is the company's packing and merchandise material environmentally sound?
4. Is the company promoting positive awareness internally to its employees as well as promoting it outside through its advertising and promotions?

Motivations vary. Certainly, some managements are more sincere than others. In each and every case, the environmental issue is further enhanced. It is not for me to be a watchdog on a business's level of sincerity. It is my purpose to show how the two dynamics now interrelate. It is important to understand how the consumer is alerted to or made aware of certain social issues when attempting to create linkage between the company and the social issues.

*Methods of Awareness*

There are two basic motivational models that increase awareness: (1) the heart motivator model, which relies on sentiment, empathy, compassion, emotion, and alignment of personal values with issues; and (2) the head motivator model, which relies more on facts, data, logic, and statistical findings. These two models are the means by which American business is attempting to reach the consumer. This thinking model applies both to the motivation of the business responding to the enlightened consumer, and to the consumer. Consumers become aware of their social responsibility

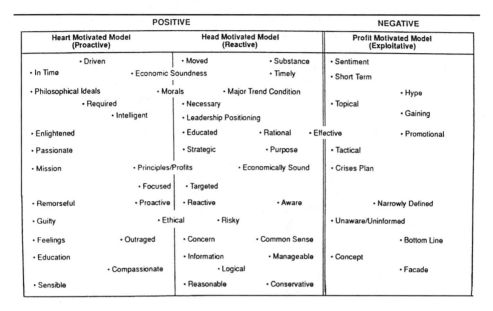

| POSITIVE | | NEGATIVE |
| --- | --- | --- |
| Heart Motivated Model (Proactive) | Head Motivated Model (Reactive) | Profit Motivated Model (Exploitative) |

Figure within table (as laid out):

| Heart Motivated Model (Proactive) | | Head Motivated Model (Reactive) | | Profit Motivated Model (Exploitative) | |
| --- | --- | --- | --- | --- | --- |
| • Driven | | • Moved | • Substance | • Sentiment | |
| • In Time | • Economic Soundness | | • Timely | • Short Term | |
| • Philosophical Ideals | • Morals | | • Major Trend Condition | | • Hype |
| • Required | | • Necessary | | • Topical | |
| • Intelligent | | • Leadership Positioning | | | • Gaining |
| • Enlightened | | • Educated | • Rational | • Effective | • Promotional |
| • Passionate | | • Strategic | • Purpose | • Tactical | |
| • Mission | • Principles/Profits | | • Economically Sound | • Crises Plan | |
| • Focused | • Targeted | | | | |
| • Remorseful | • Proactive | • Reactive | • Aware | | • Narrowly Defined |
| • Guilty | • Ethical | • Risky | | • Unaware/Uninformed | |
| • Feelings | • Outraged | • Concern | • Common Sense | | • Bottom Line |
| • Education | | • Information | • Manageable | • Concept | |
| • Compassionate | | • Logical | | | • Facade |
| • Sensible | | • Reasonable | • Conservative | | |

**Figure 47.1.** The Business Manager's Model of Social Responsibility

based on the two primary models—heart motivator and head motivator. See Figure 47.1.

With growing frequency, businesses are showing up in areas that were once reserved strictly for nonprofit groups or governmental concerns. In many cases they are reacting to issues that are affecting what the company would call *their customers.* If their customers are concerned, the company must be concerned. Just as important to attracting customers is keeping the ones you have, and should the new enlightened customer discover that your company is behaving in nonresponsible terms, the customer will have an impact on your market share. Whether consumers are responding to their feelings or their thinking, their actions will begin to have an effect on businesses. Business therefore must move beyond price, service, and quality commitments, and move toward a socially responsible commitment. The informed consumer will be concerned with the company's packaging, manufacturing processes, research methods, and its impact on human rights, the environment, health, safety, and well-being, to name a few.

Is social responsibility offensive strategy or defensive strategy for American business?

Advertising messages and statements seem far removed from the conventional communications about product or service coming from corporate America. Today, "promotional" statements are being made when, in fact, there is no product affiliation or endorsement at all other than what the corporation is bringing forth in its message. The content of their very expensive television and print advertisements will more often reflect a more dramatic social concern than a product endorsement. Advertisers will position their product behind social concerns such as the environment, teenage drinking, drug abuse, literacy, the plight of the homeless, and so on. This method of advertising is being deployed by companies in an effort to attract the consumer from a values position versus the conventional wants and needs method.

This highly effective method of reaching the consumer will be a sincere and responsible statement by some, but for others it will be only a method of hype.

Companies throughout the country are now sending this kind of message; a message of change. It is fascinating to think that this strategic tool of combining business with social responsibility may be the beginning of a new way of conducting business.

This new philosophy is spreading throughout advertising agencies and public relations firms in the United States. These enterprises can see how their clients can benefit from cause-aligned initiatives because consumers feel better about companies with a "soul" and are more likely to buy from them.

It may not be acceptable in the future for any business to sit on the sidelines of this social trend shift. Early entry companies have been rewarded with great financial success and increased prestige in the mind of the consumer. One such company, Ben & Jerry's Ice Cream, of Waterbury, Vermont, appealed directly to the enlightened consumer with their policies and philosophies of creating a direct relationship between their company's profits and their principles. This concept is a reflection of their 1960s culture of peace, love, sharing, and ideology that has unique appeal to a large group of consumers who identify with these same principles. The economic result of Ben & Jerry's principles and policies was to make them the darlings of the ice cream world, and distance them from their competition. In addition, they just happen to make great ice cream. The news media thought well of Ben & Jerry's and provided them a unique and powerful public relations machine to spread the word. This is a classic example of the power of the information society. Businesses should be encouraged to adopt approaches like Ben & Jerry's. Without some socially redeeming value, some companies may find it hard to compete.

For the purposes of fully exploring the whole universe of social responsibility, it is important to note that there are extremes. The enlightened capitalist may be seen by some as extremist. I expect to demonstrate that these companies are the mainstream of the future. Their business philosophies and the model they provide are highly effective in pure economic terms.

How did we get to this place in time? What influences shaped us? These questions should be directed back to us as a society. Let's recognize that established long-term American big business is falling into the socially responsible ranks as well. Ben & Jerry's story makes for great reading, and the company has grown in such a way that it stands for something beyond its profit statement. Its story will be told in greater detail later.

H. J. Heinz's Starkist Tuna is another of those early entries into the arena of social consciousness. Its animal rights approach to safe netting fishing practices has saved the lives of thousands of dolphins. This extremely sensitive issue touched a nerve in the American public. Consumers wanted wasteful killing of dolphins to stop. Starkist had only one valid option—take a stand with the people to save the dolphins. Millions of dollars were spent to ensure that the least possible number of dolphins would be affected. Consumers responded by increasing market share for Starkist over its competitors. Starkist's commitment can never be reversed; the effect would be devastating to the company. Starkist truly deserves the consumer and brand loyalty it has gained, and it is only one of many firms using philanthropic economics.

The findings and specifics of actual market share increase have not been made available by Starkist, but one can safely assume that very positive public relations benefited the company's revenue position. Starkist is a division of H. J. Heinz Company, a leader among socially responsible companies as defined by the Council on Economic Priorities.

### *The Council on Economic Priorities*

Alice Tepper Marlin, a 46-year-old mother of two, is the driving force behind the Council on Economy Priorities (CEP). In 1968, working as a security analyst, Ms. Tepper Marlin was asked by a synagogue to help it invest in companies that had no business interest in the Vietnam War. This request, along with others, showed her the need to create a source of information for other alternative investing managers. In response, she developed the Council on Economic Priorities. Today, her research on corporate behavior is far reaching, covering the entire area of social responsibilities.

She researches and grades corporations based on the following criteria:

- Charitable giving
- Women's advancements
- Minority advancement
- Animal testing
- Disclosure of information
- Community outreach

| Company or Product | Abbr. | Charitable giving | Women's advancements | Minority advancement | Animal testing | Disclosure of information | Community outreach | South Africa | The environment | Family benefits | Workplace issues | ALERT |
|---|---|---|---|---|---|---|---|---|---|---|---|---|
| ConAgra | CAG | ? | ✖ | ✓ | ? | ✖ | ✖ | No | ? | ? | ✖ | safe meat controversy; D.C.C.A.; factory farming |
| Coors Company, Adolph | ACC | ☑+ | ✓ | ☑ | ☑ | ☑ | ✓ | No | ✓ | ☑ | ☑ | Fair Share |
| Curtice-Burns | CBI | ☑+ | ☑ | ✖ | ? | ☑ | ✓ | No | ? | ☑ | ✓ | |
| Dep Corporation | DEPC | ? | ☑ | ✓ | ☑ | ☑ | ☑ | No | ? | ✓ | ☑ | |
| Dial Corporation | G | ? | ☑ | ✓ | ☑ | ✖ | ? | No | ? | ? | ? | |
| Dole Food Company | DOL | ☑ | ✓ | ? | ☑ | ✓ | ✖ | No | ✖ | ✓ | ✖ | pesticide sterilization suit |
| Dow Chemical Company | DOW | ✓ | ☑ | ☑ | ☑ | ☑[1] | ☑ | Yes | ✓ | ☑ | ☑ | pesticide steril. suit; nuclear weapons; on-site daycare; makes pesticides |
| Eastman Kodak | EK | ✓ | ☑ | ☑ | ☑ | ☑[1] | ☑ | No | ☑ | ☑ | ☑ | C.C.A. |
| First Brands | FB | ☑+ | ✖ | ☑ | ☑ | ☑ | ☑ | Yes | ✓ | ✖ | ☑ | |
| Flowers Industries, Inc. | FLO | ? | ✖ | ? | ? | ✖ | ? | No | ? | ? | ? | |
| GTE Corporation | GTE | ✓ | ☑ | ☑ | ☑ | ☑ | ☑ | No | ✓ | ☑ | ✓ | nuclear weapons; |
| General Electric Company | GE | ✖ | ☑ | ? | ✖○ | ✖ | ✓ | No | ✖ | ? | ✖ | nuclear weapons; INFACT boycott |
| General Mills | GIS | ☑+ | ☑ | ☑ | ☑ | ☑ | ☑ | No | ✓ | ☑ | ☑ | C.C.A. |

| Company or Product | Abbr. | Charitable giving | Women's advancements | Minority advancement | Animal testing | Disclosure of information | Community outreach | South Africa | The environment | Family benefits | Workplace issues | ALERT |
|---|---|---|---|---|---|---|---|---|---|---|---|---|
| Georgia Pacific | GP | ✖ | ☑ | ☑ | ? | ✓ | ☑ | No | ✖ | ? | ? | clearcutting; on-site day care |
| Gerber Products | GEB | ✓ | ☑ | ? | ? | ✖ | **?** | Yes | ? | ? | ? | D.C.C.A.; infant formula |
| Gillette | GS | ✓ | ☑ | ☑ | ☑Φ | ☑ | ☑ | Yes | ✓ | ☑ | ☑ | |
| Goya Foods, Inc. | GOYA | ? | ? | ? | ? | ✖ | ? | No | ? | ? | ? | |
| Grand Metropolitan PLC | GMP | ✓ | ☑ | ☑ | ☑ | ☑ | ☑ | Yes | ✓ | ☑ | ☑ | U.K. |
| Heinz Company, H. J. | HNZ | ☑ | ☑ | ✓ | ☑ | ☑ | ✓ | No | ☑ | ☑ | ✓ | C.C.A. |
| Hershey Foods Corporation | HSY | ✓ | ☑ | ☑ | ☑[1] | ☑ | ☑ | No | ☑ | ☑ | ☑ | on-site day care |
| Hormel & Co., George A. | HRL | ? | ✖ | ? | ☑ | ✖ | ? | No | ? | ? | ? | |
| Int'l Res. & Dev. Corp. | IRDV | ? | ✖ | ? | ✖○ | ✖ | ? | No | ? | ? | ? | |
| James River Corporation | JR | ✓ | ✖ | ✓ | ✖ | ☑ | ✓ | No | ✖ | ✓ | ☑ | on-site day care |
| John B. Sanfilippo, Inc. | JSAN | ? | ? | ? | ☑ | ✖ | ? | No | ? | ? | ? | |

NOTE: ☑ = Top Rating; ✓ = Middle Rating; ✖ = Bottom Rating; ? = Insufficient Information

○ Manufactures surgical/medical supplies and/or prescription drugs

1 Company tests on animals but has reduced the number used in testing by 40% or more over the last 5 years and/or has given $250,000 or more annually to alternative research through in-house or independent labs

**Figure 47.2.** Rating Criteria for Socially Responsible Consumer Goods Companies

- South Africa
- The environment
- Family benefits
- Workplace issues

Figure 47.2 is a reference guide that points out which companies are or are not doing the right things. The CEP also provides an annual awards program to recognize those companies that are making a major impact in the area of social responsibilities.

The CEP is both a consumer advocate and watchdog organization. Its focus is on mailing available information to the consumer and also recognizing and awarding companies that do the right things. Of basic importance here is the fact that there are now real measurable criteria that are easily understood by all. These measurement criteria will become the benchmark of the future and the indication that the consumer will continue to become more intelligent and socially aware.

## Note

1. For purposes of the explanation of the trend dynamics around business and social issues, I'll refer to the interest in the environmental issue as a model.

# 48

# *The Fire This Time?*

SAMUEL GREENGARD
CHARLENE MARMER SOLOMON

Is corporate America's effort to save the nation's inner cities enough, or will James Baldwin's immortal warning, "The Fire Next Time," come to pass?

The view from Peter Goldberg's 15th-floor office overlooking Newark, New Jersey, isn't pretty. Burned out buildings—ugly scars from the 1967 riots—still mar the urban landscape. Empty storefronts, dilapidated housing projects, and drug-infested alleys continue to plague the city.

It's a wrenching reminder of the extremes to which this country's poor were driven to get their problems on the national agenda: a dreadful series of conflagrations, that made Newark, Detroit, and Los Angeles' Watts district symbols for America's urban ills. And with memories of the 1992 Los Angeles riots still fresh, it's also a sobering suggestion of difficulties ahead. "Cities are an important part of the fabric of any country," says Goldberg, who, as president of the Prudential Foundation, is head of Prudential Insurance Co. of America's social investments. "The future well-being of this company, this industry and of corporate America is very much intertwined with the health and well-being of American society."

Cynics might note that such sentiments were rampant in corporate boardrooms back in the late 1960s and early '70s. Yet, some argue, so little progress has been made that when the jury announced its decision in the first Rodney King trial, it took three days and three nights of the worst riots in American history to vent the pent-up anger over social conditions. When the smoke finally cleared, upwards of $750 million in damage littered the landscape.

Many people took notice. Utility giant Southern California Edison established a $6.5 million job-training center in one of the area's hardest hit cities, Compton, and also is hiring disadvantaged youths for a wide array of community projects. State Farm Insurance invested a total of $1.2 million in three Los Angeles banks catering to minorities. Bank of America followed suit with a $1 million investment in a major African-American-owned institution. Sumitomo Bank of California pledged more than $500 million—a full 10% of its assets—for home and community redevelopment loans to neglected areas of California. And Hyundai Motors of America currently trains nearly three dozen minority youths each year to be certified mechanics. The cost? Over $10,000 per person. But as the program's assistant director, Arlene Pendleton, puts it: "We desperately need trained mechanics, and people need jobs. This program trains them for a career."

To be sure, investing in people makes the greatest sense of all. And it's the point at which human resources departments can have the most immediate impact through recruitment and training initiatives, for example. But while job-training programs are an integral part of the solution, they certainly don't solve the entire array of social ills. Creating a sense of community and giving everyone a stake in it may be the best solution of all. And that means putting money at risk in the nation's inner cities. "The same conditions that led to the Los Angeles riots exist in virtually every major American city," points out Tom Monahan of the New York City-based Committee for Economic Development. "Unless we begin to change things, we all will pay later on."

Goldberg plans to be one of those who helps to change. While other corporations flee for more idyllic pastures, Prudential remains steadfast in its commitment to the beleaguered city. Its 24-story office tower on Broad Street is in many respects the glue that holds Newark's social fabric together. "Social investing is a powerful complement to traditional corporate philanthropy because it provides access to capital and credit for community development." Goldberg says, "It's money that otherwise isn't available."

Precisely because traditional sources of funding naturally seek low-risk, high-return opportunities, America's inner cities have deteriorated beyond even the most dire predictions. Today, for those living in such areas, finding a decent job—let alone good housing and a solid education—is often next to impossible. That's because many companies and even the government, driven by fear of crime, vandalism, and a lack of skilled labor, hesitate to locate new facilities in these areas. Indeed, that sucking sound you hear is capital and jobs draining out of the inner cities. Unemployment in some urban cores now exceeds 50% and the disparity in per capita income persists. While having a tough row to hoe may not cause all of the nation's urban woes, and certainly doesn't excuse violence and crime, it explains why over 30% of the potential inner-city work force lack job skills.

Now a growing number of companies—whether driven by guilt, social responsibility, profit motives, or profound fear of a really big fire next time—are investing in America's inner cities. They are spending tens of millions of dollars opening stores, lending money, hiring residents, and providing training. "Businesses are discovering that the socially troubling problems of our cities must be attended to," says Stanley G. Karson, director of the Center for Corporate Public Involvement, a Washington, D.C. organization that helps facilitate corporate investment. "Otherwise, they threaten the stability, prosperity, even the survival of the businesses themselves." Adds Monahan: "Companies are finding that they can invest in urban areas and make a nice profit."

Not everyone agrees that those profits are nice enough to offset the risks. For public companies, the perceived added dangers of urban investments are hard to explain to shareholders and their increasingly assertive representatives on the board, especially in an era when massive downsizings and layoffs are hitting even middle-class citizens in rural and suburban America. For example, Vons Companies, Inc., Southern California's largest grocery-store chain, admits that shareholder and board concerns were partly responsible for the fact it dithered for years over whether to build supermarkets in Los Angeles' blighted core. The riots broke the logjam, and this winter the first of nearly a dozen Vons stores will open in South Central L.A. as part of the firm's post-1992-riot $100-million commitment, which will generate up to 2,000 jobs.

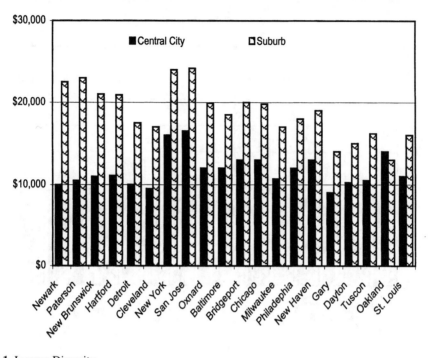

**Figure 48.1.** Income Disparity

SOURCE: Bureau of the Census, 1990 Census.

NOTE: Despite decades of private and public interventions, the difference in income between central-city residents and their suburban counterparts remains discouragingly high in most major metropolitan areas.

But the chief executive brave enough to face down shareholders is rare, and even he or she may blanch in the face of a plethora of other challenges. Public and private companies alike must overcome fear of theft, high insurance premiums, bloated land prices, absence of experienced workers, increased training and development costs, inadequate transportation, and employee resistance—all the barriers to inner-city development that often make greenfield locations far more attractive by conventional standards. "Some CEOs believe that their job is to return money to the shareholders and not be bothered by civic affairs," complains Ted Hershberg, director of the Center for Greater Philadelphia and a professor of public policy and history at the University of Pennsylvania. "CEOs who grew up in an area and continue to work there have a far greater interest in civic affairs than those who are more transient."

That's probably true, but many executives are genuinely concerned. According to a study conducted by the Center for Corporate Public Involvement (CCPI), 56% of all insurance industry respondents indicated that senior management played a critical role in the development of social-investment programs. Moreover, 44% said that the president, CEO, or chairman of the board was the key factor. And the role of senior management was further reaffirmed by the fact that at 62% of the companies involved in social investments, the decision had been made from the top.

Why did these executives feel it was necessary to make social investments in the first place? Many said they believed that a company is an important part of its community and must be involved in solving community problems. Others stated more specific reasons: deteriorating business districts and declining neighborhoods. Only 18% attributed

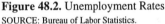

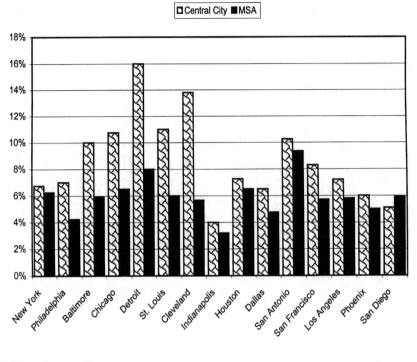

**Figure 48.2.** Unemployment Rates

SOURCE: Bureau of Labor Statistics.

NOTE: Central-city unemployment rates are uniformly higher than the average of their surrounding metropolitan statistical areas, and in some heavily industrial cities, they are more than twice as high.

their firm's actions to external influences. And, interestingly enough, three-fifths said that they were willing to accept below-market returns and take increased risks in order to effect change.

Yet, for every company like Vons or Prudential that's moving into an urban center, many more are leaving. And the fallout in human, social, and financial terms continues to worsen. States are paying out greater unemployment benefits and welfare, while crime and social problems are increasing. "Everyone has their own reason for moving away from the inner city—it may have to do with taxes or labor or a half dozen other issues—but it has a tremendous effect," says Monahan. "It moves jobs away from vast pools of people who are concentrated in urban areas."

To reverse the downward trend, some proponents of redeveloping inner cities argue that what's needed are new standards for at least some invest-

ments. Others claim that the profits already are available to those whose fears or prejudices don't blind them to the opportunities. For example, the CCPI found that 45% of firms lending money for social investments had no higher rate of default than for standard business loans. Moreover, 54% found their rate of return greater than 7% a year. And, perhaps most important, some found that what they had initially considered a social investment—a loan they thought had greater risk or a lower rate of return—actually performed more in line with a standard investment.

Prudential figures that even if it couldn't earn a return on its downtown Newark investments, the long-range benefits outweigh potential short-term losses. Over the last 16 years, the insurance company has shelled out more than $525 million for social investments—nearly 25% earmarked for Newark. It has helped build a $1.1 million six-theater cineplex, child-care facilities, the city's first central-area supermarket since the riots of 1967, affordable housing in the city's poorest neighborhoods, and now the New Jersey Performing Arts Center in Newark. "The best way to help a community grow is to involve it in its own development," Goldberg says. "The children of today are the consumers and work force of tomorrow. In Newark, we want to be able to draw from an educated, qualified work force."

Prudential isn't the only company that has learned how to profit from investments no timid chief executive would consider. Albert B. Ratner, chairman and CEO of Cleveland-based Forest City Enterprises, Inc., already has two major restoration projects under his belt. In 1980, he bought Terminal Tower—a 52-story office building—and a run-down train station in Cleveland's central district, which had been deteriorating for 50 years. His real-estate development, construction, and building materials firm then pumped $400 million into Tower City Center and by 1990 transformed it into a gleaming landmark that redefined the city's downtown. Thousands of people now work in the structure, which houses more than 100 companies (see "A City Rebuilds Its Symbol—and Rejuvenates Itself").

Four years ago, his firm managed an equally impressive feat in New York. Forest City, along with other investors, spent $1 billion to construct a 4.2-million-square-foot commercial, high-tech, and academic development on 16 acres in Brooklyn. The project, called MetroTech, has generated some 16,000 jobs and an annual payroll of over $500 million. More importantly, it helped rescue a neighborhood that had been in steady decline for years.

But Ratner doesn't let his social desires, however benevolent, get in the way of making solid business decisions. "I am a hard-nosed business person. The only justification I have for taking on a project is that I can make money. The thing that many business people don't fully understand is that you can make a profit by solving social problems."

And that's exactly how he approached Metro-Tech. At the time, former New York City Mayor Ed Koch saw his worst fears coming true: companies

fleeing Brooklyn and the outer boroughs for the New Jersey suburbs. So, Koch—and his successor, David Dinkins—worked with Ratner to stop the hemorrhaging with something more than a Band-Aid approach. With a $500 tax credit for each employee, a waiver of some real-estate taxes, and other incentives, the project went ahead. As a result, companies like Chase Manhattan, which alone had planned on moving 5,000 workers to a new out-of-state location, decided to stay.

It takes a concentrated effort to break out of the business-as-usual mentality. Back in Los Angeles, Vons had been concentrating its building efforts in the suburbs for the last two decades. After all, the guaranteed number of households in each planned suburban community took a lot of the guesswork out of site selection and facilities planning. Moreover, it's easier to develop stores where there's open land than where several parcels must be accumulated and existing structures razed. Compounding the problem, many urban landowners—upon learning Vons was interested in assembling parcels of land in urban areas—began asking inflated prices. "It was simply a matter of going where there appeared to be the easiest opportunity," explains Mary McAboy, Vons' corporate communications vice president.

But finding locations to build supermarkets is only half of the equation. Vons' HR department has found itself facing the formidable task of assembling a reliable work force. The company is hiring many people who have never before held a job, so it's working with local religious and community leaders' help to find good candidates. The California Employment Development Department provides skill-based training while Vons uses its own training program as well. It has even created a position for vice president of urban development in order to oversee the effort.

Los Angeles is not the sole recipient of this renewed fight against decay. Two-and-a-half weeks after the L.A. riots, for example, Seattle-based Seafirst Bank introduced a $2 million loan program for small businesses that wouldn't normally qualify for bank financing. The bank provided the loans of up to $100,000, with no principal or interest payment for three years. After that, borrowers pay only 5% interest for the seven-year

## BOX 48.1
## A City Rebuilds Its Symbol—and Rejuvenates Itself.

Cleveland serves as a parable: A decomposing urban center can become vital when business and government cooperate.

The Ohio city was like most old, industrial cities—only a little worse. Indeed, in the '60s and '70s it became the symbol of a decaying America. Severe social problems exploded into race riots in 1966 and again in 1968. Pollution laid thick in the air and on the river. Heavy industry was dying.

Politically, the city had become a caricature. One mayor accidentally set his own hair on fire with a torch while presiding over opening ceremonies at a bridge: another was so fanatically divisive that the city went into financial default because his administration couldn't work with the private sector on its overall finances.

By 1979, as the city moved into the most intense recession since the Great Depression, the business community of Cleveland decided enough was enough. They prevailed on then Lieutenant Governor George Voinovich to run for mayor. He agreed to the challenge in exchange for a pledge of cooperation from business leaders. After his election, he declared an era of public-private partnership, reversing the warfare.

In 1982, business leaders created Cleveland Tomorrow, a committee of CEOs of the largest corporations in the Cleveland metropolitan area whose agenda is to work on issues to make the regional economy stronger.

"Almost in one stroke Voinovich dramatically changed the way the community operated from one of constant fighting to one where everyone concluded you just had no choice but to cooperate," says Richard Shatten, formerly director of Cleveland Tomorrow.

One CEO who was instrumental in this spirit of cooperation was Albert B. Ratner. A high-stakes developer who was also known for his social conscience, his company, Forest City Enterprises, Inc., took on the city's most famous landmark: the Terminal Tower. Although a sym-

bol of Cleveland, it had been deserted for years. Ratner's goal was nothing less than to transform it into a multiuse hub of the city.

In the early 1930s, the Cleveland Union Terminal complex located on downtown's Public Square was a bustling urban magnet made up of a 52-story office building, a post office, a railroad station, department store, restaurants, and office buildings. In addition to the railroad access, Cleveland's commuter train service terminated there. Everyone came to Terminal Tower.

But, with the demise of trains and the decline of the area, the center of commerce for Cleveland shifted away from Public Square and the Terminal Tower. It degenerated into a deserted hulk of a space—a metaphor for Cleveland.

NOTE: When Forest City Enterprises bought Terminal Tower, it was a symbol of degenerated urban Cleveland.

Forest City Enterprises purchased the building and conceived an extraordinary vision: a transit station for a new generation of local rail commuters, a multilevel shopping mall with arching glass atrium, a rehabilitated tower, and a converted post office that would serve as an office building and hotel space. All were connected with pedestrian walkways.

"The project breathed extraordinary life into the city of Cleveland," says Shatten. "It was one

*(Continued)*

## BOX 48.1 (Continued)

of the linchpins in changing people's perceptions of downtown Cleveland.

It wasn't easy, though. Forest City purchased the building, but could do nothing with the structure for years because of problems with governmental agencies who were not completing street repairs and providing the necessary infrastructural support. Finally, with changes in the city's administration, with bank financing and urban development grants coming together in the mid-'80s, Forest City began reconstruction.

NOTE: The Tower now houses more than 300,000 square feet of retail shops.

It was a difficult project, says Brian Ratner, president of Tower City Retail, Inc. Getting national retailers to come to downtown Cleveland and look around was tough. Once there, however, it became easier to convince them of the economic benefits of opening stores in the shopping center because the city has good demographics. Although Cleveland had a rush to the suburbs, it had a strong base of downtown firms and enough incentives to keep Clevelanders in contact with the downtown area: 120,000 people still worked in the city, and continued to partake in the city's cultural events.

But, says Ratner, "It was an enormous risk. People were not doing development in downtown Cleveland at this point. We were believers—and Albert was right. We thought there would be a movement back to urban centers if appropriate financing was available to help the public and private sectors create projects in urban environments."

The empty space that was the Terminal Tower complex now houses more than 300,000 square feet of upscale retail shops (the Nature Company, Barney's of New York, Liz Claiborne, for example), an 11-screen movie theater, the Ritz-Carlton hotel (with over 200 rooms and meeting facilities), and several high-rise office buildings.

Tower City Center created a gigantic employment pool. They employed approximately 7,000 people during the construction phase, created over 3,000 permanent jobs, and paid an additional $4 million in a variety of taxes.

With the commitment of businesspeople such as the Ratners, civic organizations, including Cleveland Tomorrow and the Greater Cleveland Roundtable, helped complete a 7,000-seat theater renovation, development of a lake-front park, and helped create other large-scale projects such as a new baseball stadium.

Although Cleveland still has its share of significant problems, developments such as Tower City Center provide a foundation from which the city can begin to address its urban ills.

"It means a great deal," says Brian Ratner. "People respond to these types of projects. These programs don't solve social issues, but they give the city an economic base to work off of. They retain jobs, hopefully grow jobs, and provide a foundation for continuing growth."

—SG & CMS

**Figure 48.3.** Following the 1992 Los Angeles riots, Vons stopped its internal debate and launched a $100-million plan to build supermarkets in the urban core of S. Central L.A. The company plans to open a dozen stores, which will create up to 2,000 jobs.

loan. The bank uses college students—many of them minorities themselves—to serve as consultants and advocates for the borrowers.

Seafirst didn't stop there. When Seattle's mayor asked his city's businesses to hire 500 inner-city youths for the summer, bank chairman Luke Helms decided to hire more than 100 youths and teach them skills they could apply to a profession. Seafirst promptly handed out 4,000 applications at community agencies, schools, churches, and civic groups, and wound up with 350 qualified applicants from low-income households. After three days of interviews, the bank's human resources department had an ethnic cross-section of teenagers. Some were no longer living with their parents, some were having trouble at school, a few were functionally illiterate, and a handful were homeless.

During the summer, the bank put the students to work in the community earning $6.20 an hour. But when the time came for them to go back to school, Seafirst kept 95 of the 108 youths on its payroll. They worked as tellers, receptionists, and data-entry clerks. The youths put in up to 20 hours a week after school and received continuing training in broader subjects like job readiness, computers, and writing. Those who had problems with their school work also received free tutoring.

"We didn't know how supervisors would react when we asked them to take on these 108 students," says Diane Mackey, a Seafirst vice president who previously headed the youth training program. "We had to explain to them that it was a big commitment. It wasn't just an easy way to increase the size of the bank's staff. It would take a lot of hand-holding and a lot of energy. We wanted the kids to be

## BOX 48.2
## Perspectives: The Job of Reviving America's Inner Cities

*Although the 1992 Los Angeles riots stimulated a rush of corporate investments in deteriorating urban areas, neither the social problems that are the underlying causes of the violence nor investment programs aimed at alleviating those problems are new. Yet the nation's largest cities continue to lose full-time jobs while small cities gain. This month's cover story shows how both HR and financial investment programs can help.*

• In 1992, 78.7% of American cities said they were less able to meet financial needs than the previous year. Sixty-one percent reduced their capital spending.

• Two-thirds of all government leaders surveyed by the National League of Cities in November 1992 said that local governments are likely to be overwhelmed by the challenges they will face in the 1990s.

• In an assessment of conditions that have most deteriorated over the past five years, local government leaders identified: overall economic conditions, unemployment, drugs and city fiscal conditions.

• The NLC survey also found that the most important issues facing the President and Congress are: stimulating economic growth and jobs (35%); addressing the nation's infrastucture (24%); and dealing with health care needs (20%).

• Even though 80% of the respondents to the NLC survey said their communities offer only poor or fair prospects "for a young person finding a job and beginning a career," 86% described their communities as "a good place to raise a family."

• In 1990, the Center for Corporate Public Involvement, with a grant from the Ford Foundation, examined social investing in the life and health insurance industry. Surveying 78 companies, here's what they found:

• Nearly one-third of the companies that are currently making social investments have been doing so 20 years or more, while close to the same proportion have done so only during the last decade.

• The average company's social investment dollars have gone into housing, economic development, and commercial revitalization, in that order. Most of the investments have been made in their local areas.

• Most companies making such investments do not have formal programs for this purpose.

• Of the social investment companies, most are willing to accept below-market returns and take increased risks.

### Per Capita Full-Time Employment

| | Percent Change 1990-91 | Percent Change 1991-92 |
|---|---|---|
| **All Cities** | 1.0% | 2.0% |
| **Largest Cities** (pop. 300,000) | -1.5% | -1.5% |
| **Large Cities** (pop. 100,000 - 299,999) | 1.0% | 0.0% |
| **Medium Cities** (pop. 50,000 - 99,999) | 0.0% | 0.0% |
| **Small Cities** (pop. 10,000 - 49,999) | 1.0% | 4.1% |

### Per Capita Part-Time Employment

| | Percent Change 1990-91 | Percent Change 1991-92 |
|---|---|---|
| **All Cities** | 0.0% | 2.0% |
| **Largest Cities** (pop. 300,000) | 0.0% | 11.0% |
| **Large Cities** (pop. 100,000 - 299,999) | 4.8% | 0.0% |
| **Medium Cities** (pop. 50,000 - 99,999) | 0.0% | 0.0% |
| **Small Cities** (pop. 10,000 - 49,999) | 0.0% | 3.0% |

### Per Capita Total Employment

| | Percent Change 1990-91 | Percent Change 1991-92 |
|---|---|---|
| **All Cities** | 0.8 | 0.0 |
| **Largest Cities** (pop. 300,000) | 0.0 | -0.7 |
| **Large Cities** (pop. 100,000 - 299,999) | 1.7 | 0.8 |
| **Medium Cities** (pop. 50,000 - 99,999) | 0.0 | 0.0 |
| **Small Cities** (pop. 10,000 - 49,999) | 0.0 | 0.8 |

SOURCE: Bureau of Labor Statistics

*(Continued)*

---

**BOX 48.2 (Continued)**

- The experience with default risks on social investments is split, with slightly more (45%) reporting the same or lower defaults as on their standard investments and 40% reporting higher default rates.
- Twenty-five percent have earned an average annual yield of 9% on their social investments over the last five years; 29% estimate returns between 7% and 8%; 24% report returns of less than 7%.
- Commitment to corporate public involvement, community needs, and outside pressures were major factors behind the decisions to start making social investments.
- Well over 90% of the companies expect to continue to make social investments and most plan on maintaining investments at current levels.

---

successful in a work environment. Still, the supervisors' enthusiasm was great."

It wasn't always easy. Most of the teenagers had never held a job before and didn't understand basics, like calling in when they were sick or getting back from lunch on time. Others became lost in the daily routine and had trouble seeing the bigger picture of learning lifelong job skills. Regular bank employees often had to take time out from their routines to set the students straight.

But the program has achieved what it set out to. Many of the students began displaying a far greater interest in their studies, and virtually all began taking more pride in their communities. And the additional income provided many families living on marginal means with much-needed money for groceries and household goods. "We wanted to make a major impact because we recognized how great the need is," says Mackey, adding: "If we are able to get even a percentage of these kids into college or vocational school, then we have achieved a very important goal."

Another positive sign is that more and more companies make enough profit while stepping up to social problems that they can keep at it for the long haul. A case-in-point is Protective Life Insurance of Birmingham, Alabama. Since 1987, it has made loans to 13 shopping centers and business ventures that are either in predominantly African-American communities or are black-owned. One $4.8 million loan turned a group of vacant lots into an 84,000-square-foot shopping center, with a supermarket, drugstore, and the state's first black-

owned McDonald's franchise. Protective Life's senior vice president of investments, Steve Williams III, says the firm has always realized solid returns on investments that other companies shy away from.

Nobody has more experience with the subject than Prudential Insurance. It has taken a three-pronged approach to the maladies of the inner city: it makes social investments, including subsidized and low-interest loans; it provides grants to nonprofit groups through the Prudential Foundation; and it offers in-kind gifts and encourages employee volunteerism. The company's main focus has been to address problems like housing, education, drug abuse, and a debilitated business district.

The social investment program has paid dividends for everyone. Three years ago, Prudential provided $7.2 million in long-term financing to build a supermarket in Newark's central ward. Today, the market provides over 400 jobs. Since opening two years ago, the store has already turned a profit. It also has allowed locals to save as much as 30% on their grocery bills. Just down the street is the cineplex—the first neighborhood theater built in the city since 1967. And over the years, Prudential has put up funding to build dozens of low-cost housing developments and invested in a myriad of smaller businesses—pumping in as much as $15 million a shot. "Both the supermarket and the movie theater are rooted in the belief that a neighborhood must consist of more than just housing. There must be facilities—health centers, public schools, and entertainment—to keep a city going." Goldberg says: "Our challenge is to take the funding the company makes available and apply it in the most successful and effective manner we can."

*Government incentives are often necessary.* Of course, when private and public sectors work together, companies are able to address human needs as well as financial ones. And with the government's assistance, an organization is able to take a greater risk than usual.

But the ties that bind government and industry remain tenuous at best. President Clinton's proposal to create urban enterprise zones—where companies could invest and receive a tax break—has met with a lukewarm reception. Other proposals, many enacted by cities or community redevelopment agencies, have not achieved what they had planned. Some companies that want to help are discouraged by the difficulties of establishing programs, such as the constant stream of red tape. Small wonder that urban blight and ramshackle neighborhoods still abound.

There is no one solution. While small business is the primary generator of jobs in the U.S. economy as a whole, the ability of communities to foster entrepreneurs is going to be a big factor in the health of cities. At the same time, job training goes a long way to building a stable community and a future customer base. "It can be risky, it can be difficult, but the rewards can be enormous." Seafirst's Mackey says, "The fact is, everyone has to do their part."

Indeed, it is in everyone's interest to invest in our cities and people. The point isn't that a company should toss money at anyone in the inner city who needs funding. It's picking spots carefully and making sound investments that count. "Virtually every city and town in the U.S. has small companies and projects that are undercapitalized but worthy of support," points out Stan Karson, the CCPI director. "And much has been learned over the last 20 years about how to fashion long-term investments so they can work in the inner city." Says Forest City's Ratner, "There's no reason why everyone can't profit from rebuilding our cities."

# 49

# Environmental Leadership

## From Compliance to Competitive Advantage

KATHLEEN DECHANT
BARBARA ALTMAN

*Executive Overview: Contemporary environmentalism in leading companies has become an integral part of organizational strategy. Such a proactive, advantage-driven approach involves change at every level. This chapter describes the best practices of firms who have integrated environmentalism into their business planning and operations in ways that translate to bottom-line benefits. The experiences of these firms carry a clear and urgent message—companies that continue to approach environmental problems with Band-Aid solutions and quick fixes will ultimately find themselves at a competitive disadvantage.*

Recently, representatives from corporations such as Johnson & Johnson, the Body Shop, Procter & Gamble, Lever Brothers, Pitney Bowes, IBM, Olin, Colgate Palmolive, Loctite, and United Illuminating participated in a major conference on how to integrate environmental decision making into business with profitable results.[1] These organizations presented the ideas, success stories, problems, and even setbacks involved in their efforts to make environmentalism a part of the overall process of doing business and to link "green" objectives with profit goals. From their remarks, it was apparent that these firms have moved past the "why are you telling us what to do?" attitude of the 1970s when companies' environmental efforts were driven primarily by government regulation and a desire to avoid significant legal and financial liabilities. They are now in leadership positions, working hard at raising their efforts to a strategic level where good environmental management becomes a source of competitive advantage.

The efforts of these businesses epitomize the growing shift in corporate environmental thinking

SOURCE: "Environmental Leadership: From Compliance to Competitive Advantage," by Kathleen Dechant and Barbara Altman, *Academy of Management Executive,* Vol. 8, No. 3, 1994. Reprinted with permission of Academy of Management.

from a mindset in which environmentalism is viewed primarily as compliance with regulations to one that includes it as an overall part of strategic management, affecting decisions on product development, future process technology, and total quality programs.[2] This movement has been characterized as a continuum of adjustment, adaptation, and finally, innovation.[3] Accordingly, the practice of environmental management in these organizations has become an essential part of doing business, not a side issue.

## Forces for Greening

Growing pressure from a variety of sources has made environmental, health, and safety concerns a wide-reaching, long-term corporate issue for many businesses. Let's look at some of the most powerful of these forces.

### Staying Ahead of Regulations

Since 1980, there have been more than twenty major pieces of legislation which have significant implications for business.[4] The 1990 amendments to the Clean Air Act alone are an example of a set of laws which has generated a broad scope of new requirements, including an entirely new permit program, substantially tightened requirements for air pollution emission controls, and drastically increased civil and criminal liability for both individuals and companies found to be noncompliant.[5] The increase in compliance costs, in addition to the expansive liability provisions of the amendments, requires that more corporate managers across the organization become knowledgeable and involved in environmental planning as well as compliance. Such involvement demands a more strategic approach to environmental management as opposed to one characterized by fire fighting and a reliance on Band-Aid solutions.

Pitney Bowes's experience is a good case in point for moving from a piecemeal to a comprehensive approach to stay ahead of changing standards and ensure ongoing compliance. This $3.3 billion manufacturer's story is typical of many companies who initially focus on staying out of

trouble. During its start-up phase, the organization's environmental activities were predicated on the regulations in existence at the time. As a manufacturer, for example, this meant paying attention to the condition of underground storage tanks, air toxin releases, and the existence of asbestos in old buildings. As the number of regulations grew, and environmental management became increasingly more complex, Pitney Bowes found itself with a compliance program that added significantly to its costs. From 1984 to 1989 the per drum cost of hazardous waste disposal escalated fivefold, with compliance costs totaling $16.3 million. Despite its investment and effort, Pitney Bowes had no assurance that it was in full compliance at any one time. As a result, the company has embarked on a more strategic approach, which it calls "Design for Environmental Quality." The goal of this initiative is to design out environmental problems associated with a product line when it is first created. Such an approach involves choosing processes, materials, and operations in manufacturing the products that obviate the need for generating environmentally harmful wastes.

### Stakeholder Activism

Informed and concerned stakeholders such as consumers and employees are alert to environmental performance and do not hesitate to take action against companies which they perceive to be environmentally irresponsible. In his 1992 study, Dick Hare of Bruskin Goldring Research found that the general public considers environmental issues to be public health issues: "Over 80% of the people believe environmental issues affect their longevity." They expect companies to behave responsibly for the overall good of the population. This "ecological judgment" will become "increasingly harsh" as matters affecting health and longevity grow more visible or proliferate, particularly in light of the aging population. Furthermore, companies that undergo some environmental disaster recover very slowly from ensuing negative public reaction. For instance, when public perceptions of the environmental profiles of four oil companies were tested in his study, Hare found that respondents rated Exxon substantially lower than its competitors—Mobil, Texaco, and Amoco—despite the enormous amount of cleanup effort exerted by the company after the *Valdez* incident.[6]

Employees' views on a firm's environmental performance and whether it fits their values profile frequently affect their willingness to work for that firm. A 1991 McKinsey study of 403 senior executives from around the world revealed that 68% of them agreed that "organizations with a poor environmental record will find it increasingly difficult to recruit and retain high caliber staff."[7] This perspective was validated by Mike Joyce, Division Director of Environmental Affairs for Dexter Corporation, who indicated that "college graduates are looking for more than just a paycheck, they are looking for companies with which they can identify morally and philosophically."

In some cases where companies ignore or violate environmental and safety regulations, employees have been known to blow the whistle. Such incidents can tarnish a firm's reputation in addition to subjecting it to huge legal costs and potential fines. Several years ago an auditor who worked at the Hanford Nuclear Reservation of Westinghouse evaluated the company's compliance activity and subsequently urged a plant shutdown. When a senior manager refused to take this action, the employee contacted a *Seattle Times* reporter, then flew to Washington, D.C., and testified against Westinghouse before Congress. As a result, the plutonium processing facility of the plant was closed. The plant now operates as a cleanup rather than a production facility.[8]

## Competitive Pressures

As scientific understanding of industry's impact on the environment increases, organizations are expected to measure and cost out their products and processes and operate in ways that enable them to grow and maintain profitability while minimizing environmental degradation. This is the greatest single difficulty within the challenge of sustainable development.[9] From John Alvord, Manager of Customer Environmental Affairs at Procter & Gamble, we learned that "safety, value, performance, and convenience are consumer needs. The concern for the environment is a new consumer need. This

makes it a basic and critical business issue for us. If we don't build this in, consumers won't like our products and packaging as much as our competitors'."

For Procter & Gamble, this translates into redesigning a product, package, or process so that less material or less packaging is needed to achieve the same (if not better) result. Examples of this are: putting two products in one package or making dual products, using postconsumer recycled material in their packages, or designing some of their packages to be reused. For example, Tide comes with built-in bleach, Bold detergent contains a softener, and Pert is a shampoo and conditioner in one.

Alvord's job and that of others like him is to help management figure out how growth and development can be managed on a basis that is sustainable, both economically and ecologically.

## The Best Practices of Environmental Leadership

What do companies who are successful at managing environmental issues do? While there is no single set of rules that tells management how to be truly environmentally responsible, the companies we heard from engaged in five common practices.

*First: A mission statement and corporate values that promote environmental advocacy.* Environmental leaders inspire a shared vision of the organization as environmentally sustainable, creating or maintaining green values throughout the enterprise. Such values include stewardship in regard to ecology, frugality and sufficiency in regard to resources, fairness and appropriateness in relation to society, and accountability, participation, proactivity, and long-termism in regard to process.[10]

The vision can be developed as a subset of a corporate policy statement like that of Procter & Gamble (see Exhibit 49.1). It can be grounded in values that support a socially responsible approach to conducting business, such as Johnson & Johnson's "Credo," first written in the 1940s by General Robert W. Johnson, son of one of the company's founders. According to J&J's Credo,

**EXHIBIT 49.1** Procter & Gamble's Environmental Quality Policy.

Procter & Gamble is committed to providing products of superior quality and value that best fill the needs of the world's consumers. As part of this, Procter & Gamble continually strives to improve the environmental quality of its products, packaging, and operations around the world. To carry out this commitment, it is Procter & Gamble's policy to

- Ensure our products, packaging, and operations are safe for our employees, consumers, and the environment.

- Reduce, or prevent the environmental impact of our products and packaging in their design, manufacture, distribution, use, and disposal whenever possible.

- Meet or exceed the requirements of all environmental laws and regulations.

- Continually assess our environmental technology and programs, and monitor progress toward environmental goals.

- Provide our consumers, customers, employees, communities, public interest groups, and others with relevant and appropriate factual information about the environmental quality of P&G products, packaging, and operations.

- Ensure every employee understands and is responsible and accountable for incorporating environmental quality considerations in daily business activities.

- Have operating policies, programs, and resources in place to implement our environmental quality policy.

the company's first responsibility is to the people who use its products; second, to the employees; and third, to the community and environment. J&J believes that people look to the environment as an extension of their concern about their own individual health, thus the natural connection between following J&J's Credo and its commitment to neutral environmental impact.

An example of a mission statement with a strong environmental values orientation is that of the Body Shop, a British-based cosmetic chain, begun in 1976, currently with more than 600 stores in 37 countries. The company is driven by values rather than products and sees its mission as an emissary for social change. Within its mission statement is the admonition to "respect the Earth by curbing waste and energy consumption while avoiding materials from threatened species or ecosystems."[11] These values are operationalized through the training of Body Shop managers to promote environmental causes within their specific geographic locations as well as those—such as animal rights and the rights of indigenous peoples—adopted by the entire firm. The Body Shop develops and publishes an annual eco-audit to report on actions taken in support of its mission and values.

*Second: A framework for managing environmental initiatives.* Environmental leaders have well-developed approaches to environmental management which generally center around a program customized to the company's specific business and market and geared to foster change and promote internal cooperation across lines and levels. Effective environmental management consists of elements that span all aspects of an organization's operations with the goal of integrating those operations in a way which brings them in line with the environmental mission statement. The integrating framework will differ from organization to organization based on a firm's size, products, or services, and those change mechanisms appropriate to its culture.

On a smaller scale, we can point to approaches like United Illuminating's Performance Action Teams (PAT). When an accumulation of evidence and data pointed to the need for UI to address the use of chlorinated solvents in its operations, the company established a goal endorsed by top management to eliminate this family of chemicals throughout its operations. A PAT was formed comprised of workers from different geographic locations and functions, including the machine shop, engineering, safety, chemistry, and purchasing, along with a representative from middle management, who met once a month for two hours to grapple with the task. For an entire year the group researched and evaluated nine different alternatives, finally concluding that the technology required to completely replace chlorinated solvents with one universal solvent for UIs varied operations didn't exist. Instead of giving up, the team channeled its energy into finding ways to reduce the use of the problematic solvents to their lowest level possible. Within a year, the chlorinated solvents purchased at United Illuminating dropped from 3,500 gallons to one 55-gallon drum, and has, more recently, been further reduced.

On a larger scale, the effort to integrate environmental management into an organization is more complex and wide-reaching. For example, Johnson & Johnson is a very decentralized organization with more than 170 operating companies scattered across fifty countries. When the firm embarked upon its environmental program, it wanted to set standards that could be followed by every operating company regardless of its product line or location. The mechanism for accomplishing such a task at J&J is known as "The Environmental Responsibility Program." It consists of two initiatives: Environmental Regulatory Affairs, and the Community Environmental Responsibility Program.

Environmental Regulatory Affairs has oversight responsibility on a worldwide basis; it ensures that environmental regulations are carefully followed. It is also responsible for conducting environmental audits using third-party external audit teams. Finally, it serves as a conduit through which environmental policies are channeled. Such policies surface from a variety of sources but ultimately are reviewed by a cross-company council of vice presidents of operations for an assessment of impact on the business. Once approved, the policies make their way to a cross-sector task force (North America/Latin America/Far East, Europe/Africa) for implementation. As a result, the evolution and operationalization of environmental policy at J&J includes all affected and interested parties.

The second initiative, the Community Environmental Responsibility Program, is more operational in nature. It has four phases: emergency preparedness, strategy and planning, product/process development, and public affairs. The first phase has the goal of ensuring emergency readiness at J&J facilities worldwide. Each facility has people trained to respond to a variety of environmental emergencies. The second phase requires that each facility have a strategic plan with a technical component which focuses on managing the operating process from an environmental impact standpoint and a communications component that stresses the value of maintaining an open dialogue with the community in which it resides. For example, the community around an operation knows about the chemicals in use there and what J&J is doing to manage them. The third phase involves product/process development and environmental impact assessment. Consistent with a total quality approach, J&J's goal is to produce products and use processes that are environmentally neutral in their impact on the environment throughout their life cycles. The fourth and final phase looks at emerging legislation and national events and J&J's role in their evolution through contributions and project support.

*Third: Green process product design.* In organizations where TQM is in place, like the J&J example cited earlier, environmental responsibility has become part and parcel of the search for total quality. The concept that defects in production will cost more to fix once a product has been manufactured than if those defects had been prevented in the first place is at the heart of TQM. When this same concept is applied to environmental issues it translates into a "pollution prevention" as opposed to an "end-of-pipe" strategy. That is, it is less costly to prevent pollution from occurring than it is to clean up after an environmental accident or to remove pollutants at the end of the manufacturing process using end-of-pipe technologies. Quality companies strive for zero defects; green-quality companies additionally strive for zero emissions or at least continuous improvement toward that end.

Olin Corporation is an example of a chemical company that has integrated environmental management into its existing total quality process. As Charles Newton, Vice President of Health, Safety, and Toxicology, explains, TQM formed a good basis for an environmental quality initiative because "we have a common quality language across the company . . . people are very comfortable talking about customers, understanding we mean stakeholders; we talk about measures of success and try and get that out front in all our objectives." Adding the environmental quality dimension seemed a natural and simple thing to do.

Initially, the idea was to incorporate environmental quality objectives into a list of quality goals. An experiment was conducted in the Chemical Division in 1988 and two environmental goals were added to the organization's mission. The first was to reduce plant-generated hazardous waste; the second was to reduce SARA 313 releases[12] by 70%

within five years. As time went on, there was a growing realization that these two goals, while an improvement, were not producing the level of environmental quality the company had hoped for. A better integration was necessary.

Olin's "Environmental Quality Plan" was developed in 1990 by a task force whose members included divisional presidents and corporate vice presidents of manufacturing and engineering (environment, health, and toxicology), and science, along with the organization's general counsel. Following this, an intensive benchmarking study was done and a list of environmental quality performance indicators emerged as a result of this study and input from a newly formed environmental council. Categories included SARA 313 Releases, Hazardous Solid Waste, Waste Water Noncompliances, Offsite Waste Disposal Facilities, Remediation Sites, Nonhazardous Solid Waste, and Listed Reportable Emissions. The indicators were integrated into Olin's planning and processes. This year the company announced that its reportable emissions have been reduced by 70% from 1987 through the use of source reduction, recycling, treatment, and other pollution prevention techniques.

As organizations become more proficient at reducing waste, it becomes plainer that the problem may include the product, not just the process. Some products are designed without much regard for their impact on the environment. One way of addressing the issue is through green design that considers the total life cycle of a product, taking into consideration not only the extraction of raw materials used in the production process but also the ways in which products are packaged, transported, and disposed of.

IBM is a good example of one company's effort to account for the environmental aspects of a product's life cycle. In the early 1990s, it became IBM's corporate policy to operate in a way that demonstrated that products would be developed, manufactured, and marketed to be safely used, energy efficient, protective of the environment, and safely disposable. To operationalize this policy, an international task force was formed to review all aspects of IBM activity and produce environmental recommendations relative to each. J. Ray Kirby, Director

of the Engineering Center for Environmentally Conscious Products, stresses that IBM's goal is to "make every new product better than the last product environmentally."

IBM's product development cycle is driven by two objectives: (1) to build into products attributes that would be deemed environmentally conscious; and (2) to know what will happen at the end of every product's life with respect to its impact on the environment. To accomplish these goals, product development is filtered through the following set of environmental attributes:

- *Design for disassembly.* Recyclable materials are selected.

- *Use of hazardous materials.* Efforts are made to reduce or eliminate hazardous materials in the make-up of the product.

- *Reduction of chemical emissions.* Changes are made to reduce emissions.

- *Use of natural energy and resources.* Efforts are made to conserve resources, particularly in manufacture and packaging.

*Fourth: Environmentally-focused stakeholder partnerships.* Many companies recognize that the creation of partnerships with their stakeholders is one of the most expedient and cost-effective ways of solving environmental problems and accomplishing environmental goals. WHYCO Chromium Company is an example of a small business that has creatively addressed a variety of environmental issues by working with its customers and suppliers. A metal finishing company with annual sales of about $15 million, WHYCO "finishes" approximately 100 million pieces weekly. The finishing processes include painting, cleaning, plating, or polishing a variety of nuts, bolts, computer parts, and other hardware.

WHYCO is in a heavily regulated industry. Compliance efforts are time-consuming and costly. The company estimates that 17% of every sales dollar goes toward compliance. Unless small businesses such as WHYCO establish environmental management partnerships with stakeholders, they have few resources left to devote to developing ideas which yield competitive advantage.

One of WHYCO's partnerships is a joint venture with IBM. It produced a machine that performs a specialized chemical cleaning process without air and water discharge. Working with General Motors, WHYCO developed several new, more environmentally friendly multilayer automobile finishes. Once these finishes are fully utilized, cadmium will no longer be used in the exterior fastener systems of GM cars.

Degreasing—what to do with the used oil—is a perennial problem for metal finishers. One solution is to use an aqueous process and wash the parts. While this option eliminates air pollution, it still raises the question of how to dispose of the cleaners and rinsers involved in the process. Upon investigation, WHYCO found that some customers sent more oil than necessary along with their parts to prevent them from rusting while they sat in warehouses prior to shipping. By working with these clients, WHYCO was able to develop a just-in-time delivery system, reducing the amount of oil needed.

Establishing partnerships with the government is another strategy for increasing competitive advantage. The Environmental Protection Agency now engages organizations in several voluntary corporate programs in an effort to move beyond the traditional regulatory "command and control" relationship. One example is the "Green Lights" program, which offers technical assistance to corporations to help them convert existing lighting systems to energy efficient ones. Companies, like the Dexter Corporation, agree to survey and install energy-efficient lighting in 90% of their domestic facilities within a five-year period. Investment in known energy-efficient lighting systems produces rapid return on investment, reduction in utility bills, and significant pollution reduction. Since the program's inception in 1991, almost 1,000 participants have joined. As a result of the lighting upgrades already completed, pollution prevented stands at 174 millions pounds of carbon dioxide, 14 million pounds of sulfur dioxide, and 605,000 pounds of nitrous oxide. Simultaneously, electricity usage has been reduced by 126 million kilowatts annually, with $11.9 million in avoided electricity costs.[13]

In another program, the EPA has signed partnership agreements with industry-leading computer manufacturers who make 60% of the desktop computers and 90% of the laser printers sold in the United States. Under this agreement, the companies will produce equipment that will automatically power down when it is not in use to save energy. Consumers will easily recognize such energy-efficient systems because they will be identified by the EPA Energy Star™ logo. The U.S. government, the largest buyer of computer equipment in the world, has taken the lead by purchasing these systems. The EPA maintains that Energy Star™ computers could save enough electricity to power Vermont, New Hampshire, and Maine in a year in addition to cutting electricity bills by $2 billion and reducing carbon dioxide pollution in an amount equivalent to emissions from five million automobiles. According to Jim Davis, developer of IBM's energy-efficient PC, IBM is firmly committed to Energy Star™. Its "desktop prototype PC exemplifies what can be accomplished by this kind of government-industry partnership."[14]

*Fifth: Internal and external education initiatives.* Corporations have begun to take on the responsibility of environmental education with the intent of engaging employees in environmental management initiatives as well as informing the public about the company's efforts and accomplishments. Internally, education is a critical lever which can bring about a more environmentally conscious corporate culture. A recent study found that the most significant mechanism for promoting environmental awareness is the ease of access to environmental information and the use of the company's employee suggestion processes.[15] Environmental education also helps employees engage in the kind of environmental behavior to which the company aspires. Organizations are finding that once employees have been educated in environmental sensitivity, these "champions" become the best source of ideas for further environmental improvements. Much has been written about programs like Dow Chemicals' WRAP (Waste Reduction Always Pays), which was instituted in 1986. Since its inception, it has cut millions of pounds of hazardous and solid waste and emissions, resulting in annual cost savings of $10.5 million—all by means of projects suggested by employees.[16]

Externally, companies have become involved in community and consumer education to raise levels of awareness about environmental issues and to inform stakeholders about corporate activities in this arena. Positive benefits of environmental education include increased sales and improved public relations.

The Body Shop is an example of a company that has chosen as a part of its corporate strategy to serve as an external environmental educator. Employees are provided with information on environmental causes of interest to the company as well as encouraged to investigate local issues and become actively involved. Stores are used as forums for discussion and debate, distributing literature on environmental issues to their customers. Through membership in a consortium called "Act Now: Business for a Change," the Body Shop, along with companies like Ben and Jerry's, Patagonia, and Tom's of Maine, aims to use its store as a distribution center for literature telling people how to attract the attention of congressional representatives in a campaign to shift the allocation of resources from military to environmental and social programs.[17]

The issue of eco-labeling illustrates another strategy for consumer education. Procter & Gamble takes an active interest in eco-labeling, in part because of its educational impact. As explained by John Alvord, there are three approaches to eco-labeling. The first is the establishment of guidelines and standards, where marketers agree to use the same kind of labeling to explain product benefits. A label that says "this package is recyclable where recycling exists: help support recycling in your community" prompts consumers to become more aware of their local situation. Specifically, it prompts them to find out if their community has a recycling program and the type of packaging accepted.[18] A second approach to eco-labeling is the certification program, where an independent body determines whether claims are truthful, such as "25% recycled paper." A third approach is an eco-labeling program in which an independent body determines whether products are environmentally friendly; those that are receive a designated label. In Alvord's view the first of these three approaches holds the most educational value and the most potential for success because it requires consumer involvement.

## The Difficult Road to Environmental Leadership

Becoming a company which uses environmental stewardship as a competitive advantage is not an easily attainable achievement; there are countless hurdles to confront along the way, particularly in two major areas—managing change and managing human resources.

### Managing Change

In many organizations, the prevailing view of the relationship between profitability and environmental protection is that they are polar opposites. Wise governance requires making appropriate trade-offs, keeping these opposites in the proper balance. The concept of sustainable development, however, calls for moving business decisions simultaneously toward a healthy environment and a healthy economy. Such a mindset requires a fundamental rethinking of traditional notions of disposability, risk, responsibility, and the right to pollute beginning at the top of the organization and moving right through it. When companies undertake greening as a rational, strategic choice, senior management must be committed to proactive environmental goals, recognizing that short-term costs will probably be outweighed by long-term benefits. Joseph Shimsky, Director of Safety and Environmental Affairs at Pitney Bowes, reflects on the struggle that takes place in developing such a mindset:

One of the most challenging . . . but overall very rewarding aspects of my job has been educating management as to the need to integrate environmental decision making into the long-term strategic business planning process of the company. Given the current business climate it is easy to see why executive management in many U.S. companies often look to short-term results for their shareholders or why programs must have payback periods of one year or less in order to be approved. The goal of eliminating all environmental liability in a given business requires investments over the long haul and if quality results are to be realized, money has to be there to back it up. There is a little Chinese proverb that says "if you want to plan for a year, plant rice, if you want to plan for ten years, plant trees, but if you want to plan for one hundred years, educate your children."

Taking a long-term and proactive stance is further complicated by the uncertainty of decision making in this arena; that is, the technology is often unavailable, the future of legislation is unknown, and consumer preferences can shift. In an area where risk management is the watchword, it takes leaders who are risk takers to adopt a progressive stance.

In many organizations, it is easier to go along with serendipitous events or commit to contained projects that promise immediate payback. One way to illustrate the range of perspectives with respect to pollution prevention is to consider an apple tree. On the ground are those projects or "apples" which are "stumbled upon." Changes are made for reasons other than environmental ones, yet a by-product turns out to be something environmentally beneficial, like reduced air emissions. The apples on the low-hanging branches of the tree are "quick payback" projects whose strong benefits make change easy to document. Higher up the tree are the "breakeven projects" where resistance begins to take shape. At the top of the tree are the apples which are hardest to reach, the "indirect benefits" projects that companies are still struggling to gain support for and that face the most resistance. Only companies with a long-term view can "harvest the fruit" at the top of the tree.[19]

One approach to overcoming short-term cost concerns and organizational resistance is to show the economic benefits of proposed environmental modifications. For example, as part of Pitney Bowes's program, an internal task force worked with the public accounting firm of Ernst & Young to design a method to assess waste minimization

programs. Analysis of waste minimization projects is done through a seven-stage process.

The first stage of the project assessment process is strategy and organization. In this stage a task force of involved individuals such as plant superintendents and engineers is selected, and program goals are set. In the second stage a general project assessment is conducted; this includes data collection, facility inspections, and determination of whether the project commands further review. Those projects which go forward undergo a technical feasibility analysis in the third stage of the process. This analysis is conducted by a team of engineers and outside consultants, on an as-needed basis.

Those waste minimization projects that are technically feasible proceed to the fourth stage, a financial feasibility test. Assessment is conducted of the project's net present value, and indirect cost benefits. Project impacts which may be difficult to quantify, like community relations and future legislative mandates, are included in indirect cost benefits. This part of the process is the most challenging, and potentially most important, due to the unknowns and risk decisions mentioned in the previous section. Indirect benefits are forwarded to decision makers in a subjective listing, along with the quantitative analysis.

The task force's project assessment goes on to midmanagement and environmental staff for review and dialogue, and then is forwarded to upper management for approval in the fifth stage of the process. The last two stages in the Pitney Bowes Waste Minimization Project Assessment Model include implementation of approved projects, and last, reevaluation of completed projects to feed back information into future project assessments. A similar project analysis process is used annually by plant superintendents to make budget recommendations to the Vice President for Manufacturing.

Other companies overcome resistance through the proliferation of small wins. For example, Dexter Corporation achieved a small win when it successfully eliminated a toxic wet strength agent from its teabag (see Exhibit 49.2). Others have been mentioned throughout this chapter such as United Illuminating's reduction of chlorinated sol-

**EXHIBIT 49.2**  We like our tea just the way it is!!

At Dexter Corporation, one of their most popular products was a profitable grade of paper used in teabags. A wet strength agent was used to prevent the tea bag from disintegrating in hot water. Unfortunately the materials used to produce the agent accounted for 98% of Dexter's annual hazardous wastes. The product, however, had a very strong market position; its customers liked it and didn't want to change. Within the company, there was some reluctance to tamper with a popular product line. Nonetheless, a task force of employees representing the environmental, legal, research and development, and marketing departments was formed to confront the task of eliminating the agent. R&D took the role of developing an alternative to the environmentally unfriendly wet strength agent. Marketing took the role of communicating the company's intention to exit the product and convincing customers to be partners in the change. Dexter was successful in exiting the product. Customers are pleased with the substitute. Dexter increased market share and virtually eliminated hazardous wastes in the process.

vents and WHYCO's reduction of oil use. When success stories like these are communicated throughout an organization, resistance often begins to fade, allowing environmental change to take root and spread.

**Managing Human Resources**

There are three human resources issues which affect corporate environmentalism. The first is the need for a critical mass of people throughout the organization who share a common vision and are empowered to act on it. Only then are breakthroughs possible. Environmental staff must understand the business implications of environmental decision making. Likewise, operating managers need to know the environmental ramifications of their decisions.

High-level coordinating committees, such as those at IBM and Johnson & Johnson, facilitate the integration of environmental policy into the organization. The use of teams to confront environmental issues is one way used extensively to promote cross-training and participation in finding responses to environmental challenges.

The second human resource issue is the need to ensure timely and adequate training on environ-

mental issues for all employees, particularly new hires. Training of new hires can avoid costly environmental mistakes. For example, employees who are well-versed in the proper operation and maintenance of equipment can help to reduce leakage and overuse of materials. Small improvements in housekeeping practices by informed employees can reduce pollution by 25% to 33%.[20]

Training on an ongoing basis helps employees keep up to date on new regulations and community concerns. Educated employees can be the source of innovative ideas in pollution prevention technology and processes. Environmental affairs departments play a major role in developing environmental awareness across the organization. The use of various in-house media and networked information systems is also a helpful means of information sharing.

What gets measured gets done, and what gets rewarded gets done most often. The last human resource issue is the need to make managers accountable for environmental performance. This can be done by linking merit systems to targets for health, safety, and environment.

As environmental issues have become predominant, environmental staffs have taken on increasing responsibility and focus in the corporate structure. In some companies, this generally welcome development has produced an unanticipated downside. People have come to view environmental issues as strictly the job of the environmental department and not an inherent part of everyone's job. To combat this, companies such as the Dow Chemical Company peg the salaries and bonuses of their plant managers to, among other things, how well they meet environmental goals.[21] The institutionalization of environmental accountability systems can help all employees recognize that environmental performance is a part of their ongoing responsibilities even though a strong environmental staff is present.

*Toward Competitive Advantage*

Among companies in the developed world, much of the rationale for improving environmental performance is a defensive one, avoiding large fines or worse. We have made the case that sound environmental practices can be profitable. Siting new facilities will be easier when the local community perceives the firm to be one with a "clean" reputation. A reduction in toxic emissions reduces the risk of costly accidents and lowers the bill on insurance premiums. Moreover, forward-thinking companies who can anticipate the direction in which regulations are moving are more likely to capture opportunities to introduce environmental improvements ahead of their competitors. They can win time to introduce new products and processes, explore new markets, and reengineer plants. Such time advantages often cost less than if things are rushed to meet an externally imposed deadline. Finally, companies which produce products and processes that result in a cleaner environment often set the benchmark for future regulations by the government. If one company can do it, why not everyone? The standard-setting companies enjoy the benefit of a protected market which is defined by environmental standards it can meet but others cannot.

Although the path to pursuing environmentalism as a competitive advantage is a rocky one requiring time, effort, and money, the rewards can and do extend beyond the short-run negative impact on the bottom line. Ultimately, forward-thinking environmental management will set a course for higher overall business performance.

## Notes

1. Examples for this article were taken from conference audio tape recordings of "Integrating Environmental Decision-Making Into Your Business Profitably" sponsored by the University of Connecticut School of Business Administration and held at the Radisson Conference Center in Cromwell, Connecticut, September 24, 1992. Companies making presentations included IBM, Johnson & Johnson, WHYCO Chromium, the Body Shop, Procter & Gamble Company, United Illuminating, Olin Corporation, Colgate-Palmolive Company, Lever Brothers Company, Loctite Corporation, Pitney Bowes, Ernst & Young, and Dexter Corporation.

2. For further reading linking environmental management with total quality see: Frances Cairncross, *Costing the Earth* (Boston, MA: Harvard Business School Press, 1992); *Total Quality Environmental Management—The Primer* (Washington, DC: Global Environmental Management Initiative

[GEMI], 1992); and President's Commission on Environmental Quality, *Total Quality Management: A Framework for Pollution Prevention* (Washington, DC: Executive Office of the President, 1993).

3. For further reading on the developmental phases companies progress through in achieving environmental change, see: James E. Post and Barbara W. Altman, "Models of Corporate Greening: How Corporate Social Policy and Organizational Learning Inform Leading-Edge Environmental Management," in *Research in Corporate Social Performance and Policy,* 13 (Greenwich, CT: JAI Press, 1992), 3-30; Christopher B. Hunt and Ellen R. Auster, "Proactive Environmental Management: Avoiding the Toxic Trap," *Sloan Management Review,* Winter 1990, 7-18; and Thomas N. Gladwin, *Building the Sustainable Corporation: Creating Environmental Sustainability and Corporate Advantage,* document commissioned for the National Wildlife Federation Corporate Conservation Council, "Synergy '92" Conference, January 1992.

4. Kirkpatrick Sale, *The Green Revolution* (New York, NY: Hill and Wang, 1993). This book contains a chronological arrangement of major environmental laws and describes the context which served as an impetus for them.

5. P. G. Wallach, K. R. Meade, J. L. Hanisch, G. E. Hoffnagle, and Paula Schenck, *The Clean Air Act Amendments: Strategies for the 1990s,* a joint publication of Hale and Dorr and TRC Environmental Consultants (Hartford, CT, 1991).

6. For a detailed description of the making and aftermath of the oil spill in Prudhoe Bay, Alaska, by the Exxon *Valdez,* see Tom Horton, "Paradise Lost," *The Rolling Stone Environmental Reader* (Washington, DC: Island Press, 1992), 117-188.

7. Kurt Fischer and Johan Schot, eds., *Environmental Strategies for Industry* (Washington, DC: Island Press, 1993).

8. Will Nixon, "A Breakfast Among Peers: Environmental Whistleblowers Have Some Stories to Tell," *E Magazine,* 4, 5, September/October 1993, 14-19.

9. The Business Council for Sustainable Development, a consortium of fifty international business leaders, defines sustainable development as a redefinition "of the rules of the economic game in order to move from a situation of wasteful consumption and pollution to one of conservation, and from one of privilege and protectionism to one of fair and equitable changes open to all." The underlying rationale for sustainable development is the belief on the part of many experts that today's industrial societies consume too many virgin resources and degrade the environment in too many ways. The continuation of the unchecked use of resources will cause a downward spiral of social and economic disintegration. For businesses, the implication is that environmental common sense will stimulate growth and competitiveness while the lack of environmental concern will become a brake on a firm's progress. A comprehensive discussion of sustainable development can be found in Stephan Schmidheiny, *Changing Course: A Global Business Perspective on Development and the Environment* (Cambridge, MA: MIT Press, 1992). See also: Rogene Buchholz, *Principles of Environmental Management: The Greening of Business* (Englewood Cliffs, NJ: Prentice Hall, 1993).

10. Thomas A. Gladwin, "The Meaning of Greening: A Plea for Organizational Theory," in Fischer and Schot, eds., *Environmental Strategies for Industry* (Washington, DC: Island Press, 1993), 37-61.

11. Taken from an interview with Anita Roddick, founder of the Body Shop, "Retailing the Higher Ground," by David J. Fishman in *E Magazine,* II, 6, November/December 1991, 13-18.

12. SARA stands for the federal Superfund Amendments and Reauthorization Act of the federal Comprehensive Environmental Response, Compensation and Liability Act (Superfund). Under Title III of the SARA, facilities that manufacture, produce, process, or use any of the 313 designated chemicals in greater than specified amounts must report routine releases of those chemicals. The EPA reports the routine releases of these chemicals to the public.

13. U.S. Environmental Protection Agency, "Green Lights Update" (Washington, DC: EPA, July 1993). Further information can be obtained by calling 202-775-6650.

14. Information on Energy Star™ Fact Sheet, Memorandum for Understanding, List of Energy Star™ Partner Corporations can be obtained from Brian J. Johnson, U.S. Environmental Protection Agency, 501 3rd Street, NW, Washington, DC 20001.

15. Ulrich Steger, "The Greening of the Board Room: How German Companies Are Dealing With Environmental Issues," in Fischer and Schot, eds., *Environmental Strategies for Industry* (Washington, DC: Island Press, 1993), 147-167.

16. *Business: Championing the Global Environment,* Conference Board Report Number 995 (New York, NY: The Conference Board, 1992).

17. SARA, loc. cit.

18. Lever Brothers' research shows that 83% of consumers want to be informed. As a result, the company has initiated a plastics labeling program that educates and encourages consumer action. A typical label reads: *Please help! We are now using technology that can include recycled plastic bottles at levels between 25% and 35%. But to do so consistently, we need more recycled plastic. So please encourage recycling in your community.*

19. From presentation by Ernst & Young, given at "Integrating Environmental Decision Making Into Your Business Profitably" conference, September 24, 1992.

20. See note 9, loc. cit.

21. Fay Rice, "Who Scores Best on the Environment?" *Fortune,* July 26, 1993, 114-118.

# 50

# The Seven (Almost) Deadly Sins of High-Minded Entrepreneurs

ANNE P. MURPHY

In 1978, when two Vermont hippies in an unheated gas station set out to bring butterfat to the people, no one would have come to them for business advice. For Heath Bar Crunch, undoubtedly, but for a tutorial on how to build a company with a social conscience? Let's face it, we would have stuck with the cones.

More than 15 years later Ben & Jerry's, the once-funky business Ben Cohen and Jerry Green-field built into a $130-million publicly traded company, is decidedly mainstream, winning enough devotees to constitute an entrepreneurial movement of its own. Socially responsible superfounders like the two real guys in Vermont, or Anita and Gordon Roddick of the Body Shop, or Yvon Chouinard of Patagonia, or Paul Hawken of Smith & Hawken have become irresistible apologists for the notion that you can do the right thing—care for employees, suppliers, customers, and indeed, the planet—and still turn a profit to please the most capitalist of pigs.

Throughout the 1980s, prosperity and a penchant for publicity made those iconoclastic founders heroes. And like all good role models, they made it look easy. (Would we admire them if they didn't?) After a decade or two, though, the wonder years are over. Most of those founders have weathered at least one recession, an onslaught of competition, and a disappointing quarter or four. The good have grown up or grown old or grown weary. For those who would model their businesses after them, there are lessons to be drawn from their corporate histories as well as their creeds. The challenge lies not only in understanding the benefits of righteous business practice—its power as a marketing tool has been amply demonstrated—but also in anticipating its cost.

Doing the right thing can be risky business.

### The World Will Never Be the Same (Of Course, It Won't Be Entirely Different, Either)

A company, no matter how laudable its intentions, will never be good enough. The more ambitious its social agenda, the more elusive success will be. The Body Shop, which considers "changing the world" its charter, is a case in point. Its sales were $650 million last year, and it operates 1,050 shops in 45 countries. The company has opposed animal testing, embraced fair trading practices with indigenous groups, and encouraged liberal activism among its employees and franchisees. Its founders, Anita and Gordon Roddick, have become rock stars in the world of alternative business. But despite almost messianic ambitions, the Roddicks' business has yet to transform the face of the earth. "This hasn't changed the way the rain forest is being destroyed or created a vibrant economy in the Indian subcontinent," notes the Body Shop's corporate communications manager, Gavin Grant.

Indeed, the company's best efforts have taught the founders how intractable and time-consuming global disorders such as deforestation and third-world poverty can be. The politics of saving the rain forest, or trading with its native inhabitants, is itself a jungle. While leftists protest that the company does too little, those on the right complain that it proselytizes too much. "We've had to learn to manage our own expectations for success as well as everyone else's," says Gordon Roddick. Not that the Roddicks and their followers give up. They simply spend inordinate amounts of time trying not to.

Because a savior's work is never done, the Body Shop and other businesses like it must live with the same admirable goals year after year and settle for only incremental success. Instead of declaring the elimination of third-world poverty a corporate goal, "we now say that we hope to make a difference in the lives of a few hundred people at a time,"

says Roddick. "It's possible to do that. In fact, we have done that."

For companies that limit their aspirations to the banalities of financial performance, success—as they define it—is just plain easier to recognize (thanks to a crude device called a profit-and-loss statement). When you pledge your business to effecting profound social change, you can either (a) fail, or (b) not fail entirely. But you never flat-out succeed. Goal setting becomes a process of patching up the promises and trying again next year.

### Extra! Extra! Read All About Us. . . .

This just in: the press creates icons and then destroys them. These companies, which have shown no reluctance to crow about their rectitude, have benefited enormously from media exposure. "You have to declare your vision publicly if you want others to support it," says Roddick. Inevitably, however, the relationship with the fourth estate becomes complicated and occasionally perilous.

"Once you raise the bar and urge business as a whole to raise its standards, you paint a bull's-eye on your back," says Craig Cox, editor of *Business Ethics*. "The press will watch closely for signs of hypocrisy."

Even if the companies didn't invite the adulation, they have invited scrutiny. "You create a legend or a myth around the business," says Roddick. "But the press ultimately grows bored with you and starts looking around for deficiencies." Not long after a company's initial apotheosis, suspicions begin to arise that its convictions are simply marketing gimmicks, that the talk about SR is simply PR. The line between principles and image making can blur. The moment companies fall short of their own high ideals (and inevitably they do), a chorus of cynics stands ready to cry hypocrite. The Body Shop, for instance, has been publicly flogged for inadvertently violating its own animal-testing ban. It has also been charged in the press with fraud for misleading customers about its testing practices. Though the company was vindicated by the courts in the libel case it litigated last year, Roddick recommends a stoic resolve: "You have to expect you'll be held up for rigorous examination. This is not for the chickenhearted."

### We're Just One Big Happy Commune

Employees flock to these PC payrolls as pilgrims, seeking empowerment and profound happiness along with their paychecks.

"Employee expectations are often so high, they're impossible to manage," says editor Cox. "If you come to work for a socially responsible company, you expect to have more flexibility, more informal relations with supervisors, the autonomy to fashion the job the way you choose," he points out. "It can be quite a shock to find out that the visionary founder is not an attentive manager or that there's still a hierarchy and still some lousy grunt work that somebody is going to tell you to get done."

There is a secret premium exacted from employees for the privilege of living their values 80 hours a week: "Many of these companies pay less, expect longer hours, and offer harder working conditions," says Meredith Maran, a former editorial director at Smith & Hawken and now a consultant to several socially responsible companies. Outmoded equipment and relatively high rates of worker injury plagued Ben & Jerry's for years, for example.

At Smith & Hawken and Patagonia, two companies at which employees were laid off after financial crunches in the early 1990s, the disappointment was nearly terminal. "People were so stunned by how far short the company fell of their expectations," says Maran, "they started to feel afraid, powerless, and ultimately unwilling to fight for their point of view when it came to important business decisions. When fear and then resentment set in, productivity was killed by that."

### The Oath of Office:
### Now Lean to the Left and
### Repeat After Me

It is only natural that founders surround themselves with people sympathetic to their values. Who doesn't want employees who will culturally fit an organization? The problem arises when the requisites for a proper "fit" become too restrictive. Does running a politically progressive company mean you won't hire Republicans? Are meat eaters or gun owners or pro-lifers among those who need not apply? Is it possible that a conservative chief financial officer or a libertarian sales manager might be an asset and not just an anomaly in your organization? The temptation to conduct political litmus tests, even tacitly, is real. And the danger of alienating longtime customers or employees should not be dismissed. After the Body Shop issued a statement against the Gulf War, it was surprised to find fierce opposition in its own camp: no one had consulted employees with loved ones serving in Desert Storm.

### Who's Minding the Store?
### (Oh, That)

The genius in these businesses can almost always be located in their marketing or design. A visionary leader such as Chouinard or Hawken or Roddick harbors a passion for the product and for the salvific message packaged along with it. But an ardor for cash flow? Or inventory control? Or even management? The stuff of which businesses are made does not always fire the soul. A passion to do the right thing may not translate into a passion for doing things right.

Witness Patagonia, which suffered a cash crisis that eliminated as much as a third of its workforce in 1991. According to former executives, the company's infatuation with its social mission made it inattentive to, even disdainful of, the mechanics of running a business. In a year in which sales grew at a 30% rate, overhead rose twice as fast. Meanwhile, the company's finance function remained literally exiled in an outlying building. Patagonia has since reorganized and sworn off growth.

"One of the problems at Smith & Hawken," says Maran, "was that you had a bunch of people walking around with this nonprofit mentality, acting like they were working for Greenpeace instead of a direct-mail business." Smith & Hawken was sold to the CML Group last year.

## Since When Do
## Nice Guys Finish First?

The success of these companies ensures competition. Some companies, so seduced by doing good, lack the survival instincts to do well in a crowded market. Others stay and manage to fight. Yet if they respond too forcefully, they're pilloried as bullies. Ben & Jerry's withstood a barrage of criticism for aggressively shutting its competitors out of distribution (in much the same manner the Pillsbury Doughboy had earlier tried to squelch Ben & Jerry's). While other companies are free to be ruthless competitors, two ballyhooed nice guys don't have the same license.

## The Costs:
## What You Don't Count Won't Hurt You?

Virtue doesn't come cheap. It may pay off in a bonanza of free publicity or in undying customer as well as employee loyalty, but there's no avoiding hefty up-front costs and plenty of variable costs thereafter. Pollution-control equipment or day care subsidies might yield dividends in the end. But such "investments" will remain expenses for a long time first. And even when returns are realized, the costs do not necessarily abate. The Body Shop boasts an exotic collection of cost centers, including an Environmental Department, a Fair Trade Department, and an Against Animal Testing Department. The bill paid by the Body Shop, for example, to screen suppliers and enforce its animal-testing ban runs more than $100,000 a year. It is, admittedly, a small fraction of the company's revenues. But as the company grows and its network of suppliers expands around the globe, the costs will only rise. Profit margins may not.

You may succeed as a business and fail as a force for social change. But you cannot succeed as a reform movement while failing as a business.

Any business, even the most altruistic, cannot be merely a means to a social end. There must be something in the process—either making money or building an organization or producing a product—that sustains you. No matter how salutary your aim, you won't be excused from the ordinary chores of hiring and firing. You'll still have to develop a product, manufacture it, ship it, distribute it, and get paid for it. You'd better have some fun on the way to a better world.

# 51

# *The Age of Social Transformation*

PETER F. DRUCKER

A survey of the epoch that began early in this century, and an analysis of its latest manifestations: an economic order in which knowledge, not labor or raw material or capital, is the key resource; a social order in which inequality based on knowledge is a major challenge; and a polity in which government cannot be looked to for solving social and economic problems.

No century in recorded history has experienced so many social transformations and such radical ones as the twentieth century. They, I submit, may turn out to be the most significant events of this, our century, and its lasting legacy. In the developed free-market countries—which contain less than a fifth of the earth's population but are a model for the rest—work and work force, society and polity, are all, in the last decade of this century, *qualitatively* and *quantitatively* different not only from what they were in the first years of this century but also from what has existed at any other time in history: in their configurations, in their processes, in their problems, and in their structures.

Far smaller and far slower social changes in earlier periods triggered civil wars, rebellions, and violent intellectual and spiritual crises. The extreme social transformations of this century have caused hardly any stir. They have proceeded with a minimum of friction, with a minimum of upheavals, and, indeed, with a minimum of attention from scholars, politicians, the press, and the public. To be sure, this century of ours may well have been the cruelest and most violent in history, with its

SOURCE: Reprinted by permission of the author. First published in *The Atlantic Monthly*. Copyright 1994 Peter F. Drucker.

world and civil wars, its mass tortures, ethnic cleansings, genocides, and holocausts. But all these killings, all these horrors inflicted on the human race by this century's murderous "charismatics," hindsight clearly shows, were just that: senseless killings, senseless hours, "sound and fury signifying nothing." Hitler, Stalin, and Mao, the three evil geniuses of this century, destroyed. They created nothing.

Indeed, if this century proves one thing, it is the futility of politics. Even the most dogmatic believer in historical determinism would have a hard time explaining the social transformations of this century as caused by the headline-making political events, or the headline-making political events as caused by the transformations. But it is the social transformations, like ocean currents deep below the hurricane-tormented surface of the sea, that have had the lasting, indeed the permanent, effect. They, rather than all the violence of the political surface, have transformed not only the society but also the economy, the community, and the polity we live in. The age of social transformation will not come to an end with the year 2000—it will not even have peaked by then.

## The Social Structure Transformed

Before the First World War, farmers composed the largest single group in every country. They no longer made up the population everywhere, as they had from the dawn of history to the end of the Napoleonic Wars, a hundred years earlier. But farmers still made up a near-majority in every developed country except England and Belgium—in Germany, France, Japan, the United States—and, of course, in all underdeveloped countries, too. On the eve of the First World War it was considered a self-evident axiom that developed countries—the United States and Canada being the only exceptions—would increasingly have to rely on food imports from nonindustrial, nondeveloped areas.

Today only Japan among major developed free-market countries is a heavy importer of food. (It is one unnecessarily, for its weakness as a food producer is largely the result of an obsolete rice-sub-sidy policy that prevents the country from developing a modern, productive agriculture.) And in all developed free-market countries, including Japan, farmers today are at most five percent of the population and work force—that is, one tenth of the proportion of eighty years ago. Actually, *productive* farmers make up less than half of the total farm population, or no more than two percent of the work force. And these agricultural producers are not "farmers" in most senses of the word; they are "agribusiness," which is arguably the most capital-intensive, most technology-intensive, and most information-intensive industry around. Traditional farmers are close to extinction even in Japan. And those that remain have become a protected species kept alive only by enormous subsidies.

The second-largest group in the population and work force of every developed country around 1900 was composed of live-in servants. They were considered as much a law of nature as farmers were. Census categories of the time defined a "lower middle class" household as one that employed fewer than three servants, and as a percentage of the work force domestics grew steadily up to the First World War. Eighty years later live-in domestic servants scarcely exist in developed countries. Few people born since the Second World War—that is, few people under fifty—have even seen any except on the stage or in old movies.

In the developed society of 2000 farmers are little but objects of nostalgia and domestic servants are not even that.

Yet these enormous transformations in all developed free-market countries were accomplished without civil war and, in fact, in almost total silence. Only now that their farm population has shrunk to near zero do the totally urban French loudly assert that theirs should be a "rural country" with a "rural civilization."

## The Rise and Fall of the Blue-Collar Worker

One reason why the transformations caused so little stir (indeed, the main reason) was that by 1900 a new class, the blue-collar worker in manufacturing industry—Marx's "proletarian"—had become socially dominant. Farmers were loudly adjured to "raise less corn and more hell," but they paid little attention. Domestic servants were clearly the most exploited class around. But when people before the First World War talked or wrote about the "social question," they meant blue-collar industrial workers. Blue-collar industrial workers were still a fairly small minority of the population and work force—right up to 1914 they made up an eighth or a sixth of the total at most—and were still vastly outnumbered by the traditional lower classes of farmers and domestic servants. But early-twentieth-century society was obsessed with blue-collar workers, fixated on them, bewitched by them.

Farmers and domestic servants were everywhere. But as classes, they were invisible. Domestic servants lived and worked inside individual homes or on individual farms in small and isolated groups of two or three. Farmers, too, were dispersed. More important, these traditional lower classes were not organized. Indeed, they could not be organized. Slaves employed in mining or in producing goods had revolted frequently in the ancient world—though always unsuccessfully. But there is no mention in any book I ever read of a single demonstration or a single protest march by domestic servants in any place, at any time. There have been peasant revolts galore. But except for two Chinese revolts in the nineteenth century—the Taiping Rebellion, in midcentury, and the Boxer Rebellion, at the century's end, both of which lasted for years and came close to overturning the regime—all peasant rebellions in history have fizzled out after a few bloody weeks. Peasants, history shows, are very hard to organize and do not stay organized—which is why they earned Marx's contempt.

The new class, industrial workers, was extremely visible. This is what made these workers a "class." They lived perforce in dense population clusters and in cities—in St. Denis, outside Paris; in Berlin's Wedding and Vienna's Ottakring; in the textile towns of Lancashire; in the steel towns of America's Monongahela Valley; and in Japan's Kobe. And they soon proved eminently organizable, with the first strikes occurring almost as soon as there were factory workers. Charles Dickens's harrowing tale of murderous labor conflict, *Hard Times,* was published in 1854, only six years after Marx and Engels wrote *The Communist Manifesto.*

By 1900 it had become quite clear that industrial workers would not become the majority, as Marx had predicted only a few decades earlier. They therefore would not overwhelm the capitalists by their sheer numbers. Yet the most influential radical writer of the period before the First World War, the French ex-Marxist and revolutionary syndicalist Georges Sorel, found widespread acceptance for his 1906 thesis that the proletarians would overturn the existing order and take power by their organization and in and through the violence of the general strike. It was not only Lenin who made Sorel's thesis the foundation of his revision of Marxism and built around it his strategy in 1917 and 1918. Both Mussolini and Hitler—and Mao, ten years later—built their strategies on Sorel's thesis. Mao's "power grows out of the barrel of a gun" is almost a direct quote from Sorel. The industrial worker became the "social question" of 1900 because he was the first lower class in history that could be organized and could stay organized.

No class in history has ever risen faster than the blue-collar worker. And no class in history has ever fallen faster.

In 1883, the year of Marx's death, "proletarians" were still a minority not just of the population but also of industrial workers. The majority in industry were then skilled workers, employed in small craft shops, each containing twenty or thirty workers at most. Of the anti-heroes of the nineteenth-century's best "proletarian" novel, *The Princess Casamassima,* by Henry James—published in 1886 (and surely only Henry James could have given such a title to a story of working-class terrorists!)—one is a highly skilled bookbinder, the other an equally skilled pharmacist. By 1900 "industrial worker" had become synonymous with "machine operator" and implied employment in a factory along with hundreds if not thousands of people. These factory workers were indeed Marx's proletarians—without social position, without political power, without economic or purchasing power.

The workers of 1900—and even of 1913—received no pensions, no paid vacation, no overtime pay, no extra pay for Sunday or night work, no health or old-age insurance (except in Germany), no unemployment compensation (except, after 1911, in Britain); they had no job security whatever. Fifty years later, in the 1950s, industrial workers had become the largest single group in every developed country, and unionized industrial workers in mass-production industry (which was then dominant everywhere) had attained upper-middle-class income levels. They had extensive job security, pensions, long paid vacations, and comprehensive unemployment insurance or "lifetime employment." Above all, they had achieved political power. In Britain the labor unions were considered to be the "real government," with greater power than the prime minister and Parliament, and much the same was true elsewhere. In the United States, too—as in Germany, France, and Italy—the labor unions had emerged as the country's most powerful and best organized *political* force. And in Japan they had come close, in the Toyota and Nissan strikes of the late forties and early fifties, to overturning the system and taking power themselves.

Thirty-five years later, in 1990, industrial workers and their unions were in retreat. They had become marginal in numbers. Whereas industrial workers who make or move things had accounted for two fifths of the American work force in the 1950s, they accounted for less than one fifth in the early 1990s—that is, for no more than they had accounted for in 1900, when their meteoric rise began. In the other developed free-market countries the decline was slower at first, but after 1980 it began to accelerate everywhere. By the year 2000 or 2010, in very developed free-market country, industrial workers will account for no more than an eighth of the work force. Union power has been declining just as fast.

Unlike domestic servants, industrial workers will not disappear—any more than agricultural producers have disappeared or will disappear. But just as the traditional small farmer has become a recipient of subsidies rather than a producer, so will the traditional industrial worker become an auxiliary employee. His place is already being taken by the "technologist"—someone who works both with hands and theoretical knowledge. (Examples are computer technicians, x-ray technicians, physical therapists, medical-lab technicians, pulmonary

technicians, and so on, who together have made up the fastest-growing group in the U.S. labor force since 1980.) And instead of a class—a coherent, recognizable, defined, and self-conscious group—industrial workers may soon be just another "pressure group."

Chroniclers of the rise of the industrial worker tend to highlight the violent episodes—especially the clashes between strikers and the police, as in America's Pullman strike. The reason is probably that the theoreticians and propagandists of socialism, anarchism, and communism—beginning with Marx and continuing to Herbert Marcuse in the 1960s—incessantly wrote and talked of "revolution" and "violence." Actually, the rise of the industrial worker was remarkably *nonviolent.* The enormous violence of this century—the world wars, ethnic cleansings, and so on—was all violence from above rather than violence from below, and it was unconnected with the transformations of society, whether the dwindling of farmers, the disappearance of domestic servants, or the rise of the industrial worker. In fact, no one even tries anymore to explain these great convulsions as part of "the crisis of capitalism," as was standard Marxist rhetoric only thirty years ago.

Contrary to Marxist and syndicalist predictions, the rise of the industrial worker did not destabilize society. Instead it has emerged as the century's most stabilizing social development. It explains why the disappearance of the farmer and the domestic servant produced no social crises. Both the flight from the land and the flight from domestic service were voluntary. Farmers and maids were not "pushed off" or "displaced." They went into industrial employment as fast as they could. Industrial jobs required no skills they did not already possess, and no additional knowledge. In fact, farmers on the whole had a good deal more skill than was required to be a machine operator in a mass-production plant—and so did many domestic servants. To be sure, industrial work paid poorly until the First World War. But it paid better than farming or household work. Industrial workers in the United States until 1913—and in some countries, including Japan, until the Second World War—worked long hours. But they worked shorter hours than farmers and domestic servants. What's more, they worked *specified* hours; the rest of the day was their own, which was true neither of work on the farm nor of domestic work.

The history books record the squalor of early industry, the poverty of the industrial workers, and their exploitation. Workers did indeed live in squalor and poverty, and they were exploited. But they lived better than those on a farm or in a household, and were generally treated better.

Proof of this is that infant mortality dropped immediately when farmers and domestic servants moved into industrial work. Historically, cities had never reproduced themselves. They had depended for their perpetuation on constant new recruits from the countryside. This was still true in the mid-nineteenth century. But with the spread of factory employment the city became the center of population growth. In part this was a result of new public-health measures; purification of water, collection and treatment of wastes, quarantine against epidemics, inoculation against disease. These measures—and they were effective mostly in the city—counteracted, or at least contained the hazards of crowding that had made the traditional city a breeding ground for pestilence. But the largest single factor in the exponential drop in infant mortality as industrialization spread was surely the improvement in living conditions brought about by the factory. Housing and nutrition became better, and hard work and accidents came to take less of a toll. The drop in infant mortality—and with it the explosive growth in population—correlates with only one development: industrialization. The early factory was indeed the "Satanic Mill" of William Blake's great poem. But the countryside was not "England's green and pleasant Land" of which Blake sang; it was a picturesque but even more satanic slum.

For farmers and domestic servants, industrial work was an opportunity. It was, in fact, the first opportunity that social history had given them to better themselves substantially without having to emigrate. In the developed free-market countries over the past 100 or 150 years every generation has been able to expect to do substantially better than the generation preceding it. The main reason has been that farmers and domestic servants could and did become industrial workers.

Because industrial workers are concentrated in groups, systematic work on their productivity was possible. Beginning in 1881, two yeas before Marx's death, the systematic study of work, tasks, and tools raised the productivity of manual work in making and moving things by three to four percent compound on average per year—for a fiftyfold increase in output per worker over 110 years. On this rest all the economic and social gains of the past century. And contrary to what "everybody knew" in the nineteenth century—not only Marx but all the conservatives as well, such as J.P. Morgan, Bismarck, and Disraeli—practically all these gains have accrued to the industrial worker, half of them in the form of sharply reduced working hours (with the cuts ranging from 40 percent in Japan to 50 percent in Germany), and half of them in the form of twenty-five-fold increase in the real wages of industrial workers who make or move things.

There were thus very good reasons why the rise of the industrial worker was peaceful rather than violent, let alone revolutionary. But what explains the fact that the fall of the industrial worker has been equally peaceful and almost entirely free of social protest, of upheaval, of serious dislocation, at least in the United States?

### The Rise of the Knowledge Worker

The rise of the class succeeding industrial workers is not an opportunity for industrial workers. It is a challenge. The newly emerging dominant group is "knowledge workers." The very term was unknown forty years ago. (I coined it in a 1959 book, *Landmarks of Tomorrow.*) By the end of this century knowledge workers will make up a third or more of the work force in the United States—as large a proportion as manufacturing workers ever made up, except in wartime. The majority of them will be paid at least as well as, or better than, manufacturing workers ever were. And the new jobs offer much greater opportunities.

But—and this is a big but—the great majority of the new jobs require qualifications the industrial worker does not possess and is poorly equipped to acquire. They require a good deal of formal education and the ability to acquire and to apply theoretical and analytical knowledge. They require a different approach to work and a different mind-set. Above all, they require a habit of continuous learning. Displaced industrial workers thus cannot simply move into knowledge work or services the way displaced farmers and domestic workers moved into industrial work. At the very least they have to change their basic attitudes, values, and beliefs.

In the closing decades of this century the industrial work force has shrunk faster and further in the United States than in any other developed country—while industrial production has grown faster than in any other developed country except Japan.

The shift has aggravated America's oldest and least tractable problem: the position of blacks. In the fifty years since the Second World War the economic position of African-Americans in America has improved faster than that of any other group in American social history—or in the social history of any country. Three fifths of America's blacks rose into middle-class incomes; before the Second World War the figure was one twentieth. But half that group rose into middle-class *incomes* and not into middle-class *jobs.* Since the Second World War more and more blacks have moved into blue-collar unionized mass-production industry—that is, into jobs paying middle-class and upper-middle-class wages while requiring neither education nor skill. These are precisely the jobs, however, that are disappearing the fastest. What is amazing is not that so many blacks did not acquire an education but that so many did. The economically rational thing for a young black in postwar America was not to stay in school and learn; it was to leave school as early as possible and get one of the plentiful mass-production jobs. As a result, the fall of the industrial worker has hit America's blacks disproportionately hard—quantitatively, but qualitatively even more. It has blunted what was the most potent role model in the black community in America; the well-paid industrial worker with job security, health insurance, and a guaranteed retirement pension—yet possessing neither skill nor much education.

But, of course, blacks are a minority of the population and work force in the United States. For the overwhelming majority—whites, but also Latinos and Asians—the fall of the industrial worker

has caused amazingly little disruption and nothing that could be called an upheaval. Even in communities that were once totally dependent on mass-production plants that have gone out of business or have drastically slashed employment (steel cities in western Pennsylvania and eastern Ohio, for instance, or automobile cities like Detroit and Flint, Michigan), unemployment rates for nonblack adults fell within a few short years to levels barely higher than the U.S. average—and that means to levels barely higher than the U.S. "full-employment" rate. Even in these communities there has been no radicalization of America's blue-collar workers.

The only explanation is that for the nonblack blue-collar community the development came as no surprise, however unwelcome, painful, and threatening it may have been to individual workers and their families. Psychologically—but in terms of values, perhaps, rather than in terms of emotions—America's industrial workers must have been prepared to accept as right and proper the shift to jobs that require formal education and that pay for knowledge rather than for manual work, whether skilled or unskilled.

In the United States the shift had by 1990 or so largely been accomplished. But so far it has occurred only in the United States. In the other developed free-market countries, in western and northern Europe and in Japan, it is just beginning in the 1990s. It is however, certain to proceed rapidly in these countries from now on, perhaps faster than it originally did in the United States. The fall of the industrial worker in the developed free-market countries will also have a major impact outside the developed world. Developing countries can no longer expect to base their development on their comparative labor advantage—that is, on cheap industrial labor.

It is widely believed, especially by labor-union officials, that the fall of the blue-collar industrial worker in the developed countries was largely, if not entirely, caused by moving production "offshore" to countries with abundant supplies of unskilled labor and low wage rates. But this is not true.

There *was* something to the belief thirty years ago. Japan, Taiwan, and, later, South Korea did indeed (as explained in some detail in my 1993 book *Post-Capitalist Society*) gain their initial advantage in the world market by combining, almost overnight, America's invention of training for full productivity with wage costs that were still those of a preindustrial country. But this technique has not worked at all since 1970 or 1975.

In the 1990s only an insignificant percentage of manufactured goods imported into the United States are produced abroad because of low labor costs. While total imports in 1990 accounted for about 12 percent of the U.S. gross personal income, imports from countries with significantly lower wage costs accounted for less than three percent— and only half of those were imports of *manufactured* products. Practically none of the decline in American manufacturing employment from some 30 or 35 percent of the work force to 15 or 18 percent can therefore be attributed to moving work to low-wage countries. The main competition for American manufacturing industry—for instance, in automobiles, in steel, and in machine tools—has come from countries such as Japan and Germany, where wage costs have long been equal to, if not higher than, those in the United States. The comparative advantage that now counts is in the application of knowledge—for example, in Japan's total quality management, lean manufacturing processes, just-in-time delivery, and price-based costing, or in the customer service offered by medium-sized German or Swiss engineering companies. This means, however, that developing countries can no longer expect to base their development on low wages. They, too, must learn to base it on applying knowledge—just at the time when most of them (China, India, and much of Latin America, let alone black Africa) will have to find jobs for millions of uneducated and unskilled young people who are qualified for little except yesterday's blue-collar industrial jobs.

But for the developed countries, too, the shift to knowledge-based work poses enormous social challenges. Despite the factory, industrial society was still essentially a traditional society in its basic social relationships of production. But the emerging society, the one based on knowledge and knowledge workers, is not. It is the first society in which ordinary people—and that means most peo-

ple—do not earn their daily bread by the sweat of their brow. It is the first society in which "honest work" does not mean a callused hand. It is also the first society in which not everybody does the same work, as was the case when the huge majority were farmers, or, as seemed likely only forty or thirty years ago, were going to be machine operators.

This is far more than a social change. It is a change in the human condition. What it means— what are the values, the commitments, the problems, of the new society—we do not know. But we do know that much will be different.

## The Emerging Knowledge Society

Knowledge workers will not be the majority in the knowledge society, but in many if not most developed societies they will be the largest single population and work force group. And even where outnumbered by other groups, knowledge workers will give the emerging knowledge society its character, its leadership, its social profile. They may not be the ruling class of the knowledge society, but they are already its leading class. And in their characteristics, social position, values, and expectations, they differ fundamentally from any group in history that has ever occupied the leading position.

In the first place, knowledge workers gain access to jobs and social position through formal education. A great deal of knowledge work requires highly developed manual skill and involves substantial work with one's hands. An extreme example is neurosurgery. The neurosurgeon's performance capacity rests on formal education and theoretical knowledge. An absence of manual skill disqualifies one for work as a neurosurgeon. But manual skill alone, no matter how advanced, will never enable anyone to be a neurosurgeon. The education that is required for neurosurgery and other kinds of knowledge work can be acquired only through formal schooling. It cannot be acquired through apprenticeship.

Knowledge work varies tremendously in the amount and kind of formal knowledge required. Some jobs have fairly low requirements, and others require the kind of knowledge the neurosurgeon possesses. But even if the knowledge itself is quite primitive, only formal education can provide it.

Education will become the center of the knowledge society, and the school its key institution. What knowledge must everybody have? What is "quality" in learning and teaching? These will of necessity become central concerns of the knowledge society, and central political issues. In fact, the acquisition and distribution of formal knowledge may come to occupy the place in the politics of the knowledge society which the acquisition and distribution of property and income have occupied in our politics over the two or three centuries that we have come to call the Age of Capitalism.

In the knowledge society, clearly, more and more knowledge, and especially advanced knowledge, will be acquired well past the age of formal schooling and increasingly, perhaps, through educational processes that do not center on the traditional school. But at the same time, the performance of the schools and the basic values of the schools will be of increasing concern to society as a whole, rather than being considered professional matters that can safely be left to "educators."

We can also predict with confidence that we will redefine what it means to be an educated person. Traditionally, and especially during the past 300 years (perhaps since 1700 or so, at least in the West, and since about that time in Japan as well), an educated person was somebody who had a prescribed stock of formal knowledge. The Germans called this knowledge *allgemeine Bildung,* and the English (and, following them, the nineteenth-century Americans) called it the liberal arts. Increasingly, an educated person will be somebody who has learned how to learn, and who continues learning, especially by formal education, throughout his or her lifetime.

There are obvious dangers to this. For instance, society could easily degenerate into emphasizing formal degrees rather than performance capacity. It could fall prey to sterile Confucian mandarins—a danger to which the American university is singularly susceptible. On the other hand, it could overvalue immediately usable, "practical" knowledge and underrate the importance of fundamentals, and of wisdom altogether.

A society in which knowledge workers dominate is under threat from a new class conflict: the large minority of knowledge workers and the majority of people, who will make their living traditionally, either by manual work, whether skilled or unskilled, or by work in services, whether skilled or unskilled. The productivity of knowledge work—still abysmally low—will become the economic challenge of the knowledge society. On it will depend the competitive position of every single country, every single industry, every single institution within society. The productivity of the non-knowledge, services worker will become the social challenge of the knowledge society. On it will depend the ability of the knowledge society to give decent incomes, and with them dignity and status, to non-knowledge workers.

No society in history has faced these challenges. But equally new are the opportunities of the knowledge society. In the knowledge society, for the first time in history, the possibility of leadership will be open to all. Also, the possibility of acquiring knowledge will no longer depend on obtaining a prescribed education at a given age. Learning will become the tool of the individual—available to him or her at any age—if only because so much skill and knowledge can be acquired by means of the new learning technologies.

Another implication is that how well an individual, an organization, an industry, a country, does in acquiring and applying knowledge will become the key competitive factor. The knowledge society will inevitably become far more competitive than any society we have yet known—for the simple reason that with knowledge being universally accessible, there will be no excuses for nonperformance. There will be no "poor" countries. There will only be ignorant countries. And the same will be true for companies, industries, and organizations of all kinds. It will be true for individuals, too. In fact, developed societies have already become infinitely more competitive for individuals than were the societies of the beginning of this century, let alone earlier ones.

I have been speaking of knowledge. But a more accurate term is "knowledges," because the knowledge of the knowledge society will be fundamentally different from what was considered knowledge in earlier societies—and, in fact, from what is still widely considered knowledge. The knowledge of the German *allgemeine Bildung* or of the Anglo-American liberal arts had little to do with one's life's work. It focused on the person and the person's development, rather than on any application—if, indeed, it did not, like the nineteenth-century liberal arts, pride itself on having no utility whatever. In the knowledge society knowledge for the most part exists only in application. Nothing the x-ray technician needs to know can be applied to market research, for instance, or to teaching medieval history. The central work force in the knowledge society will therefore consist of highly specialized people. In fact, it is a mistake to speak of "generalists." What we will increasingly mean by that term is people who have learned how to acquire additional specialties rapidly in order to move from one kind of job to another—for example, from market research into management, or from nursing into hospital administration. But "generalists" in the sense in which we used to talk of them are coming to be seen as dilettantes rather than educated people.

This, too, is new. Historically, workers were generalists. They did whatever had to be done—on the farm, in the household, in the craftsman's shop. This was also true of industrial workers. But knowledge workers, whether their knowledge is primitive or advanced, whether there is a little of it or a great deal, will by definition be specialized. Applied knowledge is effective only when it is specialized. Indeed, the more highly specialized, the more effective it is. This goes for technicians who service computers, x-ray machines, or the engines of fighter planes. But it applies equally to work that requires the most advanced knowledge, whether research in genetics or research in astrophysics or putting on the first performance of a new opera.

Again, the shift from knowledge to knowledges offers tremendous opportunities to the individual. It makes possible a career as a knowledge worker. But it also presents a great many new problems and challenges. It demands for the first time in history that people with knowledge take responsibility for making themselves understood by people who do not have the same knowledge base.

## How Knowledges Work

That knowledge in the knowledge society has to be highly specialized to be productive implies two new requirements: that knowledge workers work in teams, and that if knowledge workers are not employees, they must at least be affiliated with an organization.

There is a great deal of talk these days about "teams" and "teamwork." Most of it starts out with the wrong assumption—namely, that we have never before worked in teams. Actually people have always worked in teams; very few people ever could work effectively by themselves. The farmer had to have a wife, and the farm wife had to have a husband. The two worked as a team. And both worked as a team with their employees, the hired hands. The craftsman also had to have a wife, with whom he worked as a team—he took care of the craft work and she took care of the customers, the apprentices, and the business altogether. And both worked as a team with journeymen and apprentices. Much discussion today assumes that there is only one kind of team. Actually there are quite a few. But until now the emphasis has been on the individual worker and not on the team. With knowledge work growing increasingly effective as it is increasingly specialized, teams become the work unit rather than the individual himself.

The team that is being touted now—I call it the "jazz combo" team—is only one kind of team. It is actually the most difficult kind of team both to assemble and to make work effectively, and the kind that requires the longest time to gain performance capacity. We will have to learn to use different kinds of teams for different purposes. We will have to learn to understand teams—and this is something to which, so far, very little attention has been paid. The understanding of teams, the performance capacities of different kinds of teams, their strengths and limitations, and the tradeoffs between various kinds of teams will thus become central concerns in the management of people.

Equally important is the second implication of the fact that knowledge workers are of necessity specialists: the need for them to work as members of an organization. Only the organization can provide the basic continuity that knowledge workers need in order to be effective. Only the organization can convert the specialized knowledge of the knowledge worker into performance.

By itself, specialized knowledge does not yield performance. The surgeon is not effective unless there is a diagnosis—which, by and large, is not the surgeon's task and not even within the surgeon's competence. As a loner in his or her research and writing, the historian can be very effective. But to educate students, a great many other specialists have to contribute—people whose specialty may be literature, or mathematics, or other areas of history. And this requires that the specialist have access to an organization.

This access may be as a consultant, or it may be as a provider of specialized services. But for the majority of knowledge workers it will be as employees, full-time or part-time, of an organization, such as a government agency, a hospital, a university, a business, or a labor union. In the knowledge society it is not the individual who performs. The individual is a cost center rather than a performance center. It is the organization that performs.

## What Is an Employee?

Most knowledge workers will spend most if not all of their working lives as "employees." But the meaning of the term will be different from what it has been traditionally—and not only in English but in German, Spanish, and Japanese as well.

Individually, knowledge workers are dependent on the job. They receive a wage or salary. They have been hired and can be fired. Legally each is an employee. But collectively they are the capitalists; increasingly, through their pension funds and other savings, the employees own the means of production. In traditional economics—and by no means only in Marxist economics—there is a sharp distinction between the "wage fund," all of which goes into consumption, and the "capital fund," or that part of the total income stream that is available for investment. And most social theory of industrial society is based, one way or another, on the relationship between the two, whether in conflict or in necessary and beneficial cooperation and balance. In the knowledge society the two merge. The pen-

sion fund is "deferred wages," and as such is a wage fund. But it is also increasingly the main source of capital for the knowledge society.

Perhaps more important, in the knowledge society the employees—that is, knowledge workers—own the tools of production. Marx's great insight was that the factory worker does not and cannot own the tools of production, and therefore is "alienated." There was no way, Marx pointed out, for the worker to own the steam engine and to be able to take it with him when moving from one job to another. The capitalist had to own the steam engine and to control it. Increasingly, the true investment in the knowledge society is not in machines and tools but in the knowledge of the knowledge worker. Without that knowledge the machines, no matter how advanced and sophisticated, are unproductive.

The market researcher needs a computer. But increasingly this is the researcher's own personal computer, and it goes along wherever he or she goes. The true "capital equipment" of market research is the knowledge of markets, of statistics, and of the application of market research to business strategy, which is lodged between the researcher's ears and is his or her exclusive and inalienable property. The surgeon needs the operating room of the hospital and all its expensive capital equipment. But the surgeon's true investment is twelve or fifteen years of training and the resulting knowledge, which the surgeon takes from one hospital to the next. Without that knowledge the hospital's expensive operating rooms are so much waste and scrap.

This is true whether the knowledge worker commands advanced knowledge, like a surgeon, or simple and fairly elementary knowledge, like a junior accountant. In either case it is the knowledge investment that determines whether the employee is productive or not, more than the tools, machines, and capital furnished by an organization. The industrial worker needed the capitalist infinitely more than the capitalist needed the industrial worker—the basis for Marx's assertion that there would always be a surplus of industrial workers, an "industrial reserve army," that would make sure that wages could not possibly rise above the subsistence level (probably Marx's most egregious error). In the knowledge society the most probable assumption for organizations—and certainly the assumption on which they have to conduct their affairs—is that they need knowledge workers far more than knowledge workers need them.

There was endless debate in the Middle Ages about the hierarchy of knowledges, with philosophy claiming to be the "queen." We long ago gave up that fruitless argument. There is no higher or lower knowledge. When the patient's complaint is an ingrown toenail, the podiatrist's knowledge, not that of the brain surgeon, controls—even though the brain surgeon has received many more years of training and commands a much larger fee. And if an executive is posted to a foreign country, the knowledge he or she needs, and in a hurry, is fluency in a foreign language—something every native of that country has mastered by age three, without any great investment. The knowledge of the knowledge society, precisely because it is knowledge only when applied in action, derives its rank and standing from the situation. In other words, what is knowledge in one situation, such as fluency in Korean for the American executive posted to Seoul, is only information, and not very relevant information at that, when the same executive a few years later has to think through his company's market strategy for Korea. This, too, is new. Knowledges were always seen as fixed stars, so to speak, each occupying its own position in the universe of knowledge. In the knowledge society knowledges are tools, and as such are dependent for their importance and position on the task to be performed.

## Management in the Knowledge Society

One additional conclusion: Because the knowledge society perforce has to be a society of organizations, its central and distinctive organ is management.

When our society began to talk of management, the term meant "business management"—because large-scale business was the first of the new organizations to become visible. But we have learned in this past half century that management is the distinctive organ of all organizations. All of them require management, whether they use the term or not. All managers do the same things, whatever the purpose of the organizations. All of them have to bring people—each possessing different knowledge—together for joint performance. All of them have to make human strengths productive in performance and human weaknesses irrelevant. All of them have to think through what results are wanted in the organization—and have then to define objectives. All of them are responsible for thinking through what I call the theory of the business—that is, the assumptions on which the organization bases its performance and actions, and the assumptions that the organization has made in deciding what not to do. All of them must think through strategies—that is, the means through which the goals of the organization become performance. All of them have to define the values of the organization, its system of rewards and punishments, its spirit and its culture. In all organizations managers need both the knowledge of management as work and discipline and the knowledge and understanding of the organization itself—its purposes, its values, its environment and markets, its core competencies.

Management as a practice is very old. The most successful executive in all history was surely that Egyptian who, 4,300 years or more ago, first conceived the pyramid, without any precedent, designed it, and built it, and did so in an astonishingly short time. That first pyramid still stands. But as a discipline management is barely fifty years old. It was first dimly perceived around the time of the First World War. It did not emerge until the Second World War, and then did so primarily in the United States. Since then it has been the fastest-growing new function, and the study of it the fastest-growing new discipline. No function in history has emerged as quickly as has management in the past fifty or sixty years, and surely none has had such worldwide sweep in such a short period.

Management is still taught in most business schools as a bundle of techniques, such as budgeting and personnel relations. To be sure, management, like any other work, has its own tools and its own techniques. But just as the essence of medicine is not urinalysis (important though that is), the essence of management is not techniques and procedures. The essence of management is to make knowledges productive. Management, in other words, is a social function. And in its practice management is truly a liberal art.

## The Social Sector

The old communities—family, village, parish, and so on—have all but disappeared in the knowledge society. Their place has largely been taken by the new unit of social integration, the organization. Where community was fate, organization is voluntary membership. Where community claimed the entire person, organization is a means to a person's ends, a tool. For 200 years a hot debate has been raging, especially in the West: are communities "organic" or are they simply extensions of the people of which they are made? Nobody would claim that the new organization is "organic." It is clearly an artifact, a creation of man, a social technology.

But who, then, does the community tasks? Two hundred years ago whatever social tasks were being done were done in all societies by a local community. Very few if any of these tasks are being done by the old communities anymore. Nor would they be capable of doing them, considering that they no longer have control of their members or even a firm hold over them. People no longer stay where they were born, either in terms of geography or in terms of social position and status. By definition, a knowledge society is a society of mobility. And all the social functions of the old communities, whether performed well or poorly (and most were performed very poorly indeed), presupposed that the individual and the family would stay put. But the essence of a knowledge society is mobility in terms of where one lives, mobility in terms of what one does, mobility in terms of one's affiliations. People no longer have roots. People no longer have a neighborhood that controls what their home is like, what they do, and, indeed, what their problems are allowed to be. The knowledge society is a society in which many more people than ever before can be successful. But it is therefore, by definition, also a society in which many more people than ever before can fail, or at least come in second. And if only because the application of knowledge to work has made developed societies so much richer than any earlier society could even dream of becoming, the failures, whether poor people or alcoholics, battered women or juvenile delinquents, are seen as failures of society.

Who, then, takes care of the social tasks in the knowledge society? We cannot ignore them. But the traditional community is incapable of tackling them.

Two answers have emerged in the past century or so—a majority answer and a dissenting opinion. Both have proved to be wrong.

The majority answer goes back more than a hundred years, to the 1880s, when Bismarck's Germany took the first faltering steps toward the welfare state. The answer: the problems of the social sector can, should, and must be solved by government. This is still probably the answer that most people accept, especially in the developed countries of the West—even though most people probably no longer fully believe it. But it has been totally disproved. Modern government, especially since the Second World War, has everywhere become a huge welfare bureaucracy. And the bulk of the budget in every developed country today is devoted to "entitlements"—to payments for all kinds of social services. Yet in every developed country society is becoming sicker rather than healthier, and social problems are multiplying. Government has a big role to play in social tasks—the role of policymaker, of standard setter, and to a substantial extent, of paymaster. But as the agency to *run* social services, it has proved almost totally incompetent.

In my *The Future of Industrial Man* (1942), I formulated a dissenting opinion. I argued then that the new organization—and fifty years ago that meant the large business enterprise—would have to be the community in which the individual would find status and function, with the workplace community becoming the one in and through which social tasks would be organized. In Japan (though quite independently and without any debt to me) the large employer—government agency or business—has indeed increasingly attempted to serve as a community for its employees. Lifetime employment is only one affirmation of this. Company housing, company health plans, company vacations, and so on all emphasize for the Japanese employee that the employer, and especially the big corporation, is the community and the successor to yesterday's village—even to yesterday's family. This, however, has not worked either.

There is need, especially in the West, to bring the employee increasingly into the government of the workplace community. What is now called empowerment is very similar to the things I talked about fifty years ago. But it does not create a community. Nor does it create the structure through which the social tasks of the knowledge society can be tackled. In fact, practically all these tasks—whether education or health care; the anomies and diseases of a developed and, especially, a rich society, such as alcohol and drug abuse; or the problems of incompetence and irresponsibility such as those of the underclass in the American city—lie outside the employing institution.

The right answer to the question, Who takes care of the social challenges of the knowledge society? is neither the government nor the employing organization. The answer is a separate and new *social sector*.

It is less than fifty years, I believe, since we first talked in the United States of the two sectors of a modern society—the "public sector" (government) and the "private sector" (business). In the past twenty years the United States has begun to talk of a third sector, the "nonprofit sector"—those organizations that increasingly take care of the social challenges of a modern society.

In the United States, with its tradition of independent and competitive churches, such a sector has always existed. Even now churches are the largest single part of the social sector in the United States, receiving almost half the money given to the charitable institutions, and about a third of the time volunteered by individuals. But the nonchurch part of the social sector has been the growth sector in the United States. In the early 1990s about a million organizations were registered in the United States as nonprofit or charitable organizations doing social-sector work. The overwhelming majority of these, some 70 percent, have come into existence in the past thirty years. And most are community

services concerned with life on this earth rather than with the Kingdom of Heaven. Quite a few of the new organizations are, of course, religious in their orientation, but for the most part these are not churches. They are "parachurches" engaged in a specific social task, such as the rehabilitation of alcohol and drug addicts, the rehabilitation of criminals, or elementary school education. Even within the church segment of the social sector, the organizations that have shown the capacity to grow are radically new. They are the "pastoral" churches, which focus on the spiritual needs of individuals, especially educated knowledge workers, and then put the spiritual energies of their members to work on the social challenges and social problems of the community—especially, of course, the urban community.

We still talk of these organizations as "nonprofits." But this is a legal term. It means nothing except that under American law these organizations do not pay taxes. Whether they are organized as nonprofit or not is actually irrelevant to their function and behavior. Many American hospitals since 1960 or 1970 have become "for-profits" and are organized in what legally are business corporations. They function in exactly the same way as traditional "nonprofit" hospitals. What matters is not the legal basis but that the social-sector institutions have a particular kind of purpose. Government demands compliance; it makes rules and enforces them. Business expects to be paid; it supplies. Social-sector institutions aim at changing the human being. The "product" of a church is a churchgoer whose life is being changed. The task of social-sector organizations is to create human health and well-being.

Increasingly these organizations of the social sector serve a second and equally important purpose. They create citizenship. Modern society and modern polity have become so big and complex that citizenship—that is, responsible participation—is no longer possible. All we can do as citizens is to vote once every few years and to pay taxes all the time.

As a volunteer in a social-sector institution, the individual can again make a difference. In the United States, where there is a long volunteer tradition because of the old independence of the churches, almost every other adult in the 1990s is working at least three—and often five—hours a week as a volunteer in a social-sector organization. Britain is the only other country with something like this tradition, although it exists there to a much lesser extent (in part because the British welfare state is far more embracing, but in much larger part because it has an established church—paid for by the state and run as a civil service). Outside the English-speaking countries there is not much of a volunteer tradition. In fact, the modern state in Europe and Japan has been openly hostile to anything that smacks of volunteerism—most so in France and Japan. It is *ancien regime* and suspected of being fundamentally subversive.

But even in these countries things are changing, because the knowledge society needs the social sector, and the social sector needs the volunteer. But knowledge workers also need a sphere in which they can act as citizens and create a community. The workplace does not give it to them. Nothing has been disproved faster than the concept of the "organization man," which was widely accepted forty years ago. In fact, the more satisfying one's knowledge work is, the more one needs a separate sphere of community activity.

Many social-sector organizations will become partners with government—as is the case in a great many "privatizations," where, for instance, a city pays for street cleaning and an outside contractor does the work. In American education over the next twenty years there will be more and more government-paid vouchers that will enable parents to put their children into a variety of different schools, some public and tax-supported, some private and largely dependent on the income from the vouchers. These social-sector organizations, although partners with government, also clearly compete with government. The relationship between the two has yet to be worked out—and there is practically no precedent for it.

What constitutes performance for social-sector organizations, and especially for those that, being nonprofit and charitable, do not have the discipline of a financial bottom line, has also yet to be worked out. We know that social-sector organizations need management. But what precisely management means for the social-sector organiza-

tion is just beginning to be studied. With respect to the management of the nonprofit organization we are in many ways pretty much where we were fifty or sixty years ago with respect to the management of the business enterprise: the work is only beginning.

But one thing is already clear. The knowledge society has to be a society of three sectors: a public sector of government, a private sector of business, and a social sector. And I submit that it is becoming increasingly clear that through the social sector a modern developed society can again create responsible and achieving citizenship, and can again give individuals—especially knowledge workers—a sphere in which they can make a difference in society and re-create community.

## *The School as Society's Center*

Knowledge has become the key resource, for a nation's military strength as well as for its economic strength. And this knowledge can be acquired only through schooling. It is not tied to any country. It is portable. It can be created everywhere, fast and cheaply. Finally, it is by definition changing. Knowledge as the key resource is fundamentally different from the traditional key resources of the economist—land, labor, and even capital.

That knowledge has become the key resource means that there is a world economy, and that the world economy, rather than the national economy, is in control. Every country, every industry, and every business will be in an increasingly competitive environment. Every country, every industry, and every business will, in its decisions, have to consider its competitive standing in the world economy and the competitiveness of its knowledge competencies.

Politics and policies still center on domestic issues in every country. Few if any politicians, journalists, or civil servants look beyond the boundaries of their own country when a new measure such as taxes, the regulation of business, or social spending is being discussed. Even in Germany—Europe's most export-conscious and export-dependent major country—this is true.

Almost no one in the West asked in 1990 what the government's unbridled spending in the East would do to Germany's competitiveness.

This will no longer do. Every country and every industry will have to learn that the first question is not, Is this measure desirable? but, What will be the impact on the country's, or the industry's, competitive position in the world economy? We need to develop in politics something similar to the environmental-impact statement, which in the United States is now required for any government action affecting the quality of the environment: we need a competitive-impact statement. The impact on one's competitive position in the world economy should not necessarily be the main factor in a decision. But to make a decision without considering it has become irresponsible.

Altogether, the fact that knowledge has become the key resource means that the standing of a country in the world economy will increasingly determine its domestic prosperity. Since 1950 a country's ability to improve its position in the world economy has been the main and perhaps the sole determinant of performance in the domestic economy. Monetary and fiscal policies have been practically irrelevant, for better and, very largely, even for worse (with the single exception of governmental policies creating inflation, which very rapidly undermines both a country's competitive standing in the world economy and its domestic stability and ability to grow).

The primacy of foreign affairs is an old political precept going back in European politics to the seventeenth century. Since the Second World War it has also been accepted in American politics—though only grudgingly so, and only in emergencies. It has always meant that military security was to be given priority over domestic policies, and in all likelihood this is what it will continue to mean, Cold War or no Cold War. But the primacy of foreign affairs is now acquiring a different dimension. This is that a country's competitive position in the world economy—and also an industry's and an organization's—has to be the first consideration in its domestic policies and strategies. This holds true for a country that is only marginally involved in the world economy (should there still be such a one), and for a business that is only marginally

involved in the world economy, and for a university that sees itself as totally domestic. Knowledge knows no boundaries. There is no domestic knowledge and no international knowledge. There is only knowledge. And with knowledge becoming the key resource, there is only a world economy, even though the individual organization in its daily activities operates within a national, regional, or even local setting.

## How Can Government Function?

Social tasks are increasingly being done by individual organizations, each created for one, and only one, social task, whether education, health care, or street cleaning. Society, therefore, is rapidly becoming pluralist. Yet our social and political theories still assume that there are no power centers except government. To destroy or at least to render impotent all other power centers was, in fact, the thrust of Western history and Western politics for 500 years, from the fourteenth century on. This drive culminated in the eighteenth and nineteenth centuries, when, except in the United States, such early institutions as still survived—for example, the universities and the churches—became organs of the state, with their functionaries becoming civil servants. But then, beginning in the mid-nineteenth century, new centers arose—the first one, the modern business enterprise, around 1870. And since then one new organization after another has come into being.

The new institutions—the labor union, the modern hospital, the mega-church, the research university—of the society of organizations have no interest in public power. They do not want to be governments. But they demand—and, indeed, need—autonomy with respect to their functions. Even at the extreme of Stalinism the managers of major industrial enterprises were largely masters within their enterprises, and the individual industry was largely autonomous. So were the university, the research lab, and the military.

In the "pluralism" of yesterday—in societies in which control was shared by various institutions, such as feudal Europe in the Middle Ages and Edo Japan in the seventeenth and eighteenth centuries—pluralist organizations tried to be in control of whatever went on in their community. At least, they tried to prevent any other organization from having control of any community concern or community institutions within their domain. But in the society of organizations each of the new institutions is concerned only with its own purpose and mission. It does not claim power over anything else. But it also does not assume responsibility for anything else. Who, then, is concerned with the common good?

This has always been a central problem of pluralism. No earlier pluralism solved it. The problem remains, but in a new guise. So far it has been seen as imposing limits on social institutions—forbidding them to do things in the pursuit of their mission, function, and interest which encroach upon the public domain or violate public policy. The laws against discrimination—by race, sex, age, educational level, health status, and so on—which have proliferated in the United States in the past forty years all forbid socially undesirable behavior. But we are increasingly raising the question of the social responsibility of social institutions: What do institutions have to do—in addition to discharging their own functions—to advance the public good? This, however, though nobody seems to realize it, is a demand to return to the old pluralism, the pluralism of feudalism. It is a demand that private hands assume public power.

This could seriously threaten the functioning of the new organizations, as the example of the schools in the United States makes abundantly clear. One of the major reasons for the steady decline in the capacity of the schools to do their job—that is, to teach children elementary knowledge skills—is surely that since the 1950s the United States has increasingly made the schools the carriers of all kinds of social policies: the elimination of racial discrimination, of discrimination against all other kinds of minorities, including the handicapped, and so on. Whether we have actually made any progress in assuaging social ills is highly debatable; so far the schools have not proved particularly effective as tools for social reform. But making the school the organ of social policies has, without any doubt, severely impaired its capacity to do its own job.

The new pluralism has a new problem: how to maintain the performance capacity of the new institutions and yet maintain the cohesion of society. This makes doubly important the emergence of a strong and functioning social sector. It is an additional reason why the social sector will increasingly be crucial to the performance, if not to the cohesion, of the knowledge society.

Of the new organizations under consideration here, the first to arise, 120 years ago, was the business enterprise. It was only natural, therefore, that the problem of the emerging society of organizations was first seen as the relationship of government and business. It was also natural that the new interests were first seen as economic interests.

The first attempt to come to grips with the politics of the emerging society of organizations aimed, therefore, at making economic interests serve the political process. The first to pursue this goal was an American, Mark Hanna, the restorer of the Republican Party in the 1890s and, in many ways, the founding father of twentieth-century American politics. His definition of politics as a dynamic disequilibrium between the major economic interests—farmers, business, and labor—remained the foundation of American politics until the Second World War. In fact, Franklin D. Roosevelt restored the Democratic Party by reformulating Hanna. And the basic political position of this philosophy is evident in the title of the most influential political book written during the New Deal years—*Politics: Who Gets What, When, How* (1936), by Harold D. Lasswell.

Mark Hanna in 1896 knew very well that there are plenty of concerns other than economic concerns. And yet it was obvious to him—as it was to Roosevelt forty years later—that economic interest had to be used to integrate all the others. This is still the assumption underlying most analysis of American politics—and, in fact, of politics in all developed countries. But the assumption is no longer tenable. Underlying Hanna's formula of economic interests is the view of land, labor, and capital as the existing resources. But knowledge, the new resource for economic performance, is not in itself economic.

It cannot be bought or sold. The fruits of knowledge, such as the income from a patent, can be bought or sold; the knowledge that went into the patent cannot be conveyed at any price. No matter how much a suffering person is willing to pay a neurosurgeon, the neurosurgeon cannot sell to him—and surely cannot convey to him—the knowledge that is the foundation of the neurosurgeon's performance and income. The acquisition of knowledge has a cost, as has the acquisition of anything. But the acquisition of knowledge has no price.

Economic interest can therefore no longer integrate all other concerns and interests. As soon as knowledge became the key economic resource, the integration of interests—and with it the integration of the pluralism of a modern polity—began to be lost. Increasingly, noneconomic interests are becoming the new pluralism—the special interests, the single-cause organizations, and so on. Increasingly, politics is not about "who gets what, when, how" but about values, each of them considered to be an absolute. Politics is about the right to life of the embryo in the womb as against the right of a woman to control her own body and to abort an embryo. It is about the environment. It is about gaining equality for groups alleged to be oppressed and discriminated against. None of these issues is economic. All are fundamentally moral.

Economic interests can be compromised, which is the great strength of basing politics on economic interests. "Half a loaf is still bread" is a meaningful saying. But half a baby, in the biblical story of the judgment of Solomon, is not half a child. No compromise is possible. To an environmentalist, half an endangered species is an extinct species.

This greatly aggravates the crisis of modern government. Newspapers and commentators still tend to report in economic terms what goes on in Washington, in London, in Bonn, or in Tokyo. But more and more of the lobbyists who determine governmental laws and governmental actions are no longer lobbyists for economic interests. They lobby for and against measures that they—and their paymasters—see as moral, spiritual, cultural. And each of these new moral concerns, each represented by a new organization, claims to stand for an absolute. Dividing their loaf is not compromise; it is treason.

There is thus in the society of organizations no one integrating force that pulls individual organizations in society and community into coalition. The traditional parties—perhaps the most successful political creations of the nineteenth century—can no longer integrate divergent groups and divergent points of view into a common pursuit of power. Rather, they have become battlefields between groups, each of them fighting for absolute victory and not content with anything but total surrender of the enemy.

## The Need for Social and Political Innovation

The twenty-first century will surely be one of continuing social, economic, and political turmoil and challenge, at least in its early decades. What I have called the age of social transformation is not over yet. And the challenges looming ahead may be more serious and more daunting than those posed by the social transformations that have already come about, the social transformations of the twentieth century.

Yet we will not even have a chance to resolve these new and looming problems of tomorrow unless we first address the challenges posed by the developments that are already accomplished facts, the developments reported in the earlier sections of this essay. These are the priority tasks. For only if they are tackled can we in the developed democratic free-market countries hope to have the social cohesion, the economic strength, and the governmental capacity needed to tackle the new challenges. The first order of business—for sociologists, political scientists, and the economists; for educators; for business executives, politicians, and nonprofit-group leaders; for people in all walks of life, as parents, as employees, as citizens—is to work on these priority tasks, for few of which we so far have a precedent, let alone tested solutions.

- We will have to think through *education*—its purpose, its values, its content. We will have to learn to define the quality of education and the productivity of education, to measure both and to manage both.
- We need systematic work on the *quality of knowledge* and the *productivity of knowledge*—

neither even defined so far. The performance capacity, if not the survival, of any organization in the knowledge society will come increasingly to depend on those two factors. But so will the performance capacity, if not the survival, of any individual in the knowledge society. And what *responsibility* does knowledge have? What are the responsibilities of the knowledge worker, and especially of a person with highly specialized knowledge?

• Increasingly, the *policy* of any country— and especially of any developed country—will have to give primacy to the country's competitive position in an increasingly competitive world economy. Any proposed domestic policy needs to be shaped so as to improve that position, or at least to minimize adverse impacts on it. The same holds true for the policies and strategies of any institution within a nation, whether a local government, a business, a university, or a hospital.

• But then we also need to develop an *economic theory* appropriate to a world economy in which knowledge has become the key economic resource and the dominant, if not the only, source of comparative advantage.

• We are beginning to understand the new integrating mechanism: *organization.* But we still have to think through how to balance two apparently contradictory requirements. Organizations must competently perform the one social function for the sake of which they exist—the school to teach, the hospital to cure the sick, and the business to produce goods, services, or the capital to provide for the risks of the future. They can do so only if they single-mindedly concentrate on their specialized mission. But there is also society's need for these organizations to take social responsibility—to work on the problems and challenges of the community. Together these organizations *are* the community. The emergence of a strong, independent, capable social sector— neither public sector nor private sector—is thus a central need of the society of organizations. But by itself it is not enough—the organizations of both the public and the private sector must share in the work.

• The *function of government* and its *functioning* must be central to political thought and political action. The megastate in which this century indulged has not performed, either in its totalitarian or in its democratic version. It has not delivered on a single one of its promises. And government by countervailing lobbyists is neither particularly effective—in fact, it is paralysis— nor particularly attractive. Yet effective government has never been needed more than in this highly competitive and fast-changing world of ours, in which the dangers created by the pollution of the physical environment are matched only by the dangers of worldwide armaments pollution. And we do not have even the beginnings of political theory or the political institutions needed for effective government in the knowledge-based society of organizations.

If the twentieth century was one of social transformations, the twenty-first century needs to be one of social and political innovations, whose nature cannot be so clear to us now as their necessity.

# X

# *Leading the New Organization*

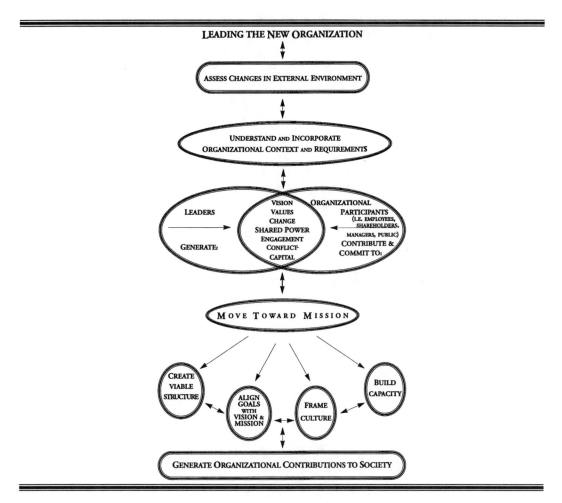

This section begins with a response to the questions raised at the end of Part IX. In the chapter "Leadership and the Social Imperative of Organizations in the 21st Century," I detail the type of leadership that is needed for new-era organizations and present a conceptual framework for generating or redesigning such organizations. The framework employs many of the concepts concerning leadership in organizations that are presented throughout this book.

The final chapter, "Leadership in the 21st Century," brings the book full circle by identifying prominent trends in the current environment, then focusing on the *purpose of leadership* for organizations, communities, and society in the 21st century. This chapter was written collaboratively by six members of the Kellogg Leadership Studies Project and represents the collective thinking of the authors and many of the participants in this project. It demonstrates why leadership is so vital for the new millennium and what purpose-driven leadership might accomplish in the interest of a global society. The challenge for all of us is to assume our role and responsibility for leading, participating in, and shaping organizations and other entities in society so that they become more supportive, sustainable, and caring than ever before in history.

# 52

# Leadership and the Social Imperative of Organizations in the 21st Century

GILL ROBINSON HICKMAN

### *A Social Imperative Emanating From the Environmental Context*

Much of our writing and dialogue as leadership scholars consists of exchanges about "good" leadership—what leadership ought to be as opposed to what it really is, as Barbara Kellerman so accurately observes. Although I strongly believe that leadership scholars should do both, I intend to provide a normative perspective for organizational leadership in the context of turbulent environments. The new era in which organizations must function is characterized by factors such as intense global concern and competition; intraorganizational relationships and collaboration; a focus on democracy, substantive justice, civic virtues, and the common good; values orientation; empowerment and trust; consensus-oriented policy-making

processes; diversity and pluralism in structure and participation; critical dialogue, qualitative language, and methodologies; collectivized rewards; and market alignments (Bennis & Slater, 1968; Emery & Trist, 1973; Toffler, 1980; Clegg, 1990; Rost, 1991; Kuhnert, 1993; ).

Consider that within a 5-year span in the political arena alone, we witnessed the fall of the Berlin Wall, reconfiguration of the former Soviet Union, and the rise of struggling democracies in previously communist societies. Events such as these link people and organizations globally in an environmental context of turbulence, unpredictability, and quantum change. Interdependencies are fostered as a way of life in environments with dynamic properties such as these.

The social imperative for organizations is to understand the interdependent nature of this new

SOURCE: A portion of this chapter was presented by the editor at the Leadership at 20 Conference, University of Maryland, College Park, Maryland, October 1997.

environment and purposely link their survival efforts to the survival and well-being of society. Can organizations be formulated or reconfigured so that social change and collective purpose have explicit prominence with profitability and productivity as their ultimate aims? A new framework is needed to help organizations meet this unique challenge. The concept of "transformistic organizations" describes *the capacity of an existing or new organization to facilitate multiple levels of transformation (individual, organizational, or societal) by partially or completely changing its human capabilities, structure, and/or functions in alignment with its core values and unifying purpose to respond to or directly inpact needs that arise from the environment.* I originated this framework to provide a means for organizations to conceptualize and configure new ways of functioning in an era that requires creative and sustainable approaches to unprecedented change.

Components of this framework already exist in some pioneering organizations. Increasing numbers of private sector and government organizations are attempting to pursue these seemingly contradictory requirements of balancing the functions for which they exist and assuming responsibility to work on problems and challenges of society. Several organizational initiatives illustrate this strong commitment to both organizational purpose and social change. For example, the Timberland Company, maker of rugged outdoor footwear and clothing, won the Corporate Conscience Award given each year by the Council on Economic Priorities. Timberland incorporates social commitment into its mission statement: "Each individual can, and must, make a difference in the way we experience life on this planet" (Will, 1995, p. 18). The company provides its employees with 32 hours of paid time off and five company-sponsored events to allow them to volunteer their services to make a difference in society. The company made a 5-year commitment of services and funding to the City Year urban "peace corps." The youth corps members teach children to read, clean up trash-strewn lots, and interact with different segments of the community. Timberland shares its private sector expertise with City Year and the youth corps provides its employees opportunities to do community service. Beyond its social commitment in the United States, the company also sets forth

international guidelines for choosing business partners based on its Standards for Social Responsibility.

In South Africa, a group of white male business entrepreneurs join together at a "walkabout" to give birth to a new nonprofit organization aimed at identifying and developing emergent leaders in black South African communities. Simultaneously, one of the entrepreneurs initiated an institute within his enterprise to develop the capacity of black South African small business owners to sustain their survival. Why are such unusual affiliations occurring? Their fates are inextricably linked.

One popular journal indicated that a number of U.S. entrepreneurs whose companies are both profitable and socially active have been moved to action by several unsettling trends including "the sharp rise in juvenile crime, the dearth of quality child care, and the plight of unskilled workers who can't get jobs" (Lord, 1994, p. 103). These are not issues that immediately affect the bottom line but can affect the future availability of workers, the location of businesses, and the quality of life in urban areas.

A major retirement system offers its contributors the opportunity to invest their retirement earnings in a fund called "social choice." The companies in this fund practice social and/or environmental responsibility in their business actions and choices. Investors have actively embraced this fund and have also received strong economic returns.

Businesses such as Tom's of Maine, Ben and Jerry's, and the Body Shop have embraced explicit organizational missions that combine profitability and productivity with specific social change efforts. For example, the mission of Tom's of Maine is to provide safe, effective, and natural products to consumers and to address community concerns locally and globally (Chappell, 1994). They support educational, environmental, and community causes through their business practices (use of natural ingredients and environmentally safe packaging), paid work time for employees to volunteer in the community, and monetary donations. One member of the board of directors commented that the company's 31% sales growth and 41% profit increase in 1992 had only been surpassed by its 50% spiritual growth (Chappell, 1994).

These examples are representative of organizations that are embracing social imperatives in their mission while meeting their organizational purpose. As organizations have incorporated these dual missions and capacity-building roles, they have encountered challenges. These organizations face the difficulties inherent in building appropriate infrastructures and capacity to generate and sustain the ambitious pursuit of organizational purpose, economic viability, and social change. Encountering challenges and even setbacks in these areas does not mean that this pursuit should be abandoned or that it is imprudent. It means that pioneering efforts into this new arena require organizational learning, concerted analysis, refinement, and corrections.

How can such efforts be prudent in a time of fierce global competition, downsizing, layoffs, outsourcing, and "lean and mean" strategizing? Downs (1995) cites a Wyatt and Company survey of 1,005 corporations that had recently participated in downsizing. The survey found that only one third of the companies reported that profits increased as much as they expected after layoff; fewer than half said the cuts reduced expenses over time, in fact four out of five organizations rehired the laid-off managers; and a small minority reported satisfactory increase in shareholders' return on investment (pp. 11-12). These tactics are temporary reactions that are often detrimental to long-term success, not responses or solutions, to larger more fundamental changes in a postindustrial/postmodern environmental context. Organizations with a social imperative that links their survival to the well-being of society may be better positioned in the long run to maintain their human and economic viability.

## The Influence of Burns on Transformistic Organizations

We are in an era that requires the pursuit of more enduring visions, purposes, and roles for organizations. Organizations may be in the most advantageous position to facilitate unprecedented advances for society and resolve highly complex problems based on their capacity to mobilize resources and often transcend political entities. The essential element is leadership—the kind of leadership that assumes elevated sights and dimensions beyond those set in previous eras.

Transforming leadership within transformistic organizations provides the potential to bring about unprecedented change. James MacGregor Burns (1978) defines transforming leadership as "a process in which one or more people engage with others in such a way that leaders and followers raise one another to higher levels of motivation and morality" (p. 20). He explains that transforming leaders engage in collective purpose linked to social change, with the ultimate objective of achieving goals that enhance the well-being of human existence. Given Burns's definition, organizational leaders who aspire to be truly transforming must generate collective purpose and transforming processes within the organization that are ultimately linked to social change.

Transformistic organizations necessitate leadership by activists who work internally and externally to bring about human and economic metamorphosis. Inside the organization they generate visions, mission, goals, and culture that contribute to the capacity of individuals, groups, and the organization to practice its values, serve its purpose, maintain strong economic viability, and serve societal needs. Externally, transforming leaders are both organizational and "social entrepreneurs" (Waddock & Post, 1991) who build interconnectedness for business and societal purposes. These individuals are frequently business executives such as those involved in Cleveland Tomorrow, Hands Across America, or the Partnership for a Drug-Free America, who recognize crisis-level social problems characterized by multiplexity (i.e., extreme levels of complexity) and mobilize activities among interdependent organizations and individuals to begin working toward new solutions. They are highly credible leaders who generate follower commitment that results in a sense of organizational and collective purpose.

How can organizational leaders develop the kind of context where human capabilities are maximized for personal, organizational, and societal good? To respond to this complex question, organizations will need to develop the ability to generate and expand human capacity at multiple levels (individual, group, organizational, societal) and

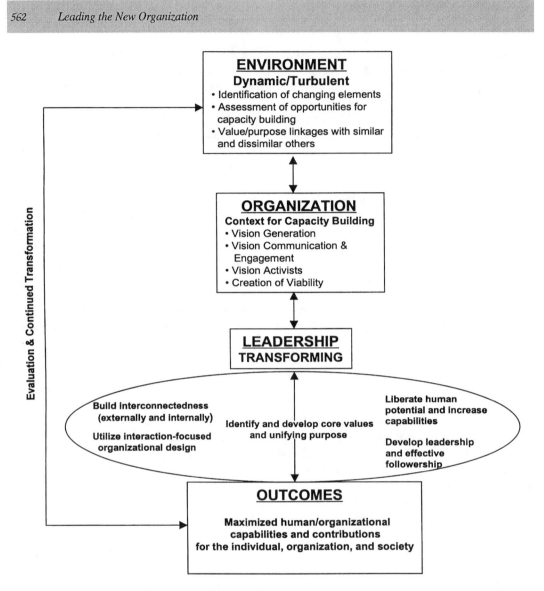

**Figure 52.1.** Transformistic Organization Framework

forge the interconnectedness among these levels.[1] The transformistic organization framework in Figure 52.1 is designed to address these issues for a new era.

As with any framework, the transformistic organization presents elements in their emergent and idealized form. However, it is intended to help us move systematically toward a more comprehensive view of the purposes, structure, functioning, and roles of organizations in a new era and to specifically examine the role of transforming leadership

in capacity building within this context. Although the elements incorporated in the transformistic framework are interdependent and mutually reinforcing, they are discussed separately for purposes of analysis.

## *The Conceptual Framework*

The framework focuses on four interdependent components—a dynamic and turbulent environment; the organization as a context for capacity building; transforming leadership that mobilizes, facilitates, and elevates human and organizational processes; and outcomes characterized by maximized human and organizational capabilities and contributions for the individual, organization, and society. Transforming leadership functions to create and sustain a context for building human capacity by identifying and developing core values and unifying purpose, liberating human potential and generating increased capacity, developing leadership and effective followership, using interaction-focused organizational design, and building interconnectedness.

## The Environment

The effects of larger societal challenges such as new markets in new democracies, changes in family structures, cultural and ethnic diversity, decline in urban environments, and environmental preservation are becoming intermeshed purposefully and often unexpectedly with organizational functioning. To build capacity in organizations, leaders are required to be as attentive to the changes and needs in the external environment as they are to the requirements of their internal environments. They must help determine the relationship between the external environment and the human and structural capacities of their organization.[2] The beginning point for structuring these relations is the identification of the organization's core values. These values provide the basis for selecting what opportunities and threats are important for the organization and which course of action to pursue.[3]

Emery and Trist (1973) described the concept of a turbulent field environment as having dynamic processes or properties created by indigenous changes emanating from the environment:

Fairly simple examples of this may be seen in fishing and lumbering where competitive strategies, based on an assumption that the environment is static, may, by over-fishing and over-cutting, set off disastrous dynamic processes in the fish and plant population with the consequent destruction of all the competing social systems. . . . It is not difficult to see that even more complex dynamic processes are triggered off in human populations. (pp. 52-53)

Implications for organizations are that traditional methods of forecasting, planning, and strategy building will be less effective, and consequences of the organization's actions or those of its competitors become more unpredictable. Collective strategies among multiple organizations linked by the recognition of "significant values" can provide a coping mechanism in this context. As discussed by Emery and Trist, significant values are methods of complexity reduction. They indicate that "values are neither strategies nor tactics and cannot be reduced to them. As Lewin has pointed out, they have the conceptual character of 'power fields' and act as guides to behaviour" (Emery & Trist, 1973, p. 69).

Upon introducing the use of values, Emery and Trist immediately recognize the problems of determining *which* values and how these values will be used in organizations. This issue will be addressed in more detail. However, the authors suggest that a means for dealing with the complex issue of values is contained in the design of the social organization. "We are suggesting that the first decisions about values for the future control of our turbulent environments are the decisions that go into choosing our basic organizational designs" (Emery & Trist, 1973, p. 71). They postulate, as does Heifetz (1994) later in his description of adaptive processes in organizations, that internally organizations must increase the adaptiveness of their individual members. Externally, they must link with like but competitive others *and* develop "some relationship between dissimilar organizations whose fates are basically positively correlated: that is, relationships that will maximize cooperation while still recognizing that no one organization could take over the role of the other" (Emery & Trist, 1973, p. 76).

In summary, the results of Emery and Trist's design principle become a responsive, self-regulating system with core values and unifying purpose as the inherent self-regulating device. The creation of such organizational contexts allows cooperative linkages with similar and dissimilar organizations in a dynamic environmental field. Existence within this environmental context, therefore, requires changes in concepts of the nature, purpose, and design of organizations, organizational leadership, relationships within and between organizations, expectations concerning human capabilities and contributions in organizations, and inherent outcomes.

## The Organization

The transformistic framework recognizes organizations as "contexts" for capacity building. Such organizations focus on human purposes and values as the driving force of the institution so that gains in economic resources become instruments for concerted human activity. This organizational focus does not mean that significant service and products do not result or that economic (bottom line) considerations and productivity are minimized. It simply means that organizations become human entities with economic interests as components of human requirements.

Building the context, which Wheatley (1994) refers to as "fields," for organizations creates an internal setting that shapes the dynamics of the organization.

In many ways, we already know what powerful organizers fields can be. We have moved deeper into a field view of reality by our recent focus on culture, vision, and values as the means for managing organizations. . . . Creating the field through the dissemination of those ideas is essential. The field must reach all corners of the organization, involve everyone, and be available everywhere. Vision statements move off the walls and into the corridors, seeking out every employee, every recess of the organization. . . . We need all of us out there, stating, clarifying, discussing, modeling, filling all of space with the messages we care about. If we do that, fields develop—and with them, their wondrous capacity to bring energy into form. (Wheatley, 1994, pp. 55-56)

Creation of such a context develops the organization's capacity for "resilience" (Wheatley, 1994) and "self-transcendence" (Carey, 1992), so that the human potential that is unleashed may be used beyond the organization for societal transformations in the external environment. When these factors are established, the organization can be positioned to create value and purpose alignments with others in the environment whose fates, in the words Emery and Trist, are "positively correlated."

Several pragmatic challenges arise for organizations moving toward such contexts including (a) how to create contexts that facilitate the liberation of human potential to maximize personal, organizational, and societal capabilities; (b) how to prepare individuals for and engage them in these new challenges; (c) how to identify, develop, and sustain core values and unifying purposes; and (d) how to align organizational values and purposes with others in the environment and/or to meet emergent needs in the environment. There are no simple responses to these challenges. However, the ability to meet them seems to lie more in a process and set of responsibilities than a solution—leadership.

## Leadership

### Leadership Structure

Changing and reframing organizations to meet the challenges of a new era require innovative leadership structures. Rost (1991) indicates that there is a definite trend toward shared or collaborative leadership. He contends that old relationships composed of one leader over many followers are improbable in the postindustrial era. Contemporary organizational leaders including chief executive officers, university presidents, government agency heads, and directors of nonprofit agencies are faced with increasing multiple demands that greatly surpass the capacity of a single incumbent. The turnover rate alone among these leaders attests to the complexity of the role and the need for new models.

Collaborative leadership, particularly at what is currently executive levels, entails a redistribution and sharing of power, authority, and position that have been relatively untested in contemporary organizations. In addition to the executive leadership team configurations, leadership might function in arrangements such as dyads, triads, representative team leaders, and many other constructs. The leadership structure, like the organizational structure, will need to be developed by stakeholders to fit the purpose, needs, and values of the enterprise.

## Leadership Role

Transforming leadership is particularly useful for the needs of this context. When Burns's (1978) concept of transforming leadership is employed in the transformistic organizational context, it is imperative that three factors maintain prominence: the focus on leadership as a *process;* the powerful and mutually reinforcing *roles and impact of leaders and followers on one another;* and the *responsibility of leaders and followers to engage in collective purpose to effect social change* while implementing the organization's purpose and remaining economically viable.

When viewed from the perspective described by Emery and Trist, transforming leadership serves to align human, organizational, and environmental values, capabilities, purposes, and needs. This form of leadership influences participants in the process to remain open to new information and inputs and move themselves and others toward the capacity for self-transcendence (Carey, 1992). It involves advancing beyond self-serving, egocentric purposes to focus on a larger perspective or greater good and serve genuine human needs.

*Identify and develop core values and unifying purpose.* One of the major roles of leadership in transformistic organizations is to engage participants in the work of identifying, developing, and employing values. Values serve as the organization's essence, stability, and guide for action. Still, the question is, which values should be used for the work of organizations and their alignment with others? In an attempt to develop the beginning of a global set of values, Kidder (1994) sought the perspectives of 24 diverse leaders and influential individuals from around the world. The values identified included love, truthfulness, fairness/justice, freedom, unity, tolerance, responsibility, and respect for life. Even in the unlikely event that these values become accepted universally, they acquire meaning only in the reality of their implementation.

Heifetz (1994) provides several significant insights concerning this issue. First, he indicates that leadership involves helping and mobilizing people to do the "adaptive work" required to address or lessen the gap between value conflicts among individuals. Second, values are shaped and refined when people must deploy them in the face of real problems. Third, success is influenced by the openness of participants to diverse and even competing value perspectives and their willingness to use creative tensions and conflict to generate new knowledge, approaches, and outcomes. He urges that leadership tackle the tough problems by allowing values to evolve without an imperialistic perspective through engaging participants in the examination and incorporation of values from different cultures and organizations.

Collective values provide a foundation for forming the organization's unifying purpose. This purpose represents the substance to which organizational participants are willing to commit. It provides meaning for the organization and in the lives of its participants (Wheatley, 1994). The pursuit of unifying or collective purposes requires an elevation of motives and values. Burns (1978) asserts that in the pursuit of collective purposes, "whatever the separate interests persons might hold, they are presently or potentially united in the pursuit of 'higher' goals, the realization of which is tested by the achievement of significant change that represents the collective or pooled interests of leaders and followers" (pp. 426-427).

Using foundational values and a unifying purpose, leaders and organizational participants can derive a shared formulation of organizational vision, culture, change efforts, relationships, and external interactions. These factors constitute the identity of an organization and position it to relate and contribute to its environment.

*Liberate human potential and increase capacity.* In transformistic organizations, engagement of the full person involves liberating human potential and capabilities to change. Transforming leadership facilitates this capacity by promoting

- Personal and emotional stability and maturity among organizational participants through establishing a culture, context, or field that supports advancement of self-knowledge, enhanced self-esteem, and emotional and physical wellness;[4]

- Development of whole-person relationships including recognition and regard for the uniqueness and diversity of individuals and the interrelated aspects of their lives (i.e., personal, professional, and relational); and
- Development of the culture and resources for continual learning to empower individuals to grow, create, and change themselves, the organization, and the environment.

The existence of these interrelated conditions provides organizational participants with the capabilities to respond to complex issues and the needs that arise in rapidly changing dynamic environments. In an earlier publication, Schon (1971) described the process that organizations must employ to gain this capacity by becoming adept at learning. He contends that organizational participants "must become able not only to transform our institutions, in response to changing situations and requirements; we must invent and develop institutions which are 'learning systems,' that is to say, systems capable of bringing about their own continuous transformations" (p. 30).

Senge (1990) later refers to this process as generative learning that enhances the capacity of organizational participants to create. He states that five essential elements must develop as an ensemble to create a fundamental learning organization:

1. Personal mastery—continually clarifying and deepening personal vision, focusing energies, developing patience, and seeing reality objectively;
2. Mental models—changing ingrained assumptions, generalizations, pictures, and images of how the world works;
3. Shared vision—unearthing shared "pictures of the future" that foster genuine commitment;
4. Team learning—aligning and developing the capacity of a team to create the results its members truly desire; and
5. Systems thinking—integrating all the elements by fusing them into a coherent body of theory and practice. (Senge, 1990)

These concepts are further developed in Heifetz's (1994) concept of adaptive work as collective learning that is stimulated during the process of leaders and followers working through hard problems together. The forms of learning described by Schon, Senge, and Heifetz require organizational participants to continually examine, synthesize, and integrate from various disciplines, perspectives, and cultures—a concept that is conceptually sound but difficult to practice. These processes must be built into the organization through planned time for dialogue (Senge, 1990), use of technology to enhance creation and problem solving (Passmore, 1988), and diligence by leaders and participants in the organization.

*Develop leadership and effective followership.* Leadership and followership in transformistic organizations are predicated less on positional authority and more on interdependent work relationships centered on common purposes. Participants are active, multifaceted contributors. Their involvement is based on shared, flexible roles.

Kelley (1995) indicates that leadership and followership are equal but different activities often played by the same people at different times. Individuals who assume leadership roles have the desire and willingness to lead as well as sound visioning, interpersonal communications, and organizational skills and abilities. Effective followers form the other equally important component of the equation and are distinguished by their capacity for self-management, strong commitment, and courage.

Organizations must be purposefully created or changed to facilitate this form of leadership and followership. They must engage participants in organizational learning processes that develop their capabilities, and especially provide greater opportunities to *experience* and *practice* leadership and effective follower roles (Kelley, 1995; Kotter, 1990). A current trend in this direction is the increasing use of self-directed work teams (Fisher, 1993; Manz & Sims, 1989, 1993) in organizations. These teams are based on "shared authority, flexible and shared tasks, and management based on information sharing and participative decision making" (Kulish & Banner, 1993, p. 27). Members must respect and use the abilities, skills, and unique contributions of each individual, and leader-follower roles emerge or are assigned with fluidity based on member contributions or capabilities.

Unprecedented advances could be made through the development of leadership and effective followership throughout the organization. Influence in this environment is multidirectional crossing of organizational boundaries. Leaders and followers have the ability to affect outcomes and effect change from any position in the organization. Advances in new information and communication technology vastly enhance these kinds of relationships.

Given the accessibility and use of technology by multiple participants who are empowered to act, new and subtler forms of power and authority are likely to emerge. In this context, power is shared and widely distributed and is defined by broader conceptions than those traditionally ascribed. As indicated by Luke (1991), power becomes "the production of intended effects, not only unilaterally but also collectively. It is facilitative power, not commanding and dominating force" (p. 40). Thus, it is critical that the organization's context, values, purpose, and human capacity are well developed so that these multiple, self-managed actors (leaders and effective followers) have clear intrinsic and extrinsic guidelines for their actions.

*Use interaction-focused organizational design.* Another vital role of transforming leadership is to create work settings and organizational design that promote the human, technical, and societal goals of transformistic organizations. Structure and work designs emerge from defining the set of human interactions that participants want to facilitate. In contrast to current practices of attempting to find an enduring fit, different forms are used and innovated by organizational participants. If participants want to promote problem solving or innovation, they need organizational designs that correspond with these activities. Technology-supported organizational design tools provide the capability for organizations to rapidly design new teams to accomplish desired program or project outcomes (Nadler, 1992). Organizational forms for the 21st century need to be fluid and transitory incorporating teams of participants from inside and outside the organization based on the requirements of the situation (Gerstein & Shaw, 1992). Structures will be formed by changing teams, partnerships, and

units who have the freedom and authority to optimize their work processes by experimenting with new flexible designs (Gerstein & Shaw, 1992).

This concept of evolving organizational form or design to support human interactions is a particularly relevant process for support of the transforming processes within organizations. It further reinforces the development of leaders and effective followers who understand how to use and advance the organization to meet its dual mission.

*Build interconnectedness.* Transforming leadership fosters boundaryless relationships to promote mutually beneficial interactions between and within organizations while maintaining the organization's core identity, purpose, and values. Luke (1991) refers to boundaryless relationships between organizations as "interconnectedness," which involves all forms of interdependencies including organizational, intergovernmental, intersectorial, and global (p. 26).

Jack Welch of General Electric describes boundaryless structures within the organization as "having no hierarchical boundaries horizontally and no functional boundaries vertically" (quoted in Rose, 1990, p. 157). Organizational designs based on human interactive requirements are indeed boundaryless and serve to establish internal connectedness while fostering fluidity of movement and relationships.

New technology will play an ever-increasing role in the flexible designs of organizations and their ability to function intra- and interorganizationally. This new technology is open and networked, modular, and dynamic based on interchangeable parts (Tapscott & Caston, 1993). It empowers users and allows them to distribute intelligence and decision making by integrating data, text, voice, and image information in different formats. They further indicate that this technology serves to blur boundaries between organizations and facilitate the recasting of external relationships.

Vital to the concept of transformistic organizations is the role of transforming leadership in fostering external connectedness with similar and dissimilar others in the environment. Gardner (1990) identified five critical skills for leaders when developing interconnectedness: agreement building, networking, exercising nonjurisdictional power, institution building, and flexibility. As previously indicated, Waddock and Post (1991) would add the skills of social entrepreneurs who bring together social alliances of multiple actors on multiple levels and by multiple means to solve extremely complex societal problems. Given the complexity of this dynamic environmental field and its accelerated rate of change, leaders must use the collective sense of organizational values, identity, purpose, and capabilities as guides to determine with whom to connect, for what purposes, and to what end. Collaboration and cooperation among organizations globally and domestically are becoming new indicators of success.

Drucker (1994) describes organizations of the 21st century as new integrating mechanisms. He indicates that together public and private organizations form the capacity that the community will need to determine how to balance two apparently contradictory requirements—the primary functions for which specific organizations exist and the social responsibility to work on the problems and challenges of the community. This, Drucker contends, is the joint work of both public and private organizations that are capable of social sector work.

The ability to collaborate among organizations domestically and globally is becoming a new indicator of success in highly dynamic environments. Society expects this form of success not only to produce profitability for those involved, but these organizations are expected to demonstrate responsibility and contribute to the collective good of the society in which they function.

## Outcomes

The outcomes of transformistic organizations are not solely exceptional products, services, or profits (although these should indeed result); they are qualitative changes in the well-being of society. Transformation of human capabilities within organizations that change the larger society could be tantamount to a new social movement for the 21st century. A comment by Edward Simon, President of Herman Miller, that "business is the only insti-

tution that has a chance . . . to fundamentally improve the injustice that exists in the world," may well apply more generally to interconnected organizations in the next century (quoted in Senge, 1990, p. 5). Although I believe these capabilities lie within organizations in various sectors, Simon's point illustrates the new thinking among organizational leaders that will make the transition to transformistic organizations a viable possibility in the 21st century.

The dynamic properties of the environment have delivered us a challenging social imperative: to prepare and position our organizations to generate unprecedented advances for society and resolve highly complex human and environmental problems. The transformistic organization framework can serve to stimulate organizational movement toward liberation of human potential to meet these unprecedented challenges.

In this context, transforming leadership itself becomes evolving and multifaceted. It evolves and shifts based on several factors:

- Influences of changes and requirements from the environment;
- Quality of adaptive work engaged in by followers with leaders;
- The level, quality, and complexity of collaboration within and across organizational boundaries;
- Ability to use technological capabilities to link participants and change environmental circumstances; and
- Deployment of economic and material resources for collective purposes.

## Application of the Transformistic Conceptual Framework

In a recent case study, I examined an initiative to establish a Leadership Training Institute (LTI) at John F. Kennedy High School (JFK) in Montgomery County, Maryland. The LTI was initiated in 1993 as the first public high school program in the country to integrate leadership into its core curriculum (The Partners, 1995). In June 1996, the first class of LTI students graduated from the program. Details concerning the LTI initiative were based on site visits; questionnaires completed by the LTI director, teachers, and seniors; and a small number of JFK students and teachers.[5]

The LTI was intended to revitalize an urban high school and serve a larger societal goal of preparing young people for meaningful roles as citizens, leaders, and directors of their own lives. Using the lens of the transformistic framework, I was able to categorize important approaches and processes that led to success while identifying critical areas for improvement. The outcome of this examination provides promise for using the transformistic organization framework in real-world organizations as a conceptual, analytical, and evaluative tool for institutions that intend transformation of individuals, structures, and forms of leadership to build increased capacity for the betterment of themselves and society.

In addition, a case study was conducted with the Timberland Company using the transformistic framework. This was the first attempt to apply the framework to a corporation. The researchers found that Timberland's intentional commitment to both meeting its organizational purpose and engaging actively in social enterprise contributed strongly to capacity building and transformation at multiple levels (individual, organizational, and societal) as indicated in the framework (Horan & Levin, 1998). Furthermore, Timberland institutionalized its social commitment through establishing a social enterprise unit in the organization. Lessons learned by participants in community projects about leadership without positional roles, building trust, and effective teamwork were brought back into the organization. Involvement in social enterprise by Timberland employees contributed strongly to the community and equally as strongly to the capacity building of the employees and company. Employees expressed a powerful sense of pride because of their ability to contribute personally and effectively to community and organizational purposes.

Responses to presentations of the transformistic organization framework in international arenas such as South Africa have supported its potential utility as a conceptual and analytical tool. The newly constituted government of South Africa rests its vision for the country on the transformation of public service organizations to continually improve the lives of the people of South Africa

(Ministry for the Public Service and Administration, 1995). To this end, it has adopted a Reconstruction and Development Program (RDP). The RDP focuses on such factors as creation of a people-centered and people-driven public service; development of new forms of leadership; creation of programs for training and education; promotion of team learning and development; facilitation of learning and skills building through diversity; devolution of decision-making power; advancement of the values of equality, human rights and dignity, fairness, honesty, democratic participation, and service; democratization of internal work procedures; building collaboration between the public sector and business, nongovernmental, and community-based organizations; and the ultimate attainment of increased capacity in the public service and improved lives of South African people. In sessions with directors of national, provincial, and local public service organizations, these factors were reconfigured in the transformistic framework to provide a means for conceptualizing, analyzing, and evaluating their transformational efforts.

## Need for Further Study

Exploration of the LTI initiative using this framework, as well as considerations of business and international governmental initiatives, suggests the need for further conceptualizing and testing to more fully define the components of the framework, test its utility, and address the issues of organizational viability and use of conflict and power. It is particularly important to focus future research efforts and analysis in organizations that have begun, with some vigor, to promote goals for simultaneous achievement of increased service outcomes or profitability, development of human potential, and enhanced societal well-being.

Transformation of human capabilities within organizations that change the larger society could be analogous to a social movement for the 21st century. Burns (1978) asserts that in the pursuit of collective purposes, "whatever the separate interests persons might hold, they are presently or potentially united in the pursuit of 'higher' goals, the realization of which is tested by the achievement of significant change that represents the collective or pooled interests of leaders and followers" (pp. 426-427).

## Notes

1. Historically, respected scholars (Argyris, 1965; Parsons, 1947/1964; Weber, 1956/1978) have employed conceptual frameworks using multilevel elements in response to changing context and requirements.

2. Classical writers such as Weber and Marx were eminently concerned with the larger environmental and societal context; however, emphasis on this context was relatively subdued in organization theory until systems theorists began to reintroduce environmental inputs into organizational analyses.

3. Earlier writers (Emery & Trist, 1973; Lewin, 1951) provided prophetic insight into the use of values in complex environments suggesting that multiple organizations might use collective strategies linked by the recognition of "significant values" as coping mechanisms in this dynamic environment.

4. This view is compatible with the concept of "personal mastery" as defined by Senge (1990) and "self-transcendence" described by Carey (1992).

5. A complete description of this study can be found in Hickman (1997).

## References

Argyris, C. (1965). *Organization and innovation.* Homewood, IL: Irwin, Dorsey.

Bennis, W., & Slater, P. (1968). *The temporary society.* New York: Harper Colophon.

Burns, J. M. (1978). *Leadership.* New York: Harper Torchbooks.

Carey, M. R. (1992). Transformational leadership and the fundamental option for self-transcendence. *Leadership Quarterly, 3*(3), 217-236.

Clegg, S. R. (1990). *Modern organizations: Organization studies in the postmodern world.* London: Sage.

Chappell, T. (1994). *The soul of a business: Managing for profit and the common good.* New York: Bantam.

Downs, A. (1995). *Corporate executions: The ugly truth about layoffs—How corporate greed is shattering lives, companies, and communities.* New York: AMACOM.

Drucker, P. F. (1994). The age of social transformation. *The Atlantic Monthly, 274*(3), 53-56ff.

Emery, F. E., & Trist, E. L. (1973). *Towards a social ecology.* New York: Plenum.

Fisher, K. (1993). *Leading self-directed work teams: A guide to developing new team leadership skills.* New York: McGraw-Hill.

Gardner, J. W. (1990). *On leadership.* New York: Free Press.

Gerstein, M. S., & Shaw, R. B. (1992). Organizational architectures for the twenty-first century. In D. A. Nadler, M. S. Gerstein, & R. B. Shaw (Eds.), *Organizational architecture: Designs for changing organizations* (pp. 263-273). San Francisco: Jossey-Bass.

Heifetz, R. (1994). *Leadership without easy answers.* Cambridge, MA: Belknap.

Hickman, G. R. (1997). *Transforming organizations to transform society* (KLSP Transformational Leadership working paper). College Park, MD: James MacGregor Burns Academy of Leadership.

Horan, J., & Levin, J. (1998). *Transforming corporations to transform society.* Unpublished senior project paper, University of Richmond, Virginia.

Kelley, R. (1995). In praise of followers. In J. T. Wren (Ed.), *The leader's companion: Insight on leadership through the ages.* New York: Free Press.

Kidder, R. M. (1994). *Shared values for a troubled world: Conversations with men and women of conscience.* San Francisco: Jossey-Bass.

Kotter, J. P. (1990). What leaders really do. *Harvard Business Review, 90*(3), 103-111.

Kuhnert, K. W. (1993). Leadership theory in postmodernist organizations. In R. T. Golembiewski (Ed.), *Handbook of organization behavior* (pp. 189-202). New York: Marcel Dekker.

Kulish, T., & Banner, D. K. (1993). Self-managed work teams: An update. *Leadership & Organization Development Journal, 14*(2), 25-29.

Lewin, K. (1951). *Field theory in social science: Selected theoretical papers* (D. Cartwright, Ed.). New York: Harper & Row.

Lord, M. (1994, October 31). Making a difference and money, too: Entrepreneurs are finding rewarding remedies for social ills. *U.S. News & World Report.*

Luke, J. S. (1991). Managing interconnectedness: The challenge of shared power. In J. M. Bryson & R. C. Einsweiler (Eds.), *Shared power: What is it? How does it work? How can we make it work better?* (pp. 25-50). Lanham, MD: University Press of America.

Manz, C. C., & Sims, H. P., Jr. (1989). *Super-leadership: Leading others to lead themselves.* New York: Berkley.

Manz, C. C., & Sims, H. P., Jr. (1993). *Business without bosses.* New York: Wiley.

Ministry for the Public Service and Administration. (1995). *White paper on the transformation of the public service* (Government Gazette No. 16838). Pretoria, South Africa: Government Printer.

Nadler, D. A. (1992). Organizational architecture: A metaphor for change. In D. A. Nadler, M. S. Gerstein, & R. B. Shaw (Eds.), *Organizational architecture: Designs for changing organizations* (pp. 1-8). San Francisco: Jossey-Bass.

Parsons, T. (Ed.). (1964). *The theory of social and economic organization* (A. M. Henderson & T. Parsons, Trans.). New York: Free Press. (Original work published 1947)

The Partners. (1995, April). *CivicQuest, 1*(1), 1-8.

Passmore, W. A. (1988). *Designing effective organizations: The sociotechnical systems perspective.* New York: Wiley.

Rose, F. (1990). A new age for business. *Fortune, 122*(9), 156-164.

Rost, J. C. (1991). *Leadership for the twenty-first century.* New York: Praeger.

Schon, D. A. (1971). *Beyond the stable state.* New York: Norton.

Senge, P. M. (1990). *The fifth discipline: The art and practice of the learning organization.* New York: Doubleday/Currency.

Tapscott, D., & Caston, A. (1993). *Paradigm shift: The new promise of information technology.* New York: McGraw-Hill.

Toffler, A. (1980). *The third wave.* New York: William Morrow.

Waddock, S. A., & Post, J. E. (1991). Social entrepreneurs and catalytic change. *Public Administration Review, 51,* 393-401.

Weber, M. (Ed.). (1978). *Economy and society* (G. Roth & C. Wittich, Trans.). Berkeley: University of California Press. (Original work published 1956)

Wheatley, M. J. (1994). *Leadership and the new science: Learning about organization from an orderly universe.* San Francisco: Berrett-Koehler.

Will, R. (1995). Corporations with a conscience. *Business and Society Review, 95,* 17-20.

# 53

# *Leadership in the 21st Century*

KATHLEEN E. ALLEN
JUANA BORDAS
GILL ROBINSON HICKMAN
LARRAINE R. MATUSAK
GEORGIA J. SORENSON
KATHRYN J. WHITMIRE

For years scholars have been trying to define or describe the nature of leadership. Today, driving forces exist that suggest that the purpose of leadership in the 21st century, rather than the definition, must be the focal point of our leadership studies.

Therefore, recognizing the context of these changing times. we propose that the *purpose of leadership* in the 21st century is

- To create a supportive environment where people can thrive, grow, and live in peace with one another;
- To promote harmony with nature and thereby provide sustainability for future generations; and
- To create communities of reciprocal care and shared responsibility—one where every person matters and each person's welfare and dignity is respected and supported.

Upon reflection it is easy to recognize that this approach to leadership will be confronted with many challenges. Among these challenges are some prominent trends that appear to be shaping thought and action for the future. A few of these challenges can be presented as dynamic trends. These are

1. Globalization;
2. Increasing stress on the environment;
3. Increasing speed and dissemination of information technology; and
4. Scientific and social change.

Our human consciousness and capacities mutually shape these trends. They illustrate the point that leadership in the future will need to be anchored in

SOURCE: Reprinted with permission of the authors.

a purposeful set of assumptions that are intended to advance human capacity and consciousness. The following narrative is intended to provide a framework for understanding the implications for leadership; it is obviously not all-inclusive.

## Prominent Trends

*Globalization.* There is an increasing global consciousness in all sectors and societies of the world. This shift in thought and action has affected all sectors of society. Instead of focusing merely on the United States, the marketing of U.S. consumer goods, manufacturing, and even entertainment has drastically expanded to worldwide status.

This globalization of manufacturing, marketing, and competition has created multinational organizations designed to compete in the broader economic playing field. The economy itself has become global. The economic challenges of Mexico, Great Britain, or any country affect the global economy. The stock markets are interdependent.

*Increasing stress on the environment.* Issues related to the environment and its ability to support the world's populations in the future are becoming increasingly challenging. While the United States may lead the world in pollution control, environmental problems do not stay within the boundaries of any one nation. Struggles between economic interests and environmental interests continue all over the world. We see this exhibited in the debate over the use of old growth forests, wetland preservation, fishing rights, and legislation on chemicals that effect the atmosphere. Concerns about our fresh-water table will probably increase as industrial runoff and other such violations challenge us. Landfills continue to be overloaded with waste, triggering increased pressure for recycling. Toxic waste, land development, and complex environmental phenomena all contribute to issues of health education and human and animal welfare.

*Increasing speed and dissemination of information technology.* Mass communication has connected the world in ways that were unheard of fifty years ago. While the Pentium chip may be the latest

addition to computers this year, just around the corner is the advent of nano-technology. Nano-technology will allow the application of techniques in every discipline from microbiology to political science that will drastically decrease the size of equipment and increase the capacity of processing and disseminating information. Today, electronic bits of information are transferred almost instantaneously. Information is rapidly disseminated throughout the world via the Internet, CNN, and major news networks. The result is that we know what has happened halfway around the world almost instantaneously. It is nearly impossible to keep information private.

Information technology is made up of "bits," and "bits" do not behave like consumer goods. Consumer goods can be stopped at country borders and their worth can be declared. "Bits" travel electronically across borders with little possibility of control. This may explain why we now have permeable boundaries among our organizations, communities, and individuals. For example, when the Chinese students were protesting in Tiananmen Square, they were also communicating by fax and other media to the rest of the world. The immediate information was very difficult, if not impossible, for the Chinese government to control. There are numerous similar examples.

*Scientific and social change.* The recent announcement of the cloning of a sheep heralds the shape of things to come from genetic engineering. Genetic engineering is just one of the scientific changes that will reshape our lives. Biomedical technology will not just continue to reveal the secrets of the gene code, but it will radically change the way we cure diseases and produce and grow our food. Social change will require new political, social, educational, and organizational structures. The perceptions of gender roles will also be reshaped and communicated widely. All of these changes will mingle with one another with little time delay.

These four trends are mutually shaped by, and interact with, the ethical and spiritual dimension of human beings. The challenge and questions for leadership then become, Can humans develop the self-discipline to choose how they currently interact with each other and the environment? Can we develop the ability to live in peace with each other? Can we learn to live in harmony with nature? Can we increase the speed at which we learn about complex, dynamic challenges and problems? Will the human race develop and support the required diversity to match and surpass the complexity of the dynamic system of the future? How far does our current consciousness extend? What is the effect of our current human capacity on the challenges of today and of the future?

While any one of these four dynamic trends would be more than enough to deal with, they cannot be treated as separate issues. They are highly interdependent and because of this it is difficult to discuss them as discrete identities. As they interact, they create an interesting set of implications that will have a powerful effect on how we practice leadership in the future.

## *Implications for Leadership*

1. *Increasing diversity in our daily lives.* Globalization has not only affected our traveling, markets, and perspective, it has also stimulated immigration and along with it population growth. This phenomenon creates a significant increase in diversity in our communities and in the workforce. Increased diversity in our lives will continue to challenge the assumptions many organizations have used to shape standards of practice. Leadership practices that recognize diversity as a positive asset of organizations and communities will need to be employed. New systems thinking will be required to design processes that increase inclusiveness and diversity in decision making.

2. *Increasing change.* The magnitude and speed of change will continue (Conner, 1992, *Managing at the Speed of Change*). The discomfort of having a decreasing amount of time to respond to change will be experienced. The complexity of change events will increase. Because the total system will be more interconnected, the number of facets that need to be considered will also increase. This will require leadership to design, support, and nurture flexible, durable organizations and groups. It will also require a systemic understanding in order to respond positively to the change events.

3. *Complexity.* As stated above our world is composed of a wide variety of infrastructures that are becoming increasingly complex and interwoven. Each one of the dynamic trends mentioned above is a complex system in and of itself. However, they all interact with one another creating a large, dynamic nonlinear system with smaller nonlinear dynamic systems nested within them. In these systems, sequential cause and effect are much more difficult to track and predict. Leadership will need to pace and intuit the changing complexity of the system. Complexity challenges every individual's capacity to fully understand or intuit the many interrelated systems. For this reason, complexity requires shared leadership and multiple perspectives.

4. *Interdependence.* This complex, changing system is also interdependent. Interdependence shapes complexity and complexity shapes interdependence. The dynamic trends of ecological stress, information technology, globalization, and scientific and social change all demonstrate the impact of interdependence and demand a total systems approach. The challenge and implication for leadership will be to initiate and practice a systems perspective.

5. *Increasing tensions around value differences.* There will be more tensions between individual rights and the common good of the larger community. We will be faced with the ethical ramifications of our organizations decisions as they influence not just the individual organization or corporation but also the community and the world. This will require that leadership be practiced with a significant ethical dimension that focuses on sustainable principles.

6. *Increasing gap between the rich and poor.* There will be continuing tension between the rich and the poor. This will affect both individuals and nations. This tension will include both economics and natural resources. This widening gap will require a leadership that recognizes justice and equity issues as well as economic and ecological concerns.

7. *Increasing requirement for continuous learning.* As stated repeatedly, these dynamic trends are continuously changing and interacting. The implication for leadership is the responsibility to encourage the speed at which individuals learn and to provide opportunities for these individuals to grow in understanding how this learning can be

brought into the changing relationship with the community or organization.

Recognizing the trends that have been articulated here as powerful forces that demand a new form of leadership, and focusing on the purpose rather than the definition of leadership, leads us to assert that a shared, collaborative form of leadership will be the most successful approach in the next century.

### Shared/Collaborative Leadership

This new leadership paradigm has been called by a number of different names: shared, participatory, collective, collaborative, cooperative, democratic, fluid, inclusive, roving, distributed, relational, and post-heroic. While consensus on the name of this "new leadership" has not been reached, there is a growing understanding that the patterns of hierarchical leadership that served us in the past are not well suited to the global complexity, rapid change, interdependency, and multifaceted challenges described above.

In the information age, the primary challenge will be to encourage the new, better-educated work force to be committed, self-managing, and lifelong learners. This "people focused" leadership has its roots in democratic traditions. It is founded on the belief that in the complex future "answers are to be found in community" (Wheatley) in group-centered organizations where "everyone can learn continually" (Senge). Followers are being transformed into partners, coleaders, lifelong learners, and collaborators.

As the demand for this new leadership grows, the command and control leaders at the top of the pyramid are being challenged to change. They are expected to become leaders who are facilitators, stewards, coaches, designers, and teachers (Senge). They are being challenged to become leaders who "walk their talk" and model the way, inspiring others, delegating and serving. Effective leaders are recognizing that every person has leadership qualities that can and must be recognized and used.

The new leadership paradigm, therefore, is restructuring our conceptual framework of what the practice of leadership is and our understanding of what effective leaders do. It is transforming the role of "followers" and revolutionizing the design of organizations for the 21st century.

A recent brochure from the Robert Greenleaf Center on Servant-Leadership captures this spirit: "The old organizational pyramids of the nineteenth century are crumbling, being replace by upside-down pyramids and circles and connections."

The term collaborative and reciprocal leadership is used here to describe the process that is at the heart of this change. Since collaborative leadership is more adaptable and fluid, focusing on relationships and the needs of people, so too, our intention is not to fixate on a definition or a set concept that describes the "new leadership." What is more important is to assist people to acquire the understanding and skills of the purpose of the new leadership and to describe for them how collaborative leadership principles can work for them in the context in which they choose to lead.

Evolution or progress requires the integration of past, present, and future. In the midst of unceasing change in an interdependent world, this recognition provides the solid ground from which to move into the uncertainty of tomorrow with an assurance that collaborative structures have served people well in the past and can show the way to collectively shape the future.

### Principles of Collaborative/Reciprocal Leadership

A basic premise of collaborative leadership is recognition that no one person has the solutions to the multifaceted problems that a group or organization must address. Leadership in this context requires a set of principles that empower all members to act, and employ a process that allows the collective wisdom to surface. These principles must be based on an understanding that people have the knowledge and creativity to respond to the problems they face. They encourage the development of organizations that support collective action based on shared vision, ownership, and mutual values.

The evolution of collaborative leadership has been deeply influenced by the natural sciences as well as history. The Newtonian concept of a mechanistic world where people followed directions and where repetitive, learned responses were sufficient has given way to an organic, systems-oriented, and dynamic understanding of how people, groups, and organizations operate. This systems perspective requires nonlinear, holistic and multifaceted approaches to leadership that stress interactive participation, open communication, continuous learning, and attention to relationships.

The function of leadership then becomes the creation of systems, structures, and environment where this interaction and learning can occur. As Wheatley has stated, "Leadership is making sure you have the right patterns in place." Senge refers to this as fashioning an environment "where everyone takes on the responsibility for learning."

While change and adaptability are key aspects of a systems approach, there are core principles that nurture the interaction and learning that are essential to collaborative leadership. Following are seven of these principles:

1. *Promoting a collective leadership process.* "Post-heroic" leadership moves away from the theory that the "great man" has the answers to a shared, distributed, and fluid concept of leadership. This is based on the belief that depending on the need, situation, and requirements, different people assume the leadership role and that everyone has leadership potential. Collaborative leaders create supportive and open environments that encourage initiation, facilitate the sharing of information, and value each person's contribution. At the same time, individuals are encouraged to learn and stretch their leadership potential. Leadership, therefore, is assisting people to grow and learn.

In Scott Peck's work on building community, for example, the "leader" is a facilitator whose role is to create and hold the "safe space" where people can discover themselves and learn to relate to one another authentically. The focus is shifted from the individual leader to the group, community, or or-

ganization. In fact, at times, the nominal leader may not even be visible.

2. *Structuring a learning environment.* An organization or group that is learner focused supports continuous self-development and reflection. Practices such as listening, promoting open-mindedness, seeking constructive feedback, sharing ideas, and viewing conflict as an opportunity for growth are embedded in the culture. People closest to the problem or opportunity are encouraged to interact and find solutions or innovative approaches. To do this, Senge believes the group must function "in a mode of inquiry, knowing that nobody knows and everybody can learn continually."

As the group or organization practices learning together, open communication, mutual trust, shared meaning, and a sense of collective ownership emerge. Senge refers to this as "communities of commitment where people are continually learning how to learn together." Thus, people can venture out of their comfort zones and take the risks inherent in managing change.

3. *Supporting relationships and interconnectedness.* In collaborative leadership, the relationships and interconnectedness of people become a primary dynamic. Values such as respect, honesty, expecting the best from others, and the ability to exercise personal choice lay the foundation for covenant relationships to emerge. These relationships are based on trust and mutual responsibility. Collaborative leadership focuses attention on building the individual's and group's capacity to live these values, to benefit from their interdependence, and to recognize that conflict and differences can foster growth and creativity.

Relationships are also strengthened through the development of a shared vision that allows people to set common directions, have mutual goals, and rise above self-interest. Shared vision and values function as a governing force where people can organize and manage themselves thereby getting the job done without the need for control or rigid policies and procedures.

4. *Fostering shared power.* For leadership to be collaborative or shared, power and ownership must

be distributed throughout the organization. Shared power implies that everyone has responsibility for leading, decision making, and learning. Groups and teams are often used to make decisions sometimes with a consensus format. Accountability and responsibility are based on individual integrity and peer agreements.

As people collaborate around common goals, partnerships and coalitions evolve resulting in lateral networks of mutual influence (Rost and Nirenberg). Kil Janow in *The Inventive Organization* describes this process as multiple relationships acting in a flexible, flattened structure based on partnerships, self-regulation, and interdependence.

In *Re-Inventing the Corporation,* Naisbitt and Aburdene refer to this as a lattice or grid where power is found in the center not at the top. Hierarchical structures are thus replaced by crisscrossing networks, overlapping, changing, and fluid boundaries. This web-like structure supports optimum participation, interaction, and empowerment.

5. *Practicing stewardship and service.* Stewardship is the cornerstone of reciprocal or shared leadership because it turns hierarchical leadership upside down. Stewardship focuses on ensuring that other people's needs are being served and not on exercising privilege, power, and control. According to Block, stewardship chooses partnership over patriarchy or hierarchy; empowerment over dependency; and service over self-interest. Thus, the leader is "in service, rather than in control."

In his landmark work, *The Servant as Leader,* Robert Greenleaf describes this commitment as "wanting to serve first. Then conscious choice brings one to aspire to lead." The litmus test of collaborative leadership is based on whether people's needs are being served. As people feel respected and valued as partners they can create a community of shared responsibility.

6. *Valuing diversity and inclusiveness.* For people to respect each other, build trust, and communicate openly, they must learn to accept and value individual differences. Valuing diversity is the rich soil that nurtures relationships, partnerships, and collaborative networks. This is reflected in the Scott Peck statement, "Perhaps the most necessary key to the achievement of community is the appreciation of differences."

Respecting each person's perspective and personal style frees them to contribute their ideas and talents so that people can learn together. Furthermore, this inclusiveness is a key aspect of transforming followers into stakeholders and nurturing collective ownership. It is an understanding that creativity and excellence are enhanced through diversity. Fostering authentic diversity can be accomplished by respecting different perspectives, fostering open-mindedness, practicing dialogue, and listening with attention and empathy.

7. *Committing to self-development.* The movement to collaborative or shared leadership is at its heart a personal transformation that is fueled by "a commitment to work on yourself first." Greenleaf believed that the motivation to serve was based on the desire for one's "own healing."

The understanding that one's inner life reflects positively or negatively on one's leadership can serve to bring authenticity and humility to the leadership process. By working on personal learning and growth, leaders model the way for others to focus on their own personal mastery and proficiency.

This authenticity and the ability to actually "live" the principles of collaborative leadership is reflected in Wheatley's statement, "We must be what we want to become, we must in every step of the way, embody the future toward which we are aiming." This resonates with the words of Mahatma Gandhi, who recognized that personal transformation was the heartbeat of leadership: "We must be the change we wish to see in the world." With the proper understanding, education, and training, every individual can begin to use the leadership gifts that they possess.

So, if these are the principles of collaborative leadership, then what are the practices or functions that collaborative leaders must practice? Based upon the premises we have stated in this document, namely,

- that as we approach the 21st century we must focus on the purpose rather than the definition of leadership,
- that the new leadership paradigm is collective and reciprocal, and
- that there are powerful trends moving us in this direction

we make the following recommendations for leadership practices for the 21st century.

## *Collective Leadership Practices in the 21st Century*

Practices are activities, customs, and ways of operating used by an individual, group, organization, or community. We view practices as an integral component of organic or natural living systems and the means by which collective leadership is exercised. Embedded and articulated in the statement of purpose and leadership practices are our values and beliefs. We think that successful leadership will model the following collective leadership in the 21st century.

### Purpose of Leadership in the 21st Century

*To create a supportive environment where people can thrive and grow and live in peace with one another.*

### Collective Leadership Practices

1. *Develop structures and processes to support collective leadership by*

   - holding shared vision and core values in trust and operationalizing them;
   - generating and supporting interdependent and interdisciplinary group processes;
   - establishing and sustaining inclusiveness of stakeholders;
   - creating and maintaining a free flow of information;
   - facilitating fluidity and flexibility in group processes and structures;
   - sharing and distributing power and authority among all group members;

- building a system of peer responsibility and accountability;
- demonstrating equity; and
- cultivating ritual and celebration.

2. *Foster human growth and development through*

   - engaging in continuous self-development and reflection;
   - enhancing and using intuition;
   - strengthening and sustaining spirituality:
   - coaching and nurturing the development of others;
   - creating opportunities for people to experience success (efficacy);
   - promoting group and community capacity building and progress;
   - expecting the best from people; and
   - celebrating individual and group success.

3. *Facilitate learning by*

   - creating learning communities;
   - including diverse individuals and perspectives;
   - fostering and demonstrating open-mindedness;
   - developing meaning and insight through individual and collective reflection;
   - seeking feedback and critique to enhance development;
   - developing creative and intuitive abilities;
   - sharing ideas through engaging in dialogue;
   - practicing deep listening;
   - using creative tension to foster change and new ideas; and
   - acknowledging and using "mistakes" as opportunities to learn, reflect, and forgive.

*To promote harmony with nature and thereby provide sustainability for future generations.*

4. *Enhance the quality of life and preservation of nature by*

   - understanding the interdependent relationship between human and natural systems and working to enhance their viability;
   - practicing "enoughness" (bigger or more is not always better);

- achieving balance in emotional, spiritual, and physical aspects of life;
- using a long-term perspective thereby creating viability for current and future generations;
- generating and supporting systems thinking (wholistic thinking) as a basis for action;
- facilitating self-organizing, self-regulating, and self-renewing systems;
- using natural conflict to foster growth and change;
- recognizing and promoting the spiritual connectedness of all life; and
- generating and sustaining peace among ourselves and aiding peace efforts globally.

*To create a community of reciprocal care and shared responsibility—one where every person matters and each person's welfare and dignity is the concern of us all.*

5. *Create caring communities of leaders and participants through*

- developing trusting relationships;
- attending to the well-being (basic needs and human rights) of others and providing opportunities for them to sustain themselves;
- supporting basic freedom for others and providing opportunities for them to maintain freedom for themselves; and
- maintaining opportunities for people to make choices for themselves that are not harmful to others, and honoring the choices they make.

6. *Demonstrate courage by*

- taking risks;
- tackling the difficult issues;
- serving others;
- challenging others when they depart from core values held in trust; and
- initiating change, transforming self, groups, and institutions.

7. *Model integrity and authenticity by*

- showing mutual respect;
- carrying out responsibilities;
- being accountable for one's actions;

- modeling integrity and authenticity (walk the talk);
- being honest with self and others;
- demonstrating equity; and
- practicing inclusiveness.

## Transition From Positional to Collective Leadership

Creating an environment where collective leadership is practiced starts with a *shared vision* supported by a set of specific values or beliefs which are integrated into the person's behavior (Wheatley & Kellner-Rogers, 1996). Some "inner work" is required for a person who wants to practice this form of leadership. Without this inner work, the practice of authentic collective or shared leadership does not occur. This inner work starts with values and beliefs. People who practice shared leadership believe that all people have the capacity to lead themselves. Further, they believe that the gifts and resources needed to accomplish a task can be found in the members of the group, not in a single leader. Therefore, the goal of positional leaders is not to direct or tell but to provide a structure that allows people to lead themselves.

This means that positional leaders distribute or *share the "power"* of their position. In this way, they enable groups to assume the responsibility and discover their own capacity to work together, decide, plan, and act. They are willing and able to share the power of their position to the maximum degree possible under the given circumstances. Their personal power remains evident, but they share their positional power. They may substitute or transmute the need for positional power into the joy of seeing the group evolve as a learning organization or community.

Another major element, after weaving the shared vision, is *modeling*. There is integrity in their vision of shared leadership that is reflected in the way they structure and respond to the development of the group. This integration of practice, vision, and modeling gives group members confidence that leaders "walk their talk" as reflected in their belief in each individual and their collective action.

Collective/Reciprocal leaders spend time *structuring the environment* as a learning environment. This may include establishing the expectation of success. Then, the group is encouraged to take risks and challenge the way things have always been done. Group members are even encouraged to challenge their own beliefs about what they can or cannot accomplish without specific direction from a positional authority.

Risk taking is supported by the creation of a safety net. The safety net creates an environment where group members believe that it is safe to challenge and exercise personal choice in achieving the mutually stated goals. Peter Block once said that people trade sovereignty or freedom of choice for safety. A step in the critical passage to the new paradigm of shared leadership requires the members of the group to practice the freedom of choice that comes with being responsible and accountable to themselves and each other (Chaleff, 1995; Kelley, 1992).

*Information is shared* with all group members so that they have adequate knowledge and understanding about the task to make an enlightened decision (Wheatley & Kellner-Rogers, 1996). Positional leaders need not be the primary source of the information. In most cases, the members need to rely on each other and on their ability to gather accurate information rather than on a positional authority. This shift in the source of information triggers greater self-sufficiency and greater interdependence. By receiving power, choice, and information, members begin to believe that they can influence the situation and the outcome. This belief is reinforced by the subsequent accumulation of actual successes.

The interdependent structures and relationships help to ensure an understanding of the distribution of different talents among group members. This facilitates the acceptance by the group of different points of readiness to practice this combination of individual responsibility and shared leadership and accountability. It also helps members discover that they can both learn with, and depend upon, each other.

These interdependent structures support group members as they work together to successfully accomplish the specified task. As groups learn this new behavior, they need the assurance that the ambiguity or the anxiety they may be experiencing due to this different way of operating is normal and that their feelings are a part of group transformation. A group often experiences ambiguity, frustration, disorientation, fear, insecurity, and a frantic desire for the positional leaders to rescue them. All this shifts the role of leaders to that of facilitators, supporters, consultants, and sometimes teachers. For group members, the result of this experience is excitement, ownership of the process and product, confidence and competence, and better ideas and learning.

All these practices, and perhaps others of which we are not aware, are needed to meet the challenges of the future as we practice collaborative leadership.

## *References*

Block, P. (1993). *Stewardship: Choosing Service Over Self-Interest*. San Francisco: Berrett-Koehler.

Chaleff, I. (1995). *The courageous follower: Standing up to and for our leaders*. San Francisco: Berrett-Koehler.

Conner, D. (1995). *Managing at the speed of change: How resilient managers succeed and prosper where others fail*. New York: Villard.

Goldstein, J. (1993). Revisioning the Organization: Chaos, Quantum Physicals and OD—An Interview With Margaret Wheatley. *Organizational Development Journal, 2*(2).

Greenleaf, R. K. (1991). *The Servant as Leader.* Indianapolis: The Robert K. Greenleaf Center.

Janov, J. (1994). *The Inventive Organization: Hope and Daring at Work*. San Francisco: Jossey-Bass.

Kelley, R. E. (1992). *The power of followership: How to create leaders people want to follow, and followers who lead themselves*. New York: Doubleday/Currency.

Naisbitt, J. & Aburdene, P. (1986). *Re-Inventing the Corporation*. New York: Warner Books.

Palmer, P. (1994). "Leading From Within: Out of the Shadows and Into the Light." In J. Conger (Ed.), *Spirit at Work.* San Francisco: Jossey-Bass.

Peck, M. S. (1987). *The Different Drum: Community Making and Peace*. New York: Simon & Schuster.

Rost, J. C. (1994). "Leadership Development in the New Millennium." *The Journal of Leadership Studies, 1*(1), 91-110.

Senge, P. M. (1990). *The Fifth Discipline: The Art and Practice of a Learning Organization*. New York: Doubleday.

Wheatley, M. J. (1992). *Leadership and the New Science: Learning About Organizations From an Orderly Universe*. San Francisco: Berrett-Koehler.

Wheatley, M. J., & Kellner-Rogers, M. (1996). *A simpler way*. San Francisco: Berrett-Koehler.

# Index

# About the Editor

**Gill Robinson Hickman** is currently Professor of Leadership Studies in the Jepson School of Leadership Studies at the University of Richmond in Virginia. Her career has involved both administrative and academic appointments. At California State University, Dominguez Hills, she served in several capacities, including founding Dean of the School of Health, Dean of Faculty Affairs, Director of Staff Personnel, and Professor of Public Administration. She has also served as interim Associate Dean of the School of Community and Public Affairs at Virginia Commonwealth University, Director of Personnel for the Ontario-Montclair School District, Personnel Analyst for the California State University system, and Administrative Assistant for the city of Inglewood, California. She has been a faculty presenter at the Salzburg Seminar in Salzburg, Austria and at the University of the Western Cape in South Africa where she presented a conceptual framework for leadership and transformation in 21st-century organizations. She is completing several books that are scheduled for publication in 1998, including *Teaching Leadership for a Diverse Society: An Approach to Including Diversity in Introductory Leadership Courses* and *Managing Personnel in the Public Sector: The Department Manager's Role.* Dr. Hickman received her B.A. degree from University of Denver in political science, M.P.A. degree from the University of California, Los Angeles, and Ph.D. in public administration from the University of Southern California.

# About the Contributors

Kathleen E. Allen
*College of St. Benedict*

Barbara Altman
*Boston University*

Bruce J. Avolio
*State University of New York, Binghamton*

Lotte Bailyn
*MIT*

Jeffrey A. Barach
*Tulane University*

Bernard M. Bass
*State University of New York, Binghamton*

Warren Bennis
*University of Southern California*

William Bergquist
*Professional School of Psychology,
    San Francisco*

Samuel E. Bleecker
*Technology Consultant*

Juana Bordas
*Mestiza Leadership Services*

Nils Brunsson
*Stockholm School of Economics*

James MacGregor Burns
*Williams College and University of Maryland,
    College Park*

Art Caston
*DMR Group, Inc.*

James Champy
*CSC Index, Inc.*

Joanne B. Ciulla
*University of Richmond*

James C. Collins
*Stanford University*

Jay A. Conger
*University of Southern California*

Gordon J. Curphy
*Personnel Decisions, Inc.*

Terrence E. Deal
*Vanderbilt University*

Kathleen Dechant
*University of Connecticut*

Max DePree
*Herman Miller, Inc.*

Gregory G. Dess
*University of Kentucky*

Peter F. Drucker
*Claremont Graduate School*

D. Reed Eckhardt
*Journalist*

L. Lawrence Embley
*Consultant*

John P. Fernandez
*Advance Research Management Consultants*

Kimball Fisher
*Belgard-Fisher-Rayner, Inc.*

John W. Gardner
*Stanford University*

Al Gini
*Loyala University, Chicago*

Robert C. Ginnett
*Center for Creative Leadership, Colorado
    Springs*

Francis J. Gouillart
*Gemini Consulting*

Barbara Gray
*Pennsylvania State University*

Samuel Greengard
*Writer, Los Angeles*

Robert K. Greenleaf (deceased)

Michael Hammer
*Hammer and Company*

Ronald A. Heifetz
*Harvard University*

James L. Heskett
*Harvard University*

Ann Howard
*Leadership Research Institute*

Jane Howell
*University of Western Ontario*

Richard L. Hughes
*Center for Creative Leadership, Colorado
    Springs, Colorado*

Robert E. Kelley
*Carnegie Mellon University*

James N. Kelly
*Gemini Consulting*

Allan A. Kennedy
*Selkirk Associates*

John P. Kotter
*Harvard Business School*

James M. Kouzes
*TPG Learning Systems*

James E. Liebig
*Wisconsin Community Capital Corporation*

Charles C. Manz
*Arizona State University*

Larraine R. Matusak
*LarCon Associates*

Alex Miller
*University of Tennessee*

Gareth Morgan
*York University, Toronto*

Anne P. Murphy
*Associate Editor, Inc. Magazine*

Burt Nanus
*University of Southern California*

Nitin Nohria
*Harvard University*

Lynn R. Offermann
*George Washington University*

Johan P. Olsen
*University of Bergen*

Patricia M. Patterson
*Florida Atlantic University of Richmond*

Jerry I. Porras
*Stanford University*

Barry Z. Posner
*Santa Clara University*

Joseph C. Rost
*University of San Diego*

Peter M. Senge
*MIT Sloan School of Management*

Henry P. Sims, Jr.
*University of Maryland, College Park*

Kenneth A. Smith
*Syracuse University*

Charlene Marmer Solomon
*Writer, Los Angeles*

Georgia J. Sorenson
*University of Maryland, College Park*

Don Tapscott
*DMR Group, Inc.*

Alvin Toffler
*Author/Consultant*

Margaret J. Wheatley
*The Berkana Institute*

Kathryn J. Whitmire
*University of Maryland, College Park*